A farewell to arms?

MANCHEStER
1824

Manchester University Press

Reviews of the first edition

'The most comprehensive guide to the Irish peace process, the most authoritative and trenchant written on the subject in recent years. A splendid volume.'
Jonathan Bardon, Chair of the Northern Ireland Community Relations Council

'This great volume rises to the intellectual challenges set by the Good Friday Agreement with the contributors succeeding brilliantly in explaining the subtlety of a still evolving Irish peace process. Its inclusivity ... sets new standards in multi-disciplinary scholarship. Superb.'
Kevin Boyle, Department of Government, University of Essex

'The long war may be over but that is not sufficient for achieving stable and agreed forms of government in Northern Ireland. All the more reason for this wide ranging and convincing survey to which we may have to return again and again.'
John Gray, Director, Linenhall Library, Belfast

'The editors have assembled an impressive range of contributors who offer a multi-faceted analysis of the Irish peace process ... A very welcome volume.'
Brigid Laffan, Department of Politics, University College, Dublin

'Essential reading for anyone wishing to understand the politics of the Irish peace process.'
Eunan O'Halpin, Trinity College, Dublin

A farewell to arms?

Beyond the Good Friday Agreement

second edition

EDITED BY
MICHAEL COX, ADRIAN GUELKE
AND FIONA STEPHEN

Manchester University Press

MANCHESTER AND NEW YORK

distributed exclusively in the USA by Palgrave

First edition published 2000 by Manchester University Press

This edition published 2006 by
Manchester University Press
Oxford Road, Manchester M13 9NR, UK
www.manchesteruniversitypress.co.uk

Distributed exclusively in the USA by
Palgrave, 175 Fifth Avenue, New York,
NY 10010, USA

Distributed exclusively in Canada by
UBC Press, University of British Columbia, 2029 West Mall,
Vancouver, BC, Canada V6T 1Z2

British Library Cataloguing-in-Publication Data
A catalogue record for this book is avalaible from the British Library

Library of Congress Cataloging-in-Publication Data applied for

ISBN 0 7190 7114 3 *hardback*
EAN 978 0 7190 7114 0
ISBN 0 7190 7115 1 *paperback*
EAN 978 0 7190 7115 7

This edition first published 2006

14 13 12 11 10 09 08 07 06   10 9 8 7 6 5 4 3 2 1

Typeset in Caslon and Frutiger Condensed
by Koinonia Ltd, Manchester
Printed in Great Britain
by CPI, Bath

Contents

List of tables

List of contributors

Arthur Aughey is Senior Lecturer in Politics at the University of Ulster and has written extensively on Northern Ireland's politics, British conservatism and constitutional change in the United Kingdom. His publications include (with Duncan Morrow) *Northern Ireland Politics* (1996). He is currently writing a book on the politics of Northern Ireland after the Belfast Agreement, which will appear in 2005.

Paul Bew is Professor of Politics at The Queen's University of Belfast. One of the best known historians of his generation, he is the author and co-author of several key works on Ireland and Northern Ireland, including *Charles Stewart Parnell* (1991), *Ideology and the Irish Question* (1994) and *Between War and Peace: The Political Future of Northern Ireland* (1997). He is currently completing *The Oxford History of Modern Ireland*.

Feargal Cochrane works at the Richardson Institute for Peace and Conflict Research at Lancaster University. A specialist on Northern Ireland, ethnic conflict and emerging peace processes, his publications include *Unionist Politics and the Politics of Unionism since the Anglo-Irish Agreement* (1997) and *People Power? The Role of the Voluntary and Community Sector in the Northern Ireland Conflict* (2002).

Michael Cox is Professor of International Relations at the London School of Economics. Formerly editor of the *Review of International Studies*, he is currently an Executive Committee member of the European Consortium for Political Research. He is the author and editor of a dozen books, including *Superpower Without a Mission?* (1995), (with Tim Dunne and Ken Booth) *Empires Systems and States* (2003) and *E. H. Carr: A Critical Appraisal* (2000; paperback 2004).

John Darby is former Director and Senior Research Fellow at the Initiative on Conflict Resolution and Ethnicity (INCORE) at the University of Ulster. He has written extensively on the conflict in Northern Ireland. His publications include *Conflict in Northern Ireland* (1976), (with Roger MacGinty) *The Management of*

Peace Processes (2000) and *The Effects of Violence on Peace Processes* (2001). He has been visiting research fellow at the Kroc Institute at the University of Notre Dame since 1999.

Brice Dickson was the chief commissioner of the Northern Ireland Human Rights Commission since its creation in 1999, serving in the role for a six-year term while on secondment from his position as professor of law at the University of Ulster. He has published in the fields of human rights, public law and comparative law.

Paul Dixon is lecturer in Politics at the University of Ulster and author of *Northern Ireland: The Politics of War and Peace* (2001). He is editor of www.nipolitics.com and is currently working on a book on the Northern Ireland peace process.

John Dumbrell, an acknowledged expert on US foreign policy, is professor of politics at the University of Leicester. His books include *The Carter Presidency: A Re-Evaluation* (1993), *A Special Relationship: Anglo-American Relations in the Cold War and After* (2000) and *Lyndon Johnson and Soviet Communism* (2004).

Sean Farren has been a member of the SDLP since the early 1970s. In 1998 he was elected to the Northern Ireland Assembly, serving as minister for further education, training and employment between 1999 and 2001 before he was appointed minister of finance. He teaches at the University of Ulster. His most cited publication is *The Politics of Irish Education 1920–1965* (1995).

Kate Fearon is a member of the Northern Ireland Women's Coalition (NIWC), and the current director of the Political Party Programme at the National Democratic Institute of the Federation Bosnia and Hercegovina. Her best-known publication is *Women's Work: The Story of the Northern Ireland Women's Coalition* (1999).

Gordon Gillespie, a graduate of the Queen's University of Belfast, has written extensively on Northern Ireland. A member of the 'Troubled Images Team' based at the Linen Hall Library in Belfast, among his publications is the best-selling *Northern Ireland: A Chronology of the Troubles, 1968–1999* (1999), co-authored with Paul Bew.

Paul Gillespie is Foreign Policy Editor and Duty Editor of the *Irish Times*, for which he is a regular columnist. He is project leader of the UK Group in the Institute of European Affairs, Dublin, and edited the publication *Britain's European Question: The Issues for Ireland* (1996) and *Blair's Britain, England's Europe: A View from Ireland* (2000).

Adrian Guelke is Professor of Comparative Politics and Director of the Centre for the Study of Ethnic Conflict at the Queen's University of Belfast. An internationally renowned expert on ethnicity, Northern Ireland, terrorism and South Africa, among his best known publications are *Northern Ireland: The International*

Perspective (1989), *The Age of Terrorism and the International Political System* (1998) and *Rethinking the Rise and Fall of Apartheid* (2004).

Fred Halliday is Professor of International Relations at the London School of Economics and one of the best-known commentators on international politics in the world today. An expert on the Middle East, the Cold War, international relations' theory, and Third World Politics, he has written several well-known studies, including *Rethinking International Relations* (1994), *Revolution and World Politics* (1999), *The World at 2000* (2001), *Two Hours That Shook the World* (2002), *Islam and the Myth of Confrontation* (2002) and (with Eugene Rogan) *The Middle East in International Relations* (2004).

Stephen Hopkins is Lecturer in the Department of Politics at the University of Leicester. He is the author of several articles analysing recent political developments in the context of post-Good Friday Agreement Northern Ireland. He has recently published 'Fighting without Guns? Political Autobiography in Contemporary Northern Ireland', in Liam Harte (ed.), *Modern Irish Autobiography: Self, Nation and Society*.

Caroline Kennedy-Pipe is Professor of International Relations at the University of Sheffield. A well-known specialist on international history, security studies, women and war, and the Cold War, her publications include *Stalin's Cold War* (1995), *The Origins of the Present Troubles in Northern Ireland* (1997) and *Russia and the World Since 1917* (1998). She is currently Chair of the British International Studies Association.

Francisco Letamandia is Professor of Political Science at the University of the Basque Country at Bilbao. He has written extensively on nationalism and Basque nationalism, and has played a key role in trying to bring peace to the Basque Country.

John Loughlin is Professor of European Politics at the University of Cardiff. His research interests include European regionalism, federalism and issues of governanace. Among his many publications are *Sub-National Democracy in the European Union* (2003) and (with Michael Keating and Kris Deschouwer) *Culture, Institutions and Economic Development* (2003).

Philip Lynch is Senior Lecturer in Politics at the University of Leicester. His most recent publications are 'The Conservatives and the Union' which appeared in *The Political Quarterly* in 2004, and (with Mark Garnett) *The Conservatives in Crisis* (2003). His is currently completing a monograph, *The End of Conservative Britain?*

Roger MacGinty works in the Department of Politics at York University where he researches conflict, peace processes and Northern Ireland. His publications include (with John Darby) *The Management of Peace Processes* (2000), *Guns and Government: The Management of the Northern Ireland Peace Process* (2001) and *Contemporary Peace Making* (2002).

Martin Mansergh was Head of Research for Fianna Fáil and senior adviser to the taoiseach on Northern Ireland before becoming a senator for Seanad Eireann in 2002. Viewed by many as one of the key architects of the Irish peace process, he has been the subject of the study by Kevin Rafter, *Martin Mansergh: A Biography* (2002).

Cathall McCall is Lecturer in the School of Politics and International Studies at the Queen's University of Belfast. His research interests address questions of civic, ethnic and cultural identity in the integrated contexts of Northern Ireland, the island of Ireland, the British Isles and the European Union. He has published widely, his most recent book being *Identity in Northern Ireland: Communities, Politics and Change* (1999).

Colin McInnes holds a personal chair in the Department of International Politics, University of Wales, Aberystwyth. He was formerly lecturer in the Department of War Studies, the Royal Military Academy Sandhurst, and special adviser to the House of Commons Defence Committee. His most recent books are *Spectator Sport War: The West and Contemporary Conflict* (2002) and (with Kelley Lee) *Health, Foreign Policy and Security* (2003).

Elizabeth Meehan is Director of the Institute for Governance, Public Policy and Social Research at the Queen's University of Belfast. Her research interests include citizenship, women, Northern Ireland and the European Union, citizens' rights and freedom of movement in the EU. Her best-known books are *Equality, Politics and Gender* (1991) and *Citizenship and the European Community* (1993).

John Morison is Professor of Jurisprudence at the Queen's University of Belfast. His books include *Reshaping Public Power: Northern Ireland and the British Constitutional Problem*, with Stephen Livingstone (1995), and *Crime Community and Locale*, with David O'Mahony, Kieran McEvoy and Ray Geary (2000).

Rachel Rebouche has studied at Trinity University in Texas and the Queen's University of Belfast. She has a particular interest in political activism in organisations of Northern Irish women that lobby for more equitable laws and policies. In 2000 she was a George J. Mitchell scholar in Ireland.

Peter Shirlow is Senior Lecturer in Human Geography at the University of Ulster. He researches culture and identity, conflict and deprivation in Ireland and Europe. He is the Irish Studies series editor for Pluto Press and in 1999 edited (with Mark McGovern) *Who Are the People? Unionism, Protestantism and Loyalism*. His most influential work has been on the increasing levels of segregation in Northern Ireland since the peace process.

Marie Smyth was Senior Fellow in the US Institute of Peace, Washington, DC, 2002–3, and founder of the Institute for Conflict Research in Belfast, where she was chief executive officer until 2003. Her publications include (with Marie Therese Fay and Mike Morrissey) *Northern Ireland's Troubles: The Human Costs* (1999) and (with Mike Morrissey) *Northern Ireland After the Good Friday Agreement* (2002).

Fiona Stephen was Director of the Northern Ireland Council for Integrated Education between 1989 and 1994 before taking up positions at the University of Wales, Aberystwyth, and then at Queen Mary, University of London in 2003. She is currently completing a study on the politics of integrated education in Northern Ireland.

Michael von Tangen Page is manager of the Security and Peacebuilding Programme at International Alert, a London-based conflict-resolution organisation. He was previously a Research Fellow at the Centre for Defence Studies and the Department of War Studies, King's College, University of London. His contribution to this volume was written in a personal capacity.

Jon Tonge is Professor of Politics at the University of Salford and has written extensively on British and Northern Irish politics. Recent works include *Northern Ireland: Conflict and Change* (2002) and *The New Northern Irish Politics* (2004). He is co-editor of the *Irish Political Studies* journal and Chair of the Political Studies Association of the UK, 2005–8.

Acknowledgements

In putting together this enlarged and greatly revised edition we owe a personal debt of thanks to the many writers who have contributed to this project, for the richness of their expertise and the readiness with which they have responded to queries from the editors.

We are also indebted to Tony Mason and the production team at Manchester University Press for carrying this expanded project through to completion. Most of all though, we must give a special note of acknowledgement to our nearest and dearest who have lived with the process and sustained us throughout. We rededicate this study to them in love and hope.

July 2004

Fiona Stephen, *London*
Adrian Guelke, *Belfast*
Michael Cox, *London*

Glossary and abbreviations

AC   Autonomous Community – of the Basque Country and of Navarre

ANC   African National Congress

ANIA   Americans for a New Irish Agenda

Anglo-Irish Agreement   Signed by Irish and British governments – November 1985

AP   Alianza Popular – Popular Alliance (Basque Country)

APNI   Alliance Party of Northern Ireland

Ard Fheis   Annual national conference held by Irish political parties

Articles 2 and 3   Articles in the Constitution of the Irish republic which laid claim to the six counties of Northern Ireland

Belfast Agreement   Otherwise known as the Good Friday Agreement, signed in April 1998

BIIC   British–Irish Intergovenmental Conference

Bloomfield Report   May 1998 report by Sir Kenneth Bloomfield into the victims of the Troubles

British–Irelish ICG   British–Irish Intergovernmental Conference

CAP   Common Agricultural Policy

CCMS   Council for Catholic Maintained Schools

CEAC   Curriculum Examination and Assessment Council

CIRA   Continuity IRA – small splinter group opposed to the peace process

CLMC   Combined Loyalist Military Command; loyalist paramilitary coordinating body formed in 1991 comprising: UDA, UFF, UVF and Red Hand Commando

CRC   Community Relations Council

CRE   Commission for Racial Equality

Dail   Lower house of the Irish parliament

DENI   Department of Education Northern Ireland

Direct rule   Introduced in 1972 following the proroguing of Stormont

Downing Street Declaration   Key document of the peace process published jointly by the UK and Irish governments in December 1993

DPP   District Policing Partnership

DUP   Democratic Unionist Party; led by Revd. Ian Paisley

EC   European Commission

EC/EU   European Community/European Union

ECHR   European Convention on Human Rights

EMU   Education for Mutual Understanding

EMU   European and Monetary Union

EOCNI   Equal Opportunities Commission Northern Ireland

EP   European Parliament

ETA   Initials in Basque for 'Homeland and Freedom'

FAIR   Families Acting For Innocent Relatives

FAIT   Families against Intimidation and Terror

FARC   Revolutionary Forces of Columbia

Fianna Fáil   Constitutional nationalist party in the Irish Republic

Fine Gael   One of the two main parties in the Irish Republic

FLNC   Fronte di Liberazione Naziunale di a Corsica – National Liberation Front of Corsica

Framework Document   Published in February 1995 by Irish and British government with purpose of bringing about an agreed settlement in Ireland

GAL   Grupas Antiterroristas de Liberación – Anti-Terrorists Liberation Group

George Mitchell   President's Clinton's special envoy to Northern Ireland

GFA   Good Friday Agreement (Belfast Agreement)

HB   *Herri Batasuna* – Popular Unity, political wing of ETA

IEF   Integrated Education Fund

IICD   Independent International Commission on Decommissioning

ILP   Irish Labour Party

INCORE   Initiative on Conflict Resolution and Ethnicity

INLA   Irish National Liberation Army; republican paramilitary group formed in

1974 as a breakaway from the Official IRA

INTERREG 1989 EU initiative to foster economic co-operation between contiguous territories of different EU countries

IRA Irish Republican Army, also referred to as Provisional IRA; formed in late 1969 after a split with the Official IRA

LVF Loyalist Volunteer Force

Mitchell Report Published February 1996 laying down six conditions for inclusive political discussions - including the renunciation of force and no resort to anything other than democratic and peaceful means.

MLA Member of the Legislative Assembly

NICE Northern Ireland Centre in Europe

NICIE Northern Ireland Council for Integrated Education

NIE Northern Ireland Executive

NIHRC Northern Ireland Human Rights Commission

NIO Northern Ireland Office, British Government Department

NIWC Northern Ireland Women's Coalition

Northern Ireland Forum Public initiative in the Irish Republic taken in 1983 to explore different possible 'solutions' to the 'Irish Question'.

OFMDFM Office of the First Minister and Deputy First Minister

Omagh Town in Northern Ireland where 28 were killed in 1998 by bomb after the signing of the Good Friday Agreement

Patten Report 1999 commission report drafted by Chris Patten advocating reform of RUC

PLO Palestine Liberation Organization

PMVO politically motivated violent offender

PNV Partido Nationalista Vasco – Basque Nationalist Party

PP Partido Popular – Popular Party (Basque Country)

PSE–PSOE Partido Socialista de Euskadi – Socialist Party (Basque)

PUP Progressive Unionist party; loyalist party closest to the UVF

Real IRA Splinter group opposed to peace process

RHC, RHD Red Hand Commando/Defenders – cover names used by the UDA groups

RTE Radio Telefis Eireann – radio and TV network in the Irish Republic

RUC Royal Ulster Constabulary – Northern Ireland police Force

SAS Special Air Services – elite regiment of the British army

SDLP   Social Democratic and Labour Party – largest nationalist Party in Northern Ireland led by John Hume

SEUPB   Special EU Programmes Body

Sinn Féin   Sinn Féin – political wing of the IRA

SSPPR   Special Support Programme for Peace and Reconciliation initiated in Northern Ireland after 1994 ceasefires

Sunningdale   Location in UK where agreement was reached that led to the formation of a power-sharing executive in 1974

Tanaiste   Member of the Dail (parliament)

Taoiseach   Official title of the Prime Minister of the Irish Republic

UDA   Ulster Defence Association – largest loyalist paramilitary Organization

UDR   Ulster Defence Regiment – locally recruited and based regiment of the British Army (renamed Royal Irish Regiment in 1992)

UFF   Ulster Freedom Fighters – proscribed loyalist para-military organization

UKUP   United Kingdom Unionist Party – led by Bob Macartney and opposed to Good Friday Agreement

UUC   Ulster Unionist Council

UUP   Ulster Unionist Party

UVF   Ulster Volunteer Force – proscribed loyalist para-military organization

UWC   Ulster Workers' Council – loyalist committee that planned the collapse of the power-sharing agreement of 1974

'Washington three'   The three conditions laid down by the British government in March 1993 for Sinn Féin joining all-party talks, which included 'actual decommissioning of some arms as a tangible confidence-building measure'

Introduction: a farewell to arms?
Beyond the Good Friday Agreement

MICHAEL COX, ADRIAN GUELKE
AND FIONA STEPHEN

With the exception of the peace process in South Africa, which seems to have been a brilliant success, peace processes worldwide since the mid-1990s fall into one of two categories: those which, like the Middle East peace process, have collapsed almost entirely; and those interesting few that have neither imploded nor as yet been able to achieve their full political potential by establishing the conditions for a final settlement. The Good Friday Agreement that was finally signed in the aftermath of the second IRA ceasefire and the election of a new Labour Government in 1997 is probably of the latter kind. Of course, one could be a pessimist – and there are more than a few of those still in Northern Ireland today – and insist that the agreement was doomed from the start by a studied ambiguity that papered over cracks and tried to resolve the unresolvable. Yet anyone who lived through the Troubles, and did not expect to see peace in the first place, cannot but be struck by how much has changed since the late 1990s. This may not yet be a society that has come to terms with its past; nor does the change render the Good Friday Agreement a perfect document – it is not. Yet, for all the political bluster and the warnings of dark days ahead, Northern Ireland feels a very different place in the early part of the twenty-first century than it did before the agreement was signed in April 1998. As we argued in the first edition – and we can see no reason to change our minds now – it was the best that was on offer then, and still remains the only game in town today.

Times and circumstances change. In the first edition of this book, published back in 2000, our primary purpose was to explain the origins of the peace process. Here, we do much more; in particular we explore the various problems involved in making peace a reality in a deeply divided society where different understandings of the past and hostile perceptions of the 'other' still make it difficult to think of there being a final resolution of that long-standing issue known as the 'Irish question'. The first edition was suitably, and perhaps fortuitously, sub-titled, 'From long war to long peace in Northern Ireland'. This second edition takes the story forward, a perspective reflected in the new sub-title, 'Beyond the Good Friday Agreement'.

The second edition has been updated and the majority of its chapters substantially revised; and we have added no less than nine new chapters, and further documents have been added to the appendices. Finally, we have reorganised the study to reflect the simple fact that much has changed since the optimistic days immediately following the signing of the original agreement. Academics are well known for their ability to predict the past while invariably failing to see the future! We hope we will not be accused of that. We made every effort in the first edition of 2000 to present the problems facing politicians in the North realistically. We always assumed that a settlement in Northern Ireland would take many years to achieve: if we are to stand accused of anything it is perhaps in underestimating how long and difficult the process would be.

Part I of the book brings together four distinguished authors who contributed to the first edition. Here we can be accused of minor revisionism, because we have transposed Marie Smyth's original and harrowing account of the human costs of the Troubles from its position around the middle of the first edition to the start – where it should have always been, as a stark reminder of what the conflict in the end was all about: the lost lives of several thousand people. Martin Mansergh – one of the crucial architects of the IRA cease-fires – follows with his very personal reflections on the origins of the Troubles and the fate of the peace process since 1998. Caroline Kennedy-Pipe continues with a much updated version of her original overview, bringing the analysis up to 2004. Paul Bew then concludes the first part with a terse reminder that, far from being a consociational (quite literally, the association of two communities) deal, the Good Friday Agreement was more directly a product of a series of transformations within the two blocs, in particular the remarkable new relationship between the British State and both the Unionist and Republican leaderships. Bew is not a thoroughgoing pessimist, though he insists that until the IRA abandons all connection with paramilitarism progress towards a final end game is always going to be compromised.

Part II discusses the politics of the Good Friday Agreement, and does so with three new essays. Jon Tonge opens the second part by looking in some detail at the balance of political power since the Good Friday Agreement, especially following the polarising Assembly elections of 2003 from which the DUP and Sinn Fein emerged as the majority parties of choice within their respective camps. He is followed by Arthur Aughey, who explores the sources of unionist anxiety – obviously a critical issue given that the agreement is now in crisis precisely because the unionist family (currently much divided) has had grave concerns about it from the outset. Sean Farren continues the discussion with a less than optimistic report on the state of play within the Social Democratic and Labour Party (SDLP), especially following the 2003 elections, a vote that many have interpreted as signalling the end of the SDLP as a serious political force in the North. Roger MacGinty goes on to assess one of the more obvious political winners since 1998: Irish republicans. In a wide-ranging essay, he assesses how and why they accepted the peace process, and what their commitment to it is likely to be in the future. Gordon Gillespie concludes part II with a somewhat bleak assessment of a divided and dispirited loyalist community, suggesting that there will indeed be no farewell to arms for it, at least not without a significant change in the wider political scenery.

Does this mean, then, that the agreement is at a crossroads? Possibly so, according to part III's contributors, who seek to show why the Good Friday Agreement has reached an impasse. Colin McInnes suggests, in his contribution on decommissioning, that republicans have moved a very long way, but clearly not far enough to assuage unionist suspicion. Brice Dickson reinforces that message in his chapter: much progress may have been made in the reform of policing and human rights law, though both issues are just as likely to divide the two communities as unite them. Philip Lynch and Stephen Hopkins in a new contribution analyse one of the less-discussed aspects of the Good Friday Agreement: the British–Irish Council, a body seen to be a sop to Unionists in 1998, but one that has already moved beyond its narrow remit to discuss problems pertaining to all parts of the UK. Michael von Tangen Page revisits an issue that was once the focus of much soul-searching: prisoner release. John Darby ends part III by reminding us of the extent to which violence inherited from the past still haunts the present.

Part IV, which is mostly new, deals in detail with civil society in Northern Ireland. Peter Shirlow's contribution is a grim reminder to optimists that political deals are all well and good, but that segregation, social deprivation and 'the spatialisation of fear' all come together to make for a most unpleasant mix on the ground – a point powerfully reinforced later by Fiona Stephen in her discussion of the role of integrated schools. More numerous they may well be since the legislation supporting them was first passed, in 1989 (against much powerful local opposition), but even in 2004 the vast majority of children continued to be educated separately. John Morrison strikes a more optimistic note, perhaps, in his analysis of the voluntary sector and the new democratic space in Northern Ireland; so too, in his own way, does Feargal Cochrane, who examines the role of nongovernmental organisations more generally and the important part they have played in making and sustaining the peace process. Kate Fearon and Rachel Rebouche go on to look at the position of women and the disappointments suffered by the Women's Coalition in the context of the broader political impasse following the Good Friday Agreement. Cathall McCall concludes part IV by suggesting that at least one of the problems facing the peace process – and an ongoing source of conflict – stems from the simple fact that whereas Irish nationalists and republicans appear to be confidently striding forward, the same can hardly be said of their somewhat sullen, inward-looking and defensive neighbours on the unionist side.

In part V we return to the theme we made almost our own in the first edition: the once much-neglected international dimension. Paul Gillespie and Elizabeth Meehan again point to the importance of the European dimension to the Irish peace process. John Dumbrell then assesses the extent to which George W. Bush has continued the initial work of Bill Clinton in an age of terror. Adrian Guelke returns to the importance of political comparisons between Northern Ireland,

South Africa and the Middle East. John Loughlin and Francesco Letamendia do the same in relation to the Basque country and Corsica, while Fred Halliday provides another panoramic examination of peace processes across the world. The section as a whole concludes on a significant note of dispute, with Paul Dixon considering the importance of the international context and Michael Cox mounting a defence of his original thesis that the Cold War made a significant contribution to making the peace process a possibility. Though in no way denying the importance of domestic factors, Cox reiterates one of the major points made in the first edition: we need an all-round approach that works at as many levels as possible if we are to explain both the origins of the peace process and why the Good Friday Agreement, in and of itself, will not necessarily remove all the reasons for division in Northern Ireland.

In our concluding chapter, we return to our point of departure – with the Good Friday Agreement itself: it is quite possible that we will have to move beyond the agreement in order to get the Democratic Unionist Party (DUP) or the Ulster Unionist Party (UUP) back to the negotiating table. That is not, however, something which recommends itself to the British and Irish governments; even less does it command a great deal of support among those who seem to have gained most over the past few years: Irish republicans. This raises an intriguing question: would any government in London be prepared to risk republicans' wrath by seeking a new or renegotiated deal that would reassure unionists? The answer for the time being would seem to be a definitive no; and, for as long as it remains so, it is difficult to imagine an easy way out of the problems currently confronting the Northern Irish peace process.

PART I
From 'long war' to long peace

1

Lost lives: victims and the construction of 'victimhood' in Northern Ireland

MARIE SMYTH

Until the beginning of the peace process of the 1990s, any attempt at a comprehensive assessment of the human impact of the Troubles was deemed premature, and such assessments were limited to statements about the total number of fatal casualties and the estimated damage to the economy. For the most part, the society functioned on the basis of denial of the extent of the damage, so any examination of such damage while the conflict was ongoing was likely to underestimate it. Auditing the resulting harm, it seems, is a task associated with the end of conflict, a task which cannot be embarked on while the conflict is ongoing and survival is often the main goal.

It was only with the advent of the ceasefires of 1994 that an evaluation of the impact of the Troubles became more feasible. Even then, such an appraisal is fraught with difficulties. So divided is the society, and so complete the bifurcation of identity within Northern Ireland – and academics are not above these processes – that to arrive at a comprehensive overview of the humanitarian costs of the Troubles in Northern Ireland presents a challenge. The identifications of the assessor with one or other side of the conflict will tend to blind them to aspects of the total picture.

This chapter provides an overview of the human consequences of the Troubles from 1969–99, the most intense period of conflict, using deaths due to the conflict as an indicator. For this reason, the assessment of the impact of the Troubles presented here uses the relatively unequivocal measure of death in the Troubles. While there are some definitional issues[1] surrounding the use of death due to the Troubles, it is the least problematic in analytical terms. Death is also a reasonably good surrogate indicator for other effects of the Troubles, such as injury,[2] and the death rate of a geographical area is correlated with reported exposure to Troubles-related violence and its psycho-social consequences.[3] An examination of the number of deaths each year compared with the number of injuries associated with the Troubles shows a correlation coefficient of 0.93. Injuries outnumber deaths by approximately ten to one but follow the same patterns of distribution. Deaths and injuries together comprise the primary human cost of the Troubles.

The second part of the chapter provides a description of and commentary on the emergence of 'victim politics' and the construction of 'victimhood' during the Northern Ireland peace process from 1994 until the review of the Good Friday Agreement of September 1999.

Analysis of deaths in the Troubles

The analysis that follows is of a comprehensive database of deaths due to the Troubles between 1969 and 1998, compiled as part of *The Cost of the Troubles Study*, which is described and analysed in greater detail elsewhere.[4]

Deaths over time

The early 1970s saw the highest death rates of any in the thirty years of the Troubles. Table 1.1 shows that 1972 was the year in which the largest number of people died. Subsequently, in the late 1970s, as a result of security policies and shifting military and paramilitary strategies, the Troubles settled into what became known as 'an acceptable level of violence', a steady, if high, level of deaths that never again reached the peaks of the early 1970s.

Just over half of all deaths occurred in the period 1971-76. If the frequency of deaths can be regarded as a good indicator of the intensity of the conflict, then these five years stand out over the entire three decades. The key events were the introduction of internment in 1971, the proroguing of Stormont in 1972 and 1974, when the power-sharing Executive was brought down by the Ulster Workers' Council strike. After 1976, despite events such as the renewed loyalist strike in 1977 and the hunger strikes of the early 1980s, the number of deaths in any one year never again reached the same level and in only seven years was it greater than 100. Data on injuries confirm the concentration of violence in the 1970s, with almost a third of all injuries inflicted between 1972 and 1977.

Just over half of all deaths due to the British Army (163 deaths, or 51.6 per cent) occurred between 1971 and 1973 compared to 15.3 per cent (7 deaths) attributable to the RUC. Republican and loyalist paramilitaries were also responsible for a large number of deaths during this time (502 and 216 respectively), although it was not their most active period. The years 1971-73 saw the most proactive security activity by the army, indicated by the number and share of the total deaths due to them that occurred in the last five months in 1971 and all of 1972-73. Paramilitary peaks of activity came later, with 40 per cent of the deaths (452 deaths) perpetrated by loyalist paramilitaries occurring between 1974 and 1976. In the case of republican paramilitaries, 47 per cent of all the deaths they have been responsible for occurred in the period 1971–76.

Table 1.1   Distribution of deaths, 1969–98

Year	Frequency of deaths	% of total
1969	18	0.5
1970	26	0.7
1971	186	5.2
1972	497	13.8
1973	274	7.6
1974	307	8.5
1975	265	7.4
1976	314	8.7
1977	117	3.2
1978	83	2.3
1979	124	3.4
1980	86	2.4
1981	115	3.2
1982	112	3.1
1983	88	2.4
1984	74	2.1
1985	61	1.7
1986	64	1.8
1987	103	2.9
1988	105	2.9
1989	81	2.2
1990	84	2.3
1991	101	2.8
1992	93	2.6
1993	90	2.5
1994	68	1.9
1995	9	0.2
1996	21	0.6
1997	23	0.6
1998	12	0.3
Total	3,601	100.0
Average no. of deaths per year	120	

Cause of death

Overall, shooting was the main cause of death, followed by explosion. Nearly 91 per cent of victims died from these causes. Deaths caused by explosions were concentrated in the 1970s, whereas deaths due to shooting were fairly evenly distributed across the entire period.

Status of those killed

Table 1.2 shows deaths which ocurred between 1969 and 1994 (the year of the first IRA ceasefire) according to the status of the individuals involved. From table 1.2 it emerges that civilians rather than members of the security forces or republican or loyalist paramilitaries form the largest category of deaths, accounting for over half of those killed. The percentage of civilian deaths decreased in the period 1972-73 during the post-internment violence and increased in 1974-76 with the proliferation of bombings and sectarian attacks. The proportion of civilian deaths increased

Table 1.2   Deaths by status of victims, 1969–94

Year	Republicans	Loyalists	RUC	UDR/RIR	Army	Civilian	Civilian % of total
1969	2	1	1			14	78
1970	5		2		1	18	69
1971	24		10	5	46	97	53
1972	77	11	16	24	108	258	52
1973	39	13	13	10	59	135	50
1974	24	6	15	7	45	204	68
1975	24	26	12	7	15	178	68
1976	25	12	25	15	15	217	70
1977	15	5	15	14	15	49	43
1978	9	1	9	7	15	40	49
1979	16	1	14	10	38	39	33
1980	5	2	9	9	12	42	53
1981	21	2	21	14	10	42	38
1982	9	5	12	8	32	39	37
1983	9	2	18	10	6	37	45
1984	16	1	9	10	10	24	34
1985	8	1	23	4	2	21	36
1986	6	2	12	8	4	31	49
1987	24	5	16	8	3	43	43
1988	17	4	6	12	23	38	38
1989	6	2	8	2	26	34	44
1990	8	1	12	8	10	41	51
1991	14	2	7	7	5	60	63
1992	14	2	4	3	4	64	70
1993	5	1	6	2	6	65	76
1994	17	2	3	2	1	38	60
Total	439	110	298	206	511	1,868	
% of grand total	13	3	9	6	15	54	

again in the 1990s, although this was due partly to relatively low levels of security casualties.

Overall, members of paramilitary organisations make up 16 per cent of the total deaths and the total security force deaths make up a further 30 per cent. In other contemporary armed conflicts, the percentage of civilian casualties is often around 80–90 per cent. The pattern is similar for injuries, with the proportion of injured security force personnel at around 30 per cent.

Gender and age

Those killed in the Troubles have been overwhelmingly male (91.1 per cent) accounting for more than nine out of ten of all fatal casualties. Table 1.3 shows that the victims were skewed towards the younger age groups.

More than a third of victims were in their twenties; those in their twenties or thirties account for more than half the total number, and one in six victims were aged 19 or less. The death risk to the 20–24 age group was more than twice as high as that of any group over 40. Just under a quarter of all victims were aged 21 or less and half were aged 22–39. Almost three-quarters of those who died were under the age of 40.

Table 1.3   Age distribution of those killed

Age	Frequency	Per cent
0–4	21	0.6
5–9	17	0.5
10–14	51	1.4
15–19	468	13.1
20–24	720	20.2
25–29	578	16.2
30–34	427	12.0
35–39	330	9.3
40–44	231	6.5
45–49	205	5.8
50–54	186	5.2
55–59	124	3.5
60–64	96	2.7
65–69	47	1.3
70–74	36	1.0
75+	23	0.6
Total	3,560	100.0

Religion or ethno-political category

The religious (or ethno-political) breakdown of deaths in the Troubles is one of the most sensitive sets of figures, since it denies or supports the claim to greater suffering made by one or other community (see table 1.4). Religious affiliation was not recorded for victims from outside Northern Ireland (NNI). Furthermore, the data did not contain religious affiliation for a high proportion of deaths among Northern Ireland security forces, explaining the bulk of the 'not known' category.

An examination of the data on deaths shows that more Catholics than Protestants have died in the Troubles. Given the smaller proportion of Catholics in the general population, Catholics have a higher death risk than Protestants. I explore this further, as follows: since the local security forces are 92 per cent Protestant, this proportion was used to redistribute the 'not known' category in table 1.4 between the two religious groups (see table 1.5); changes in the relative size of the Catholic and Protestant populations of Northern Ireland were taken into account by calculating the rate either from the base of the 1991 census or from an average of the 1971, 1981 and 1991 censuses.

Columns 1 and 2 of table 1.5 show the death rates for Protestants and Catholics calculated from the base of the 1991 census only; columns 3 and 4 show the rates as calculated using a base of the average of the population figures in the three censuses, since the deaths occurred over a period in which there were changes in the religious balance of the population in Northern Ireland.

Table 1.4   Distribution of deaths by denomination

Religion	Frequency	Valid %
Don't know	333	9.2
Protestant	1,065	29.6
Catholic	1,548	43.0
NNI	655	18.2
Total	3601	100.0

Table 1.5   Death rates by denomination (per 1,000 population)

	1991 Census		Average '71, '81 and '91	
	Catholic	Protestant	Catholic	Protestant
Civilians	2.48	1.46	3.01	1.26
Civilians and security	2.5	1.9	3.1	1.6
Excluding 'own' deaths	1.9	1.6	2.3	1.4

In the first row of table 1.5 death rates for Catholic and Protestant civilians only are shown. Using the 1991 census figures alone, the rate is 2.48 per thousand for Catholic compared with 1.46 per thousand for Protestants; using the average of the three censuses, the rate becomes 3.01 per thousand for Catholics compared with 1.26 per thousand for Protestants.

To exclude security deaths, however, omits a cohort of deaths that are largely Protestant. Since substantial numbers of security deaths had missing values for religion, we re-calculated the death ratios, attributing 'Protestant' to a proportion of security deaths in accordance with the known religious composition of the security forces. The second row in table 1.5 shows that, using the 1991 census figures alone, the rate is then 2.5 per thousand for Catholics compared with 1.9 per thousand for Protestants. Using the average of the three censuses, the rate becomes 3.1 per thousand for Catholics compared with 1.6 per thousand for Protestants.

In the third row, all deaths that were attributable to perpetrators within the same community as the victim – all Catholics killed by republican paramilitaries and all Protestants killed by loyalist paramilitaries – were removed. This gives a new rate: using the 1991 census figures alone, the rate is 1.9 per thousand for Catholics compared with 1.6 per thousand for Protestants. Using the average of the three censuses, the rate becomes 2.3 per thousand for Catholic compared with 1.4 per thousand for Protestants.

The risk for the two groups varied substantially over time. Between 1969 and 1976 (using 1971 census figures) the Catholics' death risk was more than twice that of Protestants, whereas the converse appears to be true between 1977 and 1986. For the final period, the risk for Catholics was about 50 per cent greater. Overall, however, there have been more deaths in relative and absolute terms in the Catholic community in Northern Ireland than in the Protestant community.

Responsibility for deaths

Table 1.6 shows that paramilitary organisations were responsible for 80 per cent of all deaths and more than half of all deaths was the responsibility of republican paramilitaries. For each of their members who died, republican paramilitaries killed 5.5 other individuals, whereas loyalist paramilitaries killed 8.5 people for each of their members who was killed. The figure for the British Army was just over 0.5 persons and for the RUC just less than a sixth of a person.

The categories 'republican' and 'loyalist' paramilitaries each cover a number of different organisations. Within the republican grouping, the IRA (formerly the Provisional IRA) was responsible for the greatest number of deaths (1,684, or 85 per cent of those attributed to republican paramilitaries). Other republican organisations killed substantially fewer people, with the factions associated with the Irish National Liberation Army (INLA) killing 117 people. Limitations in the data meant that it was not possible to accurately attribute the deaths due to loyalist paramilitaries to the various loyalist organisations, so 449 deaths were simply attributed overall to loyalist organisations; of these, 254 were attributable to the Ulster Volunteer Force (UVF) and 117 to the Ulster Freedom Fighters (UFF).

Table 1.6   Organisations responsible for deaths

Organisation	Frequency	Valid %
Republican paramilitaries	2,001	55.7
Loyalist paramilitaries	983	27.4
British Army	318	8.9
UDR	11	0.3
RUC	53	1.5
Civilian	11	0.3
Other	216	6.0
Total	3,593	100.0

The conflict in Northern Ireland has given rise to much political rhetoric about defence of and opposition to the presence of the British State, and to perceptions about where the greatest threat to a community lies. Table 1.7 breaks down the deaths by religion according to the organisations responsible, and its data tend to support the perceptions of the two communities as to who constitutes the greatest threat to each. The largest share of Protestant deaths has been caused by republican organisations, which are responsible for 70 per cent of the total of Protestant deaths. If the 'not known' category is treated as before (that is, 92 per cent are regarded as Protestant) then republican paramilitaries have been responsible for over 80 per cent of all Protestant deaths in the Troubles. Conversely, almost half of the Catholic deaths are due to loyalist paramilitary activity, and over a fifth of the Catholic deaths are due to security force activity, with the British Army having played the most significant role.

The size of the threat posed by paramilitaries to their own communities also is clarified in table 1.7. Nearly a fifth of Protestant deaths are the responsibility of

Table 1.7   Deaths by denomination by organisation responsible

Organisation	Don't know	%	Protestant	%	Catholic	%	NNI	%
Republican paramilitaries	278	83.5	745	70.0	381	24.7	597	91.4
Loyalist paramilitaries	25	7.5	207	19.5	735	47.6	16	2.5
British Army	4	1.2	32	3.0	266	17.2	16	2.5
UDR			4	0.4	7	0.5		
RUC	1	0.3	7	0.7	43	2.8	2	0.3
Civilian			9	0.8	2	0.1		
Other	25	7.5	60	5.6	109	7.1	22	3.4
Total	333	100.0	1,064	100.0	1,543	100.0	653	100.0

loyalist paramilitaries and over a quarter of all Catholics killings were at the hands of republican paramilitaries. This latter figure is due in part to the republican bombing campaign, during which city-centre bombs caused random civilian casualties. The paramilitaries who claim to defend each community have in fact been a significant factor in the killings that have taken place within their own communities. Furthermore, republican paramilitaries have been the most significant cause of deaths of other feuding republicans, with the execution of informers providing the rationale. The British Army has been responsible for just over 30 per cent of deaths among republican paramilitaries, while republican paramilitaries themselves have been responsible for almost all the deaths of security forces (1,070). Overall, for every organisation responsible for deaths during the Troubles, the biggest single category of victim has been civilians.

Local deaths and fatal incidents

Overall, Belfast has the highest death rate of any district council area in Northern Ireland. The fatal-incident rate in Belfast (4.69 per thousand) compared to that in Ards (0.12 per thousand) illustrates the wide variation between areas in terms of their experience of the Troubles. The overall death rate for Northern Ireland is 2.2 per thousand. In terms of the absolute number of incidents, Belfast, Newry and Mourne, Derry, Armagh, Dungannon and Craigavon stand out. In both absolute and relative terms the greatest intensity of violent deaths has been in Belfast, with the rates per 1,000 head population almost twice as high as the adjoining district, Armagh. In some other areas, for example, Castlereagh and North Down, the number of residents killed has been greater than the number of fatal incidents. This is explained either by victims' membership of the security forces or perhaps by residents killed in bombs in city centres.

Elsewhere[5] further analysis of these data show that, even within district council areas, not all communities have been equally affected. Death rates for postal districts show how particular parts of Belfast, Derry/Londonderry, South Armagh and 'mid-Ulster' have experienced high intensities of violence. In terms of postal districts, BT14, BT12, BT13, BT15 and BT11, all in north and west Belfast, have the highest number of resident victims, followed by BT47 and BT48 – Derry/Londonderry – and BT34 and BT35 constituting Newry and South Armagh. Suffering has not been evenly distributed geographically, nor indeed according to gender, religion, status or age.

Victim culture in Northern Ireland

From the beginning of the peace process, and the announcement of the ceasefire by the Combined Loyalist Military Command (CLMC) in which they express 'abject and true remorse [to] the loved ones of all *innocent victims*' (my emphasis), the battle-lines on the issue of 'victims' were beginning to be drawn. The attempts to draw distinctions between categories of victims was to become more marked following the intensification of the activities of the anti-agreement lobby.

As the peace process progressed, the advisability of addressing the issues faced by those bereaved and injured in the Troubles was recognised first by the Irish Government. Its Forum for Peace and Reconciliation devoted two hearings to the issue in November 1995 and early in 1996, though, the reluctance of some unionists to participate in this exercise limited its usefulness.

By March 1995 the British Government had paid a total of £1,119,585,000 in compensation for the Troubles, £300,516,000 in damages to property and £814,219,000 in personal injuries. Expensive though this provision was, many did not qualify for compensation and there were obvious inequities in the compensation scheme. Nor did the scheme suffice in addressing the concerns of those who had been bereaved or injured, as the prospect of putting violence in the past became more substantial.

With all the complications of the peace process, the 1996 failure of the ceasefires and their subsequent reinstatement, consistent demands for the release of prisoners were frequently voiced from early on in the peace process by both republican and loyalist parties with links to paramilitary organisations. Concessions to prisoners were seen as important confidence-building measures, and included the repatriation of Irish prisoners held in British jails in late 1997. Prisoners were a crucial part of the peace process, and their views were regularly sought during negotiations. Indeed, the secretary of state, Mo Mowlam, met with prisoners in January 1998 in order to encourage their support for the peace process. On that occasion, she apologised to those bereaved and injured, justifying her action by reference to support for the peace process. Nonetheless, television coverage of this occasion enraged many. Government anticipated that the sensitivities of those bereaved and injured would form an obstacle to the acceptance of measures such as the early release of prisoners. Politicians in the early days of implementation made many such apologies to 'victims', referring to the larger goal of peace as justification for the measures they were implementing.

It was clear from an early stage that, if an agreement could be reached, concessions to prisoners would have to form part of it. Indeed, the Irish Government had already begun the process of early release by January 1995, and continued to release IRA prisoners from that time onwards. Within the voluntary sector, concern was being publicly expressed about the plight of those bereaved and injured, and voluntary groups offering services to this section of the population were experiencing an unprecedented increase in demand for their services. The Social Services Inspectorate had already begun the first official examination of 'services to meet the psychological needs of individuals affected by civil unrest in Northern Ireland'[6] under the direction of John Park. His report was to be published in March 1998, and would find that, by and large, those affected by the Troubles did not avail themselves of statutory services. The pressure was increasing on the Government to *manage* the unfolding peace process, and therefore to address the problems of those who had been bereaved and injured.

It has been argued that government policy in relation to victims of the Troubles has been entirely driven by the need to offset concessions made to prisoners with gestures to those who had suffered at the hands of those same prisoners and others. However, there is also some evidence that unionists pressed for the needs of certain sections of victims to be addressed, and that the secretary of state in particular had some humanitarian interest in the matter. Whatever the merits of that argument, in October 1997 the secretary of state appointed Sir Kenneth Bloomfield, former head of the Northern Ireland Civil Service and governor of BBC Northern Ireland, to act as a one-man Victims' Commission. His brief was to investigate the situation of 'those who had become victims in the last thirty years as a consequence of events in Northern Ireland, recognising that those events have had appalling repercussions for many people not living in Northern Ireland'.[7]

Bloomfield, assisted by Mary Butcher, Lady Mayhew's former secretary, embarked on a series of public meetings and consultations. Significantly, Bloomfield adopted a neutral definition of the population with which he was to concern himself, one which did not exclude by definition, for example, those bereaved or injured in state violence, or those with associations to paramilitary organisations. This was not to satisfy groups in the nationalist community such as Relatives for Justice, who saw Bloomfield's lack of explicit attention to state violence as problematical, and his inclusiveness as mere lip-service. Gaining the confidence of the nationalist community was always going to be a challenge for Bloomfield, coming as he did from a background in Stormont. However, nationalist mistrust notwithstanding, in hindsight it was arguably the backlash against his attempt at a neutral approach to 'victims' that provided the impetus to the later politicisation of the victims' issue by unionists, mainly from the anti-Agreement camp. Nor did it reassure unionists when the new British Labour Government was, as they saw it, giving further concessions to nationalists, such as its announcement in January 1998 of a new public inquiry into the events of Bloody Sunday in January 1972.

Meanwhile the violence continued, albeit at a lower level, leading first the Ulster Democratic Party and then Sinn Féin to be temporarily excluded from the talks for breaches of the ceasefire. Sporadic violent incidents and deaths continued. By then, dissident loyalists and republicans – the Loyalist Volunteer Force and the Continuity IRA – had organised themselves militarily.

In the negotiations leading up to the signing of the Good Friday Agreement (GFA), signed on 10 April 1998, the Northern Ireland Women's Coalition (NIWC) tabled a section on victims of the Troubles. Paragraphs 11 and 12 on page 18 of the published Agreement show what survived the negotiations.[8]

In her speech on the GFA in the House of Commons the secretary of state welcomed the Agreement and again returned to the subject:

> It is important when we are talking about all these positive developments that we do not lose sight of the terrible price that has been paid by the victims of violence and their families. No amount of progress in the search for lasting peace will bring back those loved ones who have been lost. But I hope that Ken Bloomfield's Victims' Commission will soon be in a position to provide us with some practical

suggestions as to how we can best recognise the suffering endured by the victims of violence and their families. I cannot say better than the words in the agreement itself. 'The achievement of a peaceful and just society would be the true memorial to the victims of violence.'[9]

Bloomfield published his report in May 1998. In the Introduction he wrote: 'In more than twenty five years of public service I have never been asked to undertake a task of such human sensitivity. The letters I have read and the stories I have heard in carrying out the work of the Commission will be burned in my memory forever.'[10] The report itself made no firm recommendations on a Truth Commission for Northern Ireland, but did offer a series of exhortations to employers, social services and other agencies to improve their practices in relation to those bereaved and injured. Significantly, Bloomfield recommended that 'victims must, at barest minimum, be as well served as former prisoners in terms of their rehabilitation, future employment, etc.'[11]

Bloomfield also recommended a review of the compensation scheme. The report's launch was accompanied by the announcement of a £5 million down-payment of funding by the Government for work with those bereaved and injured in the Troubles. The amount of money allocated was disappointingly low, but some comfort was taken from the description 'down-payment'.

At the launch of the Bloomfield Report, the secretary of state announced the appointment of Adam Ingram as minister for victims. However, Ingram already held the position of minister for security, and in his first months as minister for victims the security role seemed to occupy his time almost exclusively. It was perhaps ill-conceived to give Ingram a second area of responsibility on top of the heavy responsibility of security. Whatever the official rationale, the appointment was interpreted in some quarters as yet another signal that the victims' issue was not a high priority for the Government.

On 20 May, the minister for justice and law reform in the Irish Government, John O'Donoghue, appointed former Tanaiste John Wilson to review services to those affected by the Troubles who were living in the Republic of Ireland. A Victims' Commission was established in Dublin, and began work in the months following. Meanwhile, in the aftermath of the GFA, a referendum was conducted in which 71 per cent of voters supported the Agreement. The anti-Agreement forces – the DUP and the Independent Unionist Party – seemed vanquished.

In June 1998, the Victims' Liaison Unit at Stormont was established to 'take forward the process of identifying and prioritising a packages of measures to help victims, their families and support groups'; a small team of civil servants from various departments was deployed for the purpose. By June 1998, an 'initial support package' of expenditure on victims was announced. The money was to go towards establishing a trauma unit for young people affected by the Troubles, and towards supporting local groups including Survivors of Trauma, Widows Against Violence Empower (WAVE) and Families Against Intimidation and Terror (FAIT). The total expenditure came out of the initial £5 million announced in May 1998. The allocation of money to FAIT, a group specialising not in service provision to victims, but in campaigning against punishment attacks by paramilitaries, drew the fury of one Sinn Féin assemblyman, who complained of its political nature. Anyway, the funding allocated to FAIT was subsequently withdrawn following disclosures of irregularities and conflict within the organisation.

Violence continued sporadically. Three young brothers were killed in July in a petrol-bombing incident when their home in Ballymoney was attacked. Mo Mowlam wrote an article for the *Belfast Newsletter* on 14 July 1998 in which she addressed the tragedy of their deaths, but went on to the image of 'David Trimble and Seamus Mallon standing together to condemn the killing and pledging their commitment to finding a resolution to the parades issue'. The goal of peace was still worth striving for. Yet the sectarian attack on the family was conducted by those in a section of loyalism that, increasingly, would have no truck with such images, nor with the peace process itself.

The media debate on the early release of prisoners continued. By early August, such newspaper headlines as 'He Lost Five Loved Ones in the Troubles Yet He Is For the Releases'[12] was posing the issue of prisoner releases alongside that of victims' feelings and experiences.

On 12 August, Adam Ingram announced the launch of a £250k educational bursary scheme for those who had lost a parent in the Troubles, and a memorial fund with matching funding of £1 million. Ingram also announced a formal review of the compensation scheme, which had been recommended in the Bloomfield Report.

On 20 August 1998, a massive explosion in Omagh town-centre killed thirty people including two unborn babies, and one more person was to die later. The bomb had been planted by the Real IRA. Shock and revulsion overcame the political process, and Omagh became the focus of attention on the issue of victims for a considerable period. Ministerial visits to Omagh were followed over subsequent months by announcements of various public investments in the town and surrounding area. The Omagh Fund was established, and fund-raising for it became widespread. The Omagh bombing provided a clear focus for concern about victims; furthermore, there was political unity in the condemnation of the bombing. It was reasonably clear what was needed in Omagh, and the Government and public figures could do something positive about the victims' issue. The scale of the suffering of the people in the Omagh bombing served to sideline all other victims' concerns temporarily, although the atmosphere was sustained by events such as President Clinton's visit to the town and by continued fund-raising activities.

A growing number of new groups, FAIR (Families Acting for Innocent Relatives) and HURT (Homes United by Republican Terror, later changed to Homes United by Recurring Terror), for example, had been formed over the previous months, many of them in the border regions, some of them adopting 'exclusive' approaches to membership, claiming to represent 'innocent victims', 'victims of terrorism' or 'victims of nationalist terror'. These groups began a round of meetings with politicians in which their representatives voiced opposition to prisoner releases. By November 1998, FAIR had been invited to join the Touchstone Group, established on Bloomfield's recommendation to advise the Government on victims' issues, although FAIR's delegates did not take up their seats. From another quarter, the Victims' Liaison Unit had been under pressure for some time to include prisoners in its remit, but with the increasing pressure from other quarters this became increasingly less likely to happen.

The Bloomfield Report had also drawn attention to the issue of the families of those who had 'disappeared', recommending that 'every effort should be made to persuade and enable those with information about the disappeared to disclose it'.[13] Subsequently, legislation – Northern Ireland (Location of Victims' Remains) Act 1999 – was introduced at Westminster on 26 May 1999 which limited the use of the results of forensic testing of bodies and offered protection to those coming forward with information about the location of bodies. The Victims' Commission played a key role in facilitating a number of excavations in the Republic of Ireland, in June 1999, work that stretched over a number of months. In spite of all the efforts, only 3 out of a total of 12 missing bodies were found as a result of excavations, although Jean McKendry's body was later discovered, in 2003, long after the excavations and searches had ended. Either the information given by the IRA had been inaccurate or environmental factors had intervened to thwart the majority of the searches. The period of the searches was characterised by increased tension and expectancy for the families of the disappeared, and by growing embarrassment for republicans.

The political process, meanwhile, had become stuck. On the one hand, the issue of decommissioning and, on the other, the failure to implement the Agreement and establish an executive constituted a stalemate. After the resignation of Deputy First Minister Seamus Mallon, Ulster Unionist leader David Trimble presided alone, balking at any movement on further implementation. Complaints about the status of the IRA ceasefire, and about continuing paramilitary punishment attacks, buttressed his scepticism about Sinn Féin's intentions. FAIT, a group originally considered for funding under the provisions for victims, monitored and regularly publicised such paramilitary punishment attacks, adding to the grounds for Trimble's scepticism. Added to this, recurrent media coverage of the expenditure on the resettlement of prisoners[14] promoted an increasing cynicism about the peace process and the agreement.

This ethos was further crystallised by the announcement of the campaign for 'Protestant civil rights' in the form of a 'long march'; the campaign incorporated many of the newly formed victims' groups, FAIR and HURT being among those which came together under the umbrella organisation Northern Ireland Terrorist Victims Together. NITVT campaigned for a range of demands, including: a declaration by the IRA that the war is over; decommissioning, including ballistic testing, of weapons; destruction of paramilitary weapons; disbandment of terrorist groups; and an international tribunal to investigate the role of the Irish Government in the development of the Provisional IRA. Anti-Agreement politicians, from the

DUP and the UUP, marched alongside those from the victims' groups, and other supporters, including Nell McCafferty from the 1960s' Northern Ireland Civil Rights Association.

Finally, as the UUP distanced itself from the prospect of an established Executive, its members, too, became more deeply involved with victims. Michelle Williamson, whose parents were killed in the Shankill Road bombing in 1993, was supported by the UUP in taking a court action seeking a judicial review of the secretary of state's ruling on the status of the IRA ceasefire. Were this ruling to be overturned, Sinn Féin would be excluded from the political process. David Trimble accompanied her to court.

By the end of September 1999, Fraser Agnew, United Unionist Assembly Party member, resigned from the long march campaign, saying: 'I believe innocent victims are being manipulated and exploited for political ends. It's almost like emotional blackmail.'

Definition of 'victim' and 'victim' status

It has been argued elsewhere[15] that, as a result of the particular history of Northern Ireland, the political cultures of contemporary loyalism and republicanism are cultures of victimhood. The status of victimhood brings with it certain dispensations and political advantages: the victim is deserving of sympathy, support, outside help, and intervention by others to vanquish the victimiser. The victim by definition is vulnerable and requires allies for protection or rescue from the outside. Any attack conducted by the victim can be construed as self-defence and can therefore be justified, thereby legitimising violence carried out by or on behalf of victims. It is perhaps predictable that the armed factions in the conflict, particularly those who have killed and injured others, should wish to lay claim to victimhood, for without such a status their violence is apparently politically inexplicable and morally indefensible.

The politics of both loyalists and republicans rely on their respective senses of victimisation in justifying their recourse to armed conflict. Loyalists see themselves as victims of the IRA and of the incipient threat of Roman Catholic hegemony, whereas republicans see themselves as the victims of British imperialism and of loyalist sectarianism. In the wider political dynamic of conflict, neither of the protagonist groups can afford to portray itself as the victimiser, since to do so would shift the moral ground to their disadvantage. The implications for political culture when victimhood becomes an institutionalised means of escaping guilt, shame or responsibility are far-reaching. A political culture based on competing claims to victimhood is likely to support and legitimise violence, and is unlikely to foster an atmosphere of political responsibility and maturity.

The conditions and atmosphere within which political violence takes place, and its concomitant fears and divisions, have pervasive effects, not merely on those who are injured or killed, but on a much wider section, if not the entirety of the population. The social and political institutions of Northern Ireland have been shaped by the divisions within the society and have adjusted themselves in response to ongoing violent conflict; and in that sense they can universally be regarded as 'victims'. Indeed, *all* residents of Northern Ireland – and beyond – have been adversely affected in diverse ways by the attritional effects of three decades of violence, their antecedents and consequences, and therefore could all be regarded in some sense as 'victims'. Official endorsement of this universalist definition was contained in the Bloomfield Report, which found 'some substance in the argument that no-one living in Northern Ireland through this most unhappy period will have escaped some degree of damage'.[16]

In practical terms, however, a universal definition of the 'victim' does not facilitate the targeting of humanitarian resources, and it can mask the way in which damage and loss has been concentrated in certain geographical areas, communities, occupational groups, age groups and genders. Universal definitions are therefore impracticable in social policy terms. Indeed, Bloomfield refers to the need of the Victims' Commission 'to aim its effort at a coherent and manageable target group'.[17] However, the definition in the Bloomfield Report was not narrowed in a way that excluded either those who did not support the State or those who were recipients of state violence. That was to occur in the local political arena.

The political nature and 'appropriation' of victims' issues

L. M. Thomas[18] has described the prevalent view that those who have endured great suffering, Holocaust survivors for example, are potential or actual 'moral beacons' in the wider world. In discussing the rivalry in suffering between Jews and blacks in the US, Thomas refers to what he calls the 'Principle of Job', namely that 'great suffering carries in its wake deep moral knowledge'[19] and that the victims of such suffering may become appointed or act as 'moral beacons' for the wider society. Such figures are often held up to us, overtly or by implication, to point to some higher state that we should strive for, some feat of self-transformation that we should attempt to achieve. Their stories lead us to marvel at the resilience of the human spirit, and perhaps to see something of ourselves in them. Gordon Wilson, whose daughter, Marie, was killed in the Enniskillen bombing, is perhaps the best example of a moral beacon in the recent history of Northern Ireland. He was forgiving of his daughter's killers and conciliatory in his political attitudes, although his acceptance of a seat in the Irish Senate compromised his acceptability in these terms to some unionists.

Thomas discusses who is eligible for such appointment, and it is clear that while Jews in the US have been appointed to such positions, blacks, although qualified by the suffering of slavery to fill the role, tend not to be so regarded. So suffering *per se* is not a sufficient qualification. Neither is sustaining loss in the Troubles a sufficient qualification for such a role. The widow of the alleged informer, the victim of punishment beatings or the wife of a prisoner are unlikely to qualify as moral beacons, in spite of their endurance of suffering. The suffering must be recognised as *undeserved* according to dominant values. In deeply divided societies, attitudes to suffering tend to diverge; usually the suffering of one side is not easily recognised or acknowledged by the other. The production of a 'moral beacon' about whom there is consensus is therefore problematical, since one side's suffering can be a source of the other side's triumph. Gordon Wilson's acceptance of a seat in the Irish Senate arguably disqualified him as a moral figure for sections of the loyalist community, for example. The moral beacon must be congruent with the dominant political values. The increasing political role of victims' groups which exclude sections of those bereaved or injured in the Troubles is the manifestation of this in Northern Ireland.

Moral qualifications of victims

It is often taken for granted that those who have so suffered are morally developed, in some way, by suffering and are therefore suited to a role of moral leadership. However, Vicktor Frankl's[20] description of his experiences in the death camps of the Second World War would cast some doubt on this assumption. He describes how, for example, some prisoners jeopardised others' lives in order to save themselves and how suffering can destroy moral integrity. Furthermore, the experience of great suffering, in this case in Northern Ireland's Troubles, is also commonly used to explain subsequent violent behaviour. Colin Crawford[21] thus found that 30 per cent of the loyalist prisoners he interviewed had 'members of their family' killed by the IRA – republicans – although he does not qualify the requisite closeness of relationship in his definition of 'family'. The implication that the experience of bereavement explains the motivation to violent and vengeful acts is again taken for granted.

It seems that great suffering is perceived as having one of two main – social, political and/or moral – outcomes: as motivating revenge; or, if the sufferer manages to avoid being driven towards vengeance, as morally educative, so qualifying the sufferer to act as a 'moral beacon'.

The media in Northern Ireland adopted a practice in interviews with the newly bereaved of asking immediate family members if they forgive the perpetrator – often within hours or days of the death. The bereaved person becomes a moral benchmark by which the public can read off the degree of its own entitlement to anger, desire for revenge or impulses towards retaliation. Through the victim, a message is sent to the people at large about their own state of comparative forgiveness or blame, and how they measure up to those who are most entitled to blame and seek revenge – those closest to the loss. The victim functions as a potential or actual moral beacon. It is this function that politicians have striven to appropriate. By association with victims, they bring unassailable moral authority to their cause. The entry of the 'qualified' victim onto the political stage was, perhaps, always only a matter of time.

As the political profile of so-called 'victims issues' increases, attention is deflected from the humanitarian agenda. That the poorest people have suffered most in the Troubles, that they live in communities blighted with militarism and deprivation, and that the amount of humanitarian assistance to them is paltry are no longer matters of public attention. Progress on policy development on the victims' issue in the political arena, like many other issues in Northern Ireland, is a casualty of the remaining political chasm that yawns between unionists and nationalists. Such progress may well be made, but it is to be doubted whether it will be politicians who achieve it.

Notes

1 See M.-T. Fay, M. Morrissey and M. Smyth, *Northern Ireland's Troubles: The Human Costs* (London: Pluto, 1999) pp. 126–32.
2 *Ibid.*, p. 136.
3 See M.-T. Fay, M. Morrissey, M. Smyth and T. Wong, *The Cost of the Troubles Study. Report on the Northern Ireland Survey: The Experience and Impact of the Troubles* (Derry, Londonderry: INCORE, 1999).
4 Fay, Morrissey and Smyth, *Northern Ireland's Troubles*.
5 *Ibid.*
6 Social Services Inspectorate, Department of Health and Social Services, *Living with the Trauma of the Troubles: A Report on a Developmental Project to Examine and Promote the Further Development of Services to Meet the Social and Psychological Needs of Individuals Affected by Civil Unrest in Northern Ireland* (Belfast: Stationery Office, 1998).
7 K. Bloomfield, *We Will Remember Them: Report of the Northern Ireland Victims' Commissioner, Sir Kenneth Bloomfield* (Belfast: HMSO: Stationery Office, 1998), p. 8.
8 See, for the Good Friday Agreement, Appendix 2.
9 Northern Ireland Office press release, 20 April 1998.
10 Social Services Inspectorate, *Living with the Trauma of the Troubles*, p. 6.
11 *Ibid.*, para. 5.26, p. 33.
12 *Sunday World*, 9 September 1998.
13 Northern Ireland (Location of Victims' Remains) Act 1999, para. 5.38.
14 Outrage Shock Costs of Giving Prisoners New Lease of Life', *Belfast Telegraph*, 4 June 1999.
15 M. Smyth, 'Remembering in Northern Ireland: Victims, Perpetrators and Hierarchies of Pain and Responsibility', in B. Hamber (ed.), *Past Imperfect: Dealing with the Past in Northern Ireland and Societies in Transition* (Derry–Londonderry: INCORE, 1988).
16 Bloomfield, *We Will Remember Them*, para. 2.13, p. 14.
17 Bloomfield, *We Will Remember Them*.
18 L. M. Thomas, 'Suffering as a Moral Beacon: Blacks and Jews', in H. Flazbaum (ed.), *The Americanisation of the Holocaust* (Baltimore, MD: Johns Hopkins University Press, 1999).
19 *Ibid.*, p. 204.
20 V. Frankl, *Man's Search for Meaning* (Boston, MA: Beacon Press, 1959).
21 C. Crawford, *Defenders of Criminals? Loyalist Prisoners and Criminalisation* (Belfast: Blackstaff Press, 1999).

2

The background to the Irish peace process[1]

MARTIN MANSERGH

When the Troubles finally broke out in Derry in August 1969, I was with my family in County Cork. Nightly, with other guests and locals, we crowded around the hotel's television. My brother and I discussed with my father the significance of what was happening – he had grown up in Tipperary during the war of independence and was convinced that sooner or later the IRA would re-emerge and dominate events. Having been in college during the time of student unrest and familiar with the international culture of protest of the 1960s, we argued strongly that this was about civil rights, and was completely different from old-style nationalism. With the typically critical, but not self-critical, assurance of youth, we felt that my father, who was a historian, understood the Ireland of the 1920s much better than he did the Ireland of the late 1960s. We all know who was right and who was wrong!

The tension between old and new was summarised by J. Bowyer Bell in the conclusion to his monumental book on the Irish Troubles, in which he noted that, by the end of the 1960s the newly emergent values had not had sufficient time to permeate:

> In the end the Troubles came because Ireland was improperly synchronised; it was no one's fault and not easy to predict. The old values had not eroded and the new opportunities had not attracted ... The traditional rites and rituals seemed so natural, so easy. These ways offered great benefits, Orange and Green, often unavowed, often psychological, not economic or political, often to those denied elsewhere by the existing organisation of society and the island. So there were always new and frantic believers suddenly converted to the past as the means into the future. Those who sought to act on events, to make history to history's patterns, had the legitimisation of the past as authority.[2]

The peace process has to resolve much more than the Troubles of the past twenty-five years: it has to address the whole legacy of history and the many unresolved problems inherited from the past. Those festering problems have helped to prolong and intensify the Troubles, which cost well over 3,000 lives and claimed many times more victims in terms of injuries or personal grief and trauma.

All of us must ask ourselves, as historians will ask, whether the Troubles had to go on for so long? What could have prevented them from breaking out in the first place? Could they have been channelled into more peaceful political methods? Could they have been brought to an end sooner and with the loss of fewer lives? No definitive conclusions can be drawn; nevertheless, I offer my own answers to and personal reflections on those questions.

In the period 1886–1918, the battle for home rule was fought, won and lost. The demand itself was a compromise, but deferring its implementation and conceding an indefinite derogation to six of the Ulster counties was more than it was able to bear. Whether a firmer stand by the British Government, less reckless opportunism by the Conservative opposition or a more accommodating attitude on the part of nationalists to specific concerns of Ulster unionists would have made a decisive difference is difficult to say. Nationalists of Parnell's day tended to see simply the *reactionary* elements, what A. T. Q. Stewart in 1967 called 'the last ditch stand of the Ascendancy'.[3] They were little conscious of genuine differences in political and cultural identity or of differences in economic interests between the more industrialised north-east and the rest of the island; and they were dismissive of religious fears.

What eventually emerged was the result not of democratic debate but of relationships of power. Lloyd George himself told Arthur Griffith during the 1921 Treaty negotiations that in the pre-war years, led by the instinct of trained politicians, the whole force of the opposition concentrated on Ulster: 'Ulster was arming and would fight. We were powerless. The politician who thinks he can deal out abstract justice without reference to forces around him cannot govern.'[4]

The new compromise that emerged from the crucible of conflict allowed Ulster unionists and the bulk of Irish nationalists to go their separate ways. From 1916 on, full independence and sovereignty took precedence over a unity that appeared remote, while preservation of the Union in the area where unionists were most concentrated superseded the Union as a whole, and included three of Ulster's nine counties being 'written off'.

Sir Alfred Cope, Sinn Féin's chief contact in Dublin Castle, made a fascinating proposal on 3 September 1921 (recorded in Tom Jones's diary) that Lloyd George should do one of two things: either tell the north-east publicly that they must come in or lose Fermanagh and Tyrone, and then the South would give up independence [meaning full republican status], or offer the Dail acceptance of the republic, on condition that they met other British interests.[5] In 1947, speaking in Chatham House at a time when India was on everyone's mind, my father argued that the British government had made a mistake in not accepting the external association formula in 1921.[6] Cope felt that if the Dail were offered independence, they might give up unity, or that if they were given unity, they would give up independence. It was a question of symbolism. The tragedy of the 1921 settlement was that it did not at the time clearly offer one or the other. It brought civil war in the South and sporadic violence leading to civil war in the North after a delay of fifty years. One can sometimes speculate whether, if the present consequences of the resistance to Home Rule could have been foreseen, Ulster unionists would have chosen to act any differently. I conclude, a little sadly, that the answer, with one or two exceptions, would have been 'No'.

The backdrop to the war of independence had been the doctrine of national self-determination proclaimed by President Woodrow Wilson. Ireland's right to self-determination was not overtly recognised or accepted by the British at that time. Indeed, as late as 1941, Churchill was maintaining that 'juridically, we have never recognised that southern Ireland is an independent sovereign State'.[7] The legitimacy of Irish neutrality during the Second World War was not fully accepted; indeed, until both states became members of the European Community and had to treat each other as partners in a multilateral setting, a mindset of mutual resentment lingered in British–Irish relations. Nevertheless, when the dust had settled, the 1921 settlement appeared to give southern nationalists and northern unionists broadly what they wanted. Southern unionists and Protestants for a time enjoyed special representation in the Free State Senate and a fair degree of toler-ation, even if the society was not pluralist in the modern sense; and for a further three or four decades, they still owned a lot of such wealth as there was.

The unequivocal losers were northern nationalists. Eamon Phoenix has described the disastrous divisions among northern nationalists, as they faced acute political dilemmas:[8] republican separatism in the South left them with 'little or no influence' in the North; southern policy towards the North was inconsistent and ineffective; and the Belfast boycott was a disaster, breaking the economic unity of the country with no benefit to show. Michael Collins tried to exert some counter-productive physical leverage, but the civil war relieved all serious political pressure on the North. The four safeguards in the Government of Ireland Act 1920 and the 1921 Treaty – proportional representation, the Council of Ireland, the non-discrimination clause and the Boundary Commission – were either dismantled or ignored.

In 1925, given a choice between negotiating an emancipation of the minority (and Kevin O'Higgins stated in negotiations with Baldwin, the British prime minister, and in the presence of Craig, that 'it was not just rhetoric to say that the Catholic nationalists are living in conditions of Catholics prior to Catholic emancipation'), or abolishing some of the financial obligations on the Free State under the 1921 Treaty, the Cosgrave Government eagerly grasped the latter. Craig offered occasional meetings, which never took place, instead of the Council of Ireland, and gave as evidence that there was no real problem in inter-community relations, that Lady Craig had recently been invited to a bridge evening with Catholics and that a Protestant doctor had been invited to open a Catholic bazaar![9]

A few liberal unionists, like General Hugh Montgomery, founder of the Irish Association, had serious doubts about the treatment of the minority by the unionist majority. After a long period of political estrangement, which probably reached its height during the counterproductive anti-partition campaign, the tentative rapprochement between Lemass (and later Lynch) and O'Neill touched on possibilities of cooperation between northern unionism and the southern nationalist State, without directly addressing issues of discrimination, such as the siting of the new university at Coleraine rather than Derry, which remained rampant in unionist government decisions during the 1960s. In the state of the world prior to the 1960s, with the upheavals of the Second World War in Europe, the communist blanket over Eastern Europe, and the continued existence of colonial empires, the situation of northern nationalists was not especially noteworthy.

The IRA campaigns of 1939 and 1956-62 were remarkably ineffective. Why was the experience post-1970 so different? How did the civil rights campaign give way so quickly to a campaign of terror not unlike that which followed the French Revolution? I believe two events in 1970, one in Britain, one in Ireland, had a great influence. Whatever the later merits of imposing direct rule and of Sunningdale, the change of government in Britain from Labour to Conservative replaced the initial reformist approach and sensitivity with a determination to restore order and to give clear backing to the Stormont regime, most clearly shown a year later with the introduction of internment, followed by Bloody Sunday, when fourteen unarmed civilians were shot dead in Derry in an apparently premeditated way.

In 1922 the British Government had withdrawn politically and psychologically from Ireland and its problems, and there was enormous reluctance in the late 1960s to become directly involved again. In the end, the unrest was so great – and following Jack Lynch's August 1969 broadcast there was the risk, from the British point of view, that, if they did not intervene, others might be forced to do so – that the British Army was sent in.

Initially, the hope was to resolve the problem with some limited reforms and then to withdraw again. The prospect that unionist hegemony would be propped up and that for most purposes nationalists would remain second-class citizens, despite the obvious failure of the unionist State, was enough to bring a section of the nationalist population to decide that democratic protest was ineffectual, and that it was time for the traditional recourse to arms, a solution that had never been systematically tried in the North before, but one that would complete the task begun in 1916–21.

There was little analysis of the differences between the situation in the North and the situation in the rest of the country fifty years earlier, differences that had given most of the leaders of the independence struggle pause for thought and had led them to agree, with varying degrees of conviction, that, whatever the rights of the situation, coercion of the North was not practicable. Eamon de Valera's 1957 Ard Fheis speech was particularly lucid: he said that a forced unity, even if it could be brought about, would ruin national life for generations.

The other catalyst, I believe, was the arms crisis in the South. It was then that the Irish Government, recoiling from giving any assistance for self-defence for fear of misuse, lost all restraining political influence over militant republicanism in the North, a situation that would continue for almost twenty years. Post-1970, notwithstanding certain critical moments when public emotions ran high, the South may have been secured and stabilised, but militant nationalists regarded themselves as on their own. It has taken twenty-four years to find the way back to conditions of peace.

While the British twice held discussions with republicans, in 1972 and 1975, and thereafter maintained some limited and covert channel, there was no direct line of political communication on the Irish Government's side, as far as I am aware, apart from limited, mostly indirect, contacts at the time of the hunger strikes. The prevailing orthodoxy, based on a combination of the arms crisis experience and concern about the effects of the failed British attempts to negotiate bilaterally, was that there should be no contact of any kind between governments and paramilitary spokespersons for fear of giving the latter the impression that they were winning, and also to demonstrate moral distance and, indeed, repugnance. As late as two weeks before the IRA ceasefire in mid-August 1994, Dr Garret Fitzgerald, the principal guardian of this orthodoxy, said that he was disturbed by reports that I was in direct contact with republicans.[10] All of this presupposed that the paramilitaries could be militarily defeated or forced to stop by political developments or by public political exhortation from a distance.

John Hume showed great political courage in engaging in dialogue, publicly and privately, from the second half of the 1980s. The pressures that were placed on him took a severe toll at the time, especially in 1993 and 1994. Even though Albert Reynolds met Gerry Adams for the first time only on 6 September 1994, it was the culmination of a willingness to take enormous political risks for the sake of peace, taking up the initiative begun a few years earlier by Charles Haughey. It is difficult to make omelettes without breaking eggs. All of us were conscious that in politics the dividing line between success and debacle is often a very thin one and that we had to be ready, if necessary, to sacrifice our jobs and perhaps even put ourselves at risk. To foster people's willingness to make critical strategic decisions for their movements – decisions which carried far greater risks for them – a relationship of trust had to be created, and that was all but impossible to do at a distance. In December 1993, when potentially actionable reports started to appear in the British tabloid press about meetings with IRA and UVF leaders north of the border, I recall going home at the weekend to Tipperary and feeling comforted to hear that, regardless of the truth or otherwise of those reports, everyone was behind me.

Let us consider all the factors that have contributed to the present situation. Attempts to defeat the IRA by military or security measures had failed, although there was some success in containing the violence, to the extent that, after the carnage of the early to mid-1970s, deaths from all sources settled to around 80–100 a year, what was controversially called 'the acceptable level of violence'. Events like the Enniskillen bombing in 1987, the kidnapping and mutilation of a Dublin dentist, and the Eksund arms shipment facilitated the introduction of new extradition legislation and tough security measures.

Close security cooperation was necessary, both to protect the people of this state and to prevent as far as possible cross-border attacks that might invite retaliation. While the fortunes of war continually fluctuated, the overall situation was a prolonged military stalemate, with the risk after particular incidents and at times of high tension that the situation would get completely out of hand, creating large numbers of civilian casualties. A factor in the previous few years had been the increasing intensity of loyalist violence, which was beginning to outstrip republican violence.

A second factor was the initiatives designed to achieve a political settlement between mainstream unionists and nationalists. The only one to get off the ground, Sunningdale, had its democratic legitimacy fatally undermined by the *mal-à-propos* British election of February 1974, and failed to quell either republican or loyalist violence. It was brought down by the clearest exercise of the unionist veto since 1912-14. Inter-party talks between 1975 and 1980, predicated on an internal settlement, went nowhere. From 1980, the focus shifted to the Anglo-Irish framework promoted by the two governments, a shift resisted by unionists for well over a decade. The Anglo-Irish Agreement was intended in part to galvanise the unionists into talks. The discussions between the parties, which began in 1991 under the auspices of Northern Ireland Secretary of State Peter Brooke and continued under Sir Patrick Mayhew, and the subsequent bilateral talks and preparation of the Framework Document, created the possibility that these would turn at some point into serious negotiations that would culminate in a political settlement, however remote that prospect may at times have appeared.

Despite occasional appearances to the contrary, in 1993 and 1994 the peace process and the talks process were not in conflict or competition; they were in fact complementary. Republicans felt they should be present at any real negotiations on the political future of Ireland. Not only could the Government not afford to admit defeat on the question of restarting the talks, but it had to maintain its determination to secure such negotiations. In the spring of 1994, following a three-month pause after the Downing Street Declaration, they resumed their efforts, making it clear that they were not prepared to wait on Sinn Féin's decision on the declaration. At the same time, Albert Reynolds felt that to wait for peace until some time after a political settlement between unionists and nationalists had been made, might involve waiting until kingdom come, with no guarantee that a settlement from which the direct parties to the conflict were excluded would necessarily or automatically bring an end to violence: witness Sunningdale. Understandably, perhaps, unionists were not keen to negotiate while violence was ongoing, especially with no assurance that any concessions they might make would be sufficient to bring peace.

A further factor was the power of opinion. In the North, the SDLP, with its advocacy of a purely peaceful approach, succeeded in retaining the support of a majority of nationalists, despite a strong electoral challenge from Sinn Féin following the hunger strikes, when it developed its twin 'armalite and ballot-box' strategy. The main Christian denominations, with a few individual clerical exceptions, set their face against paramilitary violence, and tried to foster better inter-community relations, with varying degrees of success. Other groups – permanent, like the trade unions, or transitory, like the peace people and similar later bodies – worked strongly for peace. In the South, despite its republican origins and aims, successive governments turned their face firmly against the use of violence, and pursued to the best of their ability, in difficult circumstances, policies of compromise and conciliation. By and large, writers and broadcasters encouraged a better understanding of the past, including a recognition of different traditions. Sometimes, though, revisionism went overboard. In consequence, there was a risk, first, of making a present of past freedom struggles to the IRA and treating them as the true successors of the founders of this State, thus in a sense delegitimising the State, and, second, of underwriting the threat of loyalist paramilitary resistance not just to imposed constitutional change but to all forms of reasonable democratic compromise.

One prominent Fianna Fáil deputy, who went on to play an important role in improving Anglo-Irish and North–South relations, told me that the turning point for him was observing the invasion of Cyprus in August 1974, which instead of ending partition cemented it. My impression is that a certain and understandable ambivalence at the start among a section of the population in the South gave way over time to a more decided rejection of methods of violence. Paramilitary-associated parties were unable to win any significant electoral support, apart from during the brief period of the hunger strikes. Even those most directly involved were horrified by some of the things that took place, whether accidentally or by way of retaliation. The truth – that in war many people not in any way involved are killed – was hammered home relentlessly by events.

The physical and material ability to carry on the long war almost indefinitely was not in doubt. Whether there was the moral capacity to do so – with no realistic prospect of a military or political breakthrough, allied to the gradual realisation that political aims cannot be advanced in this way and may even go backwards, and to a sense of responsibility towards those involved – was, however, something that had to be assessed. Paramilitary violence on both sides represented a form of political veto. While it was capable of prolonging the stalemate and frustrating political initiatives, it could advance little. As Gerry Adams has acknowledged, republicans could not achieve their aims on their own.

Apartheid and communism collapsed not so much through material default but through a loss of conviction. The value of continued struggle in the face of a gradually intensifying public hostility was open to question. I believe that, had the violence continued much longer, some of the parties in this State would have become increasingly reluctant under any conditions to sit round the table with those they held responsible – a trend in opinion that had to be taken into account. There are some dangerous myths around, accepted not only by those involved but by many independent commentators. While I do not agree that violence has never had any political effect, I see absolutely no evidence from our dealings with the British Government, or indeed its dealings with anyone else, that it was materially swayed by bombs in the City of London. The Downing Street Declaration came about for quite other political reasons; left to itself, the British Government was set to go in a different direction. The decision to situate bombs at Heathrow Airport, in March 1994, bombs which failed to explode and to which Albert Reynolds reacted very strongly, showed a serious failure in psychological understanding; *a fortiori*, anyone tempted to believe that some future political impasse could be broken by a renewed bombing campaign in the City of London would be disastrously mistaken. I also believe that, if the loyalists had bombed Dublin in 1994, far from weakening the resolve of the Government and the people to achieve an equitable peace, public anger would have intensified and determination increased. Democratic governments have no choice but to show firm resolve in the face of attempts to intimidate them by violence, and, by and large, since the 1980s governments in Europe and around the world have successfully done so. In this regard there is a solidarity among democratic governments today that bars the path to organisations using terrorist methods.

I now turn to the building blocks of the peace process: they go back a very long way, and were slowly and painfully put together. Jack Lynch in the early 1970s accepted, on a *de facto* basis at least, that unity should come about only by agreement and consent. Although the Sunningdale Agreement, with its twin principles of power-sharing and an Irish dimension, collapsed after a few months, it nevertheless defined the basic ingredients of a political settlement – even though these might be described differently today. Nationalists had to accept that unity would not come in a single step.

In the late 1970s, the Irish embassy in Washington, together with John Hume, helped to develop an active interest in democratic political progress, both at the level of the president–administration and in Congress. This came to fruition in 1985 with the creation of the International Fund for Ireland. Charles Haughey as taoiseach adjusted this policy on the ground that it was better to try to unite Irish-American opinion behind the policy of the Irish Government than to excommunicate those who sympathised to varying degrees with armed struggle in the North. There was a precedent for this, about which he occasionally spoke, in the 'New Departure' of 1878 of Devoy, Parnell and Davitt.

Another element was the putting in place of the Anglo-Irish Framework in two stages, in 1980 and 1985. At first, it was oriented more on an east–west axis, with constructive ambiguity as to whether the totality of relationships covered constitutional or merely institutional issues. Both the Downing Street Declaration and the Framework Document were also joint-initiatives by the two governments.

An interesting question is how much the Anglo-Irish Agreement concluded by Dr Garret Fitzgerald and Margaret Thatcher contributed to the peace process. At one level, its political purpose was about extending the political marginalisation of Sinn Féin which had challenged the SDLP for leadership of the nationalist community and whose growth was a particular preoccupation of Garret Fitzgerald. For Margaret Thatcher, it meant intensified cooperation against the IRA, but it

also institutionalised the Irish Government's right to be heard in relation to the
nationalist community. It reaffirmed that, if a majority in Northern Ireland voted
clearly for a united Ireland, Britain would legislate to bring it about. While this was
merely a restatement of what had been the British position since 1920–21 and was
the other side of the coin to the famous British guarantee of 1949, it was an important affirmation, coming from so pro-unionist and strategically minded a prime
minister as Margaret Thatcher. What constituted voting *clearly* for a united Ireland,
and whether it meant something more than a simple majority, was left constructively ambiguous.

The Anglo-Irish Agreement was opposed at the time by three groups, unionists, Sinn Féin and Fianna Fáil. Despite massive protests, unionists were for the
first time in no position to pull the Agreement down, but for many years they
would not begin any talks in its shadow or under its auspices. Sinn Féin felt that the
gains were incommensurate with the costs to nationalists in terms of increased
vulnerability to loyalist attacks, and the Agreement cut little ice in their heartlands.
Fianna Fáil misconstrued article 1 of the Agreement as constituting *de jure* recognition of Northern Ireland and therefore as incompatible with articles 2 and 3 of the
South's constitution. The Supreme Court in 1990 took a different view. But there
was little problem about embracing and working the institutional mechanisms of
the Anglo-Irish Conference, either in opposition or on return to office.

That opposition may have been costly in domestic political terms, but it
created opportunities from 1988, first of all *vis-à-vis* unionists, in trying to interest
them in negotiations on a new agreement that would replace or transcend the
Anglo-Irish Agreement and, second, *vis-à-vis* Sinn Féin, with whom, leaving
aside the use of violence, some political and ideological there existed some common
ground. Particularly from the time of the hunger strikes, which cost the party two
seats and the election of June 1981, Fianna Fáil in the early to mid-1980s, working
either in opposition or (as in 1982) in government, reverted under Charles Haughey
to its republican roots, in a way not seen since Eamon de Valera. This happened
not just because of the leader's northern nationalist background and his own
instincts, which were in tune with much of the party's grassroots, but also because
of a determination to hold the republican ground and not cede it to anyone else. In
the early 1980s both Fianna Fáil and Sinn Féin moved away from federalism
towards the unitary state. The reason was simple: northern nationalists were no
longer willing to accept a restored majority-rule Stormont, even in the context of a
loosely federal or confederal Ireland. It was during that period that many of the
elements of the ideological bridge, which would be of crucial importance in the
peace process right up to the ceasefire, were built.

In 1987, a Redemptorist priest from the North was in contact with the then
Taoiseach, Charles Haughey, trying to establish dialogue with a view to finding a
basis for bringing violence to an end. Only the two governments were seen as being
able to break the impasse. There was a sense of responsibility, to be found in all of
the three main churches, that they had a role in bringing shameful acts of violence

to an end, putting their moral integrity to the service of that aim. As is known, a dialogue took place in 1988 between the SDLP and Sinn Féin on the principles underlying resolution of the conflict. They were unable to agree, however, on British neutrality, following the Anglo-Irish Agreement. The Government *per se* was not involved, but the party of government was. The Fianna Fáil attitude in its two secret meetings with Sinn Féin in 1988 was more agnostic on the question of British neutrality, but would have been concerned to emphasise the unacceptability of violence, which divided and therefore weakened nationalists in the North and divided North from South, as well as opinion in America. Both the SDLP and Fianna Fáil formed the view separately that northern republicans were not then ready to end their campaign and that their primary aim in any continuing dialogue with constitutional parties was to end their political isolation and build a broad front. Under the conditions obtaining, neither Fianna Fáil nor the SDLP could accept that outcome. This particular phase was followed by the abortive Duisburg talks in 1989, which involved all constitutional parties in the North and a Redemptorist proxy for Sinn Féin.

In 1989, another element fell into place when Charles Haughey announced at his party's Ard Fheis that, if violence were to cease, he would be prepared to reconvene the forum. The New Ireland Forum, the first purely Irish initiative in response to the Prior Assembly back in 1983, had left a report that provided a valuable modern consensus formulation of the constitutional nationalist position, North and South, which northern republicans also increasingly came to appreciate.

Peter Brooke was an exceptional Northern Ireland secretary of state, the most distinguished since William Whitelaw. His Anglo-Irish background had bequeathed him a warm love of Ireland – he once proudly told me that a distant relative, the eighteenth-century poet Charlotte Brooke, had been the first to use the word 'Fenian' in the English language. His analogy with Cyprus, and his prediction that governments sooner or later end up talking to those they had regarded as terrorists, whetted interest. His subsequent statement, made in the context of the end of the Cold War, that Britain had no selfish strategic or economic interest, was to be a foundation-stone around which some of the first drafts of a Joint Declaration were built.

This Joint Declaration began to take recognisable shape in the autumn of 1991, under the direction of Taoiseach Charles Haughey, with the help of John Hume and with some input from the Redemptorist priest whose idea such a declaration was. The possibility of an initiative was mentioned at the first of the series of regular meetings starting in December 1991 between the new British Prime Minister John Major and the taoiseach. But it was not possible to obtain, through intermediaries, any firm republican endorsement either of the strategy or of the draft before Mr Haughey was replaced as taoiseach by Mr Reynolds in February 1992.

The fortnight before Mr Reynolds took office was characterised by an upsurge in violence. He brought to his office a sense of affronted decency that such things were continuing. He was determined to go for peace as an end in itself, independent of any other political agenda, pursuing an even-handed and balanced approach to issues. He picked up the threads of the proposed initiative and pushed it with vigour. It took from April 1992 to June 1993 to finalise what he called 'a formula for peace'. There were difficulties over: the republican desire for a definite timescale for agreement; reaching a common understanding of the application of the principle of self-determination and its relationship to consent; and the political realism of casting the British in the role of persuaders for unity. The Irish Government was determined not to subscribe to anything that would be clearly at variance with its international obligations, principally the Anglo-Irish Agreement. Even so, the initial draft went to the outer limits of what was acceptable. Even when difficulties of communication were *partially* overcome – and in the circumstances they were difficult enough among republicans themselves – the whole initiative was understandably treated with extreme caution on both sides. John Hume was kept informed, and, of course, he had his own dialogue and relationship with Gerry Adams, which became public in April 1993. The public Hume–Adams statements were parallel and complementary to some of the elements in the declaration, though differently expressed in a helpful and constructive manner. The attacks on them from some quarters were totally unwarranted.

In June 1993, not without much soul-searching on the republican side, the draft was handed over to the British Government by the taoiseach. To say that the British handled it with kid gloves would be something of an understatement. The Government was prepared to discuss but not negotiate it, and on several occasions in the autumn of 1993 there were those who would have preferred to put it aside. But an initiative that might bring peace was always going to be more important than attempts to restart inter-party talks or even early discussions of the Framework Document. Some progress was being made towards an understanding. Then the stakes were raised dramatically when John Hume and Gerry Adams announced that they had finished their discussions and were putting their conclusions to the Irish Government. The perception that the northern nationalist leaders were seeking to lay down conditions for peace, however, raised tensions and wild rumours in the North. The Government opened a channel to the loyalist paramilitaries through the Reverend Roy Magee to reassure them that it was seeking peace for its own sake and not seeking to impose joint authority or any other solution. Magee gave the Government a set of political principles reflecting what would be acceptable to loyalists, and this was subsequently incorporated in the Draft Declaration.

At the Brussels summit meeting at the end of October, the taoiseach agreed to create some public distance from Hume and Adams, arguing that both he and the prime minister had a broader picture to take into account, but it was on the firm understanding that the Draft Declaration would be pursued, an understanding that proved less solid than it had appeared. There followed an extraordinary series of diplomatic, behind-the-scenes, crises. The taoiseach resisted the enormous pressure on him to drop the initiative, making it clear that he would try to proceed with it in some shape or form – if necessary, recast as a purely Irish initiative. If the British

Government would not join him in the endeavour, he would not be prepared to present a collaborative front in the USA or elsewhere.

The principal obstacle proved to be the unionists, with whom the British Conservatives the previous summer had formed an informal parliamentary *alliance*. In the end – and this was a very healthy development – the taoiseach approached Archbishop Eames to communicate to him the Government's ideas and to seek his advice. Dr Eames helped to draft paragraphs 6-8 of the declaration, which were essentially about creating greater trust between North and South, and he also briefed Downing Street on the desire for peace among the majority population, provided that no major concession of principle was involved. The Alliance Party leader, Dr John Alderdice, was kept similarly informed, and was enthusiastic about the declaration when it was published. Serious negotiations took place in the first fortnight of December, and the declaration was announced on 15 December in Downing Street by John Major and Albert Reynolds. The British had finally been convinced that they had to take hold of the peace initiative, if the moral high ground were not to be lost, regardless of whether it in fact brought peace, about which they were highly sceptical. Although credit is due to Margaret Thatcher for her part in upholding the Anglo-Irish Agreement, I was always fairly clear that there was little hope of an end to belligerence in Ireland while she remained British prime minister. John Major deserves great credit for his political courage in adopting the declaration, and indeed later the Framework Document, which put at risk the unionist alliance.

What began as an Irish peace initiative, addressing the fundamental concerns of republicans, ended up, mainly at the initiative of the taoiseach and the Irish Government, addressing the fundamental concerns of unionists in an even-handed way. As a result, Ulster unionists acquiesced – Molyneaux said he did not want to be responsible for delaying peace by a single day – and the loyalist paramilitaries had no great difficulty with it either. It had unprecedented cross-party political support, except for that of Sinn Féin and the DUP.

In the end, it did turn out to be a catalyst for peace, though that hung in the balance for several months. Perhaps it should have been more explicit about nationalist rights within the North, which were being worked on in the Framework Document, rather than concentrating on just the core constitutional questions. The heart of the declaration, apart from the balancing of self-determination with consent given concurrently, concerned the achievement of agreement between the people of Ireland, North and South. Many trusted and independent advisers, such as the late Paddy McGrory, a Belfast solicitor, could see the merit of rooting the legitimacy of any new settlement in the consent and self-determination of the people of Ireland on both sides of the border.

With the declaration at last out in the open, there was an enormous task of persuasion to be undertaken. The Irish Government had no problem over providing comprehensive clarification, in public and private, but was no more than the British Government to renegotiate it. In countless speeches and interviews, at home and abroad, explaining and promoting the case for peace, Albert Reynolds was magnificent. Section 31 was lifted as a result of his alliance in government with the minister for arts, culture and the Gaeltacht, Michael D. Higgins, motivated as always by lofty libertarian principles. The taoiseach strongly supported the application by Gerry Adams for a visa to enter the USA, granted by President Clinton, where the strong support for peace among leading Irish-Americans was made clear. It was the first of a number of occasions, right up to the Washington Conference in May 1995, when President Clinton and the US administration, represented here by Ambassador Jean Kennedy-Smith (in my view the most positively influential US ambassador there has ever been in Dublin), made crucial interventions. When firmness was required of the taoiseach, it was shown – for example, in his repudiation of the attempted Heathrow bombing and the rejection of the forty-eight-hour ceasefire after Easter. Nor would he have entered into any formal pact with Sinn Féin and the SDLP, which could have been too easily represented as a pan-nationalist front. Discussions on the Framework Document were resumed.

The British Government did later provide clarification to Sinn Féin, as did the Irish Government to loyalists. I can trace no explicit suggestion on the part of the British Government that decommissioning of weapons was an additional precondition for entering political dialogue and round-table talks. The only delay envisaged was to make sure the cessation was for real. By June 1994 there was widespread scepticism about the ability of the republican movement to adopt in a united way an alternative peace strategy. There were strains within the SDLP. In July, the taoiseach warned that by the end of the summer holidays he would be forced to draw conclusions, and he also made it clear that he would reject a limited ceasefire of, say, three months, which would not make it possible to enter political dialogue or participate in the proposed forum. By the time of Sinn Féin's Letterkenny meeting, at which the Downing Street Declaration was apparently rejected, he knew that a lasting ceasefire had effectively been decided. The word 'permanent' would not be used, for ideological reasons and, no doubt, because it was what the British Government was seeking. But phrases in the ceasefire statement, 'a complete cessation of violence' and 'a definitive commitment to the success of the democratic peace process', complemented by Martin McGuinness's statement some days later that 'the ceasefire will hold in all circumstances', were meant at the time to add up to the same thing. It was a declaration very similar in effect to the ceasefire statement combined with the proclamation of Eamon de Valera on behalf of republicans in the twenty-six counties in 1923, which stated that, as the democratic alternative to force, 'the ultimate Court of Appeal for deciding disputed questions of national expediency and policy is the people of Ireland', and that 'the war, so far as we are concerned, is finished'. While some volunteers may have been persuaded that the ceasefire was merely tactical, the firm intention at the time was that it would be permanent.

Within a few days, the famous meeting between Albert Reynolds, John Hume and Gerry Adams was held at the end of August 1994 in Dublin at Government Buildings. Their joint statement affirmed: 'We reiterate that we cannot resolve this problem without the participation and agreement of the unionist people.' The loyalist ceasefire followed six weeks later on 13 October. The Forum for Peace and Reconciliation was convened on 28 October. The only deal was the one laid out in paragraph 10 of the Downing Street Declaration, which stated that, if paramilitary violence ceased permanently, the electoral mandate of those associated with it would be recognised, and they would be treated like any other political party for purposes of political dialogue.

Plans were made for the release of political prisoners and for the symbolic lifting of the state of emergency, and legislation was drafted to implement the European Convention on the Transfer of Prisoners. The British scaled down day-time troop deployments, and undertook to re-open cross-border roads. Bertie Ahern, as minister for finance, played a large role in negotiating the EU package for the North and for the South's border counties. The negotiations on the Framework Document were heading towards a conclusion, including a balanced constitutional understanding that would involve changes in both the Government of Ireland Act 1920 and in articles 2 and 3 of the constitution. Indeed, on 11 November 1994, I was co-chairing with Sir John Chilcot, permanent under-secretary at the Northern Ireland Office, a meeting on those matters, when the decision to push through the appointment of the president of the High Court, which precipitated the fall of the Government, was taken. Mr Reynolds's partner in the peace process, Dick Spring, provided continuity in the new Government under John Bruton, who was also fully briefed by the outgoing Fianna Fáil taoiseach.

It would be appropriate in this setting to mention some of those, apart from government and party leaders and clerical intermediaries, who played a key role in the early stages of the peace process. Of the Irish civil servants, Seán Ó hUiginn, head of the Anglo-Irish division in the Department of Foreign Affairs, who also had oversight of the talks process and was a principal craftsman of the Framework Document, was a key person: he has enormous understanding of constitutional nationalism in the North. Though formally retired, Dermot Nally, because of his immense experience, had continued to liaise with the British cabinet secretary in 1993, and both were on the team negotiating with the British on the Joint Declaration. Fergus Finlay was another colleague who made an important input at different times. On the British side, Sir John Chilcot, head of the Northern Ireland Office, was far-sighted and imaginative, while his deputy, Quentin Thomas, was tough-minded but unfailingly courteous; both displayed resourcefulness. On the republican side, Martin McGuinness, in effect Sinn Féin's chief negotiator, assisted by a colleague from Belfast, also played a key role in the development of the Irish peace initiative and in helping to create the conditions that brought about a complete cessation of violence in August 1994. Gusty Spence played a guiding role in the loyalist ceasefire, and in the very eloquent and courageous accompanying statement which he read out in a room in Glencairn Community Centre in the Shankill.

Albert Reynolds, speaking in September 1994 at commemorations of 1798 at Oulart Hill and of Liam Lynch at Kilcrumper, said that the tradition of physical force had come to an end because it could go no further. Far from being at the end the line, however, we were at the dawn of a new era, with the whole island poised to overcome the disadvantages that have belaboured it throughout its history, in new relationships with other countries. As Charles Haughey said on television in December 1994, the peace process was something infinitely precious; it was a time of great hope and opportunity, which must not be squandered. Provided no one tried to test, to the limit and beyond, just how much strain the peace process was capable of bearing, it would surely hold, as there could be no conceivable gain to anyone in going back, only a huge loss to both communities and to the whole island. Unlike 1968, there is today a much better understanding of the rights of a minority community in a divided society or country. The price that the South has to pay for peace is continuing engagement in the affairs of the whole island, with a particular regard to equality of treatment and parity of esteem, as well as the development of cooperation, from, at the very least, the subnormal to the normal, between neighbouring jurisdictions. The USA is seen as the ultimate guarantor of fair play, and to my mind it was no accident that the first Mayhew–Adams meeting should have taken place in Washington.

As the son of the historian Nicholas Mansergh, from whom I learnt much of what I know about Irish history, Anglo-Irish relations and the Irish republican tradition, I have been privileged to witness and participate in history being made in this country, while in the service of three distinguished taoisigh, Charles Haughey, Albert Reynolds and Bertie Ahern. In his last book, published in 1991, my father wrote: 'The fashioning of a new relationship is for another time and another pen'.[11] That was the formidable task ahead: to uphold and consolidate the peace, and to negotiate a political settlement that is, to use an evocative phrase adapted in our constitutional negotiations from the late John Kelly, 'a new dispensation'.[12]

Postscript (June 2004)

The optimism and enthusiasm began to drain away in the course of 1995, as the peace process faced increasing difficulties. Unionists rejected the Framework Document, and refused to enter negotiations without a start to decommissioning, a stance supported by John Major's Government. The Forum for Peace and Reconciliation in Dublin held useful hearings and discussions, but failed to reach consensus on crucial issues. Even US intervention failed to resolve the crisis. With evidence of further stalling – and in an attempt to prevent a split, which was only postponed until late 1997 – the IRA set off a bomb at Canary Wharf in February 1996 as part of a sporadic campaign. Multi-party negotiations were organised in the following months, but without Sinn Féin, fearing that it would face continual harassment on the decommissioning issue. It took a change of government in both London and Dublin to reinstate the IRA ceasefire. In September 1997, the UUP agreed to enter multi-party talks with Sinn Féin. To many people's surprise, all the threads of decades of political initiative and agitation were brought together in the 1998 Good Friday Agreement, which contained a far-reaching constitutional accommodation, a balanced range of partnership institutions and a radical reforming agenda in areas of equality, human rights, policing and justice, with prisoners being released. The notion of mutual consent underlay the Agreement, which was overwhelmingly endorsed by the people of Ireland, North and South, in concurrent referendums. The terrible bombing at Omagh in August 1998, by the dissident 'Real IRA', following violent deaths arising from the Orange Order's attempts to march down the Garvaghy Road from Drumcree Church, reinforced popular rejection of para-military violence, but unfortunately did not provide the impetus for decisive forward movement.

It took many government-led initiatives to break the deadlock, a deadlock that has re-emerged many times since. The Agreement came into force in December 1999, and the institutions were established, only for the Executive and the Assembly to be suspended again two months later. It was the first of many stops and starts, raising questions about good faith on both sides with regard, on the one hand, to the deeply divided UUP's commitment to power-sharing and, on the other, to the IRA's commitment to disarm and retire. At the time of writing the Assembly has been suspended since October 2002, though that has not prevented the steady electoral advance of Sinn Féin, North and South, from overtaking the SDLP, nor the DUP from overtaking the UUP. Following the Assembly elections of autumn 2003, the onus has fallen on the DUP and Sinn Féin to forge a stable agreement with the help of both governments.

A positive development has been the establishment of the new Police Service of Northern Ireland (PSNI), advocated by the Patten Report, a vital building-block in the process, which, with some improvements to the original legislation, won the support of the SDLP and the Irish Government, though not yet of the republicans.

The peace process can be divided into three phases; the long road to the establishment of the first ceasefire, from late 1987 to 1994; the manoeuvres and negotiations leading to a political settlement, the Good Friday Agreement, in 1998; and, finally, the present phase of the implementation of the Agreement. By inter-national standards, with peace marred only by a low level of violence, the Northern Ireland peace process is a success, even if those closer to it are much more critical. There is no temptation, however, to veer off on another path.

Democracy is not only about an exclusive commitment to peaceful means; it is about honouring and implementing, and not obstructing, the expressed will of the people. The democratic tradition in Northern Ireland in both regards is weak. The Good Friday Agreement is needed to strengthen it by providing a powerful sup-portive framework that combines fundamental reforms with durable institutions.

Notes

1 This chapter is based on an address made to the National Committee for the Study of International Affairs under the auspices of the Royal Irish Academy, which was published in *Irish Studies in International Affairs*, vol. 6, 1995, pp. 145–58.
2 J. Bowyer Bell, *The Irish Troubles: A Generation of Violence 1967–1992* (Dublin: Gill & Macmillan, 1993), p. 829.
3 A. T. Q Stewart, *The Ulster Crisis: Resistance to Home Rule, 1912–14* (London: Faber, 1967), p. 44.
4 Thomas Jones, *Whitehall Diary, vol. 3: Ireland 1918–1925*, ed. Keith Middlemas (14 October 1921) (London and New York: Oxford University Press, 1971), pp. 129–30.
5 *Ibid.* (3 September 1921), pp. 105–6.
6 Nicholas Mansergh, 'The Implications of Eire's Relationship with the British Commonwealth of Nations', *International Affairs*, vol. 24, no. 1, January 1948.
7 Paul Canning, *British Policy towards Ireland 1921–1941* (Oxford: Oxford University Press, 1985), p. 306.
8 Eamon Phoenix, *Nationalist Politics, Partition and the Catholic Minority in Northern Ireland 1890–1940* (Belfast: Ulster Historical Society, 1994).
9 Jones, *Whitehall Diary* (1 December 1925), pp. 241–3.
10 'Sinn Féin Must Tow the Line on Pledging Peace for Talks', *Irish Times*, 20 August 1994. However, Dr Fitzgerald made the point in the discussion following this address that the time for a shift in policy had been well chosen.
11 Nicholas Mansergh, *The Unresolved Question: The Anglo-Irish Settlement and its Undoing, 1912–72* (New Haven, CT and London: Yale University Press, 1991), p. 4.
12 *The Irish Constitutions*, 2nd edn (Dublin, 1984), p. 12.

3

From war to uneasy peace in Northern Ireland

CAROLINE KENNEDY-PIPE

The GFA of 1998 signalled a profound transformation in the politics of Northern Ireland. The stagnation that had long paralysed the region was broken up; old certainties were undermined and those engaged in Northern Ireland acknowledged it. Against the backdrop of the end of the Cold War, Sinn Féin with the backing of some (but not all) of the IRA engaged in a series of attempts to negotiate new political structures, a process which owes much to the ideas of constitutional nationalism espoused over many years by John Hume and the SDLP. The Blair Government, following the example of the previous Conservative Government, engaged in dialogue with Sinn Féin–IRA and made public its readiness to rethink constitutional arrangements in Ireland to enable new institutions with broad cross-community support to emerge. Tony Blair, as British prime minister, has gone further than his Conservative predecessors in taking the unprecedented step of acknowledging and apologising for some of the more tragic aspects of the British legacy in Ireland. The reaction of Unionism to these developments has been complex. A. T. Q. Stewart's observation, made several years ago, that a central question in Northern Irish politics has to be does Protestant Ulster have a mind?[1] has never appeared so pertinent. Groupings such as the DUP and the UK Unionist Party (UKUP) have refused to engage in negotiations with republicans, while the UUP remains divided over whether to support the political structures created by the GFA. Although David Trimble succeeded in the main in keeping his party engaged in the political process, there is within unionist ranks strong opposition to the agreement.

It is therefore an important time to take stock of the situation in Ireland. The terrorist attacks of 9/11 on the USA transformed our understanding of the threats posed by terrorist and paramilitary groups. The activities of al-Qaeda and terrorist atrocities in locations as diverse as Bali, Kenya and Madrid all heralded a new and spectacular age of violent conflict. There has been, understandably, a rush to understand the motivations of these men (and women) of violence. Yet the global profile achieved by al-Qaeda should not blind us to the rather less fashionable plight of peoples, politicians and former paramilitaries struggling over how to construct an enduring peace after years of terrorism and political deadlock in local regions such as the North of Ireland. Indeed, while the old days of terrorism in Ireland appear to have gone it is important to guard against any complacency over the future of the Irish peace settlement. It may be accurate to see Irish para-militaries and politics as rather homely in comparison to the al-Qaeda network and the struggle over the decommissioning of paramilitary materials as rather trivial compared to the potential for a weapons of mass destruction (WMD) attack on Western subways and institutions. Yet, hopes in Ireland for a permanent peace face a number of continuing difficulties. There is continued opposition to and suspicion about the settlement on both sides of the communal divide, while paramilitary activity is ongoing. There remains a substantial military presence. There is also, of course, the legacy of grief in the province for those whose families and communities have been affected by the thirty years of violence. Indeed, these victims are now expected to accept the presence in mainstream politics of some of those who perpetrated the violence. The politics of reconciliation is therefore not easy. This chapter revisits the politics of Northern Ireland to examine how and why some (but not all) of the men of violence have laid down their arms, and why many (but not all) accept a settlement which has changed the politics of the province to one of troubled peace rather than long war.

Origins and legacies

The creation of Northern Ireland in 1920 was a textbook example of a State and nation building failure.[2] The establishment of Northern Ireland marked the partial retreat of the British State from Ireland and was proof of the bankruptcy of the attempt to construct a British identity throughout Ireland. It was also, although it is unfashionable to say so, evidence of a failure of Irish nationalism. Irish national-ists lacked the resources to inspire a revolution throughout the whole island. The inability of nationalists to coerce or persuade the Protestants in Ulster to join what might be termed the 'free state' project sprang from several sources. The nationalists were weak militarily, especially in comparison to the forces of the British crown;[3] but more importantly Irish nationalism in this period defined itself in terms of opposition to the British State, the English language and Protestant denomin-ations.[4] These features were not likely to conciliate the Protestant community to the notion of a united and nationalist Ireland.[5]

Northern Ireland was also the product of *varying* political power. A 30 per cent minority in the island was able to prevent one area from seceding but this region in turn contained a 30 per cent minority in favour of the secession of the whole of Ireland. One minority had far greater political resources than the other.[6] Yet the development of the Northern Ireland 'problem' and the later Troubles was the outcome both of this 'settlement' in Anglo-Irish affairs and of the later struggle over the legitimacy of political institutions in the North.

In the years 1920–mid-1960s Northern Ireland was characterised by three features. The first was that sovereignty over the region[7] was at least in theory contested by both the British State and the Southern Irish State. Yet, Northern Ireland was not fully integrated into either and little influence was exercised by either Dublin or Westminster in the politics of the province. The South was excluded from participation in the life of the North and after 1921 Westminster withdrew from the exercise of state power, leaving Stormont to govern. The dominance of Protestants within the new Northern Ireland Government gave rise to the second feature of the regime: Northern Ireland's political institutions lacked broad support across the two communities. The unionists who governed made few efforts to win Catholic support. Unionist power depended on maintaining the cohesion of the unionist bloc and there was little incentive to make concessions to a minority. As Richard Rose has argued elsewhere, it was Catholic compliance not Catholic consent that was sought.[8] The minority therefore had little stake in maintaining or contributing to the system of government, and for nearly all of the first fifty years of government nationalist politicians refused to act as an official opposition but rather opted out of the business of government. As George Boyce has pointed out, individual Catholics were not necessarily utterly opposed to a working relationship with Northern Ireland's Government; it was the nationalist party which refused to recognise the State and preferred a policy of abstention.[9] Yet the third feature of Northern Ireland's politics, that of a disgruntled and disenfranchised minority, did not, despite Protestant fears and some street violence, unduly disturb the workings of the Stormont regime; that is, until the development of a civil rights culture in the 1960s. That change was brought about by the combined weight of external and internal factors which galvanised a burgeoning Catholic middle-class into challenging the workings of what Farrell has characterised as the 'Orange state'.[10]

Northern Ireland during the 1960s was influenced by the cross-currents in Anglo-Irish relations which arose out of the drive for greater European integration. The ongoing programme of economic modernisation in the South under Taoiseach Sean Lemass demanded an improvement in economic relations with the UK, the EEC and Northern Ireland. Southern Ireland's desire for entry to the EEC not only inspired an improvement in Anglo-Irish relations but made it increasingly difficult for Westminster – itself seeking entry to the EEC – to resist the pressure from Dublin for some reform of the minority position in Northern Ireland. For the first time, then, it is possible to argue that the Southern Irish were able to exert influence, albeit of a limited kind, over events in the North.

Perhaps more importantly, there were in the 1960s also social and economic shifts in the North brought about by the development of the post-war British State and the extension of a 'welfare state' culture into Northern Ireland. In particular, the provision a variety of welfare benefits and legislation for greater access to higher education effected a change in Catholic income and expectations. The introduction of welfare benefits made transparent the obvious disparities in living standards between the North and the South and muted much of the minority enthusiasm for joining the South. Thus far, it was imagined that the minority community would, because of its greater educational and economic opportunities, be increasingly reconciled to the Stormont regime. Terence O'Neill, Northern Ireland's prime minister, explained the benefits of the introduction of welfare programme that 'it is frightfully hard to explain to a Protestant that if you give Roman Catholics a good job and a good house they will live like Protestants'.[11] However, his comment proved rather wide of the mark: instead of reconciliation, the Catholic community sought further reform; and rather than concentrate on the politics of partition, the Nationalist Party, undergoing a period of 'revisionism', aimed to improve the economic and social conditions of the minority *within* the existing framework. This posed significant problems for unionist dominance. The rejection of 'abstentionist' politics, the pleas for equal treatment and for the reform, *not* the abolition of Stormont in themselves undermined the unionist rationale for the exclusion of the minority which could no longer be characterised simply as 'disloyal rebels'.[12]

There were other currents feeding social and political change within Northern Ireland. Although it is now almost obligatory to recognise the impact of international events such as the end of the Cold War on the politics of Ireland,[13] influence of a potent kind was exercised by the international civil rights agenda of the 1960s. In January 1967, in part inspired by civil rights movements in the USA, the Northern Ireland Civil Rights Association was founded and drew support from across both communities to bring about the abolition of discriminatory practices in the region. The slogan of 'equal rights' drew international attention and proved exceptionally damaging to the reputation of the Stormont regime.

Brian Faulkner, under pressure from the civil rights movement, Westminster, and the demands of an ailing economy instigated reforms that granted the minority a greater degree of equality in employment, housing legislation and proposed reconstruction of the security apparatus. Not surprisingly, reform met resistance from parts of the unionist community, which saw livelihood and government now threatened by the demands of an increasingly restless and articulate minority.

The first bloody encounter of the Troubles occurred in Londonderry/Derry on 5 October 1968 when civil rights marchers clashed with the police. The eruption of violence on the streets and the wholesale movement of urban populations into separate communities of Protestant and Catholics led to the formation of local vigilante groups which in turn contributed to the resurgence of paramilitary groups. The scale and intensity of the sectarian violence throughout the summer of 1969, plus the inability of the RUC to maintain order resulted in a request from Stormont to the Labour Government for the deployment of additional troops to support the police.

The Labour Government – under pressure from Dublin which threatened not to stand idly by, embarrassed by international media coverage and subject to overt appeals by a minority group whose political representatives had hitherto refused to accept the authority of the British – had little option but to respond to the crisis.[14]

Troops arrived on the streets of Belfast and Londonderry/Derry in the summer of 1969 after a period of intense deliberation by both the British military and politicians.[15] (During the spring, soldiers were deployed to protect important electricity installations because of fears of paramilitary attacks.) Initially, troops were welcomed by the Catholic community, which believed itself defenceless against sectarian attacks: 7,000 refugees were reputed to have moved across the border into the Republic of Ireland. The Lynch Government established camps for 'refugees' on the southern side of the border, called for a United Nations' peace-keeping force to be deployed and objected to the emergency legislation invoked by Stormont.[16]

The Labour Government at this point eschewed the notion of taking direct control. The deployment of troops in numbers was not intended to be permanent.[17] Attempts were made to reassure both communities that what might be termed an improved status quo would prevail: the Union and Stormont would continue, but action on discrimination would be taken. As a result of the findings of the Cameron Commission, appointed in March 1969, to investigate the causes of the violence, public housing came under the control of the Northern Ireland Housing Executive and little political power was left in the hands of local councils, which were viewed by Westminster as the source of sectarianism.[18] Lord Hunt's recommendation that an independent police authority be set up, the RUC disarmed, the USC disbanded and a new part-time force, the Ulster Defence Regiment (UDR), be set up under the general officer commanding the British Army was also implemented in the attempts to render the institutions of the North acceptable to the minority community.[19]

Such reform, however, did little to ameliorate either unionist or nationalist anxieties. Unionists resented the negative findings of the Cameron and Hunt reports, and this attitude was compounded by suspicion of a Labour Government regarded as sympathetic to the nationalist cause. Unionist anger, especially in working-class areas, was also reflected in the re-invigoration of paramilitary organisations which dedicated themselves to what Bruce has termed 'pro-state violence'.[20] On the loyalist side, the most notable or notorious were the UVF and the UDA, which, in response to republican paramilitary activity, engaged in random attacks against Catholic communities. The IRA, notable only by its absence during the early stages of the 'Troubles' (graffiti within Catholic areas had identified the IRA with 'I ran away', noting its feeble show of protecting the minority areas), re-emerged in Catholic areas.[21]

IRA impotence reflected deep-seated tensions within the republican movement over a number of issues. The subsequent split within Sinn Féin (the political wing of the organisation) and the IRA brought about the formation of the Provisionals in 1970,[22] who launched a campaign of violence against the British Army. Stormont, backed by the newly elected Conservative Government, invoked emergency legislation and, on 9 August 1971, introduced internment without trial. Special prisons were established and filled, at least initially, with Catholics, some of whom were subjected to 'interrogation in depth'. The techniques with which this interrogation was conducted inspired a public outcry.[23] Rather than containing the violence, these actions along with the use of curfews and house searches, resonant of British military campaigns in the colonies, fuelled the conflict. Internment led to a campaign of civil disobedience, prolonged street violence and an escalation of support for the paramilitaries from Catholic communities.[24] The alienation of the minority community was completed in January 1972 when members of the Parachute Regiment killed fourteen Catholics who were on a civil rights demonstration. Violence against British troops escalated. The ramifications of the events of Bloody Sunday reverberated outside the province. On 2 February, a crowd of 30,000 marched to the British Embassy in Dublin and burnt it down. This raised the prospect for Westminster that events in the North could spread disorder throughout the British Isles. International attention was drawn once again to the province and, certainly, Irish-American opinion mobilised in favour of the republican struggle with increased financial support.[25]

The initial years of crisis therefore gave rise to a bloody and multi-levelled confrontation between the British and the Provisionals and between the two communities within the North. Yet the emergence or re-emergence of the men of violence was not the whole story. Unionism itself split in the face of reform as the UUP fractured. In April 1970, those unionists opposed to violence and in favour of reconciliation left the (official) Unionist Party and formed the Alliance Party of Northern Ireland (APNI). During 1971, Ian Paisley launched the DUP to represent those Protestants dissatisfied with Stormont's reform in an attempt to recreate what Paisley termed 'traditional Unionism'.[26] In August 1970, the (predominantly Catholic) Social and Democratic Labour Party (SDLP) was founded, which, despite its aspiration to a united Ireland, had a clear reformist stance for Northern Ireland itself and replaced the Nationalist Party as the voice of moderate Catholic opinion. In June 1971, Brian Faulkner offered the SDLP positions on the opposition parliamentary committees, thus permitting nationalists a modicum of influence on the making of legislation. Nevertheless, in July 1971, after the army had killed two men during riots in Londonderry/Derry and the demands by the party for a public inquiry had been refused, the SDLP withdrew from Stormont.[27]

On 30 March 1972 Conservative Prime Minister Edward Heath signalled the end of British attempts to reform Stormont by introducing direct rule. The closing down of the only system of government which had ever operated in Northern Ireland initiated a second phase during which the British Government attempted to find new ways of governing the region.

Direct rule

Direct rule did little to solve the problems of Northern Ireland. It was a bid to *isolate* the IRA from the Catholic community and an attempt to build a moderate political centre in Ireland drawn from the SDLP, the APNI and the more liberal unionists. The prorogation of Stormont did not, however, end the violence. During 1972, there were extraordinarily high levels of violence: 103 soldiers, 41 police (UDR men), and 323 civilians were killed. In addition to the human costs, direct rule did not succeed in creating a moderate centre. Some of the initiatives taken by William Whitelaw proved controversial: the revelation that he had actually held talks with members of the Provisionals in London in July 1972 and his decision to include an 'Irish dimension' in any future settlement undermined the position taken by many in the Unionist Party who had been prepared to share power with the SDLP.

Direct rule also raised the question of Westminster's objectives in Ireland: was it in fact seeking to extricate itself from Northern Ireland? This was for many within both the unionist and republican communities an essential question. The consultative paper on the future of Northern Ireland, published shortly after the advent of direct rule, stated that no UK government had any wish to impede the realisation of Irish unity, were it come about through consent.[28] This underlined the paradox at the heart of Westminster's strategy in Ireland: the British Government had assumed responsibility for governing Northern Ireland; it was after 1972 engaged in a massive military campaign against the Provisional IRA; yet it still defined its right to rule in terms of arbitration between two warring communities in which it hoped to create the conditions for some form of devolved power-sharing.

In March 1973, a referendum was held to decide whether Northern Ireland should remain part of the UK. Catholics boycotted it: the verdict was decisively in favour of Union, but Westminster continued to promote devolution within the North. A White Paper was published proposing self-government for the region: Westminster attempted to establish a power-sharing executive and a Council of Ireland to promote North–South ties through functional co-operation.[29] In December, tripartite discussions were held to broker what became known as the Sunningdale Agreement, the principal aim of which was to create the conditions for a sufficient, and representative, number of parties to engage in local government, although a southern dimension was recognised through the creation of a Council of Ireland. While acknowledging that the majority of people in the province wished to remain within the UK, a commitment was made that if the majority of people in Northern Ireland wished to become part of a united Ireland, the British Government would support that desire.

This initiative collapsed in the face of unionist opposition. The Ulster Workers' Council strike of 1974 paralysed the province and the power-sharing executive of Brian Faulkner (with SDLP member Gerry Fitt as deputy chief executive) was brought down. Some unionists made clear their anger with certain aspects of the deal, especially the proposed Council of Ireland, perceived as a back-road to Irish unity. Harold Wilson, in power for a second time, accused the unionists of 'sponging on Westminster', but did little to break the strike: indeed the army advised against a confrontation with loyalists, which, it was feared would lead to a war on two fronts.[30] The SDLP, already angered by the failure of the British to end the process of internment, remained convinced that the strike could have been broken by a resolute action.

Normalisation and 'Ulsterisation'

The collapse of power-sharing led to a period of political stalemate during which few constitutional initiatives were attempted in Ireland. Indeed, from 1975 onwards, Britain, first under a Labour Government and then under the Conservative Government of Mrs Thatcher, implemented policies designed to redefine the problem of Northern Ireland as one of criminal activity, not one of political or constitutional struggle. Ulsterisation, or normalisation, was in many ways a logical outcome of the stated British position in Ireland. Successive British governments had refused to declare a war against the IRA and, unlike in colonial struggles in Northern Ireland, there had been no open declaration of a state of emergency.[31] Ulsterisation was designed to place the security emphasis on local forces, such as the RUC and the UDR, and to allow for a reduction in the number of British troops. This exercise was underlined by the formula, made infamous by Reginald Maudling, that 'an acceptable level of violence' had been attained in the conflict with the Provisional IRA. British politicians associated with Northern Ireland in the late 1970s and the 1980s were reluctant to use the term 'war' or even 'civil' to describe events in the region, lest in doing so they should confer a degree of legitimacy on the IRA. (This period of 'normalisation' and criminalisation was, however, also one of intensification of the so-called 'dirty war' in Ireland. While the use of special forces had been part of the British Army's campaign against the Provisionals since 1971, the deployment of the SAS in 1977 marked an escalation of the military effort to defeat the republican paramilitaries. Controversy and grievance escalated when members of the Catholic community alleged that a 'shoot to kill' policy was operated not only by the SAS but within segments of the army in collusion with the police force. Allegations of policy collusion with loyalist paramilitaries became commonplace and are still heard today.[32])

The movement away from the tacit recognition of the IRA as a legitimate opponent was evidenced by the withdrawal of special category status from paramilitary prisoners, which ended the distinction between prisons, or between ordinary and political crimes. After March 1976, prisoners convicted of terrorist offences were categorised as criminals. Up to that point 'political' prisoners had benefitted from certain concessions: they had been allowed to wear their own clothes and had been free to associate with other political prisoners.[33]

It was primarily but not only republican prisoners though who challenged the Government on this issue,[34] some of them refusing to wear prison uniform and dressing in blankets. The dispute escalated from 'blanket' protest, through a 'dirty' protest and finally, in October 1980, into a 'hunger' strikes. Bobby Sands, the leader of IRA prisoners in the H-block and a hunger striker, defeated Harry West of the UUP in a by-election for Parliament and was elected as an MP for Fermanagh and South Tyrone. (The SDLP refused to stand a candidate against Sands.) During a second hunger strike, the Thatcher Government refused to make concessions and ten strikers, including Sands himself, died. These hunger strikes were a turning point in internal, European and international perceptions of the British Government's position on Ireland. For Sinn Féin, the election of Sands confirmed the viability of entering candidates for election. Two other hunger strikers were elected to the Dail.

The management of the hunger strikes by the Thatcher Government was widely condemned. The European Commission of Human Rights (ECHR) criticised the British and, in February 1983, the European Parliament established an inquiry into the economic and social problems of Northern Ireland. The US Government too expressed it concern over the handling of the issue; indeed, the 'Irish question' began to occupy an increasingly important place in the US political process from the 1970s onwards. While scholars disagree over the reasons for the increasing attention paid to Ireland by US politicians, and here of course the issue of the Irish 'diaspora' is of note, there is also the question of the changing nature of the Anglo-American relationship in which, throughout the 1980s, Britain was arguably of diminishing importance to US foreign policy.

While the influence of the USA would become increasingly important in Ireland in the aftermath of the hunger strikes, it was the emergence of Sinn Féin as a political force which was the striking feature of that time. At its Party Conference in 1981, Sinn Féin decided to adopt an approach which can be described as 'ballot paper in one hand and an armalite in the other'. The decision to contest elections within Northern Ireland meant that Sinn Féin would be competing against the SDLP which itself had, as a result of the hunger strikes, adopted a more militant stance. In the 1983 general election, Gerry Adams was returned as Sinn Féin MP for West Belfast, defeating the sitting SDLP member, Gerry Fitt. Republicans polled 13.4 per cent of the total vote.[35] In May 1985, Sinn Féin candidates stood in local council elections; fifty-nine of them were elected and actually took their seats. This level of support for Sinn Féin, estimated as about 12 per cent of the electorate, raised the prospect of Sinn Féin supplanting the SDLP as the voice of nationalism.

The Anglo-Irish Agreement

John Hume's response to the surge in support for Sinn Féin was to arrange the New Ireland Forum – a meeting of all the Irish democratic parties: Sinn Féin was not invited. The forum took a year to agree a framework through which a new Ireland could emerge. Three specific options were offered: a unitary state; a federal system; and joint Anglo-Irish authority. This initiative served as a catalyst for thinking about Ireland. Although the three options were openly rejected by Mrs Thatcher in her now famous declaration of 'no, no, no', cabinet committees were actually discussing how to move forward with Dublin. From December 1984, senior civil servants on both sides of the Irish Sea began exploratory talks, which led to the Anglo-Irish Agreement of 1985.[36]

In his recent memoirs John Major has denied that the Anglo-Irish Agreement of 1985 represented a turning point and argued that little was achieved.[37] This is a rather churlish assessment, not least because for many engaged in the Anglo-Irish process the Agreement provided the groundwork for the view that the 'Troubles' were the business of both Dublin and London. The Agreement established a consultative forum through which both British and Irish ministers could discuss Northern Irish affairs and agreed closer Anglo-Irish collaboration on security issues. For the British Government the inclusion of the southern dimension was an attempt to stem and reverse the growth of Sinn Féin, while stabilising support for the SDLP as well as trying to encourage those within the unionist camps who supported devolution. The Agreement was opposed by the two main unionist parties and Sinn Féin.

The aftermath of the Anglo-Irish Agreement, however, exposed unionism as having lost some of its influence with the British Government over the previous decade. Although numerous methods, such as mass demonstration and a boycott of public bodies, were attempted to disrupt the Agreement, all of these failed to have the impact achieved against Sunningdale. Most notably, public servants remained loyal to government. Weakness was also attributable to the relative decline in the economic position of the unionists: industrial output had fallen since 1974 and a number of crises had beset the regional economic base. By the mid-1980s the province was sustained by a huge subvention from Britain which provided some 25–30 per cent of Northern Ireland's population's disposable income. Threats that unionism would take an independent route were less believable than they had been in the mid-1970s – there was nowhere else to go. Indeed, what constituted unionism was itself a question, as a political battle waged between the DUP and the UUP. Although an alliance had been forged between Paisley and James Molyneaux in response to the Anglo-Irish Agreement, in the ensuing years the two engaged in a struggle that Paul Arthur has characterised as a battle for dominance of the unionist electorate.[38]

If the aftermath of the Anglo-Irish Agreement revealed chinks in the unionist armour, there were sombre consequences for Sinn Féin. The popularity of the agreement in the South signalled that within the 'island of Ireland' partition had been accepted. What appeared to be the acquiescence to British rule in the North raised the question of just how strongly the people of the Republic sought reunification. The decades of the Troubles had brought home to many in the South the probable consequences of unity, of which unionist intransigence, the threat from the paramilitaries and the assumption of an economic and security burden were formidable. As Tom Garvin noted in 1988, 'If an offer of a united Ireland were to be seriously and publicly made by the British Government ... it would have devastating and possibly destabilising effects on the Republic'.[39]

There was also for Sinn Féin the problem of the 'long war'. The Anglo-Irish Agreement had improved security collaboration between North and South and raised the question of exactly how successful the IRA campaign had been. The results by the late 1980s were mixed. IRA violence had arguably played a part in persuading the British to dismantle the Stormont regime; it had kept the issue of

Irish unity on the political agenda, souring Anglo-Irish relations for two decades; and it had arguably strengthened the SDLP. But the violence had also proved counterproductive. It had led to an increase in violence by loyalists against working-class Catholics; it had alienated moderate nationalist opinion; and had done very little to dent British resolve at the governmental level. Although opinion polls demonstrated clearly that the majority of the British electorate would be glad to relinquish any claim to Northern Ireland, successive British governments had made clear that they would not and could not give way to 'terrorism'.

This was despite the evidence that the Provisional IRA, aided by supplies from Libya, set out during the second part of the decade to raise the tempo of the confrontation. During 1987–88, the Provisionals mounted a campaign in England and against British military personnel and installations throughout Europe.[40] If anything, though, the new campaign was counter-productive. Widespread outrage at the killing of eleven Protestant civilians during a Remembrance Day ceremony in Enniskillen affected support for the Republican paramilitaries. These reverses was compounded when the Provisionals killed eight off-duty soldiers in August 1988 and the Thatcher Government responded with legislation which included a broad-casting ban on Sinn Féin, a restriction already in place in the South.

Indeed, the Thatcher Government proved resolute in pursuing a counter-insurgency campaign. Although doubts must assail anyone trying to evaluate the record of the British security forces in Ireland during the 1980s,[41] the alleged 'shoot to kill' policy operated by the SAS, the supergrass trials and the strange affair of the Stalker inquiry and the subsequent refusal to prosecute anyone in the wake of the Sampson inquiry on the grounds of national security left serious question marks over the behaviour of some segments of the army and the RUC. But there is simply little doubt that by the end of the 1980s the IRA had begun to doubt its ability to push the British out of Ireland. This situation of what might be termed 'military stalemate' further compounded the process of revisionism within parts of the Republican movement, and by 1988 Sinn Féin leaders were already engaged in separate negotiations with both John Hume and, through a special negotiator, Martin Mansergh, with the Government in Dublin – the so-called 'back channel'.

Towards peace?

In discussion with Hume, Adams signalled the turn towards the idea of constitutional nationalism. He appealed for a national consensus on Irish reunification and addressed himself to Fianna Fáil in the South as well as the SDLP in the North. This was clearly articulated in the 1992 Ard Fheis when the movement adopted the document *Towards a Lasting Peace*. In this, Adams accepted that the issue of national self-determination was a complex one and that Britain might act as the persuaders of unionism, and he again opened a dialogue with Hume, which was to culminate in the 1993 peace process.

Adams's discussions with Hume had implications for the armed struggle.

There was an incompatibility, recognised all along by Adams, between armed struggle and the quest for electoral victory. The explosion of the massive bomb in the City of London, on the day in April 1993 when the Hume–Adams talks became public, gave the public the impression that the two strategies were running in tandem. However, the perceived need to continue to defend the Catholic community against loyalist attacks made it difficult for the IRA to relinquish its struggle, let alone its arms. Indeed, as Mark Urban has noted, from 1993 onwards, the conflict in the province had changed character: the British Army was not killing republicans any more; but loyalists were killing Catholics in greater numbers, and the IRA did not know what to do about it.[42] While Sinn Féin claimed that for peace to be workable in Ireland, all sides including the British military, must decommission weapons and oversee a complete demilitarisation of the region, the more pressing issue in the mid-1990s was the activities of the Ulster Freedom Fighters (UFF). Decommissioning of paramilitary weapons was to prove one of the most controversial and difficult issues for the IRA not only because of the myth of 'no surrender' to the British but because of republican fears of loyalist violence.[43]

Military 'successes' by the Provisional IRA during the 1990s, such as the bombings of the financial quarter of the City in London in 1992, were also being overtaken by IRA disasters, for example, the killing of two small boys in the town of Warrington in the spring of 1993 and the Shankhill bombing in the autumn. The problem for the Provisionals was that the political path now pursued by Sinn Féin deprived the bombing campaign of any sort of rationale. Continued violence called in the question the logic of bombing once Sinn Féin no longer sought to drive out the British, preferring to achieve recognition within the constitutional system.

John Major's Government had made clear, both through Secretary of State Peter Brooke and his successor Patrick Mayhew, that Britain, although neutral on the subject of Ireland, held that the renunciation of violence was a prerequisite for the IRA's admission to the constitutional talks initiated by Brooke. Indeed, the aim of the secret contacts opened by the British Government after 1989 was to convince the Provisional IRA to end its armed campaign. These talks marked a historic departure for the republican movement. The very fact that the Provisionals were engaged with the British government underlined their acceptance of Hume's analysis of the British position, according to which it was willing to withdraw from Ireland (or act as persuaders to the unionist population) if the right conditions could be achieved.

The influence of Hume and the SDLP was therefore considerable. Not only had Hume acted as a fundamental influence on Adams, but his long-expressed view that there were three strands to the Irish Troubles – the relationship between Catholics and Protestants, the relationship between Dublin and Belfast and the relationship between Ireland and Britain – was accepted by Brooke and by all those involved in the settlement.

The election of the Labour Government in the spring of 1997 marked a significant break with the past. Tony Blair's 'New Labour' had taken power with a determination to modernise Britain – and that included finding a settlement to the

Irish Troubles. Blair, unlike more traditional members of the Labour Party, had no inclination towards the idea of Irish unity and made clear his support for the Union. He did, however, recognised that Sinn Féin was vital to peace and the future governance of the region.[44]

Blair marked a break with the British past in Ireland in other ways, one being his recognition that the history of the Troubles affected the peace in complex ways: the re-opening of an inquiry into the events of Bloody Sunday, the establishment of both the Bloomfield Commission and the Patten Commission, plus his willingness to openly address the tragedies of Anglo-Irish relations demonstrated an awareness that the peace process should address some of the outstanding issues which had long prevented nationalists from developing a positive view of British governments. Another of Blair's departures from Britain's position on Ireland was more pragmatic: he embraced outside intervention in the affairs of Northern Ireland. Previous prime ministers had been sensitive to the importance of keeping the management of the region a domestic affair. Blair, however, actively enlisted the help of the Democratic US president, Bill Clinton, in bringing about peace. Clinton had, of course, been engaged in the affairs of Ireland since the early 1990s; indeed, much to the fury of the Major Government, he had ensured that Gerry Adams was granted a visa to visit the USA.[45] Clinton appointed former-senator George Mitchell as special envoy to Northern Ireland to co-ordinate the US economic programme. It was in conjunction with Blair, however, that Clinton played a decisive role persuading both Gerry Adams and David Trimble, the leader of the Ulster Unionists, as well as Bertie Arhern, the Irish leader, to accept the GFA of 1998, which envisaged a new assembly for Northern Ireland, a North–South Council to develop co-operation and a British-Irish council to promote relations between all parts of the British Isles.[46]

John Hume remarked of the 1985 Anglo-Irish Agreement that it provided 'a framework for a solution, not the solution itself'. The same can be said of the GFA: it was a framework designed to facilitate, not guarantee, peace in the province; indeed, it is reminiscent of the Anglo-Irish Agreement in content, and, just as in 1985, myriad problems remain. Northern Ireland remains a divided society, shaped by its past. Conflict continue to surround Orange Order parades and especially the Drumcree march. The killing of twenty-eight people by a bomb planted in Omagh by the 'Real IRA' in 1998 demonstrated the continued potency of the armed force tradition. Thus, when the new Northern Ireland Assembly eventually met it was against a backdrop of conflict not peace. Since then, the peace process has stuttered and periodically stopped. Those elected to the assembly have been embroiled in divisive issues such as policing, and, despite some evidence that the two groups could co-operate, the assembly has floundered on the issue of the decommissioning of paramilitary arms. The general elections of June 2001 saw the moderate unionists and nationalists weakened at the expense of Sinn Féin and the DUP. All of this has seemed to confirm a movement towards increasing division, and a lack of will to co-operate and compromise on the contemporary politics of the province.

Reflections

Although the politics of the province remain divided and the future of the political apparatus set up in 1998 somewhat uncertain, there has been momentous change in the province and in the politics of terrorism. During the 1970s and 1980s, an attack on a railway installation or military base in Britain or in Europe was assumed to be the work of the Provisionals. This is no longer the case. The start of the twenty-first century has seen a renunciation by most of the republican movement of violence as an agent of change. It is this ending of the military confrontation with the British that has enabled Sinn Féin to occupy a central place in representative politics. Although historians will long debate whether the IRA was actually defeated by the British Army, the decision by Adams and the Sinn Féin leadership to take the political path, accept partition and participate in devolved government was the key to a local and a wider peace. This shift by the republicans overturned the years' old conviction that the British had to be violently ejected from Ireland. Equally historic was the decision by the British Government at the end of the 1980s to include the Provisionals in discussion over the future of the province, a decision which came after years of a bloody counter-insurgency campaign in Ireland and the adoption of a counter-terrorism strategy (including emergency legislation and the use of interrogation) throughout the UK. (Of course the concentration of those whose concern is terrorism, following 9/11, is focused no longer on Irish violence but on the threat posed by Islamic fundamentalism.) It may be argued that the Blair agenda, embroiled in an increasingly controversial war in Iraq, has little room for the local politics of Ireland. Yet the problem still to be resolved is no longer how to reconcile republicanism and devolved British government but how to ensure that the unionists are not left dangerously adrift in their own land. The challenge is to reconcile unionism in its various guises to the new politics of Ireland.

Notes

1 Stewart argued that this was not an offensive question but a deadly serious one: see A. T. Q. Stewart, 'The Mind of Protestant Ulster', in David Watts (ed.), *The Constitution of Northern Ireland: Problems and Prospects*, Studies in Public Policy 4 (London: National Institute of Economic and Social Research, Policy Studies Institute, Royal Institute of International Affairs, Heinemann, 1981)
2 John McGarry and Brendan O'Leary, *Policing Northern Ireland: Proposals for a New Start* (Belfast: Blackstaff Press, 1999), p. 8.
3 David Fitzpatrick, 'Militarism in Ireland 1900–1922', in Thomas Bartlett and Keith Jeffrey (eds), *A Military History of Ireland* (Cambridge: Cambridge University Press, 1996) pp. 379-406.
4 Paul Bew has argued that there was perhaps less distinction between the 'people of Ireland' and the 'people of Britain' than this formulation allows for: see Paul Bew, *Ideology and the Irish Question: Ulster Unionism and Irish Nationalism 1912–1916*. (Oxford: Oxford University Press, 1994), p. 160.
5 Brendan O'Leary and John McGarry, *The Politics of Antagonism: Understanding Northern Ireland* (London and Atlantic Highlands, NJ: Athlone Press, 1993), p. 106.
6 *Ibid.*
7 *Ibid.*

8 Richard Rose, *Governing Without Consensus: An Irish Perspective* (London: Faber & Faber, 1971).

9 See D. George Boyce, *Nationalism in Ireland*, 3rd edn (London: Routledge, 1982), pp. 361–2.

10 Michael Farrell, *Northern Ireland: The Orange State*. 1st edn (London: Pluto, 1976).

11 See Conor Cruise O'Brien, *God Land: Reflections on Religion and Nationalism* (Cambridge: Cambridge University Press, 1988), p. 170.

12 D. W. Miller, *Queen's Rebels* (Dublin: Gill & Macmillan, 1978).

13 Michael Cox, 'The War That Came In From the Cold: Clinton and the Irish Question', *World Policy Journal*, vol. 14: no. 1, 1999.

14 For an assessment of British policy in the weeks before the deployment of troops see Peter Rose, *How the Troubles Came to Northern Ireland*, Contemporary History in Context Series (Basingstoke: Macmillan, 2000), chapter 7.

15 *Ibid.*

16 J. J. Lee, *Ireland 1912–1985: Politics and Society* (Cambridge: Cambridge University Press, 1989) p. 430.

17 James Callaghan, *A House Divided: The Dilemma of Northern Ireland* (London: Collins, 1973).

18 *Disturbances in Northern Ireland: Report of the Committee Appointed by the Governor of Northern Ireland* (Belfast: HMSO, 1969).

19 Hunt Committee, *Report of the Advisory Committee on Police in Northern Ireland*, Cmd. 535, (Belfast: HMSO, 1969).

20 Steve Bruce, *The Red Hand: Protestant Paramilitaries in Northern Ireland* (Oxford: Oxford University Press, 1992).

21 See M. L. R. Smith, *Fighting for Ireland: The Military Strategy of the Irish Republican Movement* (London: Routledge, 1995), p. 83.

22 On the legacies of the 1960s' IRA to the Provisionals see Richard English, *Armed Struggle: A History of the IRA* (Basingstoke: Macmillan, 2003), pp. 81–147.

23 See David A. Charters, 'Intelligence and Psychological Warfare Operations in Northern Ireland', *Journal of the Royal Services Institute for Defence Studies*, vol. 122, 1977, pp. 22–7.

24 P. Hillyard, 'Law and Order', in J. Darby (ed.), *Northern Ireland: The Background to the Conflict* (New York: Appletree Press, 1983).

25 English, *Armed Struggle*, p. 152.

26 John Whyte, *Interpreting Northern Ireland* (Oxford: Clarendon Press, 1990), p. 73–6.

27 Lee, *Ireland 1912–1985*, p. 436.

28 *Ibid.*, p. 442.

29 J. McGarry, 'A Consociational Settlement for Northern Ireland?', *Plural Societies*, vol. 20, no. 1, pp. 1–21.

30 Brian Faulkner, *Memoirs of a Statesman* (London: Weidenfeld & Nicolson, 1978), p. 263; Lee, *Ireland 1912–1985*, pp. 446–8; D. Anderson, *14 May Days: The Strike Which Broke the British in Ulster* (London: André Deutsch, 1975).

31 R. Weitzer, 'Contested Order: The Struggle Over British Security Policy in Northern Ireland', *Comparative Politics*, vol. 19, no. 3, 1987, pp. 293–5.

32 Peter Taylor, *The Search for the Truth* (London: Faber & Faber, 1987); John Stalker, *Stalker* (London: Harrap, 1988).

33 Michael von Tangen Page, *Prisons, Peace and Terrorism: Penal Policy in the Reduction of Political Violence in Northern Ireland and the Spanish Basque Country, 1968–97* (London: Macmillan, 1998) pp. 62–3.

34 *Ibid.*

35 W. H. Cox, 'The 1983 General Election in Northern Ireland: Anatomy and Consequences', *Parliamentary Affairs*, vol. 37, no. 1, winter 1984.

36 For a version of these events, see Margaret Thatcher, *The Downing Street Years* (London: HarperCollins, 1993), pp. 393–401.

37 *John Major: The Autobiography* (New York: HarperCollins, 1999).

38 Paul Arthur, 'The Anglo-Irish Agreement: A Device for Territorial Management?' in Dermot Keogh and Michael H. Haltzel (eds), *Northern Ireland and the Politics of Reconciliation*

(Washington, DC: Woodrow Wilson Centre Press, 1993), pp. 208–25.

39 Tom Garvin, 'The North and the Rest: The Politics of the Republic of Ireland', in Charles Townshend (ed.), *Consensus in Ireland: Approaches and Recessions* (Oxford: Clarendon Press, 1988).

40 O'Leary and McGarry, *The Politics of Antagonism*, p. 271.

41 This sentiment is expressed by Charles Townshend's 'The Supreme Law: Public Safety and State Security in Northern Ireland', in Keogh and Haltzel, *Northern Ireland and the Politics of Reconciliation*, p. 98; see Mark Urban, *Big Boy's Rules: The SAS and the Secret Struggle Against the IRA* (London: Faber & Faber, 1993).

42 Mark Urban, *UK Eyes Alpha* (London: Faber & Faber, 1996), p. 274.

43 Between 1990 and 1994, loyalist violence increased to an unprecedented level. In 1991 the formation of a Combined Loyalist Military Command was announced, and its constituent groups began to co-ordinate attacks on Catholics in response to IRA violence. The UVF and the UFF were responsible for eleven killings in 1992. Nationalists continued to claim that there was collusion between loyalist paramilitaries and the security forces. (These allegations had been previously investigated by the Stevens inquiry and in 1989 twenty-eight UDR men were arrested.) Even more ominously, loyalists claimed that it was the campaign of random assassination against Catholics which had forced the IRA to rethink its own violent campaign: see Marie-Therese Fay, Mike Morrissey and Marie Smyth, *Northern Ireland's Troubles: The Human Costs* (London: Pluto, 1999), pp. 20–1.

44 See Michael Cox, 'Bringing in the "International": The IRA Ceasefire and the End of the Cold War', *International Affairs*, vol. 73, October 1997.

45 Peter Taylor, *Provos The IRA and Sinn Féin* (London: Bloomsbury, 1977), pp. 344–5.

46 See Cox, 'The War That Came In From the Cold'; see also Jorg Neuheiser and Stefan Wolff (eds), *Peace at Last? The Impact of the Good Friday Agreement on Northern Ireland* (New York: Berghahn Books, 2002); Joseph O'Grady, 'An Irish Policy Born in the USA: Clinton's Break with the Past', *Foreign Affairs*, vol. 75, no. 3, May–June 1996, pp. 2–8.

4

Myths of consociationalism: from Good Friday to political impasse

PAUL BEW

What is the Belfast Agreement of April 1998, which was supported by 71 per cent of those voting in the referendum in Northern Ireland on 22 May 1998, and how did it come about?[1] One interpretation, by Professor Brendan O'Leary, stresses that the Agreement is in conformity with the essential principles of Arend Lijphart's notion of 'consociationalism'; it also draws attention to the long-term academic interest of the former secretary of state for Northern Ireland Dr Mo Mowlam in such a theory, as well as the fact that `at least one of her advisors has had an abiding interest in the subject'.[2] The same article concedes, however, that politicians, under the pressure of events, are capable of coming up with similar arrangements without any necessary recourse to an elaborate theoretical backdrop. The analysis of the Agreement presented here will follow this latter approach; not least because earlier research has demonstrated that the interpretation of a previous attempt at a settlement, the Anglo-Irish Agreement of 1985, as 'coercive consociationalism' was flawed.[3] This has been the approach also of writers advocating the type of settlement actually attempted in 1998.[4]

The top line of 'Heads of Agreement' of January 1998 which heralded the Stormont Agreement document was 'balanced constitutional change';[5] and now that the Belfast Agreement has been completed we can see exactly what was meant by that phrase. There will be, it is clear, significant changes both to British legislation and to the Irish constitution of 1937. The British Government has decided to repeal the Government of Ireland Act of 1920. Some republicans profess to think of this as very significant in a positive way, while some unionists are alarmed by the suggestion that in some way Northern Ireland's position within the UK is being weakened.

The nature of the constitutional deal

The Government of Ireland Act has been seen as Britain making a one-sided claim to supremacy over Northern Ireland, regardless of the views of the people living there. It sits uneasily with later solemn declarations by Britain that the Union is dependent on, and arises solely from, majority support in the province – declarations given by the British Government at the time of the Sunningdale Agreement in December 1973 and the Anglo-Irish Agreement of November 1985 and the Joint Declaration of December 1993.[6] In other words, one might say that the Government of Ireland Act represented an old-fashioned imperialist mindset and should be dispensed with.

But there is another side to this matter. As David Trimble pointed out in 1994, the controversial part of the Government of Ireland Act (section 75) is merely a 'saving clause' designed to assert Westminster's residual authority over a devolved Belfast Parliament.[7] The purpose is not to make an imperialist British claim over Northern Ireland against the wish of a majority of its citizens. The key legislation establishing the Union is, anyway, the Act of Union of 1800: that Act, as Trimble has stressed, remains in force.

The fact that David Trimble has long taken a relatively relaxed view of the significance of the Government of Ireland Act of 1920 has always suggested that he might trade it as part of a deal bringing changes to the Irish Constitution of 1937 – even though during the negotiation he often took a publicly rigid strand, such as when he wrote an article for the *Sunday Independent* (March 1999) apparently, but not actually, exhibiting a reluctance to accept change in this area.

In the new situation it will be a matter of British legislation that Northern Ireland remains part of the UK for so long as the majority there supports the Union. Thus in annex A, section 1, paragraph 1 of the Agreement it is affirmed 'that Northern Ireland in its entirety remains part of the United Kingdom and shall not cease to be so without the consent of a majority of the people of Northern Ireland voting in a poll held for the purposes of this section in accordance with Schedule 1'.[8] This is, in short, a continuation of the present reality, as most people in Northern Ireland understand it. The Belfast Agreement (Strand One, paragraph 33) contains an overt formal reiteration of British sovereignty. But what about the changes which, as part of the deal, are to be made to the Irish constitution? At present these state:

> Article 2: The national territory consists of the whole island of Ireland, its islands and territorial seas.
>
> Article 3: Pending the re-integration of the national territory, and without prejudice to the right of the Parliament and Government established by this Constitution to exercise jurisdiction over the whole of that territory, the laws enacted by that Parliament shall have the like area and extent of applications as the laws of Saorstat Eireann (the Irish State).

Increasingly, in private discussions between the two governments, the British began to challenge these articles, increasingly so after March 1990.

The McGimpsey case

In that month, Mr Justice Finlay ruled in the Irish Supreme Court in the celebrated McGimpsey case that the words 'The national territory consists of the whole island of Ireland, its islands and territorial seas', constituted a declaration of the extent of the national territory 'as a claim of legal right'. This unanimous ruling grounded the territorial claim and the 'constitutional imperative' towards Irish unity in article 2; in retrospect, however, it is clear that the McGimpsey ruling sounded the death knell for article 2.

At the margins of the European Union Summit in Corfu in June 1994 John Major pressed Albert Reynolds on two points: was the Irish Government prepared to amend its constitution to the point where its territorial claim over the North had been removed, and would the Government publicly recognise the legitimacy of British rule in Northern Ireland for so long as it reflects the consent of the majority? These two points came to be known as the 'Corfu test'. Reynolds endeavoured to reassure Major as to his good intentions, but even on the eve of the Framework Document's publication, the Fianna Fáil taoiseach was unwilling to change article 2, though he was prepared to change article 3 in a way which stressed both the consent principle and the existence of two jurisdictions in the island.[9] This represented progress of a sort, but the problem remained – the Supreme Court ruling in the McGimpsey case had been based on article 2, which remained unchanged. That explains why David Trimble and his negotiators insisted so loudly that any change to the Irish constitution had to be judge-proof; in other words, article 2, and not just article 3, had to be revised.

In the new Stormont Agreement, Mr Ahern indicated that he was prepared to go further than Mr Reynolds to meet unionist concerns – and unionist concern about this matter was one of the major irritations in the framework controversy. Interestingly, the opposition to Bertie Ahern on this matter – centred on the *Sunday Business Post* and some Fianna Fáil TDs – appears to have collapsed in the wave of euphoria following the Good Friday Agreement, though clearly Sinn Féin still have difficulties on this point.

The new article 2 will read:

> It is the entitlement and birthright of every person born in the island of Ireland, which includes its islands and seas, to be part of the Irish nation. This is also the entitlement of all persons otherwise qualified in accordance with law to be citizens of Ireland. Furthermore the Irish nation cherishes its special affinity with people of Irish ancestry living abroad who share its cultural identity and heritage.[10]

From a nationalist point of view, the *Irishness* of northern nationalists is in no way diminished by these new arrangements. Some say that Ireland is thus giving up its case in international law, but in truth Ireland has never had a case in international law – as Irish Foreign Affairs Department officials admitted privately in 1969, Dublin recognised Northern Ireland in 1925 as part of the UK and states may not undo such recognition by changing their internal constitutions at a later date.

Under this Agreement, the days of Paddy Hillery disputing at the UN the legitimacy of British rule in the North, or of Dick Spring stating, as he did in 1985, that the Irish claim to juridical sovereignty remained intact, are gone forever. Instead, the principle of consent, which is at the core of so much recent inter-governmental policy, is further enhanced. In particular, it is possible to interpret the outcome of the referendum in the Republic of Ireland, in which an over-whelming majority of voters endorsed the changes to articles 2 and 3 as part of the Good Friday Agreement, as by implication a devastating rebuke against the IRA's campaign to coerce a united Ireland.

But, of course, consent is a two-way street, and the GFA contains much that is designed to win nationalist support for a new dispensation in the North. It is in these areas that the main difficulty for unionists lies, but as far as balanced consti-tutional change is concerned unionists can now contemplate, for the first time since 1925, a new international agreement which fully recognises 'Northern Ireland's status as part of the United Kingdom' and which is not gainsaid by anything in the Irish Constitution.[11]

Structure

In its structural aspects the Agreement is three-stranded.

Strand One: the Northern Ireland Assembly

The Stormont Agreement provides for a new Northern Ireland Assembly of 108 members, 48 more than the number proposed for Wales and just 21 fewer than the Scottish Parliament's. It will have a substantial change in its freedom over domestic policy, but foreign policy stays at Westminster. The assembly was elected by pro-portional representation – single transferable vote (PR STV) using the 18 West-minster parliamentary constituencies, with each returning six members. A similar system had been used for elections to the Northern Ireland Forum in 1996, when five seats had been allocated to each constituency; the top-up system used for the forum's elections, permitting minor parties unable to secure representation in five-member constituencies to get representation in the forum, was, however, dropped.

At face value, the method of election received little attention in the negotiations. The arrangements did encounter some criticism for offending the principle of inclusivity, particularly from the Northern Ireland Women's Coalition and smaller parties to the talks, as offending the principle of inclusiveness which they wanted to retain a top-up element to the system, similar in practice to that used in the 1996 forum election or the additional-member element proposed for Scotland and Wales. Some of their proposals involved combining constituencies to give a lower threshold for election. As it was, the effect of increasing from five to six the number of members elected per constituency reduced the threshold for election from 16.7 to 14.3 per cent. It is provided in the Agreement that the executive authority of the assembly is to be discharged by a first minister and a deputy first minister, elected jointly by the assembly on a cross-community basis. On 1 July 1998, David Trimble, leader of the UUP, and Seamus Mallon, deputy leader of the SDLP, were elected by the assembly to the positions, respectively, of first minister-designate and deputy first minister-designate. This is reminiscent of the 1973 executive, with Brian Faulkner (UUP) and Gerry Fitt (SDLP) in the top two positions.

The agreement provided for up to ten ministers with departmental responsibilities, allocated using the d'Hondt system on the basis of the seats won in the assembly. Following the June 1998 elections, this meant that there would be 3 UUP ministers, 3 SDLP, 2 DUP and 2 Sinn Féin if the executive was formed without a boycott by any of the parties or the exclusion of any of the parties. This is the site of our current crisis around the issue of decommissioning.

Strand Two: North–South co-operation

Since the publication of the Stormont Agreement, Strand Two, or the cross-border co-operation issue, has been the dog that has not barked in the night. When the Framework Document was published in February 1995[12] the UUP was very upset by proposals in this area – calling them an embryonic all-Ireland government – but now the party seem relatively relaxed on the issue, and even rejectionist critics have kept their main fire for other issues such as prisoners, policing and decommissioning.

As compared to the Framework Document, the Stormont Agreement lays much more formal stress on the accountability of the North–South Ministerial Council. Indeed, it is made clear that the successful working of the North–South body is dependent on the successful working of the assembly. Instead of the remit of the North–South Ministerial Council being established simply by legislation in the Dail and Westminster, it now emerges – and this is a totally new element, marking a radical break with part of the Framework Document – that a 'shadow' Northern Irish Assembly could throughout the summer of 1998 designate the functions of a new body from a list which 'may include' animal and plant health, social welfare and fraud control on a cross-border basis, agriculture and marine matters, etc. On the face of it, this rather confirms the view of Mr Trimble's supporters that it would be possible to negotiate a 'cross-borderism' which was both accountable to northern opinion – after all, John Hume has always enthusiastically supported this principle – and limited to areas no more sensitive than those currently in process and bound to continue and expand, agreement or no agreement.

In short, the new North–South body is not 'free standing', which is hardly surprising because at no time has the Irish Government or the SDLP supported the 'free standing' aspect. But what about the other big unionist problem – the section of the Anglo-Irish Agreement which called for North–South institutions with clear identity and purpose to enable representatives of democratic institutions, North and South, to enter into new co-operative and constructive relationships to carry out delegated executive harmonising and consultative functions?

Under the terms of the Framework Document, this body was to have a 'dynamic', albeit an 'agreed dynamic'. Unionists in 1995 were outraged: they ignored the significance of agreement or consent – and anathematised words like 'executive', 'harmonising' and 'dynamic' insofar as they characterised the powers of a North–South body. These notions are absent from this new Agreement. At the Lancaster House talks session, when Jeffrey Donaldson amused and astonished the world's media by tearing up the Framework Document, David Trimble quietly pointed out the way things were going in this respect. Will there be increased or decreased cross-border activity 5 or 10 years from now if the Stormont Agreement is ratified? It is genuinely difficult to tell. The manifold areas of policy which might involve cross-border co-operation reflect the list-making capacity of the civil services, North and South; there is nothing noted in the Lancaster House paper which may not be carried out under the Anglo-Irish Agreement of 1985.

What, then, is the philosophy of the two governments on the cross-border issue? British thinking is practical and pragmatic: it notes the existence of hundreds of cross-border voluntary bodies in the sporting, religious and social fields – many of them with strong unionist participation – working harmoniously on the basis of a practicable consent principle;[13] and it hopes that an extension of this North–South activity will reduce nationalist alienation. Irish thinking is more visionary and more influenced by the notion of an 'island economy' in a European Union context. The Irish wish – the Framework Document is explicit on this point – to see harmonisation reflecting the growing integration of the two economies within Europe. British officials tend to be a little sceptical about the island economy notion: they point out both the relevant differences in the economic history of the two parts of the island and the impact in the North of the multi-billion pound subvention from London.

Anyway, Ireland will join European Monetary Union in the first wave, while Britain will not, thus slowing in some respects the integration of the two economies. Both sides meet, however, in the belief that an internal solution to the Northern Ireland problem is simply not available and that a North–South dimension is essential to any compromise. But where does all this leave us? The unionists in 1995 objected to the Framework Document on the grounds that it was allegedly an embryonic all-Ireland government.

Perhaps at that time the unionists overstated their case. After all, the Framework Document came from John Major's Cabinet, which had in a pivotal position the strongly pro-unionist Lord Cranborne – Gerry Adams, according to press reports, believed him to be the greatest enemy of the peace process – and from the Irish Government of John Bruton, known to the republicans as 'John Unionist'. Mr P. de Rossa, a cabinet minister close to Mr Bruton on the North, insisted at the time that a transitional arrangement would not provide stability.

Whatever the past, the unionists have now removed those terms which led them, and some hopeful republicans, to the assessment that the framework was inherently transitional to a united Ireland. Nevertheless, there is no escaping the fact that unionists have had to concede cross-border institutions – now described in more neutral and pragmatic terms – as the price of a deal. It is an outcome that was perhaps obvious from the first day of the talks. It is perhaps worth adding that, quite regardless of the nit-picking detail, the regular co-operation between Belfast and Dublin which will ensue has the capacity to end the internal Irish cold war which has dogged the relationship between Northern Ireland and the Republic since 1921. Indeed, a better relationship between the two political entities on the island is perhaps a more certain outcome of this deal than is a better relationship between the two communities in Northern Ireland.

Strand Three: east–west co-operation

When the Framework Document was published in 1995 even some of those intimately connected with its formulation were disappointed by the rather brief and unimaginative section on east–west relations, or Strand Three. Little was proposed in this area that was really new, but here again the Stormont Agreement marks a difference: a totally novel institutional structure is proposed, a British–Irish Council which will comprise representatives of the British and Irish governments plus devolved institutions in Northern Ireland, Scotland and Wales.

The new body has, above all, symbolic importance for unionists. It establishes a new political link with the rest of the UK – implicitly challenging the nationalist tendency to define the problem simply as an island of Ireland problem. It links Northern Ireland to the UK-wide process of constitutional reform sponsored by the Blair Government. As battles ensue, for example, over the allocation of regional public expenditure, the British–Irish Council will give the involved assemblies a forum from which to defend their material interests.

The Belfast Agreement tells us that the Anglo-Irish Agreement of 1985 is to be replaced. But what is the significance of this? Here, there is a row between the UUP and the DUP. The UUP claims credit for getting rid of the Agreement – the culmination of a long campaign – while the DUP points out that the new Stormont Agreement makes provision for a new British–Irish Agreement dealing with the totality of relations, which obviously bears a certain resemblance to the Hillsborough Accord structures. Are we really witnessing the delayed triumph of the anti-Agreement campaign of the 1980s? To the extent that unionists objected to the Anglo-Irish Agreement of 1985 on the grounds that it gave Dublin a role in the North, in the 'secretive' Maryfield Secretariat, without even the abandonment of the territorial claim – and this was a significant part of the rhetoric of the time – then the unionist case has been, in effect, conceded, with potent symbolism, the Maryfield operation is to be closed down.

Nevertheless, a close relationship between the British and Irish governments has been formed over the past thirteen years. The relationship is going to continue to be a significant feature of the Northern Irish scene even if the Irish diplomatic presence here is, as it were, regularised and put on a more 'normal' basis, as between two friendly states. This Anglo-Irish relationship is not as unproblematical as excluded unionists have tended to assume – there are often sharp disagreements. Some British officials are wryly inclined to say that Senator Mitchell's team achieved more real understanding of the local political scene in a couple of years than the Irish team had done in over thirteen years.

Nevertheless, the Anglo-Irish intergovernmental and diplomatic relationship are part of the furniture and have survived all Ian Paisley's rhetoric as well as his prediction that it could be smashed by popular resistance. This relationship will continue under the new British–Irish Intergovernmental Conference, but, at least, matters will be more open and democratic and local politicians will be involved in its working. But perhaps the greatest change here is not institutional but psychological. Although the Anglo-Irish Agreement of 1985 made reference to devolution, this was, in the view of senior British officials at the time, mere 'lip service'. The agreement was imposed and the Dublin Government given a voice in the North as a substitute for, not an incentive to, a power sharing deal which unionists at that time refused.

Gradually, and especially under John Major, the British moved back towards a policy of re-engaging the alienated unionists in the political system; this was related to a general British perception – explicitly stated in Mrs Thatcher's memoirs – that the agreement had been less than a success.[14] The new Strand Three deal protects nationalist interests by preserving a role for the Irish Government in the North, but it also protects unionist interest by healing the unionist rift with the British Government and polity.

There are, of course, other controversial aspects to the Stormont Agreement – policing, prisoners, the equality–Irish language agenda – some of which generate more understandable emotion than the actual three strands which were negotiated in the main, it has to be said, by the unionists, the SDLP, the Alliance Party, and the two governments. Some of these are not as novel as they appear. In 1921, Sir James Craig (the first Stormont prime minister) promised a police service which would be fully representative of the Catholic community.[15] After previous IRA campaigns had failed, unionist governments were relatively liberal in their prisoner-release programmes.

As long ago as the 1930s, Stormont's Education Minister Lord Charlemont instructed his ministry to recognise the Irish language in order to 'disarm criticism on the part of anti-British elements'. Finally, commissions have been established to deal with equality, policing and human rights. The Agreement has been underpinned by a radical, if controversial, programme of release of paramilitary prisoners. But the complex process of multi-layered deal-making that produced the GFA does not preclude the characterisation of the outcome in terms employed by political scientists. Thus, according to Brendan O'Leary, this Agreement meets all four of the criteria for a consociational agreement laid out by Lijphart:

- cross-community executive power sharing;
- proportionality rules applied throughout the relevant governmental and public sectors;
- community self-government (or autonomy) and equality in cultural life; and
- veto rights for minorities.[16]

Further, if use is made of the terminology developed by Sammy Smooha and Theo Hanf to describe modes of conflict regulation,[17] it may be said that Northern Ireland is on the verge of completing a transition from being an ethnic democracy (though not, I think, a state) in the 1921/72 period to being a liberal, multicultural, consociational-type political entity, assuming, of course, that the great and unresolved issue – the decommissioning of paramilitary arms – does not bring the whole system tumbling down.

Conclusion (2004)

In the event, however, this is precisely what has happened. The UUP's gamble on setting up an executive *before* decommissioning was rewarded by the slowness and secrecy with which the IRA moved on the decommissioning issue. There was also a broader failure to make the transition away from paramilitarism. This view is now the consensus of both the Irish and the British Government. The IRA's failure has been symbolised by arrests in Colombia and on 'Stormontgate', the alleged spying affair, not to mention the conviction for gun-running in Florida. As a result, despite three IRA acts of decommissioning, the executive has functioned for only nineteen months since the Agreement of April 1998. At the time of writing (early summer 2004), there is little optimism that it can be rescued within any realistic time span. The emergence of the DUP and Sinn Féin as the largest parties in the assembly has further dimmed the prospect of a return to power-sharing devolution. The report of the Independent Monitoring Commission, which made public the full extent of ongoing paramilitary activity in both communities, has, in the short term at least, made it difficult for those factions in the DUP which are said to favour a deal with Sinn Féin to actually act on that preference.

As profound a restraining factor, however, is the disenchanted non-devolutionist public mood within the unionist community; this, of course, is combined with a shift within nationalism, away from the relatively moderate and non-violent stance of the SDLP. We are brought face to face with the limitations of consociational theory in the analysis of ethnic conflict and its shifting moods. In their new book, *The Northern Ireland Consociational Engagements* (2004) Brendan O'Leary and John McGarry repeat their view that the Agreement is the product of tacit and implicit consociational thinking: this is a partial truth, applying only to the political dimension. The Agreement was a product much more directly of a series of transformations in relationships within the two blocs – in particular the remarkable new relationship between the British State and both the Unionist and Sinn Féin leaderships being absolutely central.[18] What, after all, does the consociational theory contribute to our understanding of the collapse of the power-sharing executive?

In their study O'Leary and McGarry argue that unionists should be fearful of any collapse of the Belfast Agreement's institutions because

the two governments would likely pursue the promotion of equality of esteem, reduction in the employment gap between Catholics and Protestants, and the reform of policing. Eventually there will be a shift towards direct co-sovereignty of the region. If the Agreement's core institutions are not established, then any legal challenge to the implementation of changes to Articles 2 and 3 of the Republic's Constitution is likely to be successful.[19]

But where is the threat? For 'equality of esteem' and the 'reduction of the unemployment gap between Catholics and Protestants' will be staples of government policy, whether or not there is devolution. They have been so for a generation and, indeed, very considerable progress has been achieved: the latest authoritative report[20] flags up potential Protestant disadvantage stemming from a relative lack of presence in Northern Irish universities, creating a 'brain drain' as Protestants leave for (often academically more serious) institutions in the rest of the UK and do not return. Yet the question remains: if this is a problem which requires action from a Protestant or unionist point of view, does it help to have nationalist or republican ministers of education, as in the previous executive? The 'reform of policing', too, will remain at the heart of government policy. The Patten Commission on Policing Reform had the stated objective of satisfying both Gerry Adams and David Trimble; in the end, it satisfied neither and helped destabilise support for Trimble. Policing remains a serious, divisive and debilitating issue in the context of the Agreement project. The SDLP's support for policing is the one real achievement, but that coincided with the party's loss of status as the largest nationalist party and thus greatly reduced its value. Nonetheless, the two governments have an agenda on policing reform which is unstoppable, whatever the political context – devolution or not. But it is possible that many unionists would regard devolution of policing powers to a new executive as even more irksome than the present dispensation. There is therefore no lever here either. As for articles 2 and 3, it would be difficult for any Irish government to place such a blatant irredentist 1930s' style formula back into its constitution, and there is no sign of such thinking. Even if it happened, it would not worry unionists, since the Treaty of 1925 Ireland on international law (as opposed to domestic constitutions which recognised Northern Ireland as part of the United Kingdom, and the Irish State is well aware that this recognition can not be undone.[21] The significance of the changes to Articles 2 and 3 in the 1998 referendum is that they opened the way for better North–South co-operation, as envisaged in the agreement. Such co-operation would have been impossible in the ideological context set by the tone of articles 2 and 3 of the 1937 Irish constitution, which asserted the democratic illegitimacy of partition. Incidentally, the relaxed attitude of unionists towards such co-operation today is one of Trimble's leading achievements.

But what of the sharpest thrust of all from Professors O'Leary and McGarry – the claim that the two states would inevitably move towards a system of shared sovereignty. This could be threatening to unionists, especially if Sinn Féin was represented in an Irish government. There is, however, no evidence of any British willingness to move in this direction as yet; and it is difficult to see what would be the clear advantage for London. Even more crucially, many unionists believe that they have been living under at least a form of joint authority since the Anglo-Irish Treaty of 1985. The spectre of shared sovereignty, too, ceased to frighten them: typically, polling shows that a majority of DUP voters (once the most devolutionist of parties) would prefer a form of direct rule, including those with a Dublin role, to any form of devolution involving Sinn Féin in Northern Ireland's governance. Direct rule in 2004 has brought unemployment to a record low (a mere 40,000), housing prices rise, hospital waiting lists fall, and there is peace for the vast majority. Where, then, is the impetus for change? The widespread unionist attitude to politics – one of combined cussedness and feebleness – has often been profoundly debilitating of unionism's case: it is an attitude to politics which David Trimble sought to change. Today, ironically, it has a maximum purchase on the political process. Those who continue to argue for the Agreement have to make the case that a political stand-off will not be good in the long term for Northern Ireland; but who, either in London or in Dublin, is acting in a way that will reinforce that argument? The greatest obstacle to progress has been the IRA's refusal to end paramilitary activity; that may not happen in a time-frame of less than several years, and it certainly will not happen if Sinn Féin is not reassured of a revival of the Agreement and its institutions.

Notes

1 The terms, 'Stormont Agreement', 'Belfast Agreement' and 'Good Friday Agreement' are used here interchangeably to describe the Agreement reached at Stormont Castle Grounds in Belfast on 10 April 1998.

2 Brendan O'Leary, 'The Nature of the Agreement', *Fordham International Law Journal*, vol. 22, no. 4, 1999, pp. 163ff.

3 See Paul Bew, Peter Gibbon and Henry Patterson, *Northern Ireland 1921–1996: Political Forces and Social Classes*, 2nd edn (London: Serif, 1996), chapter 6, especially pp. 213–17.

4 See Paul Bew, Henry Patterson and Paul Teague, *Between War and Peace: The Political Future of Northern Ireland* (London: Lawrence & Wishart, 1997), pp. 203–16.

5 For the text of the 'Heads of Agreement' document, see Appendix 12.

6 For the text of the Joint Declaration, see Appendix 4.

7 *Parliamentary Brief*, summer 1994.

8 For full text of Annex A, see Appendix 2.

9 For text of Framework Document, see Appendix 9.

10 For text of the new Article 3, see Appendix 2.

11 See on this point Brigid Hadfield, 'The Belfast Agreement: Sovereignty and the State of the Union', *Public Law*, winter 1998, pp. 599–616.

12 See Appendix 9.

13 For an account of cross-border activity by non-governmental organisations, see John Whyte, 'The Permeability of the United Kingdom–Irish Border: A Preliminary Reconnaissance', *Administration*, vol. 31, no. 3, 1983, pp. 300–15.

14 Margaret Thatcher, *The Downing Street Years* (London: HarperCollins, 1995), paperback edn, pp. 402–6.

15 Paul Bew, 'The Political History of Northern Ireland: The Prospects for North–South Co-operation', in Anthony F. Heath, Richard Breen and Christopher T. Whelan (eds), *Ireland North and South: Perspectives from Social Science*, Proceedings of the British Academy, vol. 98 (Oxford: Oxford University Press for the British Academy, 1999), pp. 409–10.

16 O'Leary, 'The Nature of the Agreement', pp. 1631–41; see A. Lÿphart, *Democracy in Plural Societies* (New Haven, CT: Yale University Press, 1977).

17 Sammy Smooha and Theo Hanf, 'The Diverse Modes of Conflict-Regulation in Deeply Divided Societies', in Anthony D. Smith (ed.), *Ethnicity and Nationalism* (Leiden and New York: E. J. Brill, 1992), pp. 27–34.

18 On Trimble's side, see the vitally important book by Dean Godson, *Himself Alone: David Trimble and the Ordeal of Unionism* (London: HarperCollins, 2004). This 900-page volume gives background and detail for the Unionist side which has never been given before. Its only counterpart on the republican side is Ed Molony's *A Secret History of the IRA* (London: Penguin, 2003).

19 John McGarry and Brendan O'Leary, *The Northern Ireland Conflict: Consociational Engagements* (Oxford: Oxford University Press, 2004), p. 273.

20 Bob Osborne and Ian Shuttleworth, *Fair Employment in Northern Ireland: A Generation On* (Belfast: Blackstaff Press, 2004), p. 84.

21 See Enda Staunton's neglected but authoritative article, 'The Boundary Commission Debacle', *History Ireland*, vol. 2, no. 2, summer 1996.

PART II
The politics of the Good Friday Agreement

5

Polarisation or new moderation?
Party politics since the GFA

JON TONGE

Introduction

Party politics in Northern Ireland since the 1998 GFA appear to have been characterised by polarisation, at times destabilising the peace and political processes. In
the 2003 assembly elections, the DUP and Sinn Féin emerged as the largest
representatives of unionism and nationalism, requiring a deal to be struck between
these supposed extremes for the GFA, or similar type of agreement, to become
embedded. The avowed political moderates of the UUP and the SDLP, in many
respects the principal brokers of the GFA, found themselves overtaken by centri-
fugal forces. The development might be considered startling, given that the GFA
offered much to political moderates. The UUP could point to the principle of
consent at the core of the deal. The SDLP viewed the three-stranded institutional
arrangements of the deal as the culmination of its political thinking. The centrist
APNI has seen its vote halved, despite having always advocated devolved power-
sharing as the most appropriate political arrangement.

As the GFA stumbled through various crises following its birth, the anti-GFA
DUP prospered. Despite the apparent confirmation of Northern Ireland's place in
the UK for the foreseeable future, the DUP has highlighted what it sees as a series
of unpalatable concessions to republicans during and after the Agreement, a
critique with a powerful impact on a large section of unionism. Meanwhile, the
UUP has had its divisions over whether to support the GFA played out publicly via
a succession of internal votes and there has been prominent criticism of the
leadership's pro-GFA strategy. Concurrently, Sinn Féin has prospered among the
nationalist electorate, rewarded for its movement away from armed struggle and
backed by an electorate that increasingly views the party as a better defender of the
Agreement's gains than the SDLP. Yet, as the small group of republican dissidents
are keen to point out, Sinn Féin's pre-1998 political approach was entirely at odds
with much of the Agreement's contents.

This chapter examines three aspects of post-Agreement party competition. Firstly, it explores the extent to which the electors have aligned themselves with the stouter representatives of their ethnic bloc. Secondly, the chapter considers the extent to which intra-bloc and intra-party division, evident mainly among unionists, has destabilised the GFA. Thirdly, consideration is given to how Sinn Féin has displaced the SDLP and an assessment made of the impact of this displacement on the political process. In assessing the problems of the traditional moderates, the chapter utilises evidence from a membership survey of the large ruling body of the UUP, the Ulster Unionist Council (UUC), and similar data from surveys of the entire SDLP and APNI memberships, conducted between 1999 and 2002.[1]

The changed political landscape

The growth of the DUP and Sinn Féin, and the attendant, if inflated, fears for the peace process, have been evident since soon after the GFA was reached. The 2003 Assembly elections ended UUP hegemony over unionism as the DUP overtook its rival for the first time in a non-European contest. Although, as predicted by the party's then leader David Trimble, the UUP held its seats and vote share, the DUP's rounding up of minority anti-GFA Legislative Assembly members (MLAs) ensured that the party overtook the UUP in terms of first-preference votes and assembly seats (tables 5.1 and 5.2).

The ability of the DUP and Sinn Féin to mobilise and extend their respective constituencies relegated the UUP to third place on first-preference votes. The DUP extended its support in middle-class, traditionally UUP areas, while Sinn Féin's ability to win a seat in middle-class South Belfast was indicative of the upwardly mobile demography of its vote. Furthermore, DUP and Sinn Féin voters

Table 5.1   Electoral competition, 1992–2005

Election	UUP	DUP	SDLP	SF	Other
1992 Westminster	34.5	13.1	23.5	10.0	19.9
1993 Local	29.4	17.3	22.0	12.4	18.9
1994 European	23.8	29.2	28.9	9.0	19.1
1996 Forum	24.2	18.8	21.4	15.5	20.1
1997 Westminster	32.7	13.1	24.1	16.1	14.0
1997 Local	27.8	15.6	20.7	16.9	19.0
1998 Assembly	21.3	18.1	22.0	17.6	21.0
1999 European	17.7	28.5	28.2	17.4	8.2
2001 Westminster	26.8	22.5	21.0	21.7	8.0
2001 Local	23.0	21.5	19.4	20.7	15.4
2003 Assembly	22.7	25.7	23.5	17.0	11.1
2005 Westminster	17.7	33.7	17.5	24.3	6.8
2005 Local	18.0	30.4	16.0	18.4	17.2

Table 5.2   The Northern Ireland Assembly, 2003

Party	Assembly seats	Change on 1998
DUP*	30	+10
UUP*	27	−1
SF	24	+6
SDLP	18	−6
Others	9	−9

* The DUP tally was immediately increased by 3 defections from the UUP, bringing the respective totals to 33 and 24.

were more *disciplined* in their lower-preference vote transfers under the single transferable vote (STV) system. Sinn Féin urged its voters to support all the party's candidates, then lower-preference transfer to the SDLP, and, after this, to other pro-Agreement candidates. Furthermore, as an example of how to reduce *excessive* first-preference votes for prominent party candidates, the party's president Gerry Adams canvassed strongly on behalf of other Sinn Féin candidates in West Belfast to shore up their first preferences, his own election being a formality. Four of the five Sinn Féin candidates thus topped the poll and all were duly elected. A similar example was evident in North Antrim, where DUP voters divided nearly evenly between Ian Paisley Senior and Junior and transferred two-thirds of their votes to the DUP's other candidate. In contrast, the pro- and anti-GFA faultline was apparent among UUP candidates and supporters. Less than half of anti-GFA Jeffrey Donaldson's surplus in Lagan Valley transferred to other UUP candidates, with DUP candidates receiving only 1,400 fewer transfers than those gained by the UUP. Donaldson joined the DUP soon afterwards.

Nonetheless, post-GFA voting patterns have not been based overwhelmingly on the pro- versus anti-GFA faultline. Communal voting, irrespective of attitude to the GFA, remains the norm. Even during the 1998 assembly elections, held during the 'honeymoon period' of the Agreement, when the distinction between pro- and anti-GFA unionists was stark, UUP–DUP vote transfers, and vice-versa, were easily the most common forms of transfer among unionist voters. Indeed lower-preference transfer votes to anti-Agreement unionists, undertaken by voters recording first preferences for pro-Agreement unionists, matched the figure recorded for all the other pro-Agreement parties combined.[2] In other words, pro-Agreement unionists preferred to keep their votes 'in bloc', even if this meant supporting anti-Agreement unionists. The solidarity of DUP voters was impressive, almost four-fifths transferring 'in house' but even here 44 per cent recorded lower preference votes for pro-GFA UUP candidates.[3] In 2003, when candidates were elected at the first count, only 0.8 per cent of their surplus votes transferred across the community divide.

Thus communal voting remains the norm in Northern Ireland after the

Agreement. Support of the GFA nonetheless is a marker in terms of propensity to stay with the ethnic bloc among the 858-member UUC. Unsurprisingly, its anti-GFA members are more favourably disposed to their electoral rival, the DUP, than are pro-GFA UUC members, as table 5.3 indicates.

Table 5.3 Potential lower preference vote transfers for other unionist assembly parties, according to vote in the GFA referendum among UUC members (where significant difference (<.05))

| | Vote in GFA referendum | | |
Mean (s.d)	Yes	No	N
DUP	2.65	1.52	264
	(1.14)	(.95)	
UKUP	2.72	1.46	251
	(1.09)	(.82)	
PUP	2.85	3.37	226
	(1.03)	(.86)	

Notes: 1= very likely 4 = no possibility

Pro-GFA UUC members are more hostile to the pro-GFA Progressive Unionist Party (PUP) than to the anti-GFA DUP or the tiny UKUP, equally opposed to the Agreement. This hostility to the PUP is evident even though that party helped deliver a section of the wavering Protestant working class to the 'Yes' camp during the 1998 GFA referendum. For many UUC members, the PUP's link with the UVF places the party outside of the domain of *acceptable* politics.

The DUP's substantial increase in support is explained partly by the ending of the party's willingness to step aside to allow UUP candidates a free run at SDLP and Sinn Féin seats, as happened in North Belfast and West Tyrone in 1997. From 1997 to 2001, the UUP lost 41,600 votes, whilst the DUP gained almost 75,000.[4] Despite the vibrancy of intra-unionist electoral rivalries, turnout remains substantially lower than in constituencies held by a majority of nationalist representatives, although turnout fell by more in predominantly nationalist areas in 2003 (table 5.4). The greater fall in turnout in nationalist areas might be explained as a combination of new voting procedures, a growing cynicism over Northern Ireland's politics now being extended to the nationalist community and, possibly, the urgings of dissidents to ignore the poll.

The 2003 election result confirmed diminished confidence within the unionist community over the GFA. Support had always been marginal, with only 57 per cent of Protestants backing the deal in the May 1998 referendum.[5] After this honeymoon period, Protestant support for the GFA declined, and by 2001 it had become a minority taste within that community.[6] In October 2002, as the assembly and

Table 5.4   Variations in electoral turnout in the Northern Ireland Assembly elections 2003

		%	
Constituency type	Number	Turnout	Fall in Turnout
Majority unionist	9	60.1	5.3
Majority nationalist	7	68.3	9.4
Evenly divided	2	61.6	4.6

executive collapsed, a BBC Northern Ireland *Hearts and Minds* poll reported that only 33 per cent of Protestants still backed the deal.

Nonetheless, the DUP's 2003 election triumph did not automatically spell the end of the GFA, although the British Government's emphasis was now on the deal as a 'framework' rather than as a definitive charter. The electoral arithmetic, while discouraging on the unionist side, was not as bleak as under Northern Ireland's previous experiment in consociationalism, the short-lived 1974 power-sharing executive established under the Sunningdale Agreement. In 2003, 70 per cent of voters supported pro-GFA parties, although the presence of anti-GFA UUP candidates diminished the salience of this statistic. The DUP's gains at the expense of fringe anti-GFA MLAs (often more militant than the DUP) at least offered the possibility of greater cohesion in a review of the deal. Furthermore, the DUP insisted that it was a pro-devolution, pro-power-sharing, party and came close to a deal with Sinn Féin in 2004.

Support for the political centre, as represented by APNI, fell to a mere 3.7 per cent and the Northern Ireland Women's Coalition vanished from the assembly Alliance held its seats and retained the option of supporting pro-GFA unionists in any revived assembly, assuming that designations of MLAs as Unionist, Nationalist or other were retained (a dubious prospect). Importantly, loyalist paramilitaries were still represented, in that the PUP, linked to the UVF, retained one of its two seats.

Unionist approaches to the GFA

The divisions within the UUP over the GFA, evident since the deal was clinched in 1998, have collapsed the party. Eleven special meetings of its ruling UUC have been held, each backing the position of party leader David Trimble by an average majority of 56 to 44 per cent. Trimble eventually resigned after losing his Upper Ban Westminster seat in 2005. The extent of dissent within the UUC, allied to the electoral threat of the DUP, has ensured that UUP backing for the GFA has been based on critical support and particular interpretation, the latter translated into insistence that the Provisional IRA puts its arms beyond use and clarifies that its war is over. The UUP 2003 election manifesto included a charter pledging to 'hold firmly to the requirement for acts of completion' and to 'support new powers to monitor paramilitary activity and impose sanctions'.[7] There was little indication, however, of the precise terms on which the UUP would return to government alongside Sinn Féin. This question was enlarged by the party's rejection of the IRA's third act of decommissioning, in October 2003. The refusal was costly, being followed by the British Government's agreeing to stage elections, even though the grounds for postponement remained identical to those pertaining when the May 2003 scheduled contest had been prohibited.

The UUP stressed the benefits of devolution in respect of 'bread-and-butter' issues in its 2003 campaign. Given the limited experience of devolution amid persistent political wrangling, this approach carried some risk. In defence of the Agreement, the UUP had previously highlighted how it had constructed a 'unionist veto' on assembly decisions and North–South expansion, while arguing that 'unreconstructed terrorists' would not be allowed in government.[8]

The DUP's moral opposition to such GFA items as prisoner releases and changes in policing offered a powerful political marketing device, despite the pertinence of the sardonic post-election remarks of the UUP leader that he would 'look forward to the day when he [Paisley] gets the name of the RUC restored and the released IRA prisoners sent back to jail'.[9] The DUP has strongly attacked the GFA as an immoral deal, in addition to criticising its all-Ireland element. Combined with zero-sum game appeals that the 'equality agenda' of Strand One also threatens the economic fortunes of Protestants, the party has updated its traditional twin appeal to rural evangelical or fundamentalist Protestants and to a more secular loyalist working class.[10] Indeed the party has been described as a politico-religious organisation.[11] Its leader remains the embodiment of Ulster Protestant fundamentalism, albeit assisted by more secular deputies.[12]

The DUP has oscillated between outright rejection of the Agreement and *renegotiation* of the deal, to lessen charges of negativity. Untainted by involvement in its production, the DUP has highlighted unsavoury aspects of the deal and described it as a 'failed agreement'. Nonetheless, the party does not reject power-sharing with Sinn Féin *per se*, arguing, for example, that loyalist–republican co-operation on Belfast City Council 'shows that if you have a different structure, it [power-sharing] can work'.[13] Indeed the DUP has gradually developed 'a more subtle and less hysterical critique' of the GFA.[14] The party claimed it had acquired a mandate for 'constructive change' following its 2003 election success.[15] With one-third of its supporters claiming to have supported the GFA in the 1998 referendum and half wishing the deal to work, the DUP has attempted to avoid the charge of outright rejectionism.[16] Pro-GFA fellow-loyalists have argued that emotive aspects of the package were isolated and elevated.[17] However, the DUP's critique was comprehensive, on constitutional *and* moral grounds. It outlined seven 'principles', designed to underpin any renegotiated agreement.[18] Its document *Towards a New Agreement* restated the critique evident in the party's 2001 election manifesto,

Leadership to Put Things Right.[19] Both documents criticised the presence of 'terrorists' in government; the dilution of British culture; the all-island dimension to the deal and the morally unacceptable aspects of prisoner releases and policing changes.[20]

Realigning unionism: could anti-GFA forces combine?

With the UUP in massive retreat, is there any purpose in persisting with the GFA? Table 5.5 indicates that there is only lukewarm support for parallel consent power-sharing mechanisms even within the UUP and similarly tepid backing for the attachment of cross-border bodies to the institutions created under Strand One of the GFA. It has been asserted that there is minimal difference between UUP and DUP supporters in their widespread opposition to the involvement of the Irish Government in the affairs of Northern Ireland.[21] The high standard deviations in table 5.5 indicate the presence of a large number of opponents to key aspects of the GFA even among its supporters.

Given that cross-community backing for assembly legislation and a whole-island dimension are integral aspects of the Agreement, the modest support for these aspects from those who supported the deal is perhaps perturbing. The mechanics of cross-community power-sharing have been questioned, with some supporters of the GFA opposing unionist and nationalist bloc designations within the assembly. The extent of the whole-island dimension was always set to be an arena of negotiation, with unionists successful in watering down the more substantial whole-island proposals of the 1995 Framework Document. Anti-GFA voters on the UUC are hostile to enforced power-sharing via parallel consent, with such hostility surprisingly outweighing opposition to the whole-island dimension of the GFA. The assumption, therefore, that opposition to the GFA has been primarily based on concerns over an unpalatable 'micro-agenda' of prisoner releases and policing changes, allied to greater input from the Irish Republic, may need modification.

Table 5.5   UUC vote in the GFA referendum and attitudes to dual majority voting/power-sharing with cross-border bodies

	How voted in GFA referendum		
Mean Position (s.d)	*Yes*	*No*	*N*
Assembly decisions should have dual majority	0.27 (1.31)	−1.36 (0.92)	284
Power sharing with cross-border bodies is best solution	0.30 (1.16)	−0.57 (1.14)	278

Notes: −2 = strongly disagree +2 = strongly agree

Nonetheless, as table 5.6 indicates, hostility to the prisoners and policing issues unites the pro- and anti-GFA wings of the UUC. As one would expect, opposition to the early release of paramilitary prisoners and the policing changes wrought by the Patten Report is considerably greater among opponents of the GFA.

Table 5.6   Attitudes to prisoners and policing according to vote in GFA referendum within the UUC

Mean Position (s.d)	Voted in GFA referendum		
	Support	Reject	N
Patten should	−0.66	−1.67	292
be fully implemented	(.90)	(1.20)	
Prisoner releases	−0.75	−1.54	288
releases justified	(1.24)	(1.10)	

Notes: −2 = strongly disagree; +2 = strongly agree

Whatever its flaws, the GFA was sold as the 'only show in town' by the various secretaries of state for Northern Ireland who presided over the deal. Such an argument is, unsurprisingly, not subscribed to by opponents of the GFA. Table 5.7 confirms that the integrationist wing of the UUP remains alive, drawing support, in particular, from 'No' voters.

The UUP remains a party sympathetic to integration; as such, its commitment to devolution might be questioned. The integrationist approach of anti-GFA UUP members indicates how they occupy *different* political terrain from the that of the

Table 5.7   Vote in the GFA referendum and attitudes within the UUC to political integration within the UK

Mean Position (s.d)	How voted in GFA referendum		
	Yes	No	N
Best solution:			
Full integration	−0.05	1.14	282
of Northern Ireland	(1.37)	(1.03)	
into the UK			
Direct rule	−0.98	−0.10	279
	(0.88)	(1.26)	
Electoral integration	0.00	0.30	285
(British parties to contest	(1.27)	(1.25)	
Northern Ireland elections)			

Notes: −2 = strongly disagree +2 = strongly agree

Figure 5.8   Indicative summary of policy positions within the UUC and DUP

	Pro-GFA UUC	Anti-GFA UUC	DUP
Good Friday Agreement	Pro	Anti	Anti
Devolution	Pro	Anti	Pro
Pan-Unionism	Anti	Pro	Anti
Direct Rule	Anti	Neutral	Anti
Integration	Anti	Pro	Anti
Electoral Integration	Neutral	Neutral	Not tested

DUP, which has long been a devolutionist party. The integrationist Molyneaux leadership of the UUP, from 1979 until 1995, 'recognised the fragility of belief in Stormont as a bulwark against a united Ireland'.[22] Molyneaux's aspiration was impeded by the inter-governmentalism and bi-nationalism of the 1985 Anglo-Irish Agreement. Nonetheless, despite the 'carrots' for the return of devolution offered under the Agreement, Molyneaux did not steer the UUP on a devolutionist course. Despite the arrival of a pro-devolution leader in Trimble in 1995, and notwithstanding the restructuring of the UK by the Labour Government since 1997, there is clearly still an integrationist constituency within unionism's largest party. That faction is not especially keen on the logic of integration, by which *mainland* political parties would contest elections in Northern Ireland. Meanwhile, supporters of the GFA are hostile to direct rule from Westminster, although this temporary scenario is less unacceptable to anti-GFA unionists.

The DUP's approach has been pro-devolution, anti-GFA. The party demands removal of the IRA, followed by a 'quarantine' period, prior to entering government with Sinn Féin, although its near-willingness to conclude a deal in 2004 hints at a new pragmatism. Table 5.8 indicates DUP and UUP policy positions. Traditionally, the DUP has been disdained by sections of the UUP, not least because it has been seen as a 'tribal', more working-class, loyalist party, prepared to engage in civil disobedience or dubious activity, such as involvement with the Ulster Resistance during the 1980s. Among Protestants, support for the DUP has been weakest in the professional and managerial class.[23] In contrast, the UUP has been seen as the party of the *respectable* Protestant middle-class, although survey evidence within the party indicates few occupational differences between those supporting or rejecting greater unity with the DUP. The UUP's 2005 election campaign suggested that 'decent' people vote UUP, in which case there must be a high level of indecency with the unionist community.

The nationalist ascendancy of Sinn Féin

As moderate unionism has attempted to come to terms with the GFA, moderate nationalism has also been beset by difficulties. The three-stranded arrangements of the GFA reflected much SDLP thinking, yet the party has suffered electorally since the deal. Its nationalist rival, Sinn Féin, formerly committed to armed over-throw of British colonial rule, ended its support for the IRA's campaign with entry to Stormont and the management of Northern Ireland under British rule. Sinn Féin's electoral success has masked its failure to achieve republican objectives, although these were not greatly furthered by the alternative of armed struggle. The party lacks a clear strategy on how to unite Ireland, with any faith in demographic change thwarted by the 2001 census, revealing a mere 2 per cent increase in the Catholic population since 1991. The SDLP could feel aggrieved over the apparent unfairness of it all. The Hume–Adams dialogue now appears the ultimate piece of altruism undertaken by the former SDLP leader, even if it was preceded by Adams's own secret moves towards ending the armed struggle.[24] As Sinn Féin has occupied the SDLP's political territory, the future of Northern Ireland's moderate constitu-tional nationalist party appears in doubt. Sinn Féin's new constitutionalism, allied to its successful promotion of nationalist bloc politics, is an appealing mixture to a nationalist electorate, many of whom were previously disdainful of the association of the republican movement with violence.

Nationalist convergence during the peace process had a long gestation. Although it is often traced to the Hume–Adams dialogue of 1988, it is evident that Gerry Adams, as president of Sinn Féin since 1983, wished to forge a pan-nationalist alliance, centred on a vision of Irish self-determination that might not necessarily result in physical British withdrawal from Northern Ireland. A 'greening' of the SDLP occurred after the collapse of the Sunningdale power-sharing deal in 1974, also facilitating this development.[25] The SDLP moved from its socialist origins and became less concerned with 'red' politics, instead favouring a 'greener' nationalist outlook. According to the first leader of the SDLP, Gerry Fitt, the party's aim was to be a 'social democratic and labour party that would engage the sympathies across the sectarian divide in Northern Ireland.'[26] It failed; the party's electoral support is overwhelmingly Catholic and its membership is 95 per cent Catholic. Furthermore, the party's members are more extensively nationalist than they are socialist: 88 per cent agree that the party is nationalist; only 51 per cent view the party as socialist. Despite this, only a bare majority of the SDLP membership sees a united Ireland as the optimum constitutional solution (table 5.9).

The post-1975 greening of the SDLP led to the party pressing the Dublin Government to adopt a bi-national approach to Northern Ireland. This followed the unwillingness of unionists in the 1970s to share power if a cross-border dimen-sion also existed. The New Ireland Forum of 1983–84 brought together constitu-tional nationalist forces on the island of Ireland, to argue the cases for, in order of preference:

- Irish unity
- a federal or confederal Ireland
- joint British–Irish sovereignty.

Table 5.9   Views of SDLP members on Northern Ireland's constitutional future

The best solution for Northern Ireland is ...

	SA	A	Neutral	D	SD
... a united Ireland	20.5	29.5	25.8	16.9	2.8
... joint sovereignty	6.8	27.7	21.6	26.9	8.9
... GFA/power-sharing	41.1	39.4	11.2	4.0	1.3
... remain in the UK	1.5	6.4	18.4	34.8	36.7

Notes: SA = strongly agree; A = agree; D = disagree; SD = strongly disagree.

Unsurprisingly, the British response was to concede only a slight 'Irish dimension' to political arrangements for Northern Ireland, with the Republic afforded consultative rights via the Anglo-Irish Agreement. Although a modest arrangement, the Anglo-Irish Agreement nonetheless acknowledged a bilateral dimension to any solution for Northern Ireland. The new role for the Irish Republic and the willingness of the British Government to ignore unionist opposition created mild interest among a Sinn Féin leadership already looking for a route away from violence for the republican movement. By the 1990s, a heavily watered-down version of Irish self-determination – co-determination (with a continuing northern veto) – formed the background to the peace process and eventually the 1998 GFA.

The route from violence involved the development of a pan-nationalist dialogue between the SDLP and Sinn Féin in 1988, labelled as Hume–Adams, paving the way for the development of a broad nationalist consensus. Hume, who assumed leadership of his party in 1979, offered the president of Sinn Féin a political, electoral and moral case for ending republican violence. Hume's analysis, shared by a growing number of republicans, was that the IRA was fighting an unwinnable war, as neither violence nor the post-1981 'ballot-box and armalite' strategy could force British withdrawal from Northern Ireland. The problem was not the British Government's presence in Northern Ireland, but the British people's presence, i.e. the unionists. Self-determination for all the Irish people was a legitimate demand, but would not necessarily yield a united Ireland. The electoral case advanced by Hume was altruistic and ultimately damaging to the SDLP: if the IRA ended violence, Sinn Féin's vote in Northern Ireland would surely rise. In that respect, Hume went beyond narrow sectional interest; indeed his leadership of the party was at times incidental to his wider role as statesman. The moral case was that the IRA was not fighting a just war: it was not acting against a colonial oppressor, granted Hume's argument that the British Government was essentially neutral on the future of Northern Ireland. Furthermore, the IRA did not enjoy the support of a majority of nationalists.

Is there a future for the SDLP?

Despite its 'achievement' in diluting republicanism and producing the GFA, the SDLP has electoral, organisational and image problems. The party leader's willingness to take initiatives for peace had, it was argued even by sympathisers, led to neglect of internal matters.[27] With the SDLP less able to condemn Sinn Féin's association with violence, the party needs to convince the nationalist electorate that it can offer the same benefits on the basis of the Agreement as could be extracted by Sinn Féin's form of politics. The SDLP attempts to portray itself as the party better placed to deal with post-constitutional issues through its longer experience of politics than its nationalist rival's. Differences with Sinn Féin over Europe or over the future of the nation state are scarcely designed to excite the nationalist electorate. Furthermore, with Sinn Féin ministers in charge of the key ministries of education and health in the episodic 1999–2002 executive, it was evident that the SDLP would struggle to engage the nationalist electorate and maintain its lead over Sinn Féin. The party faces a strategic quandary: is reinforcing pan-nationalist commonalities with Sinn Féin a sound tactic or will it further legitimise Sinn Féin? The SDLP held most of its ground in 2005, but that election saw Sinn Féin under pressure unlikely to be repeated.

The essential problem for the SDLP lies in the perception that it has now achieved its goals and can thus exit the stage. The GFA contained the three types of political institution seen by the SDLP as a necessary part of any political accommodation: 'North–North' arrangements, creating devolved power-sharing government in Northern Ireland; 'North–South' institutions, with cross-border bodies implementing co-operation between Northern Ireland and the Republic; and, finally, continuing 'east–west' inter-governmental relations between London and Dublin. The recycling of old SDLP ideas evident in the 1974 power-sharing experiment prompted Hume to label the new version as 'Sunningdale for slow learners'.[28] It is little wonder therefore that over 80 per cent of SDLP members concluded that the GFA achieved most of the party's objectives.

The SDLP's members also support much of the micro-agenda of the GFA so important to Sinn Féin: 59 per cent supported the early release of republican prisoners, with 18 per cent dissenting; an overwhelming 94 per cent backed radical reform of the RUC; and 79 per cent opposed Orange Order parades through nationalist areas.[29] Convergence has occurred at elite, membership and voter levels among Northern Ireland's nationalist rivals, but differences remain. Although members see their party as nationalist, the SDLP leadership regards itself as *post-nationalist*, placing the Northern Ireland problem within wider European and bi-national contexts.

The SDLP lacks Sinn Féin's structural and demographic advantages. As an exclusively Northern Ireland party, its room for expansion is limited. One possible option was merger with the Irish Labour Party (ILP) to form an all-Ireland organisation, a move advocated by the leader of the ILP, Ruairi Quinn, in an address to the SDLP's annual conference in 1998. The call fell on stony ground, only 22 per cent of SDLP members supporting merger. SDLP recruitment has not collapsed – 27 per cent of its membership claims to have joined the party between 1996 and 1999. However, the average age of a party member is 57 and working-class members comprise less than 15 per cent of the party. Sinn Féin has held its working-class base, while proving its ability to expand into a middle-class nationalist constituency.

Sinn Féin has stolen many of the political clothes of the SDLP. Nonetheless, Sinn Féin's notion of Irish unity continues to lay greater stress on territorial aspects, despite the party's tacit acceptance of a unionist right to self-determination under the GFA. The party has dropped its former opposition to the European Union, preferring a policy of 'critical engagement'. Nonetheless, Sinn Féin continues to view the nation state as the most appropriate means of territorial organisation. In that respect, Sinn Féin continues to offer a form of territorial nationalism distinct from that of its northern electoral rival. The SDLP has a difficult task in determining whether the promotion of (pan-)nationalist commonalities or post-nationalist politics offers the more promising way forward. The retirement of John Hume as party leader (replaced by Mark Durkan after the 2001 Westminster election) removed the SDLP's one highly prominent figure and his absence has added to the party's vulnerability.

With the overwhelming majority of nationalists having supported the GFA in the 1998 referendum, the electoral rivalry between the two nationalist parties is now concentrated on which of them can better deliver its full implementation. In the 2001 Westminster contest, Sinn Féin emerged triumphant over the SDLP. Fielding candidates in all 18 constituencies for the first time, Sinn Féin won 51 per cent of the nationalist vote, compared with the SDLP's 49 per cent. The accelerating growth of support for Sinn Féin was confirmed, evident since the first Provisional IRA ceasefire in 1994. In 2003, Sinn Féin was again successful in urging support for its 'peace strategy' and 'defence' of the GFA. The nationalist electorate, while supportive of the idea of decommissioning of weapons, appears to take a more pragmatic view that the IRA will disappear as electoralism finally erases redundant militarism within the republican movement as now demanded by Gerry Adams.

The SDLP has attempted to retain votes through promotion of a 'green' agenda, supporting the GFA's micro changes. SDLP supporters were anxious to see the party's nationalist rival join the Government of Northern Ireland: according to one survey, 68 per cent supported the inclusion of Sinn Féin, even if the IRA did not decommission its weapons; and only 15 per cent of SDLP supporters believed it worthwhile to form an executive without Sinn Féin.[30] The difficulty with the SDLP's adoption of a green agenda is that it fails to check Sinn Féin's advance and further legitimises the approach of the SDLP's republican rival. While the SDLP could position itself as the main repository of the APNI and 'soft' UUP vote transfers, the diminution of APNI and UUP support and continued communal unionist voting mean that such positioning has restricted utility. There was limited evidence of cross-community vote transfers in the 1998 assembly elections. Staged amid the euphoria of the aftermath of the GFA, the elections indicated an increase in the willingness of pro-Agreement electors to vote on a cross-community basis: one survey found a 5 per cent increase in unionist transfers to the SDLP;[31] 15 per cent of UUC members say that they 'definitely' or 'might' consider transferring lower preference votes to the SDLP, with a further 26 per cent describing such a prospect as a 'slight possibility'. Yet the 2001 and 2003 elections confirmed the predominance of communal voting.

SDLP gains relative to Sinn Féin's, through breaches of the sectarian divide, were always likely to be outweighed by the increasing trend for SDLP voters to transfer lower preference votes to Sinn Féin. Two-thirds of SDLP voters transferred 'in-house' in this manner in the 1998 assembly elections and in 2003 Sinn Féin was again comfortably the main repository of lower preference transfers. Whereas in the past the strength of Sinn Féin's associations with the IRA led a substantial body of SDLP supporters to vote transfer to the centrist, avowedly non-sectarian, APNI, the new moderation of Sinn Féin means this is no longer the case.

Sensitive to charges of a 'sell-out' from republican 'dissidents', Sinn Féin's agenda stresses the party's republican credentials. It demands further all-Ireland political and electoral arrangements, including the advancement of all-Ireland bodies; the right of those elected in parliamentary contests in Northern Ireland to participate in the Irish Parliament and for Northern Ireland's citizens to be given the right to participate in presidential elections and referendums in the Irish Republic. Sinn Féin demands further changes in policing, with full implementation of the Patten Report constituting the minimum demand. Sinn Féin's electoral strategy, emphasising support for the GFA, was always likely to pay dividends among an electoral base strongly favouring the accord and desirous of robust political representatives.

Structural differences between the two nationalist parties have assumed greater importance than ideological distinctions. Sinn Féin's position as the only significant all-Ireland party, consolidated by election successes north and south of the border, has made the SDLP, in comparison, look a narrow, sectional, northern nationalist party, accentuating its problems of an ageing membership, low recruitment and loss of electoral (and moral) superiority. Sinn Féin is reliant merely on a vague, unsubstantiated, 'inevitability' thesis, rather than a specific strategy, in terms of the achievement of its goal of a united Ireland. In the meantime, its vigorous participatory politics and rights-based agenda are likely to yield further gains at the expense of rivals throughout Ireland.

The crisis of the existing centre: Alliance and the bloc system

The supposed crisis of the moderates has extended to the traditional political centre. As long-standing advocates of devolved power-sharing, APNI endorsed the GFA. Its members overwhelmingly (95 per cent) backed the GFA in the 1998 referendum and 90 per cent still support the Agreement. Yet the deal posed theoretical and practical problems for Northern Ireland's main centre party. The consociational underpinnings of the GFA appeared to institutionalise a unionist–nationalist dichotomy within Northern Ireland's politics, at odds with APNI's view that the construction of *one community* was required. Since the party's establishment in 1970, it has clung to a belief that a third tradition, *post*-nationalism or *post*-unionism, could be established. APNI attempts to operate as a bi-confessional party within a confessional party system.[32] The party attracts support from Protestants and Catholics, and its members are also drawn from both communities, although only 20 per cent are Catholics. Averaging 7.5 per cent support in elections, the electoral tale is one of slow decline, from a peak of over 14 per cent in 1977 to current election levels of around 4 per cent.

The basis of APNI's thinking has been a rejection of the 'two communities' approach to politics evident in the GFA. In practical terms, the GFA threatened to further reduce the narrow centre ground farmed by APNI, moving voters away from what has been described, in any case, as a 'mythical' centre.[33] Despite a poor first-preference showing, the party nonetheless escaped unscathed with six assembly seats in 2003, as a beneficiary of pro-Agreement transfers from voters unwilling to surmount the communal divide.

The lack of a pro-Agreement unionist majority forced APNI to compromise its declared principle of being neither nationalist nor unionist. In November 2001, three APNI MLAs re-designated as unionist to ensure the re-election of David Trimble as first minister, and so bolster the GFA. The posts of first and deputy-first minister require parallel unionist and nationalist majorities. In the first contest in November 2001, Trimble failed to obtain majority Unionist support and his subsequent re-election was thus dependent on re-designation by a sufficient number of APNI MLAs. Although only temporary, these re-designations occurred against the wishes of the majority (60 per cent) of APNI's members: Re-designation, although clearly a temporary means to an end, compromised long-held APNI principles.

The party has appealed against the rigid segmental designations of the Northern Ireland Assembly which contravene the *one-community* approach of APNI and, arguably, breach its liberal principles. APNI argues that consociational institutions should be fully accommodating of parties without bloc identities. Elections and institutional representation should be based on the self-determination of the entire populace, rather than be rigidly based on representation via predetermined ethnic blocs.[34] APNI offers a vision of integrative power-sharing in Northern Ireland, attached to North–South structures. The party lays great stress on the 'democratic accountability' of North–South structures, reflective of the party's opposition to any free-standing all-Ireland dimension to Northern Ireland's political arrangements. The party's support for the GFA is based on the premiss that consociational democracy is transitional towards more integrative forms of association. APNI sees the GFA as a 'band-aid' agreement, which, in itself, will not resolve the conflict.[35]

APNI has always been anxious to avoid being labelled unionist or nationalist, though less than half (48 per cent) its members dissent from the proposition that it is a unionist party; only 7 per cent of APNI members see their organisation as a nationalist party. APNI promotes the replacement of the unionist–nationalist dichotomy with a liberal, pluralist, non-ethnic form of politics. However, there are indications from the party membership that such a position is, at best, idealised and does not conform to the membership's views of the party, let alone those of outsiders. For instance, the party leadership has asserted that 'only Alliance supporters more strongly associate with a concept of Northern Irishness ahead of Britishness or Irishness'.[36] However, this is untrue of party members themselves, among whom the largest single category of identification is *British*, but with a relative majority of Catholic members viewing themselves as *Irish*.

Surprisingly, the APNI leadership's vision of commonality, rather than unionism or nationalism, is also one not shared by many members, who are divided over whether that vision is of a single united society or of two *separate* and *equal* communities. There is, however, disagreement over APNI's vision and the mechanics of the Agreement (see table 5.10).

APNI's ideal is to see the replacement of ethnic blocs by consensual power-sharing to an extent that such blocs become redundant. Less than one-third of APNI's membership believe, however, that the GFA increases sectarianism by dividing parties into ethnic blocs, although fewer than half of party members disagree with that proposition. Almost half of the members believe that assembly votes should be taken on the basis of a simple majority.

Given APNI's avowed hostility to unionism and nationalism, compromises between ethnic blocs would not amount, in the party's view, to genuine centrist politics. However, the electorate's movement away from all types of centripetal forces – the traditional centre, the centre–unionist (pro-GFA UUP) and centre–nationalist (SDLP) – has squeezed APNI, now overwhelmingly reliant on lower preference transfers rather than outright support. Within the 1999–2002 assembly,

Table 5.10   APNI members' views of the GFA

	SA	A	Neutral	D	SD
Unionists and nationalists separate but equal	11.5	28.7	13.2	33.8	12.8
GFA increases sectarianism by dividing parties into blocs	8.8	20.9	20.4	42.2	7.6
Decisions in the assembly should require a simple majority only (*n* = 674)	11.0	37.8	12.3	32.0	6.8

Notes: SA = strongly agree; A = agree; D = disagree; SD = strongly disagree.

the temporary re-designation of APNI as unionist, to bolster overall unionist support for an unstable GFA, did little to consolidate a radical vision engendered by antipathy to both 'sectarian' ideologies. A possible shoring-up of unionist support via APNI's re-designation was again raised as a possibility after the 2003 assembly elections. Yet that would be anathema to many within the party; APNI organiser Stephen Farry argued that 'hell would freeze over' before the party's MLAs engaged in the 'false solution' of re-designation,[37] though this did not stop the party embarking on such a course in 2001. Indeed Farry, like several other APNI parliamentary candidates, effectively re-designated the party's supporters as pro-GFA moderate unionists during the 2001 Westminster election campaign. He withdrew as APNI candidate in North Down to encourage party voters (7,500 in the 1997 general election) to vote for the pro-Agreement UUP candidate Sylvia Hermon. Although the tactic was successful, facilitating the defeat of the anti-GFA UKUP incumbent Robert McCartney, it compromised APNI's avowed vision and was not repeated in 2005.

Conclusion

Post-Agreement party competition in Northern Ireland has seen a realignment of the traditional political order. The more moderate pro-Agreement parties of the UUP and SDLP have seen shifts in unionist and nationalist support to the stouter defenders of their ethnic blocs, while the centrist APNI has seen many of its supporters align themselves with a bloc. The emergence of the DUP and Sinn Féin as the main representatives of their ethnic blocs has led to much talk of a crisis of the GFA and possibly its collapse.

The assertions of crisis are to be weighed against the considerable political changes that have occurred. The mainstream republican movement has no intention of returning to violence. Encouraged by rapid electoral growth north and south of the border, Sinn Féin wishes the IRA to atrophy. There is therefore no threat to the peace process, other than from tiny groups of republican ultras who see the management of British rule in Northern Ireland and the maintenance of a 'unionist veto' as a rebuttal of all for which they fought for three decades. The peace and political processes thus require disaggregation.

With regard to unionism, discord within the UUP over tactical approaches to aspects of the GFA, notably its ambiguity over decommissioning, has assisted the DUP in marketing itself as a party which will defend robustly the interests of unionists. The DUP has moved from a position of hostility to power-sharing *per se* to one in which a far-reaching accommodation with an IRA-less Sinn Féin remains a possibility. The barriers to such a deal are not merely the obvious ones of the linkages of the near-redundant military and vibrant political wings of the republican movement: within unionism more broadly, the extent of commitment to devolution is far from absolute. Furthermore, the overarching aim of British policy has been to reduce violence, mainly via the neutralising of the IRA. A devolved settlement would be a helpful adjunct, but is not a necessary condition. For devolution to work and for Northern Ireland to develop beyond a failed political entity to a moderately stable consociational semi-democracy, the lingering reliance of a section of unionism on direct rule or belief in full integration may have to diminish.

Notes

1 One other 'moderate' pro-agreement party could have been selected; however, the centrist Northern Ireland Women's Coalition has not yet been surveyed by the author. To offer balance, the article thus uses evidence from one moderate party within each community and one 'non-aligned' centrist party. The UUC survey received 299 replies from the 858 members (36 per cent); the Alliance survey, 702 from 1,050 members (68 per cent) and the SDLP, 528 from a claimed 3,000 members (an exaggerated figure, but the response rate here is given at a low 28 per cent). The differences in response rate are acknowledged. As these are the first data sets ever constructed on party members, the extent to which replies are representative cannot be reliably gauged, even if, intuitively, responses appeared in accordance with what was expected. Attitudes expressed in the UUC replies may not replicate those found among the wider party; the results were, however, tested against a sample of 100 ordinary members, with no significant differences found, perhaps unsurprisingly, given that the vast bulk (688) of UUC members are ordinary constituency delegates.

2 G. Evans and B. O'Leary, 'Northern Irish Voters and the British–Irish Agreement: Foundations of a Stable Consociational Settlement', paper presented at the 'Elections, Public Opinion and Parties' conference, University College, Northampton, September 1999.

3 *Ibid.*

4 P. Mitchell, B, O'Leary and G. Evans, 'The 2001 Elections in Northern Ireland: Moderating "Extremists" and the Squeezing of the Moderates', *Representation*, vol. 39, no. 1, 2002, pp. 23–36.

5 B. Hayes and I. McAllister, 'Who Voted for Peace? Public Support for the 1998 Northern Ireland Agreement', *Irish Political Studies*, vol. 16, 2001, p. 73.

6 According to the Northern Ireland *Life and Times Survey*, 2001.

7 UUP, *Simply British: Ulster Unionists*, Manifesto 2003 (Belfast: UUP, 2003).

8 UUP, *Understanding the Agreement* (Belfast: UUP, 1998).

9 *Sunday Times*, 30 November 2003.

10 See S. Bruce, *God Save Ulster! The Religion and Politics of Paisleyism* (Oxford: Oxford University Press, 1986); S. Bruce, *At the Edge of the Union* (Oxford: Oxford University Press, 1994); J. Todd, 'Two Traditions in Unionist Political Culture', *Irish Political Studies*, vol. 2, 1987, pp. 1–26.

11 C. Smyth, 'The DUP as a Politico-Religious Organisation', *Irish Political Studies*, vol. 1, 1986, pp. 33–43.

12 C. Farrington, 'Ulster Unionist Political Divisions in the Late Twentieth Century', *Irish Political Studies*, vol. 16, 2001, pp. 49–72.

13 Peter Robinson, DUP deputy leader, speaking on *Hearts and Minds*, BBC Northern Ireland, 25 September 2003.

14 H. Patterson, *Ireland since 1939* (Oxford: Oxford University Press, 2002), pp. 340–1.

15 *Guardian*, 2 December 2003.

16 C. Irwin, *The People's Peace Process in Northern Ireland* (Basingstoke: Palgrave, 2002).

17 G. McMichael, *An Ulster Voice* (Dublin: Rinehart, 1999).

18 DUP, *Towards a New Agreement* (Belfast: DUP, 2003).

19 DUP, *Leadership to Put Things Right* (Belfast: DUP, 2001).

20 DUP, *Towards a New Agreement*; J. Tonge, 'Northern Ireland: A Different Kind of Election', in A. Geddes and J. Tonge (eds), *Labour's Second Landslide: The British General Election 2001* (Manchester: Manchester University Press, 2001), pp. 219–35.

21 G. Evans and R. Sinnott, 'Political Alignments North and South', in A. Heath, R. Breen and C. Whelan (eds), *Ireland North and South: Perspectives from Social Science* (Oxford: Oxford University Press, 1999), pp. 419–56.

22 D. Hume, *The Ulster Unionist Party 1972–92* (Lurgan: Ulster Society, 1996), p. 12.

23 J. Ruane and J. Todd, *The Dynamics of Conflict in Northern Ireland* (Cambridge: Cambridge University Press, 1996), p. 61.

24 E. Moloney, *A Secret History of the IRA* (London: Penguin, 2003).

25 J. Evans, J. Tonge and G. Murray, 'Constitutional Nationalism and Socialism in Northern Ireland: The Greening of the SDLP', in P. Cowley, D. Denver, A. Russell and L. Harrison (eds), *British Elections and Parties Review 10* (London: Frank Cass, 2000).

26 *Irish News*, 17 August 1995.

27 G. Murray, *John Hume and the SDLP* (Dublin: Irish Academic Press, 1998).

28 J. Tonge, 'From Sunningdale to the Good Friday Agreement: Creating Devolved Government in Northern Ireland', *Contemporary British History*, vol. 14, no. 3, 2000, pp. 39–60.

29 See J. Tonge and J. Evans, 'Party Members and the Good Friday Agreement', *Irish Political Studies*, vol. 17, no. 2, 2002, pp. 59–73.

30 *Irish Times*, 27 April 1999.

31 M. Kelly and J. Doyle, 'The Good Friday Agreement and Electoral Behaviour: An Analysis of Transfers under PRSTV in the Northern Ireland Assembly Elections of 1982 and 1998', paper presented at the Annual Conference of the Political Studies Association of Ireland, Cork, October 2000.

32 I. McAllister and B. Wilson, 'Bi-Confessionalism in a Confessional Party System: The Northern Ireland Alliance Party', *Economic and Social Review*, vol. 9, no. 3, 1978, pp. 207–25.

33 P. Arthur and K. Jeffrey, *Northern Ireland Politics* (Oxford: Blackwell, 1996).

34 A. Lijphart, *Democracy in Plural Societies* (New Haven, CT: Yale University Press, 1977).

35 S. Farry and S. Neeson, 'Beyond the Band-Aid Approach: An Alliance Party Perspective upon the Belfast Agreement', *Fordham International Law Journal*, vol. 22, no. 4, 1999, pp. 1221–49.

36 *Ibid.*, p. 1224.

37 Farry in interview with the author, 27 August 2001.

6

The 1998 Agreement:
three unionist anxieties

ARTHUR AUGHEY

This chapter reviews the experience of the period 1998–2003 and examines why it created so many stresses and strains within Ulster unionism, especially within the UUP. The chapter identifies three notable anxieties that have influenced the course of unionist politics since the Belfast Agreement of 1998. It examines the impact of these anxieties in two periods, the first from April 1998 to October 2002 and the second from October 2002 to the assembly elections of November 2003. In order to understand the responses of unionists it is important to begin by examining the ideal relationship the Agreement claimed to embody. The three anxieties for unionists can be located in the gap between that ideal and, as they saw it, the reality of its implementation.

On the making of the Agreement: three notable anxieties

The immediate origins of the Belfast Agreement can be traced to the Downing Street Declaration of December 1993 in which the British and Irish governments set out the principles for any future settlement in Northern Ireland. The wording of the declaration was that 'it is for the people of the island of Ireland alone, by agreement between the two parts respectively, to exercise their right of self-determination on the basis of consent, freely and concurrently given, North and South, to bring about a united Ireland, if that is their wish'. This obtuse formulation suggested that it was possible to conceive of self-determination as no longer a violently divisive issue between two communities but as an issue capable of consensual redescription. In other words, Northern Ireland would remain part of the UK because in that part of Ireland there was no consent for Irish unity. On the other hand, Northern Ireland's place within the UK would depend on sufficient political change to secure for it the consent of nationalists. The whole structure of the Belfast Agreement was built on the assumption that the institutionalisation of that formula of continuity and change could deliver co-operative government instead of intractable conflict. From the unionist perspective, Trimble stated the potential concisely: since the principle of consent had been accepted and since there was not going to be constitutional change, as far as anyone could see, the incentive was there now for unionists to say: 'There is not going to be a united Ireland. How can we make Northern Ireland work for all its citizens?'[1]

Yet here, amid such optimism, one finds the first notable anxiety for unionists. The distinction between the two sides of this bargain is quite important. The way in which unionist opinion moved between 1998 and 2002 reflected a deep suspicion about the balance of the deal. For *unionists*, what appeared to be on offer was a *passive* acknowledgement of the constitutional status of Northern Ireland, otherwise known as the principle of consent. For *nationalists*, what appeared to be on offer was an *active* programme of government to legislate a 'human rights' and 'equality' agenda to address their historical grievances. In other words, on the basis of unionists getting the principle of consent nationalists would be given a raft of policy commitments. Unionists put this down to 'the British establishment's rather intellectually lazy embrace of the simpler nationalist versions of Irish history'.[2] This relationship between a static condition of principle – accepting a fact that unionists thought was democratically incontestable anyway – and a dynamic set of policies – accepting claims that unionists thought were historically and morally contentious – proved to be an unstable one.

A further enticement for unionists after 1997 was the prospect of devolution as part of a general British strategy of constitutional reform. This would make self-government in Belfast part of the UK norm rather than the exception. Certainly there appeared to be a superficial commonality between the Northern Ireland case and those of the other devolved institutions in the UK which also address apparently contradictory objectives. The stated objective was to translate the historical purpose of nationalism to bring about the end of partition in Ireland and the historical purpose of unionism to strengthen the Union of Great Britain and Northern Ireland into a mutually acceptable political code. The official view was, and still is, that an acceptance of such a code means that everyone can be a winner. However, those sceptical of New Labour's constitutional changes believed that it had made optimism (or deceit) the basis of British policy. The journalist John Lloyd observed one important distinction: the centre of the reform strategy in Scotland and Wales is on difficult enough ground, he thought, even though it is designed to *defeat* the nationalist threat;[4] in Northern Ireland, because the strategy is designed to *accommodate* not only the nationalist threat but the militant wing of republicanism, Lloyd could see little prospect of success. That was precisely the view of those unionists who understood the principles of the agreement to be a big lie. Its complex arrangements, they argued, were designed to conceal the betrayal of principle which had taken place. They concurred with one New Labour commentator who wrote that, irrespective of 'Third Way' theory, the 'Irish problem, as historically defined, is not susceptible to a loserless ending'.[5] The betrayal of principle unionists identified in the willingness of the British and Irish governments to accept an equivalence between the position of the IRA and that of unionists. On the issue of guns and government, it was thought that equivalence actually meant prejudice in favour of the bargaining strength of Sinn Féin.

Thus unionist critics of the emerging dynamic of the peace process challenged the claim that it was about securing a balanced accommodation between unionism and nationalism in Northern Ireland. Experience suggested to them that republicans *certainly* and nationalists *probably* did not want a stable settlement. On the contrary, the assumption has always been that republicans, if they cannot force unionists into Irish unity, and nationalists, if they cannot manoeuvre unionists into Irish unity, desired only a dispensation that would erode Northern Ireland's position within the UK. In this sense of the political, there certainly can be no loserless ending. For pro-agreement unionists, the success of the enterprise depended on dispelling the more paranoid of these expectations of loss. Unfortunately, this was easier said than done.

This is the second notable anxiety. There emerged in the middle years of the 1990s a nationalist mantra that unionists were 'afraid of peace'. After 1998, the mantra became that unionists were 'afraid of change'. The accurate representation of opinion was that unionists were anxious about the political costs of peace and, later, about the extent of the changes that were being demanded. A situation might emerge in which an active principle of consent did not apply to the implementation of the agreement. Unionists could certainly imagine a condition in which improvement, such as a cessation of the IRA's military campaign, might be at a price which they felt to be unfair and unconscionable. This anxiety found classic expression in the original opposition on the part of critics of the Trimble leadership to the talks process with Sinn Féin. 'Without doubt', argued Robert McCartney of the UKUP, 'the whole purpose of these talks is to wring further concessions from the majority that would both undermine the strength of the Union and the quality and nature of their British citizenship and identity', a view also held by the DUP.[6] The objective of that opposition had been to prevent substantive negotiations taking place on an agenda which would lead, as one DUP statement put it, to 'the annexation of Northern Ireland by Dublin'.[7] However, there was a definite irony in this position. If the entry of Sinn Féin to the talks after the summer adjournment of July 1997 without the prior disarmament of the IRA provided the opportunity for the DUP and the UKUP to withdraw, it also provided the opportunity for a deal to be struck. As the talks chairman, George Mitchell, observed: 'No one can ever know for certain what might have been, but I believe that had Paisley and McCartney stayed and fought from within, there would have been no agreement.' Their absence, thought Mitchell, freed the UUP negotiators 'from daily attacks at the negotiating table, and gave the party room to negotiate that it might not otherwise have had'.[8]

By contrast, the attitude of the leader of the UUP, David Trimble, was to try to see the talks through to a positive conclusion. It was a delicately balanced decision and its practical outworking Trimble later admitted to have been 'a white-knuckle ride'. This dispute between unionists about the very nature of the negotiations might be called the 'Anglo-Irish Agreement syndrome'. The signing of the Anglo-Irish Agreement in 1985 had been a tremendous shock to the unionist community. But its legacy had been ambivalent: on the one hand, there remained a deep-seated suspicion of the motives and objectives of the British Government; on the other hand, the lesson of the Anglo-Irish Agreement also appeared to be that unionists could not afford to be on the outside of a process that would determine their future. It was better to be in than to be out, especially if, as many suspected, the purpose of the talks was not about reaching agreement but about apportioning blame for failing to reach agreement. As Trimble had put it in a statement on 17 September prior to entering Castle Buildings to talks which now included Sinn Féin: 'Unionism will not be marginalised. Those who walk out leave the Union undefended.' That was the first part of the syndrome. The other was his observation that without a unionist presence the Union would be left 'to the tender mercies of the British and Irish Governments'.[9] That was the second part. David Trimble's commitment to staying in the talks was, in many ways, a direct challenge to the fatalistic culture of contemporary unionism eloquently expressed by McCartney and the DUP.[10] It had its dangers.

This is the third notable anxiety. One of the demoralising aspects of unionist politics – and a strong element in its prevailing pessimism since 1985 – had been the sense of being on the fringe of strategic decisions. With a workable deal unionists would be at the heart of the new devolved institutions and so would also have the institutional leverage to ensure that their voice was not ignored. On the other hand, there was an apprehension that in return for being on the inside track unionists could get trapped in a political logic inimical to their long-term interests. Under pressure from the British, Irish and US governments, and burdened with the responsibilities of office, it might prove very difficult to resist seriously compromising the unionist position in order to preserve the peace. Five years later, the nationalist commentator Brian Feeney fed this anxiety when he revelled in Trimble's discomfiture as unionism's very own Bishop Muzorewa, 'a unionist leader carrying out a nationalist project for a British government'.[11] The three notable anxieties will be traced in greater detail in subsequent sections. However, it is necessary to set them initially in the context of popular opinion.

Judgement of the Belfast Agreement

Initial polls revealed that almost 45 per cent of unionist voters were undecided about the merits of the Agreement. In the referendum in May 1998, however, a very slight majority of the unionist electorate suppressed their anxieties and suspended their traditional fatalism for a contract with the future. More in hope than in anticipation they were prepared to accept the Agreement's promise that it was a way to end honourably the squalid violence of the previous thirty years. Here at last, perhaps, was a chance to change the code of politics in Northern Ireland from an uncivil to a civil one in the expectation that this might secure their community's long-term interests.[12] This, it must be said, was an affair of reason, not one of the heart. It had been an emotionally painful decision to accept the Agreement's whiff of appeasement and there was deep uncertainty about the prospect of Sinn Féin in government. The stilling of the three anxieties may be associated with a calculation of constitutional security and this was one of the crucial factors that swung the balance in Trimble's favour, but only just.

The referendum result, of course, was only the beginning of the battle for the hearts and minds of the unionist electorate. That battle would take place not on the ideal promise of the Agreement but on the practical implementation of the Agreement. This 45 per cent of uncertain voters was the target constituency for the future of unionist politics. The wager of Trimble and of those unionists supporting the Agreement was that the 'soft no' voters would come to see the advantages of political stability. They would come to understand that the Agreement really did lay the basis for genuine and mutually beneficial compromise, securing both the Union and promoting better relations with nationalists. As Trimble put it, with conscious reference to Lord Craigavon's famous assertion about a Protestant parliament and a Protestant state, his aspiration was to achieve 'a pluralist parliament for a pluralist people' inside the UK.[13]

Trimble was also acutely aware of the need to provide a 'soft landing' for provisional republicanism. His intention, he claimed, was not to humiliate or exclude. The Northern Ireland conflict he likened to an express train that needed to be stopped before it hit the buffers. It was understood, however, 'that time is needed to slow it down enough to come to a complete halt'. But if he were to deliver on that measured agenda Trimble needed reciprocation from Sinn Féin.[14] The wager of Trimble's opponents was that he would not get that reciprocation. His critics, both within his party and outside it, assumed that 'soft yes' voters would come to understand the implementation of the Agreement as a capitulation to a republican agenda. Implementing the Agreement would confirm the corruption of public life in Northern Ireland and 'set the seal upon an ongoing process of political warfare within an unworkable assembly and a permanently unstable society'.[15] There was also a calculation that the traditional stay-at-home unionist vote, what Peter Robinson of the DUP called the 'peacenik, one-off vote', that helped secure a small pro-Agreement vote would show little commitment to the Trimble strategy.[16] What was the political return on these wagers? The answer to that question has two parts.

First, the period from May 1998 to October 2002 witnessed a steady shift of 'soft yes' opinion into the anti-Agreement camp. The trajectory of unionist opinion can be traced in a series of polls conducted by the BBC television programme *Hearts and Minds*. At the time of the referendum in May 1998 the best estimate of unionist opinion was 55 per cent Yes and 45 per cent No. By March 1999, that balance had reversed to 45.6 per cent Yes and 57.2 per cent No. In the following two years opinion stabilised at about 42 per cent Yes and 57 per cent No. If there had been difficulty sustaining support for the Agreement equally there had been no great surge in support for its rejection, and for all the absence of enthusiasm there was, as yet, no sufficient constituency for its removal. By October 2002, however, in a poll taken shortly after the suspension of the devolved institutions because of allegations of IRA intelligence-gathering at Stormont, the figures were 33.9 per cent Yes and 67 per cent No. Only 22.6 per cent of unionists actually wanted to see the return of the power-sharing assembly.[17] While it is certainly true that the *Hearts and Minds* poll reflected the immediate anger of the unionist electorate about the behaviour of republicans, it did capture accurately a general mood of disaffection that had developed since 1998.[18]

Second, despite this widespread distaste by 2002 for the experience of the Agreement and the prospect of its institutional resurrection, there was, at first sight, a rather surprising consequence for political leaders. One would have expected that unionist opinion would blame the UUP leader for the events of the previous four-and-a-half-years. This did not happen. Trimble was still identified as the most effective leader of unionism and was given a positive rating by 41.9 per cent of unionists, slightly ahead of the 39.1 per cent support for Ian Paisley and far ahead of other immediate contenders such as Jeffrey Donaldson (12.8 per cent) or Peter Robinson (6.1 per cent). Since Paisley is of the older generation, Trimble's stature over the current pretenders for the leadership of unionism appeared even more pronounced.[19]

How may this mood be explained and how can we make sense of Trimble's position within unionist politics? Let us consider in turn the three unionist anxieties in the period 1998–October 2002.

First anxiety: passive and active contexts of the Agreement

A substantial part of unionist disaffection can be attributed to the outworking of this particular anxiety. The Conservative Party theorist Ian (Lord) Gilmour once argued that ideas and symbols are important weapons in political argument but that a party, rather like an army, marches on its stomach.[20] One could extend that analogy from a party to a political community: in other words, rational conviction can take you only so far; to be popularly persuasive reason needs to have an emotional underpinning. On the eve of the referendum, and intimating the nature of the political struggle to come, the editor of the *News Letter* suggested that unionist uncertainty was a result of people 'trying to weigh up the obvious benefits that would materialise from a long period of stability' (the pro-Agreement calculation) against 'a gut instinct that tells them that what the agreement amounts to is rather more than a tampering with the edges of their society' (the anti-Agreement calculation).[21] This struggle was not just between parties and individuals: it went on within individuals. In this light, the story of May 1998–October 2002 has a rather straightforward narrative. The edifice of rational argument that Trimble constructed around the constitutional principles and institutions of the Agreement was not so much denied (for the DUP did not seriously challenge it) as discounted by a mode of policy implementation which his own party and the wider electorate found increasingly difficult to stomach. This was an obvious problem from the beginning and one anticipated by the UUP leadership, though that anticipation did not make the problem any easier to deal with.

Ken Maginnis, for example, argued that the Agreement had secured the key constitutional objectives for which unionists would have to swallow some unpalatable concessions. In a delicate reference to the emotionally charged issues of prisoner releases, police reform and, above all, republicans in government without the disbandment of the IRA, Maginnis claimed that 'when the essentials are attained, other elements fall into place'. That was a big claim and a contested one.[22] Professor Bew, whose judgements since 1998 were at times crucial in sustaining UUP support for the Agreement, admitted that it did demand much of unionists, asking them 'to go a long way to meet the concerns of the nationalist minority'. However, his assessment was that it was in their interests to do so.[23]

Defending his support for the Belfast Agreement, Trimble argued that it 'is as good and as fair as it gets',[24] and stressed the constitutional significance of his achievement not only against both his critics outside the UUP and influential critics within, like Jeffrey Donaldson MP, who was seen by many as a leader-in-waiting. This was a constant theme of his leadership. In a speech to the Northern Ireland Forum on 17 April 1998, Trimble claimed that the Agreement had achieved the unionist goal, 'proposed separately by the UUP and the DUP in the 1992 Talks', of placing Northern Ireland's future within a wider British–Irish context than that of the Agreement of 1985. One key objective had been now achieved: 'We have sought and secured a permanent settlement, not agreed to a temporary transitional arrangement.' He cited in support of this claim the Irish Government's modification of Articles 2 and 3 of its constitution.[25] For Trimble, the achievement on North–South co-operation was a clear endorsement of these principles.

Trimble's expectation had been that the difficulties for unionists would be short-term emotional ones. The longer-term could now rationally look after itself on the basis of consent, a view shared by some academic commentary.[26] This was spelled out in the UUP's early clarification paper *Understanding the Agreement*. It noted that many of those aspects of the Agreement which were objectionable could be introduced anyway by the secretary of state. 'Unionists must make a judgement as to whether or not the features that bring us considerable constitutional gains outweigh those elements of the Agreement that we all find objectionable.'[27] The judgement was not entirely in Trimble's gift. It depended on what had proved impossible so far in Northern Ireland's history, a sense of mutual responsibility rather than a strategy of sectarian manoeuvre. This sense of responsibility was largely absent on the republican side. According to Trimble, Sinn Féin had committed itself only to an 'abstract' version of the Agreement but refused to accept the real 'responsibilities of making it work in practice'.[28] The growing judgement of the unionist voters was that the constant stream of objectionable elements, if they did not outweigh the considerable constitutional gains, significantly diminished them.

Even these objectionable elements which unionists had to stomach, for example reform of the RUC, would have been made more palatable had there been a clear indication that the IRA was in the process of disbandment, that decommissioning of illegal weapons was seriously in progress and that the republican 'war' was over. There wasn't. The reverse appeared to be true, as incident after incident seemed to confirm the IRA's disregard for exclusively peaceful methods and its contempt for democratic procedure. In his conference speech of October 2003, Trimble was still appealing to republicans to clearly commit to exclusively peaceful methods. And he addressed directly the impact of their lack of clarity on unionist support. Trimble cited focus groups research on anti-Agreement unionists that showed that these voters thought that 'the battlefield needs clearing up'. Declaring that the 'war is over', he argued, was not just a unionist demand but the expectation of everyone.[29] In retrospect it is remarkable how buoyant unionist support for the agreement did remain throughout despite the repeated evidence of republican bad faith.

An incisive explication of this major source of unionist alienation was given by the DUP MP Gregory Campbell. Reflecting on the implementation of the Agreement over four-and-a-half-years, he argued that the programme of reform pre-supposed 'unionist contentment' (i.e. passivity) and 'nationalist dissatisfaction' (i.e. activity). This, according to Campbell, had been the fundamental mistake: 'If there is no acceptance of a template that gives recognition to legitimate unionist concerns and grievances, and only begins by recognising a single set of grievances, then every attempt [at political accommodation] will fail.' Campbell articulated a profound sense of unionist dissatisfaction with the tendency of the policy agenda to assume that inequality, disadvantage and discrimination worked only one way. Moreover, he captured a growing mood of resistance to the notion that each and every nationalist demand was justified because of unionist majority-rule at Stormont between 1921 and 1972. Nevertheless, Campbell rejected the proposition that unionist hostility represented a refusal to countenance the equality agenda: 'This is not the case at all. It is because unionists are convinced that the current process disadvantages them and assists nationalists/republicanism that they so strongly resist.'[30] This was, of course, an interpretation of the facts as unspecific in its detail as was the claim of nationalist inequality. However, it was a relatively accurate interpretation of the state of unionist anxiety. Here the emotional issue of policing reform intersected with resentment about (ironically) anti-Protestant discrimination in recruitment (the 50/50 rule) to exemplify that sense of grievance about the perceived worsening of conditions for unionists in the post-agreement period.

Moreover, New Labour has often appeared insensitive to this anxiety. Tony Blair explicitly linked resolving specific constitutional issues with the unspecific resolution of nationalist grievance. In his Stranmillis speech of 15 June 1999 he declared: 'There can no longer be a Northern Ireland based on other than the principles of justice, fairness and equality and recognition that sectarianism is a thing of the past'.[31] Unfortunately, the prime minister associated the obstacle to achieving this universally acceptable vision of the future with a unionist unwillingness to form a power-sharing executive with Sinn Féin. The implication was not only that injustice, unfairness, inequality and sectarianism were features of Northern Ireland life associated exclusively with unionist politics (even though unionists had not been in office for 30 years), but that there was a moral equivalence between the IRA's refusal to disarm and the unionist refusal to share power with Sinn Féin. Nor did former Secretary of State John Reid help matters by his frequent references to 800 years of British misrule in Ireland. This concession to the republican version of history did have real effect for it confirmed the view of those who argued that 'the IRA will only disappear when the injustices that engendered support for it are addressed'.[32] Since London appeared sympathetic to that view, what incentive was there for the IRA to take seriously Trimble's calls for responsibility? The impression formed by unionist voters was that New Labour had bought into the republican definition of the problem, and this made them all the more suspicious of the appeals to unionist 'generosity'.

Second anxiety: improvement can worsen the situation

The Germans have a word for it – they usually do. That word is *Verschlimmbesserung*, which, roughly translated, means that as things get better so they also get worse. The emphasis in the word is on worsening rather than improvement, an appropriate word, one might imagine, for the vocabulary of traditional unionist pessimism. If a word can sum up for unionists the period 1998–2002, then *Verschlimmbesserung* is probably it, capturing as it does, the ambivalence of opinion within unionism as well its dynamic.

One of the greatest achievements of the last five years has been the 'peace dividend', most immediately apparent in the changing skyline of commercial Belfast and in the buoyant property market throughout Northern Ireland. Not only is the peace dividend significant for what has happened, but it is significant for what has not happened. There are hundreds of people alive today who would have been dead had the IRA and loyalist paramilitary campaigns continued with their ferocity unchecked. In both regards, the British Government has been quite correct to stress both the advantages which have accompanied the Agreement and the distance forward Northern Ireland has moved, even if it has not been quite the 'million miles further' of the prime minister's Stranmillis speech. If one acknowledges the undoubted truth that on the major indicators of political violence and material prosperity things have improved, it is also possible, on a range of other indicators, to identify things that have worsened. Indeed, one could argue that as the benefits of the peace dividend came to be accepted as the norm, concern about these other indicators became more influential in the judgement of unionists (and not just unionists) about the quality of the Agreement.

A major aspect of *Verschlimmbesserung* has been the experience of political polarisation. As Guelke observed, there has been an intensification of divisions and political polarisation during the implementation of the Agreement. While violence remains well below levels prior to the paramilitary ceasefires of the mid-1990s, 'fears of a resumption of lethal paramilitary violence and ongoing inter-communal clashes at sectarian interfaces have undermined confidence in the peace'.[33] A study by Shirlow revealed that young people in working-class areas of Belfast had become more rather than less bigoted and that the Belfast Agreement had done nothing to arrest that trend.[34] A further survey by Robinson revealed that community relations had deteriorated in the lifetime of the Agreement to 2001, 'with both sides of the community showing a greater preference to work and live apart'.[35] That academic analysis found its politicised version in the review by McCartney of the years 1998–2002. Expressing the deep unionist anxiety about the corruption of public life, McCartney argued that the Agreement had succeeded only in institutionalising sectarianism at every level of government.

> Far from providing democratic institutions affording equal rights and protection to every individual citizen, and provision for their enforcement subject to the rule of law, the Agreement gave rights to political parties sevicing the sectarian and sectional interests of the communities they purported to represent, including parties patently linked to terrorist organisations.

For McCartney, the consequence has been the worst *community* violence for twenty-five years and a growth in organised crime with which a depleted and demoralised police force cannot properly cope.[36] This was the common refrain of unionist critics of the Agreement, and it could draw on solid research to justify its conclusions.[37]

Evidence of continued paramilitary activity was only one aspect of this concern. The other was the rather contradictory condition in which electoral politics had become polarised. On the one hand, pro-Agreement UUP (and republican critics of the Sinn Féin strategy) could point to the *constitutionalising* of republicanism. Trimble did not share the view that Sinn Féin members were 'unreconstructed' terrorists and argued that involvement in the institutions of the Agreement compelled republicans to work within, even if they did not like it, a 'partitionist settlement'.[38] On the other hand, it was difficult for unionists to ignore the *republicanising* of constitutional nationalism. Sinn Féin, as the 'advanced nationalist' and *activist* party, appeared more likely to secure the catholic interest than the SDLP. As Moloney pointed out, the 'psychological advantage is now with the Provos', and 'while the SDLP have the whiff of yesterday's people, Sinn Féin will now be seen by Catholics as a party on the rise – and everyone loves voting for a winner'.[39] In the Westminster general election of 2001, Sinn Féin for the first time overtook the SDLP at the polls. In 2002, again for the first time, an opinion poll revealed that Sinn Féin best represented the views of catholics.[40] The SDLP found itself increasingly marginalised as nationalist assertion and unionist anxiety intensified. In the communal struggle of Northern Ireland politics, it tried to choose moral neutrality but soon discovered that to be neutral was to take sides with Sinn Féin. Why, then, asked Liam Clarke, 'should the unionists try to do deals with them when they are prepared to concede the decisive voice in northern nationalism to Sinn Féin?'[41] Perhaps unrealistically, most unionists had expected devolution to mean pragmatic deals with the SDLP. The apparent unconcern among all nationalists about evidence of continued IRA activity damaged trust as much as anything else, as did the willingness of the Irish Government, as Trimble graphically put it, to 'ideologically launder' republican misdeeds.[42]

One journalist expressed what many unionists felt to be a moral imbalance in the Agreement. On the one hand, there was a concern to permit 'the suspension of moral norms that shore up any normal democracy in the interests of a higher ideal – peace'. The principle was that of 'drawing a line under the past'. On the other hand, the 'peace process seems to have become the revenge process' on issues such as Bloody Sunday or collusion between loyalists and some members of the security forces.[43] However self-pitying this assumption of a differential moral agenda may have been, it had a real effect on public opinion. The psychological effect on unionism was such that the advantages of peace became less noticeable than the anxiety about the long-term effect of a polarised politics – or, to put that another way, of radicalised Catholic demands underwritten by a broader nationalist consensus. This anxiety about improvement worsening their condition compounded the (first) anxiety about the differential contexts for implementation. In a speech in November 2001, John Reid admitted that there was a strong and growing feeling that Northern Ireland might soon become a 'cold house' for unionists.[44] The growing hostility of unionists to the agreement captured well that pervasive sense of *Verschlimmbesserung*.

Third anxiety: an inimical political logic

One of the most crucial battles in politics is over who decides what is and what is not *realistic*. The definition of realism in politics is logically prior to what Rab Butler once called 'the art of the possible'. And the subsequent cultivation of the art of the possible may involve a logical unfolding of certain political objectives or the denial of others. Among unionists there developed the view that, as crunch issues emerged during the implementation of the Agreement, too often did the British Government concede that definition of reality to republicans. The result was the skewing of political expectations. The anxiety was the old one that the real engagement was between the IRA and London and that the unionists were only secondary players. Dermot Nesbitt, one of the strongest advocates of the Agreement within the UUP, put this view quite succinctly. The republican movement always said that it was impossible to conceive of IRA disbandment. 'Not long ago', responded Nesbitt, 'it was thought impossible to have Sinn Féin in Government. That "impossibility" was made a reality.'[45] In other words, unionists have been expected to confront their own impossibilities and to make them realities, but there was a political reluctance to make Sinn Féin do so. Republican and nationalist outrage at the suspension of devolution in February 2000, for example, suggested that they, too, thought that the exercise of unionist political leverage was against the spirit of the Agreement.

At first sight, this appears a rather contradictory position for a UUP spokesperson to hold. On the one hand, the UUP told its own constituency that republicans had signed up to a partitionist settlement and had lost the struggle to circumvent the principle of consent. On the other hand, it worried publicly about a logic of implementation which required of them a different sacrifice. How could these positions be reconciled? They were reconciled in two ways. First, it was thought that republicans had traded an unreal military objective for very real political gains. This may have involved an important sacrifice of principle for Sinn Féin, but, since that principle was anathema to unionists anyway, it hardly registered on their political consciousness. However, Martin McGuinness as the minister responsible for their children's education and unapologetic about the activity of the IRA certainly did register. Second, there was a profound if rather naive dismay that republicans, having lost their war, were still determined to win the argument. And winning the argument was judged to mean securing retrospective legitimacy for the IRA's campaign, achieving a republican definition of the 'equality agenda', and provoking division and ultimately implosion within unionism over the 'guns and government' issue. Here the definition of political reality threatened to prove decisive.

For example, the continued intimate relationship between Sinn Féin and the IRA could be rationalised as a necessary one. Only if the republican movement held together under Adams's leadership could peace be sustained and the transition made smoothly to an exclusively democratic politics. That rationalisation was not unpersuasive, but one consequence of its acceptance was to arrange the implementation of the Agreement to the convenience of republicanism and to permit Sinn Féin to set the parameters of what was realistic and unrealistic politics. As a critical Irish journalist observed, republicans came quickly to realise that there would never be any effective sanction on their breaching of the principles of the Agreement: 'Sinn Féin can confidently expect no serious rebuke from either the Dublin or London governments, or from their fellow nationalists' over the continuing actions of the IRA. The UUP 'cannot tolerate this farce, without being historically extinguished by the forces of Paisleyism'.[46] And so it proved. The result was to shift the costs of transition onto the shoulders of the UUP who were pressurised into accepting a power-sharing executive without an end to IRA activity. That is why it was Trimble, rather than Adams, who had such constant and exhausting problems of party management. That is why it was Trimble, and not Adams, who had to take the very public and divisive risks. It may have been the case that the Sinn Féin leadership was taking risks. However, the secrecy of its deliberations meant that it was impossible for unionists to understand, even if they wished to. Jeffrey Donaldson, responsible himself for some of Trimble's management problems, asked the appropriate question: 'Why should unionism be divided when the pressure ought to be on the paramilitaries and their political surrogates? They are the ones in default.' There really should be no need, he argued, for further divisive meetings of the UUC. The British government should hold republicans to their commitments.[47]

When the IRA was forced into acts of decommissioning after 11 September 2001, the very secrecy of the events (to accommodate republican sensitivities) had the effect of promoting more mistrust than trust. This cult of sensitivity to IRA concerns was also to produce the political debacle of 21 October 2003.

Trimble noted this problem in 1999 when he argued that the UUP's difficulty with Sinn Féin was not the timing of its entry into government but mistrust about Sinn Fein's willingness to keep its bargains. The history of implementation hitherto suggested that 'they mean to redefine the Agreement to suit their own ends'.[48] He also alluded to this concern in a speech to the British–Irish Association at Oxford in September 2000. He noted that unionist opinion was becoming increasingly hostile to the assumption that the 'logic' of the Agreement meant accepting whatever interpretation its opponents cared to put on it.[49] In the same month Trimble also told a fringe meeting at the Labour Party Conference that his party had been carrying the weight of implementing the Agreement too long and criticised other parties 'for not carrying their share of the burden'.[50] This was, of course, a reference to the decommissioning debate and those comments illustrate why that debate was so central to the question of trust between 1998–2002. In fact, if not in so many words, Trimble had proposed that republicans and unionists should set aside the objective of winning the argument about whose *reality* would prevail and should instead concentrate on sharing the political risks of managing change. 'Jumping together' (as it was called in 1999) or the principle of 'simultaneity' were different ways of avoiding the politics of blame and securing both leaderships from their respective critics. The Sinn Féin leadership did not respond, but then neither did the SDLP's or the Irish Government. What was the reason for this common nationalist attitude?

This was addressed directly by Trimble in his 2002 conference speech. He observed while that the doctrine of consent was widely recognised in Irish public life, its implications were not. 'Too many people in nationalism', he concluded, 'see unionism as a problem to be got around rather than a noble tradition to be accommodated in a spirit of genuine engagement.'[51] Moreover, much of the problem also appeared to lie in the common nationalist assumption that history is on its side and that Irish unity is inevitable. Changing demographics still underpins this assumption despite the 2001 census figures that cast doubt on a nationalist majority in Northern Ireland for the foreseeable future. Since demographics is not an argument but a statement, nationalists did not feel any great need to persuade or, to use Trimble's term, engage with unionism. Why would they encourage unionists politically when the whole point is to get them to acknowledge their historical redundancy? Far from concentrating on the constructive responsibilities which the vision of power-sharing required, both Adams and the SDLP leader Mark Durkan felt it more important to develop their respective visions of Irish unity. None of this, however unrealistic and wishful, was helpful in allaying unionist mistrust, however exaggerated or however paranoid, in the logic of the process. Indeed, it was entirely counter-productive.

The balance within unionism 1998–2003

From May 1998 to October 2002, then, unionist opinion revealed a rather para-
doxical condition. On the one hand, the polls showed a popular shift towards a
more openly critical position on the main elements of the Belfast Agreement. Even
within the UUP, Trimble's margin of support narrowed consistently, so that by the
UUC meeting in September 2002 it was questionable whether, if a vote on the issue
had been taken, he would have remained as leader. Unionist anxieties about trust
and about the implementation and direction of the Agreement had been
significantly heightened by the behaviour of republicans. Moreover, the DUP
began to exude even greater confidence about its ability to displace the UUP as the
dominant party within unionism. Following the suspension of devolution in
October 2002, it claimed that its opposition to the Agreement had been fully
vindicated.[52] On the other hand, in the course of the four-and-a-half-years since
the referendum the DUP's policy had changed from one of fundamental rejection
of the Agreement to one of arguing for its renegotiation. For some this meant that
the DUP was seeking a way to accommodate itself, with some slight modifications,
to the operation of the Agreement.[53] For others, the logic of the Agreement meant
that the DUP had no choice but to accommodate itself to the new dispensation.
Indeed, the DUP might even be the preferred vehicle to deliver the unionist
electorate to a stable settlement, the 'Nixon in China' syndrome, as one commentator put it.[54] In short, anxieties about implementation were certainly real and
growing, but this did not necessarily translate into support for a wrecking strategy.
How does one explain this ambivalence?

Part of the answer can be found in an interview Trimble gave in November
1997. It was suggested to him that most unionists were pessimistic about the
outcome of any agreement and suspected that the Paisley/McCartney analysis
about betrayal was correct. At the same time, they did not think that either leader
had an effective strategy to avoid this outcome. Trimble admitted that there was
indeed deep concern among unionists and conceded that pessimism was widespread. However, it was his view that unionists had supported the UUP's decision
to stay in the talks precisely because they were so concerned. He went on: 'I do
know that the people here appreciate the effort that we are making, know that it is
the only hope of progress, and that the Paisley/McCartney line offers no hope to
anybody.'[55] Conjuring up the anxieties was not the same thing as trying to address
them. For all their anxious observations of the last four-and-a-half-years, a large
proportion of the unionist electorate agreed with Trimble. In particular, there was
appreciation for Trimble's efforts to restore the credibility of unionist politics
nationally and internationally. In judging unionist responses in this period,
therefore, what did not happen is just as important as what did. Trimble did *not*
lose the support of his own party and crucial votes in the UUC continued to back
his strategy, albeit marginally. The UUP Assembly Party did *not* fragment and
actually exhibited remarkable solidarity under pressure. The UUP's electoral base

did *not* collapse. For all their anxieties, this latter fact suggested that unionists did *not* necessarily think there was a realistic alternative to the Agreement and did *not* think that it was entirely without merit. This pragmatic view of political circumstances, though, did not mean that they loved the implementation of the Agreement they did have.

Trimble's dogged endurance in fending off the opposition constituency within his party, in deflecting the DUP challenge and in keeping alive the possibility of an inclusive form of power-sharing has often been underestimated by those who criticised him for not *selling* the Agreement. The real problem was that Gerry Adams had not been able to sell the Agreement properly to the IRA. Following the crisis of October 2002, the conditions appeared to exist for a mode of implementation that might quell unionist anxieties. The prime minister's speech on 17 October 2002 seemed to make it plain that a republican definition of what was and was not *realistic* to expect of the IRA was no longer persuasive and that Sinn Féin was required to deliver on its responsibilities.[56] Trimble's view could be best summed up as: *Je ne regrette rien*, and he told the Party Conference in October 2002 that he did 'not regard the last five years as a mistake'. One year later and that confidence seemed seriously misplaced.

In the course of 2003 the differences within the UUP sharpened and their nature captured succinctly in an exchange on 'The future of Unionism' in the *Guardian* between Jeffrey Donaldson, Trimble's most consistent critic, and Esmond Birnie, one of Trimble's most consistent supporters. Birnie concentrated on the key claims of the UUP leadership: that the institutions of the Agreement secured the Union and, while not perfect and open to review, were rational in the sense that any revision of them would produce the same broad outline. Indeed, its flexibility in the face of republican resistance had proved that unionism could accept change, was open to sharing power, had actually delivered some IRA decommissioning and, importantly, had strengthened the influence of unionism with British and world leaders. Donaldson's response accepted that Trimble did enjoy 'popularity amongst the great and the good in high places'; but in Northern Ireland, he argued, Trimble's electoral record had been a disaster. It was the UUP that had paid a heavy price for including Sinn Féin in government. Whilst republicans continued to expand their electoral base, 'support for the UUP is crumbling and Unionist confidence generally is at its lowest for many years'. Donaldson thought it was hard to believe that Trimble could provide the leadership and deliver the support necessary to deal effectively with republicans. He asked the key political question. If Trimble continued to be in a position where he could not claim to speak for a majority of unionists 'then who will want to do business with a minority stakeholder?'[57]

That was a good question. When the British Government postponed the elections to the assembly in May 2003 it was obvious that it, too, acknowledged the question's seriousness. On the other hand, things were not entirely unambiguous for Donaldson and his colleagues in dissent, MPs Martin Smyth and David Burnside. In a critical leader, the *Daily Telegraph* noted that Donaldson did not want to overthrow the Belfast Agreement: 'rather he wants to see it implemented in full, including IRA disbandment'. It went on to argue that if 'the name of the game is playing the existing institutions', then the UUP would be better off with Trimble 'who at least had the advantage of exerting some leverage on London'.[58] Trimble's *bona fides* in London and his credibility as a broker remained his strongest cards. But what if these were to be discounted?

Discounting them had become the objective of the DUP. This involved a delicate political manoeuvre of continuing to condemn the UUP leadership for negotiating weakness, for political misjudgement and blind commitment to a failed Agreement, while at the same time moderating its tone about inclusive government and a possible accommodation with Sinn Féin. From the beginning of 2003, even Adams was acknowledging publicly a more 'pragmatic approach' on the part of the DUP.[59] As Trimble's effectiveness appeared to wane along with his credibility, the DUP began to present itself as the party that could deliver the majority of unionists to a new and renegotiated Agreement. In a very revealing exchange in the *Guardian* with Trimble's adviser Steven King, Gregory Campbell posed the question: is unionism ready to deal? He recognised that, from a 'mainland' point of view, the demise of Trimble might appear to presage 'unionism retreating back into the trenches'. There was no need to worry. Those 'who fear that the unionism they see beginning to assert itself and think that it only does so to maintain the status quo completely misunderstand the unionist perspective on present day Northern Ireland'. What unionists wanted was a better deal, not an end to dealing. They wanted, claimed Campbell, to see a better 'delivery mechanism' to address their anxieties. They also wanted to see the back of Trimble.[60]

Despite the rejection of renegotiation by the two governments, what the DUP was actually looking for in its 'seven principles' was not all that different from what the UUP was hoping to secure through discussion with Sinn Féin. The one difference was the very principle of negotiating with Sinn Féin, and even that was capable of being finessed.[61] The war of words between the UUP and the DUP defined the real struggle for primacy. For Trimble, the DUP was really looking only for a 'fig leaf' of renegotiation before accepting 'the places and power the Agreement gives' and the party's 'bombastic claims cannot cover up the hollowness of their position'.[62] For Peter Robinson, the UUP's criticism, like its policy, was simply confused, and while the DUP talks 'like a party on the way up, the Ulster Unionist Party talks like a party on the way out'.[63] There remained, however, one big problem for the DUP if it intended to pursue a more conciliatory strategy: its own support base had been so convinced by the party's rhetoric of betrayal over the previous five years that there was little support for power-sharing with Sinn Féin.[64]

Conclusion

In this contest within unionism, the significance of the fiasco on 21 October 2003 should not be underestimated. If, in the choreographed sequencing of events,

Trimble had not been misled by the IRA on the 'transparency' of decommissioning then there was every opportunity that the UUP leadership could have gone to the electorate on a positive note. As it was, the very criticisms of Trimble's leadership appeared amply confirmed. It looked as if he had been fooled yet again by republicans and his negotiating skills looked questionable. The credibility of the Agreement among UUP voters took another serious blow. Its leader had been publicly humiliated, though he could not admit that. He had been so bound into negotiation with Adams that to denounce republicans openly would have been further admission of his own gullibility. It was the worst possible position for a unionist leader. His objective of historic compromise had been compromised in historic fashion by the secretive cult of militant republicanism, the purpose of whose negotiating tactics, it seemed, had been to knock Trimble out of the game while securing hegemony within northern nationalism. As one commentator put it, the expected emergence of a DUP–Donaldson alliance would convince both governments that unionism was incapable of endorsing an inclusive future and that, in turn, would diminish the ability of unionism 'to shape the future in the North and on this island'.[65]

The result of the assembly election on 26 November 2003, then, confirmed two truths that everyone knew already. The first was that the majority of unionists were disillusioned with the operation of the Belfast Agreement. Even the small rise in electoral support for the UUP could be attributed to the strong performance of anti-Agreement candidates like Donaldson in Lagan Valley and Burnside in South Antrim. The DUP profited from an uncomplicated message that appealed to disgruntled unionists and successfully gathered up the votes of the other smaller anti-Agreement unionist parties. Moreover, the party was publicly united, and that could not be said of the UUP, which continued to fight out its own internal battles throughout the three week campaign. The DUP, with 26 per cent of the vote, nearly 8 per cent up on the 1998 result, and with 30 seats, became the largest party in the assembly. The second truth was that Sinn Féin is now the largest party within the nationalist constituency. Catholics increasingly look to Sinn Féin as the party with the energy and vitality to advance their collective interests. With, now, 24 per cent of the vote, up almost 6 per cent on 1998, Sinn Féin is drawing further ahead of their now rather demoralised rivals in the SDLP. Together these two truths suggest that Northern Ireland is in for a prolonged period of what can be called 'trial by mandate'. Standing on the legitimacy of their election successes, the DUP and Sinn Féin will confront each other with contradictory claims: the former will now argue that the Agreement must be renegotiated to satisfy unionists; the latter will claim that the Agreement is inviolable and their mandate means that Sinn Féin must be included in any executive.

Despite these mutually exclusive positions, there are those who still hope that only the extremes can deliver a deal. Now that the DUP and Sinn Féin are predominant, now that the complicating factors of a divided UUP and a weakened SDLP are out of the way, these two parties have the opportunity to make the final compromise. They both want devolution, IRA arms may be more of a handicap than an asset now to republicans and most of the deeply contentious aspects for unionists are already decided. One could argue that there does exist a logical dynamic in favour of accommodation. One cannot rule out that possibility, but it means ignoring the culture of both the DUP and Sinn Féin.[66] The result of the assembly election has probably ensured that direct rule from London will continue in the short and possibly the medium term. The condition at the end of 2003 is one of considerable unionist anxiety, articulated by the DUP, confronting considerable nationalist expectation, articulated by Sinn Féin. That is a far from stable condition.

Notes

1   'Talk of Irish Unity Is a Distraction', *Sunday Business Post*, 18 May 2003.
2   P. Bew, 'Blair Puts it Up to Adams and Backs Trimble', *Sunday Independent*, 20 October 2002.
3   A. Aughey, *Nationalism, Devolution and the Challenge to the United Kingdom State* (London: Pluto Press, 2002), ch.7.
4   J. Lloyd, 'The New Tory Federalists', *New Statesman*, 20 February 1998, pp. 18–19.
5   S. Simon, 'Trimble a Moses, Not a Judas', *Daily Telegraph*, 20 November, 1999.
6   R. McCartney, 'Talks that Won't Do the Union Any Good', *Northern Ireland Brief*, no. 14, December 1995.
7   DUP, 'Democracy – Not Dublin Rule', April 1997.
8   G. J. Mitchell, *Making Peace* (New York: Alfred A. Knopf, 1999), p. 110.
9   UUP, 'Statement by the Rt Hon. David Trimble MP on Entering Castle Buildings', 17 September 1998.
10 See A. Aughey, 'Learning from the Leopard', in R. Wilford (ed.), *Aspects of the Belfast Agreement* (Oxford: Oxford University Press, 2001), pp. 184–201.
11 B. Feeney, 'Condemned by the "Kiss of Death"', *Irish News*, 15 October 2003.
12 See A. Aughey, 'A New Beginning? The Prospects for a Politics of Civility in Northern Ireland', in J. Ruanne and J. Todd (eds), *After the Belfast Agreement* (Dublin: UCD Press, 1999), pp. 122–44.
13 D. Trimble, *To Raise Up a New Northern Ireland* (Belfast: Belfast Press, 2001), p. 79.
14 D. Trimble, 'The Commitment to Peace and Democracy', UUP Press Statement, 22 May 1999.
15 R. McCartney, 'Yes There Is an Alternative', *Parliamentary Brief*, vol. 5, no. 6, May–June 1998, pp. 16–17.
16 E. Moloney, '160,000 "New" Voters Key to Analysis of Northern Referendum', *Sunday Tribune*, 24 May 1998.
17 *Hearts and Minds* Poll, BBC News Northern Ireland; for details: http://news.bbc.co.uk/1/hi/northern_ireland/2335861.stm.
18 F. Cobain, 'Sinn Féin's Behaviour in Government Has Tarnished Powersharing', UUP Press Statement, 17 October 2002, available at: www.uup.org/current/index.shtml.
19 *Hearts and Minds* Poll.
20 Cited in P. Norton and A. Aughey, *Conservatives and Conservatism* (London: Temple Smith, 1981), p. 9.
21 G. Martin, 'Wavering Unionists Fear Havoc a Strong No Vote Could Cause', *Irish Times*, 20 May 1998.
22 K. Maginnis, 'Way Forward for Unionism Is a Yes Vote', *Belfast Telegraph*, 5 May 1998
23 P. Bew, 'The Unionists Have Won, They Just Don't Know It', *Sunday Times*, 17 May 1998.
24 D. Trimble, 'Platform', *Belfast Newsletter*, 18 April 1998.
25 UUP, 'Speech by Rt Hon. David Trimble MP to the Northern Ireland Forum', 17 April 1998.
26 B. Hadfield, 'The Belfast Agreement, Sovereignty and the State of the Union', *Public Law*, winter 1998, pp. 599–616.

27 UUP, 'Understanding the Agreement', May 1998.
28 D. Trimble, 'Sinn Fein's Irresponsibility Still Threatens Peace in Ulster', *Daily Telegraph*, 25 July 2002.
29 UUP, 'Leader's Speech at Annual Party Conference in Armagh', UUP Press Statement, 18 October 2003.
30 G. Campbell, 'Negotiating a New Agreement?', *Belfast Telegraph*, 21 October 2002.
31 Keynote speech by Tony Blair at Stranmillis, University College, Belfast, Tuesday 15 June 1999', available at: http://cain.ulst.ac.uk/events/peace/docs/tb15699.htm.
32 N. Stanage 'Trimble Puts Power Before Peace', *Guardian*, 25 September 2002.
33 A. Guelke, 'Civil Society and the Northern Ireland Peace Process', paper presented at the Annual Conference of the Political Studies Association of Ireland, Belfast, 18–20 October 2002.
34 H. McDonald, 'Belfast Youths "More Bigoted" than the Troubles' Generation', *Observer*, 23 September 2001.
35 S. McGonagle, 'Survey Reveals Schism Between Communities', *Irish News*, 5 March 2003.
36 R. McCartney, 'Counting the Cost of the "Agony Aunt"', *Belfast Telegraph*, 22 October 2002.
37 P. Shirlow ' Politics on the Streets', paper presented at the Annual Conference of the Political Studies Association of Ireland, Belfast, 18–20 October 2002.
38 UUP, 'Leader Addresses Party Conference in Londonderry', 19 October 2002, available at: www.uup.org/current/index.shtml.
39 E. Moloney, 'Election Results Put Trimble's Leadership in Doubt', *Sunday Tribune*, 10 June 2001.
40 *Hearts and Minds* Poll.
41 L. Clarke, 'A Lack of Conviction Shook Stormont's Foundations', *Sunday Times*, 20 October 2002.
42 UUP, 'Leader Addresses Party Conference in Londonderry', 19 October 2002.
43 H. McDonald 'A Treacherous Peace', *Observer*, 26 August 2001.
44 H. Patterson, *Ireland since 1939* (Oxford: Oxford University Press, 2002), p. 342.
45 'Sinn Fein's IRA Link', speech by D. Nesbitt to Northern Ireland Assembly, October 8, 2002, available at: www.uup.org/current/index.shtml.
46 K. Myers, 'The IRA Knows There Is No Plan B: It Can Do What it Likes', *Sunday Telegraph*, 6 October 2002.
47 UUP, Extracts from a speech by J. Donaldson to the AGM of Lagan Valley Unionist Association, 18 January 2001, available at: www.uup.org/current/index.shtml.
48 D. Trimble, 'There Can Be No Further Erosion of Principle', UUP Press Statement, 9 October 1999.
49 UUP, Speech by D. Trimble to the British–Irish Association at Oxford, September 2000, available at: www.uup.org/current/index.shtml.
50 UUP, Statement by D. Trimble to a fringe meeting at the Labour Party Conference, 28 September 2000, available: www.uup.org/current/index.shtml.
51 UUP, 'Leader Addresses Party Conference in Londonderry', 19 October 2002.
52 DUP, Speech by P. Robinson to Northern Ireland Assembly, 9 October 2002, available at: www.dup.org.uk/scripts/dup_s/newsdetails.
53 S. King, 'Has the DUP Changed its Spots?', *Belfast Telegraph*, 24 September 2003.
54 M. O'Doherty 'The "Nixon in China" Theory … Was There Too Much Faith in Trimble?', *Belfast Telegraph*, 22 October 2003.
55 P. Bew, 'A Not Impossible Task – Interview with David Trimble MP', *Parliamentary Brief*, vol. 5, no. 3, January 1998, p. 51.
56 *Hearts and Minds* Poll.
57 'The Future of Unionism', *Guardian*, 5 July 2003.
58 'Monitoring Sinn Fein', *Daily Telegraph*, 5 September 2003.
59 S. Doyle, '"More Pragmatic" DUP Approach to Sinn Féin', *Irish News*, 17 January 2003.
60 'Unionism – Which Way Forward?', *Guardian*, 3 July 2003.
61 W. Graham, 'DUP "Can Lead Unionists Out of the Wilderness"', *Irish News*, 26 November 2002.

62 'Trimble Launches Scathing Attack on DUP Talks Record', *News Letter*, 1 October 2003.
63 'We're the Party of Ideas, Says Robinson', *News Letter*, 30 September 2003.
64 Speech by Tony Blair, in Belfast, Northern Ireland 17 October 2002, available at: http://labour.org.uk/tbnispeech/.
65 E. Pheonix, 'Unionism Is Now Split Wide Open', *Irish News*, 22 October 2003.
66 P. Bew, 'Paisleyism Cannot Be Appeased', *Guardian*, 4 December 2003.

7

The SDLP: governing with uncertainty

SEAN FARREN

The GFA was seen as vindication of the SDLP's oft-repeated agenda for resolving the conflict in Northern Ireland. The set of three relationships which the party and, most particularly, its leader John Hume argued lay at the heart of the conflict – relationships between people and communities within the North, between North and South and between the people of Ireland and Britain – were given formal expression within the institutions to be established under the agreement. These institutions were: the new assembly for Northern Ireland; secondly, the arrangements which would bring together the executive authorities and the parliaments of North and South, the North–South Ministerial Council, and the Parliamentary Forum; and, thirdly, the British–Irish Council to link the peoples of the two countries. Together with the range of confidence-building measures which were to address matters such as police reform, prisoner releases, human rights, equality, cultural issues and, most controversially, the decommissioning of paramilitary weapons, the GFA appeared to provide a comprehensive package addressing all of the key matters to be resolved and to provide after so many years of conflict and tragedy a political and constitutional framework for a peaceful and exclusively democratic way forward.

The challenge was to implement the agreement expeditiously in such ways as would maximise confidence and deny its detractors space to mobilise opposition. Implementation began with the joint referenda of May 1998, just over a month after the Agreement had been adopted. Joint referenda had long been an SDLP proposal and were intended to provide the clearest possible expression to the principle of consent, a core principle of the Agreement. In practice, consent meant that unionists and nationalists in the North were being invited to endorse its constitutional and institutional arrangements while the electorate in the South would express its views primarily on the constitutional provisions which required amendments to Articles 2 and 3 of the Republic's constitution.[1] As the SDLP's manifesto for the referendum in the North put it, The 'Agreement provides for the democratic will of the people, North and South. This is unprecedented. The people of Ireland … will determine their own future.'[2]

The referendum witnessed the highest ever turnout by the electorate in the North, 82 per cent, and a massive endorsement for the Agreement in both parts of the country. In the South, 95 per cent of those who voted supported the agreement while in the North support stood at almost 72 per cent. The Agreement had crossed the hurdle of popular endorsement with apparently very high levels of approval. On that basis the conditions in which it could be fully implemented seemed very favourable.

By implication, the results of the referenda also addressed republican claims that the Irish people had never been allowed to speak as one entity since the last all-island test of popular opinion, the general election of 1918. Now they had so spoken, if not in a single referendum at least in two simultaneous referenda, on essentially the same issues, Northern Ireland's constitutional status and the political arrangements for its future government. The referenda results showed that the overwhelming majority of people, North and South, accepted Northern Ireland's existing constitutional status and would endorse constitutional change in favour of Irish unity only if it was to be achieved peacefully. Republicans could, therefore, no longer invoke that last whole-island election outcome to give a veneer of legitimacy to their campaign of violence, i.e. that Northern Ireland was an illegal state imposed against the will of the majority of the Irish people. On the other hand, the referenda also meant that unionists could no longer claim that nationalist Ireland did not regard as legitimate Northern Ireland's continued presence within UK for as long as a majority of the people living there wanted that presence to last.

With the constitutional issues settled and popular endorsement received for the institutional arrangements set out in the Agreement, the next implementation step was the election to the new assembly. It followed barely a month later, on the 25 June. The results punctured the optimism created by the referendum results in the North. In contrast to the outcome barely a month previously, the election results came as a sharp reminder of what the North's referendum results had concealed, namely the strength of opposition to the Agreement that existed within the unionist community. Almost 29 per cent of those voting in the referendum had voted for rejection and while it was generally assumed that the majority of 'No' votes were unionist they had not, of course, been recorded as such. The assembly election results made it clear just how significant a section of the unionist electorate this percentage represented.

Of the 108 assembly members elected 58 were unionist and 42 nationalist, with 8 others. The two nationalist parties, SDLP with 24 and Sinn Féin with 18, were strongly pro-Agreement as were the 8 others. Unionism[3] was, however, deeply divided, with only a slim majority of its members pro-Agreement. Significantly, it was never certain as to how strongly pro-Agreement all of those members were. From the outset, therefore, implementing the Agreement faced enormous challenges, most of which became focused on the single issue of decommissioning paramilitary weapons and consequently placing an ongoing question mark over the fate of David Trimble as leader of pro-Agreement unionism.

For the moment, however, all eyes were looking ahead towards the next steps, the creation of the new political institutions as set out in the Agreement. A short transition period had been foreseen following the election of the first and deputy first ministers in shadow form. The latter election took place at the first meeting of the newly elected members, the meeting being held in the very room where the agreement had been adopted just two months previously. At that meeting David Trimble, leader of the UUP, and Séamus Mallon, deputy leader of the SDLP, were jointly elected first and deputy first ministers (designate) unopposed.

The transition to regional control of the administration of Northern Ireland and to the establishment of all of the other institutional arrangements of the Agreement had begun. Ominously, the transition was initiated against a background that was not as auspicious as the referenda results had first suggested. The election results contained the seeds of grave division within unionism; moreover, on the ground, the Orange Order's marching season, which was reaching its climax, was marked by considerable violence.[4] It was soon to be overshadowed by two of the most tragic incidents of the whole of the troubles: the Omagh atrocity and the deaths of the three young Quinn boys in Ballymoney as a result of a petrol-bomb attack on their home.[5] Ironically, theirs was a denominationally mixed family and their deaths were a sharp reminder of just how great a challenge was the task of creating a tolerant, reconciled society in Northern Ireland.

Their violent deaths also served as a reminder that removing the threat of violence from a society which had become so accustomed to paramilitarism over almost thirty years was going to be no easy task. This message was devastatingly emphasised by the bomb in Omagh the following month, on Saturday 15 August 1998, which resulted in twenty-nine deaths and hundreds of injuries. It was the worst single incident in Northern Ireland during the current conflict. Not surprisingly, therefore, of all the issues to be addressed in implementing the GFA decommissioning has proved the most contentious and the one which, at the time of writing, remains unresolved.

Attempts to find a resolution predated the Agreement itself and had begun with the three-man group headed by Senator George Mitchell which produced the first report on decommissioning in early 1996.[6] The report's recommendation that decommissioning commence during talks had not been acted on; so it had been left to the talks themselves to resolve the issue. The talks did so, but what was set out in the Agreement on decommissioning was to prove almost less fruitful, if much more contentious, than what the first Mitchell Report had recommended.

Whereas much of the Agreement contains quite specific detail on how its implementation was to proceed, this one area, long signalled as crucial to the successful implementation of the Agreement, had been left quite imprecise. The wording of this section of the Agreement suggested that decommissioning[7] was to be left essentially to the goodwill of the parties, especially those associated, in one way or another, to paramilitary organisations. Parties were merely urged to work 'constructively' with the Independent International Commission on Decommissioning (IICD) to achieve the full decommissioning of paramilitary arms within two years following the endorsement in referendum North and South of the [Good Friday] agreement ...[8] More significantly, the wording set out a rather passive role for the IIDC[9] which appeared unable to act unless approached to do so by representatives of the paramilitary groups.

However, like many others, the SDLP did not believe that the lack of detail and precision was intended to leave decommissioning as a discretionary matter, something that might or might not happen. After all, from the Mitchell Report onwards, it had been made clear that paramilitary weaponry and indeed the very existence of paramilitary organisations, had to be directly addressed as part of the task of creating an exclusively democratic as well as a peaceful society in Northern Ireland. The general expectation was that weapons would have to be decommissioned in some manner and the paramilitary organisations disbanded.

While not sharing unionist demands that decommissioning was a precondition for further progress in implementing the Agreement, the SDLP recognised that decommissioning had to happen in some demonstrable way if unionists were to be convinced that IRA violence was at an end and if nationalists were to be persuaded that loyalist paramilitaries had lifted their threats against Catholics. The SDLP rested its case essentially on the will of the Irish people, North and South, expressed in the referenda. As Séamus Mallon[10] frequently put it, the Irish people had spoken and if the IRA, especially, had any regard for the voice of the Irish people it should decommission forthwith. Future leader of the party Mark Durkan emphasised the need for a clear demonstration that decommissioning was a reality and dismissed claims, frequently made, that decommissioning was a 'red herring', saying that the more it was dismissed as such 'the more people become preoccupied with the issue'.[11]

The SDLP argued that in practical terms the establishment of the Independent Commission on Decommissioning and the passing of legislation in both the Irish and British parliaments to make statutory provision for the facilitation of decommissioning, also meant that the words of the Agreement were underpinned by a very serious intent that decommissioning be a reality.

But SDLP also recognised that the sooner all of the institutions were operating the more likely it was that decommissioning would be achieved. Consequently, there was considerable frustration that as 1998 passed early progress was not achieved on making devolution a reality. Talks at assembly level and between parties and representatives of the two governments inched their way towards an outline agreement on executive portfolios and on the workings of the North–South Ministerial Council,[12] but for unionists devolution was not possible in the absence of movement on decommissioning.

In those talks the SDLP had recommended that ten government departments be established and that North–South bodies with significant responsibilities for developing co-operation in key areas be set up. The SDLP argued that ten departments would enable a better team approach to evolve within the executive. No party of the four entitled to executive membership would find itself with only one minister since each would have at least one colleague with whom to consult. Furthermore, ten departments would allow for greater scrutiny of services which, in large departments, would seldom have much public attention drawn to them.

For the North–South bodies[13] the SDLP argued that eight should be established, with a strong emphasis on bodies with an economic dimension. Hence trade and business development, training and aspects of further and higher education such as research, as well as agriculture, energy and tourism were among the areas the SDLP wished to see included under the responsibility of the implementation bodies, with the other areas cited in the Agreement to be afforded greater levels of co-operation outside of the formal structure of these bodies.

Unionists had opposed the type of executive body proposed by the SDLP with the Dublin Government's support and sought to minimise both their number and the degree of authority to be vested in them. In the event, the number of bodies agreed was six with a seventh, the tourism body, established as a limited company and so formally not counting as an implementation body.

With agreement reached on institutional arrangements, the focus for progress was now clearly on decommissioning. The UUP continued to insist on at least some firm evidence of progress on decommissioning before it would allow devolution to 'go live' by the formation of the executive, the key which would unlock all of the other institutional arrangements. Pressure on David Trimble within and without the UUP not to allow devolution to proceed in the absence of such evidence was intense. Trimble himself agued that, along with the practical arrangements for devolution, 'all those parties proposing to be in the Administration demonstrate clearly and unambiguously their commitment to the democratic process and to peaceful means'.[14] Pointing to ongoing punishment beatings and to allegations of arms' procurement by the IRA, he claimed he was not yet convinced of paramilitary intent while the absence of progress on decommissioning, even in terms of paramilitaries contacting the IICD, strengthened his case against allowing devolution to happen at an early date.

1999 opened with a good deal of hope but no greater prospects that progress on implementing the agreement would soon be achieved. The assembly continued to meet periodically in its transitional form, making what preparations it could for the transfer of power. On 16 February the proposed structures of government were endorsed by the assembly, though within the 77 'Yes' votes only 29 were unionist, while another 29 voted against. The vote was a measure of continuing unionist division and a clear indication that some progress on decommissioning was essential if devolution was to happen.

To make devolution possible pressure was put on the paramilitary-associated parties to exert greater influence to progress decommissioning. The pressure was, most notably, on Sinn Féin, which was entitled to two executive departments under the d'Hondt formula by which departments would be allocated to parties qualifying for ministerial office.[15] However, that pressure was successfully resisted despite a number of high-level attempts to resolve the issue in the first half of the year. On a number of occasions it appeared from what Sinn Féin was hinting that the IRA was coming close to accepting the goal of full decommissioning by May 2000, as indicated in the Agreement. But these hints amounted to nothing and internal IRA sources made clear that there was no prospect of decommissioning progressing at that time.[16]

Notwithstanding this situation, the SDLP, together with Sinn Féin and the Irish and British governments, believed that progress on decommissioning could be made only if the political institutions became fully operational. This was the approach outlined in *The Way Forward* document issued by the two governments following a further round of negotiations at Stormont on Friday 2 July. Devolution day was to be 18 July, with the nomination of ministers three days earlier. Decommissioning of all paramilitary arms, the document stated, would be achieved by May 2000. Should there be a failure to fulfil any of the commitments under the Agreement, the two governments would automatically move to suspend the institutions.

In the absence of what the UUP judged to be a sufficiently clear commitment from Sinn Féin that the IRA would comply with the conditions for a start to decommissioning, the party rejected the timetable on offer. Nonetheless the process of nominating ministers according to the d'Hondt procedure went ahead in the assembly as intended. With the UUP absent from the chamber and none of the other unionist parties participating in the nomination process, however, it was an all-nationalist affair. Assembly members from both the SDLP and Sinn Féin were nominated to all ten ministerial offices, but with the nominations completed the Speaker Lord Alderdice declared them void since they failed to meet the cross-community requirement of the Agreement. The drama of the occasion was then added to by a statement from Séamus Mallon as deputy first minister, in which he offered his resignation to the assembly. His reason for doing so was that the price of devolution sought by David Trimble amounted to an attempt to rewrite the Agreement.[17]

With the assembly adjourned and a review of the Agreement ordered by both governments to see if the impasse could be broken, almost six months were to pass before the parties found themselves back in the Stormont debating chamber. Senator George Mitchell was persuaded to return to Northern Ireland to undertake the review single-handed. The review was essentially directed at achieving what 'The Way Forward' document had failed to achieve, namely an acceptable start to decommissioning coinciding with devolution and the activation of the all of the other institutional arrangements of the Agreement. Discussions lasted throughout the autumn until late November, when a formula that appeared likely to work was agreed.

Although the SDLP was active throughout the review its role in these discussions was essentially secondary. Without direct influence over any of the paramilitaries, and already committed to the policy of moving ahead simultaneously on both decommissioning and institution-building, the party had no lever other than exhortation to offer. Moreover, the autumn also saw the publication of the Patten Report[18] on the future of policing, an issue to which the SDLP had devoted considerable time and attention.

Policing and criminal justice, along with human rights and equality, had been critical issues to which the SDLP had given a lot of attention during the talks. Of these, policing was the most crucial given the almost total absence of active nationalist support for the RUC, an absence most acutely reflected in the very low level of Catholic enrolment and the scale on which RUC members had been targeted by IRA assassins.

A radical report recommending a sweeping reform of the RUC, including a name-change to the Police Service of Northern Ireland (PSNI), the Patten Report went a long way towards meeting the demands of the SDLP for a new start to policing. Yet, however radical Patten's recommendations, there was a long road to travel before the party would be satisfied that it was in a position to declare the new arrangements for policing acceptable. Critically, the Patten Report had to be turned into proposals for legislation, and until that happened and the policing bill had been acceptably amended the party would be in no position to decide if it would support the new police service.

Negotiations with the British Government on the details of police reform were to last until August 2001, when the SDLP finally took the historic decision to nominate three of its assembly members to the new Policing Board and to recommend that a career in the PSNI was an honourable and worthwhile professional commitment for nationalists. The prolonged debate was over what the SDLP considered a very minimalist Bill in which many of the Patten proposals were either ignored or watered down. So, conscious that there would be only one opportunity to get policing 'right', the SDLP engaged in a line-by-line consideration of the Bill. As a result the negotiations were frequently confrontational and progress slow.

The exercise was repeated on the floor of House of Commons, and the SDLP succeeded in obtaining over ninety amendments to the Bill. The issues of concern included:

- the name and symbols of the new service;
- the powers of the new policing board, especially its rights of inquiry;
- the role of the special branch, seen by many as 'a force within a force';
- the replacement of the reserve;
- the powers and role of the Police Ombudsman;
- the human rights regime within the service;
- the right of members of the Gárda Síochána to apply for posts or be seconded for service within the PSNI, and vice versa.[19]

Implementing the new policing arrangements then became one more matter requiring considerable attention, especially since the SDLP provided the only political representation of the nationalist community on the Policing Board and on the local District Policing Partnerships eventually established in each district council area. Sinn Féin's refusal to nominate to either of these bodies left the SDLP exposed to criticism and, worse, its members on these bodies open to physical attack. In the event, despite severe criticism and attacks on the homes and property of party members serving on policing bodies, the scale of the change in policing and the progress in implementing the Patten reform programme could not have happened without the SDLP making that historic decision in August 2002. In the words of Tom Constantine, US Oversight Commissioner, who was charged with independently auditing how Patten is being implemented, 'there is good reason for optimism that all of the Patten recommendations will be fully implemented within a reasonable timeframe'.[20]

Meantime the political focus continued to be on decommissioning, with the onus by early November clearly back on David Trimble and the UUP to accept an updated version of The Way Forward, i.e. the formation of the executive to be followed by the initial steps towards decommissioning. The advance on the latter document was contained in an IRA statement that it would appoint of an interlocutor[21] with de Chastelain's IICD. There was no mention of a timetable, much less of what would actually be decommissioned. It was a statement which at best was no more than a commitment to discuss the terms of decommissioning, though admittedly with the commission responsible for overseeing the process. It was a necessary first step, but with no commitment to what might happen next, how it would happen or when it would happen, the statement did not appear sufficient and it left the UUP in a huge quandary.

Nonetheless Trimble and some of his leading colleagues were persuaded that allowing the political arrangements to 'go live' was a better option than another rejection. They were convinced in this belief by what Senator Mitchell had told them was his understanding on what would happen should the institutions be operating, namely that the IRA would begin to decommission by the end of January.[22] The pro-Agreement unionist leaders argued, therefore, that devolution would make it impossible for the IRA not to do so. After all, Sinn Féin itself had constantly stressed the importance of politics being seen to work as the only context in which decommissioning could progress.

An intensive campaign took place in the middle of November both for and against allowing devolution to proceed. The climax was at the UUC meeting on Saturday 27 November, when pro- and anti-Agreement unionists made their case to over 800 delegates. Trimble carried the vote, 58 per cent–42 per cent. But with a post-dated resignation given to the president of the UCC, Sir Josias Cunningham, which the latter would be bound to hand to Lord Alderdice, the speaker of the assembly, should decommissioning not proceed by the end of January as Trimble understood it would, the prospects of another crisis could not be ruled out. That prospect was reinforced when the Sinn Féin leader denied that there had been a deal promising actual decommissioning in the terms Trimble appeared to have understood.[23]

With the UUC vote in favour of Trimble entering an executive, the assembly was reconvened in the following week, ministerial nominations were made and devolution went 'live' at midnight on 1 December.

In the allocation of ministerial offices the SDLP had, as the d'Hondt formula determined, the second, sixth and tenth choice. Within the party's assembly group there had been considerable discussion as to which departments should be chosen, but in the absence of any firm indication from the other parties it was extremely difficult to determine which would be available when choices had to be made. The UUP had given every indication that its first choice would be enterprise, trade and investment, which meant that the SDLP would have to choose the finance portfolio. Otherwise this key department would be very likely taken by the DUP and, given its intention to nominate ministers who would not attend executive meetings, an unworkable situation would be created from the outset. Either of the education departments, health and social service, or agriculture were also high on the party's list of preferred options. In the event, the SDLP choose finance and personnel (Mark Durkan), higher and further education, training and employment (Seán Farren) and agriculture and rural development (Bríd Rodgers). A junior minister, Denis Haughey, was later appointed to the Office of First and Deputy Ministers, giving the SDLP five ministers in total, including Séamus Mallon.

Responsible for three key departments, the SDLP was determined to demonstrate that it was a party with progressive policies and lost no time in demonstrating that the executive could make a difference. The first to move was Seán Farren who indicated quite soon after taking office that a review of student financial support for those enrolling in further and higher education would be initiated as soon as possible. Bríd Rodgers very rapidly established herself as a champion of the farming and rural communities, vigorously lobbying in London but especially in Brussels on their behalf. Mark Durkan put a very authoritative stamp on the finance portfolio, directing negotiations on the next round of EU structural funds and the establishment of the Strategic Investment Body.

The North–South Ministerial Council held its first meeting in Armagh on 13 December and inaugurated the work of its new secretariat and of the implementation bodies for which it was responsible. Likewise the British–Irish Council held its inaugural meeting in Lancaster House four days later. However, the latter lacked a focus similar to that of the North–South council and its agenda did not initially amount to very much of substance.

However diligently the executive and the two councils began to address their respective responsibilities, the issue which had delayed the formation of the executive remained a time-bomb threatening to undermine the new arrangements. Decommissioning was a frequent issue of debate[24] and comment in the assembly, with all of the anti-Agreement unionists, led by the DUP, losing no opportunity to attack Trimble's position. Their case was strengthened as January drew to a close and the anticipated report from General de Chastelain appeared unlikely to signal that any significant move on decommissioning had eventuated.

Still, it seemed almost impossible that institutions which were only crossing the threshold of operation, and to which there was a widespread and positive response, would be sacrificed. But the pressure on Trimble from all sides of unionism was intense; there was also his post-dated resignation letter in the hands of the Sir Josias Cunningham. So it was that when nothing but a few informal meetings between the IRA's interlocutor and the Decommissioning Commission had taken place, and further pressure on the IRA produced nothing of substance, it was inevitable that the letter would be delivered. The need to deliver it was forestalled only by the secretary of state's move on Friday 11 February to suspend the institutions.[25]

With the situation almost back to where it had been just over two months previously, the prospects of re-establishing the institutions at an early date did not appear positive. Once again the focus was on Sinn Féin and the UUP, with the SDLP and the other pro-Agreement parties marginalised. Concerned that the GFA was now being made dependent on these two parties, the SDLP stressed the role of all of the pro-Agreement parties and suggested that their greater involvement in the negotiations would serve as a positive force in achieving a breakthrough. But neither government appeared impressed. The taoiseach dismissed the idea, claiming that it would simply provide an occasion for parties to play the 'blame game'. Sinn Féin and the UUP were likewise dismissive of an all-party approach, preferring to keep the focus of attention – and hence the glare of publicity – on themselves.

With the pressure maintained, and both governments still determined that the momentum of the Agreement not be lost, the prospect of another breakthrough rose. That breakthrough came with the proposal to invite international inspectors to regularly inspect IRA weapons' dumps to confirm that their contents were securely under lock and key and not available for use. Those invited to be the inspectors were Cyril Ramaphosa, former secretary-general of the African National Congress, and Finland's former president Martii Ahtisaari. This innovation, intended as a confidence-building, measure together with the IRA's statement that it 'will initiate a process that will completely and verifiably put IRA arms beyond use',[26] suggested that that at last decommissioning was no longer an aspiration and that it *would* happen.

Encouraged by this statement, Trimble was prepared to re-enter the executive, though it was not until after another meeting of the UUC was held on 20 May that the decision to return could be taken. Trimble again carried the vote but by a slimmer majority than previously – 53–47 per cent – figures which clearly indicated that pro-Agreement unionists were by no means out of the woods.

With the executive and all of the other institutions of the Agreement functioning again, and with the arms' inspection programme providing a breathing space, the prospects for a calmer period seemed positive. Up to a point this proved to be the case. While the next suspensions were almost purely technical, David Trimble's decision not to nominate Sinn Féin ministers to attend meetings of the North–South Ministerial Council[27] and his own resignation as first minister on 1 July 2001,[28] together with very slow movement on decommissioning itself,[29] all posed an ongoing threat to the institutions and, therefore, to the successful implementation of the Agreement.

During that period a greater focus on 'bread-and-butter' issues was able to develop alongside fundamentals like decommissioning, and to a considerable extent all parties worked hard to show that local control of services could make a real difference. The summer of 2000 saw considerable work on a programme for government. Unlike normal coalitions which take office on a pre-agreed programme, the executive had taken office first. Given those circumstances and the suspension from February to May, no time had been devoted to what it might attempt to achieve. The programme that was adopted was, unsurprisingly, heavily influenced by the existing policies of the direct rule government. Nonetheless, there were innovations driven by local considerations and the policies of the executive parties.

The SDLP already had a broad policy agenda which it was determined to advance. The previously mentioned review of student finance had continued during suspension and its report became available later in the with actual changes to the scheme in place for the 2002 enrolments.[30] But by far the biggest issue SDLP ministers had to deal with was the 'foot-and-mouth' crisis in early 2001.[31]

Agriculture and Rural Development Minister Bríd Rodgers moved decisively to close the ports to the movement of all animals, a measure which direct rule ministers would have been reluctant to take so expeditiously since it marked Northern Ireland off from the rest of the UK. Together with her general handling of the crisis, this move not only contained the outbreak of the disease in Northern Ireland, but proved a major confidence boost for the executive and highlighted the benefits of regional government. Other measures which underlined such benefits were:

- the creation of a single industrial development authority, Invest Northern Ireland;[32]
- the committee of inquiry into the school transfer procedure for 11-year olds;[33]
- the establishment of the Special Programme for University Research (SPUR);[34] and
- substantial legislation on housing.[35]

The establishment of the Strategic Investment Body marked a new determination to tackle the huge infrastructure deficit which had accumulated over the previous decades and provided Northern Ireland new revenue raising powers for capital projects such as road, school and hospital building, water services, etc.[36] In a short period of time the executive was beginning to show that, despite inexperience of government, it *could* deliver social reform and economic development.

The North–South Ministerial Council also recorded early successes with, for example, initiatives on the part of Intertrade Ireland to promote all-Ireland trade connections and new cross-border business and university links.[37] Tourism Ireland launched marketing campaigns which focus on the whole island with packages of a cross-border nature intended to bring visitors to both parts of the country. The

Languages Body created a new central funding and development body for Irish and Ulster Scots which is promoting a much greater level of contact between individuals and interest groups across the whole island. Also the British–Irish Council, after a slow start, began to identify a range of issues on which it would develop cooperation between its component regions.[38]

Notwithstanding these initiatives and the growing confidence they produced the underlying sources of instability persisted; progress on decommissioning remaining the key unresolved problem. Evidence that the IRA remained active seemed to emerge in such incidents as the Florida gun-running case, in the arrests of three IRA associates in Columbia, in a number of killings in Northern Ireland and in the Stormont espionage allegations, all of which only added to UUP anxieties about the wisdom of remaining in the executive. So, despite two acts of IRA decommissioning there was no timetable, no inventory of what was being destroyed and no indication of when the process would be complete. Meantime loyalist paramilitaries also gave evidence of their continued existence with internal feuds and killings, attacks on nationalist homes in sensitive areas and the murder of several Catholics.

The Stormont espionage allegations and the arrests of several Sinn Féin activists on associated charges in October 2002 became the straw to break unionist commitment to remaining in the executive. In the face of threatened resignations by David Trimble and his ministerial colleagues, the secretary of state suspended the assembly for the fourth time, on 14 October, and so it remains at the time of writing.

While there did not appear to be any imminent danger of a return to widespread violence it was clear that paramilitaries on both sides of the community had no intention of disbanding. There were no easy answers to how this might be brought about. Excluding Sinn Féin from the executive appeared to some to be a solution, but that would mean persuading the SDLP to vote with the UUP and DUP to provide the required cross-community majority. Such a decision by the SDLP would have had the effect of postponing indefinitely any prospect of decommissioning at a time when the process had begun, however reluctantly and however long delayed. Secondly, it would also have the effect of two governments implying that the IRA ceasefire no longer held and the dangers that entailed. Thirdly, it would require the SDLP to vote with the DUP, a party that set itself the goal of destroying the GFA; and, fourthly, it would not have placed any sanctions on parties associated with loyalist paramilitaries.

In their most comprehensive attempt to deal with the failure to progress decommissioning as well as all the other outstanding issues, the two governments convened another Hillsborough conference in early March 2003. The Joint Declaration issued at the conclusion of the conference provided the most detailed blueprint for how progress was expected to be made. Unlike the Agreement itself, the section on decommissioning is detailed and spells out in clear terms what is expected in order to see decommissioning completed and all forms of paramilitarism ended.[39] Furthermore, although not strictly part of the declaration, the two governments also announced the establishment of a proactive Independent Monitoring Commission. While this new commission would not replace the decommissioning body, it would investigate and take evidence on paramilitary activity and regularly publish its findings. Those reports were expected to have a crucial influence on future political decisions, not least the ending of suspension.

In the turmoil of suspension and its aftermath the political fortunes of the two parties at the centre of the initiative to establish and develop the new political structures, the SDLP and the UUP, suffered considerably. The parties that had done most to inhibit progress in implementing the Agreement – Sinn Féin, through the IRA's failure to advance decommissioning in a manner likely to reinforce unionist confidence, and the DUP, by its attempts to undermine the Agreement while taking advantage of ministerial office – benefited from this turmoil and the uncertainty it produced about the Agreement's future.

The first signs were in the general election of 2001 when Sinn Féin won 4 seats and the SDLP failed to gain West Tyrone, where the candidate was Bríd Rodgers, and the DUP won 5, a couple of them at the expense of the UUP; the UUP won 6, but of these several were taken by anti-Agreement MPs. The divisions in unionism were now clearly moving in favour of a more stridently anti-Agreement position.

The postponed assembly elections of 2003 saw the situation polarise even more. The SDLP dropped to 18 seats, while Sinn Féin increased its number to 24. The DUP won 30 and, following post-election defections from the UUP,[40] gained another 3. The UUP itself dropped to 27 and then to 24 seats.

With the political centre in each community reduced in strength and the suspension about to enter its third year, the gains from the Agreement are, at the time of writing, fast receding from public consciousness. More ominously, with opinion polls showing growing support for direct rule in both communities,[41] most notably within the unionist community, the prospects for an early restoration of the Agreement's institutions are not encouraging. Nonetheless, the two-and-a-half year experiment in partnership government has demonstrated that parties can work together, that the North–South and the other institutional arrangements do have considerable potential, and the wonder is that the opportunity has not been more positively and more enthusiastically seized. Is it only the will that is lacking?

Notes

1 These were the two articles to which unionists had for long taken grave exception because of their claim to territory of Northern Ireland. The amendments effectively dropped that claim and contained a statement that Irish unity could be achieved only by peaceful means.

2 SDLP, *The Positive Approach – Manifesto for the Referendum* (1998), p. 7.

3 There were several unionist groups of which the UUP, led by David Trimble, was the largest with 28 members, the DUP led by Ian Paisley Senior, with 18, the UKUP with 5, led by Robert McCartney, the PUP with 2, led by David Irvine, and a loose group of 3 independents.

4 By 8 July 1998 there had been over 400 attacks on the security forces and a Catholic police officer was murdered by loyalists.

5 The home of the three Quinn brothers was petrol bombed on the morning of 12 July 1998 at a

time when tensions across Northern Ireland were very high as a result of the continued ban on the Orange Order forbidding marching on the Garvaghy Road in Portadown.

6   Report of the International Body on Arms Decommissioning, January 1996.

7   The relevant paragraph of the agreement reads that all participants are to confirm their intention to work constructively and in good faith ... to achieve the decommissioning of all paramilitary arms within two years following endorsement in referendums ... and in the context of the implementation of the overall agreement'.

8   There are only five short paragraphs on decommissioning in the GFA, and no detail is provided as to how decommissioning was to proceed. Arrangements, such as how and when, were left to be determined by the IICD and the paramilitaries themselves.

9   The IICD was headed by General John de Chastelain, one of the co-chairs of the talks, who had been a member of the three-person group headed by Senator Mitchell which had reported on decommissioning in 1996.

10 Séamus Mallon, *Official Report of the New Northern Ireland Assembly*, vol. 1 (1998–99), p. 187.

11 Durkan, *ibid.*, p. 318.

12 The outline agreement on the North–South arrangements was reached on 18 December after all-night negotiations, the UUP having previously agreed to accept the ten-department arrangement proposed by the SDLP.

13 The Agreement had specified that at least 6 areas of co-operation be identified for development under the auspices of special implementation bodies responsible to the North–South Ministerial Council and that a further 6 be developed in the looser context of inter-departmental contacts.

14 David Trimble, *Official Report of the New Northern Ireland Assembly*, vol. 1, 1998–99, p. 340.

15 Under the formula the UUP qualified for 3 departments as did the SDLP while the DUP and Sinn Féin qualified for 2 each.

16 Report in *Daily Telegraph*, 30 June 1999, by Tony Harnden, quoting an internal IRA briefing.

17 Mallon, *Official Report of the New Northern Ireland Assembly*, vol. 1 (1998–99).

18 The Patten Report was published following detailed study and consultation by a commission headed by Chris Patten, former governor of Hong Kong and Conservative MP, who had also served as a minister in Northern Ireland.

19 See various submissions on police reform by the SDLP published over this period.

20 SDLP internal progress report on policing, March 2004.

21 IRA statement of 17 November 1999.

22 This was confirmed by Séamus Mallon in an *Irish Times* interview, 13 April 2000.

23 Gerry Adams, report on *Downtown Radio*, 27 November 1999.

24 The DUP proposed a motion demanding the handing over of all illegal terrorist weaponry and called for the process of decommissioning to verifiable, transparent and credible. It was supported by unionists of all parties and opposed by all nationalists.

25 Since suspension was not envisaged in the Agreement itself, amending legislation to the Northern Ireland Act had been rushed through the British Parliament in January.

26 IRA statement, 6 May 2000.

27 This decision affected, in particular, the attendance of Health Minister Bairbre de Brún, the lead Northern Ireland minister, at meetings of the Food Safety Implementation Body.

28 Trimble announced his intention to resign in the May in a personal statement to the assembly: *Official Report of the New Northern Ireland Assembly*, vol. 2 (May, 2001), p. 1.

29 See chapter 10 for full discussion of the decommissioning process.

30 The new package created some controversy because, instead of following the Scottish model of abolishing tuition fees, it concentrated on targeting low-income students with the re-introduction of maintenance grants.

31 Thanks to the very strict measures taken, what was an extremely serious outbreak of foot-and-mouth disease in England, Wales and Scotland was restricted to a few isolated cases in Northern Ireland.

32 Taken forward by Sir Reg Empey (UUP), minister for enterprise, trade and investment, the legislation amalgamated the Industrial Development Board, the Local Enterprise Development Unit and the Industrial Research Unit.

33 Public concern had become widespread over the effects of the so-called 11–plus transfer procedure. Minister for Education Martin McGuinness (Sinn Féin) established a committee of inquiry which eventually recommended its replacement, together with a fundamental restructuring of second-level structures, the details of which at still being worked out.

34 The SPUR measure made over £90m extra available to the two Northern Irish universities during the executive's period in office, thus helping to close the gap which had existed between them and other UK universities.

35 Taken forward by Nigel Dodds (DUP), the Housing Bill 2002 was a major updating of existing housing legislation.

36 The body was established to manage the Reform and Reinvestment Programme, under which the infrastructural deficit would be addressed, and to identify appropriate funding sources for its projects.

37 Intertrade's Fusion programme, for example, links research departments with businesses on both sides of the border through student placements focusing on product development.

38 The areas for co-operation included: drug abuse, transport, environment and cultural matters.

39 Paragraph 13, Joint Declaration of the British and Irish Governments, Hillsborough, March 2003.

40 The most notable defections were those of the long-standing Trimble opponents Jeffrey Donaldson and Arlene Foster.

41 The 2004 *Life and Times* Survey.

8

Irish republicanism and the peace process: from revolution to reform

ROGER MAC GINTY

Introduction

The preferred republican narrative of the peace process involves a largely united republican movement pursuing a coherent strategy that is respectful of traditional republican ideals but aware of the new realities of an increasingly post-nationalist Europe. The narrative involves historic compromises and magnanimous gestures in the face of obdurate opposition from truculent unionists and ungenerous British governments. In reality, the story of republican involvement in the peace process is a good deal more complex, giving rise to the questions that will form the focus of this chapter. Undoubtedly the most profound question is the extent to which republican constitutional ideals have been compromised by the involvement of the Provisional republican movement – Sinn Féin and the Provisional IRA – in the peace process. The peace process has not brought about Irish unity and indeed has muddied the waters of the simple either/or constitutional choice of a united Ireland or a United Kingdom. There are other questions: what explains the remarkable unity that the mainstream republican movement was able to maintain during the course of the peace process, and what was the relationship between the republican move-ment and the wider community of northern cultural Catholics on which it depended?

Although much in Northern Ireland is resistant to change, the peace process did usher in immense change for many institutions, groups and relationships; and republicans were at the centre of many of the transformations. Consider a single news item from July 2002: the Sinn Féin lord mayor of Belfast lays a memorial wreath at the cenotaph outside Belfast City Hall to mark the anniversary of the Battle of the Somme. Such an event would have been unimaginable 10–15 years earlier[1] and captures the extent of political and socio-cultural change in Northern Ireland in the context of the peace process and subsequent Belfast Agreement. The very fact that Belfast had a Sinn Féin lord mayor was indicative both of the party's growing electoral strength and of its increasing acceptability and legitimacy among other parties: it assumed the lord mayor's position with the aid of the SDLP and the APNI. A Sinn Féin lord mayor was also reflective of the 'greening' of Belfast and many other parts of Northern Ireland as northern Catholics became more upwardly mobile and assertive. That a Sinn Féin representative felt the need to make a nod to unionist or Protestant sensitivities (and it is worth noting that many Catholics died in service of the crown) was indicative of a change in political relationships within Northern Ireland. For much of the Troubles, republicans had regarded the British Government as the most significant 'political other' in Northern Ireland, with unionists as secondary actors. The wreath-laying ceremony indicated that republicans were taking unionists seriously. But of course political change in Northern Ireland is often slow and rarely proves straightforward. Lord Mayor Maskey laid a laurel – rather than poppy – wreath some two hours prior to the official ceremony. According to one unionist politician, his gesture was an 'insult', while for the secretary of state it was 'a sign of hope for the future.'[2]

A united Ireland?

There have been few absolutes in the peace process. For all participants it has involved a moderation of apparently irreversible positions, the adoption of a new discourse of accommodation and a complicity in a constructive ambiguity.[3] The extent to which the republican constitutional agenda has been advanced via the peace process depends on interpretation. Mainstream republicans, often prone to optimism in their accounts of the peace process, point to the all-Ireland, or federalising, aspects of the peace process and Belfast Agreement, such as the dual referendums on the Agreement, the North–South Ministerial Council and the further endorsement of the conditional status of Northern Ireland's constitutional position. Sinn Féin is also keen to stress that it is an all-Ireland party, 'the only party people can vote for, whether they live in Derry, Kerry, Wexford or Antrim'.[4] It has had considerable success in building its political representation in the Irish Republic and the clear strategy has been to forge *de facto* all-Ireland linkages even if *de jure* unity remains an aspiration. Whole-island and cross-border economic, social and functional integration feature heavily in contemporary republican discourse. Moreover, Sinn Féin notes that the peace process has moved Irish unity on to the political agenda, with the fevered anticipation of the 2001 census results illustrating how constitutional issues retained a central role on the political landscape.

Whatever the publicly articulated republican interpretation, the constitutional position prevailing as a result of the peace process was far removed from the absolutist republican rhetoric of the 1980s and early 1990s. The peace process did not amount to 'the reconquest of Ireland by the Irish people'; nor did it force 'the British government into withdrawing completely from Ireland …' thus '… rid[ding] Ireland of the decadent and mercenary system which divides us and exploits our people'.[5] Although the Belfast Agreement underlined the insecurity of Northern Ireland's constitutional position, by reinforcing the consent principle whereby

Northern Ireland's status is to be decided by its citizens,[6] the Agreement made clear that Northern Ireland's position remains inside the UK until a pro-united Ireland majority seems likely.

One of the key features of the Agreement was its ambiguity, allowing pro-ponents of the same accord to hold radically different interpretations of the document. This allowed pro-Agreement unionists to maintain that the Agreement had secured the Union and thwarted nationalist's constitutional ambitions. The UUP claimed during its 1998 referendum campaign: 'The Act of Union, the fundamental bedrock of the Union, is untouched by the Agreement and Dublin's illegal territorial claim (Articles 2 and 3) will go.'[7] But Sinn Féin and its supporters may have drawn comfort from the anti-Agreement unionist position that the Union was in peril. According to the DUP,

> [T]he Agreement will lead to a united Ireland ... The Government of Ireland Act which established the supreme authority of the United Kingdom Parliament over Northern Ireland is abolished immediately. In contrast the illegal claims in the Irish Republic's constitution are merely amended ... The Agreement takes precedence over the Act of Union.[8]

The constitutional ambiguity of the Agreement was such that republicans may have believed that their constitutional agenda had been advanced regardless of the reality. This was an easy position for republicans to find themselves in: the peace process was so complex, and contained so many apparent gains for republicans, that they may have been beguiled into de-prioritising their principal constitutional goal of Irish unification. Republican gains in two non-constitutional areas, notably in relation to security grievances and self-esteem, may have overshadowed the con-stitutional agenda.

There can be no doubt that the peace process resulted in significant advances on the republican grievance agenda, particularly in relation to security issues. Com-bined pressure from Sinn Féin, the SDLP and the Irish Government resulted in far-reaching security sector reform, including a re-organisation of the police force, the scaling down of British troop numbers, prisoner releases and the establishment of the Bloody Sunday Tribunal. This reform, and particularly the re-organisation of the RUC and partial withdrawal of the British Army in the context of the IRA ceasefire, had a real quality-of-life dividend in many nationalist communities. Alongside the republican security grievance agenda, the introduction of human rights and equality legislation and more attention to social and cultural inclusion represented a willingness on behalf of the British Government to deal seriously with the republican non-constitutional agenda. It seems unlikely, though, that the republican grievance agenda could have been so comprehensively addressed had Sinn Féin and the IRA maintained an absolutist 'united Ireland or nothing' stance. Certainly many security reforms were linked to the British Government's threat assessments in the light of the IRA ceasefire.

The second major republican non-constitutional gain from the peace process is more difficult to define. This was the perception that republicans were gaining more out the peace process than unionists. This affective republican marginal utility derived from the sense that much of the peace process was nationalist in origin and design. British Government and unionist discomfort at various junctures in the peace process served merely to reinforce the republican view that the peace process strategy was the correct one. Moreover, it was not enough for the Sinn Féin leadership to participate in the peace process; they had to have a real sense of its ownership. This apparent appropriation of the peace process, with the use of terms such as 'the Sinn Féin peace strategy', was a further switch-off factor for unionists. Many republicans internalised the peace process as a vehicle for testing the boundaries of the republican agenda rather than seeing it as a process for reaching an accommodation with Northern Ireland's other communities and the two governments. This testing of the boundaries had all the more significance since Sinn Féin had spent many years in the political wilderness, having been marginalised from mainstream political debate and banned at various times from the airwaves in Britain and Ireland. This prior exclusion established a series of esteem-enhancing propaganda milestones that Sinn Féin could exploit via the peace process, ranging from Gerry Adams's first visits to Government Buildings in Dublin, the White House and 10 Downing Street to the first UUP–Sinn Féin television debate. The cumulative impact of this procession of events helped give the impression that the peace process was a republican process.

The esteem-enhancement role of the peace process doubtless contributed to Sinn Féin's electoral rise (increasing numbers of northern Catholics wanted to back the perceived winners, Sinn Féin, rather than the perceived losers, the SDLP), yet there was something intangible and ultimately unsatisfactory about the nature of this republican gain. First, it had a diminishing return: Gerry Adams could have only one first-time meeting with the British prime minister. As the peace process progressed, Gerry Adams and Martin McGuinness seemed to troop into Downing Street more regularly than Guards' regiments marched on nearby Horse Guard's Parade. Second, esteem-enhancement was often based on the perceived momentum and achievement of the process rather than its actual momentum and achievement. As such it was open to manipulation, and cynics could claim that at times the Sinn Féin leadership seemed more intent on exploiting esteem-enhancing opportunities than the traditional republican constitutional agenda. For example, Sinn Féin invested much energy on gaining office space in Westminster following their advances in the 2001 general election. The campaign for office space seemed more closely connected with gaining recognition of the status republicans felt they deserved rather than a practical step towards fulfilling a constitutional aim.

A third reason why the republican strategy of esteem-enhancement may ultimately be regarded as inconsequential was that the perception among unionists that the peace process was largely a nationalist and republican vehicle yielded a bitter harvest in terms of unionist disaffection. A hardening of unionist anti-Agreement attitudes amid the troubled implementation of the Agreement was in large part a reaction to what were interpreted by unionists as Sinn Féin 'successes'. Although many of these 'successes' operated at the symbolic rather than the substantive level, unionist opposition to the Agreement was no less real.

Fourth, and most importantly from a traditional republican perspective, the esteem-enhancement gains seemed a poor substitute for constitutional gains, fleeting and transitory compared to the possession of sovereignty and constitutional certainties.

The charge is that mainstream republicans have been 'bought off' by the cosmetics of security reform and the tinsel of esteem-enhancement, while Northern Ireland's constitutional position has remained largely unchanged. President Bill Clinton's visits to Northern Ireland illustrate the point: he brought glitz but often left behind little more substantial than encouragement and a sense of momentum.[9] But republicans counter by contending that the constitutional and grievance agendas have been pursued simultaneously and that progress on the one increases leverage on the other. They further argue that the Belfast Agreement is a transitional document with significant federal potential, and that the meta-aim still remains Irish unity. Gerry Adams described the Agreement as 'a phase in our struggle. That stage must continue until it reaches its final phase.'[10] Yet this 'Belfast Agreement as a stepping stone to Irish unity' approach contains two significant risks for republicans. First, many in the republican movement and the wider republican support community may become disaffected with the transition, assessing that it is likely to take longer to reach a united Ireland than anticipated or that ultimately the transitional phase will be unable to deliver Irish unity. As a result they may look for more radical alternatives.

A second risk is that the Agreement may satisfy rather than maintain or deepen nationalist demands for Irish unity; in other words, the transition may become stalled as erstwhile republican supporters find that many of their aspirations are met by the Agreement and the political culture it facilitates. There is some evidence that the devolved arrangements introduced as a result of the Agreement have greatly complicated the usual binary either/or choice between a united Ireland and the United Kingdom. Despite devolution's troubled infant years, public attitudes' survey evidence suggests that an enhanced form of devolution (increased functional autonomy but remaining within the Union) draws support away from the absolutist positions of a simple united Ireland or United Kingdom.[11] Although the effect of devolution on pro-Union constitutional preferences has been most dramatic, the 2001 survey found that Catholic support for a united Ireland fell from 59 per cent to 49 per cent if respondents were also offered the option of enhanced devolution. It would seem that devolution has helped blur the constitutional agenda and that Sinn Féin played no little part in this blurring.

Sinn Féin's 2003 Northern Ireland Assembly election manifesto sets out the party's 'priorities for 2003–2008', prominent among which is the 'preparation and publication of a Green Paper on Irish Unity'.[12] This seems to sum up perfectly the transition of Provisional republicanism from revolution to reform. The overall aim of Irish unity may remain intact, but the manner in which unity is to be achieved has changed profoundly, and the very nature of republicanism has changed with it. The republicanism of the 1970s, 1980s and early 1990s was often defined by the Provisional republican movement's adherence to the primacy of physical force and its zero-sum strategy of a united Ireland or nothing. In the aftermath of the Belfast Agreement, it would seem that republicanism and republicans have changed. This is not to deny that substantial elements of continuity are present in the ideology and its principal proponent organisations (Gerry Adams was elected Sinn Féin president in 1983). But after embarking on the peace process strategy, republicans found themselves operating in new landscape of political environments and institutions, engaging with a more complex issue agenda and shouldering new responsibilities. In 1986 Gerry Adams reflected on the developing British–Irish inter-governmental relationship thus: 'The major achievement for the British government is that it has succeeded in publicly tying in the Dublin government as the junior partner in its strategy.'[13] A little over a decade later Sinn Féin and the British Government had entered into a partnership. The outsiders had become insiders and the world looked a very different place from the new perspective.

A united movement

The history of modern republicanism has been one of schism and split. The peace process presented republicans with a series of pressures and quandaries that raised questions on fundamental ideological, strategic and tactical issues. Yet the Provisional republican movement, that is Sinn Féin and the Provisional IRA, maintained a remarkable cogency as the peace process developed. The movement was presented with three major issues during the course of the peace process, any one of which had the potential to tear the movement asunder. First was the issue of whether or not to call a ceasefire and engage in the peace process. Consider the situation facing republicans in the late 1980s: they were politically isolated and IRA violence meant that they were the recipients of virtually 'surround sound' condemnation from the British and Irish governments, all other political parties on the British Isles, the media and the churches. The IRA campaign was reaching its twentieth year (an achievement in itself), but the organisation, while able to mount spectacular attacks such as large bombs in London and occupy significant British money and attention, did not have the capacity to engage in unilateral actions that would force the British Government to withdraw from Northern Ireland. Put simply: the IRA campaign had been contained, and the costs to the organisation and its support base were high.[14] In this context, the overlapping memberships of the IRA Army Council and Sinn Féin leadership explored the merits of continuing with the simultaneous strategies of violence and politics, when it was increasingly apparent that IRA violence had a counter-productive impact on the potential of political avenues.[15]

In a pattern similar to that of other peace processes, the debate in the higher echelons of the republican movement crystallised between *pragmatists* willing to explore political opportunities and *militants* favouring the maintenance or intensification of the armed campaign.[16] This was an internal debate, and one that has been the subject of much speculation, but it would seem that the pragmatists grouped around Gerry Adams and other leading republicans played a clever game in manoeuvring pragmatists into leadership positions, particularly on the IRA Army Council.[17] This was to prove crucial as the peace process developed, and the Adams pragmatists were usually able to hold sway when potentially divisive issues arose.[18]

The second major issue that had the potential to spark a major split within the mainstream republican movement was whether or not to accept the Belfast Agreement in the knowledge that it fell short of the meta-constitutional aim of Irish unification. A noticeably downbeat Gerry Adams rose from the table after the final plenary session of the multi-party talks, noting that 'we remain absolutely committed to republican objectives', but that it is 'time to draw a breath. It is time to reflect.'[19] The ensuing consultation within the republican movement resulted in substantial unanimity rather than splits.[20] Sinn Féin quickly became one of the staunchest supporters of the Agreement (albeit, and in keeping with a document with an apparently ambiguous spirit and letter, supporters of *their* version of it). The ideologically 'pure' republican position – that the Agreement amounted to a sell-out, an internal settlement, and would result in Sinn Féin ministers administering British rule in Northern Ireland – was barely mentioned.

The third major issue with the potential to divide the republican movement was the decommissioning of weapons held by militant groups. The issue dominated the peace process for long periods and many unionists interpreted the republican unwillingness to decommission as a sign of their conditional allegiance to a purely political path. Gerry Adams's 1994 aside on the IRA, 'They haven't gone away, you know', was regarded as a threat by many unionists. The spirit of the Belfast Agreement, if not the letter, makes clear that militant groups should decommission to help Northern Ireland in its transformation towards a settlement.[21] The logical extension of decommissioning was the disbandment of militant groups – an issue that gained greater salience after the Agreement was reached and the IRA was accused of intelligence-gathering and low-level violence. The disbandment of the IRA would mark the ultimate triumph of republicanism's political wing over its militant wing, but also a triumph for the British Government.

For much of the peace process the Sinn Féin leadership remained firm on the issue of decommissioning, prevaricating and obfuscating to the frustration of journalists worldwide. After the Agreement was reached, the republican position came under increasing pressure: Sinn Féin was part of the power-sharing government yet its militant cousins in the IRA retained a substantial arsenal. Eventually the IRA did cross the Rubicon and engage in decommissioning, an act of incredible symbolic worth for republicans. Weapons that had been illegally acquired, maintained and used – often at great risk to republicans – were being put beyond use. The IRA's co-operation with the IICD, in three acts of decommissioning between 2001 and 2003, may have lacked the transparency that unionists wanted, but it marked a seminal shift for physical force republicanism. (Another issue likely to place enormous strain on republicans, Sinn Féin's membership of the Policing Boards of the reformed PSNI, is looming on the horizon at the time of writing.)

Taken together, the decisions to call a ceasefire and engage with the peace process, accept the Belfast Agreement and begin a process of decommissioning mark a significant shift away from republican positions that had been tenaciously held, often at great cost, during the 1980s and early 1990s. Yet these decisions did not prompt widespread disaffection from the mainstream republican movement. The strategy pursued by the republican leadership did prompt concern and dissent, and a number of defections, but overall the movement was able to retain the vast bulk of its support. Perhaps the most visible manifestation of republican dissent came with the collapse of the IRA ceasefire between February 1996–June 1997. Frustration at the inertia of the peace process strengthened the hand of the militants within the IRA, but the moderated campaign of violence that followed the Canary Wharf bombing illustrated that the IRA did not want a return to the scale of violence that pre-dated the August 1994 ceasefire. The intention of this violence was to gain re-entry to the peace process, but a peace process modified to offer greater opportunities for republican advancement. By June 1997, the pragmatists within the republican movement had convinced their more militant colleagues that the political path was again worth pursuing. Thereafter the IRA ceasefire has remained largely intact in terms of a concerted campaign of attacks on the security forces and loyalists. But the ceasefire has become ragged on occasions, and what could be described as ancillary violence in terms of punishment attacks, intelligence-gathering and fund-raising, was largely tolerated by both the security forces and the republican political leadership.

The most serious splits from the mainstream republican movement came in the form of the Real IRA (RIRA) and the Continuity IRA (CIRA). As 'spoiler' organisations,[22] they were comprised mainly of disaffected members of the IRA who felt that the peace process strategy as pursued by the Sinn Féin leadership was a delusion and could not deliver the principal republican objective of Irish unification. Neither organisation was able to mount a military campaign similar in scale to the Provisional IRA's. CIRA emerged first, in July 1996, followed by RIRA in November 1997, with the latter attracting support from a small number of key militants in the IRA, including its chief bomb-makers. The IRA, anxious to maintain the cohesiveness of its membership and its arms stocks, and alert to the damage-potential of political violence amid the peace process, warned its members against joining its new rivals. It was reported that Sinn Féin and the IRA leadership invested considerable energy in briefing rank-and-file IRA members on the merits of the peace process, although there were occasional media reports of intra-republican abductions, fights and intimidation, suggesting some measure of dissent.

Ultimately, though, the new organisations operated at the margins of republicanism and failed to attract large numbers of IRA personnel. Crucially, they were unable to attract the community support necessary to sustain widespread or effective campaigns of violence. Many in the Catholic community wanted the Sinn Féin peace process strategy to run its course in the hope of political gains. Many others were already experiencing the benefits of the peace process in terms of less-intrusive security patrols and an end to most loyalist violence, and did not want these benefits squandered by breakaway republicans. CIRA and RIRA made little effort to provide a political rationale for their violent activities, and with Sinn Féin's increasing dominance there was little space for newcomers within republicanism. The breakaway republicans were irritants, embarrassing Sinn Féin through the use of traditional republican rhetoric and criticising the IRA for its inactivity in the face of porous loyalist ceasefires. Sinn Féin spokespersons were regularly discomforted by media invitations to condemn violence by fellow republicans, thereby appearing on the same side as unionists and the British state. But the widespread public, political and media labelling of CIRA and RIRA as 'dissident' was instructive on three counts. First, it illustrated the completeness of the Adams–McGuinness republican hegemony. Second, it suggested that many observers and political actors, including the British and Irish governments and many unionists, regarded Sinn Féin and the Provisional IRA as the legitimate representatives of a substantial section of Northern Ireland's population. Third, and related to the last point, many of these actors invested faith (albeit conditional faith) in the ability of Sinn Féin and the Provisional IRA to pursue the peace process.

Any hope that the breakaway republicans may have had of gaining broad support among northern Catholics was swept away by the RIRA's Omagh bombing in August 1998. The bomb followed a series of similar car bombs, often in majority Protestant towns and with the clear aim of goading unionists into withdrawing from the peace process. Rather than wrecking a town centre, a bungled warning meant that the Omagh bomb killed twenty-nine civilians and thus became the single worst incident in the Troubles. Coming just months after the Belfast Agreement had been ratified via a referendum, the political impact of the bombing was dramatic, mobilising Northern Ireland's nationalist and republican community, many of whom may have been ambivalent over political violence, into a rejection of the dissidents. RIRA announced a ceasefire three days after the bombing and CIRA, while not declaring a ceasefire, went to ground. CIRA attacks resumed again in 2000, but at a low level. One measure of the relatively ineffectual nature of violence by breakaway republican groups was that, while it drew unionist condemnation, the unionists' principal concern remained the IRA, although the IRA largely respected its ceasefire.

What explains the relative lack of splintering in republicanism despite the enormous internal and external pressures exerted during the peace process? An initial point to make is that for much of the peace process, the Provisional republican movement benefited from a sense of momentum and was gaining support and plaudits, with the result that many defections may have gone unnoticed. The ambivalence that characterised the republican movement during much of the peace process also meant that the movement was able to simultaneously service radical and moderate republican constituencies. As a result, limited space was left for clearly defined republican alternatives. While Sinn Féin may have moderated its language, and undoubtedly accepted a settlement well short of the traditional republican constitutional aim, the continued existence of an armed IRA may have satisfied those with more radical agendas. Possible alternatives to the Sinn Féin approach bore costs that Northern Ireland's Catholic community were unwilling to bear. It is also clear that the relative unity in republicanism was not the result of a happy coincidence: key figures in the leaderships of Sinn Féin and the IRA worked hard, through internal briefings and – in all probability – a certain amount of economy with the truth, to maintain unity.

The republican constituency

Perhaps one of the under-studied factors in the evolution of republicanism during the peace process has been its relationship with the broader Catholic constituency. The relationship between republicanism and its constituency has been symbiotic, at once presenting republicans with new opportunities but also setting limits and conditions on republican behaviour. The conventional wisdom for much of the Troubles was that nationalists voted for the SDLP and were opposed to the use of violence, while republicans voted for Sinn Féin and accepted violence as a legitimate political strategy. It is probably more useful to conceive of northern Catholic political opinion in terms of a relatively fluid continuum than in those of sharply delineated categories. Northern Ireland's cultural Catholics[23] contained a core republican constituency, ready to support the IRA and Sinn Féin through the worst of times, but there was another constituency willing to extend support to republicans *under certain conditions*. Perhaps one of the greatest accomplishments of the Sinn Féin leadership has been its ability to manoeuvre in such a way as to retain the support of the vast bulk of the core constituency while making the party more attractive to the conditionalist constituency. The extent of the core republican support base was probably illustrated by Sinn Féin's electoral support of 11.4 per cent and 10 per cent in the 1987 and 1992 Westminster elections. At this time post-Anglo-Irish Agreement British and Irish government co-operation to exclude Sinn Féin from the political mainstream was at its highest point, and was reinforced by more general political and media unity in condemning increasingly accident-prone republican violence.

As subsequent developments showed, however, the *conditional* republican support base was significant, according increasing support to Sinn Féin in the wake of the IRA ceasefire, as the party was accepted in London, Dublin and Washington, and as political optimism among Catholics spread. Clearly, both the republican movement and the conditional support base moderated their positions to some extent. While the IRA called a ceasefire and Sinn Féin promoted an 'internal settlement' (regardless of how transitory it may be), many within the Catholic community were prepared to accept republicans' ambivalence over political violence. Sinn Féin's strongest electoral showing (November 2003 assembly election) came *after* allegations of an IRA spy-ring in Stormont, the failure of the organisation to engage in transparent decommissioning, and against a backdrop IRA punishment beatings and shootings. This suggests a certain elasticity in the conditionality of the republican support base, possibly with many potential Sinn Féin supporters tolerant of low-level violence but intolerant of a full-scale resumption of the IRA's campaign. This ambivalence in attitudes towards violence (by no means unique to Sinn Féin supporters) has shaped Northern Ireland politics and explains much of the troubled implementation of the Belfast Agreement.

Sinn Féin's main rival for 'swing' Catholic support during the peace process, the SDLP deserves consideration. The SDLP was the author of many of the intellectual initiatives, procedural devices and institutional mechanisms that underpinned the peace process. In some ways the SDLP acted as a pathfinder and proxy for Sinn Féin: a pathfinder in attempting to identify the limits of nationalist politics within a constitutional framework; and a proxy in representing the Sinn Féin position by default when Sinn Féin were excluded from the formal political process. The SDLP position was characterised by a certain amount of selflessness. For example, the SDLP's post-Agreement restraint in criticising Sinn Féin's obduracy on decommissioning cushioned the republican position. Since most of the criticism came from the UUP, Sinn Féin was able to construct its discourse on the issue in nationalist versus unionist terms. When the IRA ceasefire collapsed in 1996–97, the SDLP resisted UUP invitations to press ahead with talks, instead maintaining the importance of inclusiveness. Of course the SDLP was limited in the extent to which it could move towards the centre – it needed to keep a watchful eye on its more radical rival. But often the party found itself sidelined as the media focus remained firmly on Sinn Féin and its fraught relationships with the British Government and with unionists. Support for the SDLP by no means collapsed, showing real slippage only by the November 2003 assembly election when the SDLP secured 17 per cent of the vote as against Sinn Féin's 24 per cent. Until 2003 much of the explanation of Sinn Féin's electoral rise lay in the party's ability to win the votes of new Catholic additions to the electoral register rather than taking votes from the SDLP.

Crucial to the story of republicans and the peace process has been an increasingly assertive and confident Catholic population. The British Government had considerable success, via the composition of quangos and conditions attached to regeneration investment, in co-opting some sections of the Catholic middle class during the Troubles.[24] Many Catholics though remained suspicious of the British Government. The nature of the conflict, with the almost complete bifurcation of perceptions along sectarian and constitutional lines, meant that British attempts to appear even-handed were derailed by the regular procession of atrocities, controversies and gaffes. A combination of greater Catholic socio-economic mobility, cultural confidence and political assertiveness provided a key environmental backdrop to the peace process. Evidence of this increased confidence often operated at the anecdotal level (a more prominent Catholic professional class, wider television coverage of Gaelic sports and the expansion of Catholic populations into traditionally Protestant areas of Belfast), but it was no less real for this seeming intangibility. There were, of course, headline grabbing manifestations of the further 'greening' of Northern Ireland, particularly the stance taken by Catholic residents in some areas against Orange and loyalist parades.

The evolution of the peace process left Sinn Féin and the Catholic community in a mutually reinforcing position. Catholics were emboldened by a developing peace process that they saw as capable of delivering some of the items on the nationalist agenda, and many were encouraged by Sinn Féin's position and growing status in that process. Sinn Féin, meanwhile, was emboldened by the increasing confidence among Catholics. Time series' evidence from the Northern Ireland *Life and Times* survey of public opinion offers an interesting insight into the growing confidence among Northern Ireland's Catholics.[25] The proportion of Catholic survey respondents willing to identify themselves as 'nationalist' showed a dramatic increase against the backdrop of the peace process – in the 1989–97 period, between 40 and 54 per cent of Catholic respondents identified themselves as nationalist. Following the Belfast Agreement, the percentage varied between 62–70, suggesting that the Agreement, and the attendant legitimising of the nationalist constitutional position, had a profound impact in bolstering Catholic confidence. Moreover, given that Northern Ireland's communities are often discussed in terms of a dyad, Catholic confidence was often linked with Protestant insecurity and disaffection.[26] For many unionists, the transformation of Northern Ireland into a 'cold place' for Protestants seemed dependent on it becoming more temperate for Catholics.[27]

Conclusion

Republicanism's journey through and beyond the peace process can be explained by a composite approach – a combination of internal[28] and international[29] dynamics, together with sociological factors and the strategies of the British State[30] and of other actors. Two factors in particular seem important in any discussion of republican participation in the peace process. The first concerns the changing structural context of the Northern Ireland conflict (and a number of other conflicts[31]) and its effect in convincing many leading republicans of the unsustainability of the 'armalite and ballot-box' strategy. Importantly though, the peace process offered a way out with honour: republicans were able to play a substantial role in shaping the peace process and the institutions and reforms that emerged from it. They wrought concessions from the British Government and the other Northern Ireland political parties that made a real and perceptual difference to the quality of life to their constituency. Journalist Deaglán de Brèadún, writing ten days after the Belfast Agreement was reached, captured the messy end to the war and, with it, the mix of republican loss of appetite for the armed struggle and the rewards that the peace process offered:

When this document is accepted in two weeks' time, with whatever reservations about amending Articles 2 and 3, and when, as expected, Sinn Féin enters the new Assembly not as a servant but as one of the masters of the banquet, then it can indeed be said that the war, if not over, has at least lost most of its soldiers.[32]

The second key factor in the republican involvement in the peace process lies in the increasing confidence of the northern Catholic constituency and its willingness – in a context of socio-economic advancement – to accept a republican agenda of reform rather than revolution. If the republicanism of the peace process and beyond amounts to a 'sell-out' of traditional republican constitutional ideals, then it is a sell-out that northern Catholics having willingly bought. The price for the maintenance of the armed-struggle strategy, given the alternative provided by the peace process, was higher than the community was willing to bear.

It is worth ending with two deliberately provocative points. The first stems from the contention that the principal strategic objective of the British State during the Troubles was the military defeat of the IRA. Violence on the part of other groups and political initiatives were secondary considerations. As Adrian Guelke put it in April 1994, during the tentative foundation-laying of the peace process: 'In Northern Ireland what is being sought is an end to violence without a political settlement.'[33] Clearly the extent of the peace process developed far beyond what was thought possible in 1994, but the Belfast Agreement amounts to a peace accord rather than a peace settlement.[34] It legitimises and attempts to manage (rather than confront) two nationalist sets that are incompatible on the central constitutional issue. In this context, the peace process can be regarded as a triumph for the traditional end of the British State's strategy: the end of militant republicanism. The price for the British Government was involvement in a lengthy and costly peace process, but that price was deemed more acceptable than the military one.

The second provocative point is speculative. It is becoming clear that the British security services had a stunning success in penetrating Northern Ireland's militant organisations during the Troubles. This is less surprising on the loyalist side, not least because the British State used loyalists as proxies in a classic counter-insurgency manner. But informers and agents were placed at all levels within the IRA.[35] Is it beyond the bounds of possibility that the same did not happen with Sinn Féin, that the some of the architects of the 'Sinn Féin peace strategy' were also architects of the British peace strategy?

Notes

1 See Máirtín O Muilleoir, *Belfast's Dome of Delight: City Hall Politics 1981–2000* (Belfast: Beyond the Pale Publications, 1999) for a Sinn Féin councillor's view of local government politics in Belfast during the late 1980s and 1990s.

2 'Maskey marks Somme with wreath', available online: www.news.bbc.co.uk/hi/northern_ireland (1 July 2002).

3 Richard English argues against ambiguity thus: 'You dim the lights sufficiently that the people read their own conflict preferences into the same set of political circumstances. Thus,

documents have been drafted with considerable skill in order to please everyone': 'The Northern Ireland Peace Process Reconsidered', *Eire–Ireland*, fall/winter 1997, pp. 270–6 at 74.

4 Sinn Féin, *Agenda for Government: Sinn Féin Assembly Election Manifesto 2003* (Belfast: Sinn Féin, 2003), p. 20.

5 G. Adams, *The Politics of Irish Freedom* (Dingle: Brandon Books, 1986), pp. 166–7.

6 R. MacGinty, R. Wilford, L. Dowds and G. Robinson, 'Consenting Adults: The Principle of Consent and Northern Ireland's Constitutional Future', *Government and Opposition*, vol. 36, no. 4, autumn 2001, pp. 472–92.

7 UUP, 'Say YES for the Union', Referendum Communication (Belfast: UUP, May 1998).

8 DUP, 'It's Right to Say "NO" to the United Ireland Process', Referendum Communication (Belfast: DUP, May 1998).

9 For accounts of the US role in the peace process, see A. Guelke, 'The United States, Irish Americans and the Northern Ireland Peace Process', *International Affairs*, vol. 72, no. 3, July 1996, pp. 521–36; W. Hazelton, 'Encouragement from the Sidelines: Clinton's Role in the Good Friday Agreement', *Irish Studies in International Affairs*, vol. 11, 2000, pp. 103–19; A. J. Wilson, '"Doing the Business": Aspects of the Clinton Administration's Economic Support for the Northern Ireland Peace Process, 1994–2000', *Journal of Conflict Studies*, vol. 23, no. 1, spring 2003, pp. 155–76.

10 'Adams Offers "Hand of Friendship"', available online: www.news.bbc.co.uk/hi/english/events/northern_ireland/latest_news (10 April 1998).

11 This argument is developed in detail in R. MacGinty, 'Constitutional Referendums and Ethnonational Conflict: The Case of Northern Ireland', *Nationalism and Ethnic Politics*, vol. 9, no. 2, summer 2003, pp. 1–22.

12 *Ibid.*, p. 12.

13 Adams, *Politics of Irish Freedom*, p. 106.

14 These points are further elaborated in R. MacGinty and J. Darby, *Guns and Government: The Management of the Northern Ireland Peace Process* (Basingstoke: Palgrave Macmillan, 2002).

15 M. Ryan, 'From the Centre to the Margins: The Slow Death of Irish Republicanism', in C. Gilligan and J. Tonge (eds), *Peace or War? Understanding the Peace Process in Northern Ireland* (Aldershot: Ashgate, 1997), pp. 72–84.

16 J. Darby, *The Effects of Violence on Peace Processes* (Washington, DC: USIP Press, 2001).

17 E. Maloney, *A Secret History of the IRA* (London: Penguin, 2002).

18 Paul Bew attributes the 1996–97 ceasefire collapse to the temporary re-ascendancy of the militants: see 'Why Did the Northern Irish Peace Process Collapse?', Parnell Lecture 1996, Magdalene College, Occasional Paper 15, p. 11.

19 'Time to Draw Breath, Assess the Agreement and Decide if it Answers the Questions Says Adams', *Irish Times*, 11 April 1998.

20 'Critics of SF Leaders Keep their Counsel', *ibid.*, 20 April 1998.

21 The Agreement: Agreement Reached in the Multi-Party Negotiation (no place of publication: no publisher, 1998), p. 20.

22 S. J. Stedman, 'Spoiler Problems in Peace Processes', *International Security*, vol. 22, no. 2, fall 1997, pp. 5–53.

23 For excellent accounts of Northern Ireland's Catholic community see, M. Elliott, *The Catholics of Ulster: A History* (London: Penguin, 2000); and M. Nic Craith, *Culture and Identity Politics in Northern Ireland* (New York: Palgrave Macmillan, 2003).

24 The adaptability and compliance of many northern Catholics is a key theme in Elliot's *Catholics of Ulster*.

25 Full survey results are available online: www.ark.ac.uk/ (accessed 22 January 2004).

26 Andrew Finlay, 'Defeatism and Northern Protestant "Identity"', *The Global Review of Ethnopolitics*, vol. 1, no. 2, December 2001, 3–20.

27 'Becoming Persuaders – British and Irish Identities in Northern Ireland', Speech by Secretary of State Dr John Reid, MP, to the Institute of Irish Studies, Liverpool University, 21 November 2001, Northern Ireland Office Press Archive, online: www.nio.gov.uk.

28 See Maloney, *Secret History*, and E. Mallie and D. McKittrick, *The Fight for Peace: Secret Story*

of the Irish Peace Process (London: Mandarin, 1997).

29 M. Cox, '"Cinderella at the Ball": Explaining the End of the War in Northern Ireland', *Millennium: Journal of International Studies*, vol. 27, no. 2, 1998, pp. 325–42.

30 A. McIntyre, 'Modern Irish Republicanism: The Product of British State Strategies', *Irish Political Studies*, vol. 10, 1995, pp. 97–121.

31 J. Loughlin, 'New Contexts for Political Solutions: Redefining Minority Nationalisms in Northern Ireland, the Basque Country and Corsica', in J. Darby and R. MacGinty (eds), *Contemporary Peacemaking: Conflict, Violence and Peace Processes* (Basingstoke: Palgrave Macmillan, 2003), pp. 38–49.

32 'Pragmatism Increases as Debate Continues', *Irish Times*, 20 April 1998.

33 'Promoting Peace in Deeply Divided Societies', Frank Wright Commemorative Lecture, Belfast: Queen's University, 19 April 1994, p. 13.

34 R. Wilson and R. Wilford, *Northern Ireland: A Route to Stability? The Devolution Policy Papers* (Birmingham: University of Birmingham, 2003).

35 Maloney, *Secret History*.

9

Noises off: loyalists after the Agreement

GORDON GILLESPIE

Introduction

For much of the period after 1998 the political drama in Northern Ireland centred on the formation of the executive in conjunction with the decommissioning of IRA weapons – loyalists provided the off-stage noises to the main show. Loyalists felt that their part in bringing about the Agreement had been ignored by the audience, both at home and abroad, which seemed more interested in the histrionics of the political parties. In the wake of the high-profile Holy Cross protest, continuing attacks on Catholic homes and internal loyalist feuds, however, they again found themselves portrayed as the villains of the piece. For loyalists, these problems were compounded by the apparent attempt by republicans to re-write the script to give themselves a bigger role, and this with the acquiescence of the show's directors – the British and Irish governments. Thus, by the beginning of 2003, many loyalists appeared to have either forgotten their lines or to have lost the plot completely in the great peace process production.

Early in 1998 the notoriously pessimistic loyalist community was showing spring-like signs of optimism. Loyalist political spokesmen were the darlings of the media, they had made some impact in the electoral arena and were gaining confidence, partly due to their role in helping negotiate the Belfast (Good Friday) Agreement.[1] For the loyalist community at large this confidence was under-pinned by governmental statements encouraging the view that not only was the Union safe, but political and daily life would soon be free from the threat of terrorism.

In the background, however, republican and loyalist paramilitary groups continued to operate – albeit without carrying out 'military' operations. Republicans, meanwhile, orchestrated protests and riots in opposition to Orange Order parades and attacks on isolated Protestant communities, which led loyalists and unionists to question the sincerity of republicans' commitment to making the Agreement work on anything other than their own terms.

It is impossible to understand the sense of disillusionment with the Agreement which had developed among loyalists by 2003 without examining the manner in which the Agreement was sold. While loyalists (and especially loyalist paramilitaries) and unionists may have held divergent views on issues such as the early release of paramilitary prisoners and the need for the early disarming and disbanding of paramilitary groups, on the big political and constitutional issues they shared the same concerns. It was, therefore, inevitable that any disillusionment with the Agreement among unionists would seep through to loyalists, particularly after the 'carrot' of early prisoner releases, which many loyalists supported, was completed.

From the outset, loyalist–unionist support for the Agreement was tenuous. An examination of the Northern Ireland referendum and election in 1998 found that 57 per cent of Protestant voters had voted 'Yes' in the referendum but that if those who had considered changing their vote had done so then the Protestant vote in favour would have been only 50.1 per cent. Furthermore, 44 per cent of Protestant voters said they made up their minds about how they would vote during the final week of the campaign – 12 per cent of the total on polling day itself.[2] In this light, it is evident that Prime Minister Tony Blair's interventions in the weeks leading up to the referendum were highly significant, if not crucial, in encouraging undecided Protestant voters to vote 'Yes' and, conversely, in encouraging disillusionment when those promises were not kept.[3]

The outcome of the assembly elections on 25 June proved a disappointment to the loyalist parties and, to a lesser extent, to pro-Agreement unionism generally. The UVF-linked PUP polled 20,634 votes (2.55 per cent) and won two seats in the assembly, while the UDA-linked UDP received 8,651 votes (1.07 per cent), but failed to win a seat. While the result was far from disastrous, it did not match loyalist expectations. However, while the PUP did benefit from the kudos associated with representation in the assembly, the UDP had to settle for party leader Gary McMichael's appointment to the Civic Forum instead. Given the suspicions which were to develop in the following years over the way in which the Agreement was being implemented, loyalist groups would inevitably come under increasing pressure to withdraw their support from the Agreement.

Although the PUP and UDP supported the Belfast Agreement, the fragmented nature of loyalist paramilitarism was a destabilising factor from the outset. In late 1996 the Portadown-centred Loyalist Volunteer Force (LVF) had split from the UVF and so had removed from the UVF some of those who would later oppose the Agreement. However, this split also generated a long-running feud between the two groups which, at least in part, undermined the UVF's pro-Agreement credentials and made the PUP's job more.[4]

Equally important was the historical rivalry between the UVF and UDA which had resulted in open warfare between the two organisations in the past and would do so again after 1998. In this regard the collapse of the paramilitary umbrella organisation the Combined Loyalist Military Command (CLMC), in October 1997, had been an ominous portent.

The structure of the UDA, the largest loyalist paramilitary organisation, was also a source of difficulty. It soon became clear that the various brigades had differing views on the merits of the Agreement. As early as July 1998 a worrying sign was that the UDA magazine in the north-west was already stating that 'it now appears that the promises made by Blair prior to the referendum are not going to be honoured'.[5] There were also those who had been unhappy that the CLMC had called a ceasefire in 1994, believing that they had the IRA on the back foot and were looking for an excuse to continue to attack republicans. In the autumn of 1998 these loyalist 'ultras' became active, under the cover names of Red Hand Defenders and Orange Volunteers, with attacks on Catholic-owned businesses and Gaelic sports clubs.

While the number of deaths annually resulting from the security situation fell below twenty after 1998 almost every other security situation saw a deteriorating situation. The most striking deterioration was in paramilitary attacks (often inaccurately referred to as 'punishment' attacks or beatings) and particularly in shootings. In 1998 there were 34 such attacks by loyalists – by 2001 these had nearly quadrupled to 121 (there were roughly the same number in 2002).[6]

Another destabilising factor for the political situation was that for paramilitary organisations to continue to operate they required funding to finance the costs of weapons and ammunition, communications equipment, and personnel and welfare costs. In 2002 a Northern Ireland Affairs Select Committee report estimated that the annual running cost for the UDA and the UFF was £750,000, with the UDA having an estimated fund-raising capacity of up to £1 million a year. This compared with a £1–£2 million running costs and £1.5 million fund-raising capacity for the UVF and £50,000 running costs for the LVF, compared to a £2 million fund-raising capacity.[7] However as the Northern Ireland Affairs report noted:

> Loyalist groups particularly have tended to operate within clearly defined and jealously-guarded territories: feuds have arisen as changes in the community response to the paramilitaries have made fundraising more difficult in certain areas, and put pressure on brigades to expand their territories in order to safeguard their income.[8]

With the amount of money being raised it was hardly surprising that not all of it went directly to the organisation: 'Increasingly in recent years former terrorists have used their status, connections and skills in creating and developing criminal organisations and structures. These arrangements provide the resources for comfortable – and in some instances very extravagant – personal lifestyles.'[9] A further corrupting influence was that paramilitaries often operated on the basis of 'licensing' criminals (including drugs' dealers) to operate in their 'territories' in return for a share of the proceeds of their activities.[10]

This reality stood in sharp contrast to the far-fetched claims of some former loyalist paramilitaries about how they had acquired substantial sums of money despite having spent many years in prison. This scenario has generated increasing anger among the supposed 'groundlings' in the loyalist audience who have watched some of the same individuals appearing on television to denounce the activities of drugs dealers and other criminals.[11] The continuation of these activities encouraged the belief that the paramilitaries saw themselves as being above the law and this inevitably served to undermine Protestant support for an Agreement which appeared to be encouraging the growth of a 'mafia culture.'

Decommissioning

Unlike republicans, it was difficult for loyalist paramilitaries to argue that handing over weapons could be seen as surrender since the weapons involved would be given to an independent body appointed by a government it fully recognised. Furthermore, while republicans continued to toy with the idea of the tactical use of armed struggle for political gain, loyalists had declared in their 1994 ceasefire statement that the Union was safe. The failure of loyalist paramilitaries to decommission weapons was, therefore, less about ideology than about more practical considerations.[12]

There were several other reasons why loyalist paramilitaries were not prepared to decommission weapons. Since republicans had not stated that the war was over loyalists saw no reason to unilaterally decommission. The situation has been complicated by continuing cuts in the strength of the security forces in response to what unionists perceive as a government sop to republicans. Equally there are concerns over the reform of policing, not because loyalists had an unqualified attachment to the RUC but because they believed that changes were being made to appease nationalists and republicans.

Given the intensity of intra-loyalist disputes both before and after the signing of the Agreement, loyalists also felt the need to retain weapons to defend themselves from other paramilitary groups – in some cases to maintain control over local communities or to enforce criminal activity. There was also the practical issue of determining how many guns there were and whether the leadership could rely on subordinates to hand them in. Finally there were those who believed the ceasefire and support for the Agreement were a mistake and that the 'war' against republicans should have continued.[13]

Waiting in the wings

For most of the period after the Omagh bombing until the end of 1999 public attention was focused on the arguments surrounding the formation of a Northern Ireland Executive (NIE) in relation to the decommissioning of paramilitary, particularly IRA, weapons. In these debates loyalist politicians at times seemed closer to the Sinn Féin line than to other unionists. The PUP maintained the line that weapons should be 'allowed to rust' rather than being decommissioned. The continuation of loyalist 'punishment' attacks and, increasingly, shootings not only threatened the bi-partisan approach at Westminster over the early release of prisoners but highlighted loyalist and unionist differences over the issue and made the expansion of loyalist political support less likely. The growing number of punishment attacks involving shootings also gave the lie to the argument that guns could be allowed to rust: loyalist paramilitary weapons were used to kill as well as maim. On 15 March 1999 lawyer Rosemary Nelson, who had worked for the Garvaghy Road Residents' Association, was murdered by the Red Hand Defenders (RHD) – a cover name used by UDA members; two days later former Red Hand Commando (RHC) leader Frankie Curry was shot dead on the Shankill Road amid suggestions that the UVF were involved.[14] In June Elizabeth O'Neill, a Protestant woman married to a Catholic, was murdered by loyalist paramilitaries, indicating that murders committed by loyalist paramilitaries with a sectarian motive were also likely to continue.

The IRA was similarly intent on demonstrating that it had not gone away. On 17 June IRA informer Martin McGartland was shot and wounded in Tyneside in what was widely believed to be a murder attempt by the IRA and, on 26 July, three people were arrested in Fort Lauderdale, Florida, in connection with an attempt by the Provisionals to buy weapons and export them to Ireland.

Despite these ominous signs, when the Mitchell review of the Agreement reconvened on 15 November a series of events and statements from participants led to Northern Ireland ministers being nominated and, on 2 December, power being devolved. Although this heralded a period of optimism on the wider political front there was little sign of improving relations at the grass-roots level.

While loyalist paramilitaries were involved in attacking Catholic homes republicans were also harassing Protestants and orchestrating attacks on isolated Protestant communities. The *Shankill Mirror* reported how, on 13 December, a Boys' Brigade band in Belfast city-centre to entertain late night pre-Christmas shoppers was verbally and physically attacked by republican youths.[15] Some months later, in an incident reminiscent of the later Holy Cross dispute, republicans attacked Protestant children passing through a Catholic area on their way to Springfield Primary School. The children 'had to run a gauntlet of stones, abuse and threats, including on 21st June when two grown men stopped them and told them if they were ever seen on their road again they would be dealt with'.[16]

Centre stage

The uncertainty surrounding the stability of the political institutions continued in 2000. In February the UUP left the executive over lack of progress on decommissioning, but returned in May on the basis that the IRA *would* move on the arms' issue. Two inspections of IRA arms' dumps by independent international inspectors in June and October proved enough to keep the UUP in the executive in the short term. In August, however, loyalists found themselves the centre of media attention, though, as always seemed to be the case, for negative reasons.

In July a sign of growing tensions between the UVF and the UDA manifested itself when west Belfast UDA leader Johnny Adair and members of his 'C' Company appeared at Drumcree during the 2000 parade stand-off. The television coverage of Adair and his supporters arriving at Drumcree provided an enduring – and negative – image of loyalists. As the journalist Henry McDonald noted:

> In the early to mid 1990s loyalism tried to nurture a radically different public persona. There was the articulate, well-turned-out, moderate-sounding David Ervine armed with his pipe and Lech Walesa moustache who embodied what was then fashionably known as 'new unionism'. Loyalists back then 'cared' about what the rest of the world thought of them. Since then, in terms of global perception, they have been supplanted by the shaven heads, the earrings, the baseball hats, the rippling muscles, the Alsatian dog with the T-shirt wrapped around its body – the icons of unthinking menace.[17]

The appearance of Adair's 'C' company at Drumcree also highlighted the developing links between them and the LVF, setting the scene for a future conflict with the UVF. Between January and May 2000 four people were killed as a result of a renewed feud between the LVF and the UVF. However, competition for the control of loyalist working-class areas also led to growing antagonism between the UVF and the UDA. The summer of 2000 saw the proliferation of UVF (predominantly purple) and UDA (light-blue) flags appearing as territorial markers in Protestant working-class areas. In July the tensions increased when UVF member Andrew Cairns was shot and killed by the UDA while attending bonfire celebrations in Larne early on 12 July.

In the following month this confrontation exploded into open warfare. On 19 August UDA members took part in a parade to unveil loyalist murals in the Shankill area. Although promoted as a cultural event, the march was actually a show of strength by the UDA, and particularly by Adair's west Belfast 'C' Company which, it appeared, was attempting to promote itself as the pre-eminent loyalist paramilitary group. It was suggested that Adair's group was trying to achieve this by undermining the peace process, goading republicans into sectarian violence by attacking Catholic homes and gaining control of the drugs' trade in loyalist areas.[18] With tensions between the UVF and the LVF high, the UVF believed that it had an assurance from the UFF that no LVF regalia would appear at the loyalist march; however, this proved not to be the case and a UDA colour party in paramilitary uniform carrying UDA and, crucially, LVF banners took part in the parade. According to the UDP, following an attack on a band member by the UVF, the UDA attacked and fired shots in a bar associated with UVF members, resulting in seven people being shot or injured. Later that night there were further attacks on the homes of individuals associated with the UVF and the PUP, including that of veteran loyalist Gusty Spence.

On 21 August the UVF retaliated by murdering two UDA men and firing shots into the UDP's offices on the Shankill Road. The UDA in turn attacked the PUP's headquarters on the Shankill Road. On 22 August UDA member Johnny Adair (who had been given early release under the terms of the GFA) was returned to prison because the authorities believed that he was active in antagonising the situation. Despite this, the feud continued and spread to other areas outside Belfast in the following weeks.

Between July and December 8 people died as a result of the UDA–UVF feud, while attacks on the homes of individuals associated with the rival organisations meant that by October 245 households (over 600 people) had presented themselves as homeless to the Northern Ireland Housing Executive.[19] Eventually, however, the situation became calmer and, on 15 December, the UDA and the UVF issued a statement announcing a 'cessation of hostilities'. Despite this, another loyalist was murdered only three days later, apparently in an internal UDA dispute. Like the IRA, loyalist paramilitaries appeared to be interpreting the Agreement in their own manner.

Under the spotlight

In 2001 loyalists came under the spotlight of world media attention to an even greater extent than had been the case during the UDA–UVF feud of the previous year. From the start of the year it had become clear that the UDP's nominal support for the Agreement was increasingly at odds with the activities of UDA members on the ground. In mid-January the RUC chief constable warned that the UDA had become a loose organisation, 'lacking central direction and control', and attributed an upsurge in attacks on Catholic homes to UDA members.[20]

The June Westminster and District Council elections, besides showing a swing in support to the DUP and Sinn Féin away from the centre, also confirmed the declining fortunes of the loyalist parties. Although UDP leader Gary McMichael had threatened to resign as party leader in January if the UDA withdrew its support for the Agreement his position was undermined both by the activities of the UDA and by the party's own ineptitude in failing to register as a political party (as was required by new UK legislation) leading to only three UPD members being returned as independent councillors. The PUP fared only slightly better, with 12,261 first-preference votes (2 per cent) and 4 councillors elected in local government elections and less than 5,000 votes (0.6 per cent) in the Westminster elections held on the same day.

While the PUP had a political vision (which at times appeared to be to create a loyalist mirror-image of Sinn Féin), that vision, with its nod towards Old Labour's socialist ideas was unlikely to have much electoral appeal. The UDP, on the other hand, appeared to have no long-term strategy whatever, and as UDA members increasingly turned against the Belfast Agreement the pro-Agreement UDP leadership appeared at odds with the attitudes and actions of the paramilitaries.

On the wider political front the resignation of David Trimble as first minister on 1 July, over the decommissioning issue led to round-table talks being held at Weston Park in England. Rather than leading to progress, however, the talks provided another marker in the failed implementation of the Agreement. While the British and Irish governments made further overtures towards republican demands, unionist and loyalist concerns were effectively side-lined. It was hardly surprising then that the PUP withdrew from the talks on the grounds that republicans had refused to set their terms for decommissioning and that there was, therefore, no basis on which to continue negotiations. Even more ominously, on 10 July, the UFF (and thus, effectively, the UDA) announced that it was withdrawing its support for the Agreement. With the UDP already in disarray after the June elections the latest development left their political wing worryingly out of line with the paramilitary wing and the UDP's future looked bleak. It was with a degree of inevitability that, in late November 2001, the UDP was unilaterally wound up by the UDA to be replaced in January 2002 by the Ulster Political Research Group.

The political stalemate which continued throughout the summer and autumn was resolved, at least temporarily, on 23 October with the announcement that the IRA had put some of its weapons 'beyond use' (loyalists and unionists attributed the IRA's action almost entirely to the pressure which had been exerted on them in the wake of the events of 11 September in the USA). It was not until 6 November, however, that Trimble was re-elected as first minister, and then only with the support of the small center parties.

If these developments were of the 'two steps forward and one step back' variety then, for loyalists, things seemed to be going only backwards. Despite continuing sectarian attacks by loyalist paramilitaries and intra-loyalist disputes, these problems would be overshadowed by the dispute at Holy Cross Primary School in the upper Ardoyne area of Belfast.

Passion play

In recent years few incidents have led to a portrayal of loyalists as the villains of the piece as much as did the protest at Holy Cross Girls' Primary School in north Belfast. Each day newspapers ran shock headlines, politicians made condemnatory remarks and television news carried pictures of tearful and terrified young girls running a gauntlet of abuse (and sometimes missiles) from loyalist protestors as they made their way to and from the Catholic primary school. Not for the first time, the complexity of the situation appeared lost amid the cynicism of the media circus looking for a headline or image.

The Holy Cross dispute which flared up on 19 June did not appear from nowhere. According to one loyalist report the dispute began after two men were attacked by republicans while they were putting up flags for the 12th July celebration:

> Within 5–10 minutes approximately 30 cars came up the road full of adult men, at this point both Holy Cross and the neighbouring [state school] Wheatfield primary schools were letting the children out. The men proceeded to attack the two young men again with baseball bats from the boot of their cars and parents from Holy Cross School abandoned their children, unable to resist the temptation to join in the hand to hand fighting that had engulfed the Ardoyne Road.[21]

The incident fed off the social problems of an ageing, often impoverished, Protestant community adjoining an expanding Catholic community with a better developed community infrastructure and better living conditions. For loyalists the long-contrived republican image of Northern Irish Catholics as the most oppressed people ever did not fit well with the reality of a situation where Protestants were 30 per cent more likely to live in unfit housing and 36 per cent more likely to live without basic amenities than Catholic families.[22]

The incident was also sparked by other local concerns: in an article entitled 'Why Protest Now? After Years of Ignored Abuse and Assaults – We Had No Other Choice' the Concerned Residents of Upper Ardoyne (CRUA) outlined why the protest should be maintained:

> If we called off this protest, we would shortly return to the same old routine of our local residents coming under attack from those hiding under cover of the children, our own children being assaulted, our cars scraped with nails, our homes being vandalised, our pensioners prevented from going to the local Ardoyne shops. They say we are welcome to use these shops, but if you visit the area you will see the many anti-Protestant slogans, and they have now placed large IRA placards the whole length of the shopping street. Not exactly in our opinion a friendly welcome.[23]

While the Holy Cross issue remained unresolved the UDA, or at least parts of it, appeared indifferent to anything beyond their own concerns: 2001 saw an upsurge in the use of pipe-bombs – 57 had been planted the previous year (21 exploded), 134 had been used by early August (nearly 50 exploded). These attacks were made against Catholic homes or the homes of those in inter-denominational relationships in north Belfast or heavily Protestant towns such as Coleraine, Ballymena and Larne, and were generally attributed to the UDA.[24] By this time it was evident to the proverbial dogs in the street, if not the Government, that the UDA ceasefire was over.

Inevitably this had an effect in undermining support for the Agreement and drawing other paramilitary organisations further away from their ceasefires. Worryingly, on 1 September, David Ervine stated that he believed the UVF may have been responsible for an attempted car-bombing in Ballycastle in August.

When the school year recommenced, in September, so too did the dispute at Holy Cross. The death of 16-year-old Thomas McDonald, in a hit-and-run incident which loyalists believed to have had a degree of sectarian motivation, further escalated the tension with a blast-bomb being thrown in the direction of parents and children on 5 September. In the following months Holy Cross appeared to be at the centre of events as sectarian confrontations continued across Northern Ireland.[25] With the security situation threatening to degenerate even further Secretary of State Dr John Reid ('Dr Dolittle' as he was scathingly named by unionists) finally took action and on 12 October declared the UDA, UFF and LVF ceasefires to be no longer in place. In the following month Dr Reid belatedly addressed the issue of the growing alienation from the Agreement of Protestants in a speech to the Institute of Irish Studies in Liverpool in which he plaintively noted that Northern Ireland should 'not become a cold place for Protestants'; however, by this stage more was needed to restore loyalist and unionist confidence in the Agreement than the 'tea and sympathy' offered by the secretary of state.

If the loyalist paramilitaries were in many cases the main perpetrators of violence, equally there were also many instances where loyalists were the victims of attacks by republicans. The *Shankill Mirror* reported how, on 25 September, republicans had attempted to run down Protestant children on the Ardoyne Road and then tried to entice Protestant residents towards the interface where they could be shot at by a republican gunman. The same edition of the newspaper reported on a Protestant woman being beaten by a group of republicans while waiting at a bus stop: 'she was horrified when, the following day, one of the women involved in the beating strolled casually up Ardoyne Road under her nose, and under police protection.'[26] Loyalist grievances were also fuelled by the belief that Protestant children often continued to go unprotected after being attacked by republicans as they travelled to school while massive security force protection was given to Holy Cross pupils. This led one DUP councillor to remark that '50 to 100 police and army land rovers are being provided to protect Catholic parents and pupils on the Ardoyne Road. Are Protestant pupils not equally entitled to protection?'[27] Such daily frustrations for loyalists living in interface areas stood in stark contrast to the peace and prosperity promised during the referendum campaign, and this inevitably helped contribute to a general disillusionment with the Agreement.

Although a £16.5 million housing development plan, announced for north Belfast by the NIE in November, served to ease some of the frustrations among loyalists in the area, the specific issues surrounding Holy Cross remained unresolved. Loyalists and unionists remained convinced that republicans were more concerned to milk the problem for propaganda purposes than to address the issues involved.

Reprise

If 2001 was the year in which loyalist resentment at having their concerns ignored exploded in the Holy Cross dispute then 2002 saw a return to more familiar themes. On the political stage developments were often overshadowed by acts demonstrating the hubris which had developed among some republicans, namely the break-in at Castlereagh police station, further revelations of IRA activities in Columbia and republican spying activities in Northern Ireland. On the ground, meanwhile, republicans seemed determined to demonstrate their attitude towards their Protestant fellow-Irish by continuing attacks on isolated Protestant communities in Belfast and Derry.[28] In June the unprovoked assault on the Protestant Fountain estate in Derry which followed the Republic of Ireland's elimination from the 2002 FIFA World Cup was so blatantly sectarian that it was even condemned by leading Sinn Féin members from the city – though with the qualification that the attacks were a 'reflection of the worst type of sectarianism emanating from violent unionism in Belfast'.[29]

If the summer months had seen a re-run of sectarian rioting in interface areas – increasingly with the involvement of, and orchestration by, both loyalist and republican paramilitaries, then the autumn saw a return to another well-worn theme – the loyalist paramilitary feud. Internal UDA differences were again beginning to emerge in January. Following the murder of postman Danny McColgan by the RHD on 12 January a statement issued by the UFF three days later condemned RHD's threat to teachers and postmen and gave the RHD 14 days to stand down or face 'appropriate action'.[30] On 13 September the murder of LVF member Stephen Warnock sparked another feud, with a leading east Belfast UDA man being shot and wounded three days later. On 25 September west Belfast UDA leader Johnny Adair was expelled from the organisation by the leaders of the five other UDA brigades as Adair appeared to be forging closer links with the LVF, despite the rising tension between the UDA and LVF in other areas. The final straw came with the painting of a joint UDA–LVF mural in the lower Shankill at the behest of Adair's 'C' Company.[31] The situation swiftly deteriorated into a series of tit-for-tat shootings between the UDA and the LVF with Adair's west Belfast 'C' Company apparently siding with the LVF. On 5 November UDA and LVF leaders announced that they had settled the differences which led to a feud between the two organisations, with the LVF saying that it accepted that the east Belfast brigade of the UDA was not involved in the murder of Stephen Warnock.[32]

The question of differences between the UDA and Adair's 'C' Company, however, remained unresolved. Attacks on the homes and business premises of those associated with the different factions continued towards the end of the year. Almost inevitably murders followed, and by January 2003 two people had died as a result of the latest intra-loyalist feud. On 10 January Johnny Adair's early release licence was revoked for a second time and he was re-arrested.

Conclusion

The decline in loyalist support for the Agreement after 1998s was due to structural problems within loyalism, the imbalance (both real and perceived) in the implementation of the Agreement, together with an overlapping of these factors.

Loyalists were often faced with the social problems associated with an ageing and impoverished population having a less well-developed community sector than their Catholic counterparts. These social problems were exacerbated by the activities of loyalist paramilitaries (and by the degree of fragmentation within loyalist paramilitarism), which encouraged disputes over the control of territory, promotion of criminal activity as well as sectarian attacks on Catholics. The reality of life in such areas was in sharp contrast to the supposed 'peace dividend' promised in return for supporting the Agreement.

The NIE meanwhile, with its own flawed structure, also appeared incapable of resolving social problems quickly and efficiently, though, admittedly, some of these problems would require a long-term approachs. However, the sectarian nature of the Agreement itself appeared to have done its part in helping to develop a new factory of grievances which did nothing to improve community relations on the ground.[33]

At least part of the difficulty for pro-Agreement loyalist and unionist politicians in attempting to sell the Agreement was that their position appeared to be undermined by the actions of the Labour Government (and the Irish Government) which, in continuing to move to meet nationalist and especially republican demands, reinforced the 'winners and losers' syndrome. While the British and Irish governments promised that the Agreement was a new political dispensation, in the end they colluded in helping to reinforce the old zero-sum form of politics.

Both security and social issues were inextricably linked with the implementation of the Agreement in respect of which the Government often appeared stagestruck when asked to deal with ongoing paramilitary activity. This position became even more apparent after 11 September 2001 when Blair promoted himself as the strongest international supporter of the US administration's war on terror.[34]

By 2003 Northern Ireland's loyalists appeared as divided and dispirited as they had been for many years – a position which was not conducive to achieving the aspirations of the Belfast Agreement. Although some loyalists continued to work to fulfil the aims of the Agreement and provide a new role for loyalism, it appeared that others were more than happy to continue to smile while playing the villain. At the very least it seemed clear that the uncertain political position would mean that there would be no 'farewell to arms' by the loyalist paramilitaries without a significant change in the wider political scenery.

Notes

The author would like to thank Dr Kris Brown of the Linen Hall Library, Belfast for his help in the preparation of this chapter.

1 See Roy Garland, *Gusty Spence* (Belfast: Blackstaff Press, 2001), and Gary McMichael, *An Ulster Voice: In Search of Common Ground in Northern Ireland* (Boulder, CO: Roberts Rinehart, 1999).
2 Bernadette C. Hayes and Ian McAllister, 'Who Voted for Peace? Public Support for the 1998 Northern Ireland Agreement', *Irish Political Studies*, vol. 16, 2001, pp. 73–93.
3 In a speech to the Royal Ulster Agricultural Society in Belfast on 14 May (a week before the referendum), for example, Blair stated that 'to say Yes is to say yes to hope, to peace, to stability and to prosperity'.
4 Author's interview with David Ervine, 16 October 2002.
5 *Warrior*, no. 14 July–August 1998.
6 There were also approximately 80–90 'punishment' attacks by loyalists each year after 1998.
7 The Provisional IRA was estimated to have £1.5 million running costs and a £5 million to £8 million fund-raising capacity: see Northern Ireland Affairs Select Committee report, *The Financing of Terrorism in Northern Ireland* (HC978, Fourth Report Session 2001–2), table 1.
8 *Ibid.*, para. 35.
9 *Ibid.*, para. 13.
10 *Ibid.*, para. 37.
11 The UDA in particular appeared to be in denial on this issue, seeing accusations of drug-dealing as part of a campaign in the media, 'directed by either republicans, NIO, PSNI or all of them together', *Warrior*, no. 35, October–November 2002.

12 It is worth noting that the only paramilitary organisation to hand over weapons to the IICD was the anti-Agreement LVF; it was generally recognised that its hope was that this action would lead to the early release of LVF prisoners. In 1998 the UVF at least appeared to be considering the idea of a hand-over of some weapons to the British Army provided the IRA was also prepared to decommission. It was not, however, prepared to decommission weapons unilaterally, since this would, in its view, be tantamount to decommissioning merely to put Sinn Féin into government.

13 Jim Cusack and Henry McDonald, *UVF*, rev. edn (Dublin: Poolbeg Press, 2000), p. 377.

14 Something of the intricacy of loyalist paramilitary links and rivalries can be seen in the paramilitary 'career' of Frankie Curry, who at various times was connected to the RHC, UDA, UVF, LVF and RHD. Curry, who claimed to have killed sixteen or more people, was himself shot dead in March 1999, allegedly in retaliation for his murder of another loyalist in July of the previous year. David McKittrick, Seamus Kelters, Brian Feeney and Chris Thornton, *Lost Lives* (Edinburgh: Mainstream Publishing, 1999), pp. 1468–70.

15 *Shankill Mirror*, February 2000.

16 *Ibid.*, July–August 2000.

17 Henry McDonald, 'Hannibal the Loyalist', *Observer*, 20 January 2002.

18 Nicholas Watt, '"Mad Dog" Turf War Threatens Ulster Peace', *Guardian*, 22 August 2000.

19 *Shankill Mirror*, October 2000.

20. BBC News, online: http://news.bbc.co.uk. Northern Ireland 1998–2002.

21 Anne Bill, *Beyond the Red Gauntlet* (Belfast: AB Publications, 2002), p. 28.

22 The Lessons of North Belfast', *Belfast Telegraph*, 14 August 2001.

23 Concerned Residents of Upper Ardoyne (website: www.crua.co.uk). Anne Bill described the situation more colloquially, saying: 'You can't kick a community in the teeth for thirty years and not expect them to eventually bite your foot. There are no tears for our children, no swarms of media highlighting our problems, no wails of "scum" when our pensioners are scared half to death by nationalist mobs, no condemnation when our community is battered with hurley sticks': Bill, *Beyond the Red Gauntlet*, p. 43.

24 'Police Blame UDA for Rise in Pipe Bombings', *Irish Times*, 10 August 2001.

25 A notable event during this time was the murder of journalist Martin O'Hagan by loyalist paramilitaries on 28 September.

26 *Shankill Mirror*, October 2001.

27 *Ibid.*, November 2001.

28 A well documented account of republican attacks on Cluan Place in east Belfast can be found in Peter Robinson's 'Victims: The Story of Unionists "Living" at the Interface with Republican Short Strand', DUP, 2002.

29 BBC News (http://news.bbc.co.uk) 20 June 2002, 'Trouble Blamed on Nationalists'.

30 *Warrior*, no. 31, February–March 2002.

31 On 27 September former UDP spokesman John White, who supported Adair, was also expelled by the UDA.

32 The feud led to 9 shootings including 3 murders.

33 See Robin Wilson, 'The Apartheid Thinking of the Agreement', *Fortnight*, no. 409, December 2002.

34 Roger Mac Ginty and John Darby, *Guns and Government: The Management of the Northern Ireland Peace Process* (London: Palgrave, 2002), p. 170.

PART III
Agreement at the crossroads?

10

A farewell to arms? Decommissioning and the peace process

COLIN MCINNES

The decommissioning of paramilitary (or 'illegal'[1]) weapons has been one of – and at times the most – critical and controversial issues in the Northern Ireland peace process. This is hardly surprising. The issue concerns not only weapons responsible for death and destruction but political trust. Illegal weapons in Northern Ireland are as much a symptom as a cause of tension. Even the use of the term 'decommissioning' reflects political sensitivities. For republicans 'disarmament' smacks of surrender (even though the process is one of disarmament), while for unionists 'demilitarisation' implies acceptance of the Republican agenda of 'troops out' (even though there has been significant demilitarisation in Northern Ireland since the ceasefires, including a reduction in the numbers of troops deployed). As the Mitchell Report stated, 'what is really needed is the decommissioning of mind-sets in Northern Ireland'.[2] This chapter discusses the relationship of decommissioning to the peace process,[3] from the beginnings of the process in the early 1990s through to the first decommissioning of IRA weapons in October 2001. This is not to suggest that the process is now complete, but rather that October 2001 does mark a watershed. Efforts at decommissioning continue at the time of writing, as does the wider peace process. The story does not stop in October 2001, but it did there reach a culminating point at which the IRA accepted that the political situation had changed sufficiently to allow it to decommission a significant part of its arsenal.

Beginnings

The peace process can usefully be divided into a number of stages. The first of these, from 1990 to the ceasefires of autumn 1994, saw the beginnings[4] of the process: the Brooke initiative; the Hume–Adams dialogue; and the December 1993 Downing Street Declaration. Critically, the Downing Street Declaration offered Sinn Féin the possibility of entry into political discussions about the future of the Northern Ireland, provided IRA violence stopped but without explicit reference to the handing in of weapons. After a period of 'clarification' throughout the first half of 1994, on 31 August the IRA declared a ceasefire, followed on 13 October by a similar announcement from the CLMC. Throughout this initial period the issue of decommissioning was in the background. Priority for the two governments instead lay with obtaining paramilitary ceasefires (particularly by the IRA) and on discussions over the framework of negotiations, while, in contrast, decommissioning received little public attention. Nevertheless the Irish Government raised the issue with Sinn Féin prior to the IRA ceasefire, not least in the spring 1993 'Steps Envisaged' document. Irish Foreign Minister Dick Spring also made it clear in press briefings on the Downing Street Declaration that a permanent cessation of violence had to involve the giving up of arms, although decommissioning was not mentioned in the declaration itself. Finally the issue may also have been discussed in the secret 'back channel' which operated at this time between the British Government and Sinn Féin. However, the linkage between decommissioning and participation in negotiations was left unclear in public pronouncements.

The 'Washington three'

The situation began to change in the second stage of the process, running from the 1994 ceasefires to the establishment of the Mitchell Commission in late 1995. During this period two sets of talks emerged. The first – the so-called 'strands' – examined future political structures in Northern Ireland and the latter's relationship to the Republic of Ireland and the UK; the second focused on decommissioning. Crucially, in the absence of IRA decommissioning Sinn Féin was excluded from the multi-party talks on the strands. This placed decommissioning at the heart of the peace process since, without it, Sinn Féin could not participate in negotiations on political structures, thereby rendering those talks marginal. The question of when to start decommissioning weapons proved central: should it *follow* a political agreement or should it *precede* negotiations as an indication of serious intent and to prevent the threat of a return to violence being used as leverage in talks? The British Government attempted to clarify its position on these issues when the Northern Ireland Secretary Sir Patrick Mayhew visited Washington in March 1995. Its position (expressed in what became known as the 'Washington three') was that for Sinn Féin to join the talks the IRA had to both indicate its *willingness* to disarm and actually *begin* decommissioning, thereby demonstrating its commitment to peaceful means and to engage in confidence-building. The Washington three, however, had the effect of hardening the British Government's position and turning decommissioning into *the* issue of the peace process, since Sinn Fein's participation was now conditional on prior decommissioning.

Although prior decommissioning broadly satisfied unionist concerns, it was unacceptable to republicans. In particular, the idea of the IRA handing over its weapons to British security forces before an agreement was in place smacked of surrender. The Irish Government was also beginning to suspect that the decommissioning issue was being used by London to slow progress down. This was particularly so when London's hard-line position on decommissioning was coupled to the time it took to make the 'working assumption' that the IRA ceasefire was permanent and the perceived reliance of the Major Government on Unionist MPs for its Commons majority. Although the Bruton Government in Dublin retained its own suspicions over the IRA, it was also convinced that the IRA would not accept prior decommissioning, since that would be tantamount to surrender and, as a result, Sinn Féin would remain barred from the talks. A way therefore had to be found around the decommissioning problem if progress was to be made in the negotiations on the 'strands'.

The Mitchell Report

To break the growing impasse on the issue of decommissioning, in November 1995 the two governments launched the 'twin-track initiative'. The first track involved preparatory multi-party talks to establish a framework for substantive negotiations (what became known as 'talks about talks'); the second created an independent commission, chaired by former US Senator George Mitchell, to examine the decommissioning of paramilitary arms. Decommissioning was now very much centre-stage in the peace process, and the issue of how to sequence decommissioning and all-party negotiations the biggest stumbling-block to progress. The Mitchell Commission reported in January 1996 and proposed its own solution to the key problem of *when* to decommission – that it should move alongside the all-party negotiations rather than precede or follow them.[5] The Mitchell Report argued that although 'each side of this argument [on sequencing] reflects a core of reasonable concern',[6] what was required was a compromise, with each side understanding that the other had legitimate concerns. To Mitchell, holding talks and decommissioning in parallel represented such a compromise. The report also introduced two other key developments. The first was the articulation of what became known as the 'Mitchell Principles' – six principles 'of democracy and non-violence' to which all parties involved in the negotiations should 'affirm their total and absolute commitment'.[7] Acceptance of – or 'signing up to' – the Mitchell Principles quickly became a further prerequisite to participation in the formal talks' process. Second, the Mitchell Report was the first attempt publicly to address how decommissioning might be undertaken. Despite the significance of decommissioning during much of 1995, no real thought had been paid to questions relating to the *process* of decommissioning. Technical issues such as the verification of terrorist arsenals, how to hand in weapons, and the possibility of prosecutions because weapons handed in had been involved in terrorist acts had been largely ignored in favour of the more obviously political question of *when* decommissioning should occur. This suggests very strongly that decommissioning was more important for its political meaning than for its military significance. The Mitchell Commission was the first body to publicly provide detailed answers to such technical questions, and its recommendations formed the basis of legislation introduced in both the British and Irish parliaments later that year.

Parallel decommissioning, however, proved unpopular with the unionists, who maintained their support for prior decommissioning. Nor was it embraced whole-heartedly by the Major Government. In particular John Major's decision to call elections to an assembly which would, in turn, provide the basis for representation at the multi-party talks was seen in Dublin as London's attempt to downplay the significance of the Mitchell Report. More importantly, the decision to call elections was the last straw for the IRA. From the Provisionals' perspective, the Major Government had back-tracked on its commitment in the Downing Street Declaration to allow Sinn Féin into negotiations on the sole proviso of an IRA ceasefire. With the ceasefire in place, Major had then insisted on decommissioning before Sinn Féin could participate in the talks; with the Mitchell compromise, Major had now asked for elections. This created deep mistrust within the republican community over the British Government's real intentions. On 9 February 1996 the IRA 'with great reluctance' broke its ceasefire and exploded a bomb in London's Dock-lands, beginning a campaign which later escalated in Northern Ireland. Loyalist paramilitaries formally kept to their ceasefires, though the Orange Order's and Apprentice Boys' marches in 1996 and 1997 created a series of crises which threat-ened to end the entire process. As happened in the period prior to the IRA ceasefire, so the return to violence trumped the issue of decommissioning, although the failure to resolve the decommissioning issue had been a key factor in the IRA's decision to recommence its bombing campaign. Despite the movement by the British Government from prior to parallel decommissioning, this still fell far short of the IRA's fear that to hand in weapons ahead of an agreement would constitute surrender. In contrast, unionists were unhappy about talking to Sinn Féin prior to decommissioning and, given the Major Government's weak parliamentary position, were seen as holding considerable influence over the British Government. The issue of decommissioning therefore lay at the centre of events leading up to the IRA's return to violence.

In early 1996 the Dublin Government worked hard both to get a new ceasefire and to secure a date for all-party talks to begin. On the former it failed, but on 28 February it agreed with the British Government that all-party talks should begin on 10 June, thereby moving from 'talks about talks' to substantive negotiations on the strands. In reality, however, there appeared to be little difference between the two since the parties concerned and the issues involved remained much the same. Rather 'talks about talks' merged into multi-party talks on the strands, with Sinn Féin banned due to the IRA's renewed campaign. Throughout 1996 and early 1997 decommissioning was somewhat in the background, at least for the two govern-ments. The Mitchell Report had established the basis for the two governments' positions and their priority was now on obtaining a new IRA ceasefire rather than on further developing the decommissioning issue. But Sinn Féin was rapidly losing all confidence in the two governments and in the absence of concessions from them, particularly on decommissioning, was unlikely to push the IRA for a new ceasefire. By late 1996 the process was moribund, with no real progress being made. The Major Government appeared to lose its enthusiasm for Northern Ireland, frustrated over the lack of progress. In particular the prime minister, who had been instrumental in the early 1990s in securing the political will in London to advance the peace process, had become enmeshed in internal Conservative Party politics, and Northern Ireland offered no solution to his more immediate problems, being at best a distraction and at worst a second front on which his right-wing critics could attack him.

The GFA

In the summer of 1997, new governments in London and Dublin provided the necessary impetus to re-invigorate the peace process. On 3 June the multi-party talks which had been suspended for the election campaign recommenced, with the new Northern Ireland Secretary Mo Mowlam focusing on decommissioning as the most important and sensitive issue confronting the talks.[8] On 25 June the British and Irish governments produced joint proposals on decommissioning (including a set of 'possible conclusions' on methods of decommissioning[9]), which although criticised by the unionists nevertheless indicated the two governments' intention to resolve the problem. The two governments were also discussing the establishment of an independent body to oversee decommissioning, as suggested by the Mitchell Report. On 26 August agreement was reached on the establishment of the IICD,[10] with the former Canadian general and member of the Mitchell Commission John de Chastelaine as its chair. The most important event of the summer was, however, the 19 July announcement of a second IRA ceasefire. It is clear that the ceasefire owed much to the change in attitudes of both governments, not least on decommissioning. Policy shifts were, however, relatively small. This was hardly surprising – in opposition Labour had maintained a bi-partisan consensus over Northern Ireland, including support for the Mitchell Commission's proposals on decommissioning. But within this framework the new Government appeared both intent on making progress and willing to be flexible where possible. Perhaps the key difference, however, was that, as far as Labour was concerned, once the IRA ceasefire had been re-established, the major stumbling-block to Sinn Fein's participation in talks was removed.

On 29 August Mo Mowlam announced her decision to allow Sinn Féin entry to the talks on the basis of her assessment that the ceasefire was indeed genuine, and on the sole proviso that Sinn Féin formally sign up to Mitchell's 'principles of democracy and non-violence'. In other words, IRA decommissioning was no longer a prerequisite for Sinn Fein's participation in the talks, nor indeed for that of the loyalist paramilitaries. All that was required was a ceasefire and acceptance of the Mitchell Principles. Sinn Féin signed up to the Mitchell Principles on 9 September at a plenary session of the multi-party talks, with the major Unionist parties notable by their absence. The DUP and the UKUP in particular argued that the ceasefire was a 'sham' (or, less provocatively, 'tactical') and withdrew from the negotiations unless there was decommissioning of IRA arms. Although the more moderate and larger UUP also maintained an emphasis on decommissioning, it demonstrated a greater willingness to compromise under its leader David Trimble, and entered into negotiations with Sinn Féin without IRA decommissioning.

At the end of 1997 the Maze prison assassination of Billy Wright, the leader of the paramilitary LVF, by the republican Irish National Liberation Army (INLA) threatened to spark a series of 'tit-for-tat' killings between republican and loyalist paramilitaries, undermining the peace process. With David Trimble at times appearing isolated both within unionism and even within his own party, hopes for an agreement were not high. But with the direct intervention of the prime minister and the taoiseach, and the influence of the White House (not least through the continuing efforts of George Mitchell), an agreement was finally reached at Stormont on Good Friday 1998. A key move in securing republican support for the Agreement was London's willingness to downplay the decommissioning issue. Sinn Féin repeatedly expressed its concerns that for the IRA to hand in weapons ahead of an agreement would be seen as surrender and was politically impossible. London therefore moved from parallel decommissioning being a requirement of the negotiating process to its being 'aspirational'. This in turn required a considerable compromise by the unionists who had already moved from their favoured position of prior decommissioning to one of negotiating with Sinn Féin while the IRA still possessed its full military capability. To enter into an agreement without decommissioning was an even greater step, and one which many unionists were unwilling to take – even in David Trimble's more moderate UUP. Pressure from within Northern Ireland, from London and from Washington, a sense that this was the best that would be available, together with the Agreement's commitment to decommissioning all helped to allay unionist fears, though those fears were far from being removed.

Establishing new political institutions

Decommissioning formed a small[11] but – at least in unionist eyes – significant element of the GFA. Much of what was agreed on decommissioning was presaged by the Mitchell Report and previous agreements, principally those in the second half of 1997 between the British and Irish governments. The only significant development was the inclusion of a timetable for the completion of decommissioning (within two years of successful referenda on the Agreement). Despite the successful referenda, progress on implementing the Agreement was slow, with neither the establishment of the NIE nor decommissioning occurring. Instead the summer of 1998 was dominated by two events – the Orange Order march at Drumcree and the Real IRA's bombing of Omagh. The decision by the Parades Commission not to allow the Protestant Orange Order to march down the

Catholic Garvaghy Road led to a violent stand-off between marchers and the British Army, which included shots being fired by protesters. It was widely believed that two loyalist terror groups, the UDA and the UVF, were heavily involved in the violence, while the UFF ceasefire appeared close to breaking-point. Although the situation was controlled by the security forces, Drumcree was a reminder both of the continued volatility in the province and the opposition by a large section of the unionist community to the GFA. In particular, the Orange Order had come out strongly against the GFA and saw Drumcree as an opportunity to demonstrate its strength. But linkage to specific issues in the peace process (such as decommissioning) was at best tenuous, while the Orange Order's failure to force the issue at Drumcree suggested that a repeat of Sunningdale was not likely.[12]

Events at Drumcree were, however, overshadowed by RIRA's bombing of Omagh in which 28 people were killed and 200 wounded. Once the initial horror of the attack had passed, fear for the future of the peace process quickly followed. The fear was two-fold. First, that hardline unionists would make no distinction between the 'Real IRA' – which claimed responsibility for the bomb – and the Provisional IRA, and would see the bombing as revealing the *tactical* nature of the Provisional IRA's ceasefire. Sufficient pressure might be applied to ensure that David Trimble would not be able to sit at the same table as Gerry Adams. Second, that Omagh revealed splits in the IRA and the campaign of terror might be continued by a splinter group, despite the Provisional IRA's ceasefire and Sinn Fein's signing up to the Mitchell Principles. In particular, there was concern that even if the IRA handed in its weapons, sufficient arms had been acquired by dissident republican paramilitaries (such as RIRA) that violence would continue.[13] In the event, neither fear was realised. Rather the bomb at Omagh appeared to have shaken both communities into an awareness of the costs of the peace process failing. RIRA announced that it would suspend its military activities, the INLA and LVF declared permanent ceasefires, Gerry Adams announced that violence must be 'a thing of the past – over, done with and gone',[14] Martin McGuinness was named as the link between the IRA and the IIDC, and Adams and Trimble had their first one-on-one meeting. Despite this flurry of activity, there was still little sign of decommissioning.

By the spring of 1999 decommissioning was once again a major issue, with unionists – including David Trimble – arguing that Sinn Féin could not be allowed a presence on the NIE without decommissioning, while Sinn Féin maintained that its presence would reflect a democratic mandate. The problem simmered on until Sinn Féin (with three smaller parties) rejected the Hillsborough Agreement which had been drawn up as a way forward by the British and Irish premiers on 1 April 1999. This plunged the peace process into crisis, with decommissioning centre-stage. The central problem was whether Sinn Féin should be admitted to the NIE without IRA decommissioning. The crisis was dramatically escalated when Tony Blair indicated that if there was no agreement by 30 June, when power was supposed to be transferred from London to Belfast, then he would suspend the GFA –

what became known as 'parking the car'. As the 30 June deadline approached, so negotiations became even more frantic, with calls from the Northern Ireland first minister elect, David Trimble, for the removal of Mo Mowlem, the Northern Ireland secretary, and the direct involvement of the two premiers in intensive talks at Stormont. A last-minute proposal by Tony Blair that the executive be established and Sinn Féin included, but that IRA decommissioning should follow very shortly thereafter and be completed by May 2000 under penalty of the executive being suspended, failed to satisfy the unionists. The process was therefore put on hold in a state of crisis unmatched since the second IRA ceasefire.

At the heart of this crisis was the decommissioning issue. For unionists, republican words had to be matched by republican deeds: Sinn Fein's proclamation that violence was a thing of the past had to be matched by IRA decommissioning. Already unhappy over first negotiating and then signing an Agreement with Sinn Féin without IRA decommissioning, to then allow Sinn Féin a place on a ruling executive was a step too far. For Sinn Féin, however, the IRA remained a separate body which it could not order to decommission, while a democratic mandate entitled the party to be present on the executive. Indeed Sinn Féin attempted to play down the decommissioning issue, arguing that once new political processes were established violence would slip from the agenda and decommissioning would be unnecessary. With unionists still deeply sceptical of republican intentions, however, this argument was unlikely to hold much sway. As a result the failure to resolve the issue of decommissioning stalled the implementation of the GFA and plunged the process into crisis. With the exception of a clear return to violence by a major paramilitary group, it was difficult to see any other issue – RUC reform, the release of prisoners, the establishment of cross-border bodies – having this effect on the peace process. Almost ten years into the peace process and more than a year after the GFA, there had been no significant decommissioning and, crucially, no decommissioning of IRA arms.

By the summer of 1999, the process was not so much parked as stalled. Despite the seriousness of the situation, however, the process was not in danger of being abandoned. To change the metaphor, the peace process in general and the GFA in particular formed the only show in town, and as time passed so both moderate unionists and republicans were forced to come to terms with that, despite their reservations. During the summer, however, the two sides appeared to be hopelessly separated. Unionists saw republicans 'talking the talk', but failing to 'walk the walk': that for all their fine words, there had been no substantive progress on decommissioning, while Sinn Féin had benefited from political rehabilitation, as had the IRA from the release of prisoners. Republicanism in turn was sceptical of unionist motivations, believing that decommissioning was a convenient excuse masking an unwillingness to enter an executive in which Sinn Féin was also present. In July the two governments attempted to restart the process with 'The Way Forward',[15] which proposed that the executive be established but with a failsafe mechanism should there be no decommissioning. Unionists doubted whether the failsafe mechanism would work and scuppered the process by refusing to nominate members for the executive.[16] Wrangling continued into the autumn when the Patten Report on policing was published. This added a further complication by providing another high-profile issue on which unionism and republicanism were divided. Although both were united in objecting to the report, the issues were very different for each of them. The Patten Report's publication also provided a rare occasion when the tight linkage between decommissioning and political representation was broken and a third issue threatened to intrude into the process.

Inspections and decommissioning

As the autumn passed, both sides began to realise that the process could not be stalled indefinitely and felt the need for progress. A series of minor confidence-building measures, public statements and secret negotiations slowly built up the momentum, culminating in November 1999 with the IRA nominating its representative to the IICD. But both unionism and republicanism were being stretched close to breaking point by the series of delicate compromises required. It was into this fragile process that the new Secretary of State Peter Mandelson stepped. Mandelson, a controversial figure on the mainland, was a close confidante of the prime minister and had been a key architect in Labour's rebranding and subsequent 1997 election victory. He appeared to recognise that David Trimble was a – perhaps the – key player in pushing forward the GFA. In particular, if Trimble fell to internal UUP reservations over the GFA then the process would have been dealt a body-blow from which it would take a long time to recover. Mandelson therefore devised a safety net to reassure Trimble's more moderate UUP. This took the form of legislation that would guarantee a return to direct rule if there was defaulting on either decommissioning or devolution. Although this helped Trimble, it did little to reassure republicans who did not believe they had signed up to this in the GFA. A second critical move, however, was Trimble's very public post-dated letter of resignation as first minister in the event of no decommissioning. Sinn Féin was therefore placed in an invidious position, either of accepting Mandelson's safety net and Trimble's political blackmail or refusing to join an executive and therefore delaying their first taste of power. Under these fraught conditions, the NIE was finally established on 2 December 1999. It had been accomplished without a decommisioning of IRA arms, indeed without any commitment on the part of the IRA; but decommisioning had loomed large in the establishment of the NIE and it cast a very dark shadow over its future, not least in the form of David Trimble's post-dated letter.

With the new year, the signs were not optimistic. In January the IICD reported that the IRA had yet to provide information on when decommissioning would begin, and the UVF and the UFF had indicated to the IICD that they would only follow an IRA lead in decommissioning.[17] Without significant movement on the issue, Peter Mandelson suspended the institutions rather than see the UUP bring them crashing down with Trimble's letter. Last-minute hints of movement by the IRA came to nothing as it, too, suspended relations with the IICD. Once more Northern Ireland was plunged into a round of recriminations, with decommissioning at its very heart.

As the weeks progressed, relations in public worsened as the debate over future policing began to take centre-stage. Behind the scenes, however, intensive negotiations were being conducted, particularly between the governments and Sinn Féin. This led, in the first week of May 2000, to the two governments issuing a joint statement[18] with new proposals and, more importantly, to a near simultaneous IRA statement that it would 'initiate a peace process that will completely and verifiably put IRA arms beyond use'.[19] The words 'completely' and 'verifiably', deliberately echoing the Mitchell Report, were taken by the British Government as of particular significance.[20] The IRA statement went on to say that it would resume contact with the IICD, but that 'within weeks' it would put in place new 'confidence-building measures to confirm our weapons remain secure'.[21] What emerged from this was an inspections' regime under the auspices of two respected senior international figures: the former ANC Secretary General Cyril Ramaphosa and the former President of Finland Martti Ahtisaari. The two observers had no formal relationship with the IICD, thereby enabling the IRA to avoid charges by the more extreme republicans that it was the first step towards decommissioning and surrender.[22] Nevertheless this was clearly an important step forward by the IRA. The British Army responded by closing 5 of its 71 bases in Northern Ireland, including 2 observation posts in tower blocks in nationalist areas of Belfast. But none of the loyalist paramilitary groups responded, instead becoming embroiled over the summer in a particularly violent internecine feud in the Shankill area of Belfast, which cast something of a pall over the success of the inspections' regime.[23]

The first inspection by Ahtisaari and Ramaphosa took place in June 2000, followed by another in October; a third was postponed, due to the foot-and-mouth epidemic, until May 2001. According to the Bonn International Centre on Conversion, a dual key system was used, similar to that developed in the 1990s during the UN-assisted peace process in El Salvador, which ensured that the arms' dumps remained secure and could not be opened unilaterally by the IRA.[24] This led to a degree of speculation over whether the Mitchell Report might be revisited. Mitchell had argued that decommissoning meant that weapons had to be destroyed or at least put beyond use. Might an inspections' regime, then, prove a satisfactory alternative, dealing both with IRA sensitivities over 'surrender' and unionist concerns over the possibility of a return to violence? It soon became clear, however, that for unionists and for the loyalist paramilitaries such an approach would be unacceptable. For the unionists in particular there was a sense of having compromised sufficiently and nothing short of decommissioning now would be sufficient evidence of republican seriousness of intent. This eventually culminated in October when David Trimble was once again having to fight for his political survival over the GFA, with an internal UUP vote on the peace process. Trimble won narrowly, but in so doing was forced to demonstrate his unionist credentials by imposing a series of restrictions affecting mainly Sinn Féin members of the assembly in order to put pressure on them for IRA decommissioning. Once again the peace process entered a state of crisis. The extent of the problem was indicated with an IRA statement in February 2001:

> We have never entered into any agreement or undertaking or understanding at any time what-so-ever on any aspect of decommissioning ... Those who have once again made the political process conditional on the decommissioning of silenced IRA guns are responsible for creating the current difficulties and for keeping the peace process in a state of perpetual crisis.[25]

The final visit of US President Bill Clinton in December 2000 and the appointment of John Reid in January to succeed Peter Mandelson had offered some glimmers of hope, but these were obscured by increased paramilitary violence from both loyalist groups and RIRA. Not the least of these was a car-bomb which exploded outside BBC Television Centre on 4 March 2001, widely assumed to be the work of RIRA. Later that week the prime minister and the taoiseach met with pro-Agreement parties in Northern Ireland. Despite an earlier statement from the IRA that it would recommence links with the IICD, the two premiers were unable to see the possibility of a major breakthrough before elections in June. Sinn Féin appeared reluctant to force the issue of decommissioning preferring to focus on implementing the May 2000 agreement, while David Trimble viewed the IRA statement as little more than propaganda. Once again the peace process was 'parked', this time until after the elections.

The June elections offered little immediate comfort to the two premiers: the anti-Agreement DUP increased its number of seats at the expense of David Trimble's UUP, while Sinn Féin emerged as the largest of the Catholic parties, displacing the more moderate SDLP. Worse, Trimble had once again threatened to resign unless decommisioning of IRA weapons began, a threat which he implemented on 1 July against a background of increased violence on the streets of Northern Ireland. With the peace process in crisis once more over decommissioning, the newly re-elected Tony Blair met the Irish Taoiseach Bertie Ahern at Weston Park in England. The meeting failed to find a solution, but in early August the two governments produced another decommissioning scheme, followed a few days later by a report from the IICD that the IRA had issued its own proposals which broadly satisfied the IICD. Despite this apparent progress, the overall political situation remained tense. On 11 August the British Government suspended institutions for a day and on 14 August the IRA claimed that the situation did not warrant the implementation of its own scheme, but that it would continue to monitor developments. At this point two external events unusually impinged on the peace process: the 11 September terrorist attacks on the USA and the consequent US-led war on terror; and the arrest in Columbia of three suspected members of the IRA, accused of training terrorists there, one of whom was Sinn Fein's representative in Cuba. These events, combined with tough internal negotiations, led the IRA, on 23 October 2001, to issue a statement that it had begun to decommission its arms, a statement subsequently verified by the IICD. This was followed by a second verified decommissioning of IRA arms on 8 April 2002.

Although this represented a watershed in the peace process, violence continued, not least in north Belfast. Illegal weapons continued to be found (on 19 and 20 November 2001, for example, a quantity of bomb-making materials was found during a routine search in Lurgan, County Armagh, and a car, stopped by police and army, also in County Armagh, was found to be carrying a 200lb bomb). Unionists remained sceptical of the IRA and republicanism in general over the issue of weapons; and political structures remained fragile, requiring the suspension of the assembly and a return to direct rule in October 2002. A watershed may have been reached, but the journey was far from over.

Conclusion

The fact that it had taken more than a decade of the peace process before the IRA decommissioned some of its arms indicates the difficulties and sensitivities involved. For much of this period the biggest single issue was the sequencing of decommissioning and the establishment of new political structures. The unionist position for much of the period prior to the GFA was that decommissioning should precede all-party talks. This was seen both as a signifier of the IRA's commitment to peace and as a means of preventing negotiations from being held hostage to the threat of a return to violence.[26] All of the major unionist parties initially rejected the Mitchell Report's compromise of decommissioning and talks proceeding in parallel. However the position of the larger UUP led by David Trimble shifted during 1997 towards accepting the Mitchell compromise and eventually to an agreement prior to decommissioning. Large elements of unionism, including the DUP and significant sections of David Trimble's own UUP, believed that this had been a compromise too far. Trimble was forced into a series of humiliating and politically damaging votes within his own party and continuing unionist reservations underpinned the slow establishment of the NIE, despite successful assembly elections. In contrast Sinn Féin consistently pointed to the 1993 Downing Street Declaration as the basis for its participation in talks. In that declaration the British and Irish governments appeared to state that the sole precondition for Sinn Fein's admission to talks about the political future of Northern Ireland was an IRA ceasefire – in other words that the decommissioning of weapons was unrelated to participation in political talks. The favoured republican position was to decommission arms once a political agreement had been reached, thus avoiding any sense of surrender.[27] Once agreement had been reached that position changed somewhat. The IRA attempted to put some distance between itself and Sinn Féin, arguing that it had not signed the GFA and was not therefore bound by it. Sinn Féin in turn argued that its position in the executive should be dependent not on IRA decommissioning but on the basis of its democratic mandate. The more moderate nationalist party the SDLP viewed the issue of decommissioning prior to talks as something of a red herring pursued by those parties unwilling to see progress. In particular, there was suspicion that parties associated with loyalist paramilitaries were admitted to talks solely on the basis of the loyalist ceasefire (announced shortly after the IRA ceasefire in 1994), but that the IRA was being asked to decommission its weapons before Sinn Féin could be admitted.

John Major's Government's position moved from decommissioning not being a prerequisite to negotiation (as stated in the Downing Street Declaration), to it being an essential litmus test and confidence-building measure prior to talks (its position after the IRA ceasefire), to agreeing with the January 1996 Mitchell Report's compromise of parallel talks, to its later position that Sinn Féin need only to 'address' the decommissioning issue prior to all-party talks (providing an IRA ceasefire was in place).[28] There are a number of possible explanations for these shifts in position: that the Government was demonstrating flexibility and adapting its position as required; that it was vacillating under weak leadership; or that it was not serious about peace and, beholden to the unionists for a Commons majority, it deliberately placed a series of stumbling-blocks in the path of all-party talks.

In opposition, the Labour Party had supported the Mitchell compromise that decommissioning should occur in parallel with talks about Northern Ireland's political future, with participation being subject to accepting the Mitchell Principles of non-violence and democratic means – implicitly requiring a ceasefire. In office the Blair Government demonstrated a determination to restart talks, initially retaining the Mitchell compromise as the basis for sequencing decommissioning and talks. Priority, however, lay with obtaining an agreement. Parallel decommissioning therefore became an 'aspiration', which was dropped for the greater goal of securing the GFA. With the Agreement in place, Mo Mowlam's successor Peter Mandelson ensured that it was not dealt a fatal blow by unionist scepticism over decommissioning. Labour's priority was the long game and ensuring that the process was not abandoned, even if it was sometimes stalled. It proved willing to suspend new political institutions if necessary, re-imposing direct rule, rather than see the political situation deteriorate yet further. This was clearly a gamble in that it risked alienating republican elements, but Labour also appeared sensitive to the problems of pro-agreement unionists and in particular their concerns over decommissioning.

During the peace process, and particularly in the wake of the GFA, a number of attempts were made to link decommissioning with other issues. This was perhaps unsurprising – successful negotiations require a willingness to compromise, and compromise in one area may be traded against another's concessions elsewhere. Nevertheless this can be a dangerous tactic: concessions can easily be portrayed as unequal, while points of principle may have to be abandoned for progress or tactical advantage, leading to disillusionment among those wedded to these principles. For this reason, linkage *between* issues has often been less successful than a willingness to compromise *within* an issue. The two most obvious attempts at linkage between decommissioning and other issues in the peace process concerned the early release of prisoners and participation in the NIE, both following the GFA. In order to gain unionist support in the referendum on the GFA, Tony Blair linked the early release of prisoners to progress in decommissioning. The basis for this in the Agreement was slim, resting largely on the idea that it was a package requiring progress on all issues. For short-term political reasons the British Government made what was, at best, an implicit linkage much more explicit and direct. With the referendum secure, the Government backed away from this linkage. The IRA, however, pursued a reverse linkage – that the early release of prisoners was necessary as a confidence-building measure before decommissioning could begin – while in December 1998 the LVF handed in a small number of weapons for decommissioning in an attempt to secure the early release of some of its prisoners.[29] The second major linkage concerned participation in the NIE. Unionists argued that Sinn Féin should not be allowed to participate until the IRA had begun decommissioning its weapons. The GFA is unclear on this, while Sinn Féin argued that participation should be on the basis of its democratic mandate rather than any linkage to progress in decommissioning.[30] This disagreement was the key element in the breakdown of the process in the summer of 1999. A final attempt at linkage was the somewhat half-hearted one made by Gerry Adams, who stated in 1998 that Sinn Féin would review its position on decommissioning after that summer's marches. Adams was clearly hoping for concessions over the Orange Order parades in return for progress on decommissioning.

The success of attempts at linkage has been varied. Linkage between decommissioning and the early release of prisoners may have helped secure unionist support for the GFA, though it is noteworthy that this has not been rigorously pursued beyond the referendum. The refusal of unionists to sit on an executive with Sinn Féin prior to decommissioning proved a major stumbling-block, while in contrast there is no direct evidence that Gerry Adams's attempt at linkage with the work of the Parades Commission bore fruit.[31] What is perhaps most important to note is that linkage has failed to deliver decommissioning, particularly by the IRA. The lack of decommissioning has tended to lead unionists to pursue the tactic of linkage, without any noteworthy success.

Over a decade after the inception of the peace process, a quantity of IRA weapons has been decommissioned, new political institutions have been established and elections held. Yet violence continues, within and between communities; political trust is weak; and the new institutions have been suspended on a number of occasions. The process has fluctuated between highs and lows, but throughout the linkage between violence, or the potential for violence, and political representation has been clear – despite Sinn Fein's wishes to move beyond this. As George Mitchell commented, what is needed is a decommissioning of mindsets, and that process is ongoing.

Notes

1 In contrast to legal weapons, which include not only those held by the security forces but the large number held by private citizens with official approval (members of gun clubs, for example).

2 Report of the International Body on Arms Decommissioning, 22 January 1996, para. 15. available at: www.nio.gov.uk/mitchrpt.htm (August 1997), hereafter referred to as the Mitchell Report. On the Mitchell Commission and its report, see below.

3 This is not intended to provide a detailed narrative of the peace process. Still the best, though by now dated, account is Eamonn Mallie and David McKittrick, *The Fight for Peace: The Secret Story Behind the Irish Peace Process* (London: Heinemann, 1996). A more recent narrative is to be found in Kris Brown and Corinna Hauswedell, 'Burying the hatchet: the decommissioning of paramilitary arms in Northern Ireland' (Bonn International Centre for Conversion, 2001); see also the excellent detailed chronology maintained on the CAIN website (http://cain.ulst.ac.uk/othelem/chron). Newspaper coverage of the peace process has, of course, been extensive. Excellent (if not necessarily neutral) news coverage is provided in Northern Ireland by the *Belfast Telegraph*, on the mainland by the *Daily Telegraph* and *Independent*, and in Dublin by *The Irish Times*. A reading of these has informed many of the arguments in this chapter. Most of the major political parties maintain websites with useful material, including policy statements. These can be accessed via the Northern Ireland Office's website which itself contains texts of most major statements: (www.nio.gov.uk). IRA statements often appear in *An Phoblacht/Republican News*, which is also a useful source for Sinn Féin statements and interviews.

4 For a more detailed account of the relationship between decommissioning and the peace process, see Colin McInnes, 'The Decommissioning of Terrorist Weapons and the Peace Process in Northern Ireland', *Contemporary Security Policy*, vol. 18, no. 3, December 1997, pp. 83–103; Roger MacGinty, 'Issue Hierarchies in Peace Processes: The Decommissioning of Paramilitary Arms and the Northern Ireland Peace Process', *Journal of Civil Wars*, vol. 1, no. 3, autumn 1998, pp. 24–45; see also Michael von Tangen Page, 'Arms Decommissioning and the Northern Ireland Peace Agreement', *Security Dialogue*, vol. 29, no. 4, 1998, pp. 219–30. Some of the arguments in this chapter first appeared in my 'The Decommissioning of Terrorist Weapons and the Peace Process'. I am grateful to the editors and publishers of *Contemporary Security Policy* for permission to reproduce these here.

5 Mitchell Report, para. 34.

6 *Ibid.*, para. 29

7 *Ibid.*, para. 20.

8 Address by Secretary of State at Resumption of Multi-Party Negotiations, Northern Ireland Information Service, 3 June 1997. This was reiterated in the Joint Statement by the British and Irish governments, 23 July 1997, available at: www.nio.gov.uk/press/970723d.htm (August 1997).

9 Resolving the Address to Decommissioning, Northern Ireland Information Service, 25 June 1997; see in particular the annexe 'Possible Conclusions to Item 2 (a)–(c) of the Agenda for the Remainder of the Opening Plenary'. See also the 16 July explanatory comments made by Paul Murphy, minister of state at the NIO: 'Resolving Decommissioning: Speaking Notes Explaining the Two Governments' Positions', Northern Ireland Information Service, 16 July 1997.

10 Agreement between the Government of the United Kingdom of Great Britain and Northern Ireland and the Government of the Republic of Ireland establishing the Independent International Commission on Decommissioning, Northern Ireland Information Service, 26 August 1997.

11 Section 7 of the Agreement concerned decommissioning but was less than half-a-page in length and contained just six sentences. For the text of the GFA see Appendix 2 of this book. Many of the key documents are also available on the NIO's homepage (www.nio.org.uk.htm).

12 On the BBC radio programme *Today*, David McNally, a leading Orangeman, threatened that the Orange Order would paralyse Ulster, drawing a parallel with the manner in which unionist opposition to the 1973 Sunningdale Agreement on power-sharing had led to its collapse. The arson attack on a Catholic family at the height of the 1998 Drumcree disturbances, killing three young children, led to a split in the Orange Order, with a number of senior figures

arguing that the protest should be called off. As the Rev. William Bingham, himself a senior Orangeman and a key figure in the 'proximity talks' over Drumcree stated: 'no road is worth a life'; see Toby Harnden, 'We Can Paralyse Ulster', *Electronic Telegraph*, 10 July 1998 and 'Murders Fail to End Stand-Off', *Electronic Telegraph*, 13 July 1998. It is also worth noting that the Apprentice Boys' march in Londonderry later in the year – traditionally a potential flash-point – passed off peacefully.

13 RIRA appears to have originated after a heated meeting of IRA leaders at Gweedore, County Donegal, in October 1997, where objections were raised to republican involvement in the peace process. Significantly the IRA's quarter-master general, who was responsible for its weapons, explosives and ammunition, resigned at the meeting and appointed himself chief of staff for RIRA, leading to fears that he might use his knowledge of the IRA stockpile to help equip RIRA.

14 See Sean O'Neill and Jon Hibbs, 'Violence Is Over Claims Adams', *Electronic Telegraph*, 2 September 1998.

15 '"The Way Forward": Joint Statement by the Irish and British Governments at Stormont on 2 July 1999', available at: http://cain.ulst.ac.uk/events/peace/docs/bi2799.htm (accessed 14 February 2003).

16 Under the GFA, the executive had to include cross-community representation. By refusing to nominate members, the unionists ensured that it would not be cross-community and could not therefore be formally established.

17 Report of the Independent International Commission on Decommissioning (IICD), 31 January 2000, available at: http://cain.ulst.ac.uk/events/peace/docs/iicd31100.htm (accessed 14 February 2003).

18 'Joint Statement by Tony Blair, then British Prime Minister, and Bertie Ahern, then Taoiseach (Irish Prime Minister), Issued on the Afternoon of Saturday 6 May 2000', available at http://cain.ulst.ac.uk/events/peace/docs/bio60500b.htm (accessed 14 February 2003).

19 'Statement by the Irish Republican Army (IRA), Issued (at midday) Saturday 6 May 2000', available at: http://cain.ulst.ac.uk/events/peace/docs/ira060500.htm (accessed 14 February 2003). Note that the IRA statement is signified as having been marginally preceded by the statement of the two premiers.

20 See for example the NIO's website page on 'Decommissioning': www.nio.gov.uk/issues/decomm.html (accessed 17 January 2003).

21 'Statement by the Irish Republican Army'.

22 Although reports from the two observers were sent in the first instance to the IICD; see 'Report of the Independent International Commission on Decommissioning, 30 May 2001', available at: www.nio.gov.uk/press/010530dc-nio.htm (accessed 17 January 2003).

23 R. Brown and C. Hauswedell, *Burying the Hatchet: The Decommissioning of Paramilitary Arms in Northern Ireland* (Ulster: INCORE, 2002), p. 43.

24 *Ibid.*

25 'Statement on Decommissioning Issued by the Irish Republican Army (IRA), Saturday 5 February 2000', available at: http://cain.ulst.ac.uk/events/peace/docs/ira5200.htm (accessed 17 January 2003).

26 See for example comments made by Ken Maginnis in *Hansard* (House of Commons), 16 January 1997, cols 476–7.

27 See for example 'Doherty Says Democratic Mandate is Basis for Talks Entry', Sinn Féin Press Release, 29 August 1997; 'The Republican Analysis Will Be at the Negotiations', Sinn Féin Press Release, 29 August 1997.

28 This elaboration of the Government's position appeared in the communique of 28 February 1996, the first meeting of the two premiers after the end of the IRA ceasefire. Anglo-Irish Communique for Summit on 28 February 1996, para. 12; Press Notice, 10 Downing Street, 28 February 1996.

29 Under the terms of the GFA, LVF prisoners were not eligible for early release.

30 Toby Harnden, 'Trimble Attacks Adams in Arms Row', *Electronic Telegraph*, 25 May 1998.

31 Although the critical 1998 Orange Order march at Drumcree was not allowed to pass down the Catholic Garvaghy Road, there is no evidence that this was related to the decommissioning issue.

11

New beginnings? Policing and human rights after the conflict

BRICE DICKSON

When the two governments and the various political parties in Northern Ireland reached agreement on Good Friday 1998[1] there were some key issues which still so divided the participants that they were deliberately allocated a separate resolution process. Among these were the reforms required to the criminal justice system,[2] the content of a Bill of Rights[3] and, perhaps most importantly of all, the future of policing. The parties to the Agreement recognised that it provided an opportunity for a new beginning to policing, but they went on to delegate responsibility for proposing what shape that new beginning should take to an independent commission. That commission, under the chairmanship of Chris Patten, was established on 3 June 1998. It reported on 9 September 1999 and the British Government issued its response to the report on 19 January 2000.[4] The Police (NI) Act 2000 was then enacted by the Westminster Parliament to give statutory effect to many (but not all) of the Patten recommendations, and this was supplemented three years later by the Police (NI) Act 2003. At the time of writing (February 2004) almost every last word of what Patten recommended has been implemented, and a great deal else besides. Sinn Féin remains of the view that not enough reforms have yet been implemented to justify it lending its support to the police, but such a stance is hard to square with the very substantial changes which have been wrought over the last few years. Most commentators expect Sinn Féin to lend its support for the PSNI in the near future.

Before setting out the terms of reference of the Patten Commission it is worth stressing the Belfast Agreement's recognition that if peace was to be maintained in Northern Ireland a new beginning to policing was required. Even though a new beginning does not necessarily imply that policing in Northern Ireland was in a condition that it should not have been, the very acknowledgement that a fresh start was justified was a significant concession on the part of those parties, chiefly unionist, who, throughout the thirty years of the Troubles, viewed the RUC as their first line of defence against crime and disorder, and especially paramilitary violence.

At the same time, the ambiguity in the phrase 'a new beginning' allowed observers to note that nationalists were not stipulating the complete replacement of the RUC as a precondition to any permanent reform in this area. Although both unionists and nationalists lost no time in descending into rhetoric to re-state their pre-Agreement stances on policing, epitomised on the unionist side by the DUP's insistence that no changes at all should be made to the RUC and on the nationalist side by Sinn Féin's demand that the RUC should be disbanded, the path was left open for constructive and rational consideration to be given to desirable developments in policing which would render the service, in the words of the Agreement, 'capable of attracting and sustaining support from the community as a whole'.

Indeed the participants in the Belfast Agreement had specified the features which policing structures and arrangements would need to display if support from the community as a whole were to be forthcoming:

> The participants believe it essential that policing structures and arrangements are such that the police service is professional, effective and efficient, fair and impartial, free from partisan control; accountable, both under the law for its actions and to the community it serves; representative of the society it polices, and operates within a coherent and cooperative criminal justice system which conforms with human rights norms. The participants also believe that these structures and arrangements must be capable of maintaining law and order including responding effectively to crime and to any terrorist threat and to public order problems … They believe that any such structures and arrangements should be capable of delivering a policing service, in constructive and inclusive partnerships with the community at all levels, and with the maximum delegation of authority and responsibility, consistent with the foregoing principles.

The Agreement then went on to stipulate the precise terms of reference of the commission of inquiry. By and large these fleshed out the desiderata just listed. They added, in particular, that the commission's proposals were to include *means* of encouraging widespread community support for the new arrangements, and that those arrangements should deal with matters such as composition, recruitment, training, culture, ethos and symbols (and also the retraining, job placement and educational and professional development required during the transition to policing in a peaceful society). The proposals were also to ensure that 'the legislative and constitutional framework requires the impartial discharge of policing functions and conforms with internationally accepted norms in relation to policing standards'. Finally, the terms of reference stipulated that the commission's proposals were to ensure that

> there are clearly established arrangements enabling local people, and their political representatives, to articulate their views and concerns about policing and to establish publicly policing priorities and influence policing policies, subject to safeguards to ensure police impartiality and freedom from partisan political control.

Past 'abuses'

The terms of reference of what became the Patten Commission bear the hallmarks of a rushed job. Several of their elements overlapped and in general they were very wordy; and, no doubt, several phrases were added at the behest of individual political parties. Significantly, one whole area of policing controversy was deliberately excluded from the terms of reference, namely, responsibility for alleged past abuses committed by police officers. Consonant with the whole tenor of the Belfast Agreement, there was no mechanism created for investigating or remedying real or perceived grievances involving the police's – or, indeed, anyone else's – past behaviour. Somehow, however, this simple fact was not adequately conveyed to members of the public. Thus, after the commission was established[5] and opportunities arose for people to make submissions to it or to meet with commissioners, a great deal of time was taken up in reciting the details of past incidents, only for the commissioners to reply that it was not part of their function to deal with such matters. When the commission's report was published,[6] the only reference to these alleged former abuses was in para. 1.6, which states that:

> we were not set up as a committee of inquiry with all the legal powers to call for papers and to interrogate witnesses. We were not charged with a quasi-legal investigation of the past. If there is a case for such inquiries, it is up to government to appoint them, not for us to rewrite our terms of reference. But we have naturally had to inform ourselves about past practice in order to propose future conduct.

Clearly the reason for raising such incidents with the commission was to stress that, to those submitting, the RUC was a discredited force. Many went on to argue that the force should therefore be disbanded, although some used their stories (personally hurtful though they were) simply to highlight the need for radical reform. At other meetings and in other submissions, the relatives of police officers who had been killed or injured in the Troubles told *their* stories, this time with a view to arguing that so many sacrifices had been made in the fight against terrorism that no changes at all should be made to the policing arrangements in Northern Ireland. For every call of 'Disband the RUC' there was at least one claiming that the RUC was the best police force in the world. The figure most frequently quoted, and one that does indeed deserve constant repetition, is that 302 serving officers were killed during the 30 years of the Troubles.[7]

Somehow the Patten Commission had to chart a course between these two positions. It did so, and rightly, by focusing on the future, not the past. It tried to establish mechanisms for ensuring that, if abuses *had* occurred, they could not occur in the future. It relied also on the work already done by Dr Maurice Hayes in his report 'A Police Ombudsman for Northern Ireland', which led to the inclusion in the Police (NI) Act 1998 of new provisions creating a completely independent system for investigating complaints against the police (the first of its kind in Europe).[8] And the commission further laid the foundation for a less controversial future to policing by placing at the forefront of its recommendations a commitment to ensuring that the police in Northern Ireland adhere closely to human rights standards. In its response to the Patten Report the British Government said that the commission was right to place much emphasis on human rights, but the secretary of state stressed that the Government's response was driven by respect for the sacrifices of the past as well as by the need to have a police service that was both representative and effective.

The human rights approach

Few human rights activists would have dared to predict that the Patten Report would give as much prominence as it did to human rights. Chapter 4 was devoted to the concept and made seven recommendations designed to entrench a human rights culture in the proposed new PSNI. The report called for 'a comprehensive programme of action to focus policing in Northern Ireland on a human rights-based approach' (para. 4.6); it said that this should be the philosophy of policing and inspire everything a police service did and it wanted every officer to perceive his or her job in terms of the protection of human rights (para. 4.13). The Patten Report then became more specific by recommending that a fresh oath[9] should be taken by all – new and existing – police officers, one which expressed an overt commitment to the upholding of human rights (para. 4.7). It called for a new code of ethics, integrating the European Convention on Human Rights (ECHR) within police practice (para. 4.8); moreover all codes of practice on aspects of policing were to be strictly in accordance with the ECHR (para. 4.8). All police officers, and police civilians, were to be trained (and brought up to date as required) in the fundamental principles and standards of human rights, and their practical implications for policing, and the human rights dimension was to be integrated with every module of police training (para. 4.9). Awareness of human rights issues and respect for human rights in the performance of duty was to become an important element in the appraisal of police officers (para. 4.10). At a more general level, Patten proposed that a human rights legal expert should be appointed to the staff of the police legal services (para. 4.11) and that the performance of the police as a whole with regard to human rights should be closely monitored by the new Policing Board, which was to replace the Police Authority, a body largely discredited because of its paucity of powers (para. 4.12).

Nearly all of these recommendations have been fully implemented, as is recorded by the periodic reports of the oversight commissioner, an official appointed to ensure that all of what Patten proposed was indeed carried into effect.[10] The PSNI has circulated (although not yet officially published) a Human Rights Implementation Plan endorsed by the Policing Board. The PSNI has also put in place a personnel appraisal system which incorporates a human rights component and the Policing Board has approved a scheme, prepared by its human rights adviser, for monitoring PSNI compliance with the Human Rights Act 1998. In the Police (NI) Act 2000 there is a provision requiring all new police officers to 'attest as a constable by making before a justice of the peace a declaration[11] but the requirement does not extend to existing officers – the secretary of state alluded to 'significant' (but unspecified) legal difficulties for this decision.[12] Instead the chief constable has been placed under a duty to take such steps as he considers necessary to bring the terms of the declaration to the attention of those officers and to ensure that they understand it and the need to carry out their duties in accordance with it (section 38(2)). All officers have, however, been obliged to receive human rights training (the Human Rights Commission has monitored this[13]), and from March 2003 they have been required, on pain of risking a charge that they have breached discipline, to behave in accordance with a statutory code of ethics which is solidly grounded in international human rights standards.[14] A human rights adviser was appointed to the PSNI in October 2001.[15]

Other chapters in the Patten Report are peppered with references to human rights. The non-political members of the Policing Board were to include someone from the field of human rights (para. 6.12): the members have of course now been appointed, although it is not clear which of them is from the human rights field. New legislation on covert policing was to comply with the ECHR (para. 6.43) and this was achieved through the passing (for the UK as a whole) of the Regulation of Investigatory Powers Act 2000. *As a matter of priority* all members of the police service were to be instructed in the implications of the Universal Declaration of Human Rights 1948 and of the Human Rights Act 1998, the Act which, from 2 October 2000, made the ECHR part of the law throughout the UK (para. 16.21): this was achieved through a comprehensive training programme which was evaluated (not wholly positively) by the Human Rights Commission.[16] The oversight commissioner, moreover, has complained that the PSNI has not yet provided enough information to allow him to verify and evaluate actual progress with human rights training.[17]

Much more important than the rhetoric of human rights is the practice thereof. In order to assess whether the Patten Report, and the Government's response to it, has ensured that the practice of policing will adhere to appropriate human rights standards we need to consider in more detail some of the issues covered by the report. The account which follows deals with three of the more important of these: the membership of the new service; the accountability of the new service; and the legal powers of the new service.

Membership

The PSNI replaced the RUC on 4 November 2001, although as a concession to unionists the official title of the new service was stated by statute to be 'the Police Service of Northern Ireland (incorporating the Royal Ulster Constabulary)'.[18] The recruitment[19] and training[20] of new officers began almost immediately, and the first batch of students to graduate as probationary constables did so in April 2002. Just after the establishment of the PSNI the chief constable, Sir Ronnie Flanagan, announced that he would retire from his post within a few months, and indeed he left at the end of March 2002. Mr Colin Cramphorn served as the acting chief constable for six months before the appointment of Mr Hugh Orde, a deputy commander in the Metropolitan Police who was handling the day-to-day running of the Stevens Inquiry into the murder of solicitor Patrick Finucane in 1989.[21]

Within a month of taking up his post Mr Orde had to issue a public apology for the manner in which his officers had conducted themselves when carrying out a search of Sinn Féin's offices at the Stormont Assembly. The discovery of incriminating material during that and related searches led, of course, to the British Government announcing the suspension of the Assembly on 14 October 2002. In January 2003 the plain-speaking chief constable was again in the news for apparently intimating, in a speech in Washington, DC, that not all of his senior officers were supportive of the changes initiated by the Patten Report. Later in the year he again courted controversy when he claimed to have insufficient resources to deal with current crime, let alone to deal with all the unsolved killings from the past; this has in turn prompted suggestions from various other quarters, including the secretary of state and the chairman of the Policing Board, that some kind of Truth Commission should be established in Northern Ireland.

Another important aspect of the membership question is how to ensure that Catholics are proportionally represented in the new PSNI. There is little disagreement over the need for such proportional representation, given that in 1999 only 7 per cent of RUC officers were Catholics.[22] But there continues to be considerable disagreement over how to rectify the imbalance. The Patten Report made the controversial recommendation that for at least a 10-year period an equal number of Protestants and Catholics be drawn from the pool of qualified candidates for the service: it envisaged that 370 officers would be recruited each year, 185 of whom would be Catholic and 185 'Protestant or undetermined'. This proposal was eventually reflected in section 46 of the Police (NI) Act 2000, which also made the necessary amendments to existing anti-discrimination laws to permit such 'positive' discrimination. The Government, with the support of the Irish, even secured a specific exemption for this provision in the EU's contemporaneous Framework Directive on Employment Equality. According to section 47 of the Police (NI) Act the scheme was to have a life of only three years, but could be renewed for a further such period by order of the secretary of state. A renewal order has now been made. In fact, the scheme may need to be prolonged on several future occasions, since the proportion of Catholic officers in the PSNI (on 1 September 2003) was still just 13.3 per cent, though approximately 36 per cent of all applicants to the Police Service since November 2001 have been Catholics.

Some on the unionist side argue that the 50:50 recruitment system is making it more difficult for the police to fight crime, since there are not enough officers available to do so. But the reality is that any shortfall in manpower is due not to the new recruitment system (which in fact takes in around 540 new officers each year) but to the generous severance scheme which the Government authorised for the RUC. A large number of experienced officers left the RUC with a good financial package and there are now some 1,400 fewer police officers in Northern Ireland than before the Belfast Agreement. Such was the effect on the PSNI's ability to solve crimes that in June 2003 an exception had to be made to the 50:50 recruitment system (in line with a provision inserted into the Police (NI) Act 2003) to allow the recruitment of 65 detectives, of whatever denomination, from police forces elsewhere. Noting that there were approximately 145 vacancies for detective constables at the time, which is about 25 per cent of the establishment figure, the chairman of the Policing Board, Professor Desmond Rea, said: 'There is no doubt that the loss of experienced Detectives as a result of the severance scheme has had a serious impact on the PSNI's ability to tackle crime'. A new Crime Operations Department has been created, headed by Assistant Chief Constable San Kinkaid, which has a unit called the Serious Crime Review Team that reviews murder investigations, including some of those from pre-Agreement days. Prior to taking up this role Mr Kinkaid was, among other things, the PSNI's 'human rights champion', a post now held by Assistant Chief Constable Judith Gillespie. Even the SDLP members of the Policing Board went along with this. Unionists (and APNI) believe that the 50:50 recruitment system is a breach of fundamental human rights. The Northern Ireland HRC, the Equality Commission and even the Court of Appeal (ruling in a test case[23]) disagree: they think it is justifiable affirmative action, and not therefore unlawful discrimination.

In October 2002 the Policing Board and the PSNI launched a new human resource strategy, dealing with issues such as the civilianisation of posts, the management of sickness levels and the appointment of part-time officers. It also provides for the retention of the PSNI's Full-Time Reserve until April 2005, after which date it will be phased out over an eighteen-month period.[24] The position of chief superintendent has also been recreated in the PSNI.[25] The implementation of the human resource strategy is monitored by Sir Dan Crompton, a former inspector of constabulary, and he presents quarterly reports to the Policing Board. Sickness levels are now falling, while application numbers for new posts remain at around 13:1. In October 2003 the Policing Board also endorsed the PSNI's new 'tenure of post policy', which is designed to ensure that officers do not become so highly specialised that they lose the capability to undertake 'core policing duties' during their career. Under this new policy, the minimum period that can be spent in any post will be 3 years and the maximum 7 years, officers spending at least 3 years in neighbourhood policing posts. The first transfers under this new policy will take effect during 2006.

Patten noted that to date the RUC has had stricter criteria for admission than other police services in the UK: for instance, relatively minor criminal records had disqualified applicants. No actual figures, however, were provided on how many applicants had been turned down on this basis. The Patten Report recommended in this regard that the existing admission criteria[26] should be relaxed a little:

We emphatically do not suggest that people with serious criminal or terrorist backgrounds should be considered for police service but we do recommend that young people should not be automatically disqualified for relatively minor criminal offences, particularly if they have since had a number of years without further transgressions, and that the criteria on this aspect of eligibility should be the same as those in the rest of the United Kingdom. We also recommend that there should be a procedure for appeal to the Police Ombudsman against disqualification of candidates. (paragraph 15.13)

Consistent with its stance on not making judgements about alleged past human rights abuses perpetrated by police officers, the report made no mention of whether any currently serving police officers should be disqualified from appointment to the new PSNI because of their personal histories. Obviously there should have been no serving officers who had a serious criminal or terrorist background, for any officers convicted of such offences would have been dismissed from the force; but there may have been serving officers who had been tried and acquitted of such offences, or accused or suspected but not tried. On the one hand it could be argued that those officers should not be treated any less generously that non-police officers with such a background: if the latter can be eligible for the new PSNI then so should the former – the principle against double jeopardy would require no less.[27] On the other hand it could be said that the system for bringing serving police officers to justice for crimes they have committed has historically been so flawed, and the conviction rate – in cases where prosecutions or disciplinary charges *were* brought – so low, that like is not being compared with like. In support of this second position one can cite the facts that, until the creation of the Police Ombudsman's Office in November 2000, crimes allegedly committed by the police had always been investigated by the police themselves, that case-hardening among judges is inclined to make them believe the word of a police officer over that of an accuser of a police officer and that, until the relevant regulations were recently changed,[28] the standard of proof required to be met in police disciplinary hearings was so high as to make it almost impossible to have a complaint upheld (quite apart from the fact that the persons adjudicating on the complaint were, again, fellow-police officers – an anomaly which *still* exists).

There seems to be no easy answer to this conundrum. Much may depend on the extent to which careful records have been maintained of police officers' career histories. If those files still show that Officer X was suspected of offence Y at some point during the Troubles, but was never formally charged or convicted, then it may be possible, and even desirable, provided the offence in question was a serious one involving death or more than a minor injury, for a specially convened panel to review the files in order to consider whether there is anything there which demonstrates clearly (even if not beyond a reasonable doubt, the criminal standard of proof) that the officer lacks the requisite degree of commitment to human rights which Patten is now calling for. The position of officers whose actions led to the Police Authority paying out sums in compensation to victims of those actions would be particularly vulnerable under this system: they may have escaped any disciplinary sanction prior to or at the time of the civil suit because they were not proved to have breached the code of discipline, but they could still be said to have been responsible for the actions in question. Of course many compensatory sums were paid not because the Police Authority was admitting liability but because it wished to settle the case in order to avoid further legal costs, the scandal of a court hearing or adverse publicity. In those cases the officer involved could usually *not* be shown to be legally responsible for what he or she did.

All in all, however, the chances of excluding from the new PSNI former RUC officers who have in the past been aberrant, but not found guilty of, or liable for, any crime or breach of discipline, are slim. To be equitable, any screening process applied to such officers would also have to be applied to other potential recruits: the argument that they, unlike serving police officers, are not coming from an environment in which commitment to human rights should already have been a prerequisite for the job holds no water because respect for human rights should be a *sine qua non* in every environment. Perhaps the best that can be hoped for at this stage, given that no political party seems to be campaigning against the continuance in service of former RUC officers who have a bad reputation, is that all members of the new PSNI will be required not just to make a declaration affirming their commitment to human rights but to demonstrate at an interview, or in some form of psychometric test, how committed they are to the protection of human rights – including the human rights of *criminals*. The Government, in its response to the Patten Report, stated categorically that 'there will be no question whatever of ex-terrorists joining the service',[29] but no mention was made of what would happen to those existing police officers who have a dubious past. A working group was established within the RUC to examine this aspect of eligibility. Its report was not made public (the HRC asked to see a copy, even on a confidential basis, but was refused), but apparently it did not specifically address the question of what to do with so-called 'bad-apple' officers. The latest regulations amend only slightly the ineligibility criteria operating prior to Patten: anyone convicted in Northern Ireland or elsewhere of any offence for which he or she has been given a sentence of imprisonment or detention, whether or not suspended, remains ineligible, but in most other cases a criminal conviction ceases to disqualify an applicant if five years have elapsed since it was imposed.[30]

One further dimension of elegibility for the new PSNI deserves discussion. Patten recommended that there should be no ban on officers being members of any legal organisation, provided it was clear that an officer's primary and overriding loyalty was to the values of the PSNI. The Patten Commission added, however, that all officers should be required to register their interests and associations, and that the register should be held both by the PSNI and by the Police Ombudsman (but should not be made available for public inspection). To many, this part of the Patten Report did not go far enough. In particular, they argued that there is a fundamental inconsistency between simultaneous membership of the Loyal Orders and of the PSNI. Such a stance is, however, flawed on two counts. First, it attributes to *all* members of the Loyal Orders the undoubted excesses which *some* reprobate members of those orders have committed, suggesting that mere membership of such groups automatically means that one is unable to lead a blameless life. Second, it confuses denominational commitment with professional commitment, implying that if someone holds a religious belief which is avowedly anti-Catholic he or she will be professionally unable to police the Catholic population in an impartial way. That is like saying that a lawyer with certain religious beliefs cannot properly represent a person with different beliefs, or that a teacher, doctor or social worker could not put his or her personal religious views out of mind when dealing in a professional capacity with individuals and groups holding different beliefs. In August 2003 the PSNI announced that a Register of Notifiable Memberships was being established, but no regulations have yet been issued to give effect to this. The PSNI stipulates that the information registered can be used only for very specific purposes; the register's operation will be monitored by the Policing Board as part of its overall responsibility for the code of ethics.

Accountability

The Patten Report contained many proposals for improving both the democratic and the legal accountability of the police. The former turned on the proposed Policing Board and the District Policing Partnerships (DPPs), on which no fewer than thirty recommendations were pronounced. These bodies were in due course established, the Policing Board in November 2001[31] and the DPPs in March 2003.[32] Within two months, and despite being a highly politicised entity (even without the presence of Sinn Féin representatives), the Policing Board had agreed a new emblem for the PSNI, incorporating six symbols – scales of justice, a harp, a torch, a sprig of flax, a shamrock leaf and a crown. Within a further few weeks, however, the Policing Board was rocked by the Police Ombudsman's report on the RUC's investigation of the Omagh bomb in 1998 (see below). After considering the report the board issued a set of recommendations to the PSNI and appointed three senior officials to prepare further reports. One of those officials was Sir Dan Crompton, who besides reporting on human resources was asked to review how intelligence information was handled by the PSNI's Special Branch and how it was shared with other parts of the PSNI; he reported in November 2002. Deputy Chief Constable Tonge, from the Merseyside Police, was asked to monitor how the PSNI was implementing the board's more general recommendations resulting from the Ombudsman's report; he reported in April 2003. Mr David Blakey, of Her Majesty's Inspectorate of Constabulary, was asked to examine how the PSNI conducted murder investigations; he reported in June 2003. It can be said that the Policing Board reacted professionally and efficiently to the implications of the Ombudsman's report on Omagh, which is more than some would say of the response of Sir Ronnie Flanagan at the time.

To date, in accordance with statute, the Policing Board has issued two annual policing plans and published two annual reports.[33] It is dissatisfied with the detection rate for violent crime (which at 55 per cent in 2002–3 was more than 9 per cent short of target) but happier with the PSNI's work on road crime. The Policing Board has given the green light to the construction of a new Police Training College in Cookstown, established (although only in August 2003) a Human Rights and Professional Standards Committee, chaired by SDLP MP Eddie McGrady, engaged the services of a top London QC[34] to assist with the production and implementation of a Human Rights Monitoring Framework for the PSNI,[35] overseen the establishment of 29 DPPs[36] and approved the purchase by the PSNI of 6 water cannon and CS incapacitant sprays.

The board has also conducted public opinion surveys about the PSNI and itself. A survey published in November 2002 showed that 71 per cent of the people interviewed thought that the Policing Board was working adequately, well or very well; in July 2003 it was demonstrated that for the first time more than 50 per cent of Catholics believed that the police treated everyone equally; and in December 2003 yet another survey found that 79 per cent of the people of Northern Ireland had confidence in the police. An evaluation of the work of the Policing Board was published by a non-governmental human rights organisation in October 2003[37] and the chairman of the board announced that the report would be presented to the next meeting of its Corporate Policy Committee.[38] The evaluation concludes that the board needs to make 'a number of very important changes in the way it operates if it is to improve its ability to comply with its statutory responsibility to hold the Police Service to account', and it goes on to make twenty-one recommendations to that end. One of these is that the board should 'build up its internal capacity to monitor the human rights performance of the police by attending appropriate human rights training and developing the skills necessary to fulfil this important function'.[39]

The DPPs have not yet had time to embed themselves in the policing culture of Northern Ireland. Several nationalist members have been severely intimidated by dissident republican paramilitaries, and one or two have resigned as a result. In establishing the DPPs the Government declined to empower them to purchase 'community safety services' on top of normal policing, for fear, it is alleged, that such services would become dominated by local paramilitary factions.[40] The role of the DPPs overlaps to some extent with that of the Community Safety Partnerships, which also exist in every district council area in Northern Ireland. Whether these attempts to involve local lay people in the policing of their own areas will make policing more effective, and the police more generally acceptable, remains to be seen.

It is worth remembering that lay people also serve as visitors to 'custody suites' in designated police stations in Northern Ireland and that since 1992 there has been a non-statutory official now known as the 'independent commissioner for detained terrorist suspects'.[41] Her Majesty's Inspectorate of Constabulary also carries out annual inspections of the PSNI, focusing on different matters each time. The latest published report, covering the 2001–2 inspection, states that the continued reduction in the number of officers available for deployment to operational duties has had a significant impact on the PSNI's attempts to achieve its policing objectives and confirms that the PSNI, as a whole, is failing to deliver the community policing service articulated in the Patten Report and expected by the public.[42] The newly created Inspectorate of Criminal Justice in Northern Ireland, expected to be fully operational by October 2004, will also be able to inspect the PSNI, but by statute Chief Inspector Mr Kit Chivers must not carry out inspections of an organisation 'if he is satisfied that the organisation is subject to adequate inspection by someone other than him'.[43] It remains to be seen whether the chief inspector will consider the HMI inspections to be 'adequate'.

The one aspect of democratic accountability which is less well analysed in the Patten Report is the scope of the chief constable's so-called 'operational independence' (paras. 6.19–23). The Patten Commission had been urged by, among others, the Police Authority and the Committee on the Administration of Justice (a non-governmental human rights organisation) to suggest a statutory definition of operational independence, as a way of delimiting the chief constable's freedom of action. But the commission preferred to redefine the problem rather than the concept:

> The arguments involved in support of 'operational independence' – that it minimises the risk of political influence and that it properly imposes on the Chief Constable the burden of taking decisions on matters about which only he or she has all the facts and expertise needed – are powerful arguments, but they support a case not for 'independence' but for 'responsibility'. We strongly prefer the term 'operational responsibility' to the term 'operational independence'.

The problem with this approach is that it addresses the chief constable's accountability only *ex post facto*. It requires the chief constable's conduct of an operational matter to be susceptible to inquiry or review after the event (para. 6.21), while leaving the chief constable free to decide, in advance of an operation, how exactly it should be conducted. Yet that is precisely where the difficulties have arisen in the past in Northern Ireland. Operational decisions have been taken with little or no external involvement and such scrutiny as has been allowed has been retrospective. In many instances, if independent voices had been allowed to have their say as to how the operation should be conducted, there would have been much less need for detailed scrutiny after the event. No one would seriously suggest that political majorities should be allowed to dictate to senior police officers how to conduct their business, but the range of perspectives represented, say, on the Policing Board would surely be worth taking into account – so far as it is practicable to do so – before an important operational decision is taken. One of the key consequences of the 1997 North Report on the holding of parades in Northern Ireland was the removal from the police of the responsibility for deciding whether a parade should be allowed to go ahead along a certain route, or at all. This depoliticisation of the police has generally been considered to be a sensible idea.[44]

As regards legal accountability, Patten made great play of the Office of the Police Ombudsman. He recommended, rightly, that that office needed to be fully

staffed and resourced, that its role should be to take the initiative as well as to react
to complaints, that it should compile data on trends and patterns in complaints
against the police, and should investigate police policies and practices even if the
conduct of officers were not itself culpable, and that access should be granted to all
past reports on the RUC (including, presumably, the controversial Stalker–Sampson
and Stevens reports[45]). As a result of these recommendations changes to the statutory powers of the Ombudsman were made by the Police (NI) Acts 2000 and
2003.[46]

The Ombudsman's Office has been fully operational since November 2000
and has produced a number of important reports.[47] The most controversial has
been that into the way in which the RUC investigated the Omagh bomb of August
1998; in this the Ombudsman accused chief constable Sir Ronnie Flanagan of a
failure of leadership. In other reports the Ombudsman has said that the use of
plastic baton rounds by officers was justified in the particular circumstances of the
cases examined, that police in Northern Ireland make excessive use of their batons,
that there are many allegations by practising lawyers that they have been intimidated, harassed or threatened by police officers,[48] and that RUC investigations into
the deaths of Samuel Devenney in 1969 and Sean Brown in 1997 were seriously
flawed.

Patten failed to mention two other crucial aspects of police complaints. One is
that, unless the standard of proof required for a finding of guilt in a disciplinary hearing
is reduced from that of 'beyond reasonable doubt' to something approaching 'on the
balance of probabilities' it will continue to be well-nigh impossible to achieve such
findings. The appalling record as regards complaints made by persons arrested
under the emergency laws in Northern Ireland speaks for itself in this context (from
1995 to 1998 only 2 out of 466 complaints led to charges of any kind being laid
against police officers[49]). The other is that, even with the office of the Police
Ombudsman fully operational, there are still cases where allegations of criminal
behaviour against police officers – those not resulting from a complaint by a member of the public – will be investigated by the police themselves, unless the Police
Ombudsman calls in its independent investigators *as a matter of public interest*.[50]
Such cases could range over matters such as corruption, fraud, physical abuse,
extortion, domestic violence, etc. There is a strong argument for insisting that the
responsibility for *all* criminal investigations against police officers be transferred
automatically to completely independent investigators.

Police powers

The controversy over how to formulate the legal accountability of the police in
Northern Ireland is perhaps best examined within the context of the exercise of two
contentious police powers – the power to use firearms and the power to use plastic
bullets.[51] Surprisingly, Patten says next to nothing about the use of firearms, merely
that there should be a periodic review of whether it is possible to move towards a
routinely unarmed police service (paras. 8.17 –20). He does not point to the apparent

inconsistency between the law in Northern Ireland on when police officers can use lethal force and the law as stated in the ECHR. On plastic bullets he concludes that they should not be immediately withdrawn but that better controls should be placed on their use, that research should be conducted to find a more acceptable alternative and that a range of other public order equipment should be supplied to the police so that a commander has more options from which to choose. While there is something to be said for the retention of plastic bullets as a weapon of last resort, given the police's inadequate defences against petrol-bombs and blast-bombs in such situations – indeed, that has been the policy of the Government pending the production of a less lethal alternative[52] – there is little excuse for the omission by Patten of any reference to the various international standards on the use of firearms. The UN's Basic Principles on the Use of Force and Firearms by Law Enforcement Officials, adopted by the UN Congress on the Prevention of Crime and the Treatment of Offenders in 1990, is particularly apposite here, but also relevant are the UN's Principles on the Effective Prevention and Investigation of Extra-Legal, Arbitrary and Summary Executions, a set of recommendations issued by the Economic and Social Council in 1989. Basic Principle 9 of the 1990 document, for example, specifies that 'intentional lethal use of firearms may only be made when strictly unavoidable in order to protect life'. Fortunately, this principle is at least partly reflected in the new code of ethics in force since March 2003.

It was regrettable that the Patten Report did not contain a deeper analysis of the impact of the emergency laws on policing practices in Northern Ireland. Even without delving into alleged past abuses of those laws, the commission could have examined the potential under the current emergency laws for abuse and for infection of the prevailing police culture. There is an undeniable link between perceptions of the RUC within the nationalist community and the fact that that community has been severely affected by the operation of the emergency laws through the police's powers to stop, search, arrest and detain. The unionist community has been affected too, but not to the same extent, either quantitatively or qualitatively. Patten did recommend the closure of the holding centres in Northern Ireland, which had no statutory basis anyway (para. 8.15), and the keeping of records for all stops and searches, and other such actions, taken under emergency laws. Those reforms have now been brought about. It is unfortunate, however, that the Patten Report did not recommend the repeal, or at any rate the suspension, of many of the other emergency laws. To maintain them during periods of ceasefires, even ones as tenuous as those currently in place, is quite possibly a breach of Article 15 of the European Convention, which tolerates such laws only if there is 'a public emergency threatening the life of the nation'. Of course the Terrorism Act 2000, and the even more draconian Anti-Terrorism, Crime and Security Act 2001, have ensured that severe anti-terrorist measures are to be a permanent feature of the landscape throughout the UK. In supporting the annual renewal of Part 7 of the 2000 Act – the part creating additional anti-terrorism measures specifically for Northern Ireland – the Government has repeatedly asserted that there is no question of removing these from the statute book unless and until in the assessment of the chief constable there is a stable security environment.

Conclusion

Policing remains just about the most crucial element in the political settlement proposed for Northern Ireland. If the new PSNI is to gain the kind of broad community support for which the framers of the Belfast Agreement were hoping, it must display both a deep theoretical commitment and a practicable commitment to human rights. It must at the same time be conscious of its statutory duties to have due regard both to the promotion of equality of opportunity between different sectors of society in Northern Ireland and to the desirability of promoting good relations between those sectors characterised by religion, race or politics.[53] While the PSNI is already clearly some way down the road to transforming itself into one of the most human rights-compliant police services in the world, it must be careful not to relax its commitment to that goal.

Notes

When he wrote this chapter Brice Dickson was chief commissioner of the Northern Ireland Human Rights Commission, but he has written in a personal capacity. The views expressed are the author's alone and should not be taken necessarily as representing the views of the Commission.

1 For a good explanation of how the Agreement was arrived at and a summary of what it says, see J. Ruane and J. Todd, 'The Belfast Agreement: Context, Content, Consequences', in J. Ruane and J. Todd (eds), *After the Good Friday Agreement: Analysing Political Change in Northern Ireland* (Dublin: University College Dublin Press, 1999).

2 This was referred to a Criminal Justice Review Panel, chaired by an NIO official, but with external advisers attached to it. It was due to report in the autumn of 1999 but did not do so until March 2000.

3 A task allocated to the new Northern Ireland Human Rights Commission: see the Northern Ireland Act 1998, section 69(7).

4 Through a statement to the House of Commons by Secretary of State for Northern Ireland Peter Mandelson: see House of Commons Debates, 19 January 2000, cols 845–8.

5 The chair of the Commission was Mr Chris Patten, formerly governor of Hong Kong and an ex-Cabinet minister. The seven other members were Dr Maurice Hayes (a former ombudsman for Northern Ireland), Dr Gerald Lynch (president of the John Jay College of Criminal Justice in New York), Mrs Kathleen O'Toole (a former secretary for public safety in Massachusetts), Professor Clifford Shearing (professor of criminology and sociology at the University of Toronto and also a professor at the University of the Western Cape, South Africa), Sir John Smith (a former inspector of constabulary in the UK), Mr Peter Smith (a QC in Northern Ireland) and Mrs Lucy Woods (then chief executive of British Telecom in Northern Ireland).

6 *A New Beginning: Policing in Northern Ireland. A Report of the Independent Commission on Policing in Northern Ireland* (Belfast and London: HMSO, 1999), hereinafter the Patten Report.

7 The circumstances surrounding each of the deaths are vividly described by C. Ryder, *The RUC: A Force Under Fire*, 2nd edn. (London: Methuen, 2000).

8 Sections 50–65. The Police Ombudsman – Mrs Nuala O'Loan – was appointed in October 1999. Her office began receiving complaints in November 2000.

9 The Patten Report refers to an oath but in fact RUC officers made a declaration.

10 Police (NI) Act 2000, section 67 and Sch. 4. The 9th Report of the Office of the Oversight Commissioner was published in December 2003. Tom Constantine served as the commissioner until 31 December 2003, when he was succeeded by Al Hutchinson.

11 *Ibid.*, section 38(1). The declaration is: 'I hereby do solemnly and sincerely and truly declare and affirm that I will faithfully discharge the duties of the office of constable, with fairness, integrity, diligence and impartiality, upholding fundamental human rights and according equal respect to all individuals and their traditions and beliefs; and that while I continue to hold the said office I will to the best of my skill and knowledge discharge all the duties thereof according to law.'

12 House of Commons Debates, 19 January 2000, col. 846.

13 Mark Kelly, *An Evaluation of Human Rights Training for Student Police Officers in the Police Service of Northern Ireland* (Belfast: NIHRC, November 2002). Two further evaluations, of the human rights training given to probationary police officers and of the so-called 'Course for All', are to be published by the HRC in March 2004.

14 After a lengthy and effective consultation process the code of ethics was publicly launched by the Policing Board in February 2003. It became binding on police officers by virtue of the PSNI (Conduct) Regulations 2003, SR 68, which amend the pre-existing regulations, including the RUC (Unsatisfactory Performance) Regulations 2000, SR 316.

15 This is Andrea Hopkins, a barrister and an expert on the ECHR.

16 *Report on the RUC's Training on the Human Rights Act 1998* (November 2000), available at: www.nihrc.org. It is worth noting that the PSNI has agreed a Memorandum of Understanding with the HRC in order to facilitate interaction; the Police Ombudsman's office has done likewise, but the Policing Board has not so far seen the need.

17 9th Report (December 2003), p. 15.

18 Police (NI) Act 2000, section 1(1). The PSNI maintains a good website at www.psni.police.uk. It has a section on human rights, which explains how a Human Rights Unit was set up to help prepare for the introduction of the Human Rights Act 1998.

19 See the Police (Recruitment) (NI) Regulations 2001, SR 140, as amended by SR 2002/385 and SR 2004/1 and supplemented by the PSNI (Recruitment of Police Support Staff) Regulations 2002, SR 258.

20 See the Police Trainee Regulations (NI) 2001, SR 369.

21 There was a breach of confidentiality surrounding the appointment process for which the Policing Board issued a public apology: Press Statement, 21 June 2002.

22 For the history of how this came to be the case see C. Ryder, *The Fateful Split* (London: Methuen, 2004).

23 *In re Mark Parsons*, 6 June 2003 [2003] NICA 20.

24 For the rules governing part-time reserve officers see the PSNI Reserve (Part-Time) Regulations 2004, SR 3.

25 PSNI (Amendment) Regulations 2003, SR 184.

26 As enshrined in the RUC Regulations 1996, SR 473.

27 One of the recommendations of the Macpherson Inquiry into the murder of Stephen Lawrence was that the principle of double jeopardy should be reformulated so as to allow for second trials if new evidence is forthcoming which might have led to a finding of guilt at the first trial: Cmnd. 4262–I (1999), para. 7.46. The Law Commission issued a Consultation Paper (No. 156) on the subject later in 1999 but provisionally recommended rejection of the Macpherson suggestion. However Part 10 of the Criminal Justice Act 2003 reforms the law in England and Wales partly along the lines of Macpherson's proposal. No such change has yet been made to the law of Northern Ireland.

28 See RUC (Conduct) Regulations 2000, SR 315, reg. 23(4), which requires proof on the balance of probabilities only.

29 House of Commons Debates, 19 January 2000, col. 847.

30 Police (Recruitment) (NI) Regulations 2001, SR 140, Sch. 1. reg. 12 sets up a 'vetting panel' to assess difficult cases and reg. 13 provides for an independent assessor to review decisions of the vetting panel.

31 See sections 2–13 and Sch. 1 of the Police (NI) Act 2000 and sections 3–9 of the Police (NI) Act 2003.

32 See sections 14–19 and Sch. 3 of the Police (NI) Act 2000 and sections 14–19 and Sch. 1 of the Police (NI) Act 2003. There remains a difficulty with the South Tyrone and Dungannon District Council DPP: the council is refusing to allow community background to influence its selection of candidates for the Policing Board's approval.

33 For further details of the board's activities, and copies of all its press releases, see its website: www.nipolicingboard.org.uk

34 Keir Starmer, the author of a leading textbook on the Human Rights Act 1998.

35 The Framework was issued in December 2003.

36 But see note 32, above.

37 Committee on the Administration of Justice (CAJ), *Commentary on the Northern Ireland Policing Board* (Belfast; CAJ, 2003).

38 Press Release, 31 October 2003.

39 Human Rights Monitoring Framework, p. 10.

40 House of Commons Debates, 19 January 2000, col. 846.

41 In his latest published report the commissioner, Dr Bill Norris, indicates that 236 terrorist suspects were detained in Northern Ireland during 2002, of whom he was able to visit 170.

42 The 2002 inspection report is available at: www.homeoffice.gov.uk/hmic/hmic.htm

43 Justice (NI) Act 2002, section 46(2).

44 The Quigley Report on the Parades Commission (2002) suggested that the police should be given back the responsibility for deciding whether public order requirements should dictate the re-routing of a parade, but this has met with little support. The Northern Ireland HRC, for example, has come out against such a proposal.

45 The Stalker–Sampson Reports concern allegations of a shoot-to-kill policy on the part of the RUC; the Stevens Reports (1 and 2) deal with allegations of collusion between the police and loyalist paramilitary organisations.

46 Sections 62–6 and 13, respectively.

47 These are available on the Police Ombudsman's website: www.policeombudsman.org

48 Office of the NI Police Ombudsman (ONIP), *A Study of the Treatment of Solicitors and Barristers by the Police in Northern Ireland*, Research Report 01/2003 (Belfast: ONIP, March 2003). Of 2,834 lawyers contacted, 4 barristers and 51 solicitors reported that 'at some time' they had been a victim of this form of treatment.

49 Source: Annual Reports of the Independent Commission for Police Complaints.

50 Police (NI) Act 1998, section 55(6).

51 For a useful account of the international standards relevant to this field see R. Crawshaw, B. Devlin and T. Williamson, *Human Rights and Policing* (The Hague: Kluwer Law International, 1998), especially chs 7 and 8.

52 The 4th Report of the Steering Group set up after Patten to examine alternative policing approaches to the management of conflict was published in January 2004 (it is available on the Government's website at: www.nio.gov.uk). The report suggests that an 'attenuating energy projectile' should be ready for use before the summer of 2005.

53 By section 75 of the Northern Ireland Act 1998.

12

The totality of relationships?
The British–Irish Council[1]

PHILIP LYNCH AND STEPHEN HOPKINS

The British–Irish Council (BIC) is a Strand Three institution in the Belfast (Multi-Party) Agreement and the British–Irish Agreement of 10 April 1998, its task being to 'promote the harmonious and mutually beneficial development of the totality of relationships among the people of these islands'.[2] Its members are the British and Irish governments, the devolved administrations in Northern Ireland, Scotland and Wales, plus the three crown dominions of the Isle of Man, Jersey and Guernsey.

The BIC is a novel and distinctive body, given its functions (from the exchange of information to common policies and actions in a range of policy areas), scope (the 'totality of relationships') and membership (sovereign governments, devolved administrations and crown dominions). It provides an institutional expression of the changing relationships within these islands: a British–Irish relationship no longer exclusively focused on London; intergovernmental relations in a post-devolution UK; and a new institutional architecture in Northern Ireland. Some supporters depicted the BIC as a *post-sovereign* institution that reflected the demise of the unitary state and the fluidity of identities within the islands.[3] But the UUP, early proponents of the BIC, argued that it preserved state sovereignty and located relations between Northern Ireland and the Republic firmly within a 'British Isles' context. Both agreed that it would encourage and provide a focus for emerging patterns of governance, and promote the sharing of ideas and policy models in areas of mutual interest.

The BIC has made limited progress, holding only five summit meetings and producing few concrete outputs, though it has started to establish a critical momentum. By stepping up its activity during the suspension of the assembly and the executive, the BIC may also be in the process of moving beyond the Northern Ireland context in which it originated.

The origins of the BIC

The intellectual dynamic for the creation of the BIC, as an integral part of a Northern Ireland settlement, was provided by scholars like Richard Kearney and Simon Partridge. Kearney developed a *post-national* framework for the evolution of relationships between governments, legislatures and peoples in Britain and Ireland, proposing a 'Council of Islands of Britain and Ireland' modelled on the Nordic Council.[4] Partridge also advocated the Nordic model, and focused on the myriad personal and cultural relationships within these islands.[5]

In the Northern Ireland talks, the roots of the BIC lie within the UUP and David Trimble's enthusiasm for a 'Council of the British Isles'. Trimble first articulated the idea in the 1975 Ulster Loyalist Co-ordinating Committee publication 'Ulster Unfettered', and returned to it in the 1988 'What Choice for Ulster?' pamphlet in which he was critical of a weak, power-sharing Northern Ireland Assembly.[6] In the Brooke–Mayhew talks of 1991–93, Trimble was part of the UUP team on east–west issues and tried to make headway with the idea, but other members of his party were sceptical as devolution in the rest of the UK seemed unlikely, while Ken Maginnis feared that it would give Dublin greater influence in London.[7] Trimble's view won out, however, and the UUP's 1995 'Statement of Aims' called for the creation of a Council of the British Isles that would facilitate joint action on issues of common interest. It would have a flexible structure and would include government ministers and national, regional or locally elected representatives, according to the issues under discussion. Dermot Nesbitt's paper 'Unionism Restated' elaborated, stating that 'political or constitutional aspects' should not be considered within this forum, discussions being confined to 'policies that are mutually beneficial in social, cultural or commercial terms'.[8] The ground rules for the 1996–98 negotiations included within their remit 'relationships ... between the peoples of these islands', and 'new institutions and structures to take account of the totality of relationships'.[9] The UUP formally introduced its proposals for a Council of the British Isles in the talks in October 1997.

By then, the UDP also had issued proposals for a similar body.[10] Its leader Gary McMichael introduced the idea into the Brooke–Mayhew talks process, arguing that local councillors meeting regularly across the UK could 'offer a novel and effective means of co-operation between all our peoples (without the constitutional overtones of other projects). Such a body could be a powerful pressure group within the EC on social, economic and environmental matters.'[11] As with other unionists, the UDP envisaged the body as 'an all-encompassing mechanism to deal with the totality of relationships throughout the islands, within which the North–South relationships could exist in the appropriate context'.[12] But the UDP failed to win seats in the 1998 elections to the Northern Ireland Assembly and was dissolved in 2001.

The two governments directly negotiated Strand Three matters, but consulted with the political parties. In the January 1998 Propositions on Heads of Agreement, the British and Irish governments proposed a new British–Irish Agreement establishing an east–west intergovernmental council and a North–South Ministerial Council (NSMC) which would 'operate independently in their designated areas of responsibility'.[13] Dublin had rejected British proposals that included a Council of the Isles but not a freestanding executive North–South body. Trimble continued to insist that arrangements with the Republic should be part of the larger east–west whole, with North–South meetings taking place within the Council of the British Isles framework.[14] But this stress on the primacy of the council represented a bargaining position from which, the UUP recognised, some retreat would be necessary. It also enabled the party to claim that it was shaping the talks agenda. Unionist hopes that the council would become a focus for UK intergovernmental relations were unrealistic, given its proposed membership.

The Irish Government was initially sceptical about the proposals for a Council of the British Isles, unhappy about its name (preferring 'British–Irish Council') and concerned about its relative importance *vis-à-vis* North–South institutions. Once these obstacles had been overcome, the taoiseach saw the benefits the body might bring while recognising that its primary purpose in the Agreement was to temper unionist fears on Strand Two. After the Agreement was reached, the UUP continued to claim that through the BIC, the Republic of Ireland was returning to 'a Britannic framework', confirming 'the UUP view that the British Isles, not the island of Ireland, is the natural economic and social unit'.[15] A year later, the UUP issued a detailed paper on practical co-operation.[16]

The structure of the BIC

The BIC was formally established by an international agreement between the British and Irish governments on 8 March 1999, though it did not begin to operate until the transfer of powers to the Northern Ireland Assembly on 2 December 1999. The role and structure of the BIC had been set out in the Belfast Agreement.[17] Following discussions between member administrations, and with Northern Ireland political parties, a Memorandum on Procedural Guidance and a work programme were agreed at the inaugural summit on 17 December 1999.

The BIC operates in different formats, including at summit level and in sectoral groups (tables 12.1 and 12.2). At the apex are summit meetings that should be held twice yearly, though there is no fixed schedule. Only five summits had taken place by the end of 2003. The second summit was postponed on three occasions – delayed by the death of Donald Dewar, problems in Northern Ireland and difficulties in agreeing a convenient date – before being staged almost two years after the inaugural meeting. These postponements may be viewed as a missed opportunity to generate momentum and heighten the BIC's public profile. Two summits have been held during the suspension of the Northern Ireland Assembly and the executive since October 2002, thus somewhat shifting the focus of BIC activity away from the Northern Irish context. Northern Ireland has yet to host a summit and is unlikely to do so during the period of suspension.

Table 12.1   BIC summit meetings

Summit	Host	Venue	Date
Inaugural summit	United Kingdom	London	17 December 1999
Second summit	Republic of Ireland	Dublin	30 November 2001
Third summit	Jersey	St Helier	14 June 2002
Fourth summit	Scotland	New Lanark	22 November 2002
Fifth summit	Wales	St Fagan's, Cardiff	28 November 2003

Heads of member administrations are expected to attend summit meetings but exceptions have arisen (e.g. Robin Cook stood in for Tony Blair at the New Lanark summit) because of difficulties in finding mutually convenient dates; ministers and officials from the NIO have replaced members of the NIE since its suspension.

Summit meetings are convened and chaired by the host administration, the main item on the agenda being the policy area for which it has lead responsibility (see table 12.3). They start with a report from the host member on progress in its priority area before hearing updates on progress in other areas of the work programme. Summits should provide political impetus, set the agenda for future work and raise the BIC's profile. They also play a co-ordinating role (e.g. reviewing work undertaken by officials) and perform housekeeping functions (e.g. amending the work programme and establishing which members will host future summits). Communiqués are issued after summit and sectoral meetings, and are posted on the BIC website (www.british-irishcouncil.org). Finally, bilateral meetings between

Table 12.2   BIC sectoral meetings

Meeting	Venue	Chair	Date
Environment 1	London	Michael Meacher, minister for the environment (UK)	2 October 2000
Transport	Belfast	David Trimble, first minister, and Seamus Mallon, deputy first minister (NI)	19 December 2000
Environment 2	Edinburgh	Michael Meacher, minister for the environment (UK)	25 February 2002
Drugs 1	Dublin	Eoin Ryan, minister of state for local development (RoI)	22 March 2002
Environment 3	London	Michael Meacher, minister for the environment (UK)	16 January 2003
Drugs 2	Dublin	Noel Ahern, minister of state for community affairs (RoI)	7 February 2003
Environment 4	Isle of Man	Elliot Morley, minister for the environment (UK)	20 October 2003

heads of administrations, particularly the British and Irish governments, have been held in the margins of summits.

The BIC meets regularly in sectoral group formats (see table 12.2). The environment sectoral group has made the most progress, meeting on four occasions since October 2000. The drugs sectoral group has met twice and the transport group once. The Belfast Agreement stated that appropriate ministers would attend sectoral meetings, but some delegations have consisted of officials only.

BIC activities are also taken forward in working groups of officials from relevant ministries. Over seventy meetings of officials, including BIC-sponsored conferences and seminars, had taken place by the end of 2003.

The British and Irish governments jointly provide the BIC Secretariat which prepares agendas, reports and minutes for summit and sectoral meetings, plus meetings of officials. Appropriate government departments carry out work on sectoral policies. The BIC Secretariat has been housed within three distinct Whitehall departments: initially based in the Cabinet Office, it then moved to the Deputy Prime Minister's Office (from 2001), before moving to the Department for Constitutional Affairs in 2003, where it is located with the Devolution and Crown Dependencies Division, continuing a process whereby the small group of officials working in the Secretariat are those handling UK intergovernmental relations. The Anglo-Irish Division of the Department of Foreign Affairs provides the Irish element of the Secretariat.

The absence of an independent secretariat has been a factor in the BIC's rather ineffectual start. The UUP has consistently pressed for a permanent, independent and well-resourced secretariat along the lines of the North–South Ministerial Council's Secretariat.[18] In their April 2003 Joint Declaration, the two governments indicated that they would consider establishing a dedicated secretariat.

The BIC's work programme

The BIC is primarily a consultative forum, the Belfast Agreement stipulating that it 'will exchange information, discuss, consult and use best endeavours to reach agreement on co-operation on matters of mutual interest within the competence of the relevant Administrations'. It may agree 'common policies or common actions', but 'individual members may opt not to participate in such common policies and common actions'. It 'normally will operate by consensus'. In decisions on common policies or common actions, 'it will operate by agreement of all members participating in such policies or actions'. No decisions taken in the BIC are binding on participating administrations. The Belfast Agreement also envisaged the development of 'suitable arrangements … for practical co-operation on agreed policies'. Members may develop bi-lateral or multi-lateral mechanisms to reach and implement joint decisions.

The Belfast Agreement suggested seven areas for BIC activity: transport links, agriculture, environmental issues, cultural issues, health, education and approaches to EU issues. The inaugural summit agreed the first work programme, the lead administrations, plus a supplementary list of areas for future work (see table 12.3). Of the areas identified in the Agreement, only transport and the environment were included; others dropped to the supplementary list, as drugs policy, social inclusion and the knowledge economy made the work programme. The changes reflected inputs from those members that played no role in the Belfast Agreement negotiations. Tourism, telemedicine and minority languages were added to the programme at subsequent summits.

The lead administration is responsible for taking forward work on its allocated issue, in consultation with other members, with a view to exchanging information and sharing experiences. It may adopt a narrow focus within its area (e.g. the Isle of Man leads on health but has limited its work to telemedicine), or delegate work on some issues to sub-groups led by other BIC members.

The priority areas have a cross-border dimension and have seen BIC members adopt a variety of policy models. Activity has taken the form of exchanges of information on procedures and best practice through networks of actors from member administrations. Existing policy networks (e.g. on climate change and tourism) have also gained a new dimension since the BIC began work in their fields. Progress has varied from area to area, but has generally been modest: information on policy initiatives has been disseminated in new networks, but the BIC has yet to

Table 12.3   The BIC's work programme

Priority area	*Lead administration*
Misuse of drugs	Republic of Ireland
Environment	United Kingdom
Social inclusion	Scotland and Wales
Transport	Northern Ireland
Knowledge economy	Jersey
Tourism	Guernsey
Health: telemedicine	Isle of Man
Indigenous, minority and lesser-used languages	Wales

Supplementary list: future areas of BIC work
Agriculture
Consideration of interparliamentary links
Regional issues, including links between cities, towns and local districts
Energy
Cultural issues
Sporting activity
Education
Approaches to EU issues
Prison and probation issues

produce significant action: communiqués talk of future co-operation rather than reporting concrete results.

A BIC role on the misuse of drugs was welcomed, given shared experiences and interest in initiatives in Ireland and the Channel Islands. The inaugural summit agreed to exchange information on the reduction in the supply of and demand for drugs. Initiatives on the treatment of addicts, awareness campaigns and targeting the proceeds of drug trafficking have been highlighted in a series of seminars. The prospects for inclusive joint action are, however, limited as the devolved administrations in Wales and Northern Ireland lack competence in criminal justice.

Responsibility for social inclusion is shared by the devolved administrations in Scotland and Wales. With its greater resources and more extensive competences, the Scottish Executive, which hosted the New Lanark summit, has been the more active. BIC activity has focused on financial inclusion, encouraging community-led initiatives on access to financial products and saving schemes. Scottish credit unions were highlighted as examples of best practice.

The UK is the lead administration on the environment. It is working on climate change and co-ordinating the work of sub-groups led by other BIC members. Scotland leads a sub-group on waste management, while Ireland and the Isle of Man focus on Sellafield and radioactive waste emissions. Work is also beginning on biodiversity and sustainable development. Environment sectoral group meetings have considered papers on water quality in the Irish Sea and the North Sea, waste management and the impact of climate change.[19]

The Sellafield nuclear reprocessing plant is the most sensitive issue. Member administrations bordering the Irish Sea have used BIC summit and environment sectoral group meetings to forcibly express their concerns about British policy.[20] The third meeting heard a revised paper from the Republic of Ireland and the Isle of Man, with two further papers presented at the fourth meeting, although on both occasions detailed discussions were deferred until legal proceedings, launched by the Irish Government against the UK, were concluded.

Transport might have been an especially significant issue as BIC members form a common travel area; however, Northern Ireland's lead status has created problems. The DUP held the transport portfolio in the Northern Ireland Executive, but its ministers were absent from the inaugural summit and transport sectoral meeting, having refused to attend meetings of the North–South Ministerial Council. The Office of the First Minister and Deputy First Minister took over responsibility for BIC matters from the minister for regional development, but tensions between the departments hindered progress. The sectoral group meeting identified regional air links, public–private partnerships, road safety and integrated transport as areas for the BIC to take forward. Since suspension, the mutual recognition of driver penalty points has been added to the agenda and the Republic leads a sub-group on integrated transport.

Jersey was given lead responsibility for the knowledge economy after a successful presentation at the inaugural summit, and has since hosted a summit and conferences.

Sub-groups are working on access to information technology (the 'digital divide') and e-government. The Isle of Man and Guernsey were allocated lead responsibility for telemedicine and tourism, respectively, at the second summit. On the former, the BIC aims to exchange information on the use of telecommunications technology to diagnose and treat patients; on tourism, Guernsey is looking at harmonising tourism statistics. Wales was allocated lead responsibility for minority and lesser-used languages at the third summit; it presented an assessment of existing projects at the fifth summit, which agreed to assess ways of supporting these languages.

On the supplementary list, the potential for BIC activity on approaches to EU issues is of interest as foreign policy and EU matters are reserved powers in the UK. The Memorandum of Understanding states that devolved administrations are obliged to consult the Foreign Office in advance about contacts that are 'novel or contentious', might create international liabilities or have implications for inter-national relations. But it allows the devolved administrations to engage in BIC activity on EU matters and develop bi-lateral links with the Republic.[21]

The development of the BIC

The development of the BIC will be shaped by the context in which it operates (namely the Belfast Agreement and the wider 'totality of relationships'), its institutional arrangements, and the political will and resources devoted to it by member administrations.

The Belfast Agreement

The Belfast Agreement was the primary context in which the BIC emerged and initially operated, although the latter now appears to be escaping the narrow constraints of Northern Irish politics. The BIC has established some autonomy from the Belfast Agreement by operating during the post-October 2002 suspension of the Northern Ireland Executive and Assembly. The significance of the BIC in Northern Irish politics has waned: it barely featured in the 2003 assembly election campaign or the parties' submissions to the 2004 review of the Belfast Agreement. The UUP, a key supporter of the BIC in 1998, no longer seems to claim the BIC as one of the Agreement's main achievements.

Though established by an international agreement, the BIC is part of the Belfast Agreement's 'interlocking and interdependent' institutional framework. The development of the BIC has been adversely affected by problems with the imple-mentation of the Belfast Agreement. The absence of DUP ministers from BIC meetings and Trimble's reported refusal to nominate Sinn Féin minister Bairbre de Brún ahead of a summit (ultimately postponed) provoked controversy.[22] BIC work largely ceased when the Northern Ireland Assembly and Executive were suspended in 2000.

BIC activity has, however, gathered pace since the October 2002 suspension. This had surprised some observers, though Northern Ireland minister Paul Murphy had noted in 1998 that 'nothing in the Agreement says that the British–Irish Council must wind up if the Assembly is prorogued or dissolved'.[23] Whereas the continued operation of the North–South Ministerial Council required an exchange of letters between the two governments and new legislation in the Republic, no special arrangements were required for BIC activity as it is a consultative forum without executive functions.[24] Ministers and officials from the NIO have made up part of the UK delegation since the suspension.

Any sense of UUP ownership of the BIC has been dissipated by its relative inactivity and increased autonomy from the Northern Ireland context. The UUP now shows little interest in pushing the status of the BIC up the political agenda. Pro-BIC unionists have been disappointed by its low profile and relative inactivity. The UUP believes that the east–west dimension has not been treated with the same degree of seriousness as, or afforded the resources devoted to, North–South bodies. But the executive and the UUP did not have the resources to push the BIC forward in the early period of its operation. UUP ministers recognised that the Joint Ministerial Committee was the main arena for discussions with the UK Government on devolved matters. The BIC also dropped down the list of priorities of a party concerned primarily with the implementation of other areas of the Belfast Agreement. Trimble's personal support for the BIC in the pre-Agreement talks may also have dulled support for it, given the fractious state of unionist politics. Finally, the unionist case for the BIC has weakened. The UUP had hoped that the BIC would strengthen Northern Ireland's status within the Union and bring the Republic back into a 'Britannic framework'. But some unionists now claim that the Republic's bi-lateral links with the devolved administrations suggest that the BIC may become a threat to, rather than a support mechanism for, the Union.[25]

The UUP also risks presenting the DUP with a politically open goal if it focuses too much on the BIC. As a party rooted in an Ulster Protestant identity rather than a wider British one, the DUP did not share the UUP's initial enthusiasm for the BIC. It now highlights the 'imbalanced relationship' between the BIC and the North–South Ministerial Council, describing UUP claims that the BIC was a unionist success as 'patently untrue'.[26] Lack of DUP co-operation and the suspension of the Northern Ireland Executive have also meant that the transport portfolio has been the BIC's least productive area of activity.

Although the SDLP inevitably focuses on the North–South bodies, it has been supportive of the BIC and would like to see it play a more active role in promoting multi-lateral co-operation.[27] Generally, Sinn Féin remains relaxed about the east–west dimension, though they are clearly not highly committed.

The 'totality of relationships'

The Belfast Agreement envisaged that the BIC would promote 'the totality of relationships' between peoples in its member administrations. Policy-makers have been keen to foster links between communities across the islands.[28] The post-devolution terrain offered the BIC opportunities to capitalise on a desire for multi-lateral relations, but the plethora of new institutions also made it difficult to forge a coherent identity. The BIC is clearly a junior partner to the JMC, which is the main forum for UK intergovernmental relations, and the North–South Ministerial Council: both handle issues that also fall within the BIC's remit. Nonetheless, the BIC's membership and working practices do lend it a distinct and symbolically important character. It has already become an institutional focus for the developing patterns of 'network governance', promoting a cross-fertilisation of policy ideas and co-operation in areas of mutual interest.[29]

The BIC has contributed to developing bi-lateral links between the Republic and the devolved administrations in Scotland and Wales, fostering contacts between officials as well as ministerial meetings. But the provisions in the Belfast Agreement for the BIC to promote bi-lateral and multi-lateral contact have not been fully exploited and may be a way of invigorating the BIC.[30] Bilateral relations between Scotland and Northern Ireland have not yet developed to the same extent despite the historic links between the two.

It was predicted that grievances arising from asymmetric devolution might be raised in the BIC as, for example, the Welsh Assembly Government lacks competence in some areas of Council activity.[31] The Joint Ministerial Committee and the Judicial Committee of the Privy Council are, though, the more likely arenas for the airing and solving of such problems. Indeed, the BIC may enhance the influence of peripheral regions in the UK as it allows the devolved administrations to engage in discussions with the British Government in a more equitable forum than the Joint Ministerial Committee. Future tensions within the UK may be reflected in the BIC, but the BIC itself is unlikely to be the trigger.

BIC rules and norms

The Belfast Agreement affords the BIC an important degree of institutional flexibility with regard to its areas of activity, working practices and membership. On its areas of activity, the initial work programme has already been expanded and is likely to develop further; in terms of working practices, BIC action may range from exchanges of information to 'common policies or common actions'. The differing competences of member administrations and their freedom to opt out of common policies and actions mean that non-uniform outputs are likely. Members are also encouraged to develop bi-lateral or multi-lateral agreements that do not require prior approval and will not be formally monitored.

On membership, the impact of devolution to (some) English regions may become an issue. The Belfast Agreement states that the BIC will include devolved administrations in Scotland, Wales and Northern Ireland 'and if appropriate, elsewhere in the United Kingdom'. The 2002 White Paper *Your Region, Your Choice* stated that English regional assemblies may seek to develop links with the devolved administrations, but it did not mention the BIC.[32] Any decision on membership would be for all BIC members, but some are likely to resist any influx of English regions, as this would unbalance the BIC, one of the virtues of which is that

English interests are not predominant. At present, the British Government represents English interests (and Northern Irish interests during suspension), as well as wider UK interests. So, the Department of the Environment, Transport and the Regions represented the interests of English regions on access to landing slots at London airports, but also took a UK perspective.

The Belfast Agreement encouraged BIC members to foster inter-parliamentary links, perhaps building on the British–Irish Inter-Parliamentary Body established in 1990. It expanded in 2001 and now includes delegations from all BIC members. Northern Ireland was allocated five seats, but the UUP continues to boycott the body. Despite tentative efforts by the Inter-Parliamentary Body to adapt to BIC activity, there is no formal relationship between the two.[33]

Political will and resources

The attitudes of member administrations towards the BIC and the resources that they are willing and/or able to commit to it will be key factors in the development of the BIC. The two sovereign governments are the most significant actors and have the potential to steer the BIC. The British Government has afforded the BIC significant flexibility and appears relaxed about the prospect of bi-lateral relationships. But it has not shown the same level of energy as have other members, in part because it is wary of being seen as the dominant partner. The British Government continues to conduct its core relations with the Republic and the devolved administrations in other fora.

For the Irish Government, the BIC's primary importance was its cementing of the Belfast Agreement's 'interlocking institutions' by providing unionists with an east–west counterpart to the North–South Ministerial Council. The BIC should also be placed in the context of a British–Irish relationship changed by EU membership, the end of the Cold War, Irish economic growth and UK devolution. The taoiseach has depicted the BIC as a valuable body that offers a distinctive, more equitable and potentially more fruitful forum than the strictures of an Anglo-Irish relationship with its associated historical sensitivities and fears of London dominance. The Irish Government is wary of being dragged into disputes between the devolved administrations and London, recognising that its key relationship is with the British Government.[34] Tensions over Sellafield have been aired in the BIC, where Irish concerns (but not its recourse to legal action) won some backing from other members.

The devolved administrations in Scotland and Wales have been enthusiastic and energetic members of the BIC, which offers them a platform for sharing experiences and developing multi-lateral co-operation. The small islands value BIC membership as it provides a forum for influencing multi-lateral negotiations, developing co-operation in matters of common interest, fostering bi-lateral relations and gaining information on EU developments. They also believe that membership cements their constitutional autonomy.

Scenarios

Four scenarios for the development of the Council can be identified: pessimistic, minimalist, gradualist and maximalist. The first and the last are the least likely. In the *pessimistic* scenario, the BIC does not survive the collapse of the Belfast Agreement or is put into deep freeze during a lengthy suspension of the institutions in Northern Ireland. However, the continued operation of the BIC during the present long suspension suggests that it has established sufficient momentum for it to escape the confines of the Belfast Agreement.

In the *maximalist* scenario, the BIC is an important institution sitting at the apex of extensive east–west governance networks, forging common policies and promoting closer relations between its members. Supporters of this scenario look to the Nordic Council as a model from which lessons can be drawn. Ahern speculated that the BIC 'may become in time a loose confederation, fully respecting sovereignty, like the Nordic Council'.[35] However, there are important differences between the two organisations. The UK and Ireland are the most powerful actors in the BIC, whereas in the Nordic Council the presence of five sovereign states ensures a greater proximity of resources among members. The successful evolution of the latter also reflects the high level of consensus between members, in terms of both political culture and a shared belief in the worth of the council as an arena for Nordic co-operation.[36] These factors are unlikely to be present in the case of the BIC.

That leaves the *minimalist* and *gradualist* scenarios as the more viable. At present, the BIC falls within the minimalist scenario: it has begun to forge a niche for itself, but its main activity is the exchange of ideas – though common policies or actions are a possibility. Greater political will and a reform of BIC procedures – including a more active role for the Secretariat and a firm timetable for meetings – are, however, required for it to progress to the gradualist scenario. Here, a number of BIC-badged outputs (e.g. common policies plus bi-lateral and multi-lateral action) emerge and the council establishes itself as an important player in east–west governance networks. A functionalist dynamic may be evident as low-level co-operation gathers momentum, producing concrete outcomes and extending into new policy areas. Should the BIC become a more viable institution, the British Government and the UUP may become uncomfortable with its potential to become an arena for, on the one hand, disputes between Scotland, Wales and the British Government and, on the other, closer relations between the Republic of Ireland and the devolved administrations.

After an uneasy beginning, the BIC has at last started to establish a viable programme of activity and a sense of purpose – albeit one focused on networks of contacts and exchange of information rather than substantial joint action. But the BIC has managed to extract itself from its roots in the Northern Ireland peace process. Progress in Northern Ireland is important, but no longer essential, for the successful development of the BIC.

Notes

1 The authors acknowledge the support of a grant from the Economic and Social Research Council (L327253043). We are grateful to those politicians and officials in BIC member administrations who gave their time for interviews and questionnaires.

2 *The Agreement: Agreement Reached in the Multi-Party Negotiations*, Cm. 3883. (Belfast: HMSO, 1998), hereafter referred to as 'the Belfast Agreement' (see Appendix 2, this volume).

3 G. Walker, 'The British–Irish Council', in R. Wilford (ed.), *Aspects of the Belfast Agreement* (Oxford: Oxford University Press, 2001), pp. 137–9.

4 R. Kearney and R. Wilson, 'Towards a Council of Islands of Britain and Ireland', in R. Kearney (ed.), *Post-Nationalist Ireland* (London: Routledge, 1997), pp. 92–5.

5 S. Partridge and T. Lausti, *Nordic Co-Operation: A Possible Model for British-Irish Relations* (London: Finnish Institute, 1997); S. Partridge, *The British–Irish Council: The Trans-Island Symbolic and Political Possibilities* (London: British Council, 2000).

6 H. McDonald, *Trimble* (London: Bloomsbury, 2001), p. 49 and pp. 100–1.

7 *Ibid.*, p. 121.

8 D. Nesbitt, *Unionism Restated: An Analysis of the Ulster Unionist Party's 'Statement of Aims'* (Belfast: UUP, 1995), p. 27.

9 Consultation Paper: Ground Rules for Substantive All-Party Negotiations., Cm. 3232 (London: HMSO, 15 March 1996).

10 UDP, *A Council for the British Isles* (Belfast: UDP, 1996).

11 G. McMichael, *Submission to Initiative '92* (Belfast: UOP), p. 1.

12 Gary McMichael and Niall O'Dowd, *An Ulster Voice: In Search of Common Ground in Northern Ireland* (Boulder, CO: Roberts Rinehart, 1999), p. 209.

13 Joint Statement by the British and Irish Governments, 12 January 1998, para. 5 (Appendix 4, this volume).

14 F. Millar, 'UUP Document Favours Council of the Isles', *Irish Times*, 12 February 1998.

15 T. Hennessy, *The Agreement Explained* (Belfast: UUP, 1998).

16 UUP, 'The British-Irish Council – A Work Programme: UUP Response to the Murphy Memorandum', 13 December (Belfast: UUP, 1999).

17 *Agreement between the Government of the United Kingdom of Great Britain and Northern Ireland and the Government of Ireland establishing a British–Irish Council*, 8 March, Cm. 4296 (London: NIO, 1999). On its legal status, see A. Morgan, *The Belfast Agreement: A Practical Legal Analysis* (London: Belfast Press, 2000), pp. 321–2.

18 UUP, *The British–Irish Council – A Work Programme*, p. 16; see also David Trimble's evidence, House of Lords Select Committee on the Constitution, Session 2001–2, *Devolution: Inter-Institutional Relations in the United Kingdom*, Minutes of Evidence, 10 June 2002, q. 1119.

19 The report on climate change by the Hadley Centre, part of the UK Met Office, is available at: www.british-irishcouncil.org/climatechange/index.asp.

20 See G. McKenna, 'Anglo-Irish Rift Over New Sellafield Plant Deepens', *Irish Independent*, 4 December 2001.

21 *Memorandum of Understanding and Supplementary Agreements between the United Kingdom Government, Scottish Ministers, the Cabinet of the National Assembly for Wales and the Northern Ireland Executive Committee*. Cm 5240. (London: Cabinet Office, 2001), para. D4.7.

22 On the latter, see P. Tanney, 'Putting Off Meeting Gave Trimble Fig Leaf – Sinn Fein', *Irish Times*, 23 January 2001.

23 *House of Commons Debates*, Northern Ireland Bill Committee Stage, 27 July 1998, vol. 317, cols 137–8.

24 See E. Meehan, 'Intergovernmental relations', in Constitution Unit, *Quarterly Monitoring Report: Northern Ireland, May 2003* (London: Constitution Unit, 2003).

25 See T. Luckhurst, 'The Wit of the Irish', *Spectator*, 24 February 2001, and the rebuttal by F. Millar, 'Do Our Unity Hopes Rest on the Break up of Britain?', *Irish Times*, 1 March 2001.

26 DUP, *Towards a New Agreement* (Belfast: DUP, 2003), p. 22.

27 W. Graham, 'Focus Is "Vital" for the Review', *Irish News*, 22 January 2004.
28 The British Council Ireland report, *Through Irish Eyes: Irish Attitudes towards the UK* (Dublin: British Council, 2004) reported that 81 per cent of the Irish citizens surveyed felt UK–Irish relations to be 'excellent'.
29 E. Meehan, 'The British–Irish Council', in R. Wilson (ed.), *Agreeing to Disagree? A Guide to the Northern Ireland Assembly* (Norwich: Stationery Office, 2001), pp. 95–102.
30 Evidence of David Trimble and Mark Durkan, House of Lords Select Committee on the Constitution, Session 2001–2, *Devolution: Inter-Institutional Relations in the United Kingdom*, Minutes of Evidence, 10 June 2002, q. 1116–9.
31 V. Bogdanor, 'The British–Irish Council and Devolution', *Government and Opposition*, vol. 34, no. 3, 1999, p. 298.
32 *Your Region, Your Choice: Revitalising the English Regions*, Cm. 5511 (London: DTLR, 2002), para. 8.9.
33 On the future of the BIIPB, see the documents at: www.biipb.org/biipb/member/future/fob.htm.
34 B. Ahern, 'Ireland and Britain: A New Relationship for a New Millennium', speech at the University of North London, 15 April 1999.
35 B. Ahern, 'The Western Isles of Europe at the Millennium', Lothian European Lecture, Edinburgh, 29 October 1998.
36 M. Qvortrup, 'Functionalism in Practice: Nordic Lessons for the British–Irish Council', *Regional and Federal Studies*, vol, 11, no. 1, 2001, pp. 27–38.

13

A 'most difficult and unpalatable part': the release of politically motivated violent offenders

MICHAEL VON TANGEN PAGE

One of the more controversial issues in the peace process was the problem of what would happen to the large number of prisoners who were gaoled for scheduled (terrorist) crimes. Many people found the release of terrorist prisoners repugnant. Yet to the paramilitaries the release of members was a vital, if not a core, demand if they were to sign up to a peace deal. In September 1994 there were 1,429 prisoners held for scheduled crimes in Northern Ireland's prisons.[1] There were also smaller numbers of (largely republican) prisoners held in England, the Republic of Ireland, the USA and continental Europe. In Northern Ireland the bulk of politically motivated violent offenders (PMVOs) were held in the male Maze Prison (also known as Long Kesh) south of Belfast. In this gaol prisoners were held in segregated wings, separated according to paramilitary affiliation. There were also smaller numbers of prisoners who had chosen to leave paramilitary organisations and live in an integrated wing of Maghabery Prison. Maghabery was also the site of Northern Ireland's women's prison although there were very few female scheduled prisoners.

The basic problem that these prisoners presented was that, like most aspects of the Troubles, the view taken of them depended very much on the perspective of the respective communities: to many unionists, scheduled prisoners were criminal terrorists; while to republicans, these prisoners belonged to an army of resistance against British colonial rule. Yet it was clear from a very early stage that prisoners would have to be released if a negotiated settlement that included the paramilitaries was going to be reached.

The politicians allied to the paramilitaries have always made it clear that the issue of prisoner release was central to the success of the peace process. On the eve of the Provisional IRA's first ceasefire in August 1995, Sinn Féin President Gerry Adams made a speech in which he demanded a number of concessions from the British and Irish governments, prominent among which was the introduction of an amnesty. David Adams of the UDP emphasised in a television interview several years later that the release of prisoners was important also to loyalists. He said of the link between the position of the prisoners and the ongoing negotiation process: 'we aren't involved in some sort of benign political dialogue, what we are involved in is conflict resolution. And as part and parcel of conflict resolution political prisoners must be a central issue.'[2] However, there was considerable uneasiness, especially within the unionist population, regarding the suggestion that people convicted of 'terrorist' crimes should be released. Even after a release programme was included in the 1998 Belfast Agreement many unionists continued to oppose the release of prisoners. In its 1998 Northern Ireland Assembly Manifesto the DUP, which opposed the Agreement, stated: 'All decent people recoil with moral contempt at the prospect of the mass release of those who have murdered and maimed the innocent, whilst the RUC is to be demoralised and disarmed.'[3]

Despite this level of polarisation over what should happen to conflict-related prisoners the release programme it included has been one of the few parts of the Agreement which has been implemented on time and with relatively little difficulty. It is important to look at the reason why PMVOs have become so central to the conflict before assessing the impact which their release has had on the peace process as a whole.

The importance of prisons in the Northern Ireland conflict

Historically the republican movement has always seen the prisons as an important part of their conflict with the British. This was recognised by Billy McKee, a former Provisional IRA leader, in the early 1970s when he said: 'This war will be won in the prisons'.[4] At the start of the Troubles republicans used the prisons to demonstrate their legitimacy as combatants and their status as victims of an imperialist oppressor. Over time the prisoners became an important political think-tank for the republican movement and, ultimately, in the early 1980s, the prisons became the issue on which Sinn Féin was able to launch its political strategy.

In 1972 Billy McKee led a hunger strike in Belfast Prison which resulted in the granting of 'special category status', a form of political recognition, to republican and loyalist prisoners in Northern Ireland. The prisoners were held in segregated compounds within the Maze, inside of which the various paramilitary groups would impose their own discipline and regulate affairs in much the same way as prisoners of war. By 1977, however, the secretary of state for Northern Ireland, Merlyn Rees, decided on the recommendation of a report produced by Lord Gardener to abolish special category status and attempted to class all prisoners in the region as normal prisoners. This resulted in opposition from both loyalist and republican prisoners, and to the republican protests that brought attention worldwide to Northern Ireland's prisons.

Initially the republican prisoners refused the prison uniforms which they were required to wear, instead wrapping themselves in blankets. When this failed to have the desired impact outside of the prisons or any concessions from the British the next stage of the escalation was the 'dirty' protest when republicans refused to wash or use the prison's sanitary facilities, smearing excrement to the walls of their cells instead. By 1980, after some four years of protest, the prisoners' impatience led them to escalate the dispute through a hunger strike. This protest ended when it seemed that a compromise had been reached; but it failed to materialise and a new strike began. The new strike consisted of a series of single fasts by prisoners undertaken over much of 1981 which resulted in the death of ten prisoners before its collapse. The refusal of the Government to accede to the demands of the prisoners led to widespread protests both within Northern Ireland and internationally. Once the protest had collapsed, however, the British Government introduced a number of concessions which allowed the prisoners to claim some success.

Sinn Féin used the prison issue to launch its election strategy. Initially with the hunger striker Bobby Sands as the 'anti H-Block' candidate in the Fermanagh and South Tyrone Westminster by-election, republicans were able to prove that the prison dispute had significant levels of support from the wider nationalist electorate. The election of Sands and, following his death, that of the Sinn Féin activist Owen Carron, was enough to give the Sinn Féin President Gerry Adams the ammunition he needed to launch what became know as the 'armalite and ballot-box paper' strategy which combined active support for the Provisional IRA's armed campaign with the political strategy of contesting elections.[5]

While loyalists have not attached the same mystique to prisoners as have republicans, they remain an important constituency. Like republican prisoners, incarcerated loyalists have been keen to see themselves as prisoners of war and have similarly resisted the attempts by successive British governments to 'criminalise' them. The loyalist prisoners also became a form of think-tank for their organisations outside of the prisons and were a vital ideological force behind the increased politicisation of the loyalist paramilitaries in the late 1980s and early 1990s.

Many important paramilitary strategies originated in the prisons. Most importantly, the prisoners from both the loyalist and republican wings of the Maze are widely seen as having had an influential role in the peace process.[6] It was certainly the case that when Sinn Féin was considering how the republican movement should react to the Downing Street Declaration of December 1993 prisoners on home leave under the Christmas Parole Scheme played a leading role in debates. Similarly, during the process that led to the loyalist ceasefire in October 1994, the CLMC entered the Maze to discuss the possibility of a ceasefire with their imprisoned members.[7]

On 31 August and 13 October 1994, respectively, the Provisional IRA and the CLMC announced ceasefires. Almost immediately, pressure began to mount for the authorities to reward the paramilitaries by starting to release prisoners. Leading loyalist and republican spokespersons called for the introduction of an amnesty for prisoners convicted of scheduled crimes. The Republic of Ireland was the first to announce its intention to release Provisional IRA members in late November 1994. There was, however, significant opposition to these releases from a number of police widows, who ensured that no one convicted of the murder of a Garda Síochána officer was released from the Republic's prisons at that time. The first nine prisoners were released just before Christmas 1994.[8] The Irish Government then announced a further series of early releases in 1995 which included most of the Provisional IRA prisoners not guilty of the murder of a Garda officer. The Irish Government started to put pressure on the British to also begin releasing prisoners. Prisoners allied to the republican splinter organisations CIRA or INLA, who were opposed to the peace process, were deliberately excluded from the release programme.

In Northern Ireland, the situation was not as clear-cut as in the Irish Republic. There was significant opposition to a lenient release policy from Unionist MPs and in at least one poll on early release 54 per cent of respondents in Northern Ireland indicated their opposition compared to only 34 per cent who supported the early release of prisoners. The majority was substantially higher among Protestants, who opposed the policy by 72 to 20 per cent support.[9] Given such levels of opposition within one section of the community and the opposition from unionist politicians, it was inevitable that the UK authorities would proceed with extreme caution.

The NIO found itself in a quandary, in that the paramilitaries demanded some recognition of the cessation of violence through penal policy while the politicians representing the unionist parties were hostile to any release. Given the 'democratic deficit' which has existed in Northern Ireland since the imposition of direct rule, the Government could have overruled the objections of unionists. It was, however, difficult on moral grounds to ignore the unionist community in this way on such a significant issue. Further, by the middle of 1995 the Conservative Government in Westminster was facing real difficulty in passing legislation, as its majority had declined significantly since the previous general election and the right-wing of the Conservative Party was in open rebellion against Prime Minister John Major over European policy. This placed the two main unionist parties in a powerful position in the House of Commons, at times casting crucial votes for or against the Government. To cloud the political situation further ex-premier Margaret Thatcher was indicating through political allies her own opposition to the early release of any paramilitaries in Northern Ireland.[10]

The NIO had in the past made clear that continuing political violence was a major barrier to releasing imprisoned paramilitaries. In 1986 Minister of State Nicholas Scott told the House of Commons:

> In coming to a conclusion as to whether a prisoner will or will not commit another offence outside, factors that must be taken into account are the organisation to which he or she has some allegiance and the level of violence outside the prison ... If the threat of violence were removed, that would affect our judgement of the likelihood of prisoners being caught up in a campaign of violence.[11]

This statement made it clear that the authorities, at least on one level, recognised the importance that prison release could have for the possible ending of violence. Indeed it is interesting to note that according to the former taoiseach Dr Garrett

FitzGerald the UK Government had considered offering the early release of paramilitary prisoners if political violence came to an end as early as 1985, during the negotiations with Dublin that had led to the Anglo-Irish Agreement.[12]

In October 1995, the Government moved the Northern Ireland (Remission of Sentences) Bill that restored a form of 50 per cent remission to the 417 scheduled prisoners who had, since 1989, received remission of only one-third of their sentences. While this would result in about 90 paramilitary prisoners being released in 1995, 10 per cent of approximately 900 paramilitary prisoners held in Northern Ireland at that time, the reaction of republicans was negative.[13] Sinn Féin's prison policy spokesperson Pat McGeown told *The Times* that 50 per cent remission would have 'little or no impact in terms of reducing the numbers of political prisoners in British gaols either in the next twelve months or indeed by the year 2000'.[14]

According to Secretary of State Sir Patrick Mayhew, the decision to introduce the change in the remission procedure was made possible by the fact that the ceasefires had held for over a year and that the risk of further attacks by the paramilitaries had greatly reduced. He included an important safeguard in the policy – release on licence. Rather than simply change the remission rate back to 50 per cent, which would have resulted in automatic release of prisoners after half the sentence had been served, one-third remission was retained with the remainder of the period up to the 50 per cent level being a licensed period during which a person could be re-imprisoned if his or her behaviour had not been satisfactory. In the debate, Mayhew made clear that he interpreted this to mean that if a prisoner re-offended (as with all prisoners released on remission) or if there was reason to suppose that he or she constituted a danger to the public then re-imprisonment would follow.[15]

This concession resulted in the somewhat sceptical support of the unionist parties for the policy. The Labour Party supported the move, though some of its MPs were concerned about the terms of the licence and the role that this created for the secretary of state without some form of judicial procedure. The largest nationalist party, the SDLP, was also unenthusiastic about the Bill, but supported the idea of the licensed release, even though it represented less than had existed between 1979 and 1989.[16]

The broad acceptance of the Bill meant that in November 1995 eighty-eight prisoners were released.[17] While the releases had been intended to help the peace process, the situation outside the prisons at that stage had deteriorated due to the political difficulties in reaching all-party talks. The delay in finding a compromise over the issue of the decommissioning of paramilitary arms prior to the commencement of talks created considerable republican frustration. On 9 February 1996, a large bomb exploded in London's Docklands area,[18] followed by other Provisional IRA bombs in England and Germany, and eventually the resumption of its campaign in Northern Ireland.

Outside of Northern Ireland, the transfer of Irish prisoners from British prisons to the prison system in Northern Ireland and in the Irish Republic was a source of discontent. The issue was resolved by a change in policy at the Home Office so that over forty prisoners were granted 'temporary extended' transfers to Northern Irish prisons in line with the recommendations of the 1992 'Ferrers Report'.[19] That report had argued that individuals should be transferred to prisons situated as close to their relatives as possible.[20] Temporary extended transfers gave the families better access but ensured that the prisoners were still under the control of the home secretary. However, there were complaints about the slow introduction of the new policy: Home Secretary Michael Howard was accused of being unwilling on political grounds to approve the transfers of prisoners back to Ireland.[21] However, according to the *Sunday Times*, the opposition also came from Baroness Thatcher, whose personal intervention with her successor John Major had halted the first planned transfers, in February 1993.[22] Ultimately, however, after a dirty protest by some republican prisoners at Whitemoor Prison, the policy was implemented.

There was still the problem of those prisoners from the Irish Republic who did not have links with Northern Ireland, but that situation was resolved by the Irish Republic's decision to ratify the European Convention of Prisoner Transfers in November 1995. The UK had incorporated the convention into domestic law in 1984, so that there was, in theory, little reason to prevent the transfer of prisoners to the Republic. However, there were signs that the British Government was wary of transferring prisoners convicted of terrorist-related offences, and initially only Patrick Kelly, a Provisional IRA member suffering from cancer, was transferred to the Irish Republic. This wariness dissipated to some extent in the period after the Labour Party's general election victory of May 1997 and the resumption of the Provisional IRA ceasefire in July. The new Home Secretary Jack Straw allowed several more transfers to both the Irish Republic and Northern Ireland, and indicated that by the end of 1998 only one Irish prisoner convicted of a terrorist-related crime would remain in England.

The first impact on prison policy of the resumption in violence came in the Irish Republic when, on the 10 February 1996, the Government rescinded the release of nine republicans who had been due to leave prison later that day.[23] The Government made no change to penal policy in Northern Ireland, but it was quite clear that further reforms were no longer on the cards. One reason why the British probably did not suspend the new remission policy was that the loyalist ceasefire was still holding and in the initial phase of the British response the maintenance of this ceasefire was of prime importance.

In June 1997 former Taoiseach Albert Reynlds called for further concessions by the British Government in the form of improved remission rates to convince the Provisional IRA that the newly elected Labour Government was sincere in its commitment to include the republican movement in the talks process. While that did not occur, the new Secretary of State Dr Marjorie Mowlem did give the go-ahead for a series of meetings between a Sinn Féin delegation and civil servants. The meetings resulted in the 18 July 1997 statement by Sinn Féin's President Gerry Adams, which called on the Provisional IRA to restore its ceasefire. Adams indicated that, aside from understandings regarding the participation of Sinn Féin in political talks, 'negotiations would be enhanced by specific confidence building measures'. He went on to make specific mention of the question of demilitarisation, including the issue of prisoners, as being of importance.[24] Adams's statement was rapidly followed on the 20 July 1997 by a new ceasefire.

While the British Government introduced no new initiatives in the prisons after the ceasefires, it did start the process towards the inclusion of Sinn Féin in the all-party negotiations at Stormont. However, over the December 1997–January 1998 period the prisoners again became important in Northern Ireland. After the republican ceasefire, the Irish Government began a series of confidence-building measures, including the release of Provisional IRA prisoners, while the British Government speeded up the transfer of prisoners from England to Northern Ireland and the Irish Republic. This created considerable disaffection among loyalist prisoners who felt the republican movement was gaining too many concessions while loyalists were being ignored. Further, during this period INLA murdered Billy Wright, the leader of the dissident LVF, in the Maze, resulting in a significant rise in sectarian tension. For a time the loyalist ceasefire hung in the balance, but Marjorie Mowlam entered the prison and discussed the prisoners' grievances directly with them and persuaded them to reaffirm their support for the peace process.[25]

Dr Mowlam made clear in a written presentation to the prisoners, published immediately after her visit to the Maze, that the 'prison issue' was part of the wider peace process: 'We recognise that prisoner issues are important to parties on both sides. They too need to be resolved'. However, she went on to say: 'let me be clear, there will be no significant changes to release arrangements in any other context' other than the success of the peace talks. In so doing she demonstrated that the release of prisoners would be considered, but only as part of a wider political settlement of the conflict.[26]

The Belfast Agreement and its implementation

The release of all conflict-related prisoners in the UK and the Republic of Ireland was an important part of the 'Good Friday' Belfast Agreement of April 1998. While the bulk of the document covered the structure of government for Northern Ireland it also contained a number of confidence-building measures. Alongside arms' decommissioning, which was essential for the unionist negotiators, there was the inclusion of an early release scheme as a concession to the paramilitaries. The Belfast Agreement allowed for the release of all conflict-related PMVOs in the UK and Ireland by July 2000. An independent commission was to be established to review cases on an individual basis and assess if a prisoner qualified for release. This allowed for a phased and structured release programme – over the two-year period – that also reflected the seriousness of a prisoner's crime.[27] This is not, however, an amnesty: individuals who break their release conditions by re-involving themselves in political violence will be required to serve out their sentences in full on top of any new sentence.

The Sentence Review Commission was established under the terms of the Northern Ireland (Sentences) Act 1998 to administer the release scheme,[28] and was co-chaired by the South African human rights lawyer Brian Currin and Sir John Blelloch. In order to qualify for release a prisoner has to have been a member of one of the paramilitary organisations recognised by the secretary of state to be in support of the Belfast Agreement and currently observing a ceasefire. The smooth running of the scheme meant that by the 22 January 1999 some 238 prisoners had been released.[29] The release scheme was felt to have demonstrated its worth when two prominent rejectionist groups, INLA and the LVF, announced ceasefires in order to take advantage of the release scheme. Furthermore the only decommissioning to have taken place during the first twelve months of the agreement was the LVF's handing over some weaponry to be destroyed in December 1998. This perhaps underlines the widespread unionist perception that these two issues are linked, despite the refusal of Sinn Féin to recognise this.

The continued refusal of the paramilitaries to decommission and the increase in punishment beatings resulted in increased hostility among pro-agreement unionists and the Conservative Party. In January 1999 two prominent Labour backbenchers, Harry Barnes and Frank Field, lodged an early day motion in the House of Commons calling for a slow down of the release scheme; and the Conservative Party broke with the bi-lateral approach to the Belfast Agreement by calling for the suspension of the release programme until there was an end to punishment beatings and the start of decommissioning. This hostility was further increased when on 22 June 1999 Patrick Magee, the Brighton bomber who had nearly killed Prime Minister Margaret Thatcher, was released after serving only one-third of the time the judge had recommended when sentencing him to life imprisonment. In response to this criticism a Downing Street spokesman acknowledged that the 'most difficult and unpalatable part' of the Agreement was the release of prisoners: 'It is hard to swallow. In the end, though, we have to keep the process moving forward.'[30]

The position of victims of the violence in Northern Ireland is perhaps the most sensitive confronting the issue of the release of prisoners. A number of factors were built into the Belfast Agreement in order to at least acknowledge the situation of victims. A commission was established, led by the former civil servant Sir Kenneth Bloomfield, to examine ways of addressing victims' needs. Further, with special reference to the prisoners, a couple of safeguards were built in to the Agreement and the subsequent legislation. Firstly, the families of victims had the right to request for information on the release date of the person convicted of the relevant crime. Secondly, the releases were under licence rather than an amnesty. This means that if in the future released prisoners are suspected of becoming re-involved in political violence or are reconvicted during the time they would still have been serving in prison, then they will resume their original sentences. These safeguards were intended to demonstrate to the victims of PMVOs that they were not being ignored, even if the perpetrators were being released.

Conclusion

Prisoners have played an important, if secondary, role in the process that resulted in the 1998 Belfast Agreement. This role can be divided into three significant segments.

- The prisons were vital in developing the political strategy of the paramilitaries in Northern Ireland, especially in making the paramilitaries realise that they had to negotiate and that a military victory was not possible.
- They became a factor in important confidence-building initiatives while also simultaneously being a block on agreement as many of the democratic political parties did not wish to see the release of prisoners.
- They were a vital part of the negotiation process.

These three inter-linked but separate factors were to impact significantly on the peace process. While it was clear that the release of PMVOs would not in their own right guarantee a peace agreement, it was also evident that the political parties allied to the paramilitaries could not sign up to any agreement that did not involve their release. The unionist political parties, however, had grave doubts about the release of prisoners, and while it is impossible to assess the impact that the inclusion of a prisoner release programme had on unionist voters' support for the agreement it undoubtedly played a role in fostering hostility. Similarly, the prisoners' endorsements of the political lines of those paramilitary parties taking part in the negotiations were important in aiding the 'doves' within both republican and loyalist organisations. It is difficult to see whether prominent politicians such as Gerry Adams or David Ervine could have supported the Agreement without the support given them by the prisoners. Certainly, it has been argued that the voice of ex-prisoners has been vital in maintaining support for the Belfast Agreement within hard-line communities.[31] The inclusion of prisoner release in the Agreement has also led to the decision of two previously rejectionist groups to support the peace process in order to achieve the release of their members from prison. It has also arguably been a factor in maintaining the UDA ceasefire, despite the failure of the UDP to get any members elected to the assembly. Ultimately, however, it is doubtful that the prisoners in themselves could make or break the peace process in the way that the decommissioning issue has threatened to do. On the other hand, they were a vital part of the package that persuaded the paramilitaries to sign up to an agreement which failed to completely satisfy their principal political objectives.

Despite the problems in implementing the political and security aspects of the Belfast Agreement, the release of PMVOs from prison has been broadly successful. The use of the clause to re-imprison prisoners was used famously against the leading loyalist Johnny Adair in response to his role in a vicious internal loyalist feud. Adair was variously seen as increasingly hostile to the Belfast Agreement and increasingly involved in the burgeoning trade in illegal drugs seen in Northern Ireland since the ceasefires. However, in the two years following the agreement, 428 prisoners were released. On 29 September 2000, the remaining four prisoners in the Maze were transferred to other establishments in Northern Ireland and the Maze closed. For a number of years the prison was mothballed in case there was a serious return to violence; however, in 2003 the decision was made to transfer the site to the civilian authorities for redevelopment. In March 2004 advertisements were placed for a tender to examine the history of the site to assist the developers in recognising its important role in the recent history of Northern Ireland. Whether the prison, or parts of it, will be preserved remains a matter of some debate, but it is now clear that it will never again be used as a prison. This is one of the best indicators that Northern Ireland has turned a vital corner on the road to peace and that, perhaps, it will not be necessary ever again for so many people in Ireland to spend the majority of their lives in prison for political reasons.

Notes

1 Brain Gormally and Kieran McEvoy, *Release and Reintegration of Politically Motivated Prisoners in Northern Ireland* (Belfast: NIACRO, 1995), p. 64.
2 Interview with David Adams, BBC2, *Newsnight*, 9 February 1998.
3 DUP, *Assembly Manifesto* (Belfast: DUP, 1998).
4 T. P. Coogan, *On the Blanket* (Dublin: Ward River Press, 1980), p. 73.
5 For a detailed examination of the hunger strike see P. O'Malley, *Biting at the Grave* (Belfast: Blackstaff Press, 1990).
6 *Guardian*, 21 December 1993.
7 *Irish Times*, 11 October 1994.
8 *Ibid.*, 17 September 1994 and 23 December 1994.
9 *Irish Political Studies 1996*, Vol 11 (PSAI Press, 1996), p. 274.
10 *Independent*, 21 November 1993, and *Sun*, 2 September 1994.
11 Quoted in B. Rolston and M. Tomlinson, 'The Challenge Within: Prisons and Propaganda in Northern Ireland', in M. Tomlinson, T. Varley and C. McCullagh (eds), *Whose Law and Order?* (Belfast: Queens University, 1988), p. 185.
12 *Independent*, 13 November 1994.
13 *Hansard* (House of Commons), Northern Ireland (Remission of Sentences) Bill, Second Reading, 30 October 1995, cols. 23–4.
14 *Times*, 27 October 1995.
15 *Hansard*, 30 October 1995, col. 24.
16 *Ibid.*, cols 35–45.
17 *Times*, 13 November 1995.
18 *Independent*, 11 February 1996.
19 *Civil Liberty Agenda*, spring 1993, p. 24.
20 Report of the Interdepartmental Working Group's Review of the Provisions for the Transfer of Prisoners Between UK Jurisdictions (Ferrers' Report), unpublished typescript, copy in the House of Commons Library, 1992, pp. 25–6.
21 *An Phoblacht/Republican News*, 16 December 1993.
22 *Sunday Times*, 19 December 1993.
23 P. Bew and G. Gillespie, *The Northern Ireland Peace Process: A Chronology* (London: Serif, 1996), p. 164.
24 'Adams, McGuiness urge IRA to Restore Cessation', Sinn Féin Press Release, Dublin, 18 July 1997.
25 *Independent*, 9 January 1998.
26 'Text of the Message Delivered on 9 January 1998 to Loyalist Prisoners in HMP Maze, by the

Secretary of State for Northern Ireland, Marjorie Mowlam', NIO Press Release, Belfast, 9 January 1998.

27 *The Agreement: Agreement Reached in the Multi-Party Negotiations*, (10 April 1998), Section 10, paras 1–3 (see Appendix 2).

28 Northern Ireland (Sentences) Act 1998, section 1(1).

29 'Early Releases and Christmas Home Leave – the Facts' (Belfast: Northern Ireland Information Service, 22 January 1999).

30 *Irish Independent*, 23 June 1999.

31 See for example Tracy Davanna, 'Persuaders for Peace', *Fortnight* (Belfast: February 1999).

14

A truce rather than a treaty? The effect of violence on the Irish peace process

JOHN DARBY

Ceasefires never bring an end to violence. The word itself acknowledges that there has been a truce rather than a treaty. By implication neither side has abandoned the option of returning to the use of force. At best a ceasefire may trigger a peace process which, if completed successfully, will allow violence to diminish and return to forms which can be handled by normal policing and legal procedures. The greatest obstacle to this outcome is violence itself, and the effect it may have on the process.[1] This chapter examines the relationship between violence and the peace process in Northern Ireland, presenting a chronicle of the violence, followed by an analysis. The argument advanced is that, even when political violence has been ended by a ceasefire, it has re-appeared in other forms to threaten the evolving peace process. Eight main forms of violence are identified, each of which has a different effect and requires a distinct policy approach.

A habit of violence

The conflict in the North has been exceptionally persistent: no generation since the Plantation of Ulster has escaped its heritage of violence; in Belfast alone there were nine periods of serious rioting between 1835 and 1969, and many other years where some disturbances have been recorded.[2] The recent violence was the longest and most sustained of all: it was uninterrupted, except for variations in form and intensity, from 1969 to 1994.

Many observers believed that the upsurge of violence in Northern Ireland in the early 1970s could lead only to one of two outcomes: either the belligerents would be shocked into an internal accommodation or they would be propelled into genocidal massacre. Neither occurred. The initial rioting in 1969 between Catholics and Protestants, during which eight people were killed, was soon replaced by more structured violence after the arrival of the British Army and its confrontations with the Catholic community. The emergence of the Provisional IRA, strengthened by the introduction of internment in 1971, channelled the violence to a more organised confrontation between the IRA and the British Army. During the 1990s the pattern shifted again, with loyalist paramilitaries responsible for more deaths than any other group in the years immediately preceding the ceasefires. All three main actors were both perpetrators and victims of violence.

The violence of the Troubles reached a peak in 1972, when 468 people died. In subsequent years, a succession of particularly dramatic events periodically raised the casualty rate: the killing of thirteen Catholics by paratroopers on Bloody Sunday in 1972; the loyalist Ulster Workers' Council (UWC) strike in May 1974; the activities of the 'Shankill butchers' in the mid-1970s, the IRA hunger strikes in 1981. By the 1990s there had been a gradual decline in violence to an annual average of below 100. Between 1969 and the declaration of the ceasefires by republican and loyalist paramilitary organisations in 1994, the Troubles had claimed 3,173 deaths in Northern Ireland, and a total of 235 in Britain, the Irish Republic and the rest of Europe. Thousands of people had been intimidated from their homes and thousands more injured.[3]

Inevitably, the prevalence of violence affected legal and policing procedures: there was practically a standing army on the streets after 1969. Public opinion on the State's handling of these problems was divided and subject to fluctuation during the years of violence. There was concern that the barrage of special powers infringed individual rights, that emergency powers were not exercised impartially and that the surveillance apparatus installed by the British army collected information not directly related to security concerns.[4]

Unionists often complained that security policies never amounted to more than ad hoc responses to IRA violence. With the exception of a short period in the late 1970s, security policy had largely been one of containment, maintaining what British Home Secretary Reginald Maudling called 'an acceptable level of violence'. The result was stalemate. Each set of combatants – the security forces and the paramilitaries – was able to frustrate the other, but unable to secure victory.

Violence and the peace process: a chronicle

Most people in Northern Ireland became aware that a peace process had started only when the IRA announced a ceasefire in August 1994, with the main loyalist paramilitary organisations following suit two months later. Since then, every stage in this process has been obstructed by violence, in its varied forms.

The transition from war to peace had started during the late 1980s, when elements within Sinn Féin shifted to the view that resilience was not enough to deliver a united Ireland. IRA violence was not only driving greater divisions between Catholics and Protestants in Northern Ireland, but was alienating the population of the Irish Republic. *The Sunday Tribune* (24 August 1994) voiced the increasing condemnation of IRA intransigence by the Dublin media shortly before the ceasefire: 'The IRA campaign, although not the only obstacle to this [peace] process, is now beyond all reasonable doubt the most substantial one. That is why the killing must stop.'

The British Government's entry into secret negotiation with Sinn Féin reflected a growing view that the IRA could not be defeated within the political constraints of a liberal democracy. Secret talks enabled them to test the seriousness of Sinn Féin's leadership. The nervous courtship carried an equilibrium of risk for both sides – for republicanism, the historical tendency to split at the first suggestion of compromise, and for John Major's precarious Conservative Government, the risk of alienating unionist support in parliament.

The ceasefires produced immediate and tangible benefits: 51 people had been killed during the six months preceding the 1994 IRA ceasefire, and, while paramilitary violence in Northern Ireland had not ended, only 2 people were killed as a direct result of political violence in the 6 months following that ceasefire. The euphoria did not last long. By the end of 1995 the stalemate over decommissioning – the demand that the IRA hand over its weapons – forced the British Government to agree to the establishment of the International Body on Arms Decommissioning under the chairmanship of Senator George Mitchell. The resulting Mitchell Report, published in January 1996, laid down conditions for all negotiators. Before participants were admitted to all-party negotiations they were required to agree to six principles, including their commitment to:

- democratic and exclusively peaceful means of resolving political issues;
- the total disarmament of all paramilitaries;
- ensure that such disarmament must be verifiable by an independent commission;
- renounce and oppose any effort to use force or the threat of force to influence the course of the outcome of all-party negotiations;
- abide by the letter of any agreement reached in all-party negotiations and to resort to democratic and exclusively peaceful methods in trying to alter any aspect of that outcome with which they may disagree; and
- 'take effective steps' to end 'punishment' killings and beatings.[5]

The British Government's response on the same day downplayed these main recommendations in favour of a marginal recommendation that elections should be held for a Northern Ireland Forum. Two weeks later, on 9 February 1996, the IRA ended its ceasefire by planting a bomb in London's Canary Wharf.

The IRA's justification was that the British Government had deliberately constructed a succession of obstacles to Sinn Féin's entry to political talks. For unionists the bomb simply confirmed their warning that the IRA would resort to force to resist any developments it opposed. A London senior police source alleged that what 'some people call a ceasefire' had never been more than 'a period of terrorist preparation'; others pointed to evidence that the IRA had been preparing for a resumption even during the ceasefire period (*Belfast Telegraph*, 5 January 1996). Whatever the balance of blame, the ending of the ceasefire did not lead to an immediate resumption of the IRA campaign as it had operated before the August 1994 ceasefire. The bombings were confined largely to Britain, the worst explosions having been in London (February) and in Manchester (June 1996). The loyalist paramilitary organisations decided to preserve their ceasefires, and paramilitaries from both sides kept out of the confrontations which accompanied the Orange Order's celebrations in July 1996.

The traditional July Orange parade from Drumcree Church down the mainly nationalist Garvaghy Road, which had led to serious confrontations a year earlier, was banned by the RUC. The Orange Order responded with a serious of planned demonstrations, blocking roads, bridges and airports, and converging in increasing numbers at Drumcree in the days immediately preceding the parade. Catholic families were intimidated from their homes. On 10 July the RUC reversed its decision and escorted the parade down Garvaghy Road, physically removing local protesters from the thoroughfare. That evening nationalist areas of Belfast were under curfew to prevent their anticipated protests. The sectarian confrontations of the early 1970s had returned.

The IRA declared a second ceasefire in July 1997. The orchestra unpacked its instruments and the pre-negotiation dance started for the second time, on this occasion greeted by wariness rather than euphoria. Not only had the first ceasefire collapsed, but the high level of communal and sectarian violence within the loyalist and republican communities had continued and, in some respects, intensified. 'Concerned residents' groups', fomented by Sinn Féin according to some unionists, were formed in nationalist communities to resist Orange marches. The Parades Commission was formed in 1997 to determine which marches should be permitted to proceed and which banned.

The renewed talks were directly baulked by violence. Loyalist prisoners in the Maze voted to oppose any agreement, following the British Government's refusal to release political prisoners. The crisis was relieved following a visit by Mo Mowlan, the secretary of state for Northern Ireland, to hold direct talks with the loyalists in the prison, declaring her willingness to 'take risks for peace' (*Belfast Telegraph*, 13 January 1998); within hours the loyalists agreed to continue their support for the process. The Mitchell Principles, which had been signed by all participants in the talks, were soon tested when the all-party negotiations started in January 1998. There was increasing evidence that both loyalist and republican paramilitaries were still engaging in violence. In January 1998, after the UFF admitted to three murders, the UDP was expelled from the talks. The expulsion of Sinn Féin followed in February, when the secretary of state attributed at least two murders to the IRA (*Irish Times*, 25 March 1998). Both expulsions were for a limited period – four weeks for the UDP and two weeks for Sinn Féin. This was contemptuously dismissed by Peter Robinson of the DUP as 'a spell in the sin bin' (*Irish Times*, 16 February 1998), but the expulsions were the minimum action required to justify claims that the Mitchell Principles would be enforced.

The Agreement was eventually reached on Good Friday in April 1998. The

GFA, and the referenda and elections which endorsed it, had a constitutional as well as a moral impact on Irish republicanism. Its ratification by substantial majorities on both sides of the Irish border provided an up-to-date all-Ireland mandate. This legitimation, bolstered by Sinn Féin's active participation in the negotiations, effectively undercut the traditional justification for violence for many mainstream republicans.

After two summers of violence associated with Orange parades and the protests against them, the summer of 1998 brought the GFA to near collapse. The decision by the Parades Commission to ban the march down the Garvaghy Road led to protests in many parts of the province. Supporters of the Orange Order gathered at Drumcree, apparently determined to force through the march. Public roads were blocked and sectarian killings increased; the number of families intimidated from their homes rose from 112 in 1997 to 278 in 1998,[6] while arson attacks reached alarming levels. The GFA, signed four months earlier, was seriously threatened until circumstances were changed dramatically by two violent events during the summer. On 12 July three Catholic children from Ballymoney, Richard, Mark and Jason Quinn, aged 10, 9 and 7, burned to death in one of the arson attacks in the Drumcree disturbances. Reaction to their deaths was unprecedented: support among Orangemen for the increasingly violent protest at Drumcree was severely eroded; many withdrew and some openly opposed it. The atrocity allowed those unionists who opposed the Orange Order's activities to harness the general feeling of outrage. The Drumcree protest continued, but Ballymoney had knocked the heart out of it.

A month later, on 15 August, the splinter republican group RIRA planted a bomb in the country town of Omagh, killing twenty-nine afternoon shoppers. The bombing struck indiscriminately against both communities, an action that appeared to spurn the popular wishes expressed in the recent referenda in both parts of Ireland. Consequently it allowed Gerry Adams to underline people's rejection of violence by condemning, 'without any equivocation whatsoever', a republican bomb . Martin McGuiness of Sinn Féin went even further: 'We see our job to be one of stopping the activities of these people' (*Observer*, 6 August 1998). The Omagh bomb also provided the opportunity for both governments to harmonise and toughen their anti-terrorist powers almost unopposed. This in turn allowed the unionist leader David Trimble to compliment the Irish Republic's swift decision to introduce more legislation, and even to contrast this favourably to UK provision. The British Government reacted immediately to deny the charge in a spiral of over-trumping security condemnations. In other words, Omagh licensed a number of actors who had accepted in principle the importance of making concessions to *actually* do so.

The Omagh bomb created consternation among the republican splinter groups. Within four days of the bombing the group responsible for planting it, RIRA, had declared a ceasefire. Three days later the INLA, one of the more violent republican groups, followed suit with 'a complete cease-fire'. Soon the only remaining republican group not in ceasefire was the 32–County Sovereignty Committee, and one of its leaders, a dissident IRA quartermaster, felt compelled to claim that he 'had neither hand, act nor part in this thing [Omagh]' (*Times*, 19 August). The Provisional IRA seized the opportunity to discipline other republican spoilers. They visited the houses of sixty dissidents during one September night with threats from the IRA Army Council that 'action would be taken' against RIRA if it did not disband within a fortnight (*Irish Times*, 4 September 1998). Violence, or rather spoiler violence, had become temporarily unfashionable.

The consternation caused by Omagh was not confined to republican groups: a ceasefire had been declared by the LVF a few days before the bombing. However, by 2003 the fragility of the peace process was still evident on a range of fronts: street violence, loyalist feuding, continuing tensions over decommissioning; arrests of alleged IRA associates in the USA, in Columbia and in Stormont itself. All of these were reminders that the control of violence was the central condition for the success of the peace process.

Violence and the peace process: an analysis

In 1988 Bertie Ahern, the Irish taoiseach, commented: 'it is an observable phenomenon in Northern Ireland, and elsewhere, that tension and violence tend to rise when compromise is in the air' (*Observer*, 22 September 1997). The greatest political violence in South Africa, for example, occurred during the transition to agreement between 1990 and 1994, when almost three times as many people were killed as in the previous four years. In the Middle East peace process the use of terror similarly rose dramatically while the Rabin–Peres negotiations were under way,[7] when more than two-thirds of victims were killed. In Northern Ireland, too, the Downing Street Declaration, which cleared the ground for the peace process in December 1993, led to an increase in violence: 50 people were killed in the 6 months following the declaration, up from 32 during the 6 months that preceded it.

Nevertheless, in the months following the 1994 ceasefires political violence declined significantly. It was replaced by other forms of violence, each in its own way a threat to the peace process. The eight forms identified here fall into three main categories:

- The violent activities of the paramilitaries fragmented into their component elements, which included a possible return of political violence, 'strategic violence', internal feuding and violence from splinter groups.
- Violence spread into the community at large, through a return to sectarian confrontations and a rise in conventional crime.
- New substantive issues emerged – the release of prisoners, decommissioning of paramilitary weapons, the reform of policing, as well as the dismantling of the security apparatus.

The paramilitary fall-out

Disaffection within paramilitary organisations is perhaps the most obvious threat to peace processes. Such organisations are rarely the monoliths presented by their opponents; rather, they are complex organisms performing a variety of functions and providing an umbrella for different interests. The diversity allows paramilitary leaders to assume the high moral ground by emphasising their political and civil roles, while turning a blind eye to punishment beatings and murders. It also helps to explain strategic shifts between war and negotiation, as different elements within the organisations win temporary dominance.

During ceasefire periods the varied interests sheltering beneath the para-military parasol diffused and fragmented. At least four posed separate threats to the peace process:

A return to political violence

Ceasefires may bring an official end to political violence, but they are never unanimous. The more disaffected members among militant groups may desert to splinter groups or perform individual acts of violence. The less affected may go along with the majority view, but their agreement is conditional. Their continuing allegiance depends on measurable rewards from negotiation, most notably prisoner releases and the dismantling of the security apparatus. These rewards are rarely immediate. Consequently the pendulum may swing back towards the militants, as when the London bombs ended the IRA ceasefire in 1996.

The journalist Mary Holland pointed to discontent within a number of IRA units as a more plausible explanation for Canary Wharf: 'On previous occasions since Ireland became independent, every move by the IRA away from violence and into constitutional politics has involved a split between the men of violence and the politicos. Provisional IRA was itself born from such a development' (*Observer*, 22 June 1996).

The insistence that all participants in multi-party talks sign up to the Mitchell Principles was a useful device for regulating political violence. The suspension of Sinn Féin and the UDP for breach of the principles, however temporary, was necessary to sustain credibility. Their acceptance of the suspension, however truculent, indicated their determination to remain within the peace process.

Tactical violence

The willingness of some participants to exploit violence is common during peace negotiations. When the Irish parliamentary leader Charles Stuart Parnell was jailed during the home rule campaign in the 1880s he forecast correctly that 'Captain Moonlight will take my place', thus positioning himself as the only alternative to revolutionary violence.[8]

The paramilitaries' minimum price for ceasefire was their inclusion in nego-tiations. The main concern of some constitutional parties was that their political surrogates would use the threat of violence for strategic advantage, and that the pace of negotiation would be determined by gunmen outside of the negotiating rooms. To paraphrase Clausewitz, they feared that paramilitary negotiators would approach politics as the continuation of war by other means.

Any acts of violence during the process were taken as confirmation of that fear. During the early stages of the peace process, unionists constantly warned that Sinn Féin would use IRA violence to remind other negotiators of its power. Indeed, there were occasions during the ceasefire period when Sinn Féin's leaders appeared to feed unionist fears, as when Gerry Adams drew the attention of a republican rally to the fact that 'they (the IRA) haven't gone away, you know', an implied threat that the IRA would resume the war if Sinn Féin did not profit during the negotiations. The triumphalist appearance of newly released republican prisoners at the Sinn Féin Ard-feis prior to the May 1988 referendum was cited as further evidence of conspiracy. Despite these apprehensions, however, the unwillingness of Sinn Féin and the loyalist parties to resort to tactical violence was one of the more remarkable aspects of the peace process.

Internal paramilitary violence

Punishment beatings continued throughout the peace process as both loyalists and republicans carried on what they regarded as their policing role in a number of communities. People were expelled from the community and severely beaten for 'anti-social behaviour'; alleged drug-dealers were attacked in both communities, and at least seven were killed by the IRA during the period of the first ceasefire (*Belfast Telegraph*, 5 January 1996). These and other crimes were often disowned by paramilitary sources as either unauthorised or the actions of mavericks. Mitchell McLaughlin, one of Sinn Féin's main spokesmen, protested in January 1996 that Sinn Féin was 'powerless' to stop the IRA engaging in drug-related beatings and killings (*Irish Times*, 8 January 1996), a claim regarded with scepticism by unionists.

The desire for peace encouraged, at least initially, a public toleration of paramilitary violence. The need to maintain clear water between officially condoned violence and the general lawlessness inherited from thirty years of paramilitary violence was a crucial test of the ceasefires. By 2002 struggles within loyalism, over turf controls and drugs, had strained this distinction. In January 2003 the expulsion of one segment of the UDA by others signalled yet another shift in paramilitary violence, and a new basis for post-accord instability.

Spoilers: zealots versus dealers

The very entry of paramilitary interests into negotiations implies that the purity of their cause has been compromised. It imposes strains on organisations which are essentially military, and it is difficult to find any instances when such a move was not accompanied by a split between two main groups – *zealots* and *dealers*. The Zealots often comprise radical groups who picked up the torch – sometimes literally – they believed had been surrendered by the dealers. Their aim is not to influence the content of a peace agreement but to ensure that agreement is not reached or, if reached, is derailed.

The emergence of spoiler groups was not unprecedented in Irish politics.[9] The Irish writer and IRA member Brendan Behan once said that the first item on the agenda for any republican meeting is 'the split'. The Provisional IRA itself was formed in 1969 following a split from the Official IRA. INLA had also broken away from the Official IRA in 1972, and thirteen of its members were killed during its own internal split in 1987. In 1986 the newly formed Republican IRA and Sinn Féin broke away from the Provisionals in opposition to its alleged softer line.

A new outbreak of splits followed Sinn Féin's signing up to the Mitchell Principles in October 1997. More than twenty Provisionals resigned in protest at Sinn Féin's entry to the peace process, and INLA stepped up its violence. Two new republican paramilitary groups, CIRA and the RIRA, were formed, complete with the usual political fronts, and declared their intention to resume the armed struggle. These challenges to the Provisionals' authority had some bizarre effects. CIRA accused the Provisionals of destroying one of their bombs south of the border before it could be transported to Northern Ireland. In another incident, in Derry, a member of the Provisional IRA punched and kicked a CIRA man in an attempt to stop him planting a bomb in a bank; subsequently CIRA, apparently without irony, criticised his action as placing innocent people in danger.

Spoilers were not restricted to the republican family: the growing involvement of the PUP and the UDP in the peace process also brought charges of betrayal and defection by loyalist splinter groups. The LVF, which had been formed in 1996 by dissidents from the more established groups, was further reinforced during the period of negotiations.

Violence in the community

The fragmentation of paramilitary organisations was not the only violent accompaniment to the peace process. Two other forms of violence also threatened it – the revival of direct confrontations on the streets, and a rise in the conventional crime rate.

Return to the streets

The declaration of the ceasefires was marked by a return to more direct violence between Catholics and Protestants, especially during the marching seasons from 1996 to 1998. The switch is not surprising. During a period of organised violence, paramilitaries must be dominant and disciplined to be effective; when a ceasefire is declared the discipline of the military campaign diminishes, but the underlying sectarian hatred remains, taking the form of riots and undisciplined confrontations with ethnic rivals or the police. The paramilitary representatives who entered negotiations were not divorced from the instincts and antagonisms of their communities, and some felt the need to support them. Confrontational violence hung on stubbornly into the post-accord years, marshalled around such flash points as Orange marches and protests outside a Catholic school in Belfast. By 2002 weekend confrontations between rival groups of youths and against the police had become so ritualised as to earn the description 'recreational violence'. The danger is that such confrontational violence may swing the balance from negotiation back towards a military campaign.

'Ordinary decent crime'

Was there any relationship between this confusing mixture of paramilitary violence and the 'normal' – non-security – crime rate? When the Troubles started in 1969 Northern Ireland had the lowest *per capita* prison population in Western Europe. The conventional, as opposed to politically motivated, crime rate continued to be low during the years of the Troubles. Rates of victimisation in burglaries, assaults and thefts were substantially lower than in England and Wales.[10] Initially this pattern continued after the ceasefires, in contrast to the dramatic increase in normal crime during the comparable period in South Africa. In 1997 the prison population in Northern Ireland showed a decrease for the fourth consecutive year and the crime rate was the lowest for nine years. The major exception to the low crime rate was a 22.2 per cent increase in offences against the state, mainly public order offences, reflecting the increase in sectarian violence.[11]

South Africa presents a sombre warning. By the mid-1990s the high level of conventional crime had far outpaced political violence as a destabilising factor. By 1998 the average daily homicide rate was sixty-eight and still rising. More ominously, the barrier between ordinary crime and South Africa's underlying racial tensions, never sharp, became increasingly blurred: 1,500 white farmers were attacked between 1994 and 1998, involving more than 200 murders and threatening to create a loop back from post-settlement civil violence to the racial violence familiar from the earlier struggle.

New substantive issues

Violence as an issue during negotiations

When talks began, a number of new substantive issues emerged, most of them security related. The three most notable among them were the decommissioning of illegal weapons, policing and early prisoner releases. The stubbornness of the UUP in demanding decommissioning and of Sinn Féin in rejecting it, however irritating, arose from the need of each side to keep its primary constituency on board and from the symbolic association between decommissioning and surrender. Consequently moves towards a limited decommissioning of IRA arms in 2001 and 2002 had little impact on the positions of either side. Police reform is an equally emotional issue in negotiations. It is axiomatic that divided societies require a police force which reflects the divisions. Section 195 of the 1996 South African constitution, for example, insisted that the police and defence forces 'be broadly representative of the South African people' and by 1996 16,000 former guerrillas had been absorbed into the army; it seems likely that a similar principle will apply in Northern Ireland. The agreed release of prisoners after the 1998 GFA led to an increased demand that the victims of violence should be accorded a greater priority. The establishment of a Victims' Commission failed to stem concerns than those who had suffered most had been sidelined in the drive towards a political settlement. In June 1999 the IRA revealed where their 'disappeared' victims had been disposed, but was embarrassed when police were unable to find the missing bodies. The depth of Northern Ireland's sectarianism was confirmed in July of the same year by the 'long march' on behalf of innocent victims; the protest was confined to Protestant victims of violence, and the march culminated at Drumcree during the height of the annual Orange demonstration.

The security apparatus

Thirty years of violence had absorbed a security apparatus into Northern Irish society. It had penetrated deeply into its social structures: heavy recruitment of military, police and prison personnel, emergency legislation and procedures, information gathering and sometimes abuses of power. Within six months of the 1994 ceasefire security ramps were removed and border roads with the Irish Republic, many of which had been closed by the army, were gradually re-opened. The pace quickened after the GFA. Militants were released instead of imprisoned. The security forces augmented during the violence were reduced in number. Demands were made to reform the police force, which regarded itself as the bastion against terrorism. The occasional arrest of members of the security apparatus for terrorist offences underlines the threat left after all internal wars. These issues – demilitarisation of the security apparatus and policing reform – were still at the forefront of disputes between republicans and unionists in 2003. Unless steps are taken to ease their return to civilian life, dissatisfied and well-armed professionals are as serious a threat to stability as their paramilitary counterparts.

Violence as a catalyst of peace

Occasionally, in Northern Ireland and elsewhere, certain atrocities provoke universal condemnation and galvanise popular reaction against the perpetrators. After decades of kidnappings and murders, hundreds of thousands of Basques took to the streets to protest against the murder by ETA of a Basque town councillor. During the South African peace process the murder of 28 ANC supporters in Bisho in 1992 was not followed by the same violent reaction which had followed the massacre of 48 people at Boipatong three months earlier; instead it became a stimulus for the negotiations rather than a cause for withdrawal.[12]

What is the nature of these atrocities that it converts them into catalysts of peace? Why did Ballymoney and Omagh have such a powerful effect in Northern Ireland when so many awful actions from the past had not?

War-weariness is part of the explanation, but that had been evident for years without stimulating compromise. The reason why certain violent events, at particular times, become catalysts of peace lies not in the nature or severity of the violence, but in its timing.

Support for the GFA on the part of both communities enabled public outrage to be harnessed as opposed to simply vented: it is the *harnessing* that is important. Outrage without a mechanism to enforce it fades away, as the 'Peace People' had discovered in the 1970s. In 1998 a mechanism was provided in the GFA, and it was one created by compromise between local politicians. It was notable that, during 1998 and especially after the Omagh bomb, the parties to the negotiations began to describe violence as an attack, not just on its victims, but on 'the integrity of the talks process' itself.

The point is this: courage in condemning atrocities is insufficient: what converts outrage to action is condemnation within the context, or at least a realistic hope that agreement is possible, and that further violence could threaten it. It is also clear that such moments are transitory: the often-mentioned 'window of opportunity' is barely ajar and soon slams shut. The most important effect of the Ballymoney and Omagh atrocities was not that they ended spoiler violence but that they enabled the middle grounds of unionism and nationalism to find their voice at a time when the voice of moderation could make a difference.

Notes

1 For a more comparative discussion of these issues, see J. Darby, *The Effects of Violence on Peace Processes* (Washington, DC: USIP, 2001).

2 Andrew Boyd, *Holy War in Belfast* (Tralee: Anvil, 1969).

3 Marie Therese Fay, Mike Morrissey and Marie Smyth, *Mapping Troubles-Related Deaths in Northern Ireland* (INCORE: Northern Ireland, 1997).

4 P. Hillyard, 'Law and Order', in John Darby (ed.), *Northern Ireland: The Background to the Conflict* (Belfast: Appletree and New York: Syracuse University Press, 1983).

5 'The Mitchell Principles', the Report of the International Body on Decommissioning, was published in full by the *Irish Times*, 18 February 1998; see Appendix 10 of this volume for an extract.

6 *Magill* (Dublin), November 1998).

7 Tamar Hermann and David Newman, 'The Peace Process in Israel–Palestine', in John Darby and Roger MacGinty (eds), *The Management of Peace* (London: Macmillan, 1999).

8 Parnell's Kilmainham imprisonment in 1881 was accompanied by increased agrarian and political violence; he was released the following year after the 'Kilmainham Treaty' was signed with British Prime Minister Gladstone.

9 For a fuller discussion of spoiler violence, see S. J. Stedman, 'Spoiler Problems in Peace Processes', *International Security*, vol. 22, no. 2, fall 1997.

10 R. Geary and J. Morrison, 'The Perception of Crime', in P. Stringer and G. Robinson (eds), *Social Attitudes in Northern Ireland* (Belfast: Blackstaff Press, 1992).

11 RUC, *Recorded Crime* (Belfast: Central Statistics Unit, 1998).

12 Pierre Du Toit, 'The Peace Process in South Africa', in Darby and MacGinty, *The Management of Peace*.

PART IV
Civil society

15

Segregation, ethno-sectarianism and the 'new' Belfast

PETER SHIRLOW

Within the Belfast City Cemetery there is an underground wall. The reason why such a wall exists is to separate the Catholic dead from their Protestant counterparts. In recent times the violent disputes that have taken place at Carnmoney Cemetery, on the outskirts of north Belfast, over the demarcation of the graves of Protestants and Catholics seems to confirm that even in death there is a desire to remain uncontaminated by the presence of the ethno-sectarian 'other'. The Holy Cross dispute, and other riots in places such as Short Strand and Whitewell/White City, remind us that despite a process of political change there are still problems that are evidently tied to the realities of segregation within Belfast.

There is no doubting that the paramilitary ceasefires of 1994 were preceded by the re-appearance of rioting and disorder within many of Belfast's interfaced communities. The perpetuation of ethno-sectarian conflict reminds us that, despite the onset of globalisation, cultural 'homogenisation' and the casting of Belfast as a 'normal' place, the link between ethno-sectarian separation and multiple forms of segregation remains central to the logic and explanation of violent acts and cultural opposition.[1] The capability of localised and sectarian doctrines to reproduce residential segregation is linked to the presentation of competing ideologies that are influenced by discourses of 'truth' and of mistrust and inter-community misunderstanding.[2]

Given political change and a 'decrease' in paramilitary violence it was concluded that the crossing of ethno-sectarian boundaries and a reduction in residential segregation between Catholic and Protestants would become a more evident feature of life in Belfast. Indeed both the Irish and the British State are convinced that the genius of 'conflict resolution' lies in the competence of the two states to fashion institutions which integrate order with personal, communal and spatial liberty.

It is evidently that *space* matters in understanding the perpetuation of violence and political discord. Extreme links between ethno-sectarianism and place have always been tied to the maintenance of residential boundaries and the marking of such boundaries through both symbolism and force. Space thus represents the crucial category for understanding the connections between all sorts of multiple oppressions and the possibility to mobilise around agendas framed by place.[3] The social production of space is 'an important strategic milieu for a new coalition politics of class, race, gender, sexuality, age, ethnicity, locality, community, environment, region and other sites and sources of cultural identity and the assertion of difference'.[4] Space is important also in that sites of resistance have emerged in which cultural, economic and political differences have interlocked in order to produce fractal cities comprising spatial concentrations characterised by hopelessness and alienation. Heikkila argues that this conception of space represents the key challenge to land-use planners and urban managers:

> Space matters because it mediates the experiences of people in places, and further, it shapes the structure of the opportunity set available to them. When this transpires to create a stagnant population pool of poverty cut off from the mainstream, the poverty deepens and becomes more profound in character and more potent in its ability to sustain itself over time.[5]

In analysing the impact and effect of segregation it is asserted that the type of radical political adjustment needed to positively alter the nature of ethno-sectarian practice remains under-developed. Given the nature of residential segregation and the impact that it has on spatial mobility it is argued that the capacity for *normalised* social relations remains, in the short to medium term, unlikely.

This chapter highlights how segregation influences the localised nature of the politics of territorial control and resistance, where the imperatives of communal difference, segregation and exclusion still predominate over the politics of shared interests, integration, assimilation and consensus. I chart and explain the relevance of ideologically constructed space in the reproduction of highly politicised identities, which are linked to notions of *besiegement*, cultural dissipation and fear. It is argued that despite significant political morphology, the technical instruments of ethno-sectarian discord are still being reproduced within what are termed 'interface areas'. Those arenas, predominantly socially and economically deprived, are separated by both physical and mental constructions: arenas within which violence between Catholic and Protestant communities is ongoing; places within which prejudice and avoidance of the ethnic 'other' are commonplace and daily occurrences. However, as argued by Horowitz[6] and Smith,[7] much work on residential segregation tends to overplay the cataloguing of peoples and ignores the nature of political heterogeneity in ethno-sectarian groups. It is important to note that the violent ultural and political acts which aid the reproduction of segregation should not be read as supported by all residents of segregated communities within which inter-communal violence is of concern. Moreover, the reluctance to enter areas dominated by the 'other' ethno-sectarian group can be influenced by threats, both imagined and real, levied against people by members of their *own* community.

In sum, segregation should be understood as a set of atavistic relationships not just *between* places but *within* places themselves.

The construction of ethno-sectarian landscapes is influential, but does not convert all those who live in such places towards an acceptance of homogenous senses of belonging and affiliation. In simple terms, many people who live in highly segregated communities do not support a uni-dimensional logic that their dreads and prejudices are sourced merely from elements that exist outside of their own community. However, this does not mean that such persons are completely against the ascendant political representations that exist within their own community. It could instead be argued that highly segregated communities contain diverse populations which reject, or partly reject–partly accept or accept symbolic representations and discursive hegemonies that are related to ethno-sectarianised discourses. It could also be predicted that devotion to and rejection of ethno-sectarian discourses are temporal.

Segregation and the city

The relationship between residential segregation and the enactment of violence and political discord is contingent on a series of relationships such as the environments of everyday life, violence (both imagined and real) and political manipulation.[8] The presentation of fear of the other community by certain political entrepreneurs has been a central element in the fabrication of ethno-sectarian tradition in a range of urban environments. In some cases socially and politically dominant groups can claim ownership of a community's fears, phobias and traumas in a desire to impose particular political discourses.

As shown in table 5.1, the majority of Catholics and Protestants, and those whose community background is either Catholic or Protestant, live in places that are at least 81 per cent Catholic or Protestant: 67.3 per cent of Catholics and 73 per cent or Protestants live in such places. A mere 10.7 per cent of Catholics and 7.0 per cent of Protestants live in places that are between 41-60 per cent Catholic or Protestant or places that could be described as 'mixed'. Some commentators and organisations such as the Northern Ireland Housing Executive have maintained that within Belfast 92 per cent of social housing stock is located within what are known as single-identity estates; they also claim that that segregation within the social housing stock is increasing. Evidently social class is tied to levels of segregation; but there is anecdotal evidence that as socially mobile Catholics move into middle-income areas some Protestants move out in response.

There is no doubting that during the 1970s and 1980s segregation was intensified by the impact of violence.[9] The increase in segregation had the effect of conditioning a series of emotional and cultural concerns between communities. Anxiety is an obvious outcome given the history and reproduction of violence within segregated areas; phobia, insecurity and uncertainty remain due to low levels of social trust and an inability to control the nature and direction of violent acts.

Table 15.1   Segregation in Belfast by community background

% Population Bands	Community background	
	% of total Catholic population in band	% of total Protestant population in band
0–20	4.7	3.4
21–40	3.6	7.3
41–60	10.7	7.0
61–80	13.8	9.3
81–90	9.3	28.4
91–100	58.0	44.6

Source: Census of Population, 2001.

Fear and mistrust are linked to understandings of risk, doubt and behavioural responses that are influenced by the assessment of threat. The feeling of being threatened may not be directly related to levels of violence, given that interpretations of risk and threat can be more extreme than contemporary levels of violence would justify. Some atavistic attitudes towards the 'other' community, in particular, are influenced by the representation of information and the collectivisation of memories in a desire to present the 'other' community through discourses of danger, purity and impurity.

The effects of politically motivated violence in Belfast are obvious. Between 1969 and 1999, around 1,200 people were killed and over 20,000 injured by paramilitary and state violence. Fear of being a victim of such attacks meant that many people living in arenas of conflict developed a comprehensive knowledge of *safe* and *unsafe* places. Furthermore, mental maps created a process of consciousness that was intensified through narratives of fear, victimhood and risk. Between 1969 and 2003, around twenty euphemistically labelled 'peace-lines' (interfaces) were constructed around those areas in which patterns of the most excessive violence occurred.[10] Interface walls aimed to restrict mobility by sundering the built environment, and such structures had the effect of clearly appointing an 'opposing' community as a menacing spatial formation. As Feldman noted: 'the wall itself becomes the malevolent face of the people who live on the other side'.[11]

One-third of the politically motivated attacks resulting in fatalities between 1966 and 2001, took place within 250 metres of an interface; over two-thirds of deaths (but representing only 53 per cent of Belfast's population) occurred within 500 metres. More than three-quarters of deaths occurred in areas which were over 90 per cent Catholic or 90 per cent Protestant. In overall terms death was closely tied to places that were highly segregated, militarised, close to interfaces and socially deprived. Segregation provided a physical demarcation of space that aided the process of targeting Catholic and Protestant communities.

A central goal among those political entrepreneurs who supported ethno-sectarian discourses was to destabilise established patterns of inter-community relations. The enactment of violence and the assault on pluralist discourses were closely tied to paramilitaries, and the State's identification of certain communities as a permanent threat. Fear was constructed not only around the experience of violence but through the use of urban space in order to de-territorialise inter-community linkage. For those who accepted ethno-sectarian apportionment the belief grew that the ethno-sectarian 'other' was committed and remains committed to harming them. Thus, reciprocation was founded on violent acts which, in certain instances, sought to maximise the losses of 'other' groups. Violence undoubtedly created feelings of mistrust and harm, which manifested themselves, in Belfast's most violent arenas, as a condition of constant or intermittent anxiety. The re-appearance of violence in the 1960s highlighted the importance of developing a reading of threat and risk required in order to remain 'safe'.

The complexity of fear and prejudice

My work on ethno-sectarian enclaving and the reproduction of ethno-sectarianised fears in Belfast is based on a survey of 1,800 individuals living within interface communities in Belfast; the survey collected data on households, and in sum information on over 4,500 individuals is available.[12]

The surveys aimed to determine the level of spatial interaction between inter-faced Catholic and Protestant communities. Given that each of the six pairs of communities studied share similar socio-economic profiles and is adjacent it would be expected that there would be a similarity in terms of public- and private-sector based usage. However, the level of socio-economic interaction between communities is low. A mere one in twelve people worked in areas dominated by the religion of the 'other'. Seventy-eight per cent of respondents could provide examples of at least three publicly funded facilities that they would not use simply because it was located on the *wrong* side of an interface. The disruption to everyday living in such places is even more alarming when it is acknowledged that interfaces are areas which contain the most excessive forms of social dislocation in Belfast. Somewhat depressingly, the evidence suggested that around one in eight people forgoes healthcare for himself or herself and younger members of the family rather than use the nearest health facilities because those facilities are located in areas dominated by the other community. Other material collected via the surveys indicated that 82 per cent would not enter an area dominated by the other community at night; while 48 per cent would travel through an area dominated by the other community during the daytime. Furthermore, the reality that spatial divisions are reproduced, especially among younger respondents, indicates that spatial separation remains unchallenged.

In overall terms a mere 18 per cent of respondents undertook weekly consumption activities in areas dominated by the other's religion. Such low levels of interaction were explained by the finding that 58.9 per cent of respondents would not undertake journeys into areas dominated by the other community due to fear of either verbal or physical violence. Around 9 per cent stated that they would not undertake such journeys because they wished to avoid spending money in areas dominated by the other community. The findings given in table 15.2 would seem to suggest that fear of being attacked by the other community dictates low levels of cross-community contact. However, a subjective reading of such information masks a series of relationships complexified by age, gender and intra-community threat.

Fear, as shown in table 15.2 is a much stronger determinant in the choice of facilities than is loyalty to the home community. However, 13.5 per cent of respondents would not undertake journeys into areas dominated by the other community for fear of being ostracised by their own community for so doing. A similar number stated that fear of the other community was a motivating factor in the refusal to enter areas dominated by that community. Fear of 'my own community' was directly linked to the belief that entering areas dominated by the other sectarian group would lead to individuals being 'punished' by members of their own sectarian group. As such fear stems from both an inter- and intra-community understanding.

The interviews conducted following the survey produced a series of complex cultural and demographic positions. Pensioners were those least likely to perceive the other community as a menacing spatial formation. Table 15.2 shows that pensioners are less likely to fear the other community than are younger age-groups. For pensioners fear of 'my own community' or fear of both communities were more palpable than among those aged 16–44.

Almost all of the able-bodied respondents of pensionable age used facilities in areas dominated by the other community. Interviews among the pensioner group disclosed that the majority are not afraid to enter 'alien' territory for four main reasons:

- social relationships that existed prior to the contemporary conflict have tended to endure and older people visit the other community in order to maintain such friendships;
- pensioners were three times as likely as the other age-groups to have either Catholic or Protestant relatives within each community, suggesting that inter-marriages were more numerous prior to the present conflict;

Table 15.2 Percentage share, by age and reason, of those who do not use facilities in areas located in the other community

Age	Fear of the other community	Fear of my own community	Fear of both communities	Loyalty	Other
65+	45.6	20.2	20.2	8.5	5.5
45–64	49.6	16.2	14.2	13.5	6.5
25–44	64.6	9.4	9.2	8.8	8.0
16–24	75.8	8.4	6.2	5.6	4.0
Av.	58.9	13.5	12.4	9.1	6.0

- older people tended to be repulsed by violence, which they contended had destroyed a previous society within which community relations were relatively *normalised.*

Although the pensioner group conceded that its communities had been victimised by sectarian violence it was also contended that those communities had been involved in transgressive sectarian behaviour. A fourth issue to emerge was that of religious conviction and the belief that it is immoral to judge whole communities as abnormal and inauspicious. It is apparent that lived social histories, in which there has been extensive cross-community linkage are capable of diluting the rationale of sectarian sentiment and as a result fear of the other community is tempered by more experienced cultural understandings.

Stronger and more distinct sectarian attitudes were located among those – comprising 86 per cent of all respondents – aged 16–55. Few within this group undertook by choice any form of inter-community linkage or visits to areas dominated by the 'other' religious group. For the 16–55-year-olds the experience of residential segregation was channelled via a framework of exclusive and sectarian representations and ideological 'tradition'. Sectarianism and fear of the 'other' community were viewed not as repressive relationships but as an articulatory process which enshrined spatial segregation. Space, for those who articulate sectarian discourses, was seen to function as an object that hosts historical 'truths' and collective communications. Community and history, for this group, served as micro-territorial constructions which reinforced the way in which geography presents sectarian hostility as a valid politicisation of space. Among those who advanced sectarian discourses, the materialisation of residential segregation into spatial constructs was imperative in order to functionalise and advance topographic conflict. At every point of conversation among those who maintain sectarian narratives it was acknowledged that all social space is coded through a sectarian analysis. In those interviews of people with sectarian views, it was commonly understood that urban space is fabricated by both ideological and physical separation. However, one of the most pronounced factors that distanced the sectarian group from those who were non-sectarian was the manner in which they eulogised, through the expression of topophilia, the communities in which they lived. Each member of the sectarian group discussed his or her community via utopian discourses of integrity, loyalty, kinship and symbolic purity, whereas non-sectarians were more likely to indicate that their communities contained multiple forms of impurity, transgression and deviance.

The interviews conducted among the sectarian group produced passionate sectarian narratives and a most pronounced sense that the other community was abnormal, antagonistic and uncompromising. The share of those who had experienced physical harm at the hands of the sectarian other was similar to that among pensioners (40 per cent and 38 per cent, respectively). Unlike non-sectarians, members of this group tended to maintain that they could not rationalise why their communities had been objects of sectarian violence and tended to assert that their communities were victimised and that the perpetrators of such attacks were odious representations of a complete community. The failure, by the majority of these respondents, to recognise that analogous threats are an encumbrance on the other community meant that ethno-sectarian separation was comprehended through a uni-dimensional ethno-sectarian logic.

Fear, in this sectarian group, was explained in terms of *reproaching* the other community, the result of which is that sectarianised readings are constantly linked to an acknowledgement of spaces of fear and the location of unsafe places. Within such a climate of ethno-sectarian cognition and telling, cross-community contact was discussed through tales of violence and aggression. Violence from within the 'home' community which had been directed at the other community was nearly always articulated as a strategy of defence or in terms of rational patterns of reprisal.

Without doubt paradigms of ethno-sectarian purity and impurity predicate social relations to such an extent, and with such power, that the capacity exists to silence a dialogue capable of challenging ethno-sectarian discourses. This implies that telling, violence and the reproduction of fear are based on sectarianised relationships which aim not only to reproduce residential segregation but to suppress any belief system which identifies ethno-sectarian purity as a socially constructed and imagined set of relationships. Preserving the capacity to control the propaganda of ethno-sectarian belonging is facilitated by spreading the myth that the other community is to be feared. Ensuring that sectarianised relationships will continue to be achieved by endorsing the morality of cultural and political sectarianism.

Segregation: one side to every story

The violent activities of paramilitaries and the British State have been examined by the sociology of deviance.[13] Violent behaviour has been both celebrated and castigated in the dogmatic struggle over 'truth' and political legitimacy. Violence in Northern Irish society has been paralleled by multifarious forms of felon-setting which has aimed to present the violent activities of opposing groups as dangerous, aberrant and irrational. Despite political change, as articulated in the Belfast Agreement, it is obvious that political protagonists continue to uphold the rationale and integrity of previous violent activities.

There is an ongoing refusal among those who see violence as legitimate to fully understand that violent acts have been unwarranted and excessive, and that the failure to recognise the harm done thereby significantly reduces the capacity for meaningful political exchange. This is due in part to violence being understood via a uni-dimensional community logic. There is no doubting that many individuals who were involved in paramilitarianism are now working via community organisations to build some form of inter-community linkage and in so doing aim to reduce the potential of violent acts. Yet there remains an inability to challenge wider narratives of resistance and interpretations of violence that point to the legitimacy of that violence. Apologies have emanated from within loyalism, republicanism and the British State, but such 'repentance' has always been tied to a selective understanding of victims. The growth in demands for inquiries and truth commissions highlights the reality that victimhood remains as a symbolic and ideological battleground. Politics, despite change, still works on the mobilisation of unionist–loyalist and republican–nationalist communities and, in some instances, on exploiting the narratives of violence and harm that have been created over the past thirty odd years of political turmoil. Within such an intensely divided society it is evident that mobilising harm done *to* a community as opposed to recognising the harm done by that community remains a key political weapon. Violence may well decline but that does not mean that its memory is not used to mobilise wider ideological commitments.

The media and the British and Irish states have aimed to censure the violent behaviour that has emerged from Northern Ireland's most politicised and violent communities. The violence that has emerged and continues to emerge from republican and loyalist communities is denounced as deviant, pathological and criminal. Irish republican groups view their engagement in violence as necessary for the protection of their areas and the development of 'anti-colonial' strategies. For such groups it was and is the violence of the British State and of Loyalists that is viewed as illogical and based on illicit political depictions. Loyalist paramilitaries have argued that their violence was similarly based on a determination to shield loyalist places: they present their violence as a 'legitimate' and historically constituted right to safeguard their political links with the UK. The British State generally remains silent when it, too, is cast as an abuser of military force.

The perpetuation of political and ideological conflict between Northern Ireland's political groups ensures that the complexities of segregation and the perpetration of violence have been generally left unexamined. The desire to champion political discourses and violence as 'veritable', 'virtuous' and 'legitimate' has led to a conspicuous failure to recognise how ethno-sectarian conflict has reproduced spatial enclosure and behavioural practices that are partly dictated by near universal fears and prejudices.

In political terms the attempt to undermine the discourse that fear of and prejudice against the other community sustained violent acts was undertaken in order to encourage the belief that all violent practices articulated by the other group are unwarranted, apolitical and ethically repugnant. Presenting the other community as fearsome and pathological was employed as a tactic that aimed to homogenise communities and as such to reinforce spatial enclosure. Spatial enclosure via segregation was less about creating boundaries between Catholic and Protestants as it was concerned with building relationships within segregated places that promoted a resistance culture and the development of an unwavering community-based political logic that tended to see only 'one side' to any story. The primacy of such a selective sectarianised argument led, in extreme instances, to an inadequate understanding of the fears and anxieties that existed among those who resided within the other community. Therefore, it is not surprising that political representatives who are trying to take their community towards more pluralist modes of reasoning find it difficult to truly engage in cross-community dialogue, especially dialogue which seeks apology and recognition of victimhood and hurt.

Communities thus championed the case that they were the *bona fide* victims of violent conflict. The refusal or inability to recognise that harm was done to those cast as antagonists remains a prevalent feature of political argument. Accepting the victimhood of the other community is, within the context of sectarian opposition, politically inappropriate as it would emasculate ideological integrity and encourage a process of accepting responsibility for violent acts, a political shift that would incapacitate the legitimacy of political *resistance*. It is important to stress that, in recent years, the decrease in politically motivated violence has been accompanied by an intensified process of claiming and *owning* victimhood. Without doubt, and despite that fact that such a logic undermines political progress, claiming the *cognomen* of having been the most persecuted community helps to perpetuate the rectitude of political justification.

The reality that political righteousness has been tied to sectarian and residential segregation means that there is a need to present those opposed to one's political logic as still determined to reject true political progress. In terms of representations that emerge from the media and the British and Irish states the fact that many people, most of whom lived in the most socially deprived and violent communities, felt unprotected, fearful and threatened has been conveniently ignored in the profiling of communities as either *deviant* or *trustworthy*. Of course, the presentation of those labelled deviant and transgressive cannot now be counterposed by an acceptance that they were themselves victims of politically motivated violence. The whole edifice of political belonging would be severely tested if communities and the British and Irish states were to accept an alternative belief system, one which recognised that the ideologically constructed 'bad' suffered at the hands of the ideologically constructed 'good'. Remaining blameless is thus a key component in the perpetuation of sectarian atavism in Northern Ireland.

In the context of the peace process and more recent violent events it is clear that the comprehensive desire to circulate an image of stability means that those engaged in violence must remain categorised as an atavistic cabal intent on destroying political progress. Recognising that many people involved in ethno-sectarian and violent acts experience disproportionately high rates of fear and exposure to risk is rarely seen as a motivating factor for the perpetuation of inter-community discord.

Conclusion

Fear and residential segregation impede the search for work, the uptake of training and education, and the use of public services. In addition, fear creates socio-spatial burdens which are endured mostly by socially deprived communities. The potential to reconstruct Northern Ireland's production and consumer arenas so that they respond to equality of opportunity and parity of esteem is a major factor in the creation of long-term political stability. Few, if any, of the policies which aim to challenge socio–economic dislocation link the realities of spatialised fear to the reproduction of social deprivation and communal polarisation.

Even though the Belfast Agreement identified the spatialisation of fear as a policy priority for a number of territorial and economic developmental departments, there is no evidence that it has become a key issue in policy formation. This is not simply due to gaps in data and methods; the political sensitivites outlined above have played their part. In reality most public sector agencies have actively downplayed the inter-connectedness of rigid residential segregation, rising sectarian tensions and ethnic territoriality. As is the case in all Western societies, the downplaying of social and political exclusion remains a feature of neo-liberal governance. Furthermore, the lack of consensus among political parties and the nature of sectarian disputation that exists between them means that the articulation of pan-community concerns is severely hampered.

A significant body of policy is now emerging which aims to solve problems relating to segregation, compounded by fear and restricted social mobility. Yet policies tend to be attached to the central features of crisis management, the key principle of which has been to imagine that abnormal problems can be solved via normal policy-making strategies. Evidently the desire to collect information on the degree and nature of sectarianised habituation remains negligible, especially given that the reading of such data would be undermined by highly sectarianised interpretations. The reality that there are no policies directly linked to the acknowledgement of sectarianised fears is located in the 'policy blindness' and, indeed, resistance of government departments to challenge the edifice of sectarian opposition.

The analysis of fear and prejudice provided above underpins the need to translate policy and political rhetoric around segregation into practice and to connect practice with the reality of sectarianised habituation. Given the sectarian nature of political control in Northern Ireland much of the normative commentary dedicated to challenging segregation and ultimately the reproduction of fear is ambiguous and difficult to distinguish in the detail of policy-making instruments.

Notes

1   A. S. Adair, J. N. Berry, W. S. McGreal, B. Murtagh and C. Paris, 'The Local Housing System in Craigavon, N. Ireland: Ethno-Religious Residential Segregation, Socio-Tenurial Polarisation and Sub-Markets, *Urban Studies*, vol. 37, 2000, pp. 1079–92.
2   P. Shirlow, '"Who Fears to Speak": Fear, Mobility and Ethnosectarianism in the Two Ardoynes', *Global Review of Ethnopolitics*, vol. 3, no. 1, 2003, pp. 76–92; P. Shirlow and B. Murtagh, 'Capacity Building, Representation and Intra Community Conflict', *Urban Studies*, vol. 41, no. 1, 2004, pp. 57–70; S. Maguire and P. Shirlow, 'Shaping Childhood Risk in Post-Conflict Northern Ireland', *Children's Geographies*, vol. 2, no. 1, 2004, pp.69-82.
3   P. Shirlow and M. McGovern, 'Language, Discourse and Dialogue: Sinn Féin and the Irish Peace Process', *Political Geography*, vol. 17, no. 2, 1998, 171–186.
4   E. Soja, *Postmetropolis: Critical Studies of Cities and Regions* (London, Blackwell, 2000).

5 E. Heikkila, 'Identity and Inequality: Race and Space in Planning', *Planning Theory and Practice*, vol. 2, no. 3, 2001, p. 266.

6 D. Horowitz, *Ethnosectarian Groups in Conflict* (Berkeley: University of California Press, 1985).

7 A. Smith *Nations and Nationalism in a Global Era* (Cambridge: Polity Press, 1991).

8 R. Pain and P. Shirlow, 'The Geographies and Politics of Fear', *Capital and Class*, vol. 60, 2003, pp. 15–25.

9 J. Whyte, *Interpreting Northern Ireland* (Oxford: Clarendon Press, 1990); T. Wilson, *Ulster: Conflict and Consent* (Oxford: Basil Blackwell, 1969).

10 In certain places walls were not erected between places in which violence acts took place; such places were in many instances already divided by railway tracks, the construction of new road systems or slum clearance.

11 A. Feldman, *Formations of Violence: The Narratives of the Body and Political Terror in Northern Ireland* (Chicago, IL: University of Chicago Press, 1991).

12 The communities, listed by the Catholic place first, were Ardoyne/Upper Ardoyne, New Lodge/Tiger's Bay, Manor Street/Oldpark, Lenadoon/Suffolk, Whitewell/White City and St James'/Village.

13 N. Jarman, *Material Conflicts: Parades and Visual Displays in Northern Ireland* (London: Berg Publishing, 1998).

16

Constitutionalism, civil society and democratic renewal in Northern Ireland

JOHN MORISON

Conventional constitutional thinking in the UK used to consider 'Westminsterism' the most developed form of constitutionalism and would stress the role of Britain as the mother of parliaments, bequeathing democracy to lesser nations. Now such ideas seem quaint, as the UK struggles to update its essentially seventeenth-century constitution to the twenty-first century by way of a various reforms which elsewhere generally were accomplished in the nineteenth century.[1] Meanwhile there has been a sea-change in the site of public power and the way in which it is now exercised. Much of this is captured by ideas of globalising power, notions of the state being engaged in rowing rather than steering, or by the move from government to *governance*. Government does not now take place only within a single unified national territory or by means of a unified single system: the effects of globalisation mean that territory, like economy and culture, are increasingly multiple and plural rather than unified and national. In this context government acts not so much by simply issuing commands or making law as by developing strategies, techniques and procedures which operate across the countless, often competing, value systems and concentrations of power that exist across state and non-state institutions and centres of power and expertise. Ideas of multi-level government have evolved from a simple recognition that there are layers beyond the national state to more sophisticated ideas of how power is dispersed into a multiplicity of sites, constituting nodes in a heterarchical network, rather than layers in a hierarchical pyramid, which operate in a relationship of mutual influence rather than one of control.[2] Ideas are emerging according to which the activity of government is complex and multi-*format*, too: there are now many more agencies and bodies of civil society, the private sector as well as of government and quasi-government, and they operate at every level from the local, the regional, the national and the European to deliver both the policy and the services of government.

Orthodox constitutional thinking in the UK is struggling to accommodate these changes.[3] The structures envisaged by the Belfast Agreement and the

Northern Ireland Act 1998 illustrate this general point very well. While the motives of the various governments involved may be high-minded, the result is a settlement that is politically brokered by higher forces and imposed through a constitutionalism made up of conventional ideas of the state, of assemblies and executives and, most of all, of the sovereignty of laws passed by parliament. As the Northern Ireland Act 2000 (which has been used on four occasions to suspend the institutions of devolution) demonstrates all too well, such a settlement can be revoked with a stroke of the same sovereign power by which it was instituted. Indeed, in many ways the Northern Ireland Act 2000 marks out the boundaries of British constitutionalism generally and the limits of even the modified consocial version developed in Northern Ireland.[4] The whole idea of building an ever-more elaborate institutional edifice to include all political elements, while at the same time drawing on the language of rights to reserve certain matters from the agenda of short-term politics as a method of resolving the problems arising from a wider politics of disagreement, comes to a natural conclusion in the difficulties that have surrounded the Northern Ireland Act 1998 and the Belfast Agreement.

That even this most sophisticated structure remains highly problematical suggests that constitutional regeneration at a much more profound level is probably necessary – at least as an additional underpinning of what has been achieved so far. Whatever the eventual political fate of the GFA, what is required is arguably a genuine *constitutive* change: a transformation at the ethical level where it is the conduct of conduct that is being agreed. Such an idea of constitutional regeneration must be different from and subtler than simply adding on new layers of representation or holding together what is already there through impasse-favouring or consensus-requiring arrangements in an assembly. While the institutions of formal government may not provide a solution to the political/constitutional issue of 'Who governs?' they can provide at least a place to 'park' the problem.

Meanwhile, however, there is still the more deep-seated issue about *how* to govern. It is here that ideas of governance and in particular the role of the voluntary sector are of interest. It may be that new forms of civil society involvement developing beyond the formal State and its institutions provide an indication of how the values behind the settlement can be developed in all the realities of governance as it now actually takes place. Such understandings will require new models of constitutionalism that far exceed even the limited reform model that is presently being rolled out in the UK generally.

In seeking to make this argument this account briefly reviews the settlement's structures and suggests that the role of government has changed since last there was devolution in Northern Ireland. Next the history of involvement of the voluntary sector in governance in the Northern Ireland context is outlined to indicate its particular potential for development. Finally, the positive advantages of opening up a new democratic space by developing the role of the voluntary sector in the processes of governance are reviewed and the value of a more fundamental constitutional *renewal* project considered.

The structures of the settlement and the changing role of government

The constitutional solution to the historical problem of Northern Ireland is in many ways unique; at the same time, parts of it remain thoroughly traditional.[5] It is a British solution, *mutatis mutandis*, of which the chief aim is to restore institutions of representative democracy in order to provide a democratic space where accountable self-government can take place against a background of what hopefully will be an economy and society growing in stability and self-confidence in the absence of endemic conflict. The brokering of an agreement is generally viewed as a triumph of (UK, US and Irish) political will in securing a deal in the unpromising circumstance of recalcitrant local politics. Achieving agreement has required a number of interesting additional structures, such as those for North–South co-operation, intergovernmental relations between Britain and Ireland, and relationships among all the people of these islands. It has also necessitated an important human rights and equality agenda (and this is where the uniqueness of the settlement largely lies).[6] A reading of the Belfast Agreement alongside the Northern Ireland Act 1998 also shows the novel feature of a constitutional settlement which recognises that issues of devolved government in Northern Ireland have an associated (and troublesome) additional political agenda of weapons decommissioning, prisoner release, and the reform of policing and criminal justice.[7] However important and unique these features are (and the equality and rights agenda are of particular value), it is undeniable that the main tangible result of the settlement is a structure – the Northern Ireland Assembly.

In some contrast to devolution elsewhere, the Assembly of Northern Ireland is an example of very traditional representative government. In fact, it is not only very traditional but also very representative. There seems to be a view that all possible voices must be accommodated within some sort of idealised public space provided in an assembly building. Here everyone is to be heard (although none can dominate, as a result of the elaborate cross-community mechanism for 'key decisions' and the power-sharing requirements for executive office). Indeed the baroque (or perhaps even rococo) nature of the constitutional architecture of the settlement's structures almost seems to indicate a reckless abandoning of concerns about cost and convenience as every conceivable political viewpoint and relationship is factored into an ever-more complex edifice of government. Currently there are 18 members of the Westminster Parliament, 3 MEPs as well as the 582 members of the 26 local councils, in addition to the 108 members of the assembly. There are 12 government departments in addition to the 18 government agencies (such as the Planning Service, Road Service and Child Support Agency), and over 65 executive non-departmental public bodies (NDPBs), including the 5 education and library boards and 4 health and social services boards, which together consume more than half of the devolved budget. There are more than 20 advisory NDPBs and a network of tribunals and other bodies which contribute to what may be regarded as a hugely over-governed population of only 1.6 million.[8] It is important not to cavil at cost, but it is noteworthy that the estimated monthly cost of the Northern Ireland Assembly while operational is £2.64 million (£1.93 million while suspended).[9] Of course, such expenditure is better than a violent alternative, but since the conclusion of the GFA the period for which the assembly has been suspended now far exceeds that for which it has been operational.

More important than the cost of government is the fact that what is now possible and what is expected of governments generally have changed. One of the more resonant contemporary descriptions of the Belfast Agreement and the structures it promised was that it amounted to 'Sunningdale for slow learners'.[10] The reference here is of course to the not dissimilar package of legislative assembly, power-sharing executive and all-Ireland bodies that had a very short life in 1974. But while the structures are redolent of that previous exercise in devolution, it is important to remember that the whole project of government generally has changed radically since the 1970s. No longer do governments anywhere expect to fund, plan and deliver the whole range of social goods to their citizens within their defined territories. The general move from government to governance, with its emphasis on globalisation and the hollowing out of the nation state, is well documented.[11] There is now not only multi-level government but also multi-form (or multi-format) governance too where the actions of states are augmented by interventions from elsewhere in the market or the voluntary sector. Government in a 1970s model of parliamentary institutions and departments of state which tax widely, spend highly and make big choices has been replaced everywhere by notions of governance where opportunities for making big changes are more limited and the emphasis is on partnership, and *steering* rather than *rowing*.[12] Northern Ireland cannot be expected to be exempt from worldwide changes. Indeed it has been argued elsewhere that although the structures of settlement may provide a more or less satisfactory answer to a *political* problem, they do not offer a very satisfactory solution to a *governmental* problem.[13]

The *problem* of government has changed during the period in which the search for an answer to the complex constitutional problem was being made. Indeed, the public sector and its technologies of government are still changing. Now the driver is best described under a general rubric of 'modernisation', a worldwide trend which has several common elements based essentially on developing consumer focus, improving public sector performance and taking advantage of new information and communication technology.[14] In Britain this is a complex, constantly changing and somewhat indistinct phenomenon. It encompasses much of what is more or less straightforward reform, such as the modernisation of parliament and reforms to political party funding. It also provides a *brand* to describe general processes of change in the health service, education and, particularly, local government. In addition, however, it involves a more general orientation in the organisation of government, one requiring a new approach, or *style*, in government operations. This is oriented essentially around re-invigorating public services by bringing in different understandings of efficiency, including elements of private sector efficiency, but without ceding control to the same extent as happened with earlier versions of privatisation. Ideas of partnership are key: government is to be the enabler, facilitator or regulator rather than a main provider. Targeting resources, monitoring and enforcement, and measuring satisfaction are important; bench-marking and performance management are particular features. Initiatives are typically project-based, cross-cutting and joined up. The original key document, the White Paper *Modernising Government* (Cm. 4310 1999) outlines the 'overall vision', which sees the public sector 'with a culture of improvement, innovation and collaborative purpose' (para. 10), and suggests that this culture can be achieved by the twin goals of seeking to meet users' needs more effectively and improving departments' performance. The overarching aim is to 'build upon the many strengths in the public sector to equip it with a culture of improvement, innovation and collaborative purpose' so that it might be 'as efficient, dynamic and effective as anything in the private sector' (para. 11). Indeed, this emulation of the private sector is a signature aspect of the overall programme.

For the second term the delivery mechanisms for modernised government have changed but the emphasis on public sector reform has intensified. Now the initiative is supported by the Prime Minister's Delivery Unit and the Office of Public Services Reform. The new document *Reforming Our Public Services: Principles into Practice* (March 2002), offers 'four principles of public sector reform', which turn out to involve national standards, devolution and delegation, flexibility and the expanding of choice.[15] This in turn has been reinforced by a number of key speeches by the home secretary, David Blunkett, and by Alan Milburn, MP, who have talked in terms of the future of public services in a third Labour term being predicated on actively engaged citizens who take responsibility for their own communities in a programme of civil renewal where delivery of public services are responsive to a public empowered by broadened choices.[16]

Even in Northern Ireland, where the peace process has a brought significant surplus of government, there are new mechanisms of service delivery which replicate those developing in Great Britain. There government has increasingly re-oriented itself around the voluntary sector as one of the significant players in terms of service delivery. Now it seems that consultation with the sector is important not only to policy development and its expression in law, but to the actual delivery of services, particularly in the modernised and partly marketised forms that these are presently taking. Services are provided by a range of state and non-state agencies in a variety of quasi-public, partly private and market-based formats which require citizens to act as consumers in exercising a degree of accountability and control consonant with their status as customers. This ambitious strategy for changing the basis on which public services are delivered involves developing earlier ideas of the Citizen's Charter into programmes such as Service First, with its quality networks, charter marks and public sector benchmarking schemes. In particular, ideas about 'best value' in providing services involve the sector not only in competition to provide services but in the consultation to determine exactly what best value actually is in any given situation, establishing key best value priorities and in devising the performance indicators to ensure that it has been delivered. This duty to consult with users and user groups is itself of particular value and importance in creating a democratic space of real involvement beyond the formal halls of the Northern Ireland Assembly. However, there is also clearly potential for 'quality' to be defined so as to include more democratic elements requiring, for example, further consultation, fair employment practices, improved community relations, more transparent and accountable organisation, and so on. The role of the sector here, and indeed in seeing that quality is delivered, is potentially significant and may allow it to assist in mainstreaming a democratic agenda within elements of basic service delivery.

While arguing for a view of government, and of the constitution, that accommodates this more sophisticated understanding of the limits and potential of public power and the changing nature of modernised government, this account focuses on the role of the voluntary sector in the governance of the new Northern Ireland. After considering the already highly developed nature of the sector in the context of pre-settlement mechanisms of rule, the capacity of the sector to provide an engine of renewal in addition to the Northern Ireland Assembly and its various structures is assessed.

The evolution of the voluntary sector in Northern Ireland

There is a long history of voluntary activity in Ireland, where it has been developing since the end of eighteenth century.[17] Some have speculated that this degree of development was brought about by a politics of exclusion from the formal State, with the result that alternative structures emerge among the nationalist community, this in turn bringing a response from the Protestant community.[18] Certainly, voluntary activity is now perceived to be highly developed in Northern Ireland. The Northern Ireland Council for Voluntary Action (NICVA) maintains a list of some 5,000 organisations on its data base.[19] In the recent past the voluntary–community sector performed a *different* and *wider* role in Northern Ireland than did its counterparts in Great Britain, and this ranges through service provision to a more engaged policy development role.

The voluntary sector as an adjunct to direct rule: 'civil servants without ties'?

The system of direct rule which continued for more than twenty-five years, with only a limited interruption occasioned by the brief restoration of devolution in 1973–74, offered particular opportunities to the voluntary sector in Northern Ireland. Characterised, as it was, by the absence of a nexus between the local political process and mechanisms of government, direct rule in some ways allowed the sector to act as an alternative site of politics and as an unofficial opposition. In the absence of a local assembly and with only very limited local council involvement,[20] direct rule was characterised by a number of negative features. Legislation was made by orders in council with the effect that law that was primary in substance was made by means that were secondary in terms of the level of scrutiny and debate involved.[21] Much legislation was passed as a 'read across' from Great Britain and arguably did not benefit from local input. Epithets like 'helicopter rule' or 'consular government' capture something of the flavour of a mechanism of government whereby a secretary of state from the Westminster administration, holding a seat in an English parliamentary constituency, was brought in to head up a governing structure that depended for local information on Northern Ireland's Civil Service rather than local politicians.

To counter these negative features, and the perceived democratic deficit that they brought, the voluntary sector was encouraged to become involved to some degree in government. In part the sector could offer its local expertise and knowledge, and also may have brought a degree of legitimacy to state action, particularly in politically sensitive areas. From the sector's point of view, such a relationship with government had certain advantages. General efforts at depoliticising service delivery by removing it from local government control and distancing it from direct rule mechanisms provided an opportunity for the sector to become involved in a service delivery role.[22] Some parts of the sector, particularly those staffed by individuals who elsewhere might well have entered political life but who were not attracted by the local political scene, may have welcomed the opportunity to become more closely involved in a policy development role. Indeed there are suggestions that successive secretaries of state, even those from the Conservative Party, may have found voluntary sector personnel less distant and easier to deal with than local party politicians.

While the relationship was not always easy, expressing it at its strongest direct rule presented parts of the sector with an opportunity to engage with the NIO departments and other structures of direct rule. Government engaged in policy dialogue with non-governmental organisations and empowered them to deliver services and advance conflict-resolution strategies. Of course there always remained an imbalance in the relationship in so far as government generally was the funder and the sector was in the role of applicant. However, there were alternative funders and a range of other arenas in which politics could develop. European institutions and structures, in particular, afforded the voluntary sector opportunities to bypass domestic government institutions and engage in politics on different terms.[23] At its very highest this may have amounted to a sophisticated form of governmental dialogue or a 'communicative constitutionalism' in which the sector was one important element among the many involved in governance in Northern Ireland.[24]

The voluntary sector and the new democratic space of representative politics

It seems clear that the voluntary sector had a distinctive role and a particular opportunity during the time of direct rule. The British Government's strategy centred on policing the crisis while awaiting the moment of grand-scale political agreement which could then be rendered in institutional form in a devolved assembly that simultaneously guarantees the Union and recognises and legitimises an all-Ireland dimension, while ameliorating the excesses of majoritarian government. Tactics varied around the key elements of security, economic support and community relations. While the security agenda could always trump the others, there were nevertheless conditions where the voluntary sector (along with others) could have a particular role both in getting the business of government done in difficult circumstances and in developing new forms of governance and conflict resolution. The GFA secured in April 1998 represented the historic achievement of British aims to resolve the (Northern) Irish issue and, of course, changed the agenda completely.

In the post-Agreement situation the voluntary sector is in a different position. The exact nature of the role that the sector will play in the future remains unclear. There is a Taskforce, established by the Department of Social Development, to explore the future of the sector. Its 2005 report, *Investing Together*, recognises the essential role of the sector within the new politics of Northern Ireland and argues for the development of a longer-term community investment model and modernisation strategy.[25] There are, however, others, particularly some of those presently holding elected office, to whom it may appear that there is now little need for a voluntary sector operating in an enhanced role: with the political process restored, normal service has been resumed and the sector can be dismissed to the background.[26]

Such a view is unrealistic. As has been argued already, it is not a 1970s-style government that has been restored: the project of government everywhere has changed. Modernised versions of government now engage with a range of other actors engaged in the business of government – in terms both of service provision and the production of policy. This realisation of the limits of traditional representative democracy may not yet have quite come in the early excitement of restored devolutionary government (and its subsequent suspension). However, in some ways it should not be a surprise. If the local politicians presently waiting offstage to re-occupy the offices of government were to look at developments in governance elsewhere they would notice a reduction in capacity that comes both from a rolling back of the state that now manifests itself in multi-level and multi-form governance, and from attempts to involve others in the operation of governance in an effort to, in the words of Anthony Giddens, 'democratize democracy'.[27] Furthermore, a proper understanding of the past and present role of the voluntary sector in Northern Ireland itself, combined with an accurate reading of the full implications of the GFA and the Northern Ireland Act 1998, would show the centrality of ideas of consultation and participation, and suggest that the voluntary–community sector's role as an alternative democratic space beyond formal politics is more likely to increase than diminish. Each of these features must be briefly considered.

New patterns of governance transferring to Northern Ireland

The experimentation with new formats for governance to fill the spaces left by the rolling back of the State that has occurred in Great Britain has been reproduced to some extent in Northern Ireland. The voluntary sector is thought especially appropriate to deal with some issues, particularly social exclusion, which are beyond the reach of government and outside the interest of the private sector. In recognition of the important potential of the sector, the Government is attempting to build a new relationship with the voluntary–community sector which involves both a recognition of its increasing role and the formalising of the association between parts of the sector and the State through the development of a series of 'compacts' in all four constituent parts of the UK.[28] Much of this is directly transferred to Northern Ireland. Interest in developing 'joined up' government has led to increased voluntary sector involvement in statutory plans and in community plans which seek to factor in all local stakeholders and providers from the public, private and voluntary sectors. There is a series of policy initiatives in Northern Ireland ranging from New Deal for Communities and Health Action Zones to the Safer Communities initiative which involve the sector directly. Other initiatives, such as the development of Community Interest Companies and the instigation of a social economy, envisage a particular role for the voluntary and community sectors.[29]

Indeed, it may legitimately be argued that ideas of partnership governance, which are rapidly gaining in popularity in Britain, are in fact more developed in Northern Ireland than elsewhere. Ideas of partnership provide one of the basic tenets of the GFA,[30] which is, of course, unique in that section 56 of the Northern Ireland Act 1998 provides for a formal role for the voluntary–community sector through the Civic Forum. Although this is currently suspended along with the other institutions, it does provide an interesting recognition of the sector in Northern Ireland and its partnership role.[31] There are, however, other, less formal, ways in which the new politics established by the GFA build in a special role for civil society. There are the District Partnerships, mentioned above, which in spending European funding must operate co-operatively. Further funds (termed 'Peace II' funding) are available until 2006, and they have significant potential to develop further the sorts of structures and practices of partnership governance that grew up with the earlier funding. Partnerships are needed, too, to bid for certain additional funding from, for example, the Single Regeneration Budget.

Governance and GFA: developing new democratic spaces

Having earlier characterised the GFA and the Northern Ireland Act 1998 as mainly about institutions and restoring traditional representative democracy, it must be acknowledged that suffusing the whole structure are the elements of human rights, equality and indeed partnership. While some of this is about creating further institutions, such as the HRC and the Equality Commission – and there may be an element of ritualistic obeisance to the new totem of rights and equality – there are significant features, too. Important aspects of these may involve the voluntary sector in creating and operating within a new participatory space.

It has been mentioned already that partnership is described as being central to the GFA and, indeed, it is present in some form in the consocial aspects of the formal arrangements for government. Also, partnership (in the more developed sense of working with civil society and others) is an important element in proposals on policing,[32] and it is there, too, to a degree, in relation to criminal justice.[33] However, it is in pursuit of equality values and human rights that partnership and participation can be seen as having most application to the voluntary sector and its role in developing a forum beyond traditional politics where many voices can be heard in a participatory act of genuine *constitution*.

In addition to the other consultation requirements, discussed above, that relate to governance structures everywhere,[34] there are clearly some that are unique to the Northern Ireland settlement. Building on the earlier Policy Appraisal and Fair Treatment scheme, section 75 of the Northern Ireland Act 1998 imposes a statutory duty on public authorities to promote equality of opportunity.[35] This requires public authorities to consult with persons likely to be affected by the scheme and with representatives of such persons. This brings the voluntary sector into the heart of the consultation process in a way that is not equalled elsewhere. Voluntary sector bodies are to be involved, too, in consultation with regard to enforcement.

There is a whole range of other features that indicate the potential of the GFA to deliver democratic process (rather than merely structure). There is the debate about a Bill of Rights for Northern Ireland which has come about as a result of the HRC being charged by the GFA with consulting widely on rights appropriate to Northern Ireland and supplementary to those in the ECHR such as should be included in Westminster legislation. While in some ways the actual experience of this consultation may be seen as an opportunity lost, with rather inconsequential consultation simply adding to the burden of participation and overstretching the patience of those being continually consulted, in other ways there has been an opportunity for a genuinely participatory process where the voluntary sector has a vital role in both establishing and then operating within, an additional democratic space.

It is vital that the issue of rights, and the use to which those rights will be put in the new Northern Ireland, are not decided by the political parties alone (or even by elite groups of activists and scholars drawing on international best practice). Rights must be fully constitutive of the new society, the foundation for participation on an equal basis, and by all groups and individuals within society, with an equal voice that is worthy of respect. Rights must not be seen as belonging to one or other tradition, or even as something of short-term value in smoothing over the aftermath of the conflict. Rights emphasising participation, as well as the usual safeguards against arbitrary power, are an important foundation for a proper civic dialogue about the way in which people in Northern Ireland wish to live together.

If political discourse is to be widened beyond the debating chambers of the Northern Ireland Assembly, where politicians register their tribal affiliation and must struggle to act in ways that transcend it,[36] then a widening of the political space is required. This can be achieved in part by defining a rights base that provides the foundation on which individual citizens can take part in dialogue within safe limits and where their voices will be guaranteed to be heard in a deliberative process. The voluntary sector, which is largely outside the traditional limits of politics, is central in ensuring that the sorts of rights considered appropriate are those that guarantee real and effective participation. There are other instances, too, of consultations offering civil society a particular role in government. The consultation that has occurred around the *Shared Future* initiative which asks fundamental questions about whether Northern Ireland's future as a pluralistic society provides a further 'constitutive moment' in the life of the community.[37]

All of these new democratic spaces require consultation and dialogue that involves hearing voices from outside of traditional politics. The voluntary–community sector has a special role as a champion of various unheard interests in all the 'best value' consultation exercises and partnership mechanisms, and in these important dialogues, too. Indeed, there is evidence that the voluntary sector may well have a particular role to play on a number of issues such as gender equality, social exclusion and rural development where affected groups might otherwise have to struggle too hard to get their voice heard. Participatory democracy will involve the voluntary sector generally in more long-term projects of planning and peace-building. The short-termism and problem-fixing of politicians, although necessary, is not particularly suited to address issues such as what the new society should look like in twenty years time. Civil society is particularly important in times of transition, and there are jobs which, arguably, belong there most of all.[38]

More generally, there is the main argument that democracy cannot work effectively without alternative spaces. The general project of reviving politics and democratising democracy factors in an important role for civil society and the voluntary sector, and can be an important addition to state action. Ideas from a range of theorists relating to the way in which a revived participatory politics can be developed open up possibilities for an enhanced role for the voluntary sector both within Blairite 'third way' thinking – and beyond it. Thus, for example, accounts range from those who require simply a more participatory form of politics – where the sector with its links to groups that perhaps are not given adequate voice in the sectarian politics of traditional representative politics can have a particular role – to those theories which identify as necessary wider ideas of community, sympathy and compassion. In this way ideas of participatory politics shade into more fundamental notions of a politics of association.

New forms of constitutionalism

At this stage we clearly require a better version of constitutionalism, one that moves beyond simply reforming institutions and giving formal representation, albeit now within devolved administrations. Older ideas of (particularly British) constitutionalism with their focus on parliament, sovereignty and pragmatic solutions are unable to accommodate this new turn satisfactorily. We must look instead at ways of thinking about public power that cut across the traditional boundaries and reflect better how governance now actually occurs. Ideas of *governmentality*, developed from the work of the French theorist Michel Foucault, inform us that power is exercised indirectly and at a distance by a whole range of active subjects who not only collaborate in the exercise of power but actually shape and inform it.[39] With this understanding it can be seen that the democratic quality of governance depends on a raft of other agencies beyond the formal State and the orthodox public sphere. Indeed, as ideas of governmentality demonstrate, just as the notion of 'a unified solidary social domain ... is displaced by images of multiple communities, plural identities, and cultural diversity', so too has there been a recasting of the role of national governments which 'no longer aspire to be the guarantor and ultimate provider of security', but instead should 'be a partner, animator and facilitator for a variety of independent agents and powers, and should exercise only limited powers of ... [their] ...own'.[40] Issues are framed by many perspectives with citizens being 'responsibilised' in relation to a wide range of schemes, modalities and rationalities, ranging from individual morality and organisational rationality to more formal audit and legal controls. Individuals have multiple identities, the State has been rolled back and the complex consequences of globalisation and localisation, privatisation and marketisation, as well as consumerisation and a host of other redesignations, have the effect of altering the whole project of government and what is to be governed.

Understandings of government and of power that develop these insights are important in developing new ideas of constitutionalism that transcend traditional Westminsterism. While the still-evolving constitution of Northern Ireland has many of the features of old-fashioned, institution-based, British constitutionalism, it also has indications of the way that new forms of constitutionalism may evolve both there and more widely in the rest of the UK. This is a constitutional revolution that should be watched closely.

Notes

This chapter is a modified, shortened and updated version of earlier work which appears in C. Harvey (ed.), *Human Rights, Equality and Democratic Renewal in Northern Ireland* (Oxford: Hart, 2001) and 21 *Oxford Journal of Legal Studies* 287 (2001).

1 See further J. Morison, 'The Case Against Constitutional Reform?', *Journal of Law and Society*, vol. 25, no. 4, 1998, pp. 510–35; and D. Oliver, *Constitutional Reform in the UK* (Oxford: Oxford University Press, 2003).

2 See, for example, N. Bernard, *Multilevel Governance in the European Union* (The Hague and New York: Kluwer Law International, 2002), or M. Keating's account of the 'reterritorialisation of politics' as involving 'a dual process of sub-state mobilisation and supra-state integration' and a 'search for new levels of political action', in 'Europe's Changing Political Landscape', in P. Beaumont, C. Lyons and N. Walker (eds), *Convergence and*

Divergence in European Public Law (Oxford: Hart Publishing, 2002), p. 7.

3 See further N. Bamforth and P. Leyland (eds), *Public Law in a Multi-Layered Constitution* (Oxford: Hart Publishing, 2003).

4 See J. McGarry and B. O'Leary, *The Northern Ireland Conflict: Consocial Engagements* (Oxford: Oxford University Press, 2004).

5 See further C. McCrudden, 'Northern Ireland, the Belfast Agreement and the British Constitution', in D. Oliver and J. Jowell (eds), *The Changing Constitution* 5th edn. (Oxford: Oxford University Press, 2004).

6 See further C. Harvey (ed.), *Human Rights, Equality and Democratic Renewal in Northern Ireland* (Oxford: Hart Publishing, 2001).

7 See further C. Campbell, F. Ni Aolin and C. Harvey, 'The Frontiers of Legal Analysis: Reframing the Transition in Northern Ireland', *Modern Law Review*, vol. 66, no. 6, 2003; and K. McEvoy and J. Morison, 'Beyond the Constitutional Moment: Law, Transition and Peacemaking in Northern Ireland', *Fordham International Law Review*, vol. 26, no. 4, 2003, pp. 961-95.

8 There is currently an OFMDFM Review of Public Administration being carried out whose terms of reference are to consider the arrangements for the delivery of public services by all those bodies not established by the GFA The options for the future set out in the consultation paper are remarkable for their highly traditional outlook and almost complete disregard of developments elsewhere in the UK where government increasingly is seen as only one player among many others from the private and voluntary sector who are responsible for delivering services in partnership. See www.rpani.gov.uk

9 According to the Paul Murphy, secretary of state for Northern Ireland, in response to a question from David Burnside, MP (House of Commons, *Hansard*, Written Answers for 15 December 2003, col. 740W).

10 This remark is generally attributed to Deputy First Minister Seamus Mallon.

11 For recent work on the now familiar idea of governance, see M. Bevir and R. A. W. Rhodes, *Interpreting British Governance* (London: Routledge, 2003) and the special issue of *Public Administration*, vol. 81, 2003; see also J. Pierre (ed.), *Debating Governance: Authority, Steering and Democracy* (Oxford: Oxford University Press, 2000).

12 This phrase comes from the influential book by D. Osbourne and T. Gaebler, *Reinventing Government: How the Entrepreneurial Spirit is Transforming the Public Sector* (New York: Plume, 1992).

13 See further J. Morison, 'Constitutionalism and Change: Representation, Governance and Participation in the New Northern Ireland', *Fordham International Law Journal*, vol. 22, no. 4, 1999, pp. 1608-27.

14 For the phenomenon of modernisation generally see B. Charlton and P. Andras, *The Modernization Imperative* (London: Imprint Academic, 2003); and for modernisation worldwide see the Organisation for Economic Co-operation and Development policy brief *Public Sector Modernisation* (2003) (available at: www.oecd.org/publications/pol_brief). For its application to UK government see www.pm.gov.uk/output/page249.asp and J. Newman, *Modernising Government: New Labour, Policy and Society* (London: Sage 2001).

15 See further www.number-10.gov.uk/output/page5624.asp.

16 As Alan Millburn put it recently, these changes will 'refashion the relationships between government, services and citizens [where] the overall presumption should be towards a more diverse, more devolved, more flexible system of governance … [with] more choice for users. It should no longer be about central government acting as the proxy for the choices of local communities but for local communities themselves to be empowered to make those choices': see 'Active Citizenship: The Ten Year Agenda' (2004) available at: www.alanmilburn.co.uk; see New Local Government Network (NLGN) *Making Choices: How Can Choice Improve Public Services?* (2004); D. Blunkett, 'Civil Renewal: A New Agenda', Edith Kahn Memorial Lecture (London: Home Office, 2003) and 'Active Citizens, Strong Communities' (London: Home Office, 2003).

17 See further A. Williamson, 'The Origins of the Voluntary Action in Belfast', in N. Acheson

and A. Williamson (eds), *Voluntary Action and Social Policy in Northern Ireland* (Aldershot: Avebury, 1995) pp. 161–80.

18 J. Schense, 'Creating Space for Change: Can the Voluntary Sector Help End Northern Ireland's Troubles?', *Harvard Human Rights Journal*, vol. 11, spring 1998, pp. 149–85.

19 Department for Social Development, *Consultation Document on Funding for the Voluntary and Community Sector* (Belfast: DSD, Northern Ireland, April 2000) suggests that the sector provides employment for 33,000 people and has a gross annual income of £500 million, while the Northern Ireland Council for Voluntary Action State of the Sector III (2002) survey pointed to an annual income of £657 million and argued that the sector employed more than the agriculture, financial or local government sectors.

20 Local authorities, seen by civil rights campaigners of the 1960s as epitomising unionist domination and abuse of powers, were effectively stripped of all powers except for the most minor in areas of environmental health, tourism, recreation and refuse collection in the McCrory Review of 1972.

21 See further, for example, B. Hadfield, 'Legislating for Northern Ireland at Westminster' in M. Connolly and S. Loughlin (eds), *Public Policy in Northern Ireland: Adoption or Adaptation* (Belfast: Policy Research Institute, 1990), pp. 55–75.

22 See for example how provision for personal social services developed through statutory bodies, quangos and voluntary organisations: (B. Caul and S. Herron, *A Service for the People: Origins and Development of the Personal Social Services of Northern Ireland* (Belfast: December Publications, 1992).

23 The role of the sector in the District Partnerships established by the European Special Support Programme for Peace and Reconciliation with its budget of €44.2 million with matching government funding indicates, too, how successful the sector became in enmeshing itself in governance at all levels; see further J. Hughes, C. Knox, M. Murray and J. Greer, *Partnership Governance in Northern Ireland: The Path to Peace* (Dublin: Oak Tree Press, 1998).

24 See J. Morison and S. Livingstone, *Reshaping Public Power: Northern Ireland the British Constitutional Crisis* (London: Sweet & Maxwell, 1995), pp. 138–49.

25 See further www.taskforcevcsni.gov.uk and the Government response in *Positive Steps* (2005).

26 See R. Wilford and R. Wilson, *A Democratic Design? The Political Style of the NI Assembly* (London: Constitution Unit, 2000), pp. 55–7 and 64–5.

27 A. Giddens, *The Third Way: The Renewal of Social Democracy* (London: Polity Press, 1988), pp. 70–8; T. Blair, *The Third Way: New Politics for the New Century* (London: Fabian Society, 1998), especially chs 4 and 5.

28 See further J. Morison, 'The Government–Voluntary Sector Compacts: Governance, Governmentality and Civil Society', *Journal of Law and Society*, vol. 27, no. 2, 2000, pp. 98–132.

29 See Department of Enterprise, Trade and Investment's consultation paper on community interest companies 'Developing a Successful Social Economy: Community Interest Companies' which can be accessed via www.detini.gov.uk.

30 See the foundational 'Declaration of Support' that appears at the beginning of the GFA's document (Appendix 2, this book), where it states 'we are committed to partnership, equality and mutual respect as the basis for relationships' (para. 3). Indeed partnership ideas can be observed all over structures in Northern Ireland. North, South, West and Greater East Belfast all have partnerships for development and there are Rural Development Partnerships and numerous Local Action Partnerships.

31 See further C. McCall and A. Williamson, 'Governance and Democracy in Northern Ireland: The Role of the Voluntary and Community Sector After the Agreement', *Govenance*, vol. 14, no. 3, 2001, pp. 363–83 and V. Bell, 'Spectres of Peace: Civil Participation in Northern Ireland', *Social and Legal Studies*, vol. 13, (2004), pp. 403–28.

32 *A New Beginning: Policing in Northern Ireland*, Report of the Independent Commission on Policing for Northern Ireland, 1999, (Patten Report), which contains ideas about 'a real partnership between the police and the community – government agencies, non-governmental organisations, families and citizens' (para. 1.16).

33 In a rather thin section on rights and principles, the Criminal Justice Review Group identifies

as one of the 'common values' of the criminal justice system an idea of 'partnership between the criminal justice system, the community, and other external bodies': *Review of the Criminal Justice System in Northern Ireland* (Belfast: Stationary Office, 2000), p. 30.

34 See the Northern Ireland Department's Consultation Register at www.consultationni.gov.uk for a list of these structures.

35 See C. McCrudden, 'Mainstreaming Equality in the Governance of Northern Ireland', *Fordham International Law Journal*, vol. 22, no. 4, 1999, pp. 1696–775, for discussion of the origins and development of this initiative.

36 Under the standing orders of the Northern Ireland Assembly each member must formally declare himself or herself as a unionist, nationalist or other. This has particular importance with regard to certain 'key decisions' where cross-community support is required.

37 See *A Shared Future: Improving Relations in Northern Ireland*, available at: www.asharedfutureni. gov.uk/consultationpaper.htm

38 Walzer argues that 'no state can survive for long if it is wholly alienated from civil society ... The production and reproduction of loyalty, civility political competence, and trust in authority are never the work of the state alone, and the effort to go it alone – one meaning of totalitarianism – is doomed to failure': M. Walzer, 'The Civil Society Argument', in R. Beiner (ed.), *Theorizing Citizenship* (Albany, NY: SUNY Press, 1995), pp. 153, 168.

39 This governmentality approach is based on key writings of Michel Foucault and some subsequent work including, particularly, N. Rose, *Powers of Freedom: Reframing Political Thought* (Cambridge: Cambridge University Press, 1999). Much of this thinking has been developed in a criminological context but it can be usefully applied to law and constitutional issues where it sets an important agenda for constitutional scholarship and practice.

40 N. Rose, *ibid.*, pp. 323–4.

17

Two cheers for the NGOs: building peace from below in Northern Ireland

FEARGAL COCHRANE

Transnational advocacy networks have been instrumental in shaping global decision-making, persuading and pressuring governments to ban landmines, endorse international environmental agreements and denounce female genital mutilation. These and countless other citizen initiatives, campaigns and movements are ushering in an era in which governing is no longer left only to governments. The operative word now is 'governance' – a process that is more inclusive, participatory and democratic than in the past.[1]

It is well established that volunteering empowers people. It contributes to building trust and solidarity, encourages participation and ownership, creates networks of reciprocity and reinforces a sense of collective responsibility ... It is a vital component of the community development process and to the functioning of a democratic, inclusive and cohesive society.[2]

Many of this volume's chapters focus on political dynamics in Northern Ireland at the track 1 level; to put it another way, they focus on the political parties, paramilitary factions, government policies and international interventions at the top of society. This is of course entirely appropriate as it has been primarily governments, political parties and paramilitary groups that have driven both the conflict and the 'peace process' in a direct sense. It is the contention of this chapter, however, that these elite actors have not *exclusively* determined the dynamics of conflict and peace in Northern Ireland, and that other groupings within society, from the business community and trades union movement, to the Churches, the media and individual NGOs, have played a role in shaping the political environment in the region. The focus of this chapter therefore, is how politics functions at a community level and the interventions that have been made in what is often referred to as civil society before, during and after the GFA of 1998.

Politics in Northern Ireland is not restricted to the political elite but reaches down through society via influential groupings within civil society to the community level. While many citizens at the grassroots level may feel undervalued, disempowered and disenfranchised by the political process, they nevertheless exert an indirect influence on the dynamics of conflict and peace in the region. One needs to think only about community conflict over contested Orange parades such as Drumcree or the attacks on children at the Holy Cross Primary School in Ardoyne in 2003 to understand the impact of ordinary people on the political process.

Defining civil society

The term 'civil society' has become *de rigeur* in recent years within academic and policy-making discourse and is frequently referred to today as an essential ingredient of stable liberal-democratic states. What lies behind such thinking is the notion that civil society is a force for stability, civic engagement and, fundamentally, for non-violence. Thus, a vibrant civil society, where citizens are moved to take an interest in their communities, join NGOs and informal voluntary associations, vote in elections; and so on, will augment what might be referred to as the 'contentment index' in the regime, increase social cohesiveness and thus reduce alienation and the proneness of the region's inhabitants to conflict. Robin Wilson, director of the Belfast-based think-tank Democratic Dialogue – itself a component of civil society – explains:

> It has become a truism to say that politics has become disconnected from real people, that we inhabit an 'anti-political age' in which mass parties no longer conduct social change. Perhaps nowhere more so than in Northern Ireland, where the fault lines of division have in the past rendered the parties prisoners of the conflict rather than authors of an alternative political project. Yet it has also become increasingly evident that governance – the *business* of government, at all levels – does matter. There is growing evidence that regions which are economically successful are socially cohesive, and that their political viability depends on an active culture of civic life.[3]

Allusions to the positive potential of civil society have become increasingly prevalent in recent years: Western governments, anxious to combat declining levels of trust and participation in the democratic process, and international organisations, eager to find some means of tackling protracted social conflicts and ethnic violence, make frequent reference to it. However, while 'civil society' has become relatively commonplace in recent years, it has a theoretical pedigree which in Western thought extends 'from classical times in Greece and Rome, through the faith-based medieval period, and up to the start of the 21st century'.[4] While it may have become more fashionable after the democratic changes in Eastern Europe at the beginning of the 1990s, the concept of civil society has been a strong undercurrent in western political thought throughout the twentieth century, and it has been used by everyone, from revolutionary socialists to British Prime Minister Tony Blair, in defending their political manifestos for change.

Given its widespread usage, it is important to define the limits of civil society in the context of Northern Ireland and to acknowledge that it can be used to justify and defend a multiplicity of political values and objectives. Contemporary uses of 'civil society' too often cherry-pick associations and NGOs that are deemed to be 'good' rather than 'bad', positive rather than negative. Thus, the notion of civil society is deconstructed to incorporate the churches, the media, academia, the trade unions, the business sector, NGOs and so on. When NGOs are mentioned in the same breath as civil society, the focus tends to be on campaigning, advocacy or service delivery groups, human rights organisations, community regeneration projects and reconciliation groups. However, these constructions often place more emphasis on what is deemed to be *civil* than on what is understood by *society*, and may, in consequence, have little bearing on the actual patterns of association in these communities. Thus, while people may well feel the urge to associate around parent–teacher organisations, re-cycling campaigns and neighbourhood-watch groups in stable communities, the drive to associate in unstable communities, such as Northern Ireland's, can focus just as easily on sectarian societies, partisan community groups and, ultimately, paramilitary organisations.

This chapter prefers an *inclusive* understanding of civil society in order to reflect the positive *and* the negative aspects of society itself, and to underline the fact that the line between what is deemed to be positive and negative in a society like Northern Ireland's is itself a value judgement, one that may change over time and may differ depending on one's particular political agenda.

Consequently, the term 'civil society' is here used to refer to the groups, associations and individuals from trade unions, churches, business communities, educational sectors, cultural organisations, NGOs, media groups, the arts, peace groups and other pressure groups that mediate between the individual and the State. While my focus is primarily on the non-governmental individuals and groups that make a *positive* engagement with the society, it does not exclude those sometimes perceived as exerting a negative and destructive influence. Paramilitary organisations, such as the Provisional IRA and the UDA, and ethnocentric cultural/religious organisations, such as the Orange Order and the Gaelic Athletic Association, are some of the most powerful and important constituents of civil society in Northern Ireland, and thus are not to be excluded if the political and social dynamics of the region are to be properly understood. What is deemed to be an 'effective' or 'successful community' may say more about the values of the person making the assessment than about the community in question. 'Successful according to what criteria? Effective for whom? The measurement of social capital needs to go beyond a rehearsal of data relating to crime, unemployment, teenage pregnancy, school achievement and so on.'[5]

The emergence of civil society in Northern Ireland

During the 1960s the conflict in Northern Ireland gave rise to a polity in which normal democratic politics scarcely existed. The Government at Westminster was largely disinterested in Northern Ireland other than in security terms, the nationalist community having opted out of the formal political system due to a combination of its sectarian exclusion from effective citizenship and poor political leadership. The Government at Stormont meanwhile was partisan in its favouring of the unionist section of the population and operated levers of local governance that had little responsibility or power.

Following the suspension of devolved government in 1972, most of the day-to-day policy-making was in the hands of powerful civil servants and quangos. The resulting 'democratic deficit'[6] saw space opening up for the voluntary and community sector. That sector grew consistently, its influence and the scope of its responsibilities continually widening. As opportunities for participation in conventional political structures declined, the voluntary sector emerged as an alternative site for citizen activism, and there was a discernable shifting of human energies away from party politics and into civil society. To put it simply, those who wanted to make a contribution in the areas of social or economic policy during the 1970s and 1980s were more likely to be attracted to NGOs rather than to political parties, which were deadlocked and relatively powerless, their focus almost exclusively on the constitutional debate. Clem McCartney provides an accurate summary in observing that:

> the early period of the Troubles saw a flowering of local community activity and the development of community leadership. Those involved tended to reject conventional politics and community action provided an alternative stage from which to work for social change … It was also true that in other sectors of civil society there was a great deal of disillusionment with politics throughout the 1970s and 1980s. Many who did not support the predominant system of sectarian politics found their sphere of activism in the trade unions, churches, and neighbourhoods, but they had little impact on the overall political situation. Most sectors of society, including the churches, were themselves divided about the most appropriate response to the conflict, and in these circumstances intransigent voices were dominant.[7]

At the level of community-based NGOs, civil society groups developed differently within the unionist and nationalist sections of the population. From its formation in 1921 until the suspension of devolved government in 1972, Northern Ireland's Government was dominated by the unionist community, which consequently regarded government, in a general sense, as a competent deliverer of social services and as something of a large-scale community development organisation. Unionists, on the whole, saw a direct correlation between their concerns and votes, on the one side, and the activities and social programs that *their* government undertook, on the other. The experience of the nationalist community was rather different. Nationalists felt little allegiance to a post-partition state after 1921 from which they felt excluded. While some nationalists deliberately opted out of the State and its structures because they were ideologically opposed to it, successive Unionist Governments did little to persuade nationalists that they were an integral part of the State. Unionists often treated nationalists with suspicion, excluding them from both the political process and the workplace. As a consequence, the nationalist community could not rely on the State to satisfy all of its needs and soon developed its own service delivery mechanisms based on community co-operation and self-help initiatives. Some of these, such as the St Vincent de Paul Society, were associated with the Catholic Church, while others, such as the credit union movement, were secular initiatives motivated by economic need. By the early 1970s it had become difficult to disentangle the socio-economic from the political grievances that lay behind both nationalist and unionist community action. As this disagreement became increasingly violent, and as central government's reach and authority decreased within urban working-class areas, unionists and nationalists alike had to rely on their own resources to fulfill some of the services the State had once provided and to satisfy emerging needs. NGOs therefore developed to populate political and economic spaces. These tended to conform either to service delivery groups, such as relief centres for those who had been forced out of their homes and community development initiatives of various kinds, or to campaigning groups, such as the Peace People, formed in 1976 to oppose sectarian violence from republican and loyalist paramilitary organisations.

Civil society and the peace process

The low-intensity political conflict over the last thirty years has seen the evolution of a unique and highly diverse civil society in Northern Ireland. In addition to the business sector, trade unions, media, vibrant arts and educational sectors and the range of influential church organisations, a large array of NGOs has emerged that focus, either directly or indirectly, on peace and conflict resolution and/or community development activity. This diversity is a result largely of the sector's lack of regulation and structure while at the same time being reasonably well resourced for the size of the population. Funding from the EU's Special Support Programme for Peace and Reconciliation (SSPPR), the US and the British Government (the NIO, in particular) has facilitated development and growth in the NGO sector. In a society with just over 1.7 million people, NGOs abound in Northern Ireland, a recent estimate putting their number between 4,500–5,000 groups with a turnover of £657 million in 2000–01. During the same period, the general public donated an estimated £147 million to the voluntary and community sector, an monthly average of £12.17 per person.[8] This is a serious level of commitment by any reasonable standards. In a survey conducted by NICVA, meanwhile, it was found that in September 2002 alone the voluntary and community sector advertised at a cost of approximately £75,000 a total of 139 jobs, evidence of the size of the sector within the economy.[9]

This monetary support is indicative of a general concern to improve good social, cultural and community relations between and within Northern Ireland's divided communities, and to encourage reconciliation and conflict-resolution activities in the region. The EU and the British Government, and various non-state-based philanthropic funding bodies, see civil society (or specific elements of it) as *a good thing*. One of the anomalies of the NGO sector within Northern Ireland, particularly the peace-promoting and conflict-resolution organisations and community development groups central to civil society there, is the extent to which they are funded by the British Government. Knox and Quirk point out: 'Since the government is perceived by one section of the community to be a key protagonist in the conflict, [its] motivation is regarded with a degree of suspicion.'[10]

Since the early 1990s, successive governments have been eager to fund community development and community relations groups. They had two reasons for doing this. Firstly, it suited the developing ideology of state contraction and the privatising of the provision of services. Thus, statutory agencies were encouraged to contract out to the NGO community, funding and co-opting community groups to undertake what had been the responsibility of statutory agencies. Some academic commentators (e.g. Robson 2000) have claimed that another motive for contracting out to NGOs was to blunt their radicalism and force them into the position of service deliverers rather than advocates of social change.[11] This trend was common in Northern Ireland in the 1980s and 1990s. While many groups formed around a radical conscious-raising agenda based on a critique of the existing political or economic system, some, in practice, found themselves sucked into service-delivery functions that converted them into extensions of the very public statutory bodies they had been formed to challenge or respond to. This view was summed up by a member of Dove House Resource Centre, the Derry-based community development group, who suggested that the organisation's participation in the ACE scheme in the 1990s, while enlarging the scale and human resources of the organisation, had de-radicalised the NGO and, by taking on functions previously provided by statutory organisations such as the Training & Employment Agency (e.g. advising the unemployed on how to fill out benefit forms) had actually disempowered the very people it had been set up to enable. This activist saw the ACE scheme as responsible for 'mission drift' within the organisation and making it complicit in state-driven schemes for providing cheap labour.

> ACE was an awful system of workfare that didn't aid unemployment, didn't provide people with greater skills, and was just cheap labour basically, and cheap labour which tied groups like Dove House, and other groups, into an administrative system which actually diffused the energy and the potential creativity to address some of the problems people were having.[12]

The amount of resources funnelled into the voluntary and community sector over the last thirty years in Northern Ireland has to some extent rebounded in public attitudes to it. Some people have reacted against what they perceive to be the professionalisation of the voluntary sector, and refer disparagingly to the community relations 'industry'. A recent NICVA survey found that more than 200 voluntary and community organisations had a turnover in excess of £1 million a year.[13] The influx of money from the EU during the 1990s through the SSPPR, and the growth of core funding from the statutory sector during the same period, opened up the voluntary and community sector (and the funders themselves) to accusations of wastefulness and of ineffectual direction of resources. Reports that the Northern Ireland transport company Translink was to receive £75,000 from the EU SSPPR in 2003 may have fuelled such perspectives.[14] The total expenditure within the first three years of the SSPPR (1995–97) amounted to £350 million.[15] While this programme was generally seen as a welcome shot in the arm for the voluntary and community sector and delivered in a variety of innovative ways, the second tranche of money in the programme (known as 'Peace II', to run from 2000–4) has been less critically acclaimed, due in part to its economic and infrastructural focus and, more pointedly, the bureaucracy associated with its administration:

> Groups out there are crying out for money, at times living from hand to mouth, closing down or choking back good projects yet money has been available and has not met its target ... Clearly there are many reasons for delays in this Programme including the length of time of negotiations with the European Commission, the stop/go nature of devolution and changing Ministers but a large part has to be administrative. It is noticeable that the over-burdensome bureaucracy associated with the Programme ... is getting out of hand. Reports regularly come into NICVA of what can only be described as petty, bureaucratic monitoring fixated with counting sandwiches and checking to the [nth] degree.[16]

Some of those active in less well resourced community development initiatives, echo the criticism that the sector has become a community relations industry, invaded by professional managerial classes with a nine-to-five commitment to the areas concerned and the problems they face. Thus, rather than seeing high profile state-funded initiatives as contributions to the region's social capital, some sceptics view them as projects with a top-down drive populated by middle-class outsiders who do not understand, or are unresponsive to, the real demands and needs of the community. This view contends that such initiatives are built on shaky foundations, and will sink as soon as the project funding/political interest in them declines. There has been a fierce debate, therefore, even between those actively working in civil society groups and networks in Northern Ireland as to the kinds of voluntary and community groups which are likely to make a contribution to conflict prevention, social capital and democratic change.

Northern Ireland today is a highly complex region, with a sophisticated, politically literate and vibrant civil society. Many of its constituent elements – educators, religious organisations, the media, business leaders and trade unions – have played their part in encouraging the peace process that resulted in paramilitary cease-fires in 1994 and the GFA in April 1998. The result of several years of negotiation between the main political actors, mediated by the British, Irish and US governments, the GFA produced a set of political principles and institutions that would restore democratic accountability to Northern Ireland on an agreed basis and a new system of power-sharing between the unionist and nationalist communities. Unfortunately, its implementation has been beset by problems and thus far it has failed to transcend political differences or promote a shared sense of community values within the region.

Many of the influential actors of Northern Ireland's civil society (the business sector, trades union movement and the main Churches, to cite only three) became active advocates of the peace process and made determined efforts to support – and at times to critique – the efforts of the major political parties to secure a negotiated political settlement.

While the business community was initially wary of expressing views on the political situation, it became more vocal during the 1990s in response to progress in the formal political process. In 1994, the Northern Ireland CBI published *Peace – A Challenging New Era*, labelled by the media the 'peace dividend' paper, an influential document that spelled out in detail an economic rationale for peace based on stability, investment and economic prosperity through the reduction of security costs and the increase in tourism and external investment.[17] The publication of this document provides a good example of the virtuous circle that civil society can help to generate, as the phrase 'peace dividend' was taken up by politicians, and has been used extensively ever since. In 1996, the CBI joined with six other trade and business organisations to create the 'Group of Seven',[18] the central message of which from its foundation has been that political stability by means of a negotiated and properly implemented settlement is essential for the economic well-being of Northern Ireland and all of the people within it. The Group of Seven has been an active supporter of the peace process and of the GFA itself, lobbying for progress on political issues linked to the troubled implementation of the latter and instances of community sectarianism such as the Drumcree protests. Following Drumcree 4 in 1998 and the deaths of three children following a firebomb attack in Ballymoney, the Group of Seven was forthright in once again linking political instability with the economy:

> The present madness cannot continue. Northern Ireland cannot credibly, on the one hand, hold itself out as a prime location for investment and tourism and, on the other, indulge in behaviour that gives the investor and the tourist every reason to shun us. There is no future for a society that does not respect the rule of law.[19]

While most business organisations would shy away from aligning themselves with particular party-political viewpoints, those like the Group of Seven have been eager to point out the economic advantages that political stability offers to Northern Ireland and to issue warnings about the negative impact on jobs and investment that political instability will bring. Trade unions such as the Irish Congress of Trades Unions became increasingly vocal during the 1990s over the need to support a negotiated settlement and preserve the ceasefires of the main paramilitary organisations, while the main Churches and elements of the media also added their weight to the efforts of those involved in the political negotiations in 1997–98. A noticeboard outside St Anne's Cathedral in Belfast displayed the pithy remark in support of the negotiations 'You can play a part in the political talks. Drop in and say a prayer'.[20]

While acknowledging that civil society and its constituent parts have been of indirect rather than immediate importance to the peace process, it could equally be claimed that its role in contributing to progressive social and political change in Northern Ireland has nevertheless been an important one over the last thirty years of low-intensity conflict in the region.[21] As NICVA's Director of Research Frances McCandless suggests, 'it is clichéd, but nonetheless true, to say that over the past 35 years, the voluntary and community sector has provided much of the glue that held Northern Ireland society together'.[22] These groups have varied from high-profile NGOs such as the Peace People, that tried in the 1970s to mobilise mass public support against paramilitary violence through vigils and street demonstrations, to groups in the 1990s such as Initiative '92, New Agenda and Democratic Dialogue, that lobbied for progressive political and social change through reports and conferences seeking to influence the policy-making community rather than public opinion more generally.

> Perhaps one of the most significant civic contributions was Initiative '92, which described itself as a citizens' inquiry ... Opinions vary on its impact. Its findings may not have been particularly original, and its lasting contribution may have been its efforts to encourage community groups and individuals to think and discuss the options for the future.[23]

While often unacknowledged by the political class, these groups have had a slow-burning impact on the political debate in Northern Ireland, were integral to the 1998 negotiations that resulted in the GFA and saw this influence reflected in post-GFA political structures such as the establishment of the Civic Forum. They have therefore played, and continue to play, a role integral to the governance of the region. The Civic Forum was heralded by some as Northern Ireland's equivalent of the Blairite vision of 'joined-up government', a 'third-way' form of governance capable of connecting society to produce a more sophisticated form of politics. A working paper published by the NGO New Agenda in 1998 summarised the hopes that some people held out for this revolutionary institution:

> The traditional concept of government, in which administrations do things to economies and people, is being replaced by the concept of governance which depends on utilising the knowledge and skills present in society through a wide range of partnerships and networks. The Civic Forum has the potential to nurture the effective governance of Northern Ireland through marrying the skills and knowledge of the sectors it represents with those of elected representatives, the public administration and wider society.[24]

During a Northern Ireland Assembly debate on the Civic Forum on 25 September 2000, Deputy First Minister Séamus Mallon heralded the new institution as integral to the GFA. 'The Forum is one more step in the realisation of the vision of the Good Friday Agreement ... It is in keeping with the new era in which we are now operating that, through the Forum and the other institutions of the Good Friday Agreement, we embrace these progressive and positive developments in inclusive democracy.'[25]

Predictably however, the Civic Forum (specifically its composition) became yet another site for sectarian squabbling between the political parties with both Sinn Féin and the DUP complaining about the balance of those nominated to it. The following enquiry from the DUP's Sammy Wilson to First Minister David Trimble on 25 September 2000 was probably rhetorical:

> As one reads through the list [of nominations], it is significant that it is made up of the membership of the Ulster Unionist Party, political failures, IRA terrorists, and yes-men. Does the First Minister agree that this kind of cronyism is probably the kind that would make even Tony Blair blush? What credibility can an organisation that is made up of cronies, failures and IRA bomb-makers possibly have when it comes to its public announcements?[26]

While the Civic Forum was to a large degree a product of the influence of civil society pressure for inclusion in any new political dispensation and, formally at least, brought the voluntary and community sector into the political process, in practice it has been a disappointment to many. Since the Civic Forum was established, in October 2000, its public profile has been low and its political impact limited. While it held out the prospect of a new constitutional model that connected the formal political sector to the voluntary and community level, its achievements have been minimal, even within the context of a dysfunctional assembly.[27] In the event that devolution is reconstituted from the detritus of the November 2003 assembly elections, the role of the Civic Forum is unlikely to be a major aspect of future public debate or a critical sticking-point in negotiations between the main political parties.[28]

After the GFA had been agreed by the main political parties, several key elements within civil society came together to advocate a 'Yes' vote in the subsequent referendum of May 1998. This culminated in the establishment of a non-party political 'Yes' Campaign, populated in the main by trade unionists, voluntary and community activists and academics. A nucleus of activists drew together the various strands of civil society, mobilising support from church leaders, educators, journalists, actors, local sporting heroes and business leaders. Quintin Oliver, director of the 'Yes' campaign, was aware of the risks that were being taken by a coalition of individuals normally expected to remain outside of the political fray. 'But who were we – other than a group of friends and colleagues, some drawn from the voluntary sector and others from the business sector – and what was our legitimacy? We knew we had none, in electoral terms, but we felt we had rights as citizens and as inhabitants of Northern Ireland – and, indeed, a duty to help the political process along.'[29]

It would be fair to conclude that without the efforts made by civil society initiatives and specifically by the independent 'Yes' Campaign, the result of the referendum[30] would have been significantly closer and the GFA would have received a much smaller mandate which would have weakened it from the outset. While civil society initiatives and campaigning NGOs have had little direct impact on the political process before or after the GFA, the sector as a whole has exerted an important influence on society in other ways: it contributed to the 'mood music' prior to the 1997–98 negotiations which helped to create a climate for constructive discussions to take place; it acted as a resource for individuals who had been directly affected by the conflict; and the sector helped support the political parties in the risky business of searching for a settlement. While much of this contribution was indirect, intangible and osmosis-like in operation, it was nevertheless vital in oiling the wheels of the peace process.

Following the GFA in 1998, attention naturally centred more intensely on the formal political process specifically on unionism's internal battles, and the debate between the UUP and Sinn Féin over the decommissioning issue and the other terms of the GFA. The focus (limited though it was) therefore shifted away from the role of civil society and towards the stop–start–stop again political institutions that were the product of the 1998 negotiations. Notwithstanding the weak achievements of the Civic Forum during the post-Agreement period, civil society generally has continued to play an important role in supporting the GFA. The business sector has repeatedly made the connection between political stability and economic prosperity, while trade union groups and the voluntary and community sector more generally have continued to condemn sectarianism within the community. The Northern Ireland Economic Development Strategy Steering Group for instance, produced *Strategy 2010*, a report which promoted the link between political stability, peace and economic growth. The following statement from the report,[31] is typical of the desire of business leaders to promote stability, and by inference the GFA, as an economic opportunity, rather than on the basis of the GFA's strengths and/or weaknesses as a political settlement in itself:

> The establishment of a stable political environment in Northern Ireland will be of critical importance to the speed and scope of the development of the economy. The civil unrest of recent years has adversely affected business confidence, leading to delay in or cancellation of investment strategies. It has also clearly had an effect on our ability to attract inward investment projects into the region, and this in turn has restricted our integration into the wider European and global economies [...]
>
> A lasting political settlement will represent a significant opportunity in both the social and economic context. It will strengthen our ability to attract international investment and provide the right environment for our indigenous firms to realise their full growth potential. The potential for the tourism sector is particularly significant in terms of increased employment in the sector itself and significant spin-off employment in the retail, leisure and entertainment fields. We will need every sector to maximise the economic benefits of peace.[32]

Influential NGOs such as NICVA, meanwhile, have taken a leading role in denouncing violence, supporting the peace process and engaging with devolved Government formed in the wake of the GFA. NICVA has developed a draft policy manifesto in which it deals directly with issues surrounding political conflict in Northern Ireland:

> Sectarianism ... is present throughout society at all levels. Effective long-term peace-building and conflict resolution must involve all sectors and communities. The voluntary and community sector has a crucial role to play in healing social divisions, empowering local communities and striving to develop a just, anti-sectarian and stable society.[33]

These are laudable goals, articulated by one of the largest and most influential NGOs in Northern Ireland. The problem, however, is one of selling this message to the diverse and complex range of civil society organisations at the micro-level, against the backdrop of community conflict and interface tension. Many community groups were formed and now operate within this nexus of low-intensity conflict, in which notions of 'community' are often narrow and parochial and conceptions of 'rights' can differ to an alarming degree. In an effort to tackle the ingrained sectarianism of Northern Ireland society, Kenneth Brannagh, NICVA's honorary president, helped launch One Small Step in March 2003. The Belfast-born actor endorsed this latest effort by civil society:

> This campaign builds on the work of many organisations in Northern Ireland which are committed to working for the common good and towards a peaceful future based on equality and mutual respect [...]
>
> At this stage we are asking others to reflect on what they can do for peace in 2003. One small step from everyone can take us a long way.[34]

The campaign was endorsed by other groups in Northern Ireland's civil society, including the CBI, the Irish Congress of Trades Unions and, more exotically, the Belfast Giants ice-hockey team. Such initiatives have found it difficult to sustain public interest in the post-GFA period and to demonstrate short-term impact in the face of community tension and outbreaks of sectarian violence at interface areas of Belfast.

Frequently during the post-GFA period, sectarian murders and intimidation by paramilitary organisations have been met by rallies and demonstrations organised by civil society organisations. Trade union groups, business leaders and the main Churches have taken a very public role in efforts to promote anti-sectarianism, and several high-profile demonstrations and vigils have been directed at ending sectarian violence.[35] NICVA Chief Executive Seamus McAleavey, meanwhile, issued a press statement in September 2003 condemning recent paramilitary death-threats to members of the Policing Board and the DPP.

> There is no place in our society for the threats, violence and intimidation which are being directed at members of the Policing Board and District Policing Partnerships in Northern Ireland. It is particularly invidious that independent members, many of whom are associated with voluntary and community groups, and our sector, are being targeted because they want to make a positive contribution to our society. NICVA and many voluntary and community organisations

take a community development approach to our work which often means striving to ensure that ordinary people are involved in the decisions which affect their lives and in the delivery of our public services. This is exactly what DPP members are doing on behalf of the public ...

In the past NICVA has had to call on those issuing threats against community workers to lift those threats. We do so again.[36]

Conclusion

Demonstrating the positive impact of civil society on the peace process in Northern Ireland in purely *quantitative* terms is a difficult task. Nevertheless, this chapter has tried to raise at least *two* cheers for the indirect role of civil society over the last 30–35 years of community conflict in Northern Ireland, suggesting that the political elites alone have not determined the dynamics of conflict and peace in Northern Ireland and that the contribution of the rich array of organisations outside of the formal political sector deserves recognition. Many of these individuals and groups have worked tirelessly in Northern Ireland's civil society to promote peace, reconciliation and community development, often against a backdrop of vicious conflict within those same communities.[37]

Returning to the nature of civil society, it has often been this sense of *community* which has motivated both the positive *and* negative components of civil society in Northern Ireland. Ironically, perhaps, the motivations behind the establishment of human rights organisations, reconciliation groups, church-based peace groups and community development organisations were similar to those behind the main paramilitary factions in Northern Ireland. The sense of *community values* and the desire to defend, protect or augment that community's position have led to a strong (though dichotomous) community cohesiveness in Northern Ireland. In a society of 1.7 million people, with somewhere in excess of 4,500 active NGOs and numerous interventions by other civil society actors such as church leaders, trade unionists and business leaders, people are falling over one another to do something for their communities. However, in a divided society like Northern Ireland's, 'the community' is a contested concept and those who are overly con-cerned about to which community they belong, have sometimes been prepared to kill those they have determined to belong to the *other* community. While a plethora of civil society groups have been working for peace and reconciliation over the last thirty years, many forms of community association have resulted in uncivil activities and outcomes. The motives of those concerned have often been articulated as the pursuit of civil rights or the protection/defence of their community's cultural heritage/identity. Unfortunately, unionist and nationalist communities have understood political, legal and cultural rights so differently that mutual exclusivity rather than interdependence has been encouraged.

While the main Churches have supported initiatives by the political parties, notably the GFA of 1998, they themselves remain an obvious source of division within the community. The mainstream media have been broadly supportive of the

GFA, though they, too, have been accused of fuelling the conflict by concentrating on division and difference, rather than on more positive stories.[38] The major trade union and business sector groups have often condemned sectarian violence, although they have given vocal support to political initiatives only in recent years. Notwithstanding the limitations of such efforts, and those of individual NGOs, and despite the influence of what might be termed 'negative' aspects of civil society, the indirect impact of this sector on the peace process over the last thirty years has been considerable. While the restoration of devolution and workable political institutions to Northern Ireland is likely to be difficult to achieve in the years ahead, we can be confident that many elements within civil society will play a positive role in all efforts to do so.

Notes

1 *Civicus World*, 'Civil Society and Good Governance', (March/April 1999, at: www.civicus.org.
2 J. R. Kearney, 'Bowling Along Together', *Scope*, April 2003, p. 18.
3 Democratic Dialogue, 'Making Democracy Work: Participation and Politics in Northern Ireland', Working Paper commissioned by NICVA, February 1998, at www.democraticdialogue.org/working/democracy.htm.
4 R. A. Couto, 'The Third Sector and Civil Society: The Case of the "YES" Campaign in Northern Ireland', *Voluntas*, vol. 12, no. 3, 2001, pp .1–20.
5 Gordon McCullough, 'A Sack of Analytical Potatoes', *Scope*, October 2003, p. 21.
6 For a fuller discussion of this term, see A. Pollak (ed.), *A Citizen's Inquiry: The Opsahl Report on Northern Ireland* (Dublin: Lilliput Press, 1993).
7 Clem McCartney, *Striking the Balance*, Accord Series, at http://cain.ulst.ac.uk/events/peace/docs/accord99.htm.
8 Figures from NICVA, *The State of the Sector III*, at: http://www.nicva.org/resources/Publications/article.asp?ArticleID=1185
9 *Scope* , 'Charities hit with £300,000 bill', March 2003, p. 11.
10 C. Knox and P. Quirk, *Peace Building in Northern Irlenad, Israel and South Africa: Transition, Transformation and Reconciliation* (London: Macmillan, 2000), p. 82.
11 T. Robson, 'Northern Ireland: Community Relations and Community Conflict', *Developments*, vol. 43, no. 3, 2000, pp. 66–71.
12 Representative from Dove House Resource Centre, interview with author, 7 October 1997. From F. Cochrane and S. Dunn, *People Power? The Role of the Voluntary and Community Sector in the Northern Ireland Conflict*, (Cork: Cork University Press, 2002), p. 145.
13 *Scope*, April 2003, p. 9.
14 *Scope*, March 2003, p. 6. In its defence, The EU SSPPR, (known as Peace II), which runs from 2000–4, was targeted at economic development in an effort to complement the Peace I (1995–99) prioritisation of social inclusion projects.
15 Knox and Quirk, *Peace Building in Northern Ireland, Israel and South Africa*, p. 80.
16 Seamus McAleavey, 'Peace II – We Lose £100 Million?', *Scope*, July/August 2003, p. 20.
17 *Peace –A Challenging New Era*, (Belfast: 1994, CBI Northern Ireland, p. 4).
18 The Group of Seven includes the CBI, the Hotel Federation, the Institute of Directors, the Northern Ireland Chamber of Commerce and Industry, the Northern Ireland Growth Challenge, the Northern Ireland Economic Council, and the Northern Ireland Committee of ICTU. It has recently been joined by the Federation of Small Businesses.
19 Statement by the Group of Seven, the Northern Ireland Chamber of Commerce and Industry, and the Federation of Small Businesses, 'Northern Ireland is on Self-Destruct: Action is Imperative', 9 July 1998.

20 F. Cochrane, *Unionist Politics and the Politics of Unionism since the Anglo-Irish Agreement* (Cork: Cork University Press, 1997), p. 360.

21 For a full examination of the nature and impact of NGO activity in Northern Ireland, see: F. Cochrane, 'Unsung Heroes? The Role of Peace and Conflict Resolution Organisations in the Northern Ireland Conflict' in J. McGarry (ed.), *Northern Ireland and the Divided World* (Oxford: Oxford University Press, 2001), pp. 137–56, and 'Beyond the Political Elites: A Comparative Analysis of the Roles and Impacts of Community-Based NGOs in Conflict Resolution Activity', *Civil Wars*, vol. 3, no. 2, summer 2000, pp. 1–22; also Cochrane and Dunn, *People Power?* and Knox and Quirk, *Peace Building in Northern Ireland, Israel and South Africa*.

22 Frances McCandless, 'Funding and Sustaining the Sector', *Scope*, March 2003, p. 12.

23 McCartney, *Striking the Balance*.

24 From website of *Democratic Dialogue*: http://www.democraticdialogue.org/working/newagenda. htm

25 Deputy First Minister Seamus Mallon MLA, Northern Ireland Assembly debate, 20 September 2000, available at: http://www.nics.gov.uk/Press/ofmdfm/000925d-ofmdfm.htm.

26 Sammy Wilson MLA, *ibid.*

27 When this chapter was being written even the website of the Civic Forum was offline.

28 While the SDLP and the Women's Coalition asked in January 2004 for the Civic Forum to be reconvened as part of the review process of the GFA, in the SDLP's case this may relate more to its concern that the structures of the GFA are not altered during this review than it reflects SDLP satisfaction with its activities and achievements.

29 Q. Oliver, *Working for 'Yes': The Story of the May 1998 Referendum in Northern Ireland* (Belfast: 'Yes' Campaign), p. 9.

30 The referendum in Northern Ireland was held on 22 May 1998; 71 per cent voted in favour of the GFA while 29 per cent voted against it.

31 *Strategy 2010* is the report of the Northern Ireland Economic Development Strategy Steering Group which was commissioned in 1998 to review economic development in Northern Ireland and devise proposals for economic progress. The review aimed to provide advice to the new Northern Ireland Assembly and was established as a result of the GFA in 1998.

32 *Strategy 2010*'s assessment of how 'peace' could impact on the Northern Ireland economy can be read in full online at: http://www.edfni.com/strategy2010/strategy2010.pdf.

33 NICVA, Draft of Policy Manifesto, available at: www.nicva.org/policy/PolicyManifesto 3rdDraf290802.pdf.

34 *Scope*, April 2003, p. 16.

35 Several thousand people took part in a rally against sectarian violence at Belfast City Hall on 2 August 2002. This followed the killings of a Catholic teenager and a Protestant construction worker , the latter murdered while working at the Territorial Army base in Derry. Bob Gourley, speaking for the ICTU, emphasised ICTU's opposition to sectarian violence: 'The evil purveyors of bigotry have declared war on us all and wished to ensure that the legacy of hatred continued.' The rally was also supported by the four main churches in Northern Ireland. For a news report, see: http://news.bbc.co.uk/1/hi/northern_ireland/2167440.stm.

36 NICVA Press Release, 19 September 2003; available online www.nicva.org/news/article. asp?ArticleID=8513.

37 See M. Sutton, *Bear in Mind These Dead: An Index of Deaths from the Conflict in Northern Ireland 1969–1993* (Belfast: Blackstaff Press, 1994); M. Smyth and M. T. Fay, *Personal Accounts from Northern Ireland's Trouble: Public Conflict, Private Loss* (London: Macmillan, 2000).

38 The impact of the media on the conflict in Northern Ireland has been widely debated: see D. Miller, *Don't Mention the War: Northern Ireland, Propaganda and the Media* (London: Pluto Press, 1994); B. Rolston, *The Media and Northern Ireland: Covering the Troubles* (Basingstoke: Macmillan, 1991); G. Spencer, *Disturbing the Peace? Politics, Television News and the Northern Ireland Peace Process* (Aldershot: Ashgate, 2000).

18

Integrated schools: myths, hopes and prospects

FIONA STEPHEN

An essential aspect of the reconciliation process is the promotion of a culture of tolerance at every level of society and includes initiatives to facilitate and encourage integrated education and mixed housing.[1]

One of the least expected peace settlements in recent times was that which finally culminated with the signing of the GFA on 10 April 1998.[2] Long in gestation, and carefully worded in content, the agreement had what has accurately been described as a most 'difficult birth'. But in spite of its problematical origins, it was endorsed just over a month later by electorates on both sides of the border (albeit with significant disaffection registered by northern unionists), and it looked to many as though this particular bargain at least – unlike that struck back in 1974 – 'could and would stick'.[3] Indeed, such was the euphoria that greeted what one observer later referred to as this 'major agreement'[4] and another as 'this extraordinary achievement'[5] that one might have been readily forgiven for thinking that the Troubles had finally come to an end. As time passed, however, it became evident that while the new deal may have at least offered one way out – and perhaps the only one available – from one of the more intractable of conflicts in Western Europe, it also bore within it the seeds of future misunderstanding. It was not so surprising, therefore, that within only a few short months of its signing the end of the 'long war' apparently signalled by the GFA seemed to be turning into a very acrimonious peace.[6] The political reality of on the one hand having to share power in a devolved government with those who had for so long been identified as the 'enemy' and on the other of having to address such issues as police reform, weapons' decommissioning, and cross-border bodies (issues that were more likely to further divide the two communities than unite them) only highlighted the obvious fact that although the GFA provided some sort of framework within which both sides could try to manage their differences without resorting to violence, it was neither an all-purpose solution to existing tensions in Northern Ireland nor, by any stretch of the imagination, a complete solution to the 'Irish question'.

Yet if there is no obvious and immediate answer to the big problem, there are some signs of limited progress having been made in the area of schooling. It is, of course, important not to overstate the case, for while there has been much earnest talk about the need to build bridges and to overcome divides, there has been little to indicate that the two communities have moved especially close to each other. In reality, as Shirlow shows in chapter 15, many areas have become more entrenched in their segregated isolation rather than less.[7] Even the GFA itself, with its positive nod in the direction of reconciliation, still assumed two blocs co-existing on the basis of parity rather than a serious expansion of the narrow ground in the middle.[8] That said, there are some factors which point to perhaps less pessimistic conclusions; and one of the more interesting indicators of change in Northern Ireland over the past few years has been the continued growth of integrated schools. Certainly, in a society where the hand of the past has weighed so heavily on the present,[9] any move that looked like offering some way forward was bound to attract a great deal of attention. Although numerically feeble at the outset,[10] and playing what even its most ardent of admirers would accept was a relatively insignificant role in the larger peace process – despite being identified as an essential aspect of the reconciliation process according to the GFA – the attempt to build a 'third way' in education in Northern Ireland has generated both hope and a not insubstantial literature.[11] This has included, among other things, an early attempt to think about integrated schools in the broader framework of community relations,[12] a subsequent and more popular study concentrating on the 'story of integrated schools',[13] a great number of more specialised research pieces looking in the main at the practices of integrated education at the level of the school itself, and more recently four rather more substantial assessments of the implications of the expansion in integrated education for education in Northern Ireland as a whole.[14] For a such a comparatively small phenomenon (in 1990 there were but 10 integrated schools in Northern Ireland and by 2000 only 45), there can be little complaint that integrated education has been ignored.[15]

The interest which integrated education has generated tells us much about the important role which education has played (and is perceived to have played) in shaping the character, and thus the history, of Northern Ireland. Few would go so far as to argue that there is bound to be enmity between children who are educated separately; yet many (and not only those within the integrated education movement[16]) would insist that while there are multiple causes for the 'Troubles' in Northern Ireland, the effect a segregated school system has on the development of children's attitudes should not be ignored. In a 2002 study of 3 to 6-year-olds which focused on political and cultural awareness, researchers found that the number of children beginning to identify themselves with one or other community and making sectarian remarks increased rapidly at ages 5 and 6, coinciding with the first two years of formal schooling.[17] Indeed, even those who accept that a system of segregated education is more a symptom than it is a cause of the conflict, nevertheless concede that if the integration of education is 'not the answer' it has to be 'part of the solution' to the problems which face Northern Ireland'[18] – a view endorsed by the 2003 Ulster Omnibus survey which found that 81 per cent of people polled believed that integrated education was important to peace and reconciliation within Northern Ireland.[19] This conviction has also been expressed by politicians and commentators outside of Northern Ireland, most recently by the All-Party Group for Integrated Education.[20] Incidents such as the internationally publicised Holy Cross School conflict in north Belfast,[21] and the continuing Northern Ireland political impasse, have only reinforced the view that even if schools are not political answers in their own right, their role in shaping a community's outlook is not to be discounted. Indeed, what is true of Northern Ireland is true elsewhere, especially perhaps 'across the water' where the search for suitable models to bring together culturally divergent groups has received a fresh impetus in a post-9/11 Britain, unnerved by race riots and cultural and religious segregation in areas such as Oldham and Burnley. [22]

Nevertheless, the idea of using education to shape beliefs has, until recently, tended to give rise to alarm in democratic societies where such a proposal has been regarded as 'social engineering'.[23] In fact, even the concept of 'integration' has been regarded with some suspicion by members of the two communities of Northern Ireland. Here we confront an obvious paradox. On the one hand, there would appear to be a vague but real level of support for integrated schools; on the other, many – including some very powerful interest groups on both sides of the divide – would seem to regard the idea of integration as constituting either some form of accommodation with the 'other' that over time is bound to lead to a loss of cultural identity in a shared 'melting pot',[24] or a false solution to the Irish question which assumes that the conflict is not the by-product of measureable inequalities created by the imposition of partition on the Irish people, but the result of community divisions. These associations have often meant that suggestions of integrating education in Northern Ireland have been greeted with a good deal of suspicion, even though repeated opinion polls have indicated that there is a consistently high level of public support for integrated schools and integrated education.[25]

Two of the charges frequently levelled at integrated schools in Northern Ireland are that they are too few in number to be relevant, and too socially exclusive to be politically significant. Let us deal with each charge in turn.

On the question of the low numbers the picture is far more complicated than critics imply. First, there is the simple issue of supply and demand. Every year now a substantial number of parents apply for places for their children in integrated schools, only to have their request turned down because of the lack of available places:[26] in 1998, 1,000 applications had to be turned down by integrated schools because there were no more places.[27] Not for nothing has the integrated sector talked quite openly of an over-subscription 'crisis', claiming that while 'parental demand for integrated places continues to grow there are simply not enough places or schools available to soak up the demand'.[28] Making the matter worse has been the failure of the Northern Ireland Department of Education (DENI) to increase enrolment to anywhere near the level required – quite often because of organised opposition. In a number of cases new requests for additional places have in fact been strongly opposed by either the regional Education and Library Board (ELB) or the local district council. A member of one ELB argued in response to the proposed increase in numbers at Erne Integrated College that 'something needed to be done about the growth of integrated education' because it was destroying the whole education system in Fermanagh.[29] DENI has not been entirely unhelpful. However, the evidence points overall to an expedient rather than a principled official approach, one that seems more interested to transform existing schools than to create new ones,[30] partly because of cost and partly to avoid appearing to be positively discriminating in favour of new integrated schools.

On the socio-economic profile of school enrolments the picture is a less privileged one than opponents suggest. One of the better measures is to see how many pupils in integrated schools (compared to those elsewhere) are entitled to free school meals. The statistics published by DENI make for interesting reading. As table 18.1 shows, though the Catholic-maintained school sector has a significantly greater proportion of pupils entitled to free school meals than either the controlled or integrated sector, integrated primary schools do have a slightly higher percentage of free school meal entitlement compared with the predominantly Protestant-controlled school sector representing pro-rata enrolments of pupils from the full range of society.

A much bigger problem perhaps concerns the new schools themselves. Here there is a very real issue because an increasing number of the more recent additions have arisen as a result of the *transformation* of controlled state schools to integrated status. Indeed, all schools that have opted to transform to integrated status have come from the state sector, representing in the eyes of Protestant opponents, a loss to their community. This sense of loss risks being compounded by the shifting balance between Protestant and Catholic school-age pupil numbers, with the former's pupil numbers now appearing to be lower than the latter's enrolments (see table 18: 2).

Table 18.1   Entitlement to free school meals: comparison by school sector, 2000–3

School Sector	% free school meals 2000 –1	% free school meals 2002–3
Integrated primaries	19.4	17.7
Controlled primaries	17.3	16.0
Maintained primaries	30.2	27.4
Integrated colleges	22.5	22.2
Controlled second level	24.7	22.4
Maintained second level	39.3	37.0
Northern Ireland average	22.5	23.7

Table 18.2   Pupils in integrated, primary, secondary and grammar schools[a] by denomination and type of school, 2001–2

	Catholic	Protestant and other	Not recorded	Total
Integrated schools	5,901	7,367	1,358	14,626
'Catholic' schools	151,905	1,368	356	153,629
'Protestant' schools	7,276	135,994	14,531	157,801
All schools	165,082	144,729	16,245	326,056

Note: [a] Including preparatory departments.
Source: Department of Education statistics, Press Release, 30 April 2002.

But how in the end do we measure genuine progress? Is the glass half empty or half full? It very much depends on perspective. Judged by where the schools once were back in the very early days when the sector hardly existed, enormous strides have been made. In September 2001 for example the total of officially 'integrated' schools rose to 46 (including 13 transformation schools) with places for 15,069 children, or 4.5 per cent of the total Northern Ireland school population.[31] These numbers at the end of the second decade of the existence of integrated schools represented an impressive increase[32] – particularly during a period of overall decline in school enrolments. On the other hand, this still left over 95 per cent of all school children in the North being educated separately. However, the incremental expansion, year by year, still suggests that progress is being made, with 5 more new integrated schools scheduled to open in September 2004 and another 2 transformed schools starting on the path to fully integrated status. Of these 7 projects, admittedly only 6 had received ministerial approval, while the seventh – Lir School, Ballycastle – opened with support from the Integrated Education Fund.[33] This rate of growth is remarkable, particularly as the legislative provision for integrated education contained in the 1989 Education Reform Order (ERO) was intended primarily to sustain the original ten financially precarious integrated schools and to provide for further expansion only through the process of transformation of existing schools to integrated status.

From the integrated education perspective, the 1989 ERO has a particular significance: on the one hand, it had the effect of raising the level of public expectation of improved and easier access to integrated schools; on the other, it increased anxieties among the integrated education membership that local perceptions of integrated schools as 'agents' of Westminster strategy, would undermine what standing they had within the two communities. Certainly, for many parents, it was a surprise to discover that the responsibility for the setting up of a new integrated school still rested with them and that the process remained quite arduous, with government approval and funding being far from automatic.[34] Integrated schools remained a do-it-yourself project for parents and not an off-the-shelf option, or a readily available basic right.

A decade on and the devolution of government to the Northern Ireland Assembly and the appointment of Martin McGuinness as minister for education were landmarks, which brought with them both fresh uncertainty and new possibilities.[35] That Sinn Féin chose the education portfolio for Martin McGuinness in 2000 may perhaps be seen as an indicator of the political importance attached to education, not to mention the media-friendly opportunities it provided for 're-branding' the image of the republican leader as a man of the people, a grandfather concerned about fair access to education for all. In any case, McGuinness provided welcome reassurance for the integrated schools almost immediately with his approval for the Ulidia Integrated College in Carrickfergus and the Millennium Integrated Primary School in Carryduff. The number of letters of support for the latter from a wide range of political sources, was also a welcome change, including messages from the PUP and the UDP, as well as more predictably, perhaps, the Northern Ireland Women's Coalition and the APNI. Such support provided a piquant contrast with news stories from the previous summer, such as 'Parents Express Opposition to Suggestion of Status Change' in which Iris Robinson, DUP, was quoted criticising the Government for 'throwing money' at integrated educa-tion.[36] In his announcement of approval for the two integrated schools, the minister stressed that his guiding principles would be 'equality, choice, accessibility and excellence', but that transformation had to be the preferred option in pursuing further expansion.

The stop-start (and now stop again) nature of the political power-sharing arrangement has meant that any continuity of administration and policy has depended heavily on the civil servants in DENI. While the Civil Service would reject any suggestion that it is in control,[37] it is difficult to think otherwise, particularly when it continues to provide the continuity from one minister to the next, plus the briefings and advice to both Westminster and local politicians on aspects of education policy. Following the suspension of the Northern Ireland Executive, the civil servants, once more, find themselves in a holding position, under the direction of ministers in Westminster.

Political stalemate does not necessarily spell disaster for integrated education, which in fact has received its two biggest boosts to date in terms of the number of new school approvals at times – 1989/90 and 2003/4 – when there has been an impasse at the top.[38] This is perhaps one reason why the planned integrated school model, developed by ordinary people as a response to the frustrations and political powerlessness of life within a divided and conflict-ridden society, has aroused a good deal of interest among those involved in peace-building and conflict resolution in other parts of the world. As a legal entity and structure, the model offers a formula that might work equally well, integrating groups with divergent interests, in other contexts. As a case study, the adoption of the integrated schools by government also highlights some of the issues involved when the status quo is confronted with an expression of the will of a nascent civil society, in this case that of cross-community groups of parents of varying religious beliefs, political views and, in many cases, a multiplicity of personal motivations. In each instance, however, a common purpose was established and a viable school built, according to a set of underpinning principles, arrived at by consensus, with the stated purpose of contributing to the development of peace and reconciliation in Northern Ireland through the opportunity for children from *opposing* sides of the community to get to know each other by sharing the same education and school experience. For the parents though the path was never a smooth or easy one. Indeed, the process of arriving at consensus on keenly disputed issues has often been long and exhausting. The diversity of personal and political perspectives, and the high level of parent participation in the management of schools, have often produced highly contentious meetings.[39] A representative of one of the major charities even remarked that he had never attended such fiercely contested meetings as he had in connection with the integrated school sector in Northern Ireland.

At first sight these observations seem to run counter to the claim that integrated education is about contributing to the development of peace and reconciliation. However, as Michael Walzer has observed, perhaps the most valuable thing that people learn as they become more deeply involved as *participants* in civil society is 'how to live with the many different forms of social conflict'.[40] In Northern Ireland and other deeply divided societies, perhaps the significant value lies in the transformation of conflict defined by political groups and reflected in community violence into more individualised social conflicts within a shared sphere of participation. It seems often to be overlooked and under-appreciated that conflict *per se* is a normal part of life, a feature of healthy human interaction. *How* that conflict is expressed and the *means* by which it is resolved are what defines conflict as 'healthy' or 'unhealthy'. Thus, for individuals and communities with experience of extreme conflict, there is a tendency to avoid issues likely to be contentious or offensive when they are in 'mixed' company.[41]

It has been observed that the model on which the integrated schools have been established since the first school was opened does not seem at all dissimilar to the consociational model on which the Northern Ireland Assembly and Executive is supposedly based. The premiss for both is two blocs predominant within the society they each seek to serve. Both are structured with carefully designed checks and balances to guard against one interest group dominating the other. Where they differ, though, is in the basic assumptions on which the institutions are based. With the Northern Ireland Assembly, the 'realist' consociational solution to the deep divisions has been to accept the situation and build a power-sharing system on the basis of established political blocs. This expedient approach to government has the sole purpose of making it possible for long-term opponents to establish some form of *modus vivendi*, rather than bringing about significant change in the political and social structures underpinning the bi-polar blocs. Critics of the model suggest that without a longer term reconciliation strategy, the 'solution' guarantees a perpetuation and reinforcement of the political divisions.[42] The planned integrated schools' model is based on an approximate balance between Catholics and Protestants, and while the integrated schools talk in terms of a plural society and the need for 'equality' and 'democratic and open procedures' as essential elements in the philosophy of planned integrated education, the emphasis has been on putting the principles into practice in a shared environment. In the wider society, if recognition of and respect for the 'other' is something practised from behind a high fence, it becomes altogether more notional.

The encouragement of mutual respect must be a crucial aim of democratic education. Bolstering self-esteem by fostering (or even reinforcing) group identity is not the way forward. Self-esteem that is compatible with mutual respect and trust has to be earned by individuals working either co-operatively or alone. Multicultural education uninformed by civic values discriminates between citizens on the basis of their group identities, as Amy Gutman has identified.[43] An integrated school claims to be 'democratic and open in procedures and promotes the worth and self-esteem of all individuals within the school community'.[44]

In this context, the continuing expansion and increase in number of integrated schools is an encouraging indicator. Each new-start integrated school may be seen to represent a public commitment from adults within a local area to work for peace and reconciliation through a form of co-operation and cross-community dialogue which introduces the prospect, however limited, of some tangible change in inter-community relationships. Critics of the model frequently question how effective integrated schools can be, operating as they do at the level of the individual rather than of the wider community. The response from those involved is that it is better to start somewhere than it is to contribute to the perpetuation of a divided system – 'If you're not part of the solution you're part of the problem.' Findings from a survey of former pupils of integrated school (conducted as part of a major study sponsored by the Nuffield Foundation[45]), confirm the positive impact of integrated schooling on cross-community friendships, and mixing with the other side in social and work situations.

Ultimately, however, the supporters of integrated schools cannot ignore financial exigencies; and in spite of the 1989 ERO, all new-start integrated schools are confronted with the need to borrow the necessary money to purchase a site and provide school buildings for the early years of the project. After three years, such a school can expect to receive government funding for its buildings provided it has demonstrated a steady enrolment pattern and, more problematically, that there is sufficient money available in DENI's budget for the capital grant to be paid, without its seeming to priviledge integrated education. With the escalating cost of new buildings, and the need to appear even-handed in the distribution of resources, it is little surprise that DENI (or the Department of Education under the Northern Ireland Executive), would prefer to see more existing schools being transformed to integrated status rather than more 'new-start' integrated schools emerge. The UN Committee on Economic, Social and Cultural Rights in its 1997 report stated: 'The Committee is of the view that current government policy, which appears to consist of a willingness to consider the conversion of existing Protestant or Catholic schools into integrated schools, if that is the wish of the majority in a given school, is ineffective and likely to preserve the status quo'.[46]

Yet, integrated education continues to move forward in spite of its critics – and despite a government strategy that, while supportive, can hardly be characterised as generous. Indeed, if an integrated education 'sector' exists now, it is entirely due to the activity of parents who, instead of being intimidated by the forces arraigned against them, continued to press on. In fact, one of the paradoxes of the integrated sector is that it has flourished not in spite of but because of opposition and material constraints – even now when the future of the GFA would appear to be in some doubt. Pessimism about the future of 'high politics' therefore should be tempered by an acknowledgement that on the ground, at least, strides (if not giant ones) continue to be made. This is very much one of those cases about which we should be saying – along with Fergal Cochrane (chapter 17) – two cheers for the NGOs and their supporters!'

Notes

1 Strand Three, Article 13 , Belfast Agreement, 10 April 1998 (see Appendix 2, this book).
2 Otherwise known as the Belfast Agreement. The Agreement was composed of three main strands: Strand One dealt with 'Democratic Institutions in Northern Ireland'; Strand Two with 'The North/South Ministerial Council' and Strand Three with 'The British–Irish Council'.
3 Rick Wilford (ed.), *Aspects of the Belfast Agreement* (Oxford: Oxford University Press, 2001), p. v.
4 Brendan O'Leary, 'The Character of the 1998 Agreement: Results and Prospects', *ibid.*, p. 49.
5 Lord Alderdice in J. Neuheiser and S. Wolff (eds), *Peace at Last? The Impact of the Good Friday Agreement on Northern Ireland* (New York: Berghahn Books, 2002), p. xii.
6 For further discussion on the peace process see Michael Cox, Adrian Guelke and Fiona Stephen (eds), *A Farewell to Arms? From 'Long War' to Long Peace in Northern Ireland* (Manchester: Manchester University Press, 2000).
7 See also David McKittrick, 'Concern Grows in Ulster as Divisions Continue', *Independent*, 22 March 1993.
8 John McGarry, in his Introduction, 'The Comparable Northern Ireland', in John McGarry (ed.), *Northern Ireland and the Divided World: Post-Agreement Northern Ireland in Comparative Perspective* (Oxford: Oxford University Press, 2001), presents a clear and concise survey of the key political theoretical models with reference to Northern Ireland and the search for a political solution.
9 See Feargal Cochrane, 'The Past in the Present', in Paul Mitchell and Rick Wilford (eds), *Politics in Northern Ireland* (Boulder, CO: Westview Press, 1999), pp. 1–28.
10 Even in 2000, integrated schools still educated only 13,924 pupils: see IEF, *Integrated Education Development Fund: Ten Year Development Plan* (Belfast: Integrated Education Fund, 2000), p. 5. By 2002 the number had increased to over 15,000, according to the September 2002 enrolments provided by Northern Ireland Council for Integrated Education (NICIE).
11 See Lesley Abbott, Seamus Dunn and Valerie Morgan, *Integrated Education in Northern*

Ireland: An Analytical Literature Review, DENI Research Report Series no. 15 (Belfast: DENI, 1999), for a summary of the issues covered and a detailed bibliography.

12   Chris Moffatt (ed.), *Education Together for a Change: Integrated Education and Community Relations in Northern Ireland* (Belfast: Fortnight Educational Trust, 1993).

13   Fionnuala O'Connor, *A Shared Childhood: The Story of Integrated Schools in Northern Ireland* (Belfast: Blackstaff Press, 2002).

14   See Grace Fraser and Valerie Morgan, *In the Frame. Integrated Education in Northern Ireland: The Implications of Expansion* (Coleraine: University of Ulster, 1999); Julie McGonigle, Alan Smith and Tony Gallagher, *Integrated Education in Northern Ireland: The Challenge of Transformation* (Coleraine: UNESCO Centre, University of Ulster, 2003); Tony Gallagher, Alan Smith and Alison Montgomery, *Integrated Education in Northern Ireland: Participation, Profile and Performance* (Coleraine: UNESCO Centre, University of Ulster, 2003); and Alison Montgomery, Grace Fraser, Claire McGlyn and Tony Gallagher, *Integrated Education in Northern Ireland: Integration in Practice* (Coleraine: UNESCO Centre, University of Ulster, 2003).

15   By 2001, there were 46 integrated schools educating 15,097 pupils: NICIE, *Going for Growth: Annual Report 2000–1* (Belfast: NICIE, 2001).

16   'Children being brought up in a plural divided society should be educated in a context where they will come to know, understand, respect and appreciate those who differ from them and to recognise what they hold in common as well as what divides them': 'Statement of Principles', approved and adopted by NICIE's Board of Directors, 19 December 1991.

17   P. Connolly, A. Smith and B. Kelly, *Too Young to Notice: The Cultural and Political Awareness of 3-6 Year Olds in Northern Ireland*, (Belfast: Community Relations Council, 2002).

18   Statement by the actor Kenneth Branagh on the cover of IEF, *Integrated Education: Educating Children Together* (Belfast: Integrated Education Fund, 2002).

19   *Milward Brown Ulster Omnibus 2003* (formerly *UMS Omnibus*).

20   See, for example, the editorial 'Beyond the Bombs', *Guardian*, 5 January 1993, in which forced integration of schools in Northern Ireland (as apparently was adopted as policy in the USA) was proposed; see also James Callaghan, *A House Divided: The Dilemma of Northern Ireland* (London: Collins, 1973), who suggested that some gradual process of bringing pupils together, perhaps initially at sixth-form level with sixth-form colleges, would be a desirable strategy.

21   In 2001 and again in 2002 Catholic parents and children were attacked by local Protestant residents as they took their young daughters to school in a loyalist area. Demographic changes had separated the Catholic primary school from its catchment area, and the original incident escalated into terrifying and protracted violence necessitating armed police escorts for children and parents for several weeks, and spreading to more loyalist attacks on other Catholic schools in north Belfast. For an interesting insight into the Holy Cross situation see Richard N. Haass, 'The Northern Ireland Peace Process: Remarks to the National Committee on American Foreign Policy', New York, 7 January 2002; available online www.state.gov/s/p/rem/7300.htm

22   The report 'Four Religions' Plan for Multi-Faith School Aims to Establish a Trend', *Guardian*, 8 July 2002, is one example.

23   Historically, the term 'social engineering' has been associated in Western consciousness with education as a tool of communist ideology, whether in the former Soviet Union or in China, under Mao Tse Tung, where, it was once argued, the 'uneducated man was a blind man'.

24   Originating from North America, the 'melting pot' was the popular metaphor for the creation of a society drawn from the ethnically diverse groups of people who combined or blended to form American culture; see the seminal study by Nathan Glazer and Daniel P. Moynihan, *Beyond the Melting Pot* , rev. edn (Cambridge, MA: MIT Press, 1970), for a detailed account and analysis. For a critique of multi-culturalism in the context of Northern Ireland, see Bill Rolston, 'What's Wrong with Multiculturalism?' in David Miller (ed.), *Rethinking Northern Ireland* (London: Longman, 1998), pp. 253–74.

25   Since 1965 most social surveys have found significant support (60 per cent and over) for integrated education: Peter Stringer and Gillian Robinson (eds), *Social Attitudes in Northern*

Ireland (Belfast: Blackstaff Press, 1991); Seamus Dunne and Ed Cairns, 'A Survey of Parental Opinion on Education in Northern Ireland: A Consultants' Paper Presented to the Standing Advisory Commission on Human Rights', plus numerous surveys carried out by *Fortnight, the Sunday Times, Irish News* and most recently (April 2000) the *Belfast Telegraph* .

26 For example, see IEF, *Integrated Education Development Fund: Ten Year Development Plan*, p. 8. The IEF claims that there are three factors illustrating a continuing demand: insufficient places available in existing integrated schools; lack of accessibility to integrated education because of the uneven geographical distribution of integrated schools within Northern Ireland; and the level of demand recorded in opinion polls.

27 'Chief Executive Officer's Report', in NICIE, *Annual Report* 1998–99 (Belfast: NICIE, 1999).

28 'Integrated Schools Face Over-Subscription Crisis', *Integrated News*, vol 2. no. 2, 1999, p. 2.

29 *Ibid.*

30 IEF, *Ten Year Development Plan*, p. 8.

31 NICIE figures.

32 According to NICIE's 1991 report 'The Growth of Integrated Education: An Outline' (Belfast: NICIE, 1991), in 1991, exactly 10 years after Lagan College opened, there were 14 integrated schools with 2,608 pupils amounting to approximately 0.75 per cent of the total Northern Ireland school enrolment.

33 The Integrated Education Endowment Fund was established in 1992 with funding from the Joseph Rowntree Charitable Trust, the Nuffield Foundation, the EU structural funds and DENI to provide support for the development of integrated education in the early stages when it was unable to receive government funding.

34 Some new integrated schools have had to open without government approval and consequently have been completely unfunded from day one: e.g. Oakwood Integrated Primary School (1996), Belfast; Strangford Integrated College (1997), Newtownards; Ulidia Integrated College (1997), Carrickfergus; Lir IPS, Ballycastle (2004).

35 See O'Connor, *A Shared Childhood*, p. 48.

36 *Star*, 18 June 1999.

37 In 'Politicians Find Civil Service Veterans Slow to Change', *Irish Times*, 20 April 2001, tensions were reported between locally elected politicians in the new Northern Ireland Assembly and senior civil servants.

38 Integrated education may be seen as one of a raft of prgrammes in the community relations-linked 'soft' agenda. It is worth noting that Building Common Ground, a Housing Executive-linked community development programme, was launched in spring 2004, suggesting that there is a fresh recognition – if not a degree of desperation – that something needs to be done to encourage a more positive climate at grassroots level.

39 See O'Connor, *A Shared Childhood*, pp. 117–30, for a discussion of some of the issues and conflicts.

40 Michael Walzer, ' Equality and Civil Society', in S. Chambers and W. Kymlicka (eds), *Alternative Conceptions of Civil Society* (Princeton, NJ, and Oxford: Princeton University Press, 2002). p. 38.

41 See Frank Wright, *Integrated Education and new beginnings in Northern Ireland* (Coleraine: Corrymeela Press, 1990), pp. 11–12; also Joanne Hughes, 'Prejudice and Identity in a Mixed Environment', in Adrian Guelke (ed.), *New Perspectives on the Northern Ireland Conflict* (Aldershot: Avebury Press, 1994), pp. 86–103.

42 See Rick Wilford, 'Inverting Consociationalism? Policy, Pluralism and the Post-Modern', in Brigid Hadfield (ed.), *Northern Ireland: Politics and the Constitution* (Buckingham: Open university Press, 1992), pp. 29–46; also Rupert Taylor, 'Northern Ireland: Consociation or Social Transformation?' in McGarry, *Northern Ireland and the Divided World*, pp. 37–52.

43 Amy Gutman, 'Challenges of Multiculturalism in Democratic Education', in Robert K. Fullinwider (ed.), *Public Education in a Multicultural Society* (Cambridge: Cambridge University Press, 1996), pp. 156–79.

44 NICIE, 'Statement of Principles'; also quoted in *What's What in Integrated Education: A Guide for Teachers* (Belfast: NICIE, 2001), p. 20.

45 The research was carried out under the auspices of the UNESCO Centre at the University of Ulster; see *Report 2: Integrated Education in Northern Ireland*, pp. 40–4.

46 UN Economic and Social Council's Committee on Economic, Social and Cultural Rights, *Consideration of Reports Submitted by States Parties under Articles 16 and 17 of the Covenant, Concluding observations of the Committee on Economic, Social and Cultural Rights, United Kingdom of Great Britain and Northern Ireland*, E/C. 12/1/Add. 19, 12 December 1997, para. 18.

19

What happened to the women? Promises, reality and the Northern Ireland Women's Coalition

KATE FEARON AND RACHEL REBOUCHE

Introduction

This chapter begins by describing the role played by the Northern Ireland Women's Coalition (NIWC) in the talks process that led to the GFA of 1998.[1] It then identifies those provisions that explicitly address women or gender equality issues as well as highlighting the related issues in the GFA that are of special interest in relation to women. The second section explores what happened when the provisions in the GFA were translated into legislation in the form of the Northern Ireland Act: what got left behind; what remained as new aspirations; and what became new actualities. The process of constructing the new institutions, in particular the Equality Commission, an amalgam of the existing equality agencies, is examined. We then briefly examine both how these changes have been realised to date and some of the obstacles confronting women in implementing the promises of equality in the GFA. We argue that though the GFA extended great potential for change for ordinary women and men in Northern Ireland, and while some of that potential has been realised, the non-implementation of the GFA and the social, economic and political priorities debated in the Northern Ireland Assembly militated against more substantive change occurring. In particular, assembly debates illustrate an inherent conservatism in the Northern Irish political culture, irrespective of political or religious background. The role of the NIWC in challenging this conservatism in the first assembly is examined, as is the role of other women assembly members.

Although this chapter cannot hope to fully address the ways in which the GFA has affected women and women's issues in Northern Ireland, it seeks to examine how the GFA can still serve as a vital tool in securing equality rights. To succeed in this task, however, the GFA must be supported not only by a change both in public institutions and in the political mindset.

NIWC and the talks process

NIWC had been formed specifically to contest the elections that determined delegates to the peace negotiations (the talks) chaired by Senator George Mitchell. It had a deliberate cross-community base and organised an 'ethical framework' which included three core principles – human rights, equality and inclusiveness. From the outset, the NIWC declared that it would not defend a fixed constitutional position: it was concerned with the *interests*, not the *positions* of others, and how those interests might be accommodated within the NIWC's ethical framework. For NIWC it was better to have a different view of what was possible in the given political norm, and to work towards it, than it was to declare the probable and wait for others to share that view.

Parties to the negotiations had a tendency to spend most of their time and effort determining *whether* any agreement was possible, rather than trying to devise a comprehensive and creative agreement. NIWC engaged with other parties as advocates and protectors of the process which placed an unequalled emphasis on the importance of getting the process right and of believing in it. While patently process should never impede progress, NIWC always raised the issue of *how* the process was being conducted. NIWC always believed there would be an agreement, even in the face of negative observations from all political commentators, and, in late 1997 and early 1998, a dangerous climate on the streets as a consequence of the UDA–LVF murder campaign.

NIWC exercised its belief in the possibility of consensus both inside and outside of the talks process. By engaging in a communicative loop that involved the British and Irish governments, the talks' chairpersons, other members of civic society, from grassroots community organisations to businesses and trade unionists, NIWC was always well briefed on what was, or might be, acceptable to the different sectors on any given question. This constant communication with the external community allowed NIWC to provide resources for the talks on two planes. First, members of NIWC became a trusted source of information and advice for the independent talks' chairpersons and assisted them in presenting general options for the participants. Second, NIWC submitted its own ideas for refinement to those persons outside of the official process who were most likely to be affected by what was being decided within the talks. Many members of NIWC had come from or were working in the community and voluntary sector, and their contacts were optimally utilised. What the coalition lacked in size it made up for by forming and maintaining strategic alliances both inside and outside the formal process. It was able to minimise the stunting effect of 'group-think' precisely because of its heterogeneity and the ethical framework that guided its participation.

Gender issues in the GFA

As the second draft of what eventually emerged as the GFA was being prepared, all of the participants were lobbying energetically, pushing for their priorities to be included in the text. This would entail discussions between various parties and the government representative who was drafting the text, not necessarily between the parties themselves. Once included, however, parties had to ensure that their proposed language would stay in, and thus the focus would then shift to persuading others not to lobby to have it excluded. Traditional parties tended to push for traditional demands. For instance, Sinn Fein advocated the release of all politically motivated prisoners; the UUP argued for the securing of the position of Northern Ireland as an integral part of the UK. NIWC had adopted a counter-traditional approach to resolving the conflict's fundamental questions by pursuing an agenda that not only covered these questions, but went beyond them.

NIWC, as a party formed to highlight the paucity of women in politics and, specifically, around the negotiating table, was keen to make the GFA as inclusive and accessible a document as possible, enabling the public to claim some ownership of the provisions it contained. One such provision was that 'against the background of the recent history of communal conflict' the participants affirmed a series of basic rights, including the right to free political thought, freedom to express religious beliefs, and freedom from sectarian harassment. Added to this list of fundamental freedoms was 'the right of women to full and equal political parti-cipation'.[2] It was an uphill struggle to ensure the drafters understood the rationale for inserting such a principle in the historic document, and it became properly clear only when a NIWC delegate suggested that women had been living in an 'armed patriarchy' and that such a clause was necessary. Once included, none of the other parties lobbied to have it excluded.

The final GFA was a complex, ambitious and ambivalent document produced by myriad discussions. More than seventy separate 'action points' were signalled in its various paragraphs and clauses, responsibility for the implementation of which lay with sponsors vested with different degrees of authority. Some sponsors were explicitly named (like the British and Irish governments, in respect of establishing new international treaties), and other action points were referred to more vaguely as the responsibility of all the participants (like the affirmation to the principles of partnership, equality and mutual respect). The British Government was specified as the premier body with responsibility for implementing specific aspects of the GFA. Those aspects may be arranged under three categories of action:

- promoting principles of, for example, equality of treatment;
- giving practical effect to new institutions and initiatives; and
- policies that would complement the principles.

The British Government committed itself, in the period before devolution of powers to the Northern Ireland Assembly, to pursuing 'broad policies for sustained economic growth and stability in Northern Ireland and for promoting social inclusion, including in particular community development and the advancement of women in public life'.[3] The British Government also incorporated two extant public consultations dealing with equality issues within the GFA: the merger of the existing equality agencies; and the creation of a statutory obligation on public bodies to carry out all functions 'with due regard to the need to promote equality of opportunity in relation to religion and political opinion; gender; race; disability; age, marital status; dependants; and sexual orientation'.[4]

Additionally, throughout the GFA, there were numerous pledges committing various parties to a strengthening of human rights. For example, both the British and Irish governments pledged to incorporate the ECHR into domestic legislation.[5] The new assembly would be obliged to make assembly legislation consistent with the ECHR. Without prejudice to this, there was provision for a Bill of Rights for Northern Ireland. Further, the Irish Government pledged to 'take steps to further strengthen the protection of human rights in its jurisdiction', including the implementation of enhanced equality legislation and the introduction of equal status legislation.[6] When ministers are again eventually appointed to their posts, their Pledge of Office commits them to 'act in accordance with the general obligations on government to promote equality and prevent discrimination'.[7]

Political aspiration to legislative fact

How well the GFA actually serves the needs of women depends on how it is implemented and the level of commitment political and civic actors have invested in strengthening equality between women and men. However, repeated commitments to 'inclusiveness' by the new institutions are without substance if they fail to take account of the inclusion of women in particular. Some of the institutions prescribed by the GFA, such as the Equality Commission, the Northern Ireland HRC and the Civic Forum, as well as initiatives for equality reform as set up by the Northern Ireland Executive and Assembly, and civil society have taken hold. These changes are only part of the broad institutional change needed to adequately implement the GFA.

The GFA's policy promises

During the process of drafting legislation to implement the GFA's various political principles, lobbies to give legislative effect to the right of women to full and equal political participation proved unsuccessful. This remains a principle that parties to the GFA have affirmed – and no more. In the event of further review of the GFA, however, the willingness of parties to put forward female candidates and to include women in the upper echelons of party decision-making may be one measure of its performance. Pledges by the Government on pursuing policies that promote social inclusiveness are more difficult to assess. In what seemed like an early indicator of its action, the British Government provided 'listening' space;[8] several legislative changes were announced during 1998 that were welcomed as positive steps toward fulfilling this commitment, like the extension of maternity leave from 14 to 18 weeks, the introduction of the right to parental leave and the increase in child benefit.

Other areas of government policy, however, militated against women's interests early in the GFA's first years. Joan Smyth, chair of the then Equal Opportunities Commission (EOCNI), writing in the *Belfast Newsletter*, highlighted other issues that fell into this category.[9] The Government's New Deal programme, for instance, signposted the potential gender gap in the working families' tax credit. The New Deal as a benefit-based programme was believed to be biased against women because access depends on receipt of the Jobseekers' Allowance (JSA). Women are less likely than men to receive JSA and have accordingly less access to the training and work opportunities provided for under the programme. Inadequacy of childcare in all of the New Deal options compounds these difficulties.[10]

Beyond these early efforts, implementation of the policy and principle aspects of the GFA are difficult to police. Those components that are principle-based have no named authority to champion them – they remain the responsibility of all the participants of the Agreement process, and require political leadership to embed them. Those components that are policy-based are generally the responsibility of the British government. In looking at UK wide policies, no particular effort appears to have been made to craft these policies in the general context of a society emerging from conflict, or in the specific wake of the commitments undertaken in the Agreement.

GFA promises outside of the legislature

Most of the promises that relate to women in the GFA are not binding, being phrased more in terms of aspirations. The human rights, equal opportunities and civic participation initiatives signalled have, however, been put on a legislative footing in the Northern Ireland Act in the form of a newly created HRC, Equality Commission and Civic Forum. Explicit in their remit is a commitment to gender equality and by implication, women's participation in public life.

NIHRC has attracted more scrutiny than has the Equality Commission. Early research seems to suggest that NIHRC's effectiveness is weakened by the limited scope of its powers (particularly in bringing cases on human rights abuses) and by its restricted budget and small number of staff.[11] What NIHRC has meant for women in progressing the equality agenda has not been similarly analysed. Much of NIHRC's work in the area has been in terms of research and investigation, although it has made submissions to the Convention on the Elimination of All Forms of Discrimination Against Women (CEDAW) Committee on some of the issues facing women in Northern Ireland,[12] as well as including a gender dimension in reports whose subject matter is varied.[13]

Perhaps, though, one of the most important contributions NIHRC has made to date is its work since 2000 on a Bill of Rights for Northern Ireland on which it has been actively engaged in drafting preliminary advice to the secretary of state.

The Bill, a stipulated duty of the GFA, contains 'rights supplementary to those in the European Convention on Human Rights', as covered by the Human Rights Act 1998, that address the 'particular circumstances of Northern Ireland, drawing as appropriate on international instruments and experience'.[14] NIHRC published a consultation document in September 2001 which included a section relating to the rights of women in Northern Ireland, with four proposed rights to gender equality, freedom from violence, reproductive health care and political participation. The justification for the women's rights chapter relies heavily on the need to fulfil commitments under the GFA, particularly in discussion on the right of women to participate in public life and the right to equality of opportunity.[15]

At present, the future of the Bill of Rights is uncertain, failing to gain support from unionist parties and facing substantial criticism from nationalist parties. The arguments range from the practical to the political: rights are too costly, and, if defined too broadly, may be unenforceable; rights may lead an overly litigious society, and, so it is argued, may deepen divisions in Northern Ireland. Opinions diverge as to whether the Bill should deal only with issues typically thought of as pertinent to the conflict (such as rights in the criminal justice system, victims' rights, identity rights and equality rights) or whether it should also incorporate rights that are arguably important in securing as a stable future for Northern Ireland. This issue should be of real concern to women as their rights have been historically (and, we would argue, incorrectly) seen as tangential to the conflict.[16]

The Equality Commission, largely because of its structure, has had a more visible role in relation to gender equality issues. The Equality Commission absorbed the work of the Fair Employment Commission and the Equal Opportunities Commission, both of which dedicated substantial portions of their work to gender discrimination. In addition, the Equality Commission 'equality proofs' the work of public bodies under section 75 of the Northern Ireland Act, described in more detail below, where gender is one of the categories of prohibited discrimination, and is active in research into gender issues.[17] In the fall of 2002, it helped launch a cross-border programme to review women's experiences of inequality in both Northern Ireland and the Republic, built largely on the work of the North–South Research Collaboration Group. Together with Opportunity Now, the Equality Commission launched the Equal Pay Forum 'to give employers, employer and business organisations and trade unions an opportunity to share the difficulties and the successes they have experienced in dealing with gender pay issues'.[18] Under the Northern Ireland Act, the commission also has the power to bring cases and support claims under the Sex Discrimination Act. Its choice of cases, however, suggests that preference is given to those that *test* the blurred areas of discrimination law or those that attract public attention. This might well be a strategy developed by the commission in the light of its limited financial resources and thus its inability to support every discrimination claim brought to its attention.

The two main legislative initiatives of the Equality Commission have been drafting a Single Equality Bill (SEB) and reviewing the equality schemes of public bodies under section 75. The SEB is currently slated for completion and full implementation by 2006.[19] However, for our purposes, the development of section 75 is of crucial importance in evaluating how the GFA is working 'on the ground'. There is undoubtedly a substantial gain, symbolically, in making public authorities responsible for monitoring the equality impact of their policies. However, some critics suggest that, for many organisations, the process of assessing their policies, consulting other organisations and putting together reports is costly and time-consuming, especially because consulted organisations receive no additional financial support.[20] The organisations which are meant to review and advise a public authority on their policies are often not able to give a fulsome critique due to time and finance constraints. This perpetuates a system whereby only the organisations that can afford to engage in the consultation can do so effectively, depriving the public authority of the expertise of smaller and under-resourced groups.[21]

The Civic Forum, as an institution of the GFA, is perhaps the most difficult to assess, particularly in terms of its impact on women's rights. The Civic Forum is composed of representatives from ten public sectors and is intended to be a more participative way of strengthening democracy in a deeply divided society.[22] It has the potential to provide more opportunities for people to get involved in politics because, unlike what happens in elected politics, the nominating bodies must adhere to guidelines, one being gender balance, when selecting representatives. The first Civic Forum seemed to deliver on that promise, with 38 per cent of its membership being women. Although there has been no formal study of the forum's effectiveness in creating an inclusive complement to assembly structures, early evidence suggested that the forum fell into some of the same traps as the assembly, becoming redirected by arguments between members affiliated with either unionist or nationalist politics.[23] The stalls and stops in the forum's debates, due largely to sectarian politics' domination of discussion, did not help create a more open and progressive arena for women's issues. The Civic Forum was prorogued with the most recent assembly suspension. Unlike the North–South bodies and other institutions which have their genesis in the GFA, the Forum was afforded no special legislation by the governments to keep it in existence; and no moves have been made to appoint new members or to establish a shadow Civic Forum subsequent to the November 2003 elections. It is arguably in times of a political vacuum that the Civic Forum should be fortified rather than diminished.

As for the other mechanisms recommended by the GFA, these have had little direct consequence for the pursuit of women's rights. The Criminal Justice Review did not directly address the issue of women's representation on the bench. The final product, the Justice (Northern Ireland) Act 2002, included the requirement that the committee responsible for judicial appointments be 'representative of the community'.[24] This statement, when taken in the light of the findings of the Criminal Justice Review and the rest of the Justice (NI) Act, indicates representation of the two main communities and not of other groups. The Policing Board and the Parades Commission have also not dealt with issues directly related to women's interests. Worth noting, however, is that the Parades Commission, when first formed, had no female members. In one instance, a female applicant lost her challenge, failing to convince the High Court that the appointments were discriminatory and offended the principles of the GFA.[25]

Women in public office

Statistics for public appointments find Northern Ireland marginally ahead (at 34 per cent) of the rest of the UK but the number of women in elected office is far behind that elected to Westminster. Northern Ireland has only three women MPs and/or MEPs, whereas in Great Britain 18 per cent of MPs and 24 per cent of MEPs are women, as tables 19.1–8 illustrate. Around 19 per cent of councillors in local government districts are women and, in 2001, of the twenty-five district councils only four had a woman as mayor/chair, with a further five having a woman as deputy mayor/deputy chair. Of the 108 members of the first assembly (1998-2003), only fifteen were women, constituting 14 per cent of members.[26] They are divided amongst the parties as shown in table 19.3. Though there are eighteen women now elected to the as yet convened second assembly, none of them is a

Table 19.1   House of Commons 2001 election results by gender and party

Party	Women	Men	% women
Labour	95	317	23
Conservative	14	152	8
Liberal Democrat	5	47	10
SNP	1	4	20
UUP	1	5	17
DUP	1	4	20
Sinn Fein	1	3	25
Other	0	9	0
Total	118	541	18

Table 19.2   Northern Ireland local election results 2001 by gender and party

Party	Women	Men	% women
UUP	27	127	18
DUP	19	112	15
SDLP	31	86	26
Sinn Féin	17	91	16
APNI	11	17	40
Other	0.3	41	7
Total	108	474	19

Table 19.3   Assembly seats by party, 2001

Party	Total seats	Women
UUP	28	2
SDLP	24	3
DUP	20	1
Sinn Fein	18	5
APNI	6	1
NI Unionist Party	4	0
Ulster Unionist Assembly Party	3	0
PUP	2	0
NIWC	2	2
UKUP	1	0
Total	108	14

Table 19.4   Assembly seats by party, 2003

Party	Total seats	Women
DUP	30	2
SF	24	7
UUP	27	2
SDLP	18	5
APNI	6	2
PUP	1	0
UKUP	1	0
Independent	1	0
Total	108	18

NIWC representative. We do not know how many of them will sit on committees, nor what issues they will chose to prioritise on the floor.

A Northern Ireland Civil Service (NICS) survey carried out in January of 2001 showed that only 13.4 per cent of senior-level officials were women, indicating that women are not well represented in the service's higher level. As noted in table 19.5, women still comprise the substantial majority (72 per cent and 61 per cent, according to position) of administrative or secretarial work. The areas in which the majority of women in the civil service were employed beyond this, namely, education-related, childcare and social services, correspond to areas traditionally associated with 'women's interests.'

Outside of elected politics, women seem to fare no better on publicly appointed bodies: of the 134 bodies in Northern Ireland, women held 39 chair and 8 deputy chair posts – the survey results do not account for bodies with multiple chairs.

The fifteen women MLAs of the first assembly, however, were dispro-

Table 19.5 Gender breakdown of NICS by grade, January 2001

Grade	Women	Men	% women
Grade 5+	29	189	13
Grade 6/7	0.236	864	21
Deputy principal	0.412	1307	24
Staff officer	0.701	1524	31
Executive officer grade 1 and 2	3218	3681	47
Administrative officer	5062	1947	72
Administrative assistant	1648	1015	61
Total	11306	10527	52

Table 19.6 Gender breakdown of NICS by department, January 2001

Department	Women	Men	% women
Agriculture and Rural Development	1182	1775	40
Culture, Arts and Leisure	110	225	33
Education	342	234	60
Enterprise, Trade and Investment	544	616	47
Finance and Personnel	1198	1309.	48
OFMDFM	150	146	51
Higher and Further Education, Training and Employment	908	515	64
Health, Social Services and Public Safety	410	464	47
Environment	768	767	50
Regional Development	1024	1868.	35
Social Development	238	204	54
Social Services Agency	3528	1832.	66
Child Support Agency	904	572	61
Total	11306	10527	52

portionately busy relative to their male colleagues, each of them holding either ministerial office or a seat on a departmental committee and several sitting on at least two committees. Tables 19.7 and 19.8 show the gender breakdown by departmental and standing committee.

It can be seen from table 19.7 that the committee with the highest proportion reflects what is commonly thought of as an interest of women: health, though this may be a reflection either of some autonomy on the part of women members on what position they wanted or else a lack of interest on the part of their male colleagues in becoming members of this committee.

Table 19.7   Assembly departmental committee seats by gender, 2002

Departmental committee	Seats	Women
Agriculture and Rural Development	11	0
Education	11	1
Culture, Arts and Leisure	11	0
Employment and Learning[a]	11	3
Enterprise, Trade and Investment	11	3
Environment	11	3
Finance and Personnel	11	2
Health, Social Services and Public Safety	11	5
Regional Development	11	0
Social Development	11	1
Ministers[b]	11	2

Notes: [a] Formerly Further and Higher Education, Training and Employment.
[b] There have been three women ministers – Bairbre de Brunn, Bríd Rojers and Carmell Hanna – though only two of them have been in office at the same time

For Standing Committees, the statistics are similar:

Table 19.8   Assembly Standing Committee seats by gender, 2002

Standing committee	Seats	Women members
Procedures	11	0
Business	13	3
Centre	17	4
Public accounts	11	2
Standards	11	1
Audit	11	0

Assembly debates: changing the nature of politics

In addition to the policy promises, the new institutions of the GFA, and the electoral outcomes of post-Agreement government, there is the performance of the centrepiece of the GFA, the assembly, in dealing with women's issues to consider. As noted, women made up just under 13 per cent of the first assembly and just over 16 per cent of the second. Early research, however, seems to indicate that women MLAs do not differ radically from men in the voting pattern, and their interests are not that dissimilar to their male counterparts.[27] For example, of those interviewed in a recent study, an almost equal percentage of men and women listed education, a children's commissioner, and health policy as important to Northern Ireland's future development; they also ranked as a top priority helping constituents receive the services they need. However, the study did show one significant difference in their attitudes: women MLAs were more likely than men MLAs to recognise gender imbalances and to argue for an equal responsibility in caring functions.[28]

The problem we note is that NIWC, the only party to have overtly prioritised gender equality and looked for gender implications in each policy, no longer has a voice in the assembly. One need only consider how a number of issues were debated in the first assembly – for example the matter of divorce, various initiatives before the Health Committee and the establishment of a children's commissioner – to see why this fear is justified.[29]

NIWC's agenda tended to differ from those of the other parties, and on some symbolic matters was successful. Prior to suspension, for instance, the assembly approved family-friendly hours as well as provisions for child care expenses for members (£15 per month) – both measures introduced by the NIWC, though not implemented with its oversight.

Often it was NIWC's representatives who provided a radical voice in assembly debates, the underlying conservatism of Northern Irish parties surfacing readily on social issues that disproportionately affect women. The debate on the Second Reading of the Family Law (Divorce, etc.) Bill in 2002 provides a graphic illustration of this point.[30] The Bill, introduced by Sean Farren, sought to update the law on divorce in Northern Ireland by absorbing adultery into the category of unreasonable behaviour, making it no longer a stand-alone 'fact' that had previously been used to define irretrievable breakdown of marriage. It also proposed to reduce the separation time required to prove irretrievable breakdown from 5 years to 3 years. At the same time the minister's speech was careful to telegraph that the 'Bill does not make divorce easier' and that it did not 'seek to change' the only ground for divorce in Northern Ireland.

Even though the minister stated that the bill would not 'bring about root and branch reform but will refine and hone existing legislation', the subsequent interlocutors were unconvinced. Of the seven MLA's that responded to the minister, only Monica McWilliams of the NIWC gave unequivocal support to the Bill. Francie Molloy of Sinn Fein, then chairperson of the Committee for Finance and Personnel, said that the 'Committee is concerned about the permanence of marriage, and its [sic] perception of the ongoing effort of groups to undermine the sanctity of marriage. The Committee wishes to be reassured that the intention is not simply to provide a facility for quicker divorces'.[31]

Esmond Birnie (UUP) stated his concern over 'what may be the unintentional by products of the Bill and their possibly negative consequences'.[32] He feared that the reduction in separation time would make it easier to get a divorce, 'whatever may be argued to the contrary'.[33] The Reverend Ian Paisley (DUP) also spoke in defence of marriage, stating that he would be laying amendments to the Bill, as 'the needs of the people are not served by legislation that will weaken the sanctity of marriage. The need of the people is to strengthen marriage, not to undermine marriage or to make it easier to depart from the solemn obligations entered into by those who are married'.[34] Though supporting the Bill, Patricia Lewsley (SDLP), the only other woman speaking on this issue, noted that 'while facilitating those people faced with divorce, we should continue to strive to promote marriage'.[35] Seamus Close of the ostensibly liberal APNI cited his own experience, having been married for more than twenty-four years, stating: 'If we further undermine the institution of marriage, future generations will be all the poorer for any failure to adhere to the clear definition, meaning and understanding of what marriage is about ... We do not need quickie divorces: they are not in the interest of the people of Northern Ireland ... The Bill undermines the importance of the state of marriage.'[36].

In contrast, Monica McWilliams's speech focused much more on the practicalities involved in relationship breakdown than any philosophical discursive on the social role and sanctity of marriage: 'Rather than the words we have heard from some Members about keeping the family together at all costs, they should be asking – for the sake of the children – at what cost should the family be kept together?'[37] She challenged the concerns expressed by the other Members regarding the five to three year reduction: 'Members who have done any work in this area or who have interviewed those affected will know why the Bill seeks to reduce the five year requirement to three years. As public representatives, they will have had women in their constituency offices telling how their husbands have said, 'If I can't have you, no one else will.'[38] Thus the only non-conservative views, apart from the minister's, emanated from the NIWC, no matter the political–ethnic origin of the speaker. The question for the future is who will provide the radical voice, the non-conservative perspective, particularly for women, since there are no longer NIWC representatives at the assembly level.

Women's issues were also the focus of a motion put forward by MLA Jim Wells to prohibit any future motions to extend the 1967 Abortion Act to Northern Ireland.[39] NIWC tabled an amendment to have the abortion issue discussed in detail by the Health, Social Services and Public Safety Committee. The amendment was defeated by a vote of 14 to 53, and the motion was subsequently passed without further amendment. Some members supporting the motion rejected outright the notion that they could not represent women's interests in the abortion debate, as stated by MLA Wells: 'As Dr McCrea said earlier, I resent the view that because I am only the father of three children, rather than the mother, I have no right to have a say on this issue. Like Mr Bradley, another Member for South Down, I represent the overwhelming majority view of the people of South Down on this issue.'[40]

But this view is problematical when considered in terms of the entire debate on the motion. Members in support of the Bill claimed to have the broad support of their communities, without offering any evidence of such unanimous abhorrence of the 1967 Act. Furthermore, most chose to focus on the so-called rights of the unborn rather than women's health. MLA David Ervine (PUP) summarised the difficulties in his statement: 'The Member who introduced the motion set the scene clearly when he described the foetus as "he" "he" "he".'[41] It would seem that the members' claim to equally represent women's health interests is hollow if not complemented by substantive analysis of how abortion law affects women in their constituencies. Their comments do not suggest how to reduce the number of unwanted pregnancies and do not suggest how to deal with the current physical, financial and emotional burdens which the law places on women dealing with unwanted pregnancies.[42] The PUP, like NIWC, sustained losses in the November 2003 elections, further reducing the capacity for alternative perspectives in the regional legislature.

There are also examples of NIWC representatives initiating and directing discussion on policy change from within assembly committees. For example, NIWC introduced the issue of the lack of funding for residential and secure accommodation for children, resulting in an inquiry by the Health and Social Services (HSS) Committee.[43] The Report on the Protection of Children and Vulnerable Adults Bill[44] was also published as a direct result of NIWC's intervention on the HSS Committee, as were the official reports on the Children (Leaving Care) Bill (NIA Bill 05/01) and the Delivery of Cancer Services in Northern Ireland.[45]

One issue, although appropriated by the larger parties, demonstrates a major contribution to the legislative accomplishments. In April 2001, NIWC proposed the first ever non-executive piece of legislation – a Private Member's Bill in the names of Monica McWilliams and Jane Morrice for the establishment of a children's commissioner.[46] Hitherto, the executive had not prioritised the issue of children's rights, even though the first Programme for Government had made reference to the Chancellor's Children's Fund.[47] However, although published with a schedule for further readings, the Bill was never given a second reading. OFMDFM then published a consultation paper stating that 'legislation to establish the post of Commissioner for Children will be brought forward in the next session of the Assembly; the ultimate aim being that the Commissioner will be in post by spring 2002'.[48] This schedule was not adhered to and Monica McWilliams raised the issue again as a Parliamentary Question on 17 May 2002, asking when the OFMDFM planned to provide legislation for the establishment of a children's commissioner. In June 2002, a Children's Commissioner's Bill was proposed in the names of Jim Wells (DUP) and Roy Beggs (UUP) and the Committee of the Centre discussed the Bill at meetings in June and September. Due to another suspension, the Bill subsequently passed as an Order in Council through the Westminster Parliament in February 2003 and a children's commissioner was appointed in July 2003.[49]

Thus, the overall outcome of the NIWC's Private Members' Bill and subsequent lobbying was the appointment of a children's commissioner. However, whereas in the talks process NIWC did not necessarily claim individual initiatives as its own, the *realpolitik* of the assembly was that a party's contribution would become easily lost in the minds both of the public and of the other political parties if not claimed.

Beyond the legislature: the general social and economic backdrop

What of life outside of the legislature? What impact does the establishment of these new institutions, principles and practices have on the lives of women in Northern Ireland? What does the GFA mean in real terms for women? In the past fifteen years, the general position for women in most areas of life – with the exception of the political arena – has been steadily improving, due in no small part to the extent of the lobbying and campaigning undertaken by women activists in the community and voluntary sector.

In 2002, the number of economically active women had increased by 29 per cent since 1984 (there are now 340,000 economically active women and 443,000 economically active men in Northern Ireland) as compared to the 20 per cent increase for women in the rest of the UK.[50] The number of women in employment had increased by 41 per cent from 228,000 in 1984 to 322,000 in 2002, compared to an increase of 12 per cent for men. Of those currently employed in 2003, 44 per cent were women (compared to 45 per cent of women in the rest of the UK).[51] The earnings' gap is also narrowing, with women's weekly earnings now standing at 81 per cent of men's. Women are, however, much more likely to be working in the service sector, particularly in clerical/secretarial and personal/caring occupations, and in positions lower on the management ladder than their male counterparts. Furthermore, the number of women who are self-employed was substantially lower than that of their male counterparts: in 2002, 17.8 per cent of men, the highest rate in the UK, were self-employed, compared to only 4.2 per cent of women.

Though the economic activity rate typically decreases as the number of dependent children increases, child-care provision has increased vastly. Day-care places from 1992 to 2002 have increased by 39 per cent, as have the number of registered childminders. These figures, however, do not depict the numbers of women relying on family members for child-care support nor do they reflect the percentage of women who can afford the child-care offered. The average weekly amount paid for child-care was £70.46, whereas the credit received through Working Families' Tax Credit was £46.66.

The outlook for young women prior to entering the labour force is decidedly bright, though as detailed above, this prospect dims as women try to advance in the workplace. Young women tend to leave school better qualified than their male counterparts and are more likely to go on to further or higher education: 70 per cent of girls leaving school progressed to further or higher education, compared to 50 per cent of boys in 2000–1 and 59 per cent of students in further education colleges and 59 per cent of students at university were women in the academic year of 2000–1. There is some evidence that women are making some breaches in the barrier between 'hard' and 'soft' subjects at undergraduate level, accounting for almost 40

Table 19.9   Domestic incidents in Northern Ireland, 1996–2000

	1996	1997	1998	1999	2000
Domestic incidents attended by PSNI	6,727	8,509	14,429	15,304	14520
% Female Victims	89	90	89	88	88
Murder	2	8	10	7	3
Rape	4	10	21	20	13
GBH	26	51	60	86	63
Breach of order	184	472	603	723	580
Harassment			147	427	421
Common assault	1,758	1,899	3,223	3,784	3488

Source: PSNI domestic violence statistics compiled by NI Women's Aid Federation.

per cent of those enrolled for science courses at university, 35 per cent in mathematics and computing and 17 per cent in engineering. In 2003, 81 per cent enrolled in medicine- and dentistry-related subjects were women, while in the social sciences, almost 62 per cent of students enrolled in first-year courses are women.[52]

Yet higher education participation and attainment levels at the second level do not necessarily mean all is well in the workplace, where there continues to be a large number of legal complaints and enquiries regarding sexual harassment made to the Equality Commission, as well as similar numbers of complaints regarding maternity and pregnancy rights, and recruitment and selection procedures.[53]

The period coinciding with a lessening of violence on the streets has not resulted in reduced violence against women in or outside of the home. Police Service (NI) statistics show that the number of 'domestic' incidents attended by police has more than doubled during 1996–2000, with a slight decrease evident only in 1998–2000; incidents involving harassment have increased dramatically from when first reported in 1998 (see table 19.9).

The number of deaths related to domestic violence, which was rising sharply until 1998, has been decreasing, with only three deaths in 2000. However, police may exercise discretion in classifying murders and assaults as domestic violence, which may suggest that there are incidents not recorded here.[54]

The impact of political progress

It is against this patchy backdrop that one should examine whether or not the peace process has impacted the opportunities of women, and, if so, what the nature of this change has been. The *Life and Times Survey* in 2001 suggests that acceptance of the GFA and awareness of women's rights are declining in public opinion. Women were marginally more likely than men to have voted for the GFA in May 1998.

However, answers to a survey question asking how the respondent would vote for the GFA showed that support was declining, with 50 per cent indicating a 'Yes' vote as compared to the 55 per cent in the survey who actually voted 'Yes' in 1998. There seems to be little difference in the numbers of women (50 per cent) supporting the GFA and men (51 per cent), while there appears to be a growing disillusionment with the GFA's capacity to effect change. Other responses showed that 45 per cent of people said that if the GFA stays in place prosperity would increase; 33 per cent thought that if the agreement ended the level of violence would stay the same and 11 per cent responded that they thought it would actually decrease.[55]

Looking at how people feel about equality and women's rights, the results are not much more heartening. Although 63 per cent disagreed or strongly disagreed that there was 'no need' for equality laws, only 4 per cent of respondents thought that women generally were unfairly treated as compared to other section 75 groups; 33 per cent of respondents stated that women were treated better than they were 5 years ago, and 58 per cent thought women were treated no differently.[56] The difficulty with this type of survey is that it does not illuminate *why* respondents held these opinions. Some indicators suggest that women's rights are improving: economic access is increasing, more women were elected to the assembly in 2003, and rights-based bodies, like the NIHRC and the Equality Commission, are still in operation. Added to this, it has been pointed out that the method of consultation on equality issues (for example, as found in section 75) is unrivalled in the rest of the UK.[57]

There is, however, a long way to go in ensuring that the mechanisms set up by the GFA work in practice for women. In assessing the capacity to deliver on the promise of women's equal participation in public life, some have pointed to the nature of party politics in Northern Ireland and the gap between formal and informal political processes as an obstacle to reform.[58] This suggests that, unlike in Scotland where many of the initiatives to promote women's participation in politics came from established political parties, there are no firmly established commitments within each party to ensure that women are better represented in public life. As suggested of the NIWC, its position as a rival party opens it up to the criticism and scrutiny of other parties, done 'with little fear of alienating their own members'.[59] This in turn does little to challenge the dominant party positions in Northern Ireland and, more importantly, does not bode well for parties taking women's representation seriously. As argued by Margaret Ward, although parties have made claims to promote equality and diversity, they have not put women forward for 'winnable seats' in the 1998 assembly elections and in the 2001 elections for local and Westminster government, with NIWC being the notable exception.[60]

As noted, however, the November 2003 elections returned eighteen female MLAs, the highest in the history of devolved government in Northern Ireland. While this should be applauded as a step forward in women's political participation more generally, we are concerned that the shift does not necessarily signal a change in the ethos of the political debate in the assembly, nor does it reflect deep changes in how parties put women forward for election. It is difficult to decide whether the parties deliberately placed women candidates in more winnable seats, though gains by women in nationalist parties like Sinn Fein and the SDLP, even in the face of a broader SDLP defeat, would suggest that women's political participation is something given consideration by those parties. This could be due in part to NIWC's agenda and the positive role models of the three women ministers.

Yet the gain of only four women MLAs and the loss of representation by a party committed to women's rights highlights broader problems of promoting women within parties that reflect institutional obstacles to change. The attitudes of political parties, and indeed Northern Irish society, reflect the deeply ingrained conflict between the two communities, which, to the disadvantage of feminist politics, has narrowed the scope of political dialogue, making it more difficult to situate women's issues in the political spotlight.[61]

Despite a tradition of a strong community movement for women's rights and the creation of NIWC, feminist politics in Northern Ireland is still very much in transition.[62] There is a need for a radicalised voice in the assembly, one which supports the implementation of GFA principles as well as helping to secure a broad commitment to the human rights and equality agenda. The defeat sustained by NIWC in the November 2003 elections means the loss of representation by the only party that prioritised gender equality in its mission and which vocalised a radical perspective on a range of gender-relevant social issues.

Conclusion

It is too early to tell whether or not all of these new institutional and administrative arrangements will have any long-term and substantive impact on women's lives. The GFA has accelerated the already growing awareness of the true cost of the Troubles, and provided a safer environment in which research exploring this could be publicly undertaken. Greater stability and economic growth should mean that women, particularly young women, will be well placed to benefit economically.

However, as the assembly's suspension in autumn 2003 has indicated, the GFA hangs in a precarious balance and depends on the negotiations of political parties. If it is implemented in full, women stand to make enormous gains in terms of political visibility and influence: the agreement has been the catalyst for women asserting *rights* to full and equal political participation. There is now more than ever a need to safeguard the GFA, and in that process infuse further negotiations with a sense of the importance it has for Northern Ireland's marginalised and vulnerable communities.

The GFA's provisions go beyond the stock constitutional questions in Northern Ireland and look at how equality, human rights and parity of esteem are important to a stable future. The heavy electoral defeat sustained by NIWC and other parties in November 2003, which seek to further this part of the GFA's agenda, highlights the urgency of the current political situation. In an election where the electorate was highly polarised, parties offering a more nuanced perspective were made invisible by those parties offering a more familiar political worldview. This is not to imply that NIWC did not make tactical and strategic mistakes: NIWC, with an eye on women's political participation, probably took valuable resources away from the key constituencies of North Down and Belfast South by running too many candidates in constituencies that would be unlikely to return NIWC members. In addition, NIWC's message could have emphasised to better advantage its work with and continuing commitment to the peace process, and its success with 'bread and butter issues' during the assembly's life.[63]

The outlook for women's rights at the assembly level is murky at this point. As for NIWC, at an assessment meeting held on 13 March 2004, it determined a new three-pronged approach to its continued existence, an existence to which McWilliams looks forward because 'we were so taken up with electoral politics over the last five years that we never got a chance to breathe. It was one election after the other and we fought all of them, because we felt that we needed to keep our name out there. Now we have a breathing space. I think sometimes that when you are outside electoral politics you can actually be more radical.'[64] NIWC has decided to focus on being a radical policy think-tank and a pressure group that will provide policy alternatives to the political debate and to the lack of implementation of equality issues in the GFA. It plans to contest future elections, at both the assembly and local council levels.[65] Avila Kilmurray, a leading political strategist within NIWC, suggests that the envisioned NIWC will develop a new grading framework for policies – likely to be those policy areas the other parties neglect – on which it will comment and likely to be from a much more radical position than those taken by the other parties.[66]

Kilmurray also sees an opportunity to involve women currently unassociated with NIWC in developing such alternative positions. It may be the case, she thinks, that the current diminution of NIWC's voice will again provide opportunity for the diversity of women's activism on the ground to re-emerge. When NIWC was represented at assembly level, there was a tendency for the media to approach it as *the* voice of women in Northern Ireland. Kilmurray suggests that one of NIWC's unintended successes was taking 'the radical and profile edge off other women's groups'.[67] She feels there is now an opportunity to revisit grassroots women's organisations and assess their views on the impact of NIWC on their work and on issues of gender equality since 1998.

If politics are 'normalised' then there will be, once again, space for NIWC to successfully carve out a place for itself in electoral politics.[68] However, the 2003 and 2005 elections prove that it is only during times of political progress and optimism that NIWC stands any chance of 'changing the face of politics' in Northern Ireland.[69] Both elections were the consequence of political bargaining over and insecurity in the GFA. The emphasis on constitutional issues, decommissioning, policing and the mainstays of Northern Irish politics does not bode well for parties seeking to change the terms of political engagement. Kilmurray and others look forward to a time when NIWC again has representatives at the assembly level, particularly in light of McWilliams missing her seat by only 120 votes, and Morrice by less. The lessons from 1998 to 2005 suggest that to receive any attention at all, issues of equality and human rights need persistent representation at government level. Without representation, the constitutional struggles of today are likely to be replaced with conservative policies for tomorrow. The retreat to and strengthening of a 'politics as usual' discourse does not bode well for the GFA's institutions and aspirations, which seek to change politics, such as NIHRC's work on of a Bill of Rights, the Equality Commission's work on section 75, or the emergence of a non-sectarian and vibrant Civic Forum. The absence of NIWC is an absence both of active and robust women legislators and of a centre-left political voice in Northern Irish politics. And without an established Agreement Implementation Committee, composed of parties with the specific and powerful brief of ensuring that the whole GFA, in both letter and spirit, is implemented, the potential it will not be realised by the women and men of Northern Ireland.

Notes

1　Both authors have been closely involved with NIWC: Kate Fearon was a founder member of NIWC for which she worked as a political advisor during the talks process and the first assembly; and Rachel Rebouche was an active member and participant in policy and election committees.
2　*Agreement Reached in the Multi-Party Negotiations* (Belfast: Stationery Office, 1998), Stand 3 (see Appendix 2, this volume).
3　*Ibid.*, p. 19.
4　*Ibid.*, p. 16.
5　In 1998, the Westminster Parliament passed the Human Rights Act, which incorporated most of the articles in the ECHR. The Human Rights Act became effective in Northern Ireland in 2000. The Republic of Ireland, at the time of writing, has not yet agreed on a bill to incorporate the ECHR into Irish domestic law.
6　*Agreement Reached in the Multi-Party Negotiations*, 'Rights, Safeguards and Equality of Opportunity'.
7　*Ibid.* at Annex A, Strand 1.
8　Most notably, the Government sponsored the 'Listening to Women' conference held in Belfast Castle in April 1998, chaired by Baroness Jay.
9　'Government Lends Open Ear to Issues', *Belfast Newsletter*, Business Section, 4 May 1999, p. 23.
10　ECNI, *Annual Report* (Belfast: ECNI, 1999), p. 9.
11　Stephen Livingstone, 'Northern Ireland Human Rights Commission', *Fordham Law Journal*, vol. 22, no. 4, p. 1465.
12　Northern Ireland Human Rights Watch, Submission to the CEDAW Committee, 1999.
13　See, for example NIHRC reports on the rights of older people, transgender individuals and children in police custody, online: www.nihrc.org.
14　*Agreement Reached in the Multiparty Negotiations*, p. 18.
15　NIHRC, 'Making a Bill of Rights' (Belfast: NIHRC, 2001), 35.
16　Adrian Little, 'Feminism and the Politics of Difference in Northern Ireland', *Journal of Political Ideologies*, vol. 7, no. 2, pp. 163–77.
17　See recent papers on the discriminatory effects of pension policies for women, for example, Elizabeth Evanson, 'Women and Pensions'; available at: www.equalityni.org.
18　Speech by Joan Harbison, chief commissioner, Equality Commission, Equal Pay Forum Launch – 24 March 2003; available at: www.equalityni.org.

19 The European Directives, agreed in 2000, will be fed into the SEB, with race, religion and belief, sex and sexual orientation non-discrimination laws implemented first, and followed by the implementation of age and disability discrimination laws by 2006.

20 Tahnya Donaghy, 'Mainstreaming: Northern Ireland's Participative–Democratic Approach', Centre for the Advancement of Women into Politics, Occasional Paper no. 2 (Belfast: Queen's University, 2003); see also Ruth Tallion, *Where to From Here? A New Paradigm for the Women's Sector in Northern Ireland* (Belfast: Northern Ireland Voluntary Trust, 2001).

21 The need for a review of the workings of section 75 consultation was mentioned in the Joint Declaration by the British and Irish governments published in April 2003, in which the British Government undertook to consider whether the definition of a public body should be expanded and to examine the effectiveness of equality monitoring: Joint Declaration by the British and Irish Governments, April 2003, Annex 3, p. 22. It is clear that the ECNI would need resource support to conduct an investigation of the effectiveness of section 75 in house.

22 'The various sectors were allocated the following number of nominations: business (7), agriculture and fisheries (3), trade unions (7), voluntary/community (18), Churches (5), culture (4), arts and sports (4), victims (2), community relations (2), education (2), first and deputy first minister (6). The nominating bodies were advised to adhere to guidelines on gender balance, community background, geographical spread, and age, and to the principles of public appointment: equal opportunity, merit, openness and transparency': S. Elliott and W. D. Flackes, *Northern Ireland: A Political Directory, 1968–99* (Belfast: Blackstaff Press, 1999); available at: http://cain.ulst.ac.uk/issues/politics/elliott99.htm.

23 Cathal McCall and Arthur Williamson, 'Governance and Democracy in Northern Ireland: The Role of the Voluntary and Community Sector After the Agreement', *Governance*, vol. 14, no. 3, 2001, p. 363.

24 Justice (Northern Ireland) Act, 2002, part 1, section 3, para. 7.

25 *In the Matter of an Application by Evelyn White for Judicial Review* (2000), NIQB.

26 Annie Courtney was the replacement for John Hume on his retirement, so that while there were 14 women elected, by the end of the first assembly there were 15.

27 Kimberley Cowell-Meyers, 'Women Legislators in Northern Ireland: Gender and Politics in the New Legislative Assembly', Centre for the Advancement of Women into Politics, Occasional Paper no. 3 (Belfast: Queen's University, 2003).

28 *Ibid.*, at pp. 5–7.

29 There was no assembly committee established to look at equality or gender equality specifically.

30 Northern Ireland Assembly Official Report, Tuesday 17 September 2002, at www.ni-assembly.gov.uk/record/reports/020917.htm.

31 *Ibid.*, p. 17.

32 *Ibid.*, p. 18.

33 *Ibid.*, p. 18.

34 *Ibid.*

35 *Ibid.*, p. 19.

36 *Ibid.*, p. 21.

37 *Ibid.*, p. 22.

38 *Ibid.*, p. 23.

39 Official Report of the Northern Ireland Assembly, *Hansard*, 20 June 2001, at www.ni-assembly.gov.uk/record/000620.htm.

40 *Ibid.*

41 *Ibid.*

42 See Mary Sexton and Anne Rossiter, *The Other Irish Journey: A Survey Update of Northern Irish Women Attending British Abortion Clinics, 2000/2001* (London: Marie Stopes International, 2001).

43 HSS Committee, Inquiry into Residential and Secure Accommodation for Children in Northern Ireland (Belfast: HSS Committee, 2000), vol. 1 and 2.

44 NIA Bill 22/01, 9 October 2002.

45 Both in the 2001–2 Session.

46 Children's Commissioner Bill, NIA Bill 14/00; the Bill was drafted by Kate Fearon.
47 On 8 December Joan Carson (UUP) asked the OFMDFM regarding the detail of these plans via a Parliamentary Question.
48 'Foreword to Consultation paper', at www.allchildrenni.gov.uk/consultation.
49 The Commissioner for Children and Young People (NI) Order, 2003.
50 DETI, *Northern Ireland Labour Force Survey: Women in Northern Ireland*, January 2003; available at: www.detini, gov. uk.
51 *Ibid.*
52 *Ibid.*
53 See www.equalityni.org.
54 This underreporting was suggested to us by a staff member of the Northern Ireland Women's Aid Federation; for more information about domestic violence in Northern Ireland, see www.niwaf.org.
55 The difference in the percentage of men and women's responses was negligible: Northern Ireland *Life and Times Survey*, 2001.
56 *Ibid.*
57 Fiona Beveridge, Sue Nott and Kylie Stephen, 'Mainstreaming and the Engendering of Policy Making: A Means to an End?', *Journal of European Public Policy*, vol. 7, no. 3, 2000, pp. 401–5.
58 Alice Brown, Tahnya Barnett-Donaghy, Fiona Mackay and Elizabeth Meehan, 'Women and Constitutional Change in Scotland and Northern Ireland', *Parliamentary Affairs*, vol. 55, no. 1, 2002, pp. 71–84.
59 *Ibid.*, p. 81.
60 Margaret Ward, 'The Northern Ireland Assembly and Women: Assessing the Gender Deficit', *Democratic Dialogue*, December 2000; (2002) 'Women and the Local Government Elections', Briefing papers, *Democratic Dialogue*; www.democraticdialogue.org/womenlocal. htm.
61 See Monica McWilliams, 'Women in Northern Ireland: An Overview', in E. Hughes (ed.), *Culture and Politics in Northern Ireland* (Buckingham: Open University Press, 1991); Rosemary Sales,*Women Divided: Gender, Religion and Politics in Northern Ireland* (London: Routledge, 1997).
62 Adrian Little, for instance, argues that there is an essentialism plaguing feminism and the pursuit of women's rights in the province. In this way, the NIWC has appealed to what women have in common and negotiated from that vantage point. However, as has proved problematical with any women's movement, this essentialism can detract from a dialogue that emphasises the fullness of women's diversity: see Adrian Little, 'Feminism and the Politics of Difference in Northern Ireland', *Journal of Political Ideologies*, vol. 7 no. 2, 2002, pp. 163–77.
63 In the view of Monica McWilliams, 'We, in the assembly, made bread-and-butter issues our forté, but people didn't see normalised politics here, and by the time the assembly was down for a year and it was time for elections it was going to be impossible for us to keep that message': onterview with Monica McWilliams, Belfast, 18 March 2004.
64 *Ibid.*
65 The June 2004 European elections and most probably the expected 2004/5 general elections will not be contested by the NIWC.
66 'We almost absorbed any energy that was around in terms of those other women's groups, and it may have de-radicalised them somewhat': interview with Avila Kilmurray, Belfast, 18 March 2004.
67 *Ibid.*
68 At the moment there is one member of the NIWC in political office – Patricia Wallace, on the North Down Council. She has chosen to dedicate all her time to work on the council, even though it is an unpaid position. Council elections next year will be interesting in gauging the potential for NIWC to once more make electoral gains.
69 NIWC election campaign slogan, November 2003.

20

From 'long war' to 'war of the lilies': 'post-conflict' territorial compromise and the return of cultural politics

CATHAL McCALL

Whose culture shall be the official one and whose shall be subordinated? What culture shall be regarded as worthy of display and which shall be hidden? Whose history shall be remembered and whose forgotten? What images of social life shall be projected and which shall be marginalized? What voices shall be heard and which silenced? Who is representing whom and on what basis? This is the realm of cultural politics.[1]

Introduction

State territory has been at the heart of the British–Irish ethno-national conflict in Northern Ireland; justice, equality, police reform and cultural representation have been secondary interlocking sources of conflict. The civil rights' campaign of the late 1960s was based on an Irish Catholic claim to equality. When Ulster Protestant reaction to that claim sparked an escalation in violence, the conflict quickly deteriorated into a 'long war' over the territorial status of Northern Ireland.

The Belfast/Good Friday Agreement of 1998[2] involved a territorial compromise by conflicting Irish nationalist/republican and Ulster British unionist/loyalist ethno-national groups, and the UK and Irish governments, bringing to an end three decades of politically motivated violence.[3] Thus, the 1998 GFA was a milestone in a concerted collective effort aimed at ending a violent territorial conflict. John Hume, then leader of the SDLP in Northern Ireland, was central to the process of conflict resolution and the creation of a political framework for stability. He was the principal architect of the three-strand (Northern Ireland, North–South and British–Irish) institutional infrastructure provided by the 1998 GFA.[4] He used his considerable influence with the Irish Government, which in turn had developed a close co-operative relationship with the UK Government regarding Northern Ireland conflict resolution, to ensure that this design formed the basis of institutional arrangements.

Signatories to the 1998 GFA observed three principles, advocated by Hume, for underpinning the new institutional infrastructure. These principles were:

- *transterritorialism*, embodied in structures of governance that reach beyond the territorial border of the state;
- *consent*, whereby the constitutional position of Northern Ireland in the UK cannot be changed without the agreement of the majority community (currently the unionist/loyalist community);[5] and
- *inclusivity*, whereby previously marginalised groups, primarily Irish nationalists and republicans, are brought into the system of governance.[6]

The shifting thresholds of the 'state' in the EU, a changing international context, a repositioning and strengthening Irish nationalist/republican community, and violent stalemate and ceasefires provided the impetus for pro-Agreement unionist and republican elites to contest their respective traditional ideologies based on territory and subscribe to an institutional infrastructure that transcended the territorial source of the conflict. However, although territorial compromise at state level signalled the ending of politically motivated violence, the issues of police reform, communal equality, justice and cultural representation emerged to become the primary sites of post-Agreement ethno-national conflict in political mode. This chapter focuses on cultural representation in and of Northern Ireland as a source of continuing conflict.

Culture is a site of struggle and contestation wherein meanings are continually negotiated.[7] Cultural politics in Northern Ireland involves issues of power, ideology, language, symbols and consciousness. Irish nationalists and republicans have traditionally thrived on a rich seam of cultural (re)invention and political innovation: adapting traditional cultural forms to contemporary (global) conditions; placing emphasis on territorial, transterritorial, equality, justice or cultural resources of identity depending on their potential for making political capital. Ulster unionists and loyalists, on the other hand, have traditionally emphasised the *status quo* based on communal dominance, territorial control and the exclusion of nationalists and republicans from the structures of power in Northern Ireland.

The unionist culture of parading has traditionally served to symbolically assert unionist territorial control in Northern Ireland. However, in the past, unionist leaders have tended to disavow engagement in cultural politics, perceiving it to be the preserve of nationalists and a distraction from the essential reality of the Union between Great Britain and Northern Ireland. Yet, during the 1990s peace process, and particularly after the 1998 GFA, unionists of all hues came to regard cultural politics as a key battleground for their identity and the identity of Northern Ireland generally. They have paid increasing attention to cultural politics because, in the aftermath of territorial compromise, it determines the way in which Northern Ireland is represented, particularly in relation to the Republic of Ireland.

This chapter examines the making of the territorial compromise and the way in which it has signalled an intensification in the culture war over the representation of North and South as one and the same or as separate places.

Territorial compromise

Some scholars contend that the development of the EU has lead to a softening of modern nationalism, the nurturing of liberal nationalism and the reconfiguration of national identity.[8] The EU challenges the claim of the nation state to exercise legal, political and popular sovereignty within a specific territorial domain. While popular sovereignty remains the preserve of the nation state, it has relinquished a measure of legal sovereignty to the *supranational* EU level. Though the extent to which political sovereignty has been transferred from member states to the EU is disputed, the EU represents an extension of political space beyond the territorial boundary of the nation-state and, as such, is taking the form of a transterritorial non-state polity.[9] To promote the economic and cultural well-being of the nation in these changing structural circumstances, liberal nationalists challenge the primacy given to territorial boundedness in modern nationalism and promote the virtues of transterritorial interconnection for the nation.

Informed by the civil rights consciousness of the 1960s, John Hume and the SDLP articulated and developed a liberal nationalist discourse in the Irish context during the 1980s and 1990s. This discourse eschewed the emphasis of modern nationalism on territorial absolutism, secure borders and centralised power in favour of a concentration on communal civil and cultural rights, a commitment to cross-border co-operation and a pooling of sovereignty in the EU context. Throughout this period, the liberal Irish national narrative of the SDLP contested the traditionalist Irish republican national narrative articulated by Sinn Féin which was centred on a modern territorial imperative.[10] This contest provided a vivid demonstration of Homi Bhabha's articulation of the nation as a product of fluid narration that constructs meanings, influences actions and provides self-conceptions.[11] Hume promoted the idea of transterritorialism and its implications for the reconstruction of the Irish national narrative and, consequently, for Northern Ireland conflict resolution. In 1995 he asserted that the Irish nationalist exclusive attachment to territory had changed: 'The nation-state is based on two problematic concepts, territory and the feelings of superiority of one people over another. In Ireland, the nationalist mindset was a territorial mindset. But we have changed. Our position now is that people have been divided, not a territory'.[12] Hume's argument was that the principles of transterritorialism, inclusion and consent associated with European integration had gradually seeped into the Irish nationalist identity represented by the SDLP, rendering it liberal nationalist. He also argued that these principles should form the basis of Northern Ireland conflict resolution.[13]

The 1985 Anglo-Irish Agreement was a milestone in the contestation of the Irish national narrative between liberal nationalists and militant republicans. By emphasising the communal equality and cultural rights' issues, as well as securing a role for the Irish Government in the affairs of Northern Ireland, the Anglo-Irish Agreement represented a success for SDLP liberal nationalism and stymied the electoral rise of Sinn Féin following the appeal of the 1981 IRA hunger strikes to

Irish nationalism's myth of sacrificial martyrdom. Conciliatory noises coming from the UK Government and the failure of the IRA's 'long-war' strategy to deliver political dividends were additional factors that instigated the emergence of Sinn Féin's peace strategy.

In 1989, a series of meetings between Hume and Sinn Féin President Gerry Adams helped to develop this strategy, leading inexorably to ideological revision. In the 1992 policy document *Towards a Lasting Peace in Ireland*, Sinn Féin began to address the unionist 'other' as well as the developing EU context. By the end of the decade, Sinn Féin had abandoned whole swathes of militant republican ideology and signed up to the 1998 GFA.[14] Ideological change was underlined by compromise on the republican principles of collective self-determination for the Irish people as a whole and modern territorial sovereignty for an all-Ireland state. In subscribing to the consent principle of the 1998 GFA, Sinn Féin leaders accepted that the constitutional position of Northern Ireland in the UK could not be changed without the consent of a majority unionist community.[15] Significantly, Martin McGuinness, Sinn Féin MP and figurehead of the republican struggle, took his oath of ministerial office in the Northern Ireland Executive with the words: 'I affirm the Pledge of Office set out in schedule 4 to the Northern Ireland Act 1998.'[16] In doing so, he symbolically recognised Northern Ireland as a legitimate administrative territorial entity.

Sinn Féin's ideological change was accompanied by a political strategy that successfully stole the SDLP's liberal nationalist clothes and used them to help secure electoral dominance in the northern nationalist/republican community. In particular, this strategy concentrated on issues of equality, justice and cultural rights, and emphasised their communal and national contexts. At the same time, Sinn Féin leaders withheld endorsement of police reform proposals. However, radical ideological development over the previous decade and the ability of the Sinn Féin leadership to maintain a largely cohesive republican community indicated that the Irish republican identity represented by Sinn Féin had become fluid, non-essential and mutable, and that the future acceptance of a reformed police service could not be ruled out.[17]

In contrast to Irish nationalist and republican identities, Ulster British unionists and loyalists have a predilection for the *status quo*, that is, Northern Ireland as an integral part of the Union of Great Britain and Northern Ireland expressed through secure state borders, especially the one with the Republic of Ireland. This position has led unionists to emphasise the territorial resource of their identity and neglect the role of cultural (re)invention in providing a political fillip for communal identity. Indeed, the unionist identity has relied on a strict formal–legal interpretation of state sovereignty to give it meaning.[18] Such reliance rendered the unionist identity fixed, essential and immutable. However, a number of factors militated against a unionist position underscored by this reliance. Firstly, UK sovereignty is diminished because the right to leave the UK is invested in a majority of the people of Northern Ireland rather than the State.[19] Secondly, the Anglo-Irish Agreement

(1985) impinged on UK political sovereignty because it granted the Irish Government an influential role in Northern Ireland's affairs. Thirdly, European integration
and the development of a 'post-sovereign' EU polity have potentially ominous
implications for modern legal and political conceptions of state sovereignty underpinned by territorial boundedness. Unionist Euro-scepticism has emanated largely
from the belief that the source of SDLP enthusiasm for European integration was
the threat that it presented to the sovereignty of the UK State. Unionist antipathy
to integration was bolstered by the fact that the 1985 Anglo-Irish Agreement,
which brought an infringement of sovereignty directly to the Irish border, had
traceable Euro-roots.[20]

In the 1980s, changes associated with the Anglo-Irish Agreement and the EU,
and a repositioning and strengthening Irish nationalist 'other', left unionists
vulnerable to increased insecurity and crisis. The unionist response was to establish
a joint DUP–UUP Task Force which produced a 1987 document entitled *An End to
Drift*. It laid the basis for the subsequent ideological shift by pro-1998 GFA
unionists because it offered negotiations on a wide spectrum of issues.[21]

In their quest for security, pro-GFA unionists attempted to contest the
established unionist ideological orthodoxy based on exclusion and the territorial
border with the Republic of Ireland. They accepted the principle of inclusiveness
regarding the participation of Irish nationalists and republicans in the governance
of the region. Furthermore, they acquiesced to the establishment of cross-border
institutions aimed at political, economic and cultural co-operation and co-
ordination between Northern Ireland and the Republic of Ireland. In essence, this
ideological shift was based on the assumption that, in order to maintain their
political position *vis-à-vis* Irish nationalists and republicans, unionists needed to
enter into a partnership with them via territorial compromise, political accommodation, respect for cultural diversity and cross-border co-operation. However,
this attempted ideological shift was, in turn, contested by significant sections of the
unionist political élite and community.

In common with Irish nationalist and republican identities and ethno-national
identities generally, Ulster British unionist and loyalist identities derive from an
'imagined community' in which individuals identify with other people whom they do
not know personally.[22] This 'intimacy of strangers' is socially, politically and culturally
constructed, as well as internally (and externally) contested in terms of its constitution and political action. The 1990s peace process and the GFA provided the context
for the internal contestation of the Ulster unionist narrative. The pro-Agreement
faction hesitantly began sharing power with Irish nationalists and republicans in
Northern Ireland and participated in transterritorial, cross-border co-operation
between Northern Ireland and the Republic of Ireland. The anti-Agreement
faction wished to exclude Irish nationalists and republicans from governance, and
reassert Northern Ireland's formal–legal sovereignty within the UK.[23]

The transterritorial nature of EU governance was reflected in the system of
governance provided by the GFA. Its most important transterritorial institutional

provision was for the establishment and operation of the North–South [cross-border, island of Ireland] Ministerial Council and its implementation bodies. The importance of these North–South arrangements was highlighted by the mandatory nature of the implementation bodies. They concentrated on the specifics of cross-border, whole-island co-operation in the areas of food safety, minority languages, trade and business development, aquaculture, waterways, as well as EU programmes.[24] Meanwhile, the North–South Ministerial Council met regularly to discuss wide-ranging cross-border co-operation. These meetings involved ministers with sectoral responsibility for education, health, transport, agriculture, the environment and tourism. Moreover, the GFA stipulated that the territorial Northern Ireland Assembly could not survive indefinitely without the transterritorial North–South Ministerial Council. Irish taoiseach Bertie Ahern highlighted the developmental potential of this North–South axis during the inauguration of the North–South Ministerial Council on 13 December 1999, when he declared that 'there is no area of our economic and social life without the potential for enhanced cooperation and common action'.[25] The North–South Ministerial Council enjoyed a measure of autonomy in pursuit of these goals, providing agreement was reached among participants that included Ulster unionist political elites. However, decisions reached in the council that were 'beyond the authority of those attending' had to be consented to by both the Oireachtas (Irish Parliament) and the Northern Ireland Assembly.[26]

The working of the North–South Ministerial Council and the implementation bodies was hampered by major difficulties experienced during the implementation of the GFA. These difficulties resulted in: periods of suspension for territorial and transterritorial institutions; a ban, imposed by David Trimble, then first minister of Northern Ireland and leader of the UUP, on the participation of Sinn Féin ministers in North–South Ministerial Council meetings; and a later refusal by UUP ministers to attend any North–South Ministerial Council meeting that included Sinn Féin representatives. There were also teething problems involving staff and resource transfer, and the shift of responsibility from existing territorial bodies to the transterritorial implementation bodies. However, when operational, the North–South Ministerial Council proceeded in a businesslike manner, with both ministers and civil servants appearing keen to develop an effective and accountable North–South infrastructure. Consensual decision-making, on both the North–South axis and the unionist–nationalist axis was held to be key to success for this transterritorial venture. In this regard, every sectoral council meeting involved a northern minister from each community, one with sectoral responsibility and a 'shadow minister' to ensure transparency and build confidence between nationalists and unionists.[27]

Pro-Agreement unionists accepted territorial compromise in the form of the North–South Ministerial Council and the implementation bodies on condition that articles 2 and 3 of the 1937 Bunreacht na hÉireann (Irish constitution) – which laid claim to the territory of Northern Ireland – were deleted and an east–west,

British–Irish Council established. Unionists hoped that the British–Irish Council would provide a vehicle for countervailing co-operation and common action on the east–west axis and so strengthen the economic, political and cultural ties between Northern Ireland and the rest of the UK. However, two factors suggested that this would not transpire. Firstly, the absence of east–west implementation bodies and the failure to have the fate of the British–Irish Council tied to that of the Northern Ireland Assembly rendered the British–Irish Council weak in relation to the North–South Ministerial Council. Secondly, it did not seem plausible that representatives from the Scottish Parliament and the Welsh Assembly would have UK interests at the top of their respective agendas for British–Irish Council meetings. Instead, it appeared likely that these politicians would seek to capitalise on any further leakage of power from the central seat of UK governance at Westminster in an evolving British–Irish transterritorial context.[28]

The GFA also provided for a transterritorial British–Irish Intergovernmental Conference (IGC) between UK and Irish governments to co-operate on non-devolved matters including prisons, policing and criminal justice. This IGC replicates, and even enhances, the 'more than consultative but less than executive' role conferred upon the Irish Government by the 1985 Anglo-Irish Agreement, with continuing consequences for UK political sovereignty. In the British–Irish IGC, the Irish minister for foreign affairs shares the chair with the secretary of state for Northern Ireland. An intensification of co-operation on non-devolved matters is envisaged; indeed, in the event of a prolonged period of suspension for the assembly, it is likely that the British–Irish IGC will extend its remit to previously devolved matters and become much more prominent as a result.

With varying degrees of success, the new transterritorial institutions began to deliver on the transterritorial promise of the GFA. However, with an annual budget of approximately £7 billion, the Northern Ireland Executive and Assembly were the vital territorial structures of the new system of governance.[29] While power was devolved to Northern Ireland on 1 December 1999, the Northern Ireland Executive and Assembly, like the other institutions of the GFA, suffered periods of suspension, principally because of the failure of the IRA to 'decommission' (or dump) its weaponry and disband (or disperse) to the satisfaction of pro-Agreement unionists.

The attempted ideological challenge by pro-Agreement unionists in response to structural change created a significant schism within the unionist body politic and the broader unionist community, with exclusivist anti-Agreement tradition-alists securing just under half of the unionist vote in the 1998 Northern Ireland referendum on the GFA. Support for the anti-Agreement position strengthened as the implementation of the GFA's provisions proceeded. A number of factors were responsible for this strengthening support, including:

- the early release of paramilitary prisoners;
- the actuality of Sinn Féin leaders occupying ministerial positions;
- police reform;

- the prolonged failure of the IRA to 'decommission' its weaponry; and
- the unionist perception that the implementation of the GFA entailed an agenda for emaciating the Britishness of Northern Ireland.

The unionist sense of insecurity was not alleviated when the details of three acts of arms' decommissioning by the IRA – in June 2000, October 2001 and October 2003 – remained confidential. Indeed, these factors combined with charges of IRA intelligence-gathering activity in Northern Ireland and guerrilla-training activity in Columbia to maintain and even intensify the unionist sense of threat. Consequently, they helped to undermine the pro-agreement unionist ideological shift from exclusion to inclusion regarding nationalists and republicans in the governance of Northern Ireland, as well as the institutions themselves.

Surprisingly, the territorial compromise embodied in the establishment of Northern Ireland, North–South and British–Irish institutions did not feature as a major source of alarm for unionists; neither did the suggestion that ultimate political authority is invested in the people of the island, a suggestion made by holding simultaneous North–South referenda on the GFA in May 1998. This was surprising because unionism is state-orientated and the primary features of a modern state are the maintenance of the territorial border and the monopoly of effective violence.[30] Two years prior to the signing of the GFA, the Cadogan Group, an influential unionist think-tank, emphasised the priority of maintaining the UK territorial border, especially the one with the Republic of Ireland.[31] On occasion, Peter Robinson, DUP deputy leader, attempted to inject a note of controversy on the issue of institutionalised North–South co-operation. For example, in remarks to the 2002 annual conference of the Young Democrats, the DUP's youth-wing, he claimed that the North–South bodies posed the 'greatest long-term threat' to the Union.[32] However, the issue failed to ignite unionist concerns. The GFA's provision for substantial police reform and its implications for the unionist monopoly of violence were a much more potent source of unionist state-orientated concern.[33]

The return of cultural politics

Together with issues of police reform, equality and justice, cultural representation gained in significance as a site for the unionist–nationalist conflict after the territorial compromise signalled by the 1998 Agreement. Pro- and anti-Agreement unionists engaged in cultural politics to boost the cultural resource of their identity, and also to pursue their ideological aims of inclusion and exclusion respectively. However, with their perception that the Britishness of Northern Ireland was at stake, it was not always clear that 'inclusivist unionists' pursued inclusivist cultural goals. What did become clear when the UUP nominated Michael McGimpsey for the position of minister for culture, arts and leisure was that UUP leaders finally recognised the importance of culture for identity and politics in Northern Ireland.[34]

The nomination confirmed that UUP political elites now understood that sovereignty is more than just the sum of its formal–legal parts and also has important political and cultural dimensions.[35]

During his tenure, McGimpsey devoted considerable time to aspects of unionist culture such as Ulster Scots, as well as the Act of Union commemoration (2001) and the Golden Jubilee celebration (2002). However, he also made some inclusivist remarks. In his speech to the conference, 'Partnership for Diversity – Forum 2000', he said:

> For too long in Northern Ireland, active support for a lesser-used language, whether it be Ulster-Scots, Irish, sign language or one of the many others which have arrived recently on our shores, has often tended to label an individual as belonging to one particular tradition. Similarly, there are some who believe that support for one language devalues another. This should not be the case. We are extremely fortunate to be able to boast such a diversity of language and I believe that it is an inheritance which everyone should share, treasure and preserve for the benefit of future generations.[36]

The cultural conflict in Northern Ireland has been concerned primarily with the relationship between the Irish language and culture and the Ulster Scots language/dialect and culture. In the 1990s, the Irish language secured funding from the UK Government to aid its revival as a medium of education and cultural enrichment. At the same time, the cultural signifiers of unionism, particularly the traditional British identity in the mould of Protestantism, empire, world war and remembrance appeared to be in terminal decline. Devolution for Scotland in 1999 was another alarming development for unionists because it suggested the possibility of the dissolution of the UK. The response of unionist cultural entrepreneurs to these political and cultural developments was to reinvent the Ulster Scots language/dialect and culture.

McGimpsey's objective – to place Ulster-Scots in the inclusive mould of respect for diversity and the shared cultural heritage of Northern Ireland – was echoed by others.[37] For example, at the opening of the first Institute of Ulster-Scots Studies in January 2001, Vice-Chancellor of the University of Ulster Professor Gerry McKenna maintained that 'its work will contribute to the culture of pluralism upon which our social and economic future depends'.[38] However, some unionists have contested the representation of an Irish cultural identity in Northern Ireland and the ideal of a shared cultural heritage. For them, Ulster Scots presents a means of limiting the representation of the Irish language and culture in Northern Ireland by offering an Ulster British unionist/loyalist language and culture that can compete for already scant resources. For Nelson McCausland (DUP MLA) and director (Heid Yin) of the Ulster Scots Heritage Council (Ulster Scotch Heirskip Cooncil), Ulster Scots provides unionists with a cultural identity that enables differentiation and separation from Irish culture, which he believes to be culturally imperialist in nature.[39]

Contemporary unionist cultural separatism has a modern historical precedent. At the beginning of the twentieth century, unionist elites mobilised culture to contest the Irishness of the North of Ireland. The Irish cultural revival, which straddled the nineteenth and twentieth centuries, provided the catalyst for a less distinguished Ulster Protestant cultural revival that celebrated the Ulster dialect and the role of the Scots-Irish in the USA. Unionist histories of the 1920s and 1930s also dwelt on the stereotype of the 'Ulsterman' who was dour but honest, God-fearing but shrewd, and straight-talking but in an incomprehensible dialect. In contrast, the Irish 'other' was often portrayed as superstitious, lazy, uncivilised, and lacking in moral courage. After the First World War the 'Ulsterman' stereotype was encouraged and embellished by unionist historians such as the amateur Ernest Hamilton and the academic W. A. Phillips. The First World War had intensified the isolation felt by unionists and the 'Ulsterman' stereotype served as a cultural bind to strengthen unionism against the real and perceived threats of Irish nationalism and the UK Government's perfidy.[40] At the beginning of the twenty-first century, Ulster Scots offers a contemporary cultural bind to unionists faced with increased alienation from 'mainland' Britishness. Perhaps more importantly, it can be mobilised to challenge the cultural assertion of Irish nationalists/republicans in Northern Ireland and their contestation of Northern Ireland as British. However, the anti-Agreement DUP MP Gregory Campbell has argued that lip-service is given to Ulster Scots to airbrush the new political dispensation with the colours of cultural equality: 'the present political system is built on the implicit acceptance that nationalists get a raw deal when it is unionists who are left behind in the equality stakes'.[41]

With the implementation of the GFA, pro- and anti-Agreement unionists complained increasingly that a concerted effort was being made to undermine the Britishness of Northern Ireland – the 'Britishness of Northern Ireland' being a direct reference to the political and cultural substance of UK sovereignty. Consequently, Northern Ireland was becoming a 'cold place for unionists',[42] and language was a major cultural issue. However, state-orientated unionists were arguably even more exercised by government proposals to downgrade the symbols of Britishness associated with state institutions such as the police and the courts.[43] This attempted downgrading, in order to re-create Northern Ireland either as a neutral public space or as one that reflects the region's cultural diversity, had a detrimental effect on unionist attitudes towards the GFA and its implementation.

Flags provided a particular focus for unionist concern during the implementation of the GFA and had a direct bearing on the stability of its institutions.[44] The flying of the Union flag over government buildings was objected to by nationalist and republican leaders because they believed it to contravene the bi-communal ethos of the GFA. They argued that both the Union flag and the Irish Tricolour should be flown, and if unionists could not agree to this proposition then no flags should be flown. Pro- and anti-Agreement unionists were incensed, believing it to be a symbolic challenge to the Britishness of Northern Ireland. For unionists, the two flags' option represented joint British-Irish sovereignty over Northern Ireland. In October 2000, Northern Ireland Secretary of State Peter Mandelson intervened and used his reserve powers to order the flying of the Union flag on a limited number of 'designated days' associated with British royal family members' birthdays, much to the chagrin of nationalists and republicans.[45]

Flowers have also been the subject of the unionist–nationalist culture war. In April 2001, the placing a vase of Easter lilies in the great hall of Parliament Buildings at Stormont forced an emergency debate and the recall of MLAs from the holiday recess. Easter lilies had become a symbol of republican struggle after the Easter Rising of 1916 and the subsequent execution of fifteen republican revolutionaries by the UK State. Sinn Féin leaders had wanted to commemorate the Easter Rising with a floral display and a eulogy in the great hall to laud the work of the National Graves Association which takes care of republican graves.[46] In doing so, they employed this invented floral tradition to camouflage ideological deviation from traditional republicanism, since symbols have the immediate appeal of uncomplicated imagery and can provide camouflage for internal group contradictions and contestations.[47] That this floral display also challenged symbolically the Britishness of the new political dispensation was an added bonus for Sinn Féin's leaders.

In the event, the cross-party committee that dealt with the running of the Northern Ireland Assembly proposed a compromise in the form of a small floral display without accompanying eulogy. Pro- and anti-Agreement Unionist assembly members supported the motion against the display, but it failed because it did not have cross-community support. Jim Wells, the DUP MLA who forced the emergency debate, proclaimed: 'For the first time in the history of the United Kingdom a government building will be used to display symbols which honour IRA terrorists.'[48] In the event, the 'war of the lilies' served to highlight the fact that the effort to re-create Northern Ireland as a neutral public space, or one that reflects equally its two main communities, is undermined by conflicting political and cultural claims.

Commenting on cultural representation in Northern Ireland, Jeffery Donaldson (DUP MP),[49] has argued that the increasing recognition and support for Irish culture requires commensurate recognition and support for Britishness:

> If bridges of co-operation are about recognising the Irish dimension ... then equally it is important for unionists that there is the maintenance of, and respect for a vibrant British dimension. That's why there is a concern that people have a sense that their Britishness is being diminished, whereas the Irish dimension is being promoted and enhanced. You see that in many and varied ways, especially through the promotion of the Irish language. There has been a belated response with the development of Ulster-Scots language and culture, but that is not the essence of Britishness. Language is not a main feature of Britishness in Northern Ireland. It tends to be expressed much more in an affinity with the Crown and the symbols of the British state.[50]

Problematically, however, these manifestations of Britishness require expression as the state representation of Northern Ireland. Therefore, recognition of Britishness in Northern Ireland necessarily requires recognition of the Britishness of Northern Ireland, a position which serves as a linchpin for the unionist–nationalist culture war. It also acts as a potential cultural stumbling block for the transition of unionism from territorialism and exclusion to transterritorialism and inclusion.

Conclusion

By signing up to the GFA, pro-Agreement unionists and republicans demonstrated that they had made significant shifts in their ideologies and political strategies. Sinn Féin leaders recognised the legitimacy of Northern Ireland as an administrative unit and accepted that changes in the constitutional status of that territory required the consent of a unionist majority. However, alleged post-Agreement IRA activity and Sinn Féin's hesitation in endorsing police reform earned the party the epithet 'the slightly constitutional party', one also used to describe Fianna Fáil in the early years of the Irish State.

Pro-Agreement unionists acquiesced in transterritorial co-operation between Northern Ireland the Republic of Ireland. They also committed themselves to the principle and act of political inclusion by sharing power with Irish nationalists and republicans. The low-profile nature of post-GFA cross-border co-operation downgraded the importance of state territory and the Irish border in the unionist–nationalist conflict. However, the territorial compromise at state level shifted the focus of the unionist–nationalist conflict to the areas of police reform, equality, justice and the representation of culture in and of Northern Ireland. The unionist perception that the implementation of the GFA involved the erosion of the Britishness of Northern Ireland lead to pro-Agreement unionist difficulties in embracing the principle of cultural inclusiveness and had the potential to give rise to territorial recidivism.

Culturally, Irish nationalists in Northern Ireland have appeared to be vibrant, dynamic and outward-looking, whereas, the primary cultural resources of the Ulster British unionist/loyalist identity – traditional Britishness, Ulster Protestantism and its corollary Orangeism, as well as Ulster Scots – have appeared to be either in decline or parochial and meaningless outside (and even inside) the unionist community. Therefore, post-GFA efforts to recreate Northern Ireland as a neutral political and cultural space, or one that reflects the two main communities, are feared by unionists to be part of a campaign that capitalises on their relative cultural weakness, strips the region of its Britishness and represents North and South as one and the same rather than as separate places.[51] Consequently, after the territorial compromise reached in 1998, culture has become a primary site for the perpetuation of the unionist–nationalist ethno-national conflict.

Notes

1 Glen Jordan and Chris Weedon, *Cultural Politics: Class, Gender, Race and the Postmodern World* (Oxford: Blackwell, 1995), p. 4.

2 Hereafter referred to as the GFA.

3 Signatories to the GFA included leading members of the UUP, the political representatives of the Irish nationalist/republican community in Northern Ireland (Sinn Féin and the SDLP), those from more minor political groupings (including those associated with loyalist paramilitary groups) and the UK and Irish governments. DUP representatives walked out of the multi-party talks leading to the GFA on the entry of Sinn Féin negotiators to Castle Buildings, Stormont, on 21 July 1997. Sinn Féin formally joined negotiations on 15 September 1997.

4 The institutional infrastructure of the GFA included a territorial Northern Ireland Executive, Assembly and Civic Forum, and a transterritorial North–South (cross-border, island of Ireland) Ministerial Council and its implementation bodies, as well as a transterritorial British–Irish Council and British–Irish Intergovernmental Conference.

5 Article 1, paragraph (ii) of the GFA states that the two governments 'recognise that it is for the people of the island of Ireland alone, by agreement between the two parts respectively and without external impediment, to exercise their right of self-determination on the basis of consent, freely and concurrently given, North and South, to bring about a united Ireland, if that is their wish, accepting that this right must be achieved and exercised with and subject to the agreement and consent of a majority of the people of Northern Ireland'. Ulster British unionists/loyalists currently represent approximately 52 per cent of the Northern Ireland voting population and Irish nationalists/republicans approximately 45 per cent.

6 Provision for the nominal inclusion of non-governmental participants in this system of regional governance, by means of consultation, was also made through the establishment of a Civic Forum as part of the GFA's infrastructure.

7 Jack Goody, 'Culture and its Boundaries: A European View', *Social Anthropology*, vol. 1, no. 1, 1992, pp. 9–33.

8 Yael Tamir, *Liberal Nationalism* (Princeton, NJ: Princeton University Press, 1993); Malcolm Anderson, *States and Nationalism in Europe since 1945* (London: Routledge, 2000).

9 Ben Rosamond, 'Discourses of Globalization and the Social Construction of European Identities', *Journal of European Public Policy*, vol. 6, no. 4, 1999, pp. 652–68 at 666–7; Jo Shaw, 'Postnational Constitutionalism in the European Union', *Journal of European Public Policy*, vol. 6, no. 4, 1999m pp. 579–97 at pp. 583–7; William Wallace, 'The Sharing of Sovereignty: The European Paradox', *Political Studies*, vol. 47, no. 3, 1999, pp. 503–21 at pp. 503–6 and pp. 511–12; Dimitris N. Chryssochoou, 'Civic Competence and the Challenge to EU Polity-Building', *Journal of European Public Policy*, vol. 9, no. 5, 2002, pp. 756–73.

10 To a greater or lesser extent, the liberal national narrative is shared by the main political parties in the Republic of Ireland including, Fianna Fáil, Fine Gael, Labour and PDP.

11 Homi Bhabha, 'Introduction', in Homi Bhabha (ed.), *The Nation and Narration* (London: Routledge, 1990), pp. 1–7.

12 Quoted in the *Independent*, 28 April 1995.

13 John Hume, *Personal Views: Politics, Peace and Reconciliation in Ireland* (Dublin: Town House, 1996).

14 Cathal McCall, 'The Production of Space and the Realignment of Identity in Northern Ireland', *Regional and Federal Studies*, vol. 11, no. 2, 2002, pp. 1–24.

15 John Coakley, 'Conclusion: New Strains of Unionism and Nationalism', in John Coakley (ed.), *Changing Shades of Orange and Green: Redefining the Union and the Nation in Contemporary Ireland* (Dublin: University College Dublin Press, 2002), pp. 132–54 at p. 148.

16 Northern Ireland Assembly, 29 November 1999, available at: www.ni-assembly.gov.uk/record/991129.htm

17 Fringe dissident republican groups continue to observe an essentialist attachment to the modern territorial principle of sovereignty. One such group – the 32 County Sovereignty

Movement – makes this explicit in its constitution and objectives (www.geocities.com/thirtytwocounty/constitution1.html).

18 Arthur Aughey, 'Unionism', in Arthur Aughey and Duncan Morrow (eds), *Northern Ireland Politics* (London: Longman, 1996), pp. 31–8.

19 James Anderson, 'Rethinking National Problems in a Transnational Context', in David Miller (ed.), *Rethinking Northern Ireland: Culture, Ideology and Colonialism* (London: Longman, 1998), pp. 125–45 at p. 134.

20 DUP, *The Surrender of Maastricht: What it Means for Ulster* (Belfast: DUP, 1992); UUP, *Westminster General Election Manifesto.* (Belfast: UUP, 1992).

21 Coakley, 'Conclusion', pp. 143–4.

22 Benedict Anderson, *Imagined Communities: Reflections on the Origins and Spread of Nationalism* (London: Verso, 1991).

23 In its 2004 policy document *Devolution Now: The DUP's Concept for Devolution*, the anti-Agreement DUP appeared to shift towards more inclusive models for the governance of Northern Ireland (www.dup2win.com/pdf/DUPDevolution_lo-res.pdf). However, its subsequent espousal, together with the SDLP, of a 'voluntary coalition model' was indicative of an exclusivist ideology since it sought to exclude Sinn Féin.

24 The Special EU Programmes Body (SEUPB) is the implementation body with managerial responsibility for the EU Peace II Programme (2000–6) and oversight responsibility for other EU programmes such as INTERREG. Peace I (1994–9) and Peace II had a number of priority areas, cross-border co-operation among them (www.eugrants.org/peace_summary.pdf). Voluntary groups, drawn from local nationalist and unionist communities, have been involved in projects funded under this priority. The support given to such activity has been aimed at re-enforcing at the 'grassroots' level the cross-border co-operation initiative taken at the political elite level. It is significant that a substantial number of projects funded under this priority emanate from the unionist and loyalist communities.

25 Quoted in the *Irish Times*, 14 December 1999.

26 The GFA, Strand 2, para. 6.

27 Andy Pollak, 'The Policy Agenda for Cross-Border Co-operation: A View from the Centre for Cross-Border Studies', *Administration* vol. 49, no. 2, 2001, pp. 15–22 at p. 16.

28 Vernon Bognanor, *Devolution in the United Kingdom* (Oxford: Oxford University Press, 1999), p. 298.

29 A Northern Ireland Civic Forum was also provided by the GFA (Strand One, para. 34). It was to act as a consultative body for the devolved assembly and executive, so enhancing the prospects for the institutionalisation of participative democracy. However, with an annual budget in the area of £370,000 (the sum allocated for the first year of its operation), it appeared that the Civic Forum faced a difficult task in becoming an effective conduit between civic society and the new political administration.

30 Charles Tilly, *The Formation of National States in Western Europe* (Princeton, NJ, and London: Princeton University Press, 1990), at p. 1.

31 Cadogan Group, *Square Circles: Round Tables and the Path to Peace in Northern Ireland* (Belfast: Cadogan Group 1996), p. 24.

32 Quoted in the *Irish Times*, 18 February 2002.

33 While post-Agreement transterritorial, cross-border co-operation itself has largely evaded controversy, there is some evidence to suggest an increasing political and cultural definition of borders in Northern Ireland. The 1991 census revealed a sharp increase in Northern Ireland's east–west demographic divide between Protestants and Catholics, a divide shown by the 2001 census to have been maintained in the intervening years. The 2001 UK general election resulted in Sinn Féin candidates claiming the two remaining unionists seats west of the River Bann. Consequently, the Bann, which follows a course that runs roughly through the middle of Northern Ireland from North to South, became a heightened symbolic border between unionists and nationalists. Meanwhile, internal Northern Ireland North–South divisions between Catholic nationalists and Protestant unionists have also become apparent in counties Armagh and Down. Borders in Northern Ireland are particularly clear in the urban working-

class and under-class areas of Belfast. Prior to the 11 September 2001 Islamic fundamentalist attacks in the USA, television screens were filled with the images of distressed Catholic primary-school children who were running a daily loyalist gauntlet in the Ardoyne area of north Belfast because their school was situated in a 'loyalist area'. The underlying reason for the action of the loyalist protesters was that the Catholic (mainly nationalist/republican) population of the area was on the increase while Protestant (mainly unionist/loyalist) numbers were dwindling, leaving them insecure territorially. The situation was exacerbated by almost nightly 'tit-for-tat' violence between the communities and suggested that the territorial compromise reached at state level had done little to appease territorial conflict at the street level.

34 This was one of the three Northern Ireland ministries that the UUP was entitled to in the share out of ministries among the major parties.

35 Brigid Laffan, Rory O'Donnell and Michael Smith, *Europe's Experimental Union: Rethinking Integration* (London: Routledge, 2000).

36 Michael McGimpsey, 'Breaking the Moulds: A New Future for Linguistic and Cultural Diversity in Northern Ireland', paper presented to the Partnership For Diversity Forum, 2 February 2001: www.dcalni.gov.uk/press_releases/2001.

37 For an examination of the initiative to place Irish and Ulster Scots in the context of respect for diversity and a shared cultural heritage as detailed in the 1998 Agreement see my paper 'Political Transformation and the Reinvention of the Ulster-Scots Identity and Culture', *Identities: Global Studies in Culture and Power*, vol. 9, no. 2, 2002, pp. 197–218.

38 www.ulst.ac.uk.news/releases/2001/280.html.

59 Interview with author, 26 June 2000.

40 David Fitzpatrick, *The Two Irelands, 1912–1939* (Oxford: Oxford University Press, 1998), p. 220; Gillian McIntosh, *The Force of Culture: Unionist Identities in Contemporary Ireland* (Cork: Cork University Press, 1999), pp. 51–2.

41 Gregory Campbell, 'How Unionists Might View 2002', *Belfast Telegraph*, 8 January 2002.

42 See, for example, the two-part article 'Northern Ireland: A Cold Place for Unionists', *Irish Times*, 14 and 15 January 2002.

43 Disillusionment also had a substantive institutional focus in the form of new commissions to deal with parades, human rights and equality issues. These new commissions are the product of the GFA and are assumed by many unionist politicians to be anti-unionist in nature.

44 Robin Wilson, *Flagging Concern: The Controversy Over Flags and Emblems* (Belfast: Democratic Dialogue, 2000).

45 *Irish Times*, 25 October 2000.

46 Paul Tanney, 'Unionists Fail to Stop Stormont Easter Lilies', *Irish Times*, 11 April 2001; Nicholas Watt, 'A Bunch of Lilies Does Not Seem Like a Problem, But in Ulster Nothing is Simple', *Guardian*, 11 April 2001.

47 Anthony P. Cohen, *Self Consciousness: An Alternative Anthropology of Identity* (London: Routledge, 1994), pp. 16–20.

48 Quoted in David Sharrock, 'Unionists Fail to Block Assembly's Easter Lilies', *Daily Telegraph*, 11 April 2001.

49 Donaldson lead the anti-Agreement faction of the UUP until he jumped ship to the DUP in January 2004.

50 Interview with author, 3 December 2001.

51 There is some evidence to suggest that political elites and sections of society in the Republic of Ireland imagine North and South as economically, politically and culturally separate: see Andy Pollak, 'Why North–South Co-operation Makes Perfect Sense', *Irish Times*, 17 February 2004; and Behaviours & Attitudes, *Through Irish Eyes: Irish Attitudes towards the UK* (Dublin: British Council of Ireland, 2004), a report commissioned by the British Council of Ireland and the British Embassy in Dublin (www.britishcouncil.org/ireland/interior.pdf). However, the creation of Tourism Ireland Ltd under the GFA for the promotion of tourism on an all-Ireland basis supports the representation abroad of North and South as one and the same.

PART V
Bringing in the international

21

From Anglo-Irish to British–Irish relations

PAUL GILLESPIE*

Four themes have dominated relations between Britain and Ireland from 1969 to 2004. There was, first of all, a decisive shift from dependence to interdependence between the Republic of Ireland and the UK; their relationship becoming more equal, despite the evident asymmetries of size and power. This transformation is best understood as a process of internationalisation within the context of the EC and relations with the USA – the second major theme. Without that process there would not have been the confidence to tackle the transition from unity to astability based on inclusiveness and consent as the primary focus of the Republic of Ireland's policy towards Northern Ireland – the third theme. This culminated in the Belfast Agreement (GFA) and is closely related to the normalisation of relations between Britain and Ireland – the fourth theme – which is occurring, crucially, at a time when the larger island is undergoing its own process of constitutional change, 'fundamental alterations in the arrangements of the United Kingdom, which amount to a reshaping of the British state'.[1] The GFA directly involves Ireland in this historic process through the link-ups it has put in place with devolved governments in the UK.[2]

Taken together, these changes may be described as a transition from Anglo-Irish to British–Irish relations.[3] Such is the argument of this chapter, which first looks critically at Anglo-Irish relations as conventionally described and written about and then goes on to examine each of these four themes in turn, with particular reference to the Northern Ireland peace process. This is not, therefore, a chronological narrative of Anglo-Irish diplomatic relations over these thirty-five years but a thematic commentary on them in the light of the peace process and the changing relations between Britain and Ireland.

Anglo-Irish Relations

Anglo-Irish relations have been described as a 'label of convenience which confuses two distinctions, the first between nationalities and the second between geographical entities'.[4] The fact that both the nationalities involved in Anglo-Irish relations are themselves undergoing changes of identity transforms the geographical relations between Britain and Ireland. Scotland and Wales have been brought into the foreground by devolution and European regionalism, as well as being promised a potentially fruitful new set of identities by developing their relations with Ireland through the British–Irish Council. The very reduction of the English domination of Britain following the end of the empire and the Cold War and the emergence of an Anglo-British question as it is constitutionally rearranged can facilitate the resolution of traditional British–Irish quarrels – partly by offering dual or multiple identities as the GFA does and which is central to Scottish and Welsh relations with England. Historically and geographically Irish nationalism's quarrel was more with south-east England and its imperial governing class than it was with the British peoples over whom the latter ruled. The term *Anglo-Irish* connotes the Anglo-Irish ascendancy which was so integrated with that discredited socio-geographical system. British–Irish represents these new political realities more accurately.

Traditionally Anglo-Irish relations have taken for granted that the two nationalities in question were the English and the Irish before and after the Treaty settlement. This presumption about nationalities made sense so long as the inherently ambivalent relationship between Englishness and Britishness was resolved practically by the unproblematical concentration of political power in London, Westminster and Whitehall. Such centralisation was a function of imperial rule and the development of the twentieth-century big state through war, welfare, economic production and regulation. Inter-state relations between independent Ireland and the United Kingdom of Great Britain and Northern Ireland were automatically conceived as involving contact between the British and Irish governments in London and Dublin. That remains true despite the changing international context in which Britain now finds itself following the demise of the empire and after a Cold War which had frozen many of its political structures in a centralist mode.

Relations between Britain and Ireland in the years 1922–69 must, therefore, be put in the context of a British State the structure and nature of which was for the most part taken for granted, even as argument about what it should do and how the resources it could command should be distributed dominated British politics. This coincided pretty well exactly with one of the principal motivations of British policy with regard to Ireland: the desire to ensure that the Treaty settlement removed the Irish question from domestic British politics – 'disengagement was the objective and for the better part of a half century, from 1922 to 1969 … and was achieved to an extent that would have seemed inconceivable before the Great War';[5] Ireland 'was best managed with a barge pole'.[6] Hence the shocking realisation in 1969 that direct involvement would reintroduce Northern Irish affairs centrally to Westminster politics.[7] After direct rule was introduced in 1972 a great deal more parliamentary and political time was taken up with Irish issues. One can plainly hear in several of Tony Blair's comments a desire to see that reduced to more normal proportions in order to concentrate on other issues – including the development of closer relations with the Republic of Ireland in the context of the European Union. As he put it in his speech to the Oireachtas in 1998: 'Northern Ireland is now helping to bring us together. But I do not believe Northern Ireland can or should any longer define the relationship between us. Our common interests, what we can achieve together, go much, much wider than that.'[8]

Anglo-Irish relations in the period 1922–69 have been studied extensively and there are a number of outstanding diplomatic and political histories, concentrating on inter-state relations conducted relatively secretively at the highest levels of government. The main themes include the development of *dominion* status, the economic war, neutrality and the Second World War, and the crisis leading to the declaration of the Republic of Ireland in 1949.[9] There are also fine studies of Anglo-Irish relations since 1969[10] and a flow of memoirs and autobiographies[11]– especially on the British side; but there are relatively few attempts to theorise or compare the relationship.[12] From the perspective of British–Irish relations – or, in the Hegelian phrase first inserted in the 8 December 1980 statement following the Thatcher–Haughey talks, the 'totality of relationships in these islands' – the narrow focus of this literature is unsatisfactory. It leaves too little room for the extensive social, economic, sporting and cultural interaction that continued and deepened after independence, creating one of the most intimate relationships between neighbouring states anywhere in the world.[13] This is more apparent after the GFA's definition of the British–Irish Council's task, which is 'to promote the harmonious and mutually beneficial development of the totality of relationships among the peoples of these islands'.

The extent to which the relationship continues to be dependent, post-colonial and politically contested obviously affects this literature and remains a central concern of the debate on historical revisionism.[14] That debate has broadened studies of British–Irish relations insofar as they are intended to give a comprehensive account of how the peoples of the two islands relate to one another. But it also highlights their scattered disciplinary nature, sub-divided between history,[15] economics,[16] sociology,[17] politics,[18] constitutional law,[19] international relations,[20] literary and critical studies.[21] With some notable exceptions, such as the volume edited by P. J. Drudy in 1986,[22] there has been little attempt to bring them together. It was, extraordinarily, not until 1999 that an Institute for British–Irish Studies, with a wide brief to examine the relationship and an active programme of conferences, meetings and research, was set up in University College, Dublin, despite the proliferation of Irish studies' courses throughout the English-speaking world and beyond it. But this is probably symptomatic of a post-colonial dependence on Britain and its intellectual mindsets which took that relationship so much for granted.[23] Thus it has been precisely the relative escape from Anglocentricity over the period 1969–2004 that has enabled a more comprehensive approach to emerge in everyday life, as well as in policy-making, the media and the academy – a point that Hegel would have appreciated.

From dependence to interdependence

It helps to draw a distinction between *independence* and *sovereignty* when considering relations between Britain and Ireland. While British governments have traditionally been preoccupied with territorial sovereignty in the EEC/EU context, Irish ones have been readier to recognise that independence can be enhanced by pooling sovereignty. Thus sovereignty is of little use if its exercise inhibits the pursuit of influence in a more interdependent world. That is, above all, the lesson to be drawn from Ireland's experience of European integration.

For the first two generations after independence it had been taken for granted that political sovereignty would facilitate national economic development, even as arguments continued over whether it was best pursued by open or protectionist means. Neutrality in the Second World War was the ultimate assertion of independence and sovereignty in formal terms. 'When Ireland was dependent upon Britain, neutrality was the policy to which it aspired; when it became independent, neutrality was the policy it practised; and when Ireland and the United Kingdom became interdependent, military neutrality was a policy Ireland would still not relinquish.'[24]

Ireland's dependence on Britain in the period 1922–69 has been characterised as follows: 'The British influence on Ireland stemmed from the demographic fact of the unequal numbers of inhabitants, the geographical fact of nearness, the historical fact of political dominion and social and economic dominance, and the intellectual context of similarity of language and cultural blanketing.'[25] Paradoxically, all this was reinforced by neutrality and its aftermath of international isolation in the 1950s, insulated from Europe by Britain – an island behind an island – and preoccupied politically by the border and partition. Nonetheless political independence, international boundaries and institution-building ensured that dependence did not amount to re-absorption. The Republic and the North also grew apart; de Valera, no less, was to remark in 1963 that 'France was France without Alsace and Lorraine … Ireland is Ireland without the North'.[26]

From 1922 until EEC accession Ireland remained Anglocentric economically. Ireland's was little more than a regional economy within the wider British economy in the 1920s, with 92 per cent of its exports and 78 per cent of its imports to or from there, making Ireland a part of Britain's informal empire; by 1937 these figures were still 91 per cent and 50 per cent respectively, despite the economic war between the Fianna Fáil Government and Britain. It suited Britain to bring it to a close because Ireland was its second best market and a highly profitable one, surpassing Australia, Germany and the USA – and it remains by far the most important recipient of British exports on a per capita basis.[27] Agricultural goods in particular were bound up with the British market and its policy of inexpensive food. Many Irish-owned businesses traded exclusively with the British market, while sterling parity meant that Ireland's automatically devalued with the UK's, most dramatically so in 1967. As a result Ireland had little option but to join Britain in applying, again, for accession to the EEC. Joint accession confirmed Ireland's economic dependence, but was anticipated to reduce it – such has become the accepted interpretation of the Anglo-Irish Free Trade Agreement of 1965.

And this is indeed what happened in the economic sphere, so that by 1995 exports to the UK had reduced to 26 per cent and imports to 37 per cent.[28] Over the period 1970–93 the Ireland–UK trade ratio declined from 60 to 31.[29] Such overall figures admittedly conceal the continued existence of a dual economy, divided between largely domestically owned firms for which Britain is the largest trading partner (although diversification is happening in that sector as well) and the extensive new multinational sectors which trade only marginally in that market.[30] Tension between their interests has been central in Ireland's strategy towards EMU; within the euro group Ireland has the greatest exposure to sterling volatility and the rate at which it would enter the single currency. Official policy assumes Britain will eventually join the euro; adjusting to the delay in deciding on this was made easier by the Celtic Tiger economic boom from 1994–2002 and by the euro's weakness against the dollar and sterling during those years.

These changes represent a qualitative break from post-colonial economic dependence on the UK, confirmed by the decision in 1979 to join the European monetary system without Britain and, in 1999, similarly to join the euro. While argument continues as to whether one set of dependences have merely been substituted by others – on the larger European Union powers for overall macro-economic policy or the USA for investment[31] – Irish capitalism has definitely diversified and developed away from what was a debilitating and exploitative relationship with the UK. The term *interdependence* best expresses the level of equality involved, in a framework of EU integration expressly geared to re-balance smaller and larger states by a system of international law and regulation that enmeshes nation states together in a new system of governance.[32]

That such interdependence works its way through and transforms strong bi-lateral relationships, as well as multi-lateral ones, was recognised by British Foreign Secretary Douglas Hurd, in a speech to the Institute of European Affairs in Dublin: 'For the Irish membership in 1972 was about Ireland's place in history, confirming Ireland's position in Europe as a modern state ... and its decisive shift away from the embrace of Britain'.[33] That decisive shift was felt in the political and diplomatic spheres as well as in the social and psychological ones. Politically, Ireland's perspectives were broadened by participation in a multi-lateral setting of the EU, as was its diplomacy. Membership provided a setting in which British and Irish ministers could meet on an equal basis;[34] in recent years no European Council has been complete without a meeting of taoisigh and prime ministers about Northern Ireland on the margins – notably between Bertie Ahern and Tony Blair, who developed an extraordinarily close relationship during the ups and downs of implementing the GFA, making the Republic effectively an arbiter and co-manager of the northern conflict. In the same way Ireland's and Britain's relations with the USA broadened and intertwined over this period. Social change, too, fed into a transformation of traditional social and cultural structures, as a new middle class asserted liberal and gender rights, consumer values and more secular attitudes.[35] All these interacted with the economic in a complex re-orientation of Ireland's public policy and popular attitudes away from such a central preoccupation with and dependence on Britain. Disparities of size and power often have their own psychological repercussions – and the British–Irish relationship has been marked historically by a superiority complex on the British side and an inferiority complex on the Irish one. There are similar asymmetries in the degree to which each is fixated by and knowledgeable or informed of the other in the media[36].

Since a central aspect of unionist ideology concerned the supposed superiority of British political culture over Ireland's, as well as the superiority of British economic performance, of which the industrial North used to be such an integral part, it is not surprising that these changes profoundly influenced British–Irish relations. They inverted most of the presuppositions on which such judgements were based, including the supposed backwardness of the southern economy (it has in recent years caught up with the per capita income of the UK, surpassed that of the North, out-produced and out-sold the North industrially); the supposed clericalist nature of southern society (after the undermining of the Catholic Church's authority in a welter of scandals); and the exclusivist nationalist identities on which it is perceived to be based (after the retrieval of its hybrid and genuinely republican as well as its cosmopolitan ambience – not to mention its Anglo-American popular culture which sits uneasily with its supposed European orientation).

Internationalisation

The Republic of Ireland now has one of the most open economies in the developed world: imports and exports come to over 150 per cent of gross national product and the Republic topped the list of the most globalised states in the world published by the Washington-based *Foreign Policy* magazine in 2003 and 2004. This openness developed rapidly over the period of the Troubles, although it is based on processes originating before they began, in the Lemass period. Coinciding with the economic opening there has been a political one: 'In order to understand the future evolution of Irish politics, it will be essential to see the state as a "small open polity"'[37] as well as a small open economy. That this affects Northern Ireland as well as the Republic is increasingly recognised. The internationalisation process in fact includes the State's northern policies, which have drawn on it systematically over the period 1969–2004. Arthur suggests that this should be examined under several headings, including the consequent reduction of dependence on Britain: the more dynamic influence of the Irish diaspora; the evolving debate on how to govern the North and contain its violence, which requires innovation in developing relations between Dublin and London; and the pervasive if usually indirect influence of the European Community as a model and a field for the transformation of contemporary political sovereignty.[38]

All this has transformed traditional Irish identities based on territorial sovereignty and has added a certain post-national aspect to the new ones set out in the GFA. Indeed the principles built into it, including consent, parity of esteem, recognition of diversity and power-sharing, amount to a lexicon of contemporary identities and make it something of a model that other conflicts may follow.[39] Despite the evident hybridity that has characterised Irish identity over millennia, in the twentieth century we experienced a classic set of exclusionary nationalisms and their associated essentialisms. That identity be defined as de-Anglicisation – Ireland as not-Britain, and Britain as Ireland's 'Other' – was inscribed canonically by Douglas Hyde as the task of Irish cultural nationalism in the following significant terms: 'But you ask, why should we wish to make Ireland more Celtic than it is – why should we de-Anglicise at all? I answer because the Irish race is at present in a most anomalous position, imitating England and yet apparently hating it.'[40] This was perfectly understandable in the context of imperial power and cultural renaissance. But in Ireland as in Britain there has been a struggle between ethnic and civic nationalisms,[41] and effectively – as in many other European states – they became intermingled. The achievement of the civic modernisation project of the last two decades of the twentieth century has been rather through Europeanisation and Atlanticisation substantially to reduce Ireland's Anglocentricity. Diversification of economic, political and cultural life away from preoccupation with and over-dependence on Britain over that period of EC/EU membership has accomplished whatever independence is possible in a post-Westphalian world. As Tom Garvin has eloquently put it:

> In these islands, Europe symbolises the end of empire and, therefore, the obsolescence of the ancient English–Irish quarrel. I would argue emphatically that that has been the true European achievement in Ireland, an achievement which far outweighs the undoubted benefits of the Common Agricultural Policy, the Brussels cornucopia of grants or even European free trade. The odd thing is, we have scarcely noticed that the 800–year war is over, dying quietly and unmourned sometime between 1972 and 1998.[42]

Precisely because Ireland has been happier with this process than has Britain, and *a fortiori* than have unionists wedded to a zero-sum notion of sovereignty,[43] Dublin has had a certain advantage in pushing open the doors of political innovation involved in the GFA by experimenting with a new liberal or cosmopolitan nationalism; thus integration and nationalism have reinforced each other, unlike in Britain.[44]

Europeanisation has awakened longstanding memories of the previous engagement with the Continent.[45] It has led to a greater realisation that Ireland's experience is more akin to Central and Eastern European nationalisms thrown up by the collapse of empires there after the First World War. The role of majorities and minorities is another similarity, which Frank Wright's pioneering study put in the context of ethnic frontiers.[46] Another is the triadic structure of political interaction between nationalising states, external homeland nationalisms and national minorities in Central and Eastern Europe, uncannily reflected in the structure of the GFA.[47] This experience was reinforced during the two referendums on the

Nice Treaty in 2001 and 2002; had the second one not voted in favour the enlargement to take in eight new states from Central and Eastern Europe, as well as Malta and Cyprus, would not have taken place. The fact that Ireland welcomed them into the EU on 1 May 2004 during its presidency added to the mutual identification, as has those states' desire to emulate Ireland's economic development based on effective EU participation.

Ireland's engagement with Britain must be seen historically not only on a bilateral basis but in its wider European setting. As Fanning reminds us, 'crises in Anglo-Irish relations often either originated in or were subsumed by larger international crises in which British governments subordinated concern for harmony in Anglo-Irish relations to perceptions of what constituted their more vital national interests.'[48] That this applies as much to the ending of the Cold War and the collapse of the Soviet Union as it does to previous major European convulsions is increasingly recognised by analysts. With the ending of the Cold War the strategic issue that for hundreds of years determined Britain's presence in Ireland had fundamentally changed: 'When the Soviet Union ceased to exist as a legal and geopolitical entity in December 1991 it was to mark the beginning of the most dramatic change to Anglo-Irish strategic relations since the Act of Union in 1800.'[49]

Peter Brooke's important speech on 9 November 1990, in which he said that 'the British government has no selfish strategic or economic interest in Northern Ireland', was specifically intended to influence Sinn Féin's thinking in its dialogue with John Hume at the time;[50] so were the suggestions that other regional conflicts, in South Africa or the Middle East, for example, would be more amenable to resolution after the ending of the geopolitical conflict. The balance of forces in the special relationship between Britain and the USA was also profoundly changed by the ending of the Cold War: without that, it is hard to see how President Clinton would have been willing to offend the British so deeply by agreeing a visa for Gerry Adams to visit the USA in February 1994[51] – despite the increasingly significant involvement of the US in Irish affairs during the Carter and Reagan presidencies, which abrogated the diplomatic fiction that Northern Ireland was an internal UK affair. The Irish diasporic involvement was central to that story and is a growing feature of contemporary internationalism. Clinton regularly invoked the GFA as a model for the resolution of other ethnic conflicts and regarded it as one of his principal foreign policy achievements. The Bush administration, while less active, continued a close involvement in the peace process.

From unity to stability and consent

Over the time of the Troubles there was a definite evolution of attitudes towards the conflict in Northern Ireland among the voting population of the Republic. This gave political leaders the space to reach compromises on Northern Ireland and to co-operate closely with the British Government – these leaders had become more confident in that respect after the internationalisation of Ireland's economics and politics during the 1970s and 1980s. Articles 2 and 3 of the Irish constitution claiming jurisdiction over Northern Ireland, which was found by the Supreme Court to have a legal imperative, were central features of the traditional political culture. But from 1986 to 1996 there was a fall from about 70 per cent to 30 per cent in the number of the Republic's voters who identified a united Ireland as their preferred political settlement.[52] In that same poll only 7 per cent agreed that the Border is worth fighting over, 47 per cent that it mattered but is not worth fighting over, and 42 per cent that it was not even worth arguing about.

These were dramatic findings, given the long history of propaganda and conflict about partition and sovereignty in British–Irish relations in the twentieth century. It would be a mistake to interpret the figures as an abandonment of the aspiration towards Irish unification, however. This remained as a general but weak and shallow aspiration, based roughly on the assumption that 'partition was damaging and destructive to the whole of Ireland and reunification would bring certain benefits'.[53] A devolved, reformed, power-sharing arrangement in the North with links to Britain and the Republic is still seen as a stepping-stone to eventual unity of the island, at least as a Pascalian wager. An opinion poll for the *Irish Independent* published on 31 December 1999 found 86 per cent to support a united Ireland, with nearly half expecting it within 10 years, a further 21 per cent within 20 years. But 85 per cent reject the condition of higher taxation for unity, 59 per cent Ireland returning to the Commonwealth, 42 per cent joining NATO and 25 per cent having unionists as part of a united Ireland government. The crisis certainly exposed the layers of unexamined attitudes in the Republic towards sectarianism, partition and the British role in Ireland – and also the sheer ignorance and prejudice about the North that had built up during the years of partition.

Opinion shifted from unity to stability, based on the consent of the Northern Ireland majority and the inclusion of republicanism in negotiations as the primary focus of the Republic's policy towards Northern Ireland. There was often a failure to articulate this or a refusal to accept that the shift had occurred. As Fergus Finlay, special advisor to Dick Spring during the successive coalition governments from 1992–96, puts it in his political memoir: 'So far as I was concerned, this was never about unity. The process of 25 years, and the new process I was being invited into [in 1992], was about stability and peace.' He added that 'both governments had to work together'.[54] Despite the unitary rhetoric – and whatever the inherent merits of a united Ireland – the logic of events and negotiations drove politicians of various tendencies to accept a formula based on consent, devolution, power-sharing, North-South bodies and a growing realisation of the need to institutionalise relations between the Dublin and London governments.

That was the context within which the New Ireland Forum was convened in May 1983. Its deliberations involved a crucial rethinking of Irish nationalism after fifteen years of conflict in the North. Its three options – the unitary state, a federal/confederal Ireland and a joint authority solution – set the scene for negotiation of the Anglo-Irish Agreement in 1985. The forum report and the subsequent agreement with Britain took due account of two central features of the state's response to the Troubles: the need to protect it from paramilitary subversion;[55] and 'to strengthen constitutional nationalism in the North as an alternative to republicanism by offering it moral and political support and by pressing for reforms. Successive Irish governments hoped for a return to peace and stability'.[56] The possibility that the British might actually have contemplated withdrawal had created alarm in the coalition after the collapse of Sunningdale.[57] It was to prove an enduring motive for governmental caution in dealing with paramilitary violence and subversion or relaxing the media censorship directed against them. It also played to a potent mood of public disenchantment with things Northern Irish within significant sectors of Irish public opinion, anxious to protect itself from destabilising spill-over and in any case increasingly disgusted by violent methods of pursuing Irish unity.

Inclusion of republicans was the other principle on which the emerging policy was predicated. Contacts between Mr John Hume and the Fianna Fáil Government with Sinn Féin were communicated to the British Government and were taken up enthusiastically by Albert Reynolds, who had, as Mansergh says, 'a warm personal relationship' with Mr Major; this was confirmed in Major's autobiography, in which he says: 'the great point about my relationship with Albert Reynolds was that we liked one another, and could have a row without giving up on each other'.[58] There has been a similar relationship between Bertie Ahern and Tony Blair. Three arguments developed by John Hume in his dialogues with Gerry Adams were central:

- the British are 'neutral' as between unionism and nationalism, which undermines the case for armed struggle;
- European developments erode traditional notions of sovereignty; and
- the Irish people could choose to accept the principle of consent within Northern Ireland and the Republic as a valid exercise in self-determination.[59]

Normalisation of British–Irish relations

The notion of *normality* in inter-state relations craves definition – all the more so when the two states in question are as intimately linked as Britain is to Ireland. It means a mutual recognition based on rights, justice and a flow of information and interaction capable of realising the full potential of their close relationship. Britain and Ireland share certain features of asymmetry comparable with other pairings of large and small neighbours – Austria–Germany, Canada–USA, Finland–Russia/Sweden, Norway–Sweden, or Estonia/Latvia/Lithuania–Russia spring to mind. But most of these others did not have the precise combination of metropolitan and colonial interpenetration and domination, nor the same agonising setting of precedents on the theme of imperial decline that Ireland has had for Britain this century. The title of Erich Strauss's classic study – *Irish Nationalism and British Democracy* – captures another dimension of the relationship: the intimate connection between popular political mobilisations in the two countries over the whole period 1770–1922.[60]

Keatinge's study[61] is, surprisingly, the only systematic and detailed attempt to examine the modern relationship between Britain and Ireland in the light of comparative international relations theory and research. He looks at realist, or power, models of inter-state relations and contrasts them with the development of integration theory as applied to the EC/EU. In between them is the study of complex interdependence proposed by Keohane and Nye, and especially their application of the model to relations between Canada and the USA.[62] Keatinge finds this more relevant than power models which emphasise conflict and the potential use of force (which is questionable in the light of Northern Ireland and the suggestion made above that dependence characterised the relationship until the late twentieth century). He looks empirically at British–Irish relations in terms derived from the Canada–USA comparison under the headings of the patterns of interaction between the two states, the political processes employed and the types of outcome that generally occur.

Examining the *patterns of interaction*, he finds a case of very complicated interdependence, using multiple channels of contact. Taking similar categories twenty-three years on from his study one can readily see that this complex interdependence has both deepened and become less dependent and more normal – which is, indeed, 'healthy for both partners as it substitutes a greatly wider embrace for what had been an excessive intimacy'.[63] This applies in trade, finance and investment migration, short-term mobility (business or personal visits, tourism[64]), churches, trade unions, sporting[65]or other networks that straddle the border; media and cultural penetration, especially television;[66] the free travel area and common citizenship provisions.

These contacts show that the extent of direct human and family ties is probably unprecedented between two independent states, even if it is now more diversified than hitherto:

- 7 per cent of people born in Britain have at least one Irish parent, so that nearly 4 million people qualify automatically as Irish citizens;
- the 1991 UK census showed 830,500 people born in Ireland and living in Britain (174,000 from Northern Ireland and 656,500 from the Republic);
- 25 per cent of Britons have an Irish relative;
- only 6 per cent consider those who come to Britain from Ireland to be foreigners;
- and the social class profile of the Irish in Britain is nearly identical to that of their British counterparts.[67]

The volume of passenger traffic between Ireland and Britain is 70 per cent of the total travel from Ireland, although movement to the Continent has been increasing in recent years: an estimated 9 million people travelled in 1997, a daily and vivid affirmation of normalisation, involving some 25,000 journeys daily across the Irish Sea.

In terms of the *political processes* involved, governmental goals and the intergovernmental agenda have been made much more explicit with the Anglo-Irish Agreement (1985), the Downing Street Declaration (1993), the Framework Document (1995), the GFA (1998) and the Weston House agreement (2002). These were negotiated at summits prepared by officials from cabinet offices, the Anglo-Irish division of the Department of Foreign Affairs, the Department of Justice and the NIO (less so the Foreign and Commonwealth Office). The role of personal relationships between taoisigh and prime ministers – and between officials – has been crucial. Policy instruments used vary from the summit meetings; the institutionalised Anglo-Irish Intergovernmental Conferences;[68] systematic use of meetings on the margins of European Councils since they were inaugurated in the mid 1970s – these deserve a separate study of their own; and complex networks between government departments looking after bi-lateral and EU business.[69] On the margins of the European Council at Luxembourg in December 1997 both governments issued a progress report on developing east/west relations, which covered almost every area of public policy, ranging from education to transport, crime, drugs, immigration, homelessness, defence, tourism, agriculture, health, trade, finance and arts and culture.[70] Co-operation was driven and co-ordinated by a joint steering group co-chaired by the Department of the Taoiseach and the Cabinet Office. The secretariats of the British–Irish Council set up under the GFA carry on that work.

Alliances and concertation of policy within the EU are increasingly common, given the converging agenda between the two states and the British policy of pursuing selective bi-lateral alliances to amplify its European influence. In his Oireachtas address, Mr Blair suggested that 'increasingly we share a common agenda and common objectives', including: completion of the single market and structural economic reform; better conditions for growth and jobs in Europe; successful enlargement; and co-operation on the Schengen agenda of crime, drugs and illegal immigration. He also included the need for flexible, open and accountable institutions. Irish governments since then have shared many of these perspectives, including resistance to tax harmonisation; there is general agreement among policy-makers that it is in Ireland's interest to have Britain participating fully in the EU, both to balance the other large states, especially France and Germany, and to ease the path of British–Irish relations. But there is also concern that Mr Blair's preference for intergovernmental methods could herald a return to a *directoire* of the larger states rather than developing the supranational institutions which have so modified traditional balance of power politics in Europe. There are different interests on agriculture and structural funds, both of which are expected to play out as closer relations are built up with Scotland, Wales and Northern Ireland.

There is, however, little evidence of explicit issue linkage.[71] Nonetheless security and defence policy became a relatively open issue in bargaining between Haughey and Thatcher in 1980–81[72] (and relations were undoubtedly soured by Ireland's refusal to renew EC sanctions against Argentina in the Falklands/ Malvinas war). The issue has not been opened explicitly since then, although Bertie Ahern raised relations with the UK and the USA in a general sense in the light of his support for Ireland's membership of the Partnership for Peace.[73] Ireland could sign up to a European defence arrangement if it is agreed, despite military neutrality;

in the Seville Declaration of June 2002, following rejection of the Nice Treaty in June 2001, there is a commitment to hold a referendum if it does. From 1989 Irish governments based policy on the assumption that Britain's commitment to NATO would block the development of a more ambitious European defence and security policy. That premise changed following the British agreement with France at St Malo in December 1998, agreements in 1999 to develop it more comprehensively following the Kosovo war, culminating in the development of an EU Rapid Reaction Force and the adoption of Security Stretegy in December 2003. While there is little suggestion of a linkage with the Northern Ireland peace process, Ireland's security policy is converging towards the European norm. This is a considerable test of its residual commitment to sovereignty.

As for the *types of outcome* that generally occur, a crucial consideration in the study of interdependence is the extent to which political co-operation has been institutionalised in a particular type of international regime, formally or informally. The Anglo-Irish Agreement of 1985 is a case in point. But many other aspects of British–Irish relations are worth examining from that point of view, including those organised under the Anglo-Irish Intergovernmental Council established by Thatcher and FitzGerald in November 1981, informal contacts between policy elites in the annual British–Irish Association meetings, between civic and political leaders in Encounter (which has been funded by the two governments since 1983) and in the British–Irish Inter-Parliamentary Body since 1990. They have endeavoured to overcome the inherently asymmetrical relationship and in many cases have been successful in doing so. This will be all the more important as relations are built up between the devolved assemblies and executives in Scotland, Wales and Northern Ireland, whether bi-laterally or through the British–Irish Council. Comparative inter-state relations remain relevant. The Nordic Union is one possible analogue, with provision for concertation of policy across a wide span of issues; but it differs substantially in that a greater number of sovereign states are involved and the process is firmly rooted in inter-parliamentary contacts based on a wide popular consensus.[74] In time, however, such features could grow from the GFA.

It will be important to understand these processes, because if the GFA fails or has to be parked for a prolonged period, as was the case when the Northern Ireland Executive was suspended in October 2002, it will be up to the two governments to continue their close co-operation in administering Northern Ireland by implementing those substantial aspects of it that do not necessarily depend on the setting up of an executive. It must be remembered that British policy-makers and businesses look at Ireland as a whole: the balance of their interests, political stability, their international reputation and need for EU co-operation all give priority to closer co-operation with Dublin. This confirms the argument that 'the two sovereign governments are primarily concerned with maintaining good relations with *one another*, rather than with working for the achievement of more fundamental objectives such as Irish unity or preservation of the Union'.[75] Symmetrical withdrawal of such sovereign concern for Northern Ireland on the part of the British and Irish governments has helped to create the conditions on which an autonomous political settlement can be based; but, equally, it can facilitate executive implementation of change if agreement is not reached to share power within Northern Ireland.

Conclusion: from Anglo-Irish to British–Irish relations

This chapter has traced the changing relations between Britain and Ireland over the last thirty-five years under four headings: the transition from dependence to interdependence; internationalisation; the shift from unity to stability as the major norm in Irish policy-making; and the normalisation of relations between the two sovereign governments. There is a great deal of interpenetration and overlap between these different categories. Interdependence implies normalisation and internationalisation reinforces the appeal of stability. But they do tap into various dimensions that have been left relatively unexamined in the British–Irish relationship because of the understandable concentration on Northern Ireland. Without these changes the GFA would not have come about. The British Government has a major interest in creating new institutional arrangements capable of reducing the crisis management aspect of the relationship and transferring them to political or bureaucratic routine in order to clear space for other business.

That is part and parcel of the ambivalence, perhaps the uniqueness, characterising the relationship between the two countries – as to whether they are genuinely *foreign* to one another or not. The ambivalence of identity is reinforced by uncertainties created by two transformations which profoundly affect the British–Irish relationship: the constitutional changes introduced by the Labour Government; and its efforts to bring Britain to the heart of Europe. Britain's crisis of state and political identity after the ending of the Cold War operates in four dimensions: the international, transatlantic and global; the European; its internal constitutional arrangements; and its relations with Ireland.[76] They are interlinked and are being addressed by the Labour Government. But there are tensions among them, notably between the desire to maintain the special relationship with the USA and to integrate more with Europe; to devolve power within Britain while maintaining strong central control over the process; and whether and when to commit the UK to join the euro.

This chapter has examined British–Irish relations largely from the Irish point of view, in what could be a methodological shortcoming given the asymmetries involved, since there is an inherent temptation to exaggerate the reciprocal response of the larger state to the necessarily persistent preoccupations of the smaller one. It is therefore important to understand the pressures bearing on the UK in this period of transition. Will they lead to the break-up of the UK or to its regeneration? What would the consequences of that be for relations between the two sovereign governments? The Taoiseach disappointed members of the Scottish National Party by his failure to endorse independence when he spoke in Edinburgh in October 1998.[77] The question arises as to whether that would be in Ireland's interest.

Arguably it would not be, given the close relationship built up through the peace process between Dublin and London.

Symbols are vitally important aspects of political reality in the relations between Ireland and Britain, none more so than the monarchy. The improvement of relations has been calibrated by state and private visits to Britain by Presidents Robinson and McAleese and that of Prince Charles to Ireland in June 1995 and subsequently. It would take a firm implementation and bedding down of the GFA to enable a state visit to the Republic by Queen Elizabeth II – that would be a real sign that abnormal business had been finished in the eyes of official Ireland. Other symbols play a role. On the eve of Tony Blair's address to the Oireachtas in 1998 Bertie Ahern suggested that a debate should open on whether Ireland should rejoin the Commonwealth, in order to avail of its networking and to indicate to unionists that reconciliation with British institutions is sincere and normalisation complete.[78] There was surprisingly little political reaction to the call; but a number of letter writers to the *Irish Times* argued in sharp terms that they felt such a move is premature, because it would be seen internationally as confirmation that Ireland is returning to the British fold.[79] This seemed to be daily confirmed in the retail and sporting spheres as a strong sterling and an undervaluation of Irish shares based on the persistent if mistaken belief in the City of London that the Celtic Tiger was a bubble economy were suspected of making Irish firms vulnerable to takeovers. Since then investment both ways and strengthened economic relations have reinforced the British–Irish economic relationship. Policy convergence based on a mutual preference for economic models based on Boston rather than Berlin created an impression elsewhere in the EU that Ireland was becoming closer to UK positions and influence. Insofar as British–Irish normalisation alters the dynamic of *othering* on which Irish nationalism has traditionally been based this could be so – although it is reproduced in the contrasting attitudes of both states towards the EU, which were reinforced during Ireland's successful presidency of January-June 2004.

In these circumstances the letter writers continue to have a point. If the case put forward in this chapter is sound, it can be seen that Ireland has finally attained independence from Britain by pooling sovereignty in the EU and participating effectively internationally, especially by creating its own special relationship with North America. Until Britain resolves its dual sovereignty and identity questions – by participating fully in Europe and constitutionally rearranging itself – such a normalisation would signify reabsorption rather than genuine interdependence. It is very much in Ireland's interest that this British participation and rearrangement happens. Until it does so Irish policy would serve that normalisation best by sticking to its path of achieving de Valera's objective of external association through European integration, in what has been aptly described as a policy of 'interdependent realism'.[80] That would also best serve the Republic's new relationship with Northern Ireland.

Notes

1   Robert Hazell (ed.), *Constitutional Futures, A History of the Next Ten Years* (Oxford: Oxford University Press, 1999), p. 4.
2   Elizabeth Meehan, 'The Belfast Agreement: Its Distinctiveness and Points of Cross-Fertilisation in the UK's Devolution Programme', *Parliamentary Affairs*, vol. 51, no. 1, 1999, pp. 19–31. Philip Lynch and Stephen Hopkins, 'The British–Irish Council: Structure, Programme and Prospects', *Irish Studies in International Affairs*, vol. 12, 2001, pp. 133–50.
3   External Affairs was not renamed the Department of Foreign Affairs until 1972 ; and a specific Anglo-Irish section was not set up in it until the Troubles broke out in 1969, notwithstanding its responsibility along with the Office of the Taoiseach for conducting relations with London from the beginning of the State: see Patrick Keatinge, 'Unequal Sovereigns: The Diplomatic Dimension of Anglo-Irish Relations', in P. J. Drudy (ed.), *Ireland and Britain since 1922* (Cambridge: Cambridge University Press, 1986). Likewise in London, relations with Ireland were with, first, the Dominions Office (until 1947) and then the Commonwealth Office, which was merged with the Foreign Office in 1968.
4   Keatinge, 'Unequal Sovereigns', p. 139.
5   Garret FitzGerald, Paul Gillespie and Ronan Fanning, 'Britain's European Question: The Issues for Ireland', in P. Gillespie and G. FitzGerald (eds), *Britain's European Question: The Issues for Ireland* (Dublin: Institute of European Affairs, 1996), p. 29.
6   Brendan O'Leary and John McGarry, *The Politics of Antagonism: Understanding Northern Ireland* (London: Athlone Press, 1993), p. 143.
7   Ronan Fanning, 'Anglo-Irish Relations: Partition and the British Dimension in Historical Perspective', *Irish Studies in International Affairs*, vol. 2, no. 1, 1985, pp. 17–19. See also coverage of the State Papers, *Irish Times*, 1 and 3 January 2000.
8   *Irish Times*, 27 November 1998.
9   Among them Nicholas Mansergh, *The Irish Question 1840–1921: A Commentary on Anglo-Irish Relations and on Social and Political Forces in Ireland in the Age of Reform and Revolution* (London: Allen & Unwin, 1965) and *The Unresolved Question: The Anglo-Irish Settlement and its Undoing 1912–1972* (New Haven, CT: Yale University Press, 1991); David Harkness, *The Restless Dominion* (London: Macmillan, 1969); Deirdre MacMahon, *Republicans and Imperialists: Anglo-Irish Relations in the 1930s* (New Haven, CT: Yale University Press, 1984); Paul Canning, *British Policy towards Ireland 1921–1941* (Oxford: Oxford University Press, 1985); Robert Fisk, *In Time of War: Ireland, Ulster and the Price of Neutrality 1939–1945* (London: Andre Deutsch, 1983); John Bowman, *De Valera and the Ulster Question 1917–1973* (Oxford: Oxford University Press, 1983); D. G. Boyce, *The Irish Question in British Politics, 1868–1996* (London: Palgrave Macmillan, 1996).
10 Notably Paul Arthur, *Special Relationships: Britain, Ireland and the Northern Ireland Problem* (Belfast: Blackstaff Press, 2000); Keatinge, 'Unequal Sovereigns'; Ronan Fanning, note 12; James Downey, *Them and Us: Britain–Ireland and the Northern Question, 1969–1982* (Dublin: Ward River Press, 1983).
11 Garret FitzGerald, *All in a Life: An Autobiography* (Dublin: Gill & Macmillan, 1991); Edward Heath, *The Course of My Life* (London: Hodder & Stoughton, 1998); Margaret Thatcher, *The Downing Street Years* (London: HarperCollins, 1993); John Major, *The Autobiography* (London: HarperCollins, 1999).
12 See Joseph Ruane and Jennifer Todd, *The Dynamics of Conflict in Northern Ireland, Power, Conflict and Emancipation* (Cambridge: Cambridge University Press, 1996); Frank Wright, *Northern Ireland, A Comparative Analysis* (Dublin: Gill & Macmillan, 1987); Adrian Guelke, *Northern Ireland: The International Perspective* (Dublin: Gill & Macmillan, 1988); Patrick Keatinge, 'Unequal Sovereigns'; Brendan O'Leary and John McGarry, *The Politics of Antagonism: Understanding Northern Ireland* (London: Athlone Press, 1993); John McGarry and Brendan O'Leary, *Explaining Northern Ireland: Broken Images* (Oxford: Blackwell, 1995); Patrick Keatinge, 'An Odd Couple? Obstacles and Opportunities in Inter-State Political Co-operation between the Republic of Ireland and the United Kingdom', in Desmond Rea (ed.), *Political*

Co-operation in Divided Societies (Dublin: Gill & Macmillan, 1982); Ronan Fanning, 'Small States, Large Neighbours: Ireland and the United Kingdom', *Irish Studies in International Affairs*, vol. 9, 1998, pp. 21–30 and note 80.

13 See the study conducted by the British Council, based on a public opinion survey and focus groups: BCNI, *Through Irish Eyes: Irish Attitudes Towards the UK* (Dublin: BCNI, 2003).

14 D. George Boyce and Alan O'Day (eds), *The Making of Modern Irish History: Revisionism and the Revisionist Controversy* (London: Routledge, 1996); Ciaran Brady (ed.), *Interpreting Irish History: The Debate on Historical Revisionism, 1938–1994* (Dublin: Academic Press, 1994); Stephen Howe, *Ireland and Empire: Colonial Legacies in Irish History and Culture* (Oxford: Oxford University Press, 2000).

15 Roy Foster, 'Anglo-Irish Relations and Northern Ireland: Historical Perspectives', in Dermot Keogh and Michael H. Haltzel (eds), *Northern Ireland and the Politics of Reconciliation* (Cambridge: Cambridge University Press, 1993).

16 Dermot McAleese, 'Anglo-Irish Economic Interdependence: From Excessive Intimacy to a Wider Embrace', in Drudy, *Ireland and Britain since 1922*; M. Gallagher and D. McAleese, 'Ireland's Trade Dependence on the UK', *Irish Banking Review*, spring 1994.

17 John Archer Jackson, *The Irish in Britain* (London: Routledge & Kegan Paul, 1963); Mary Hickman and Bronwen Walter, *Discrimination and the Irish Community in Britain* (London: CRE, 1997).

18 Arthur, *Special Relationships*.

19 Alan J. Ward, 'A Constitutional Background to the Northern Ireland Crisis', in Keogh and Haltzel, *Northern Ireland and the Politics of Reconciliation*.

20 Michael Cox, 'Bringing in the "International": The IRA Ceasefire and the End of the Cold War", *International Affairs* vol. 73, no. 4, October, pp. 671–94.

21 Terry Eagleton, 'Ascendancy and Hegemony', in *Heathcliff and the Great Hunger, Studies in Irish Culture* (London: Verso, 1995).

22 Drudy, *Ireland and Britain since 1922*.

23 J. J. Lee, *Ireland 1912–1985: Politics and Society* (Cambridge: Cambridge University Press, 1989), pp. 627–8.

24 Fanning, 'Small States, Large Neighbours', p. 25.

25 Basil Chubb, *The Government and Politics of Ireland*, 2nd edn (London: Longman, 1982), p. 329.

26 Bowman, *De Valera and the Ulster Question*, p. 312.

27 Gillespie and Fitzgerald, *Britain's European Question*, p. 9.

28 *Ibid.*, p. 23.

29 Gallagher and McAleese, 'Ireland's Trade Dependence on the UK'.

30 Seamus Bannon, 'EMU and Ireland's Sterling Trade', paper presented to the Statistical and Social Inquiry Society of Ireland, 28 March 1996.

31 See Denis O'Hearn, *Inside the Celtic Tiger: The Irish Economy and the Asian Model* (London: Pluto Press, 1998).

32 Brigid Laffan, Michael Smith and Rory O'Donnell, *Europe's Experimental Union: Rethinking Integration* (London: Routledge, 1999).

33 Gillespie and Fitzgerald, *Britain's European Question*, p. 7.

34 Brigid Laffan, 'These Islands and the European Dimension', in Ben Tonra and Eilis Ward (eds), *Ireland in International Affairs: Interests, Institutions and Identities* (Dublin: Institute of Public Administration, 2002); Clodagh Harris, 'Anglo-Irish Elite Cooperation and the Peace Process: The Impact of the EEC/EU', *Irish Studies in International Affairs*, vol. 12, 2001, pp. 203–14.

35 P. Clancy, S. Drudy, K. Lynch and L. O'Dowd (eds), *Irish Society: Sociological Perspectives* (Dublin: Institute of Public Administration, 1995); J. E. Goldthorpe and C. T. Whelan (eds), *The Development of Industrial Society in Ireland* (Oxford: Oxford University Press, 1992); Dermot Keogh, *Twentieth Century Ireland,: Nation and State* (Dublin: Gill & Macmillan, 1994), pp. 243–388; Hilary Tovey and Perry Share, *A Sociology of Ireland*, 2nd edn (Dublin: Gill & Macmillan, 2003).

36 Garret FitzGerald and Paul Gillespie, 'Ireland's British Question', *Prospect*, vol. 12, October 1996, pp. 22–6.

37 Patrick Keatinge and Brigid Laffan, 'Ireland in International Affairs', in John Coakley and Michael Gallagher (eds), *Politics in the Republic of Ireland* (Galway: PSAI Press, 1992), p. 220.

38 Paul Arthur, 'Anglo-Irish Relations and Constitutional Policy', in Paul Mitchell and Rick Wilford (eds), *Politics in Northern Ireland* (Oxford: Oxford University Press 1999) pp. 244–6.

39 Paul Gillespie, 'Multiple Identities in Ireland and Europe', in *The Expanding Nation: Towards a Multi-Ethnic Ireland* (Dublin: Department of Sociology, Trinity College, 1999), pp. 8–16; Cathal McCall, *Identity in Northern Ireland, Communities, Politics and Change* (Basingstoke: Macmillan, 1999).

40 Douglas Hyde, 'The Necessity for De-Anglicising Ireland', in Charles Gavan Duffy, George Sigerson and Douglas Hyde, *The Revival of Irish Literature* (London: Fisher-Brown, 1894).

41 Hugh Kearney, 'Contested Ideas of Nationhood', *Irish Review*, vol. 20 winter/spring 1997, pp. 1–22.

42 Tom Garvin, 'The French Are on the Sea', in Rory O'Donnell (ed.), *Europe: The Irish Experience* (Dublin: Institute of European Affairs, 1998), p. 43.

43 See chapter 22 in this volume by Elizabeth Meehan.

44 See James Goodman, 'The Republic of Ireland: Towards a Cosmopolitan Nationalism?', in James Anderson and James Goodman (eds), *Dis/Agreeing Ireland: Contexts, Obstacles, Hopes* (London: Pluto Press, 1998); James Goodman, *Single Europe, Single Ireland? Uneven Development in Process* (Dublin: Irish Academic Press, 2000).

45 Brigid Laffan and Rory O'Donnell, 'Ireland and the Growth of International Governance', in W. Crotty and D. Schmitt (eds), *Ireland and the Politics of Change* (London: Longman, 1998).

46 Wright, *Northern Ireland*; Paul Gillespie, 'Optimism of the Intellect, Pessimism of the Will: Ireland , Europe and 1989', *Irish Studies in International Affairs*, vol. 11, 2000, pp. 163–78.

47 Rogers Brubaker, *Nationalism Reframed: Nationhood and the National Question in the New Europe* (Cambridge: Cambridge University Press, 1996).

48 Fanning, 'Anglo-Irish Relations', p. 2.

49 G. R. Sloan, 'Geopolitics and British Strategic Policy in Ireland: Issues and Interests', *Irish Studies in International Affairs*, vol. 8, 1997, p. 134; see also G. R. Sloan, *Geopolitics of Anglo-Irish Relations in the Twentieth Century* (Leicester: Leicester University Press, 1997).

50 Michael Cox, 'Northern Ireland: The War that Came In from the Cold', *Irish Studies in International Affairs*, vol. 9, 1998, p. 78. Mrs Thatcher refused to allow Brooke to make the speech prior to the ending of the Cold War because of her concern to protect British nuclear submarines passing near Northern Ireland, according to Nicholas Watt: see his 'Thatcher Gave Approval to Talks with IRA', *Guardian*, 16 October 1999.

51 See contributions by Michael Cox, John Dumbrell and Adrian Guelke to this volume (see chapters 23, 24 and 28). For a vivid account of the story, see Conor O'Clery, *The Greening of the White House* (Dublin, Gill & Macmillan, 1996).

52 *Irish Times*/MRBI Poll, 2 February 1996.

53 Ruane and Todd, *Dynamics of Conflict in Northern Ireland*, p. 250.

54 Fergus Finlay, *Snakes and Ladders* (Dublin: New Island Books, 1998), pp. 182–3.

55 Eunan O'Halpin, *Defending Ireland: The Irish Free State and its Enemies since 1922* (Oxford: Oxford University Press, 1999), pp. 342ff.

56 Ruane and Todd, *Dynamics of Conflict in Northern Ireland*, p. 262.

57 FitzGerald, *All in a Life*, pp. 244 ff.

58 Martin Mansergh, 'The Background to the Peace Process', *Irish Studies in International Affairs*, vol. 6, 1995, p. 153; see also Kevin Rafter, *Martin Mansergh: A Biography* (Dublin: New Island, 2002), pp. 196–265.

59 Finlay, *Snakes and Ladders*, p. 184.

60 E. Strauss, *Irish Nationalism and British Democracy* (London: Greenwood Press, 1994 [1951]).

61 Keatinge, 'An Odd Couple?'

62 Robert O. Keohane and Joseph Nye, *Power and Interdependence: World Politics in Transition* (Boston: Little Brown, 1977). Keohane and Nye have recently revisited their study of complex interdependence in the light of the information revolution, in 'Power and Interdependence in the Information Age', *Foreign Affairs*, vol. 77, no. 5, September/October, 1998, pp. 81–94. They

agree that realist assumptions about the dominance of military force and security issues remain
valid – 'information does not flow in a vacuum but in political space that remains occupied';
and power is distributed through communications facilities in such a way that relations
between large and small states are not fundamentally affected. Keohane pays tribute to the
contribution which the literature on international regimes, neo-institutionalism, transnational
actors, networks, game theory, and bargaining and globalisation has made to the study of
interdependence: Robert O. Keohane, 'International Institutions: Can Interdependence
Work?' *Foreign Policy*, vol. 110, spring 1998, pp. 82–96). There has been little attempt, however,
to apply them to Britain and Ireland, whose relationship remains a very special one in
comparative terms.

63 The phrase comes from Eamonn Gallagher, 'Anglo-Irish Relations in the European Community', *Irish Studies in International Affairs*, vol. 2, no. 1, 1985, p. 35.

64 Elizabeth Meehan, *From Inverted Commas to Capital Letters; Ireland's Choice to Prioritize Free
Movement with the United Kingdom Over Free Movement in the European Union* (Dublin: The
Policy Institute, 2000).

65 Michael Holmes, 'Symbols of National Identity and Sport: The Case of the Irish Football
Team', *Irish Political Studies*, vol. 9, 1994, pp. 81–98; Mike Cronin, *Sport and Nationalism in
Ireland* (Dublin: Gill & Macmillan, 1999).

66 BCNI, *Through Irish Eyes.*

67 James O'Connell, 'British Attitudes to Ireland and the Irish: A Special Relationship', *Irish Post*
survey reported in 10 parts, 19 November 1994–4 February 1995 (cited in Simon Partridge, *The
British Union State: Imperial Hangover or Citizens' Home?* (London: Catalyst, 1999), pp. 12–13).
This is not to say the Irish in Britain do not have their problems. They do, as recent studies
demonstrate: 50 per cent of the 20,000 ill-educated and marginalised people who emigrate
from Ireland go to Britain, where 'they experience high rates of unemployment and illness, a
low rate of upward social mobility, live in poor housing, enter unrewarding occupations, suffer
a distinct level of discrimination and present high rate of social problems, including alcoholism
and suicide', according to the Irish Episcopal Commission, as reported in *Irish Times*, 19 May
1999. See also the report of the Task Force on Policy regarding Emigrants to the Minister for
Foreign Affairs Mr Brian Cowen, TD, *Ireland and the Irish Abroad* (Dublin: Department of
Foreign Affairs, August 2002).

68 Their communiqués are recorded in successive issues of the journal *Irish Studies in International
Affairs*, starting in 1986.

69 The former British ambassador in Dublin, Mrs Veronica Sutherland, referred to the complications of diplomacy when prime ministers and taoisigh are in direct touch by telephone on
Anglo-Irish and European business, as are governmental departments, sometimes without
contacting the embassy: see Maol Muire Tynan, 'Departing Envoy Admits Concern about NI
Peace', *Irish Times*, 16 January 1999.

70 *Progress Report on Co-operation between Ireland and the United Kingdom: Developing East/West
Relations*, 12/13 December, 1997; Mark Brennock, 'Report Shows Wide-Ranging East–West
Links Being Forged', *Irish Times*, 13 December 1997.

71 An exception is the abortive attempt by Anthony Crosland to link fishery issues with broader
co-operation: recorded in FitzGerald, *All in a Life*, pp. 172–5.

72 Patrick Keatinge, *A Singular Stance: Irish Neutrality in the 1980s* (Dublin: Institute of Public
Administration, 1984), pp. 77–83.

73 Bertie Ahern, speech to European Movement Seminar on PfP, 29 March 1999.

74 *The Nordic Council: Lessons for Council of the Isles* (London: Constitution Unit, University
College, 1998).

75 See Feargal Cochrane, 'Any Takers? The Isolation of Northern Ireland', *Political Studies*, vol.
42, 1994, pp. 378–95, and the exchange between Cochrane and Paul Dixon in vol. 43, 1995, pp.
497–508.

76 Paul Gillespie, 'Constitutional Politics', in Paul Gillespie (ed.), *Blair's Britain, England's
Europe: A View from Ireland* (Dublin: Institute of European Affairs, 2000).

77 Bertie Ahern, 'The Western Isles of Europe at the Millennium', the Lothian European

Lecture, University of Edinburgh, 29 October 1998.

78 Interview with Bertie Ahern, *Times*, 26 November 1998; see also Bertie Ahern, Address to Kevin Barry Fianna Fáil Cumann, University College, Dublin, 13 January 1999; text in *European Document Series* no. 22 (Dublin: Institute of European Affairs, 1999), pp. 6–9.

79 *Irish Times* Letters page, 10, 18, 21, 23, 24 December 1998; 7, 9, 20, 25 January, 5 February 1999.

80 Ronan Fanning, '*Raison d'Etat* and the Evolution of Irish Foreign Policy', in M. Kennedy and J. M. Skelly (eds), *Irish Foreign Policy 1919–1966: From Independence to Internationalism* (Dublin: Four Courts Press, 2000).

22

Europe and the Europeanisation of the Irish question

ELIZABETH MEEHAN

One of the striking things about the Belfast Agreement is that, to anyone who knows the European Union, one immediately recognises that it was written by people who also know the EU and have worked its systems quite extensively.[1]

Introduction

The links between Europe and the Europeanisation of the Irish question are complex and disputed. First, 'Europe' as the ECHR co-exists with 'Europe' as the European Union – and both have some part in the Europeanisation of the Irish question. Secondly, the significance of the EU on the Irish question was complicated by the coincidence in the timing of the imposition of direct rule and of negotiations by the UK and the Republic of Ireland to join the EC in 1972. This both *domesticated* the Europeanisation of the Irish question in the Northern Ireland conflict and promoted it as a new factor in its potential resolution. Thirdly, insofar as the literature on Northern Ireland attends to the EU's effects, it comes to contradictory conclusions.[2] Most commentators agree that common EU membership helped the Irish and British governments to co-operate effectively in the quest for a solution. But there is disagreement about the EU's impact on North–South co-operation and on sectarianism.

Assessing the impact of Irish and British membership of the EU on Northern Ireland is complicated by the interaction of four factors. These are that

- unlike Ireland, the UK has been ambivalent towards European integration;
- in Northern Ireland, direct rule overshadowed UK and Irish accession to the EC;
- most unionists, however, saw direct rule and UK accession as a twin blow; and that
- constitutional nationalists, not only reversed their previous indifference to the European Community, but, from the early days of direct rule, looked positively on it as a means of transcending conflict over territory and sovereignty.

In impinging on one another, these factors led the question of EU influence to become politicised rather than a matter of disinterested intellectual enquiry. That is, prior outlooks on Northern Ireland affected the extent to which people were able or willing to *see* actual or potential EU influences on conflict resolution. The thesis of this chapter is that there *has been* some Europeanisation of the Irish question – before, during and after the reaching of agreement in Belfast on Good Friday 1998 (see Appendix 2). The chapter begins with the sphere where most commentators do accept a degree of Europeanisation; that is, the EU context for a transformation of east–west relations in which British and Irish governments have become able, more readily than before, to co-operate over Northern Ireland.

It might be expected that attitudes on the part of the two states towards European integration and its role in Northern Ireland would have found parallels locally in the 'two communities'. The chapter thus explores the extent to which the centrality of the EU to Ireland's interests and the UK's ambivalence about it are reflected in nationalist and unionist outlooks in Northern Ireland. Here, it is suggested that, prior to direct rule, attitudes in Northern Ireland did not simply parallel those of the two states with which the 'two communities' identify. The imposition of direct rule changed this, dividing unionist opinion on Europe more fundamentally than before on its import for Northern Ireland[3] and providing the circumstances for nationalists to promote the EU as a factor in bringing about 'an agreed Ireland'.

The chapter then moves to areas in which there is less agreement about EU influence and/or its desirability. It deals first with North–South co-operation. On the one hand, it can be argued that the first steps towards potential co-operation pre-dated Irish and British membership, thereby demonstrating its irrelevance. It is suggested here, however, that the very existence of the European Economic Community (EEC) and the European Commission, even without Ireland and the UK as members, prompted consideration of closer links between the two parts of the island. However, the main impact came as the EC/EU itself began to develop a more systematic regional policy on integrated development in internal and cross-border regions and to provide Northern Ireland with a Special Support Programme for Peace and Reconciliation (SSPPR), which has a cross-border element. Here, it is argued that unionists moved considerably but that their heightened awareness of the *spill-over* effects in neo-functionalist explanations of European integration has made them wary of a similar logic in North–South co-operation resulting in 'rolling reunification'. All the same, pro-GFA unionists accept that such co-operation is a corollary of nationalist acceptance that Northern Ireland remains, for the time being, British – and that there is a legitimate EU dimension to this.

Next, the chapter discusses the impact of the EU on relations within a still British Northern Ireland, suggesting that, though the EU's impact may be disputed in terms of the budgetary significance of structural funding, the conditions of eligibility for support have contributed to new forums for inter- and cross-community participation. This was relevant to the changing climate of the 1990s and can be seen in the way in which the devolved institutions approach (inadequately, according to some) the role of the EU in Northern Ireland and Northern Ireland's place in the EU.

The chapter, having – by and large – followed the three strands of the GFA, closes by touching on matters beyond them. It is here that the ECHR's influences are most apparent, and it is concluded that while the influence of the EU (and the ECHR) should not be overstated, it is equally a mistake to minimise the impact of external developments.

The Europeanisation of British–Irish relations and east–west institutions[4]

In the early 1960s, both states sought to accede to the EEC. Though one opinion in Ireland favoured entry irrespective of any British decision,[5] the general view was that simultaneous accession would suit Ireland's interests, given existing dependence on British markets (shaped by a cheap food policy) and its aim to reach other export destinations where higher prices were paid. Ireland pursued accession wholeheartedly because membership was expected also to raise its international status. As in the case of the Benelux countries before it, *pooling* sovereignty would be the means of escape from the shadow of a single dominant neighbour. In the course of actual membership from 1 January 1973, Ireland's economic and political expectations were vindicated and the EU is now a core Irish interest. Conversely, the UK's decision to try to enter was taken reluctantly, part of coming to terms with the decline of empire and its position as a world power. From the British–Irish point of view, the greater equality of status between the two states contributed to their ability to act jointly to *pacify* Ireland by pooling sovereignty[6] (to a certain extent) over Northern Ireland. This process was helped by the familiarity between each state's civil servants, induced by their interaction in the EU and by the opportunities at the interstices of intergovernmental meetings for discreet high-level exchanges of political views.

Early Irish speculations about a possible EEC impact on the status of the whole island took place prior to direct rule and, hence, were more North–South than east–west in focus (thus, discussed later). British Prime Minister Edward Heath's overriding determination during 1970–72 finally to succeed in joining the EC made the Northern Ireland crisis at best a distraction and at worst a threat to his European policy.[7] The main EU impact on a seriously joint British–Irish focus on Northern Ireland began in 1980, when there was a 'dawning of a new era in Anglo-Irish relations',[8] and continued during the 1990s, a period coinciding with the consolidation of EU regional policy and one in which the experience of European integration enabled even traditional states to acknowledge that sovereignty now encompassed interdependence.

Anglo-Irish intergovernmentalism, starting with Taoiseach Charles Haughey and Prime Minister Margaret Thatcher, survived tensions over the hunger strikes in 1981, the lack of an Irish dimension in a proposal for a new Northern Ireland

Assembly in 1982, Ireland's attitude to the Falklands War, and the preference in the New Ireland Forum report of 1983 for re-unification. It was given an overt European gloss by Taoiseach Garret FitzGerald in his hope for 'a new and dynamic relationship with both communities in Northern Ireland, with the British Government and with our European friends', and in his determination to use the 1984 Irish presidency of the EU 'to smooth the path of Anglo-Irish rapprochement'.[9]

The 1985 Anglo-Irish Agreement has been described as a 'compromise between Irish demands for joint authority and British reluctance to cede sovereignty'.[10] Even so, 'spill-overs' from pooled sovereignty at the European level can be seen in the Agreement's institutionalisation of cross-border relations and the expansion, from 1989, of areas for co-operation. The Intergovernmental Conference report of 1993 refers to the relevance of the Single European Market and, in general, shows that membership of the EU 'increasingly encroached upon the work of the IGC' and that EU programmes were used to develop to functional agenda of the Anglo-Irish Agreement.[11] On the political front, British antipathy to joint authority, as symptomatic of ceding sovereignty, became less obvious as negotiations proceeded through the 1991 talks and the governments, together, produced the Joint Declaration of 1994 and the New Framework for Agreement Document of 1995. The institutions and responsibilities outlined in the 1995 document refer in some detail to the EU, including how the two governments might try to reach an agreed approach for the whole island in respect of EU interests. Versions of these references are reflected in the 1998 GFA. Since devolution, the EU dimensions of North–South co-operation, and areas of co-operation previously agreed by the two governments under the Anglo-Irish Agreement, have been taken over by the North–South Ministerial Council and its implementing bodies (see pp. 467–8).

Before dealing with attitudes in Northern Ireland to the EU and with the EU aspects of North–South co-operation, however, it should be noted that the GFA reflects the culmination of new relations between Ireland and the UK initiated by their rapprochement under the umbrella of EU membership. That is, Anglo-Irish relations have become British-Irish relations. The term 'Anglo-Irish relations' is a legacy of the Anglocentricity of the historical relationship between the two islands and of the empire that was still intact at the birth of the Irish Free State (see chapter 21 by Paul Gillespie). Now, the machinery of the so-called Anglo-Irish Agreement has been replaced by two innovative institutions with new names. These are the British–Irish Intergovernmental Conference (BIIC) and the British–Irish Council. Whereas the negotiation of the old Anglo-Irish Intergovernmental Conference gave nationalists informal access to the Irish Government while it did not give unionists access to the UK Government, the decisions of the new BIIC are informed by consultation with the Northern Ireland Executive/Assembly (when not suspended).

The other innovation, the British–Irish Conference, reflects a new Britain on the British arm of the intergovernmental relationship. It consists of representatives of the two governments, the devolved institutions in Northern Ireland, Scotland

and Wales, the Isle of Man, the Channel Islands and, if they are established, devolved assemblies in England. Though the analogy is imperfect (as only two of the members are independent states), the proposed institutional relationships and functional responsibilities bear the hallmarks of that sense of interdependence underlying the pooled sovereignty arrangements of the EU.

The BIC arose, first, from proposals by unionists to offset the North–South Ministerial Council, but it is difficult to see how it and the BIIC could have come about without changes beyond the confines of Northern Ireland; that is, a more relaxed British understanding of sovereignty, acknowledging interdependence in the EU context and permitting devolution at home. Two potentially significant features of the BIC are that it may discuss EU issues and that any two, or more, of its members may enter into agreements with one another on matters within their competence. This, together with North–South arrangements which are stronger on the EU front (see p. 268), introduces a novel development in sovereignty by permitting a non-sovereign sub-state government in the UK to interact with the government of another sovereign state on matters of bi-lateral interest. On the other hand, the terms of reference of the Joint Ministerial Committee, Memorandum of Understanding and Concordats,[12] brought in to co-ordinate devolution within the UK, expressly state that the devolved administrations must channel all matters relating to foreign governments and the EU through the UK Foreign and Commonwealth Office. To add to the confusion, the co-ordinating documents state that they are not to be read as contradicting the GFA on Northern Ireland – which, of course, they do in that one restates the vertical convention of sovereignty and the other introduces a horizontal model. The seeming contradiction *might* be partially resolved by reference to prior legislation, passed in response to Ireland's becoming a republic, stating that, under British law, Ireland is not a 'foreign' country.[13]

Northern Ireland: the Europeanisation of the Irish question or the *domestication* of the European question?

As noted at the start, it might have been expected that Irish enthusiasm for and British ambivalence about accession to the EU would be reflected in a similar contrast between nationalists and unionists in Northern Ireland. There is a certain truth in this; but patterns of support for and opposition to European integration, in itself and in respect of its potential to ameliorate domestic conflict, have varied.

Superficially, unionists look like the last defenders of the imperial values that led Winston Churchill and Ernest Bevin to be for European integration but against UK participation in it. There is some overlap of personnel among Tory Eurosceptics and Friends of the Union, and it is sometimes rumoured that the leader of the UUP David Trimble might seek common cause with Euro-sceptics in the Conservative Party. There is a common thread here in a concern to highlight the significance of borders for the preservation of national sovereignty and identity and, hence, the danger, especially for a disputed territory, of membership of a body whose *raison d'être* is to make them more permeable. Such disquiet is fuelled by the mirror-image approach of modern nationalists. Since the 1970s, John Hume has used the resolution, through the EU, of the Franco-German territorial conflict as a metaphor for Northern Ireland and has promoted the idea of a 'Europe of the regions' as the means of resolving conflict over territorial sovereignty. In the early 1990s, his party took the further step of proposing that the EU play a part in the governance of Northern Ireland – a suggestion opposed by unionists and by the Conservative Government because of the implications for UK sovereignty over Northern Ireland (albeit to be exercised in consultation with Ireland).[14]

However, at the time of the first UK efforts to join the EEC – prior to direct rule – unionists, though divided over prospective membership, were more enthusiastic than the Nationalist Party (predecessor to the SDLP) and republicans. Unionist policy simply sought certain safeguards, especially the preservation of the Stormont legislation on the Safeguarding of Employment[15] (which prohibited the recruitment of Irish nationals normally resident in the South). Conversely, nationalists and republicans maintained the then conventional nationalist aspiration of autarky.[16] Direct rule altered that pattern and, to some extent, domesticated Europe as an additional aspect of polarisation within unionism and between it and nationalism.

Moderate unionists tended to remain pro-European, especially the then new APNI which has shown consistently high levels of support for the EU ever since. But *hard-line* unionists took the view that unionist values and interests had been doubly betrayed by the two events. The complex interaction of European integration and Northern Ireland's constitutional status is perhaps illustrated by two boycotts of a banquet in Belfast in 1983 to celebrate ten years of EU membership. Dr Ian Paisley (DUP) stayed away because of the presence of the Irish taoiseach and John Taylor (UUP) refused to attend because of the presence of Edward Heath.[17]

On the other hand, the young SDLP began to espouse European integration. In 1973, it adopted a policy of 'a United Ireland in an EC context',[18] an endorsement hardly likely to endear the EC to unionists. Over the years, it has come to match APNI's enthusiasm for European integration. Reflecting a more post-national, or postmodern nationalist, outlook, one which takes account of interdependence, than is to be found among republicans, John Hume has declared that 'the days of the [autarkic] nation-state are gone'.[19] Republicans in the North (they have not really become pro-EU in the South) were more opportunistic converts to the EU, their strategists being forced by the 'Europeanisation of Ireland' to reformulate their ideas of Irish nationalism and their planning for Northern Ireland.[20] The reluctance of the shift is illustrated by Bernadette McAliskey's retort to John Hume – that she had not yet had her nation state – and in the fact that Sinn Féin supporters still tend to be more similar on EU issues to the DUP than to other nationalists.[21]

In the post-GFA period, the Northern Ireland Executive speaks and behaves as though its members share the view that European integration is good for

Northern Ireland and that Northern Ireland can and should begin to contribute to the well-being of the EU (see p. 50). Though in the assembly, Dr Paisley sometimes portrays the GFA, especially its North–South dimensions, as an EU 'plot',[22] 'Europe' is, once again, less domesticated into the local conflict. However, as explained in connection with North–South co-operation, acceptance of a European dimension is accompanied by an awareness of competing theories of integration – functionalism and neo-functionalism. These different understandings of integration *do* coincide with unionism and nationalism.

The Europeanisation of North–South co-operation

The impact of the EU on North–South relations has economic and political dimensions. As noted, Irish opinion in the early 1960s favoured simultaneous accession to the EEC by Ireland and the UK. Though this did not stem from Ireland's northern interests (see above), a European Commission report on regional economies occasioned a passing reference in 1962 to the possibility of 'the 32 counties being designated as one region'.[23] While unionist policy did not oppose UK efforts to join the EEC, the prime minister of Northern Ireland, Lord Brookeborough, raised the stakes by alleging during an election campaign that the taoiseach, Seán Lemass, had told his party that Irish entry into the EEC would effectively end partition.[24] The taoiseach himself claimed to have been more modest and to have suggested only that 'the gradual disappearance ... of the Border as a barrier in the economic and many other fields ... would, in time, tend to promote a common desire to remove the political barrier also'. In explaining his remarks, he drew upon the late Lord Craigavon's words: 'In this island, we cannot live always separated from one another. We are too small to be apart or for the border to be there for all time.'[25]

The first two applications by both states to join the EEC were unsuccessful but, it was observed, in or out of it, the 'establishment of the European Community ... affected both Irish and Northern Irish States'.[26] This was the background to a number of proposals which prefigured the areas of co-operation that are now accepted. They were initiated by Secretary of the Department of Finance T. K. Whitaker, familiar with the thinking of northern politicians, and pursued in 1965 by the Taoiseach and the new Prime Minister of Northern Ireland Terence O'Neill.[27] But the *dynamism* of the mid-1960s disappeared during the Lynch premiership in the wake of renewed suspicions in the North about the possibility of a political agenda hidden behind functional co-operation, the arms smuggling scandal implicating the Irish Government, escalating violence in Northern Ireland and the imposition of direct rule.[28]

As noted already, the coincidence of direct rule and EC accession divided unionists. Terence O'Neill and Brian Faulkner were excoriated for their 'un-Ulster values' of 'compromise, cross-border dialogue with the annexationist Irish Republic and power sharing with Republicans'.[29] This was compounded during British renegotiation of the terms of membership and the 1975 referendum. Prospects for North–South co-operation remained stymied by the domestication of the European question, especially as the European Parliament (EP) sought in the mid-1980s to intervene in political, as well as economic, affairs relating to internal and North–South matters.[30]

Change began with the development of European regional policy in the late 1980s and 1990s, which provided a more comprehensive basis for the potential seen by the SDLP in a 'Europe of the regions'. The first INTERREG programme (now in its third manifestation) started in 1989 and was intended to foster 'bottom–up' initiatives reflecting the common interests of contiguous territories in different member states throughout the EU. There is a common chapter in the structural funds programmes for Northern Ireland[31] and the Republic of Ireland. And there is a cross-border dimension to the SSPPR or Peace I and II), initiated for Northern Ireland in the wake of the 1994 ceasefires.

This is not the place to assess the details and intrinsic merits of these programme or the projects funded by them.[32] The point is to consider the extent to which they have Europeanised the Irish question. Commentators are agreed that, because of centralisation and weak local government in Ireland and the UK, INTERREG I and II were not, in the words of McCall and Williamson,[33] a 'radical catalyst in the redefinition of relationships for the governance of the border region' (i.e., bottom–up joint administration). But the INTERREG initiative, they suggest, activated local interest among business people, councillors and the voluntary sector in cross-border networking, administration and policy delivery. The bottom–up approach, they argue, became more successful in Peace I and II. Perhaps because of the first experience, the early stages of INTERREG III, according to Laffan and Payne,[34] show more potential than its predecessors for the introduction of an element of cross-border multi-level governance, or, to put it another way, to Europeanise the Irish question, at least in the border counties.

The lifespan of these programmes coincides with a shift in some post-direct rule unionist ideas about cross-border co-operation. At first there was opposition to it – which continued among hard-line unionists. Moderates thereafter began to accept its legitimacy, provided that it was spontaneous, market-led or otherwise voluntary but with no administrative superstructure.[35] In the early 1990s 'a remarkable upsurge in business enthusiasm for North–South economic integration' was noted.[36] At the same time, hard-line unionists berated a leading local banker[37] and others for pursuing the idea of a 'North-South economic corridor' – even without a superstructure. At the same time, however, moderate unionists began to accept the idea that there could be some administration in joint – local – hands. The UUP was prepared in the 1992 talks to concede the sense of some cross-border bodies, provided the remit of their joint management was functionally specific and limited to those functional objectives.

Strand Two of the GFA reflects an emergent recognition among unionists of the legitimacy of the nationalist interest in co-operation (in the absence of a majority for re-unification); and that for unionists, too, there are some common North–South interests. The GFA gave rise to the North–South Ministerial Council and a set of implementing bodies: Waterways Ireland (navigable waterways); the Food and Safety Promotion Board; InterTrade Ireland; the Language Body (Gaelic and Ulster Scots); Foyle, Carlingford and Irish Lights (including not only lighthouses, but also commerce, recreation, fisheries, acquaculture, marine tourism); and the Special EU Programmes Body (SEUPB). The North–South Council also oversees co-operation between the tourist boards of the two parts of the island and has assumed responsibility for areas of co-operation previously agreed by the two governments: animal and plant health; teacher qualifications and exchanges; strategic transport planning; environmental protection, pollution, water quality and waste management; and accident and emergency services. In addition to the SEUPB, responsible for relevant EU programmes (those mentioned above and URBAN, LEADER, etc), the North–South Council may also consider the EU dimension to all areas of its activities. It was promised that ways would be found to ensure that the views of the Council were represented at relevant meetings of the EU Council of Ministers. The North–South Council has only recently begun to tackle this aspect of what it may do, calling – just before the October 2002 suspension – on its secretariat to provide a paper on the topic.[38]

The design and remit of the North–South Council are reminiscent of those of European institutions. In plenary form, it is a *quasi*-European council, led by the first minister and deputy first minister of Northern Ireland and the Irish taoiseach. Like the Council of Ministers, it meets in sectoral format under the leadership of ministers from both sides according to the topics under discussion. Its remit goes beyond discussion: it is meant to attempt to reach agreement on the adoption of common policies where there is a mutual interest or a whole island benefit, subject to the competences of both administrations; it is supposed to take decisions for implementation separately in each jurisdiction where each side is accountable – rather like EU directives. Something like the EU's Economic and Social Committee can be seen in a North–South consultative forum, mooted in the GFA and about which discussions were taking place before the October 2002 suspension.

This was a difficult part of the GFA on which to reach consensus. Both sides had to come a long way: nationalists from immediate re-unification and unionists from opposition to a political–administrative superstructure which they believed would be a Trojan horse for a re-united Ireland. The DUP, apparently, still believes this.[39] While EU initiatives may have helped to *normalise* North–South co-operation, awareness of different theories of integration also complicated matters during the negotiation period.[40]

For the same reason that theorists of functionalism prefer the allocation of collaborative functions to a variety of bodies rather than to a single body (and, perhaps, remembering older proposals for a Council of Ireland), unionists originally preferred North–South co-operation to be carried out by several bodies set up for narrowly defined and specific purposes. In conceding in the negotiations to the overarching North–South Council, they would have preferred it to have been given an advisory role rather than to be required, in EU style, to develop common policies for implementation in the two jurisdictions. Nationalists have a more neo-functionalist way of thinking – that, as people are accustomed to co-operation in one area, the habit will spill over into others, as implied in the earlier noted speculations by Seán Lemass and references by John Hume to the EU's origins and development. Even so, they are puzzled by what they see as a lack of unionist confidence in being able to say 'No' to some future proposal or another. But unionists observe neo-functionalist spill-overs leading, in theory and actuality, to 'ever closer union' in the EU. This means that they expect their potential 'No' responses to be seen as irrational and dysfunctional to the full benefits of co-operation. Hence, the rashness of the comment during the negotiations by David Andrews, then Irish foreign minister, that the proposed North–South Council would be 'a kind of government'.[41]

One account[42] of the North–South dimension in what was finally agreed is sceptical of both 'irredentist nationalist hopes' and corresponding unionist fears that the EU will bring about 'rolling integration' by neo-functionalist means. But its authors do suggest that North–South economic co-operation could 'square the circle' between nationalism and unionism' within a still 'British Northern Ireland'. And – perhaps curiously, given how much was at stake in different ways to the different parties – the North–South Ministerial Council was quickly judged by the governments and by the Northern Ireland Executive to have become a success, save, that is, for the DUP, which boycotts it because of the participation of Sinn Féin ministers.

The impact of Europe on relations within a *still* British Northern Ireland

Some commentators argue that the EU has had no impact on how the communities view each other or on 'the warring factions' within Northern Ireland.[43] Irrespective of the EU, community relations have deteriorated since the GFA.[44] Nevertheless, EU initiatives did provide pretexts for people from different parties and communities to interact with one another – sometimes enhancing mutual understanding as well.

Despite the domestication, in the 1970s, of the European question, the coming about in 1979 of direct elections to the EP brought about an 'unsuspected opportunity for common cause'[45] among Northern Ireland's MEPs to maximise the benefits of EU programmes. Objective 1 funding requires the inclusion of social and local partners (as well as regional, national and European) at all stages of the life of a project. The first round of structural funds planning within Northern Ireland was criticised as too state-driven. But, over time, according to Hodgett,[46] the special problems of Northern Ireland encouraged the then Conservative governments to permit a degree of popular participation in policy-making that was not regarded as suitable in Great Britain. Peace I and II institutionalise cross-community partnership – which, with some changes, will survive the ending of EU support.[47] Peace I led to the setting up of twenty-six District Partnerships as one of three sets of bodies to which applications for project funding could be made. The others are statutory agencies and intermediary funding bodies, usually voluntary sector organisations and often, themselves, partnerships. The District Partnerships originally comprised of equal proportions of elected councillors, people drawn from business and trade unions, and members of the community and voluntary sectors. They, like the intermediary funding bodies, judge project applications on the basis of their capacity to address the legacy of the conflict and the opportunities of the peace process. Such projects may sometimes be directed primarily at a single community particularly affected by the conflict, but they are required to justify this or to show how they may begin to open out to 'the other community'.

In 1997, it was suggested that the District Partnerships and associated projects would not bring about 'the big solution' but had 'the potential for making a solution more possible'.[48] This is borne out by research findings. In assessing the District Partnerships and IFBs, Williamson, Scott and Halfpenny found that, even during times of high tension between 1996 and 1998, 'the extent of co-operation between members of opposing parties and members of different communities is quite remarkable'.[49] Similar findings were made by McCall and Williamson in comparing the impact of the peace and INTERREG initiatives in the border areas.[50] There is also an example, known to this author, of two ex-prisoners from different communities working together in a District Partnership who were also on the talks teams of the parties representing their communities.

Another European dimension to community politics and the peace process comes about through women. Women are particularly visible in community action and negotiation with the statutory sector over the politics of everyday life; for example, in respect of employment conditions and a wide range of social policy issues. During the 1990s, women became increasingly alert to the potential of the EU, pointing to their considerable experience of and skills in the partnership approach. Moreover, there seemed a greater appreciation in EU circles, not only of women's effectiveness in participation, but of their right to participate.[51] The EU, through the Northern Ireland Women's European Platform, provides a network, operating internally and at the interstices of the EU and in the international human rights policy community associated with the UN. Combined with local community networks, this was the basis on which NIWC was brought into being.[52] It was NIWC which proposed the Civic Forum at the talks to conserve, in a form inspired by the District Partnerships, experience of participation but now within a new democratic framework.[53] NIWC's talks team deliberately examined the workings of the EU Economic and Social Committee and institutions in other European countries in considering the details of what to propose and what to avoid.

The Civic Forum may be construed as a kind of power-sharing initiative in that it grafts the politics of inter-community action or cross-community participation onto the *pillared* political representation of the two communities. But power-sharing in its formal sense belongs to the chamber of elected representatives, and that, too, has a European dimension. The practice of consensual decision-making, or coalition politics, elsewhere in Europe informed the thinking of the Executive of the short-lived Northern Ireland Assembly of 1973.[54] APNI leader Oliver Napier pointed out that power-sharing was 'the rule rather than the exception throughout Europe',[55] and, when the assembly was on the brink of being brought down, Brian Faulkner warned that 'Europe's eyes will be upon us to see if we can pull together'.[56] In contrast, the assembly's opponents equated 'softness on Europe' with 'softness on power sharing'. Power-sharing was not wanted at any level, 'within Northern Ireland, between Northern Ireland and the Republic of Ireland … or within Europe.'[57]

Twenty-six years later, however, linking the EU and power-sharing negatively did not figure in the negotiations leading to the GFA and the EU is not invoked in new difficulties over power-sharing.[58] Whereas past controversies were about whether unionists would agree to share power with the SDLP, current problems are about sharing power with Sinn Féin. The DUP, though in government, does not participate in a normal fashion because of the presence of Sinn Féin without the prior completion of decommissioning by the IRA. The UUP at first agreed to share power in anticipation that decommissioning would take place but, until its completion, is unwilling to continue to do so. Power-sharing, as practised in Northern Ireland, also gives rise to disquiet for those who would otherwise regard it as legitimate – based on their awareness of its practice in other European countries. As noted elsewhere in this book, the two systems of weighted voting institutionalise the rights of the 'two communities' but not those who decline to label themselves as either nationalist or unionist. The lack of provision for the so-called 'others' means, in this view, that power is still based on sectarianism instead of reflecting a new form of equality that moves beyond 'parity of esteem' to one based on diversity and pluralism.

Though devolved government in Northern Ireland often has been interrupted as a result of disputes about sharing power between unionists and Sinn Féin, the EU has figured quite prominently in Northern Ireland's Executive and Assembly business. The new executive inherited the negotiation of further rounds of EU funding, and this was carried out by the UUP's first minister, the SDLP's deputy first minister and the SDLP's minister for finance and personnel.[59] Increasingly, the OFMDFM has begun to speak of Northern Ireland's becoming a 'forward and outward looking region'[60] which can begin to move from being assisted by the EU to making a contribution to European integration. Marks of this ambition can be seen in the hosting of delegations from the Committee of the Regions, attendance by Northern Irish ministers at the Cohesion Forum, and in high-level visits by the first minister, the deputy first minister and relevant departmental ministers to France (received by President Chirac) and Germany (received by Foreign Minister Joschka Fischer). The OFMDFM also took steps to make a contribution to the debate on the future of Europe. The junior ministers, in particular, in the

OFMDFM firmly and frequently state that devolution gives Northern Ireland (as a 'constitutional region') a stronger and more self-confident base from which to act in the EU, especially in co-operation with the devolved administrations in Wales and Scotland.

The assembly has held two enquiries into EU issues. In one, cut short by the October 2002 suspension, the Committee on Finance and Personnel had begun to examine the spending of EU monies; in the other, the Committee on the Centre reviewed the capacity of the OFMDFM and the new Executive Office in Brussels to handle EU affairs and itself to hold the executive to account on European issues.

The OFMDFM's linking of devolution with European integration and its aim of being a 'forward and outward looking region' are consistent with the conclusions of a report in December 2002 by the House of Lords Select Committee on the Constitution.[61] The Committee concluded that the devolved administrations of the UK had better opportunities than many regions in other states to promote their interests in EU institutions. It expressed some concerns about how the Joint Ministerial Committee system operates in respect of EU issues, about the secrecy of discussion between devolved ministers and central government on the development of joint UK policy positions, and about communication (or lack of it) between UK negotiators and the devolved executives at the final bargaining stages in the Council of Ministers. On the other hand, the committee suggested that proximity and close working relationships between the executive offices of the devolved administrations in Brussels and UKREP[62] could ensure that variations in interests or situations could be taken into account at early drafting stages. It also argued that there were benefits to regions in the possibility of their ministers being permitted to lead UK representation at the Council of Ministers. While such ministers are obliged to present the policy stance of central government, the occasions can be used for mutual familiarisation with officials and counterparts from elsewhere. The committee also noted that the capacity of the UK's devolved administrations to interact with others elsewhere, viewed positively by OFMDFM ministers for Northern Ireland, is also advantageous for central government, enabling denser relations at a level of government where UK ministers cannot go directly.

However, the House of Lords Select Committee on the Constitution's optimism may have to be tempered by the possibility that institutions in Northern Ireland are not yet fully able to take advantage of these opportunities. The report by the Committee on the Centre[63] was highly critical of arrangements in the OFMDFM and the Executive Office in Brussels. The latter, it felt, was inadequately resourced to promote networking among other Northern Irish actors in the EU, such as its three MEPs and members of the Committee of the Regions and the Economic and Social Council, and with counterparts from other European regions. The committee regretted the paucity of secondments from the Northern Ireland Civil Service to EU institutions and the infrequency, compared to Scotland, of Northern Irish ministers seeking to lead at the Council of Ministers. It also noted its own difficulty in securing sufficient and timely information from the

Northern Ireland Executive for consideration in the assembly; it called also for a designated Northern Ireland Assembly Committee.

Many of the committee's findings coincide with other research. Kennedy and Murphy[64] are pessimistic about the preparedness of subject-based departments overseen by ministers other than those in the OFMDFM. Papers presented at the conference 'Forging Regional Links' on 17 June 2003, organised by the OFMDFM, indicated that the Scottish Executive Office in Brussels has travelled much farther in establishing agreements with regions elsewhere in Europe. And, whether or not as a result of the alleged defects of the Northern Ireland presence in Europe, the previously concerted activities of MEPs seems to have dissipated and there appears to be little networking among politicians at the various levels of governance. As Phinnemore[65] points out, no Northern Ireland MEP sat on the EP's Constitutional Affairs Committee prior to 2004, and none was a delegate or alternate on the EP's delegation to the convention. Moreover, Northern Ireland members of the House of Commons are less assiduous than their Scottish and Welsh counterparts in taking part in the scrutiny process in the UK's Parliament. Of the 29 MPs on the Standing Committee on the Convention, none was from Northern Ireland, compared with 4 from Scotland and 2 from Wales; there is no Northern Irish MP on the European Scrutiny Committee, compared to 5 and 1, respectively, from Scottish and Welsh constituencies. UUP member Dr Martin Smyth sits on Standing Committee C of the three Standing Committees on European Scrutiny; of the 40 MPs on the 3 committees, 6 are Scottish and 3 are Welsh. Such is the price of the larger parties' preoccupation with domestic constitutional and security issues – and the consequence, perhaps, a less general view than exists in Scotland and Wales that the EU is an important factor for self-determination even within a *still* British State.

Conclusion

There are other aspects of the politics of Northern Ireland and British–Irish relations to which Europe is relevant. Three issues – freedom of movement between Ireland and the UK, police co-operation and EMU – are important. Freedom of movement dates from the founding of the Irish Free State and, to some extent, is made more complicated by the EU.[66] The EU now formalises a habit of police co-operation which took place over the same period.[67] The introduction of the euro into Ireland and the rapidity with which it became used in the North,[68] especially in the border towns, occasioned a motion in the Assembly to ask the UK Government if Northern Ireland could be a parallel currency zone.[69] But these are matters covered by reserved or excepted powers and cannot be acted on at the present time by the Northern Ireland Executive.[70]

Several issues, not mentioned so far, in Strands One to Three of the GFA and outside them show signs of the Europeanisation of the Irish question or, at least, the interaction between indigenous ideas and developments elsewhere. For example, assembly legislation has to be 'equality proofed' and must comply with ECHR standards. The two governments are strengthening human rights standards to meet those of the ECHR and to match one another: for example, in provisions for minorities and their languages, the status of women, and socio-economic equality regardless of class, religion, disability or ethnicity. A charter of human rights for the whole island is mooted.

Acceptance of some harmonisation of standards of rights owes something to both the ECHR and the EU. That discrimination against homosexuals is unlawful in both parts of the island (affirmed in the GFA explicitly by the UK and implicitly by Ireland) stems from actions in the respective courts which led, eventually, to rulings in the European Court of Human Rights. The EU has long been argued to have contributed to the emergence of commitment in Ireland to sex equality and its reinforcement in the UK. Legislation to incorporate the ECHR in the UK and proposals for human rights legislation in Ireland were completed and introduced, at the same time as the ratification of the Amsterdam Treaty. The first text of that Treaty, drafted by the Irish presidency in 1996, declared that ECHR principles are also the EU's fundamental principles – and this remained in the final version, notwithstanding some disagreement in other member states about how strong such a declaration should be.

It has not been the intention of this chapter to overstate the European dimension to the reformulation of the Irish question and answers to it. Obviously the roots of the Irish question long pre-date European integration; and it has been shown that moves similar to provisions in the GFA were on the agenda in the 1960s, before either state belonged to the EU. But, if Europe was irrelevant to the causes, it *is* relevant to the solution: Europe is a new factor in the context in which an answer was and is being sought. Even in the 1960s, the existence of the EEC, although the UK and Ireland were not in it, was considered significant to the well-being of both parts of the island.

This proposition became less persuasive in mainstream Northern Irish unionism as a result of direct rule, of nationalist hopes that the EU could *blur* the status of Northern Ireland and of an overlap between unionists and Euro-sceptics at Westminster. But such forces did not eliminate a Northern Ireland unionist sense that the EU could have beneficial effects. The GFA, as indicated in this chapter, shows that an EU impact has been accepted, albeit on a less ambitious scale than speculated on in Ireland in the 1960s and envisaged in subsequent SDLP aspirations. In everyday life, the EU has become a palpable reality to people in community politics. My only claim is that the language, conventions and institutions of EU policy-making have contributed to the creation of spaces for contending parties in formal and informal politics to discuss solutions to old problems in new ways, to do so in a context in which the states with which they identify have become more equal partners than before, and to act on that opportunity. Northern Ireland as a 'forward and outward looking region' may yet be a slightly implausible slogan but it is a signifier of a sense of the prizes at stake.

Notes

1 Rory O'Donnell, 'Fixing the Institutions', in Robin Wilson (ed.), *No Frontiers: North-South Integration in Ireland* (Belfast: Democratic Dialogue, 1999), pp. 70–3 at p. 7.
2 In addition to works cited here, other (mostly) brief reference works dealing with the EU and Northern Ireland are reviewed by Elizabeth Meehan in her E. H. Carr Memorial Lecture, University of Wales, Aberystwyth – published in the *Review of International Studies*, January 2000.
3 Paul Hainsworth, 'Northern Ireland in the European Community', in Michael Keating and Barry Jones (eds), *Regions in the European Community* (Oxford: Clarendon Press, 1985), pp. 121–3.
4 See also Paul Gillespie's contribution to this book (chapter 21).
5 Letter from Garret FitzGerald to T. K. Whitaker, secretary of the Department of Finance, 29 April 1961, D/T SI6023C/61.
6 John McGarry and Brendan O'Leary, *Explaining Northern Ireland* (Oxford: Blackwell, 1996), esp. pp. 279–82, 302–6.
7 Hainsworth, 'Northern Ireland in the European Community', p. 130.
8 Etain Tannam, *Cross-Border Cooperation in the Republic of Ireland and Northern Ireland* (Basingstoke: Macmillan, 1999), pp. 75–6.
9 Quoted by Hainsworth, 'Northern Ireland in the European Community', pp. 128, 130.
10 Tannam, *Cross-Border Cooperation*, pp. 77, 83, 85.
11 *Ibid.*
12 Presented to parliament by the Lord Chancellor in July 2000 and available on the Northern Ireland Government website: www.northernireland.gov.uk/mou/index.htm
13 The Ireland Act 1949, section 2; see also the Nationality Act 1948 and subsequent British nationality legislation under which Irish nationals are 'not aliens': discussed in Elizabeth Meehan, *Free Movement Between Ireland and the UK: From the 'Common Travel Area' to The Common Travel Area*, Studies in Public Policy 4 (Dublin: Policy Institute, Trinity College, in Association with the Department of Justice, Equality and Law Reform, 2000), chapter 2.
14 Paul Bew and Elizabeth Meehan, 'Regions and Borders: Controversies in Northern Ireland about the European Union', *Journal of European Public Policy*, vol 1, no. 1, 1994, pp. 95–6; Tannam, *Cross-Border Cooperation*, p. 95.
15 Letter from the Irish ambassador in London to the secretary of the Department of External Affairs, 24 November 1961, D/T S15273B.
16 Michael Cox, 'Bringing in the "International": The IRA Ceasefire and the End of the Cold War', *International Affairs*, vol. 73, no. 4, 1996, pp. 671–3.
17 Hainsworth, 'Northern Ireland in the European Community', p. 122.
18 *Ibid*, p. 123; see also Cathal McCall, 'Postmodern Europe and the Resources of Communal Identities in Northern Ireland', in *European Journal of Political Research*, vol. 33, 1998, pp. 398–411, esp. 397–8.
19 James Anderson, 'The Shifting Stage of Politics: New Medieval and Postmodern Territorialities?' *Environment and Planning D: Society and Space*, vol. 14, 1996, pp. 133–53, esp. pp. 137–8, from where the statement by John Hume is taken; also see McCall, 'Postmodern Europe', on the impact of postmodernity and developments in the European state system on Irish identity.
20 Cox, 'Bringing in the "International"'.
21 See Anderson, 'The Shifting Stage of Politics', pp. 689–92, on McAliskey and, on Sinn Féin (as well as the other parties), Gavin Adams, 'The Impact of European Integration on Northern Irish Politics', PhD thesis submitted at Queen's University Belfast, 2001.
22 Elizabeth Meehan, sections on the EU in Rick Wilford and Robin Wilson (editors and main contributors), Monitoring Devolution, quarterly reports. Research project led at the Constitution Unit, University College London, funded by the Leverhulme Foundation and the ESRC. Northern Ireland's Quarterly Reports are available at: www.democraticdialogue.org.
23 File note to Taoiseach, 4 January 1962, D/T SI6877X/62.
24 *Irish Press*, 31 February 1962.

25 *Dáil Debates*, vol. 194, 5 April 1962, cols 1427–8, D/T SI7246E/62. He attracted public correspondence about whether or not Lord Craigavon had actually said such a thing: *Irish Times*, 11 and 13 April 1962, D/T SI7246F/62.

26 Tannam, *Cross-Border Cooperation*, p. 51.

27 *Ibid.*, pp. 50–7.

28 *Ibid.*, pp. 58–60, 83–4.

29 Hainsworth, 'Northern Ireland in the European Union', p. 122.

30 E.g. the 1983 Haagerup Report which recommended joint British–Irish responsibilities, as well as cross-border co-operation and also attempted in Strasbourg to debate the Anglo-Irish Agreement in 1985; Tannam, *Cross-Border Cooperation*, pp. 174–5, and Hainsworth, 'Northern Ireland in the European Union', pp. 111, 129.

31 Objective 1 and Transitional Objective 1 ('Building Sustainable Prosperity'). Objective 1 status is being phased out and the peace programmes will be, too. Some version of the latter may continue, according to a consultation paper by the British Government: *A Modern Regional Policy for the United Kingdom*, HM Treasury, Department of Trade and Industry, Office of the Deputy Prime Minister (London: Stationery Office, March 2003), also available on the websites of the three departments. Peace II will leave a legacy for the structures of governance in Northern Ireland, of which more later.

32 Accounts are available in: Tannam, *Cross-Border Cooperation*, chapters 4–7; Cathal McCall and Arthur Williamson, 'Fledgling European Union Social Partnership and the Irish Border Region', *Policy and Politics*, vol. 28, no. 3, 2000, pp. 397–410; James Corrigan, 'Cross-Border Programmes', in Mary Browne and Dennis Kennedy (eds), *Northern Ireland and the European Union: Discussion Papers on the Intergovernmental Conference and other European Issues* (Belfast: Institute of European Studies, Queen's University, 1996), pp. 35–6.

33 McCall and Williamson, 'Fledgling European Union Social Partnership', p. 402; see also Tannam, *Cross-Border Cooperation*, chapters 4–7.

34 Brigid Laffan and Diane Payne, *EU Cross-Border Co-operation After the Good Friday Agreement* (Armagh: Centre for Cross Border Studies, 2001)

35 Anderson, 'The Shifting Stage of Politics'.

36 Respondent to Opsahl Commission; A. Pollak (ed.), *A Citizens' Enquiry: The Opsahl Report on Northern Ireland* (Dublin: Lilliput Press and Initiative 1992, 1993), p. 75.

37 Dr George Quigley, chairman of the Ulster Bank and former senior civil servant, introduced the idea of a corridor, an economic and political critique of which is provided by Paul Bew, Henry Patterson and Paul Teague, *Between War and Peace: The Political Future of Northern Ireland* (London: Lawrence & Wishart, 1997), chapter 7.

38 This was initiated in the summer of 2002 and was beginning to come to fruition, but the latest development took place just five days before the institutions were suspended. Executive Press Release, 11 October 2002.

39 See note 22.

40 Tannam, *Cross-Border Cooperation*, deals with this from the standpoint of an observer, though politicians themselves also use these categories and theories: see Anderson, 'The Shifting Stage of Politics', p. 136, on how they have done so in the past; and Bew, Patterson and Teague, *Between War and Peace*, pp. 192–5 on the present; see also McCall, 'Postmodern Europe', pp. 393–4.

41 Rory O'Donnell , 'Fixing the Institution', p. 73, alludes to postmodern political theories that state power now seeps outwards, downwards and upwards to a variety of non-governmental semi-public bodies and supranational regimes by saying that 'one smiled' at this 'unfortunate phrase' – 'because nobody knows what a government is like nowadays'. This fits in with post-nationalist ideas but unionism is, perhaps, still 'modern'; see works referred to in note 19.

42 Bew, Patterson and Teague, *Between War and Peace*, esp. p. 199.

43 McGarry and O'Leary, *Explaining Northern Ireland*, pp. 198–9.

44 There have been notorious street conflicts between the two communities and within the loyalist community; segregation is increasing. Opinion polls indicate markedly different attitudes between the 'two communities' about their experience of the GFA and sense of what

the future holds: see Joanne Hughes, Caitlin Donnelly, Gillian Robinson and Lizanne Dowds, 'Community Relations in Northern Ireland: The Long View', Occasional Paper (Belfast: ARK [Northern Ireland Social and Political Archive, www.ark.ac.uk] 2003), which draws on the Northern Ireland *Life and Times* Survey, available at: www.ark.ac.uk/publications/occasional/occpaper2.PDF. On the other hand, others, especially politicians, point to the reduction in sectarian killings, the open doors of hotels and shops, and the greater presence and bustle of people in the city-centre streets at night.

45 For example, action by John Hume (SDLP), supported by Dr Ian Paisley (DUP) and John Taylor (UUP), led to the Martin Report by the EP which called for special assistance for Northern Ireland. Throughout the 1980s, various single initiatives or problems (agriculture, lobbying for Objective 1 status, additionality) attracted the combined attention of the three MEPs (John Taylor replaced by Jim Nicholson). In the 1990s, the MEPs co-operated in helping to secure (and renew and enlarge), Peace I; see Hainsworth, 'Northern Ireland in the European Union', pp. 110 and 128. Local politicians also found common cause in joining together under an initiative started by the Law Society and the private sector to set up and fund the Northern Ireland Centre in Europe (NICE). Political co-operation arises in part from perceived defects in constitutional conventions (Bew and Meehan, 'Borders and Regions', pp. 105–6) which, despite the high profile of Northern Ireland secretaries of state (Hainsworth, 'Northern Ireland in the European Union, pp. 113–4), are seen by unionists, as well as nationalists, as rendering Northern Irish interests poorly defended in the Council of Ministers. According to Dr Paisley, the three MEPs work together so closely that, on seeing this, their colleagues in the EP 'thought they had worked a miracle': interview in Bew and Meehan, 'Regions and Borders', p. 103.

46 Susan Hodgett, *Community Infrastructure: The Northern Ireland Voluntary Sector and European Union Regional Policy* (Belfast: NICVA, 1998).

47 They have been reformulated as Local Strategy Partnerships (LSPs) with half the positions being filled by the district councils on an institutionalised basis rather than through individual councillor membership. They are to have a wider role in socio-economic development.

48 Paul Sweeney, then director of the Northern Ireland Partnership Board, the 'umbrella' for the twenty-six boards, quoted by McCall and Williamson in 'Fledgling European Union Social Partnership', p. 408.

49 Arthur Williamson, Duncan Scott and Peter Halfpenny, 'Rebuilding Civil Society in Northern Ireland: The Community and Voluntary Sector's Contribution to the European Union's Peace and Reconciliation District Partnership Programme', *Policy and Politics*, vol. 28, no. 1, 2000, pp. 49–66, statement quoted from p. 57.

50 McCall and Williamson, 'Fledging European Union Social Partnership'.

51 *Women and Citizenship in Northern Ireland: Power, Participation and Choice* (Belfast: Women's Education and Resources Centre and Equal Opportunities Commission, 1995), a report produced by a research team accommodated by WERC and Belfast EOC.

52 Bronagh Hinds, 'Women Working for Peace in Northern Ireland', in Yvonne Galligan, Eilis Ward and Rick Wilford (eds), *Contesting Politics. Women in Ireland: North and South* (Boulder, CO: Westview Press and Political Studies Association of Ireland, 1999).

53 APNI proposed a kind of civic forum in the 1980s; communication with author.

54 Hainsworth, 'Northern Ireland in the European Union', p. 122.

55 *Ibid.*

56 *Ibid.*

57 *Ibid.*, p. 123.

58 On the other hand, a negative association between the two is implicit in manifestos for the European elections, especially those of the DUP. These tend to convey the electoral contest as a plebiscite on the constitutional status of Northern Ireland. Notably, the European election of 1999 was presented as a competition between pro- and anti-GFA forces, an agreement that has at its heart the notion of power-sharing.

59 See Meehan, *Monitoring Devolution*, which also provides accounts of the other activities which follow.

60 The name of one of the funding measures under Peace II.

61 House of Lords Select Committee on the Constitution, *Devolution: Inter-Institutional Relations in the United Kingdom*, Session 2002–03, Second Report, HL Paper 28 (London: Stationery Office, 17 December 2002), esp. paras. 172, 174–9, 183, 196.

62 The acronym for UK Representation to the EU, the permanent delegation of officials which, with other delegations, considers proposals for legislation that will eventually be decided upon by the Council of Ministers and, increasingly, the EP.

63 Debated in the Northern Ireland Assembly on 8 April 2002, *Official Record*, 8 April 2002.

64 Dennis Kennedy and Mary Murphy, '*Plus ça change*: Stormont, Devolution and the European Union', paper presented at the European Policy Forum, Democratic Dialogue and the Institute of European Studies, Queen's University Belfast, 2001; see also Mary Murphy, 'The European Union Dimension to Devolution in Northern Ireland; Continuity and Change in the Policy-Making Process', PhD thesis, Queen's University Belfast, 2002.

65 D. Phinnemore, 'The Draft Treaty Establishing a Constitution for Europe: Implications for Northern Ireland': paper presented at the conference 'From Convention to Constitution: Northern Ireland and the Future of Europe', Queen's University Belfast, 18 September 2003. On the other hand, as Phinnemore also points out, MEP Jim Nicholson (UUP), is one of the eighteen signatories (including Jens-Peter Bonde, Georges Berthu and Dana Rosemary Scallion) of the Earl of Stockton's statement, 'Reaffirming the Aims of the Laeken Declaration', CONY 808.03, 16 June 2003. This criticised the convention for failing to entrench the position of the nation state as the means of bringing democracy closer to the people. Conversely, Sinn Féin and the SDLP have taken steps to address, within Northern Ireland and/or at the Irish National Forum on Europe, the future of the EU.

66 Meehan, *Free Movement Between Ireland and the UK*.

67 Jason Lane, 'The Development of Irish Cross-Border Police Cooperation: Influences and Effects of the European Union', PhD thesis, Queen's University Belfast, 1999.

68 Nicola Byrne, 'You Can Keep the UK Out of the Euro, But it Seems You Can't Keep the Euro out of the UK', *Scotland on Sunday*, 13 January 2002. And Chris Ashmore, 'Strabane Sells Itself as the Most Euro-Friendly Place in NI', *Irish Times*, 4 January 2003.

69 Introduced in December 2001 by Jane Morrice, MLA, Northern Ireland Women' s Coalition (NIWC). It was not voted on, ostensibly because currency is outside the assembly's competence. But probably what was more important is a division of party attitudes, albeit that the executive did pledge in its first Programme for Government to develop an agreed policy on the euro. In fact, only the SDLP of the larger parties is a relatively straightforward supporter. The UUP is largely silent on the matter, while the DUP thunderously opposes it, describing a visit by Jack Straw to Belfast to discuss Valery Giscard d'Estaing's review of the future of Europe as really a 'touting exercise' for the prime minister's 'back door agenda' on the euro: *Newsletter*, 28 September 2002. Sinn Féin has got itself into a tight corner, being Euro-sceptical in Ireland but having to compete for voters who support a pro-EU party in the North. Previously, it deflected questions about the euro by referring to the importance of the US. In its party conference in March 2003, it restated its preference for 'democratically controlled economy on the island of Ireland'. However, it noted that the euro was a 'reality'. In the interests, therefore, of an 'all-Ireland currency', it too called for the euro to be a 'co-equal currency', with sterling, in 'the Six County area'.

70 Though policing could become a devolved matter.

23

The new American connection: President George W. Bush and Northern Ireland

JOHN DUMBRELL

Prior to the 1990s, interest in the American connection to the conflict in Northern Ireland concentrated on fund-raising and support for the republican cause. Attention focused on the main, largely Roman Catholic, Irish-American organisations, ranging from the Ancient Order of Hibernians, the traditional Irish defence body, to the Irish National Caucus (the lobby group led by Father Sean McManus) and the Irish Northern Aid Committee (NORAID, the main US fund-raiser for the Provisional IRA). Observers of the US connection to the Troubles also concerned themselves with US sources of IRA arms and with the articulation of positions on Northern Ireland within Congress. The Congressional Ad Hoc Committee on Irish Affairs was set up in 1977 as an organisation sympathetic to republican agendas within the national legislature. Of special significance in the 1970s and 1980s, of course, were the stances taken by three key congressional Democrats: House of Representatives Speaker 'Tip' O'Neill and Senator Edward Kennedy, both of Massachusetts, and Senator Daniel Patrick Moynihan of New York. Along with Democratic Governor Hugh Carey of New York, these three constituted the influential 'four horsemen' group: a body, very responsive to diplomacy conducted from Dublin, broadly committed to a constitutional nationalist version of the peace process.[1]

Before Bill Clinton's election as president in 1992, with two modestly important exceptions, American chief executives had not become involved to any significant extent in Northern Irish issues. The conflict was remote from the concerns of the Cold War and was, in any case, the prior business of London, Washington's major Cold War ally. The two exceptions were Presidents Jimmy Carter and Ronald Reagan. Carter's post-Vietnam War global human rights agenda led him to express a substantive US interest in Northern Irish peace in a 1977 statement on the province. Interest was maintained during the years of the Reagan Administration by William Clarke, Reagan's second national security adviser. Washington's stance, under both Carter and Reagan, was that US investment would follow progress broadly along the lines favoured by Dublin, the 'four horsemen' and the Friends of Ireland (a Congressional grouping in the 1980s committed to constitutional nationalism). The Reagan Administration played an important role in advancing the Anglo-Irish Agreement of 1985.[2]

Such precedents notwithstanding, Clinton's activism on Northern Ireland was of an entirely different order. Clinton was, perhaps even more than his predecessors, responsive to Dublin's diplomacy. He had a strong personal commitment to Irish issues – a legacy of his family background and his student days at Oxford. His activism reflected the strand of Irish-American opinion represented by business-orientated Americans for a New Irish Agenda.

His new agenda, central to the peace dynamic of the 1990s and in particular to the achievement of the 1998 GFA, was also the product of the ending of the Cold War and a new insouciance about upsetting the working norms of the US–UK 'special relationship'. In 1994, Gerry Adams was granted a visa to visit the USA. As Sidney Blumenthal reports: 'Clinton was pushing new diplomacy whether [Prime Minister John] Major approved or not.'[3] Washington was accused of aligning itself with militant republicanism: according to Raymond Seitz, US ambassador to London between 1991 and 1994, Jean Kennedy Smith, sister to Edward Kennedy and Clinton's first ambassador to Dublin, was 'an ardent IRA apologist'.[4] Like most US politicians who involve themselves in Irish affairs, Clinton was also accused of – in the words of Michael Mates – 'cynical playing to the green Irish vote'.[5] In fact, Clinton's initiative did involve a strong effort to include moderate loyalism, or at least to drive a wedge between different brands of unionism. Concerned to avoid a repetition of the solid loyalist opposition to the Anglo-Irish Agreement, the Clinton White House facilitated the opening of a dialogue in the early 1990s between official unionist leader James Molyneux and Vice President Al Gore. Clinton's activism also involved a far greater commitment of political time, energy and capital than can be convincingly explained in terms of likely electoral benefit. At the heart of Clinton's Irish initiatives lay the desire to establish, in conditions which did not risk the loss of American lives, internationalist precedents for American peace promotion in the post-Soviet era.[6]

Tony Blair's 1997 victory brought to Downing Street a positive and welcoming attitude towards Clinton's Irish agenda. The dynamic which had been inaugurated in 1993, with a White House policy review undertaken in response to the Downing Street Declaration, accelerated. Clinton's interventions were important to the 1998 peace agreement. The pivotal, facilitating role played by Senator George Mitchell, originally named by President Clinton as special Northern Irish economic envoy in 1994, is also almost undisputed. As author of the report on decommissioning, chairman of the negotiations of 1998 and reviewer of the process subsequently, Clinton's one-time economic envoy was at the living centre of the process.[7]

By the end of Clinton's second term, the nature and extent of the US dimension to Northern Ireland's problems and prospects had been transformed. Presidential interest and involvement, including actual visits to Belfast, had become familiar.

Catholic Irish-Americans now gave money to Sinn Féin, which was allowed openly to raise funds in the USA from 1995, rather than to NORAID. Economic involvement in Northern Ireland, much of it co-ordinated through Clinton's economic envoy (initially Mitchell, subsequently Jim Lyons), had also made a considerable impact. According to some estimates, by 2001 around 20 per cent of private sector jobs in Northern Ireland were linked to American companies or their subsidiaries.[8] With the new century, however, came a new party in the White House, and with it new foreign policy priorities.

The presidential election of 2000 saw little serious or extended debate on the foreign policy choices facing the US. To an extent, however, the election was a referendum on Clinton's record, and Northern Irish success was claimed (for example, on the White House website) as a visible and important part of the foreign policy record. The general stances taken by candidates Al Gore and George W. Bush also had implications for Northern Ireland. Vice President Gore strongly defended the internationalist, interventionist and 'liberal hawkish' dimensions of President Clinton's foreign policy legacy. The Bush team presented an 'Americanist' analysis of foreign issues, promising to conduct policy according to a realist calculus of the national interest: principles of nation-building, 'foreign policy as social work', idealistic democracy promotion and assertive humanitarianism would be rejected in favour of a 'humble' foreign policy which did not tilt at windmills of little direct or obvious relevance to rather narrowly conceived US interests. One of the very few direct comments on Northern Ireland from George W. Bush occurred during his primary campaign, when the future president implied that Clinton had allowed his desire for popular approval to distort the clear identification of national interest. Asked about Clinton's 'brokering the peace' in Northern Ireland, Bush expressed his generalised support for the policy, but, having noted current setbacks in peace process, he continued: 'And, hopefully, they'll be able to get talks back together again – as in the Middle East – but the danger is that any president allow … public opinion in the United States to drive or standing in the public opinion polls to drive the US to dictate terms of peace'.[9]

The new administration seemed unlikely to continue Clinton's energetic Irish commitment. When Secretary of State for Northern Ireland Mo Mowlam visited Washington in early 2001, she found National Security Adviser Condoleezza Rice genuinely 'uncertain then as to what their strategy was going to be'. (Mowlam, contemplating US policy in Colombia, felt that 'a position of "not our problem" might be the least bad option for N. Ireland from this presidency'.[10]) Committed to a foreign policy of 'not Clinton', the new regime seemed likely to favour disengagement from the province's affairs. Despite President Reagan's involvement in the politics of the Anglo-Irish Agreement, there was also a widespread assumption that Irish activism was largely a characteristic of US Democrats. It was also evident that few senior Bushies had any significant personal stake in Irish affairs. As Richard Haass, adviser to the Bush campaign, put it later: 'I will be the first to admit that shamrocks were not exactly a family tradition where I grew up.'[11]

In Northern Ireland, as in the Middle East, the early Bush policy was one of relative disengagement. To an extent, this disengagement mirrored the new 'Americanist' orientation of foreign policy and the desire to be anything-but-Clinton. In a sense, however, just as Middle Eastern disengagement was a response to the collapse of the Clinton–Barak proposals, so Northern Irish quietism merely reflected the changed conditions in the province. In this line of interpretation, Bushite disengagement involved a tacit recognition that Clinton's Irish initiative had run its (largely successful) course. Sandy Boyer thus argued in September 2001 that US attitudes were traceable, not to 'the de-greening of the White House' but to the realisation that 'the US had essentially done its work'. Clinton had successfully strengthened the cause of peace and compromise in Irish republicanism and had produced the GFA. Now, it was simply up to Washington to refrain from doing anything to damage the prospects for peace. Boyer noted that Washington had, in early 2001, conveniently 'looked the other way when the IRA was caught running guns from Florida in violation of their ceasefire'.[12]

In fact, it was clear even quite early on in 2001 that the new administration did wish to maintain an active interest in Northern Irish affairs, and that its spokesmen were actually not especially concerned to distance their approach from that of the Democrats. The key event here was the appointment, in time for St Patrick's Day 2001, of Richard Haass as (in his own phrase) 'the Administration's point-man for Northern Ireland'.[13] The significance of Haass's designation can be overestimated: he remained director of policy planning at the State Department, and was closely involved in a range of policy arenas. Nevertheless, Haass soon emerged as the clear setter of the administration's policy on Ireland. A strong opponent of unilateralism in economic sanctions policy, Haass was prepared to state publicly the case for multilateralist internationalism and to contest the position of neo-conservative 'Americanists'. A high-profile academic commentator, Haass, who also served in the first Bush administration, had published a study of regional disputes in 1990, arguing that American intervention was appropriate only if and when internal conditions for conciliation were 'ripe'.[14] In late 2000 he argued for a co-operativist foreign policy: 'If negotiations were the centrepiece of Cold War diplomacy, consultations will characterize the age of global relationships, that defy definition and vary by situation.'[15]

Explaining US interest in Northern Ireland, Ambassador Haass appealed to principles of internationalism that clashed noticeably with the priorities being advanced elsewhere in the administration. Speaking in January 2002, Haass explained:

> In some ways, my role mirrors that of the U.S. government within the peace process: impartial advisor, honest broker, and firm supporter of the Good Friday Agreement. We are not central to implementation of the process agreement ... But because of the many strong links between our country and the island of Ireland – including the 44 million Americans with Irish ancestry – we are immensely interested in and strongly committed to an enduring peace ...[16]

In a St Patrick's Day 2001 speech, the president himself was prepared to acknowledge that Irish peace fell within the remit of his newly 'Americanist' foreign policy: 'Peace in Northern Ireland', declared Bush, 'is in American's strong national interest.'[17] The administration actually, perhaps uniquely in the instance of Northern Ireland, did not seriously attempt to distance itself rhetorically from Clinton's legacy. Asked in a radio interview in Dublin how US policy on the province now differed from the days of Clinton, Haass responded: 'I don't really think it differs much at all.'[18] In October 2001, Democratic Senator Christopher Dodd of Connecticut agreed, commending George W. Bush 'for continuing President Clinton's policy of prodding all the parties to move forward to implement the Good Friday Accords so that Irish weapons will be silenced once and for all'.[19]

It is a feature of American post-Cold War foreign policy that various attempts to follow a relatively disengaged, 'national interests' foreign policy have broken down in the face of international pressures for US engagement – Clinton's pre-1995 Balkans' policy is the best example of this process. President Bush's Northern Irish policy became increasingly less disengaged during 2001. The Real IRA was designated a 'foreign terrorist organisation' under US law by the State Department in May; and Richard Haass issued statements approving the Patten Report's recommendations on policing and urging full implementation of the GFA, including decommissioning, demilitarisation and widespread support for the Northern Ireland Assembly and Executive.

Unquestionably, it was the arrest in Colombia, in August 2001, of three members of the Provisional IRA which gave the new US connection to the Troubles a clear focus and direction. The arrests severely damaged the reputation of both political and military wings of the Provisionals. An editorial in the *Washington Post* on 16 August reported that the IRA members detained in Colombia had 'assisted that country's drug-trafficking terrorists in mastering explosives'. The newspaper indicated that Gerry Adams was scheduled to visit Latin America, calling on 'Fidel Castro, a longstanding ally'. Adams had friends in Washington, continued the *Post* editorial, 'but their band is dwindling now'.[20]

Haass visited Dublin and Belfast in early September and seemed newly determined to pressure Sinn Féin and the IRA on weapons decommissioning. His focus on this issue was markedly sharper than it had been in his previous trip to the province in June. Haass's pressure was reinforced by statements from influential Irish-Americans: for instance, Bill Flynn, chairman of the Mutual Bank of America and leading figure in the reconfigured Irish-American lobbies which had supported the Clinton initiatives, warned that corporate donations to Sinn Féin might cease. Flynn told the *Observer* that it 'wasn't just me', that a 'number of executives saw those relationships with the Colombians as devastating. Colombia is a place that peddles drugs into this country.' On the very morning of 11 September, Haass was reported as threatening Adams, in a face-to-face meeting, that visa and US fundraising rights would be withdrawn if the IRA failed to move on arms decommissioning.[21]

11 September and after

With Sinn Féin receiving around $1 million annually in declared donations from the US, Haass's and Flynn's threats were always likely to draw some sort of positive response. As it was, the afternoon of 11 September 2001 saw the demise of the post-Cold War era, the onset of the war on terrorism and a seismic shift in US foreign policy unmatched in scale since Pearl Harbour. Sinn Féin changed its public language on decommissioning almost immediately, and the IRA announced in October that it was prepared at least to begin decommissioning 'to save the peace process and to persuade others of our intentions'.[22] The announcement followed further face-to-face meetings between Haass and Sinn Féin leaders, and a meeting in New York between Martin McGuiness and Bill Flynn.

The most obvious change, unintentionally engineered by the 11 September terrorists for Northern Ireland, involved a new US sense of urgency and alarm regarding terrorism, even in its non-Islamic guise. As Richard Haass declared in early 2002: 'September 11th obviously had a profound change on the people ... and on this administration. If I may borrow a phrase from the War on Drugs, there is "zero tolerance" in this country for terrorism of any sort.'[23] Less than a month after the terrorist attacks, the State Department's co-ordinator for counter-terrorism described to a congressional sub-committee how the IRA was implicated in a 'narcoterrorist' internationalist network involving the Revolutionary Forces of Colombia (FARC) and possibly Basque separatists.[24] Justice Department officials included information about RIRA in testimony concerning loopholes in US immigration procedures.[25] In Senate Judiciary Committee hearings in December 2001, IRA arms acquisition in the US was discussed in the same context as the ability of Islamic extremists to gain access to weapons in America.[26]

Clearly, US tolerance for Irish republican terrorism had decreased sharply in response to the events of 11 September. In April 2002, the House International Relations Committee scheduled hearings on 'international terrorism, its links with illicit drugs as illustrated by the IRA and other groups in Colombia'. The deputy co-ordinator for counter-terrorism testified that he could see no links between the IRA and either al-Qaeda or Hezbollah. Several committee members, however, commented on the IRA's links with Cuba, while Chairman Henry Hyde (Republican) of Illinois, deemed it an 'insult to our intelligence' to accept that the IRA members had been in Colombia for peaceful or 'eco-tourist' purposes. (Gerry Adams wrote a letter to Hyde, denying that there was any terrorist link between FARC and Irish republicans.) The post-11 September mood was well illustrated by the comments of Congressman Peter King (Republican) of New York. King, the author of a novel on the Troubles in Belfast, had for many years been a strong sympathiser with a wide range of Irish republican causes on Capitol Hill. His April 2002 outburst on the IRA–FARC links spoke volumes about the shift in outlook which had taken place since 9/11:

> I think it is important that those in the republican movement and all its manifestations, realize that something like this can never ever be allowed to happen

again. That they are going to be serious players in the Irish peace process. Serious players on the international scene. This has to be ended once and for all ... you're only allowed one mistake in this business.[27]

The Irish dimension of the US post-11 September debate over terrorism landed its participants in some rather predictable tangles. Peter King, unsurprisingly, was prepared to allow that the IRA's Colombian connection was due more to 'negligence' than to complicity in international narcoterrorism; 11 September damaged rather than extinguished the traditional reservoir of pro-IRA sentiment among some Irish-Americans. It was difficult to imagine, however, that Sinn Féin's fundraising would not be severely impaired by the events of August–September 2001; or that, especially younger, Irish-Americans would not find it difficult to see the IRA in anything but a very unfavourable light. The widespread debate over visa waivers, under which some RIRA personnel certainly had entered the US, also pointed up the difficulties of calibrating degrees of terrorism. The administration, in its post-11 September homeland security measures, was keen to send the message that terrorism is a seamless robe. Old adages about the problems of distinguishing 'freedom-fighters' from 'terrorists' were forgotten in the immediate reaction to the 11 September attacks. President Bush's November 2001 Military Order, outlawing and establishing penalties for even unwittingly 'aiding and abetting' terrorism was extremely broad in scope. Although most Americans probably saw it as applying simply to Islamic terrorism, Lawrence Tribe of Harvard Law School argued in December 2001 that the order had the *potential* to pull in 'many supporters of Irish nationalism'. Though enforcement was difficult and unlikely, it seemed in its breadth to cover not only support for RIRA (designated a terrorist organisation) but for the Provisional IRA (certainly if the connection with FARC were established).[28]

Richard Haass found it very difficult to apply the 'with-us-or-against us' Manicheanism of the president's response to 11 September. In his interview with Eamon Dunphy, for example, Ambassador Haass struggled to defend his dialogue and contacts with Sinn Féin and, indeed, with the political representatives of some loyalist paramilitaries. Haass's responses involved an tacit denial of President Bush's absolutist condemnation of terrorism, and appealed to the difficulty of defining the key term: 'What we've made clear is that again we have no tolerance for ongoing terrorism. The groups we deal with are obviously political groups.'[29]

If the most obvious Irish consequences of 11 September was this new (if still not completely unnuanced) US attitude to terrorism, another involved the growing stature in Washington of Tony Blair. It is difficult to recall that, prior to 11 September, Blair was not especially well known or influential in the US capital. He was seen as a Clinton crony, or, as Mark Steyn wrote in February 2001, simply acknowledged 'as the fellow who wants to ban hunting'.[30] By the middle of 2003, following his support for US military action in Afghanistan and Iraq, Blair was due to receive the Congressional Medal of Honour. Washington's new immersion in the war on terrorism was unlikely to involve a radically new prioritisation of Irish issues. However, Washington was also extremely likely to wish to back Blair in his efforts to revive and nurture the peace process. Haass's comments evinced a strong commitment to cross-community even-handedness. In January 2002, he announced – in words which echoed sentiments coming from Downing Street – that a 'new paradigm' existed in Northern Ireland: 'much more complex than the old one of minority discrimination'. Bush's envoy quoted Secretary of State for Northern Ireland John Reid's comment that the province 'must not become a cold place for Protestants'. What was needed, declared Ambassador Haass, was 'a house that is warm for all those who live there'.[31] Conor Murphy, a Sinn Féin member of the Northern Ireland Assembly, was denied a visa in February 2002 to attend a NORAID fundraising event. When devolution faced collapse in October 2002, Haass noticeably toughened his line, criticising both the IRA for its tardiness on decommissioning and Unionist leader David Trimble for setting a deadline to quit power-sharing. In April 2003, Tony Blair succeeded in attracting President Bush to Belfast, primarily to consult on Iraq but also to act on Irish peace, where he presided over an extraordinary mass meeting of Sinn Féin, SDLP, APNI, UUP and PUP leaders.

By April 2003, the US administration was also regularly citing the experience of Northern Ireland as a pointer to progress in the Israeli–Palestinian conflict. In his joint press conference in Belfast with Blair, Bush said that the British leader's agenda for Northern Ireland was 'the same vision we need to have in the Middle East'. The problems of apparently equating the Irish peace process with the moves towards a two-state solution in the Middle East were raised during press conference questioning.[32] It was also pointed out that the Northern Irish peace process had involved compromises and deals with the forces of terrorism. Haass, on 8 April 2003, described the Middle East and Northern Ireland as like 'apples and oranges', but cited the former as a 'tragic reminder of what happens when the boulder gets rolled up the hill, leaders don't seize the opportunity, and then the situation gets worse'.[33]

Conclusion

George W. Bush's administration was happy to identify with a peace process in Northern Ireland which, certainly by international standards, can be judged a major success. The administration's interest in Northern Ireland however was considerably less than that of its predecessor. This was due to a variety of factors: its worldview, generally; the post-11 September preoccupation with Islamic terrorism; the perception that the time for decisive intervention had passed anyway; and the desire to act (at least after 11 September) only on London's approval. Clinton's activism and energetic commitment rapidly assumed the appearance of rare phenomena, distinctly characteristic of the post-Cold War pre-11 September era. A striking indication of the Bush Administration's relative lack of commitment to Irish issues occurred in connection with the president's foreign budget request released in March 2003. The requested amount was $8 million, compared to around $25 million in preceding years. The administration indicated that the cut reflected the decreasing unemployment in Northern Ireland.[34]

The years 2002–3 saw some interesting and important developments in the history of US involvement in the affairs of Northern Ireland. In contrast to the pre-1993 era, the attention of interested parties remained locked on the White House, rather than on Congress and the Irish-American support groups. As in so many other regions, the US hegemon found it difficult to sustain a tone of disengagement, even as Ireland slid down its list of priorities. The reputation of Sinn Féin and the IRA in the USA suffered considerably in the wake of the Colombian arrests, revelations about Sinn Féin links to Cuba and 11 September itself. The suspicion that US presidential activism on Northern Ireland was essentially a vehicle for the interests of the IRA would henceforth be difficult to substantiate. Bush's appointment of Richard Haass, a very high-profile foreign policy operator, was an indication that Washington did favour continued Irish involvement at the highest level. The characteristic hesitancy in criticising Clinton's Irish adventures also illustrated the degree to which the commitment, though certainly diminished, had become bi-partisan. Following 11 September, Washington moved closer to London, and apparently further away from Dublin. The political manoeuvring here, of course, was affected by the geopolitical backwash of the US war on terrorism and the 'axis of evil'. Dublin remained officially neutral in the Iraq war, although – following a parliamentary vote and large anti-war demonstrations – US military aircraft were allowed refuelling rights in the Irish Republic. As we have seen, Bush's absolutist approach to terrorism did raise complications and paradoxes in the case of Northern Ireland. The president's meeting with paramilitary political representatives in Belfast during the Iraq conflict was also replete with irony. Haass was forced to defend apparent double standards towards the forces of terrorism, while Sinn Féin leaders at Hillsborough had to run a gauntlet of their own supporters, who opposed any meeting with the leader of American imperialism.[35] Of the interested Northern Irish parties, Sinn Féin and the SDLP strongly opposed the Iraq war, while David Trimble strongly supported it. America's war on terrorism will no doubt continue to affect the politics of Northern Irish peace in strange and unpredictable ways.

Notes

1 On the Irish-American groups and Congress, see Jack Holland, *The American Connection: US Guns, Money and Influence in Northern Ireland*, rev. edn (Boulder, CO: Roberts Reinhart, 1999); R. J. Thompson and J. R. Randolph, 'Irish-Americans in the American Foreign-Policy-Making Process', in M. E. Ahrari (ed.), *Ethnic Groups and US Foreign Policy* (Westport, CT: Greenwood Press, 1987); A. J. Wilson, *Irish-America and the Ulster Conflict: 1968–1995* (Belfast: Blackstaff Press, 1995).

2 See John Dumbrell, 'The United States and the Northern Irish Conflict, 1969–96: From Indifference to Intervention', *Irish Studies in International Affairs*, vol. 6, 1995, pp. 107–25.

3 Sidney Blumenthal, *The Clinton Wars: An Insider's Account of the White House Years* (London: Viking, 2003), p. 447; see also Conor O'Clery, *The Greening of the White House* (Dublin: Gill & Macmillan, 1996).

4 Raymond Seitz, *Over Here* (London: Weidenfeld & Nicolson, 1998), p. 299.

5 Michael Mates was a Northern Ireland minister under Prime Minister John Major. His remarks on Clinton were published in the *Mail on Sunday*, 25 August 1996.

6 See Michael Cox, 'The War that Came In From the Cold: Clinton and the Irish Question', *World Policy Journal*, vol. 16, no. 1, 1999, pp. 59–67; Adrian Guelke, 'The United States, Irish Americans and the Northern Ireland Peace Process', *International Affairs*, vol. 72, no. 3, 1996, pp. 521–36.

7 See George J. Mitchell, *Making Peace* (London: Heinemann, 1999).

8 See Tim Lavin, 'Yankee Dollar', *Fortnight*, no. 392, February 2001, p. 8.

9 See Jacob Heilbrunn, 'President Gore's Foreign Policy', *World Policy Journal*, vol. 27, no. 2, 2000, pp. 48–55; Bush's remarks come from a transcript of the Jim Lehrer *News Hour* programme, 16 February 2000.

10 Mo Mowlam, *Momentum: The Struggle for Peace, Politics and the People* (London: Coronet Books, 2002), p. 302.

11 Address to the National Committee on American Foreign Policy (NCAFP), 9 January 2002; available at: www.usembassy.org.uk/nil67.html.

12 Sandy Boyer, 'Dubya's Dubious Credentials', *Fortnight*, no. 398, September 2001, p. 7.

13 Address to NCAFP.

14 See R. N. Haass, *Conflicts Unending: The United States and Regional Disputes* (New Haven, CT: Yale University Press, 1990), especially pp. 27–8, 122–37.

15 R. N. Haass, 'Foreign Policy in the Age of Primacy', *Brookings Review*, vol. 18, no. 4, 2000, pp. 2–7 at 7.

16 Address to NCAFP.

17 Quoted in Haass, 'Foreign Policy in the Age of Primacy', p. 7.

18 Interview with Eamon Dunphy, 6 March 2002; available at: www.usembassy.org.uk/nil69.html.

19 *Congressional Record*, 23 October 2001, 510873.

20 'Fidel's Irish Friends', *Washington Post*, 16 August 2001.

21 *Observer*, special report, 'How America Held the IRA Over a Barrel', 28 October 2001.

22 Quoted in *ibid.*, p. 23.

23 Interview with Eamon Dunphy.

24 Testimony of F. X. Taylor to the House of Representatives Committee on International Relations, Sub-committee on the Western Hemisphere, 10 October 2001 (available via LexisNexis).

25 Testimony of G. A. Fine to the Senate Judiciary Committee, Sub-committee on Technology, Terrorism and Government Information, 12 October 2001 (available on LexisNexis).

26 Hearings before the Senate Judiciary Committee, 'The Department of Justice and Terrorism', 6 December 2001 (available on LexisNexis).

27 Hearings before the House of Representatives Committee on International Relations, 'International Terrorism, its Links with Illicit Drugs as Illustrated by the IRA and Other Groups in Colombia', 24 April 2002 (available on LexisNexis).

28 Testimony to the Senate Judiciary Committee, 4 December 2001 (available on LexisNexis).

29 Interview with Eamon Dunphy.

30 Mark Steyn, 'Bomber Blair Goes to Washington', *Spectator*, 24 February 2001, p. 12.

31 Address to NCAFP.

32 Glenn Frankel, 'Bush Sees a Model for Mideast Peace', *Washington Post*, 9 April 2003. David Russell of Democratic Dialogue pointed out that Protestant paramilitaries have flown Israeli flags and that the Provisional IRA has supported the PLO (*ibid.*). 'On the Iraq War', *An Phoblacht: Republican News*, 27 March 2003, attacked the Bush policy as 'unnecessary, unwise and illegal'.

33 'Visit of President Bush to Northern Ireland, April 7–8, 2003', available at: www.usembassy.org.uk/ni.html.

34 See E. D. Henry, 'Byline', *Roll Call*, 13 March 2003.

35 'Iraq and Bush muddy NI loyalties', BBC news, 8 April 2003; available at www.bbc.co.uk/1/hi/northern ireland/2928751.stm.

24

Political comparisons: from Johannesburg to Jerusalem

ADRIAN GUELKE

One of the more striking features of politics in Northern Ireland since the start of the peace process has been the role that comparison with other societies has played in political discourse. Analogies with other places have had a place in the politics of Northern Ireland since the start of the Troubles and even before that during the era of the civil rights movement. However, in the past, comparison, generally speaking, appealed more to nationalists than it did to unionists. Typically, unionists insisted on Northern Ireland's uniqueness and argued that lack of understanding disqualified outsiders from commenting on the political situation. Only after they became opponents of the status quo in the wake of the Anglo-Irish Agreement did this attitude change. The unionists' campaign against that Agreement included comparison of their cause with the battle of Solidarity for trade union recognition in Poland and with the campaign against the Marcos dictatorship in the Philippines.

Use of comparison for polemical purposes is, of course, by no means peculiar to Northern Ireland. Indeed, such political comparison has become so much a part of political discourse that it tends to be taken for granted. When major decisions are about to be made, all manner of analogies are employed to support this or that point of view. To the immense irritation of historians, 'lessons of history' are commonly invoked to lend extra weight to the action being contemplated. The debate in Washington in the summer and autumn of 2002 over whether the USA should go to war over the issue of Iraq, with or without UN authorisation, provides a relatively recent example of the phenomenon. The coincidence of this debate with reflections over the Cuban missile crisis forty years earlier provided a reference point for both doves and hawks. For hawks, President Kennedy's conduct during the crisis could be used to legitimise Bush's stance that Iraq's presumed possession of weapons of mass destruction could not be tolerated, while doves pointed to Kennedy's rejection of a course of pre-emptive military action urged by some in the military.[1]

Political comparison

If political comparison can be used to justify particular courses of action or specific policies, it also plays its part in the prediction of political developments. Thus, ever since George W. Bush's razor-thin victory in the US presidential elections of 2000, the question of whether this would be the start of a trend towards the right in elections across the Western world has been the subject of political commentary. In fact, especially since the attacks on America on 11 September 2001, such a trend seems to have been in evidence so that in the course of 2001 and 2002 left or left of centre governments were voted out of office in Norway, France, Portugal, the Netherlands and Denmark. This run of success for the right ended in September 2002 with the victory of the Social Democratic government in Sweden and, even more significantly, with the re-election by a narrow majority of the Red–Green coalition in Germany in October 2002. The main exception to this trend was the landslide victory of Labour in the UK in June 2001.

Of course, *identifying* a trend is not the same as *explaining* it. There is a considerable divergence in how political commentators and academics approach this issue. A common explanation in journalistic commentary is of voters responding to the choices made elsewhere, copying what others have done or taking their cue, as an article in *The Times* put it in May 2001 in relation to the trend to the right in European elections. That is not an explanation one would be likely to find in any academic journal of comparative politics. There is a methodological reason for this. When countries are compared to measure the impact of particular variables, almost of necessity the assumption is made that what happens in one country does not exercise a significant influence on what happens in the other or vice versa. This is because such influence would undercut treating them as separate cases.

This is by no means the only reason for academic hostility towards political comparison. Another is the wish that tendentious or false analogies ought not to influence political behaviour. Further, scholars tend to dislike the simplification and even distortion of the evidence that may take place when analogies are created between two or more political situations, despite the fact that academics often play a part in establishing the credibility of particular comparisons in the first place. Thus, academics took the lead in the systematic comparison of the conflict in Northern Ireland with those in South Africa and Israel–Palestine. What attracted academic attention was the seeming intractability of the conflicts in the three cases. A difference between the cases in the early years of Northern Ireland's Troubles was that conflict over South Africa and Israel manifested itself principally at the international level. That changed in South Africa as a result of the Soweto uprising of June 1976 and in Israel as result of the first *intifada* in December 1987. A workshop of the European Consortium on Political Research held in Freiburg, West Germany, compared the three cases plus that of Lebanon in 1983. A report on the workshop in a South African newspaper concluded that the crisis of governability in South Africa was not quite as far advanced as in the other cases.[2] A conference devoted to the cases of Northern Ireland, Israel–Palestine and South Africa was held at the initiative of South African academics in 1989 in Bonn, West Germany, one product of which was the book *The Elusive Search for Peace*.[3] A key theme of the book was that what the three cases had in common was the lack of a solution to the political impasse which gripped each of them. Ironically, this conclusion was being overtaken by events as the book was being printed.

The basis of the academic comparison at Bonn was, however, stronger than a quickly falsified assumption as to their future. It was that they were all examples of deeply divided societies with a high potential for inter-communal violence. South Africa seemed to many the most intractable and insoluble of the three cases. Consequently, the very fact that the land of apartheid embraced a peace process in the 1990s, which ultimately culminated in the country's transition to a non-racial democracy in 1994, provided encouragement to the process of change in the other two societies. This positive basis for the comparison dominated Northern Ireland during the 1990s. In the early to mid 1990s the main focus was on the contribution of the South African transition to the Northern Irish peace process. In the late 1990s Northern Ireland's own miracle in the form of the GFA came to be seen as a model for the resolution of conflict in other deeply divided societies, providing the inspiration in particular for peace processes in the Basque Country and in Corsica. Further, despite the difficulties that implementation of the GFA encountered, the example of the settlement in Northern Ireland was seen as particularly relevant also to the continuing quest for peace between Israelis and Palestinians in the Middle East.

The impact of Sharon

That continued to be the case in the first decade of the new millennium. The breakdown of the peace process, following the Camp David summit on a final settlement in July 2000, prompted successive pleas by the British prime minister, both before and after the events of 11 September 2001, for the parties to return to the negotiating table. Blair invoked the example of Northern Ireland as a model for the Israelis and Palestinians to follow. However, in areas of Northern Ireland affected by continuing inter-communal violence a quite different response was prompted by events in the Middle East. This became evident as the last vestige of any peace process appeared to have been destroyed with the launch of the Israeli offensive against Palestinian areas at the end of March 2002. A column in the *Observer* in May 2002 captured the spirit of the response in working-class strongholds of Northern Ireland's paramilitaries:

> Israel has found a new ally in its war against Yasser Arafat and the Palestinian Authority – Johnny Adair's dog. Rebel, Adair's pet Alsatian, has become the latest member of the Ulster loyalist community to display support for Ariel Sharon's assault on the West Bank and Gaza. Last Monday afternoon the UDA commander's four legged friend was seen being taken for a walk along Belfast's Shankill Road with the Star of David flag wrapped around its body. Rebel, a Zionist version

of Superdog with his Israeli flag turned into a cape, was paraded along just days before his master was released from prison.

In UDA redoubts such as the Lower Shankill and Tigers Bay it seems every lamp-post is now festooned with the Jewish State's flag. In response Palestinian flags have been put up in large numbers across Republican strongholds. The INLA in particular has been keen to express support for the PLO and even more extreme forces in the Palestinian controlled areas. 'Victory to Jenin' and 'We support the suicide bombers' are commonplace on the walls of Duncairn Gardens, Newington and Ardoyne.[4]

These reactions need to be seen in the context of increasing violence at Belfast's sectarian interfaces. The unmistakable message on the loyalist side was that loyalists preferred Sharon's war process to Blair's peace process; on the republican side that loyalist actions would elicit an aggressive response from republicans. At a slightly more sophisticated level than the display of Israeli flags unionist politicians reinforced the same point that was being made by the loyalist paramilitaries, by denouncing the Government's failure to treat republican terrorism in the same way it treated international terrorism. At the same time, Blair's advocacy of military action against Iraq put him in a weak position to deny the political efficacy of the use of physical force in dealing with one's enemies.

What significance ought one to attach to the extraordinary display of support for Israel from a community with little historical basis for such sympathy? Indeed, from a historical perspective it could be argued that Zionism had more in common with both Afrikaner nationalism and Irish nationalism than it did with the pro-empire sentiments of the Protestant community in Northern Ireland. However, such reversals of historical sympathies are quite common and by no means indicate that the attitudes currently displayed are not strongly felt. Yet it might still be argued that there has been an element of political opportunism in the current displays of support for Sharon. The point can be illustrated by the fact that when a loyalist neighbourhood of Belfast hosted a visit by supporters of the British National Party, the slogans in support of Israel abruptly disappeared from the walls of that neighbourhood.[5] What the story underlines is the desire of loyalists to cultivate support within the UK from any segment of mainland opinion, no matter how marginal, willing to give it. But it remains the case that in general loyalists find it easier to identify with the situation of Israelis than with the extreme right-wing groups that give them support from time to time.

In the past, the absence of any desire on the part of Israelis to identify with the unionist cause in Northern Ireland has acted as a dampener on the comparison with the Middle East. This has also affected republican identification with the Palestinian cause, in so far as figures such as Yasser Arafat have found it expedient to play the notion of links of any significance between the Palestinians and Irish nationalism in its militant forms. The factor that has given added impetus to the comparison among loyalists in 2002 is the link to 11 September and the war against terrorism. In the immediate aftermath of 11 September, there had been speculation that Sharon would come under US pressure to enter into negotiations with the Palestinian Authority. That prompted Sharon's 'We will not be Czechoslovakia' speech. Another dimension of Israel's response was a poster that presented Osama bin Laden and Yasser Arafat as twins.[6] This proved effective. The difficulty of justifying to US opinion a different attitude towards suicide bombers in Israel to that adopted towards al-Qaeda carried the day. The Bush Administration made no effort to put pressure on Sharon and reserved its criticism for the beleaguered and increasingly powerless figure of Arafat.

The sight of Sharon discarding the Oslo peace process with its principle of land for peace by presenting the Israeli Government as being engaged in a war of survival against the forces of international terrorism presented a vision attractive to unionists seeking to overturn the GFA. Anti-GFA unionists had at the outset denounced it as constituting nothing less than appeasement of terrorism. In the context of the settlement of a number of regional conflicts in the aftermath of the Cold War, that language had seemed dated. In the wake of the attacks on the USA it acquired a new lease of life. The Israeli Government was not alone in seeking to exploit the new mood. The Spanish Government of Aznar sought to capitalise on the post-11 September climate of opinion in its approach to the continuation of the conflict in the Basque conflict following the collapse of the region's short-lived peace process in the late 1990s. So too did the new Government in Colombia in the wake of the collapse of that country's peace process. Both situations had relevance to the Northern Irish peace process because of links between Colombian and Basque militants with the Provisional IRA.

South Africa and Ireland

The plethora of Israeli and Palestinian flags across Belfast overshadowed the comparison that had dominated the peace process prior to 2002, that of South Africa. As in the case of Israel–Palestine, the comparison went back to a time when the lines of sympathy were very different from what they are today. At the start of the twentieth century, it had been Irish nationalism and Afrikaner nationalism that had been paired as engaged in a similar struggle against British imperialism. The appeal of the comparison was sufficiently potent to inspire both Irish nationalists and Irish-American sympathisers to volunteer to fight on the Boer side in the Anglo-Boer War of 1899–1902.[7] Even more significant was the role that the comparison played after the war. In February 1906 Boer War General, Jan Christiaan Smuts had a meeting in London with Sir Henry Campbell-Bannerman who had become prime minister in December 1905 and whose Liberal Party had just won the ensuing general election by a landslide.

Smuts wrote the following in his diary about the meeting: 'I put a simple case before him that night in Downing Street. It was in substance: Do you want friends or enemies?' Smuts set out the advantages of friendship and warned the prime minister that the alternative was 'possibly to have another Ireland on your hands'.

Smuts's appeal worked. 'That talk', the diary entry concluded, 'settled the future of South Africa.'[8] In the immediate aftermath of Smuts's visit, the British Government agreed to the granting of self-government to the Transvaal and the Orange River Colony on the basis of the same whites-only franchise that had been in operation in the defeated Boer Republics. This effectively paved the way for the creation of the Union of South Africa under white minority rule. Smuts's threat of another Ireland would hardly have possessed the potency it did if the analogy had not already been widely prevalent. Smuts repaid his debt to the British Government by acting as an intermediary between the British Government and Irish nationalists, while urging the latter to accept dominion status. He also wrote the conciliatory speech delivered by King George V on the opening of the Northern Ireland parliament in June 1921.

The reversal in the lines of sympathy between Afrikaner and Irish nationalism occurred in the 1960s, an episode in 1960 providing a bridge between the two eras. In that year the Conservative Government planned to hold exhibitions across the UK to celebrate the existence of the British Commonwealth. The Government wanted the South African high commissioner to open the Belfast exhibition, but the Unionist Government refused to give its consent. Unionist hostility towards hosting the South African envoy derived, in part, from memories of the Anglo-Boer War and, in part, from the determination of the Verwoerd Government to hold a referendum to turn South Africa into a republic. However, one of the younger unionist ministers struck an altogether different note. Faulkner stated his objection as follows: 'The word "apartheid" had already been maliciously applied to conditions in Northern Ireland. Some sections of the national press might mischievously use the South African association with the Belfast Exhibition to make misleading and damaging comments.'[9] Faulkner's words proved prophetic.

A landmark in the development of the comparison as part of nationalist political rhetoric within Northern Ireland was a speech made in 1963 in the South African Parliament by Minister of Justice B. J. Vorster. Vorster offered to exchange the Bill he was presenting to parliament for one clause of the Northern Ireland Special Powers Act. The opposition, drawing most of its support from English-speakers, had criticised the powers in the Bill as draconian and unprecedented in a Western liberal democracy. The speech got picked up by the civil rights movement in Northern Ireland which was campaigning to get rid of the Special Powers Act. Thus civil rights leaders were able to claim that the Act was the envy of the fascist Government in South Africa. In short, the comparison was being used for very different purposes in the two societies. However, Vorster's use of the comparison was not especially significant. Another comparison held sway in South Africa in the 1960s, and it was 'Look what happened in the Congo'. This became the rallying cry of whites throughout Southern Africa in their effective opposition to African majority rule.

Thus, whereas at the start of the 1960s it had seemed inevitable that majority rule would engulf Southern Africa, by the 1970s, particularly in South Africa, the only prospect for political change seemed to lie in finding an alternative to majority rule. It was in this context that first the white opposition and then the Government itself discovered the writings of Arend Lijphart. Lijphart's theory of consociation-alism seemed to offer the possibility of democracy without majority rule. Further it seemed especially justifiable in a divided society. Consociationalism provided the basis for comparing South Africa with societies outside of Africa, including Northern Ireland. Northern Ireland was especially attractive for the purpose of comparison. Consociationalism was widely seen outside of Northern Ireland as the only realistic basis for creating stable government in Northern Ireland.

In 1985 the South African Ambassador to London Denis Worrall made an extra-ordinary visit to Belfast. APNI and the SDLP refused to see him. The unionists, who did meet him, criticised APNI and the SDLP for supporting majority rule in South Africa but not in Northern Ireland. The extraordinary denouement of the visit was a press conference the ambassador gave at the end of his visit in which he declared: 'Northern Ireland and South Africa are examples of societies in which majority rule cannot work.' He also revealed that he had sought a meeting with Sinn Féin.[10] Ultimately the National Party's hopes for a consociational settlement in South Africa were to be dashed, though Joe Slovo's sunset clauses helped to sugar the pill of majority rule.

Republicans in Ireland arrived at the comparison with South Africa by a very different route. In the mid-1970s the republican movement abandoned its expecta-tion that just one more push would persuade the British to withdraw, and it adopted what it called 'the long war' strategy: the war was going to have to go on until the middle of the twenty-first century, if necessary. In this context the sustainability of the armed struggle in the long run became more important than the amount of violence at any one time. However, justifying violence became more difficult. This is where comparisons with other places came in, and two of them proved especially attractive to the republican movement – the comparison of the IRA with the African Nationalist Congress (ANC) and with the PLO.

Peace processes and comparison

One might have thought that the initiation of peace processes in the 1990s would have undercut these analogies. On the contrary, those processes reinforced the use of the two comparisons as they became the basis for legitimising the republican movement's adoption of a peace strategy. To a degree, the analogies themselves forced the republican hand. After February 1990 in South Africa and the release of Mandela, and after September 1993 and the handshake on the White House lawn between Arafat and Rabin, the inevitable question of journalists to Gerry Adams was: 'Where is your peace process?' After the British and Irish governments launched their peace initiative with the Joint Declaration of December 1993, the two governments pressed the case for a positive response from the republican movement by emphasising the analogies.

For a variety of reasons, the South African analogy gradually became the principal one used by republicans. The most important of these reasons was the much weaker political position of the Palestinians compared to that of the black majority in South Africa. That made the former comparison much less attractive to Sinn Féin leaders seeking to convince their followers that participation in the peace process was not tantamount to defeat. Another reason was the lesser interest in Northern Ireland of the Middle East. Thus, Israelis, whether supporters or opponents of the Oslo process, had little reason to identify with the unionists in Northern Ireland. By contrast, South Africans showed considerable interest in both the peace process in Northern Ireland and the use of South Africa as a model for political progress. Thus, the IRA ceasefire was greeted with the banner headline 'IRA Takes SA Option' in the country's leading evening newspaper, *The Star*.[11]

The use of the South African analogy put the peace process in the context of the republican movement's conception of the conflict in anti-colonial terms. The ANC was flattered by the comparison and has provided support for Sinn Féin through different stages of the process. Gerry Adams visited South Africa in 1995 at the invitation of the ANC. In 1997 after the breakdown of the peace process in 1996 the South African Government invited all the parties to a conference on the lessons of South Africa's transition. The purpose was to assist the leadership of the republican movement to secure a renewal of the IRA ceasefire, and thereby to facilitate a resumption of the negotiations among the parties on a political settlement. When the GFA was reached in 1998, leading members of the ANC were on hand to help Sinn Féin leaders in persuading their followers to take a positive view of the deal. After suspension of the Northern Ireland Executive in February 2000, South African intermediaries were credited with convincing the IRA of the need to open up arms dumps to international inspectors, including the ANC's chief negotiator during the South African transition, Cyril Ramaphosa. Following the further suspension of the executive in October 2002, Martin Ferris, Sinn Féin TD for North Kerry, briefed ANC leaders on the difficulties in the peace process on a visit to Cape Town in December 2002.

However, the ANC's continuing engagement with the peace process in Northern Ireland does not mean that the outcome in either South Africa or Northern Ireland has been what the parties who initiated the comparison of the two cases have sought. In fact, the irony of the outcomes is striking. The National Party in South Africa looked to Northern Ireland to get a consociational outcome, but what it in fact got, after a brief transitionary period, was majority rule. By contrast, the republican movement in Ireland looked to South Africa to get an anti-colonial outcome and what it got was the consociational settlement of the GFA. However, the consequences of the comparisons for the parties that promoted them have been very different. The National Party fared well in the general election of 1994. However, as the New National Party it lost two-thirds of its vote in the general election of 1999. After an abortive merger with the Democratic Party in 2000, it has survived as a very junior partner of the ANC. By contrast, Sinn Féin has flourished as political party both in Northern Ireland and in the Republic of Ireland.

The differing consequences for the parties can be seen as a reflection of the different nature of the outcomes in the two cases. The South African transition resulted in a new dispensation that to all intents and purposes is irreversible, so that whatever the future holds for the country it is extremely unlikely to involve the restoration of the political power of the white minority. By contrast, the future both of the GFA and of Northern Ireland as a polity remains uncertain. However, just as the South African miracle provided inspiration to people engaged in peace processes in other conflicts, including that in Northern Ireland, the GFA has provided inspiration for other peace processes, including processes initiated or proposed in the Basque Country, Corsica, Kashmir and Sri Lanka and this despite its own fragility. As the breakdown of the Basque process has, however, underlined, imitation has by no means assured success.

Conclusion

Imitation is difficult to get to grips with analytically but its importance in political discourse is obvious and that provides at least a starting-point for examining its hold. At times people will insist that the conflict in their country is unique; at other times there may be a greater openness to comparison, and of course different communities within a society may have different responses to this issue. In peace processes comparisons tend to be particularly important for a number of reasons. Firstly, there is a widespread perception of the need to legitimise new arrangements, new institutions, new processes of decision-making, and comparison assists in this. Secondly, comparison can provide an overarching framework for viewing the changes necessary to the success of the process. Thirdly, comparison may provide reassurance that a successful outcome to a process of difficult negotiations is possible. Fourthly, in almost all peace processes it is vital to secure external support; consequently, meeting international standards looms large in such situations: models of what the international community considers legitimate inevitably matter.

It is also important to recognise that failed peace processes can provide the basis for a negative set of lessons. These are that appeasement is a foolish policy, that the demands of the other side are impossible to meet and that measures adopted to promote the peace process tend to enhance insecurity if the process breaks down. On the basis of the climate of international opinion after the events of 11 September 2001, it might seem likely that it is the latter, negative, set of lessons that will be seen by the parties to the process as most relevant to the situation in Northern Ireland. Such a conclusion would seem to fit in with the displacement of South Africa by Israel–Palestine as the main focus of comparison in 2002. The existence of a war against terrorism is quite obviously not the ideal backdrop for the conduct of peace processes. Further wars demonstrating the potency of military force as an instrument of political power are unlikely to discourage belief in political violence as an effective political instrument.

It would be wrong, however, to suggest that the consequences of war are necessarily and inevitably negative in all situations. Developments that run against the grain of events elsewhere are possible and indeed have been demonstrated by the progress of the Sri Lankan peace process after 11 September 2001. Thus, with regard to Northern Ireland, one can make a case that in the short term, at least, 11 September gave a boost to the peace process because it put overwhelming pressure on the IRA to start the process of decommissioning on 23 October 2001. But the benefit to the peace process did not prove long-lasting as fresh areas of difficulty arose in the peace process. Though these are not directly related to 11 September, their impact has been affected by the new climate of opinion, so reversing the initially positive impact of 11 September on the peace process. That effect has undoubtedly been compounded by the decision of Prime Minister Tony Blair to prioritise his role on the world stage over securing the success of the GFA.

In fairness to Blair, in the course of 2003 he did attempt to reclaim a positive basis for comparison between Northern Ireland and the Middle East. As President Clinton had been fond of doing when he was in office, Blair suggested that the relative success of the Northern Irish peace process provided a model for Israelis and Palestinians to follow. President Bush's visit to Northern Ireland, primarily for the purpose of a war summit on Iraq, created the occasion for Tony Blair both to reiterate the comparison and to secure President Bush's endorsement of it. Bush declared:

> Prime Minister Blair and I are committed to implementing the road map toward peace, to bring closer the day when two states – Israel and Palestine – live in peace and stability. Peace in the Middle East will require overcoming deep divisions of history and religion. Yet we know this is possible; it is happening in Northern Ireland.[12]

The impact of this attempt to relaunch the Israeli–Palestinian peace process was, however, slight. It was not helped by the fact that a settlement of the difficulties in the Northern Irish process that Blair had hoped to announce in the same week did not materialise.

Notes

1 See, for example, Joseph Nye, 'Owls Are Wiser About Iraq Than Hawks', *Financial Times*, 21 October 2002.
2 'There's a Pretty Long Fuse on South Africa's Ticking Time Bomb', *Sunday Times* (Johannesburg), 17 April 1983.
3 Hermann Giliomee and Jannie Gagiano (eds), *The Elusive Search for Peace: South Africa, Israel and Northern Ireland* (Cape Town: Oxford University Press, 1990).
4 Henry McDonald, 'Rebel With a Confused Cause', *Observer*, 19 May 2002.
5 Ciaran Barnes, 'Israeli Flags Taken Down for Fascist Visit to the Village', *Andersonstown News*, 11 November 2002.
6 A photograph of the poster was published in the *Irish Times*, 4 October 2001.
7 See Donal P. McCracken, *The Irish Pro-Boers, 1877–1902* (Johannesburg: Perskor, 1989).
8 Quoted in W. K.Hancock, *Smuts: The Sanguine Years, 1870–1919* (Cambridge: Cambridge University Press, 1962), p. 215.
9 Quoted in Bryan A. Follis, 'Friend or Foe? Ulster Unionists and Afrikaner Nationalists', *Southern African-Irish Studies*, vol. 3, 1996, p. 172.
10 Worrall's visit is described in the *Irish Times* and the *Belfast Telegraph*, 11, 12 and 13 April 1985.
11 *Star* (Johannesburg), 1 September 1994.
12 *Irish Times*, 9 April 2003.

25

Learning from other places: Northern Ireland, the Basque Country and Corsica

FRANCESCO LETAMENDIA AND JOHN LOUGHLIN

Of all the cases of violent conflict that have arisen in Western Europe over the past 4 decades, 3 regions stand out by reason of the longevity and degree of political organisation of the armed groups involved and their challenge to the traditional nation state: Northern Ireland, the Basque Country and Corsica. Today, each of these regions is lurching towards some kind of peace settlement, although in all three the obstacles to its obtainment are formidable. The Northern Ireland case is the most advanced; Corsica is still on the way; while the Basque Country seems to have taken several steps backward with the collapse of the ETA (*Euskadi ta Askatasuna* – Basque for 'Freedom') ceasefire at the end of 1999.

The three cases are very different in many respects: the historical origins of the conflict, the issues at stake, the composition and political orientations of the regional populations, and even the degree of organisation (or disorganisation) of the armed groups all vary considerably. Nevertheless, all three illustrate the problems associated with a notion of the nation state whereby this is supposed to integrate minority groups into the national system and to exercise absolute sovereignty over every piece of its territory. The existence and activities of the IRA, ETA and the FLNC (*Front de Libération nationale de la Corse*), in their various manifestations and guises, demonstrate the limitations of these supposed attributes of nation states. Each of these movements challenges the legitimacy of the state to exercise a complete monopoly over the means of violence. In all three cases, the groups have gone through a historical development, in more or less the same period, during which they passed from regionalism or federalism to a position of adopting the unitary state as their final goal. Thus, all three movements have, in the past, defined their objectives in terms reminiscent of the stato-nationalism of the state which they oppose: each sought a nation state independent of the state in which it is included (or from which it felt excluded). This development involved in the three regions a use of Marxist ideology sometimes consciously borrowed from Third World liberation movements in the 1960s and 1970s, sometimes drawing on internal colonialism analyses. Each of the movements has managed to garner sufficient support from the local population, although varying considerably from case to case, to continue in existence over a long period of time and to ensure that, at least in these territories, the writ of the state did not run completely smoothly. Furthermore, each of the three movements exercised a kind of negative veto over attempts to pacify the region and, in this way, swayed the public and political agendas in its area. Finally, the armed movements in each region have, over the past several years, declared a willingness to seek a non-violent approach to achieving their objectives, through a process of dialogue and alliance with other political forces.[1]

It is clear that these developments coincide with changes at the level of the nation state itself.[2] Globalisation, Europeanisation, the application of 'new public management' approaches to public administration systems and the emergence of sub-national authorities as policy actors in their own right have all considerably altered the nature and significance of nation states, at least in Western industrialised countries.

It is outside the scope of this chapter to go into these changes in detail but one of the more important consequences has been the decoupling of the concept of *nation* and *state* that was developed at the time of the French Revolution and has been the basis of modern liberal democratic systems ever since. This concept postulated that nations ought to have states and states ought to be co-terminous with nations, and has underlain nationalist mobilisation right up to the present day. Irish, Basque and Corsican nationalisms, at least in their more extreme separatist manifestations, as represented by the IRA, ETA and the FLNC, have also been driven by this desire to gain (or recover) a state appropriate to each of their *nations*. However, if, today, the concept of the *nation state* itself is being called into question, then this quest has become less meaningful.

Nationalist movements are being forced therefore to reformulate anew their basic ideological concepts – *nation, sovereignty, self-determination*, etc. – as well as their strategy and tactics. This is most strikingly illustrated in the Northern Ireland case, where a strategy of dialogue among nationalists (SDLP, Sinn Féin and Fianna Fáil) coincided with a process of devolution in the UK that made a real breakthrough possible. UK devolution itself was made possible both by new ways of thinking about the state and by the new context of European integration which the reformers have embraced with much more enthusiasm than any previous British government. These developments have rippled across Europe and have influenced both the Basque Country and Corsica. There is not a direct causal link between the Irish peace process and these two regions. However, Ireland has provided a boost and an example to already existing political forces seeking a new way of resolving their conflicts. This chapter outlines the main features of these situations of conflict and the recent moves towards peace, while emphasing that the peace processes in these countries are far from solidified and there is still plenty of scope for the continuation of violence.

The Basque problem

The Basques are an ancient people with a unique language, occupying a territory at the western end of the Pyrénées straddling the French and Spanish border, so that there are, in fact, two parts to the Basque Country.[3] Most of the violence has taken place in the south, although there have been some violent groups in the north,[4] and militants from the south have used the north as a refuge and a base for conducting military operations in the Spanish State. The southern Basque Country is, however, divided politically and administratively between the Autonomous Community (AC) of the Basque Country and the Autonomous Community of Navarre which nationalists claim as part of their territory. The Basques in Spain, as a people occupying the border with France, have had, since the Middle Ages, privileges known as the *forals*, or the right to a certain fiscal independence, which lasted into the modern period but were abolished by the Franco regime.

The Basques thus developed a strong sense of identity based on their linguistic uniqueness, the mystery surrounding their origins and their special position within the medieval Spanish monarchies.[5] At the end of the nineteenth century, they differentiated themselves from the rest of Spain because of their high degree of industrialisation. This attracted Spanish immigrants who settled in the cities, joining socialist and trades union movements, while traditional Basque society was faithful to the Catholic Church.[6] This dichotomy worried early Basque nationalists such as Sabino Arana, the founder of the Basque Nationalist Party (*Partido Nacionalista Vasco* – PNV) in 1896, who formulated the early doctrine of Basque nationalism in terms more racist than linguistic or cultural and was quite opposed to this intermingling. Fortunately, this aspect of Arana's doctrine was quietly abandoned by later nationalists.[7] Nevertheless, Basque nationalism offers an interesting contrast to Catalonia where the emphasis is much more on culture and language as identity markers.[8]

During the Spanish Civil War, the majority of Basques of all political tendencies opposed Franco.[9] In the 1960s, the PNV re-emerged but some members of its youth wing founded ETA in 1959. ETA was a coalition of different groups, some of which emphasised political actions, while others were more inclined to military action. We can thus distinguish three political blocs in the Basque Country at the time of the transition to democracy (1976–78):

- a moderate nationalist bloc represented by PNV;
- a radical nationalist bloc represented by the various groups emanating from ETA such as *Herri Batasuna* (Popular Unit – HB), created in early 1978; and
- a pro-Spanish bloc, represented by the Spanish political parties such as the Spanish Socialist Workers' Party (*Partido Socialista Obrero Español* – PSOE, or Socialists) or the Right-wing parties such as the UCD (now defunct) and the Popular Alliance (*Alianza Popular* – AP) which would later become the Popular Party (*Partido Popular* – PP), and attracting supporters either from the working-class constituencies of non-Basque origin[10] or from some sections of the industrial and financial bourgeoisie.

The moderate nationalists of the PNV have ruled the Basque Autonomous Community since its inception in 1980, sometimes alone, sometimes in coalition with the Basque Socialist Party (*Partido Socialista de Euskadi* – PSE–PSOE). Most Basque nationalists, however, are unenthusiastic about the 1978 constitutional settlement which, in their eyes, divided the southern Basque Country by creating two distinct Communities and did not go far enough in recognising its national character. Another source of dissatisfaction has been the failure to implement fully the *foral* laws which would allow the Basques to gain control over their fiscal and tax regimes.[11] Basques feel that they pay too much to the central Government to subsidise the southern Spanish ACs.[12] Even more intense has been the conflict between PNV and the various radical nationalist groups clustering around ETA and HB. But radical nationalists have also been bitterly divided into different factions.[13]

The radical nationalists succeeded throughout the 1980s in shaping the political agenda of the Basque Country and, to some extent, of Spain itself.[14] This provoked a repressive response from the Spanish State which sometimes used its own anti-terrorist organisations of dubious legality, such as the Anti-Terrorist Liberation Groups (*Grupos Antiterroristas de Liberación* – GAL), responsible for more than twenty-five deaths.[15] By the mid-1990s, however, ETA was in a position similar to that reached by the Provisional IRA in the mid-1980s – it could only disrupt the system but could not achieve a positive outcome for any of its declared aims. In order words, it could not go forward politicially, but neither could it abandon the armed struggle. This was especially important as there were a considerable number of prisoners in different parts of Spain outside the Basque Country, and to give up the armed struggle would have seemed like abandoning them. Nevertheless, by the 1990s, it was clear to many Basques that nationalists needed to go beyond the armed struggle.

Richard Gillespie lists six factors which led to the 1998 ceasefire:

- political setbacks experienced by ETA and HB;
- decline in ETA's military capacity with more members in prison than active outside;
- isolation of the militarists from the mainstream of Basque society;
- generational change in which younger militants were less convinced by the old Marxist discourse;
- the changing international context, especially Europe and the Irish peace process; and, finally,
- developments within Basque nationalism as a whole.

This author also points to the influence of the Irish peace process and the close links between Sinn Fein and HB which encouraged the latter to follow a similar path.[16]

The Basque peace process

The peace process began with a series of developments originating from within the moderate nationalist movement. In 1988, the parties represented in the Basque parliament, PNV, PP and PSOE, but excluding HB, signed the *Pacto de Ajuria-Enea* (henceforth – the Pact), which had two aims: to oppose both ETA violence and the radical nationalism of HB; and to create the conditions that would permit the full implementation of the Basque Country's statute with the transfer of more competences from the centre.

To achieve the first aim, the Pact's signatories sought the co-ordination of extant peace movements opposed to ETA violence, such as *Gesto por la Paz* (Association for Peace – close to the PNV) and the creation of new ones. The traditional pacifist groups rejected ETA as a partner in political negotiations since renouncing violence was a prerequisite to finding a solution. In 1992, however, the *Elkarri* movement, made up of environmentalist groups close to radical nationalism, and describing itself as the 'Social Movement for Dialogue and Agreement in the Basque Country' (*Movimento Social por el Diálogo y el Acuerdo en Euskal Herria*), came into existence. It sought to overcome the multiple cleavages within the Basque Country through dialogue involving all the protagonists.[17]

After an initial hostile reception from the pacifist organisations involved in the Pact, contacts between the two movements developed in the 1990s. From 1993, PNV, like its coalition partner EA (*Eusko Alkartasuna* – Basque Solidarity), was embarrassed by the use of the Pact by PP and PSOE simply to pressure radical nationalists and not for completing the transfer of competences promised by the Basque statute of 1979. Gesto por la Paz shared the PNV's disappointment and moved closer to Elkarri. Then, in 1994, the revelation of the activities of the GAL, brought Elkarri and Gesto por la Paz closer together and they began to collaborate on concrete initiatives.

PNV initiated its own, distinct, peace process, involving a rapprochement with HB through a 'dialogue without limits' to find a solution to the Basque conflict. PNV's position was made known at a Peace Conference in 1995: the Basque problem was a political one; PNV was ready to engage in a dialogue with ETA; it would support a reform of the Spanish constitution recognising the right of self-determination; and, finally, this should lead to sovereignty and thence to peace. Constitutional Basque nationalists modelled this approach overtly on both the Downing Street Declaration and the dialogue between SDLP and Sinn Fein. Alongside this rapprochement between moderate and radical nationalists was a series of actions by two Basque trade unions – ELA (ELA-STV, *Solidaridad de Trabajadores Vascos* – Basque Workers' Solidarity) and LAB (*Laugile Abertzalean Batzordeak* – Nationalist Workers' Union), close to radical nationalism.[18] In early 1995 ETA published *Alternativa Democrática*, which took account of these developments and advocated a new approach from one of dialogue between ETA and the Spanish State, to one that would give a voice to ordinary citizens and other social and political forces within the Basque Country, while insisting that the State recognise the right of self-determination and the entire territory of the Basque people.

Despite these burgeoning peace movements within the heart of radical nationalism, the latter remained deeply divided for a further three years. While HB attended Elkarri's Peace Conference in 1995, increasingly indiscriminate military actions on the part of ETA led to increased tension between HB and Basque society. ETA, hounded by the Spanish and French police after the arrest of its leadership in Bidart, in the French Basque Country, intensified the armed struggle attacking both Basque and Spanish politicians. PP representatives in the Basque Country were assassinated in retaliation for the prisons policy of the PP Government in Madrid after its election in 1996. These actions set off alarm bells among constitutional nationalists who feared they would lessen their capacity to influence the further implementation of the Basque statute. At this point, the *lehendakari* (president of the Basque Government) José Antonio, denounced 'the political bartering' through which the parties in power in Madrid exchanged support in the Spanish Parliament for the transfer of a few powers, and the 'political prejudices' of those parties in favour of a symmetrical and homogenous state.[19] In October 1997, ELA organised a meeting in Guernica attended by the leading figures of all the Basque nationalist parties, during which its secretary, General Elorrieta, while criticising the ongoing campaign of ETA, announced that 'the Statute [of the Basque Country] was now dead'.

In 1998, discussions continued among the nationalist parties and, in September of that year, the Declaration of Lizarra was signed by PNV, EA, HB and *Ezker Batua* (Basque branch of the Spanish coalition *Izquierda Unida*, or United Left, led by the Communist Party), by ELA and LAB, and by social movements such as Elkarri and *Bakea Orain* (*Paz Ahora*, or Peace Now – a pacifist organisation).[20] The declaration was signed partly under the influence of the Belfast GFA and, indeed, the meeting was known as the 'Irish Forum'.[21] Even if the central State and the centralist political parties become entrenched in immobilism, it was felt that Basque political and social actors should build their own national consensus. An indefinite ceasefire should be the beginning and not the end of the peace process. The declaration invited all the interested parties, including the Madrid Government, to participate in the agreement, though their presence was not an essential precondition to begin the process. The Declaration of Lizarra recognised the existence of a political conflict between the Basque Country and the Spanish State involving unresolved questions of territory, decision-making and sovereignty. It laid out a negotiation process open to all actors in conjunction with Basque society. Following an initial phase of multi-lateral discussions without preconditions, there would be a final phase of negotiation which would tackle the reasons for the conflict. However, these negotiations could happen only following a complete and permanent cessation of violence. This should lead to a resolution of the conflict without any imposition or coercion which would respect the *pluralism* of Basque society and treat all political positions on the basis of equality. The Spanish and French governments were asked to respect the declaration, which envisaged not definitive and closed scenarios but an open and innovative approach.

In the AC elections in October 1998 and the municipal (local) elections in the spring of 1999, the parties which had signed the declaration triumphed;[22] in the Basque AC elections, they won 65 per cent of the vote and, if Navarra is included, the entire southern Basque Country (that is, in Spain), this comes to 55 per cent. HB, which had stood under the name *Euskal Herritarrok* (Basque Citizens), saw a spectacular increase of over 30 per cent in the numbers voting for them.

At the end of 1998, the Spanish Parliament unanimously approved a resolution which requested the PP Government to modify its policies towards Basque prisoners. With the formation of a Basque Government consisting solely of a coalition between PNV and EA, Basque radical nationalists had, for the first time, to take on responsibilities within the political system and to subscribe to a programme of government with the governing parties. Doubtless, the peace process in the Basque Country was unlike what had happened in Northern Ireland. The Spanish right-wing Government, fearful of the questioning of national sovereignty which the Declaration of Lizarra implied, adopted an immobilist position, and were supported in this by the opposition Spanish Socialist Party, which shared the same fears. It ignored the massive street demonstrations in the Basque Country at the beginning of the year in favour of the declaration. It dragged its heels on the moving of prisoners closer to the Basque Country. The PP Government declared that it would not pay any price for peace, which really meant that it refused to discuss any change in a political model clearly opposed by a majority of Basques. The French Socialist Government, which regarded with suspicion the demand for a unified Basque *département* in the French part of the Basque Country, shared Spain's obstructionist attitude. French Minister of the Interior Jean-Pierre Chevènement continued to collaborate with the Spanish police in arresting ETA militants as if the latter had not declared a ceasefire. Those arrested included a woman who had taken part in the only meeting between ETA and the Spanish Government in Switzerland in May 1999.

The intransigent centralism of the Spanish authorities is reminiscent of the attitude of John Major's Government during the first IRA ceasefire of 1994 and, like this, has contributed directly to the breakdown of ETA's ceasefire in December 1999. It has also irritated the Basque Government and certainly slowed down the peace process. This casts a shadow over the future and whether there can be a negotiated solution to the Basque problem. Groups of young radicals who are sympathisers but not members of ETA have carried on a low-level campaign of violence against public buildings and property belonging to Socialist and PP activists. The Spanish and French police have also intercepted, at the end of 1999 and the beginning of 2000, several large car-bombs primed and ready to explode. On the political level, Euskal Herritarrok took a decision, in contrast to the other signatories of the Pact, not to stand for the Spanish general elections which took place in 2000 – one of their assumptions being that the GFA model of multi-lateral negotiations was not viable.

In November 1999, ETA announced the end of its ceasefire. All the Basque political organisations, except HB, denounced the new situation as contrary to the spirit of the Declaration of Lizarra. The reasons alleged by ETA gave rise to surprise and concern among the radical nationalists. According to ETA, the reason for the breaking of the ceasefire was not the stubbornness of the Spanish Government, but the failure of PNV and EA to comply with the agreements that these parties had previously concluded with ETA. These had promised to break all links with the Spanish parties and a commitment to make nationalist unity the driving force behind Basque sovereignty, calling for single-constituency elections to be held in the whole of Euskal Herria. The other Basque nationalist parties denied having signed these agreements.

In the six months that followed the breakdown of the ceasefire, ETA killed four people: a member of the Spanish Army; the Basque socialist leader Fernado Buesa and his police escort, and an intellectual, who was also a member of the Forum of Ermua, an organisation which stood against the Declaration of Lizarra. As a result of these attacks, the Basque governmental parties, PNV and EA, broke off their political agreement with Euskal Herritarrok. Since then, the dynamics of Lizarra and nationalist unity have been seriously affected, and there has been little movement on bringing Basque prisoners closer to the Basque Country. In Spain as a whole, support for the immobilist position of PP, has grown in public opinion which has laid the responsibility for what happened firmly on the camp of moderate Basque nationalism. For the first time in the history of the Spanish political transition, a central government has managed to mobilise the police, politicians and media resources to condemn Basque radical nationalism as responsible for those deaths, and the nationalist parties, and PNV and EA, along with the Autonomous Government presided over by them, as their moral accomplices. This was one of the factors that led to the triumph, by an absolute majority, of PP in the general elections of March 2000. PP's hopes that constant undermining of the Basque nationalist Government, will force early elections in the Autonomous Community that can make the current Spanish home secretary, the Basque politician Mayor Oreja, the next *lehendakari* of the Basque Government.

Nevertheless, not everything is negative in the Basque peace process. In the spring of 2000, there developed for the first time in the heart of the radical nationalist movement an organised current against street-fighting and ETA's armed struggle. Recently, reports have appeared of further conversations between PNV and EA, on one side, and Euskal Herrtarrok, on the other, aimed at restoring the circumstances that gave rise to ETA's ceasefire in September of 1998. These reports have sparked off a new wave of accusations by the central Government against the supposed co-existence between the Basque governmental parties and ETA. The PSOE, finally, although with differences between Spanish and Basque Socialists, and within the Basque Socialist Party, as well, has of late jumped off PP's bandwagon and has proposed an open dialogue without exclusions of interlocutor parties.

The Corsican problem

Corsica's position in the French State differs radically from either Northern Ireland or the Basque Country. It is an island in the western Mediterranean and was a colony of the city state of Genoa for several centuries. It came under French control in 1769 following a forty-year revolt by Corsicans. During the second half of this revolt (1749–69), Corsicans, led by Pascal Paoli, set up an embryonic democratic republic whose constitution was inspired by Jean-Jacques Rousseau. The French monarchy intervened at the request of the Genoese and quelled the revolt. The Genoese then *leased* the island to France, but Corsica became fully French at the Revolution when most Corsicans expressed a desire to be fully incorporated into the French State rather than return to Genoese rule. However, Corsican culture, language and society owed more to Italy than to France. Even as late as the nineteenth century, many mayors of villages conducted their official business in Italian while the spoken language of the people was Corsican, closely related to Tuscan Italian. There were, in fact, two Corsicas: the Corsica of the towns built – mostly by the Genoese[23] – around the coast-line and the village Corsica of the interior, and they reflected two kinds of society and ways of life. Bastia was originally the capital and was oriented toward Italy. Ajaccio, the birthplace of Napoleon, became the capital during the second empire when Bonapartism was at its height. It developed a way of life typical of a French provincial town. In the mountainous interior, society resembled that found in southern Italy, Sardinia and Sicily, with their traditions of family honour, banditry and the vendetta. This dichotomy is a pointer to the ambivalences of Corsican identity, which is both French and Italianate.

Throughout the nineteenth and twentieth centuries, most Corsicans identified with the French State which they perceived to be the source of their continued survival as an island community. Corsicans joined the army, the police, the customs service, and other branches of the French Civil Service and as administrators or soldiers identified strongly with France's imperialist expansion. Identification with France reached its apex during the First and Second World Wars when thousands of islanders gave their lives for *la patrie*. They rejected identification with the surrounding Italian regions and islands, which they regarded as inferior.[24]. Furthermore, Corsica had exactly the same political and administrative institutions as the rest of France, with only some minor fiscal advantages granted as a result of its geographical situation. On the other hand, the island, despite its rejection of Italianateness, bore a strong resemblance in its culture and society to its Italian neighbours in southern Italy, Sardinia and Sicily. French political institutions were recast into a mould of clientelism and patronage, and were operated by the political clans of the island,[25] which were basically powerful political families who divided the island among themselves. They adopted the official labels of the French political parties, usually of the left and the right, although their political practices were fundamentally similar to each other and far removed from those of mainland France. The clans acted as mediators between the local society and the State, ensuring the loyalty of the local population in return for resources of various kinds channelled in a clientelistic manner from the State to the locality. It was an exaggerated form of the *système notabiliaire* which operated in other parts of the French periphery.

While the system worked well it went largely unchallenged either by Corsicans or by state officials such as the prefect. During periods of economic crisis, however, as at the end of the nineteenth century, in the 1930s, and after the Second World War, regionalist groups emerged to criticise and challenge the clan system. They blamed the economic crisis on the clans and the French State. Until the most recent period, regionalist groups tended to be right- or even extreme-right-wing. During the Second World War, some of their number collaborated with the Italian and Fascist occupants of Corsica.[26] However, the economic crisis of the 1950s, when Corsica was in a state of ruin and collapse, led to a much more broad-based regionalist mobilisation, this time led by the Communists and Socialists but containing under its umbrella more radical autonomist and nationalist tendencies.

The traditional French response to Corsican problems was one of benign neglect. However, following the success of Breton regionalists in obtaining a Regional Action plan[27] in the 1950s, Corsica was also granted such a plan in 1957. This emphasised tourism and agricultural development related to the tourism industry. It failed, however, to satisfy the more radical Corsican regionalists. When De Gaulle came to power in 1958, the plan was shelved at first, but was resurrected following Algerian independence in 1962. In effect, around 17,000 *pieds noirs* returned to Corsica, where many had family contacts and where the climate and landscape resembled North Africa. Most integrated without difficulty or moved on to mainland France. However, about 500 *pied noir* families were granted under the Regional Action Plan farm land which had been cleared for use by Corsican farmers. Not surprisingly, Corsicans reacted vigorously to this and that reaction was the immediate reason for of the emergence of the first violent clandestine groups in the mid-1960s, with bombings of *pied noir* property and crops.[28]

It is unlikely that these early groups had clear political aims, such as greater autonomy or independence. On the contrary, the evidence suggests that they were actually close to the *Algérie française* movement which fought against Algerian independence. However, the *pied noir* question and a number of other *affaires* led to the emergence of more radical regionalist movements in the 1960s and early 1970s.[29] Some of these, such as the autonomist UPC (*Unione di u Populu Corsu*), sought greater autonomy within the French Republic and recognition of the existence of a distinct Corsican *ethnie*.[30] Others, such as the *Front Régionaliste Corse*, created in 1973, mainly by students on mainland France, adopted a more Marxist analysis and espoused the then fashionable internal colonialism model to explain Corsica's backwardness. Violence continued in the background to these more overt political movements. The autonomists of UPC, led by Edmond and Max Simeoni, engaged in more symbolic violence, one-off spectacular events, such as the occupation in 1974 of the wine-cellars of a *pied noir* wine-grower. UPC soon afterwards renounced the use of violence because of deaths caused by this incident. This was not the case of the more radical nationalists.[31] Several groups, such as *Fronte Paisanu Corsu di Liberazione* (1973–76) and *Ghjustia Paolina* (1974), existed until *Fronte di Liberazione Naziunale di a Corsica* (FLNC) was created in 1976, becoming the main clandestine group until 1990, when it split into several competing factions.

These movements never attracted the support of the majority of the Corsican population, which continued to support the main French parties. Nevertheless, they did succeed in dominating the political agenda on the island and, to a lesser extent, in France, and provoked several responses from the French Government. Until the election of François Mitterrand to the French presidency in 1981, the response was a mixture of repression and concessions which were usually too little and too late. The Socialists, however, launched their decentralisation programme in 1982, part of which involved setting up elected regional governments. Corsica received special treatment through a *statut particulier* which recognised its specificity through a regional assembly (rather than a regional council) and some extra committees related to culture and economic development because of its island status.

Decentralisation deeply divided the nationalist and autonomist movements, some of which participated in the new institutions, while others continued to boycott them. In fact, the violence increased in both quantity and intensity.[32] There followed several years of splits and then feuds between rival groups. However, all nationalists and autonomists were in agreement that the *statut* did not go far enough in recognising the existence of a Corsican *peuple*, let alone a Corsican *nation*. The Corsican Assembly also failed to function well, with continual crises due to the fissiparous nature of the political groups elected to it. There were problems of electoral fraud and financial corruption. Meanwhile, the economic situation deteriorated further, adding to the sense of foreboding and crisis on the island. Social movements and trade unions launched strikes which left the island isolated from France and the outside world. We should not exaggerate the extent of this crisis or the effect of the violence, which never reached Northern Ireland proportions. Nevertheless, it was sufficient to prevent the economic development of the island and contributed to the failure of the political institutions to function in a democratic manner.

A first step toward resolving the problem came in 1991 when the Socialist Minister of the Interior Pierre Joxe promulgated a revised version of the *statut particulier* which raised its legal status to the same level as that of the *Territoires d'Outre-Mer*.[33] The Bill setting up the new sssembly also recognised the existence of 'the Corsican people, part of the French people'.[34] The Bill passed through the French National Assembly with a small majority, but was struck down as unconstitutional by the Constitutional Court (*conseil constitutionnel*) on the grounds that the constitution recognises only the 'French people' and not the 'Corsican people'. Nevertheless, the new institutions were set up and began to function, but the refusal to recognise a Corsican people further radicalised the nationalist movement.

But radicalisation was accompanied by more dramatic splits and an increase in internal feuding.[35] This was related, at least in part, to control of different kinds of criminal activities engaged in by some of the clandestine movements. French governments both of the right and of the left tried at various points to enter into negotiations with different factions to meet some of their demands, but these usually ended in failure and infuriated the groups left out of the dialogue. The final straw for the Government came with the assassination of the prefect, Claude Erignac, in 1998, as he left the prefecture in Ajaccio.[36] This created a wave of revulsion among the majority of French people, similar to the reaction of people in Britain to IRA activities. A parliamentary commission published a report on the use of public funds in Corsica which was highly critical of mainstream Corsican politicians on the island, who it accused of corruption. The Jospin Government dispatched a hard-line prefect, M. Bonnet, who favoured a harsh law-and-order crackdown, though this backfired when it emerged that the prefect had sent some senior policemen to burn down a restaurant which had been erected illegally! Bonnet, in turn, was arrested along with the policemen and detained in custody. Relations between the island and the mainland reached its lowest point ever, with criticisms coming from mainstream Corsican politicians as well as nationalists and autonomists, most of whom were beginning to realise that Corsica's institutional and political relationship to the French State needed to be re-appraised.

A Corsican peace process?

Despite these problems, there developed, in the 1990s, a willingness to come to grips with the Corsican problem and a dialogue opened up between nationalists, autonomists and some mainstream political groups on the island. The IRA ceasefire and peace process also exercised an important influence on the radical nationalists of the various armed groups emanating from the FLNC. John Hume's role was particularly admired by the autonomists of UPC (roughly the equivalent of the SDLP).

At this point, a project was launched by the European Centre of Minority Issues[37] who invited a group of Corsican politicians and activists to the conference 'Island Regions in the New Europe', held on the Åland Islands in Finland.[38] This conference seems to have been a turning-point in internal Corsican relations for two reasons. First, Corsicans as bitterly opposed as nationalists and unionists in Northern Ireland came together for the first time and found themselves largely in agreement on a whole range of issues. Thus a dialogue among Corsicans was begun that would not have been possible on the island itself. Second, by couching the Corsican problem in terms of European regions and in the context of European integration, the vocabulary of Corsican politics began to change.[39] The word 'autonomy', hitherto taboo in the political lexicon of certain traditional French parties, now began to be used more freely. Mr Paul Giacobbi, president of the Conseil Général of Upper Corsica and heir of the Radicaux de Gauche political clan,[40] caused a sensation at the conference by declaring that he was in favour of many positions hitherto espoused by the regionalists. In fact, he demanded a statute of 'regional citizenship'[41] for Corsica and a radical reduction of the island's political and administrative institutions.[42] The conference participants, including Pierre Joxe, referred on several occasions to the Northern Irish peace process. On Corsica itself, some time after the conference, following the success of nationalist lists in the March 1999 elections to the Corsican Assembly,[43] fifteen nationalist groups came together, declared a common programme and renounced violent acts against each other – the Declaration of the Fiumorbu. There was a great willingness to engage in a constructive and open dialogue with the French Government and other political forces on the island.

On a visit to Corsica in September 1999, Prime Minister Lionel Jospin failed to respond positively to most of these demands.[44] This was probably expected, given the strong Jacobin factions within his own party, such as the Mouvement des Citoyens led by Minister of the Interior Jean-Pierre Chevènement, bitterly opposed to anything which seemed to threaten the unitary State. The instransigence on the part of the French Government and parliamentary reports which criticised the functioning of the island's legal system soured relations between the islanders and the mainland. Some nationalists stepped up the violence, with car-bombs exploding during the day in the centre of Ajaccio. The entire political class in Corsica, including the Gaullist chair of the regional executive, Jean Baggioni, and the centre-right chair of the assembly, José Rossi, felt alienated from the hard-line position of the Government. Rossi, in particular, was engaged in dialogue with the nationalists and both politicians called for further modifications to the island's institutions. At first, the Jospin Government, under pressure from its own hard-line Jacobins, refused to engage in dialogue with elected representatives unless these first condemned the use of violence. However, in December 1999, Jospin appeared to adopt a less intransigent line by dropping this demand and inviting representatives of the main groups elected to the Corsican Assembly to an open-ended dialogue on the island's future to take place in Paris. Eight of the nationalist groups which had signed the Fiumorbu Declaration came together under the umbrella of a group called *Unita* in order to participate in this dialogue. The Paris round-table was, by all accounts, a great success and marks a step further in the process outlined in the Åland Islands conference: first, dialogue among Corsicans; second, dialogue between Corsicans and the French State. The only group to seriously question this process was the hard-line Jacobins in the Socialist Party close to Jean-Pierre Chevènement.[45]

Discussions continued throughout 2000 both on Corsica and between Corsican political representatives and the Government. In the Corsican Assembly, two groups crystallised around each other: one group, including RPR, Communists, some Socialists and independents, around Emile Zucarelli; the other, including DL, the Paul Giacobbi faction of the Radicaux de Gauche, some Socialists and the nationalists, around José Rossi. Debate has revolved around two issues: first, whether the Corsican statute should be *upgraded* to give the assembly primary legislative powers – the traditional Jacobins of Zucarelli opposing this, the neo-autonomists approving it; and, second, whether this should be ratified in a referendum. At the time of writing, neither issue has been resolved; nevertheless, despite setbacks, the dialogue is continuing and seems likely to result in some kind of modification to Corsica's institutional set-up, although the change will probably be less radical than the nationalists are hoping and less timid than the rejectionists would like.

Conclusions

The three cases of Northern Ireland, the Basque Country and Corsica have many features that differentiate one from the other. What is remarkable, however, is that the phasing of the different conflicts seem to correspond quite closely. moving from early regionalism to separatist nationalism. However, while the armed struggle did influence the political agenda, in none of the three cases was it capable of achieving the nationalists' political goal of setting up an independent state.

From the late 1980s onwards there has been a very different context. Today, political activity is no longer confined to the nation state but occurs in a system of European governance marked by a complex variety of public actors. Regions and local authorities, despite their great diversity throughout European states, have found a new role as political actors within this new European system, for example in the Committee of the Regions.[46] Small nations such as Catalonia and, more recently, Scotland and Wales recognise that this new situation offers them windows of opportunity that had not existed before. Moderate nationalists have been quick to exploit these opportunities, often as a way of putting pressure on central governments such as Madrid. Furthermore, the new context radically changed traditional conceptions dear to nationalism, such as sovereignty, which, confronted by both globalisation and a more integrated European Union, is barely meaningful. It is this broader context which, combined with the realisation by republicans that armed struggle had reached its limits, made it possible to redefine the nature of the Northern Irish problem in such a way that republicans could extricate themselves from the cycle of violence while saving face in the eyes of their own followers.

The same processes have been at work in the Basque Country, with the rapprochement between PNV and HB, and in Corsica between radical nationalists and traditional parties of the left and right. The path trodden by the Irish and the British has been an important stimulus to the Corsicans and the Basques in finding an alternative to political violence. It is difficult at this point to say what the direct influences have been – certainly, there have been some, such as a visit by Gerry Adams to the Basque Country and of John Hume to Corsica. However, it is probably true to say that the influence of the Irish peace process has been more indirect, encouraging radical nationalists especially to rethink their political project and to study the *method* which led to the GFA. One key difference, however, is in the attitude of the national governments involved. Neither the French nor the Spanish feel much desire to emulate the initiatives taken by Blair's Government, fearing that this might encourage further separatist trends. Another difference lies in the nature of the nationalist movements. The Provisional IRA is, by and large, a unified

movement with a solid base in almost half of the Northern Irish Catholic community. They have shown a remarkable discipline in holding to the ceasefire. In the
Basque Country, and especially in Corsica, the nationalist movement is deeply
divided and finds it difficult to present a unified front to enter into dialogue with
both the Government and other regional political forces.

Postscript

This chapter was written at a time when there seemed to be some progress towards
peace, at least in Northern Ireland and Corsica, while the Basque Country completely stalled under the Aznar Government. Events subsequent to its initial writing
have not fundamentally changed the basic argument of the chapter. Northern
Ireland is still lurching towards a settlement. Even the victories of the DUP and
Sinn Fein in elections in 2003 have not signalled a return to the earlier violent years.
On the contrary, both parties continue to play the game of what passes for politics,
and negotiations have not completely broken down. It may even be the dominance
of these two hard-line parties that will facilitate a more lasting settlement.

In Corsica, the Matignon process really achieved quite a lot, with legislation to
refound the Corsican Assembly by bestowing certain powers to modify parliamentary legislation which would affect the island (but stopping short of the Corsican
Assembly itself having legislative powers) and making teaching of the Corsican
language to some extent compulsory in schools (although parents would have been
able to opt out if they so wished). Unfortunately for those seeking a settlement, this
was rejected by a small majority of the islanders when it was put to them in a
referendum on 6 July 2003. In effect, the Corsican issue provoked a wide debate in
France on the nature of the French State and its constitution which divided those
who wished to see a more pluralist state and those, called *souverainistes*, led by
politicians such as Jean Pierre Chevènement, then a government minister. The
souverainistes were opposed both to any form of political regionalisation that
infringed the principle of the one and indivisible Republic of France and to moves
towards greater Europeanisation.

The situation in the Basque Country worsened until the al-Qaeda bombings
in Madrid, which claimed the lives of over 200 people in March 2004. Ironically,
this atrocity may have opened the way to a softening of the relations between the
central Government and the Basque separatists in ETA. The Aznar Government
initially, without any real proof, attributed the bombings to ETA, and continued to
insist on this despite mounting evidence of an al-Quaeda link. In the end, the PP
Government was punished in the subsequent general elections as the majority of
Spaniards were outraged at what they saw as this deception by the Government,
even though PP was on target for another election victory. Before the bombings,
the Basque PNV Government had moved away from a Northern Ireland-type
solution to a Quebec model of sovereignty association, which was even less likely to
win the approval of PP centralists. With the accession to power of the Socialists led

by Zapatero, however, there has been a certain lessening of tensions and it appears that feelers have gone out between the two sides with a view to recommencing negotiations. Undoubtedly, PSOE has not totally shed its centralist views, but the current Government does at least seem to be willing to open negotiations rather than completely close the door, as was the case with previous Government. It is still too early, however, to say whether this will produce another ceasefire by ETA.

Notes

1 In Northern Ireland and the Basque Country, the radical nationalists have done so with the moderate nationalists in the SDLP and PNV, while in Corsica, the radicals are in dialogue with non- and anti-nationalist groups such as elements of the French centre-right or sections of the Socialist Party.

2 See John Loughlin, 'The "Europe of the Regions" and the Federalization of Europe', *Publius: The Journal of Federalism*, autumn, 1996.

3 These are usually referred to as the Spanish Basque Country and the French Basque Country. Basques, however, especially those in Spain, tend to use the terms the North Basque Country (in France) and the South Basque Country (in Spain).

4 See John Loughlin, *Regionalism and Ethnic Nationalism in France: A Case-Study of Corsica* (Florence: European University Institute, 1989).

5 See J. Cara Baroja, *Los Vascos* (Madrid: Minotauro, 1958).

6 See Daniel-Louis Seiler, *L'exemplarité du nationalisme basque: une perspective comparée.* (Iruña: Fundación Sabino Arana, 1996).

7 See Francesco Letamendia, 'Basque Nationalism and the Struggle for Self-Determination in the Basque Country', in B. Berberoglu (ed.), *The National Question* (Philadelphia: Temple University Press, 1995).

8 This is understandable given the high percentage of Catalans who speak Catalan and the ease with which a Castilian immigrant can understand and learn the language, while Basque is much less accessible. An excellent comparison of the two nations may be found in Daniele Conversi, *The Basques, the Catalans and Spain: Alternative Routes to Nationalist Mobilisation* (London: Hurst & Co., 1997).

9 The upper bourgeoisie and the Spanish military stationed in the Basque Country supported Franco.

10 This needs to be qualified by stating that many Basque nationalists and even members of ETA and HB are also from this group of immigrants.

11 The *foral* laws give the Basque Country and Navarre a great deal of financial autonomy. The *Foral* Deputation, not the Spanish State, first collects taxes of various kinds; these are then divided according to a complex formula between those which remain in the AC and those which go to the central State.

12 The sentiment on the part of richer regions that they are subsidising the poorer is not confined to the Basque Country and may be found also in Italy's northern regions, such as Lombardy.

13 See Joseba Zulaika, *Basque Violence: Metaphor and Sacrament.*, (Reno: Nevada University Press, 1988).

14 They have been responsible for over 800 deaths and many bombings in different parts of Spain.

15 See Francesco Letamendia, *Juego de espejos: Conflictos nacionales centro-periferia* (Madrid: Ed. Trotta, 1997).

16 Richard Gillespie, 'Peace Moves in the Basque Country', *Journal of Southern Europe and the Balkans*, vol. 1, no. 2, 1999.

17 See M. Uranga Gomez, I. Lasagabaster, F. Letamendia and R. Zallo (eds), *Un nuevo escenario: democracia, cultura y cohesión social en Euskal Herria* (Bilbao: Instituto Manu Robles Aranguiz, 1999)

18 See F. Letamendia, *Juego de espejos*.

19 Whereas Basque, Catalan and Galician nationalists argued in favour of an 'asymmetrical state'.

20 Twenty-three groups and parties signed the declaration; see Gillespie, 'Peace Moves in the Basque Country', p. 125.

21 *Ibid.*

22 *Ibid.*, p. 127 and Gomez *et al.*, *Un nuevo escrenario*.

23 Ajaccio, Bastia, Calvi, Bonifacio etc. were built mostly by the Genoese; Ile-Rousse was built by Pascal Paoli during the revolt against the Genoese as a means by which to gain access to the sea.

24 Italians came from different Italian regions to work on Corsica and were referred to pejoratively as '*I Lucchesi*', even if few actually came from Lucca in Tuscany.

25 See Jean-Louis Briquet, *La Tradition en mouvement: Clientélisme et politique en Corse* (Paris: Belin, 1997); and John Loughlin, *Regionalism and Ethnic Nationalism in France*.

26 *Ibid.*

27 This was basically the introduction of a regional dimension to the National (Economic) Plans, invented by Jean Monnet, which covered France as a whole.

28 See John Loughlin, 'Les Pieds Noirs en Corse', in *La Guerre d'Algérie et les Français* (Paris: Fayard, 1989).

29 See Loughlin, *Regionalism and Ethnic Nationalism in France*; E. Bernabéu-Casanova, *Le Nationalisme corse: Genèse, succès et échec.* (Paris: L'Harmattan, 1997).

30 Some members of this movement were, in fact, old-style regionalists and nationalists who did not wish to use this terminology, given the discredit it had earned because of the collaborationist activities referred to above.

31 There was a shift from *regionalism* to *nationalism* on the part of these groups in defining the nature of Corsican society; see J. Loughlin, *Regionalism and Ethnic Nationalism in France*.

32 Much of the early FLNC violence had taken the form of *propagande armée* (symbolic actions) rather than *lutte armée* (armed struggle). The latter involved more serious destruction of property and led inevitably to the taking of human life. There was also an intense campaign against non-Corsican French people (*les continentaux*) who had settled on the island as teachers, civil servants, etc.

33 See Helen Hintjens, John Loughlin and Claude Olivesi, 'The Status of Maritime and Insular France: The DOM-TOM and Corsica', in J. Loughlin and S. Mazey (eds), *The End of the French Unitary State: Ten Years of Regionalization in France (1982–1992)* (London: Frank Cass, 1995). The TOMs are in fact, ex-colonies and have the right to independence if they so wish. Although the French State refuses to place Corsica in this category of being a colony, the Joxe statute goes some way towards recognising its special circumstances.

34 Article 1 of the Law of 13 May 1991 (*Loi no. 91–428 Statut de la collectivité territoriale de Corse: Journal officiel de la république française en date du 14 mai 1993*, p. 6318–29) on the Special Statute of the Corsican Region reads: '*La République française garantit à la communauté historique et culturelle que constitue le peuple Corse, composante du peuple français, les droits à la préservation de son identité culturelle et à la défense de ses intérêts économiques et sociaux spécifiques. Ces droits liés à l'insularité s'exercent dans le respect de l'unité nationale, dans le cadre de la Constitution, des lois de la République et du présent statut.*' ('The French Republic guarantees to the historical and cultural community constituted by the Corsican people, component of the French people, the right to preserve its cultural identity and to defend its specifc economic and social interests. These rights related to insularity are to be exercised with respect for national unity, in the framework of the Constitution, of the laws of the Republic, and of this present statute.')

35 An organigramme of the different nationalist and autonomist groups may be found in John Loughlin and Farimah Daftary, *Insular Regions and European Integration: Corsica and the Åland Islands Compared*, ECMI Report no. 5 (Flensburg: European Centre for Minority Issues, 1999), p. 62.

36 This was the only occasion, at least since the Second World War, when a French prefect was assassinated.

37 ECMI, based in Flensburg, Germany, and financed by the Danish, German and Schleswig-

Hosltein governments, is an institute devoted to the study of, but also to contributing to, peaceful solutions to minority conflicts. John Loughlin, co-author of this chapter, and Claude Olivesi, a Corsican academic and politician, acted as academic and political advisors to ECMI on this project.

38 Also present were Pierre Joxe (in a private capacity), several French and Corsican journalists, and politicians and administrators from Finland and the Åland Islands. A full report of the conference may be found in John Loughlin, Claude Olivesi and Farimah Daftary (eds), *Autonomies Insulaires: Vers une politique de différence pour la Corse?* (Ajaccio: Albiana, 1999).

39 It is true that many Corsicans, such as Claude Olivesi, had begun to speak in these terms, but this was the first time that the language was used by such a diverse gathering of political tendencies.

40 His late father, François, had been the chief of this political clan and was bitterly opposed to nationalism.

41 'Regional citizenship' was the basis of the Åland Islands' autonomous State and could be obtained only if one possessed Finnish nationality, was resident on the islands for at least five years, and had a mastery of the Swedish language, spoken by 95 per cent of the islanders; see John Loughlin *et al.*, *Autonomies Insulaires*.

42 Besides the regional assembly, there are two departments with all their cantons and about 350 communes for a population of around 220,000.

43 In the second round, the list *Corsica Nazione*, led by Jean-Guy Talamoni won 16.77 per cent of the vote and 8 seats, third behind the centre-right list *Rassemblement pour la République* (RPR, *Démocratie Libérale* (DL), which won 27.9 per cent of the vote and 17 seats and the left-wing list *Gauche 'Plurielle'*, which obtained 22.7 per cent and 11 seats.

44 While the prime minister affirmed his support for the recognition of Corsican specificity and of the island's language and culture, in his speech to the Corsican Assembly on 6 September 1999, he ruled out any political or consitutional developments while violence persisted.

45 Chevènement, as Minister of the Interior, attended the ninety-minute meeting between Jospin and the Corsican political groups, but apparently did not utter a word – a symbol of 'republican vigilance'.

46 See John Loughlin, 'Representing Regions in Europe: The Committee of the Regions', *Regional and Federal Studies: An International Journal*, vol. 6, no. 2, summer 1996.

26

Peace processes in the late twentieth century and beyond: a mixed record

FRED HALLIDAY

The charms of singularity

The purpose of this chapter is to examine the peace negotiations in Ireland of the 1990s in a broader, comparative, context, that of the world-wide set of peace agreements and settlements, partial and plenary, which marked the decade following the ending of the Cold War. The points of comparison are the peace processes which, on self-evident grounds, appear most like Ireland's – those of the Basque Country, Corsica and, at a stretch, Palestine. It is, in the first instance, comparison of this kind which has attracted the attention of those who have sought to cast light on the Irish conflict by an analysis of fragmented societies.[1]

Such international contextualisation of the Irish case can also examine the ways in which the broader changes from the late 1990s to the early part of the twenty-first century have impacted on the Irish case. There is, of course, much resistance to this in Ireland, where such comparison encounters a good deal of scepticism. Unhappy nations, like unhappy people, feel themselves to be unique – nationalism would have it no other way. The first step may, however, lie in reducing that sense of singularity, and uniqueness, to which all inter-ethnic, and nationalist, conflicts are easily prone, even while avoiding any facile reduction of any individual case to a broader international pattern.[2]

Comparison is often more easily made from outside. Certainly there are those in such contexts who, for one reason or another, look to Ireland for their own inspiration: in Palestine, both Arabs and Jews have in the past sought succour from the Irish case, the Jews taking, at various times, the Catholics and Protestants as their model.[3] In the Basque Country and Corsica, but not Sardinia, the matter is simpler – a generalised sympathy for the 'Irish' cause, meaning Sinn Féin, is evident in both contexts. Those seeking peace have also looked to the Irish peace agreements for support: 'Stormont en Euzkadi?' was the title of one such, hopeful, article published after Good Friday 1998.[4]

The Cold War, however, and its termination presents a particular problem, since, in comparison with many other international processes that did influence Ireland – Reformation, industrial revolution, Mazzinian nationalism, the First World War, the European Union, to name but some – the Cold War seems not to have affected Ireland in an overt manner. Ireland's conflict, along with Cyprus and the Iranian revolution, has been one of those that had only a tangential relation to the Cold War. Communism was weak in both the North and the South; indeed, the Republic did not even have diplomatic relations with Moscow until 1973. The North's role in NATO's Atlantic strategy was without direct political impact on the island; while the Republic, for its part, did play its role as a neutral State, be it through the promotion of a co-operative European neutrality, or by participation in peace-keeping. (The extent of this should not be exaggerated – NATO membership did not prevent the Danes or the Norwegians from playing their role in peace-keeping, and neutrality was, in Cold War as in World War, as much a ticket to free-ride as to play an effective alternative international role.[5] When violence returned to the North in 1969 it was striking that it had little or no Cold War component, the adoption of some Third-Worldist rhetoric by sections of the republican movement aside.

This apparent insulation is, however, open to some challenge. The argument as to the relevance of the ending of the Cold War itself to the Irish process has been made elsewhere, and to great effect.[6] If not the end of the military and ideological Cold War, then the broader international context of economic interdependence, and the demilitarisation and de-ideologisation of politics, had a partial role in promoting negotiation in the 1960s. Here I make another kind of relation, showing how, in a comparative perspective, this general record of peace negotiation and enduring conflict in the 1990s may throw light on the progress, and certain limits of progress, in the Irish case.

Peace processes and the Cold War

The record of peace negotiations in the Cold War was, in large measure, a reflection of the degree of incorporation of local conflicts into strategic rivalry. Where the conflicts had a clear Cold War character, or where local states were closely allied to, or dependent on, the Cold War rivals, agreement of a kind was sometimes possible: ceasefires in Korea and Vietnam, and in the successive Arab–Israeli wars reflected the ability of Washington and Moscow to impose peace on their local allies. The neutrality of Austria and Laos, in 1955 and 1962, reflected similar understandings. It was significant, however, that in the main these agreements, like agreements on arms control, were reached through direct, bi-lateral, negotiations between the major states, not through the UN or other multi-lateral fora. The UN, however, had a role, in various forms of peace process, provided this was an area in which the Cold War antagonists were willing to allow the involvement of other parties.

The UN often found its activities undermined by the collapse of local agreements – as was the case in the Congo in 1961 – or marginalised as local forces decided to prosecute their wars irrespective of the UN presence – as in the Lebanon. Elsewhere, a UN presence may have kept, or helped to keep, the peace, as in Kashmir and Cyprus, even as the overall conflict was very much frozen, not resolved. In the context of the 1990s there was a temptation to look back at the classic peace-keeping of the Cold War, at some kind of 'golden age', when mandates were clear, peace-keeping was independent of 'great power' involvement and the peace-keepers represented benign smaller states. There was no golden age, in a world beset with regional and local conflicts, and overshadowed with the threat of nuclear annihilation, a threat itself increased by the initiatives of local states and political forces.

Peace processes after the Cold War

The period following the ending of the Cold War saw an apparent transformation in the character of peace processes, at first in an optimistic sense, then in more doom-laden vein. In the first place, the proclamation of a new collaborative spirit between the USSR and the USA, and then of a new collaboration between the West and post-Soviet Russia, led to a set of substantial, and interrelated, peace initiatives. Gorbachev, in his 'new thinking', proclaimed a set of new principles for dealing with what he termed 'regional' issues: de-ideologisation, reduction in arms supplies, 'national reconciliation', an end to the zero-sum approach by international and local forces. Bush, in 1991, proclaimed a 'New World Order', a term much misused and abused, but which had, at the time, a limited, and relevant, meaning, namely active collaboration between the two major powers to resolve, and if possible prevent, conflicts.

The elements of this new positive approach were evident in several respects. At the UN itself the US and the USSR, and more broadly the permanent five members of the Security Council, began to collaborate more actively and to shed Cold War antagonism. The result was a set of peace agreements that were brokered, in whole or in part, through the UN: Namibia, long ruled, in the face of international condemnation, by South Africa, attained independence in 1991; in Mozambique, years of war between Frelimo and Renamo were ended by a compromise peace in 1992; in Cambodia, where war had been raging since the 1960s, the UN negotiated a compromise agreement in 1992, which in time brought the Khmers Rouges to a political settlement; in Central America – in El Salvador, Guatemala and Nicaragua – peace agreements, followed by elections and by internationally backed 'peace-building' (a term that came into fashion in the 1990s), ended decades of civil war;[7] in South Africa, international pressure, and participation in negotiations, produced the settlement of 1994.

In three of the most dramatic international conflicts of the 1980s there were also negotiated settlements. In 1988 Iran and Iraq reached a ceasefire agreement, after eight years of war – an event preceded by a letter from Khomeiny urging Gorbachev to embrace Islam. In Afghanistan, the USSR agreed, in April 1988 to withdraw its forces, a process completed, on schedule, in February 1989. In the Arab–Israeli dispute, a Palestinian recognition of Israel in November 1988, as much under US and Swedish as under Soviet pressure, led to the Madrid conference of 1991 and, in time, to the Oslo Accords of August 1993. Elsewhere, and with all sorts of local variations and prevarications, agreements, and/or ceasefires, occurred: in Western Sahara, POLISARIO and the Moroccan Government agreed on a ceasefire in 1991, to be followed by a referendum to determine the territory's status; in the two major armed conflicts of Western Europe – Ireland and the Basque Country – ceasefires were proclaimed in 1994 and 1998, respectively; in Corsica, most of the fragments of the armed cause took the hint as well.

The optimistic perspective on peace was confirmed by three other developments in the aftermath of the Cold War. One was the Kuwait conflict of 1990-91: here a clear act of aggression by one state against another led to an unprecedented action to expel the aggressor. All political entities act in the light of past failures, and international organisations are no exception: the UN response to the Iraqi attack on Kuwait owed much to a realisation, drilled into UN officials during the long Iran–Iraq War, that the Security Council's failure to act in September 1980, when Iraq attacked Iran in clear breach of the Charter, had antagonised Iran and so greatly prolonged the war.[8] Now, with broad US–USSR agreement, the UN could, and did, act: it appeared that this form of action at least, of which there had been rather few instances in modern times, would be prevented.[9] The subsequent allied action to protect the Kurds of northern Iraq, in effect occupying part of Iraq in defence of the human rights of the inhabitants, appeared to confirm this trend, as did the unprecedented, intrusive, arms' control regime subsequently imposed on Iraq. Resolute, and co-operative, enforcement was now, it seemed, possible.[10]

This optimism was reflected in the statements of the UN Secretary-General Boutros-Ghali himself, and above all in his statement *Agenda for Peace* of 1992,[11] in which he outlined the possibility of a more secure world. The essay stressed several measures to maintain the peace which were, in the secretary-general's view, now possible:

- a greater emphasis on pre-emptive diplomacy to prevent conflicts breaking out;
- a more secure financial base for peace-keeping operations;
- a permanent standing force to act as a rapidly deployable peace-keeping force; and
- a greater investment in post-conflict action, what was now termed 'peace-building', in countries where precarious agreements had been reached.

All of this optimism from above was accompanied by a wave of what one may term 'optimism from below'. In a convergence of neo-liberalism from the right and the promotion of social movements and civil society from the left, greater roles were being allocated for private, non-governmental and social forces in societies.

Much of this remained confined to national societies, but an increasing interest was shown in transnational or global civil society – in the work of human rights and development groups, in the activities of ecological and feminist organisations. At the same time, and across several continents, there was a wave of democratisation, a process that not only removed authoritarian, and often violent, regimes at the top, but which encouraged a mellowing, and pacification, of opposition from below: armed struggle had lost its 1960s romantic appeal, but it was only in the late 1980s that those who had taken up the gun in Latin America, Africa and the Middle East were able credibly to contemplate entering the political arena.[12]

Before entering a cascade of pessimism, it is worth noting that much of this optimistic scenario held true. The record of agreements, bringing peace in whole or in part to a dozen countries, was substantial enough in itself. The threat of strategic nuclear war did recede. Military expenditure in major states declined between 1985 and 1995 by, in real terms, around 20 per cent.[13] The process of democratisation, and of promotion of civil society in a broad sense, sustained itself, in Eastern Europe, though not the former USSR, outside the Baltic states, and in Latin America, with even hold-outs like China changing substantially. In the field of international humanitarian law, there was significant progress – from the establishment of an International Criminal Court, to the tribunals for war criminals, to the arrest of Pinochet in October 1998.

The unravelling of peace

In retrospect, however, the turn to peace was far from being the whole picture. In the first place, the record of peace agreements was a very partial one. Some agreements were, in the context of the ensuing decade at least, broadly successful: Namibia, Mozambique, Lebanon, Central America. The UN (in effect US) intervention in Haiti did promote, if not conclusively stabilise, a democratic transition. Other processes were shaky, perhaps emperilled, but by no means returning to war, or the *status quo ante*: in South Africa and Palestine, matters did not proceed as planned, or expected, but nor did the whole process break down – the phrases 'on a knife's edge', and 'in serious danger of collapse' were too readily used. Elsewhere, however, serious regression occurred. In Afghanistan, the USSR's withdrawal and the collapse of the People's Democratic Party of Afghanistan regime in 1992 led to new and unprecedented levels of killing and savagery, culminating in the seizure of Kabul by the *taliban* in 1996. In Sri Lanka, despite many mediation attempts, war between the state and both its Tamil and Sinhalese foes continued. In the Horn of Africa the apparent resolution of Africa's longest war, that between Eritrea and Ethiopia in 1993, with the Ethiopian assent to the restoration of Eritrean independence, was followed five years later by the outbreak of a new murderous border war between these two former guerrilla allies. In Angola a UN-brokered peace process did not prevent UNITA from relaunching its war. In Cyprus and Sahara there was a cold peace, but no diplomatic movement. In Sudan,

Somalia and Colombia, wars that had begun in the 1980s or before intensified in scope and fatalities. In Turkey the Kurdistan Workers' Party's insurrection, begun in 1984, continued through the decade, until 1999.

The balance-sheet of the old, Cold War, agenda itself was therefore mixed. But the overall balance-sheet of world peace and conflict was placed more in deficit by the new conflicts that emerged after, and in considerable measure as a result of, the end of the Cold War itself. These were located, above all in two areas. One was in what had been multinational communist countries – the former USSR, and the former Yugoslavia. In the first, there were wars in the independent Transcaucasia (Ossetia, Nagorno-Karabagh, Abkhazia) and in the northern Caucasus, still part of the Russian Federation (Chechenya, Dagestan), in Tajikistan, and in Moldova. In the Balkans the secession of Slovenia in 1992 was followed by – some would argue led to – the brutal wars of Croatia and Bosnia (1992–95) and Kossovo (1998–99). The second arena of conflict of the 1990s was Africa: in the Horn every significant state was affected; in the Maghrib, Algeria was riven by civil war, along indeterminate battle lines; in West Africa, civil conflict ravaged Liberia and Sierra Leone; in Central Africa, the massacres of Rwanda in 1994, in which an estimated 700,000 people died, were followed by an internationalisation of conflict in the Congo, drawing on a range of regional states: from Sudan in the north-east to Angola in the south-west, Africa was, it seemed, at war.

Nor was the sense of regression confined to such a proliferation of small and local wars: as was the case after the end of other great, strategic, conflicts an initial period of great power co-operation and trust appeared to be yielding, as the 1990s wore on, to a new and more antagonistic pattern of inter-state competition. The consolidation and expansion of the NATO–EU bloc in the Atlantic occasioned growing anxiety in Russia, at both state and popular levels. In the Far East, the triangle of China, Korea and Japan, the locus of the inter-state strategic military rivalry that had, a century before, presaged the wars of the twentieth century, was once again witnessing growing tension, as China and Taiwan failed to resolve their differences, and internal political and social tension in China prompted a resort to greater nationalism. In the Gulf, there was no resolution of the unstable, triangular, inter-state conflicting involving Iraq, Iran and Saudi Arabia. Most immediately, and with the greatest possible potential for promoting a return to world-wide military competition, the decision by India to explode a nuclear device, in May 1998, followed by a similar action by Pakistan, marked the start of a new defiance of international non-proliferation that stimulated states throughout Asia, from the Middle East to the Far East, to follow suit. As far as inter-state military competition was concerned, the first post-Cold War decade ended on a note of more ominous uncertainty.[14]

A crisis of international peace-keeping

This proliferation of war and uncertainty led some to argue that the world had, in some significant way, entered a new and more ominous period of conflict, one that perhaps posed greater threats than did the conflicts of the Cold War period itself. For some writers, the post-Cold War period was indeed marked by a greater degree of global disorder, anarchy, chaos, in which nationalism and the growing independence of economic and financial activity from state control, contributed to producing a dangerous instability, a 'new middle ages'.[15] Robert Kaplan wrote of a new period of savagery and anarchy that threatened to consume the West.[16] Michael Ignatieff, in books covering the rise of ethnic nationalism and the disregard by contemporary military forces of the traditional restraints of war, stressed the dangers of these new conflicts.[17] Mary Kaldor and others analysed the nature of the *new* wars in which the traditional aim of controlling territory was replaced by the dissemination of fear, in which political goals were linked to narco-trafficking and other forms of transnational financial activity, aided and often encouraged by powerful disasporas, in which the majority of casualties were civilians, in which traditional codes, and boundaries, seemed not to operate. Beyond the hatred generated thereby, such wars acquired their own dynamic and were, therefore, all the more difficult to control and conclude.[18]

This sense of growing chaos was fuelled by an apparent weakening of precisely that new intergovernmental co-operation that had marked the early post-1989 period. The critique of international institutions, starting with the UN itself, had begun well before the end of the Cold War, and encompassed a range of concerns – lax managerial standards, corruption, a tendency to rhetoric. In British diplomatic circles it was common to talk of two kinds of international institutions, the *talking* and the *doing*. The hope expressed by many was that, with the ending of the Cold War, and a general bracing air of institutional reform, these difficulties could be overcome. There was also, in the new managerial spirit, much talk of decentral-isation – of encouraging regional organisations and influential states to play a leading peace-keeping role, or of a range of institutions, not just the UN, being responsible for security. The initial post-1989 years seemed to bear this out: the UN's involvement in a range of peaceful settlements, and the operations over Kuwait and the Kurds, seemed to confirm optimism. There was even talk of reviving the Military Staff Committee, mentioned in the UN Charter but never implemented. In the run-up to the fiftieth anniversary of the UN, in 1995, there were many proposals, building on *Agenda for Peace*, for a strengthened peace-keeping capability.

All of this was, however, overtaken by events. In the first place, the traditional resistances to reform of the UN continued to prevail. The permanent five did not want to see their prerogatives diluted by Security Council reform or the creation of a standing military force. The regional organisations encouraged by the Charter and the secretary-general did, to some measure, operate, but they did so in a way that appeared to highlight the dangers of allowing regional hegemons to act: one person's devolved peace-keeper became another's bully on the bloc – be it Nigerian troops in West Africa, Japanese in Cambodia, Russians in Georgia and Moldova, let alone NATO in former Yugoslavia. Throughout the developed world, i.e. in those countries from which the troops and/or funds for peace-keeping would disproportionately be drawn, there was widespread resistance to the despatch of such forces, and to the casualties peace-keeping might entail. The *de-bellicisation* of developed societies came to act as a major constraint on the international operations of these countries.

More significantly, the optimism about UN peace-keeping itself that had culminated in *Agenda for Peace* was to crumble in the face of a series of cases where the UN proved ineffective. Two of these were themselves relics of the Cold War: Afghanistan and Angola. Despite long-term UN involvement in peace-making, and the deployment of observers and advisers, the local parties pursued their conflicts, at great cost to their own countries and to the neighbouring regions. In two African cases the UN proved ineffectual: in Somalia an initial deployment, in 1992, for 'humanitarian' purposes, in the sense of providing food and basic services, degenerated into a military and political conflict with local forces, and an abject retreat; in Rwanda, the outbreak of violence in 1994 between Tutsi and Hutu – one long foreseen by diplomats and UN officials – prompted no effective international response. In the neo-liberal language that had become fashionable in the 1990s, 'there were no takers for Rwanda'.

Most sustained and visible, and most evocative of the weaknesses of the whole UN machinery, were the wars in South-East Europe. It was one of the unexpected ironies of the post-1989 period that UN peace-keeping, which had hitherto been confined to the Third World or the remoter European periphery, was now concentrated on the mainland of Europe itself. Whereas in 1987 there were 5 UN peace-keeping operations, with 10,000 personnel, in early 1994 there were 17 such operations, with 72,00 personnel, military and police. The majority of these personnel were now deployed in Europe, which also became the theatre for the proliferation of institutions called for in the new neo-liberal institutional doctrine: in contrast to a monopoly of one, the UN, on the classical model, there were now at least seven such international security organisations involved.[19] The changed character of peace-keeping was evident, also, in a shift in the composition of the forces involved: during the Cold War the major powers had stayed out of peace-keeping, even if they provided logistical, financial and diplomatic support; now they participated, in a leading role, obstructive or constructive.

The nemesis of the new peace-keeping optimism was to be, first, Bosnia, then Kosovo. In the end, of course, action was taken – in support of Bosnia in 1995, in support of Kosovo in 1999, but the story of these operations underlined the limits of the UN and other diplomatic actors. First, the inability of the UN to prevent the outbreak of war demonstrated the limits of what had become one of the leitmotifs of the early 1990s' optimism, pre-emptive diplomacy: put simply, foresight and preemptive diplomacy had little impact where one, or all, of the local actors wished to proceed with war. This was the case with Serbia, as it was with India and Pakistan and their nuclear tests, and with Ethiopia and Eritrea. It is doubtful what difference it would have made in, say, June 1990 if Western and Arab capitals had realised, as they did not, that Saddam Hussein was going to occupy Kuwait.

Second, the delays in action over Bosnia and Kosovo highlighted the gap between rhetoric and action in UN, and more general diplomatic, policy. It is easy to suggest, with hindsight, what should or could have been done, but even the best-intentioned of critics would notice how confused, mixed and ineffectual was the response of the international community to these crises. All too often resolutions passed with solemn authority in New York were ignored, or proved ineffectual, on the ground. Many times the Serbs were solemnly warned to cease their activities, to no avail. In 1995 sanctuary was offered by the UN to thousands of Moslems at Srebrenica: nothing was done to prevent the massacre in which thousands of Bosniak (Moslem) males were killed.

The problems highlighted by Bosnia and Kosovo were not, however, only those of determination and co-ordination: there were very real quandaries, of policy and principle, involved here which no amount of coherence at the policy level could automatically have resolved. When, for example, does an ethnic group have the right to secession? What of the rights of minorities? How far should the pursuit of justice, including the arrest of suspected war criminals, be carried if this undermines agreements to keep the peace? What levels of corruption are tolerable, among local political elites and peace-keepers themselves? These are problems which arose in the Bosnian and Kosovar cases, but they were by no means specific to them. The problems associated with UN activities in Bosnia were on occasion blamed imprecise mandates and 'mission creep': but others say this was inevitable or even desirable – reference was made to 'robust' peace-keeping, or to 'Chapter Six and a Half', a constitutional position somewhere between peace-keeping and peace enforcement.

The cost of these accumulated problems was, however, substantial and widespread: the optimism of the early 1990s was dispersed, the institutional fragmentation and paralysis intensified. At the end of the 1990s, and without accepting the more dramatic claims about historical regression or the prevalence of new forms of anarchy, the crisis of international peace-keeping, and of global governance with regard to peace and security, was arguably greater than it had been a decade before.

The limits of peace agreements

It may well be asked what relevance all this has to the Irish case. For all the temptations of comparison, instrumental or even well-intentioned, it is evident that in many key respects the Irish case is distinct from, and largely insulated from, this history of expectations, rising and falling. The Irish conflict, most importantly, was not created by the Cold War, nor did it to any significant extent acquire a Cold War character. Its course after 1969 was not, in any significant way, the subject of attempts at international negotiation, nor was any international organisation, the UN or any other, directly involved in seeking a solution. Even in those cases most conventionally associated with Ireland there were significant differences: in contrast to the two other main Western European cases, Corsica and, even more so, the Basque Country, there was no rise of social movements to oppose the armed struggle and unite different communities – the history of civil society in the Northern Irish conflict is recurrent, but intermittent, strangely silent, when not silenced. The women's movement of the 1970s petered out: there was, for example, no counterpart to demonstrations for peace organised by trades unions and other groups, or the mass rallies in the Basque Country, in July 1997, after the murder of the PP's Municipal Councillor Miguel Angel Blanco.[20]

Yet, as Michael Cox has argued, there were in three respects international changes that did affect Ireland: the decline of national liberation as a legitimate goal; the changed nature of the Anglo-US relationship; and the enticements, economic and civil, of Europe. Such a survey of peace, and war, in the post-1989 world therefore prompts a revised version of Winston Churchill's famous question.[21] If, in this case, after the Cuba missile crisis, the Korean and Vietnam wars, and the rise and fall of the Berlin Wall, the twin steeples of Fermanagh and Tyrone, the dismal streets of the Falls and the Shankill, will indeed rise again. We cannot be sure, and for a conflict that has gone over 800 years, going back, as I once remarked to an Arab audience, to the time of Saladin and the Abbasid empire, the Cold War may appear as just a blip.

On the side of caution, if not pessimism, there are five lessons which this comparative panorama of the 1990s may suggest as far as Ireland is concerned. First, if Ireland is to be set in the international context of the 1990s this is not a context in which peace and the resolution of problems have overwhelmingly prevailed. The record is, as I have said, a mixed one, and the implications for Ireland are also, therefore, mixed. Ireland is, to be sure, located in a region of the world where military conflict, between and within states, has been overcome more than anywhere else in the world, but the mixed character of the global pattern, including certain parts of Europe, suggests a degree of caution as far as invocation of world trends is concerned. We do not have to buy into the more exaggerated talk of a *new* world anarchy, or of *new* nationalisms or wars, to see that there are several patterns which Ireland could, arguably, fit.

Second, the conditions for lasting peace are neither wholly internal nor external. Both are necessary conditions. A change in the international environment, and active international involvement, are not, on their own, sufficient to guarantee peace: there are, simply, limits to what outsiders, be they states, facilitating individuals or NGOs, can do. Neither threat nor money are on their own sufficient. To criticise the failure of the international community anywhere, in Ireland, Afghanistan, Sri Lanka or Rwanda, is to imply that *on its own* such changes or mediations can resolve the conflict. They cannot. In the Irish case the range of external circumstances, and not least an active US involvement, were propitious: but as in Palestine, or Angola or Cambodia, such an external involvement is not on its own sufficient.

Third, when it comes to internal conditions, the central issue remains the intentions of the main military and political players. Peace does not come, as many in the rush of 'civil society' expectations of the early 1990s may have hoped, through the replacement of nasty people with nice people: would that it did. Protest, denunciation and scorn may play a role, but this not enough to sway 'hard' men and women, *duros* and *duras*. It comes through a decision by the nasty people that it is, at a particular moment, more advantageous to pursue peace than to pursue war. The term 'hurting stalemate', pioneered by William Zartman to refer to a situation in which a party decides it cannot attain its maximum goals, identifies such a decision.[22] It was obvious that this is what occurred in, say, Afghanistan, Palestine, Bosnia. In the Irish case it would seem evident that, at some point the republican leadership realised it could not achieve a purely military victory: there was no 'last push'. What else was rethought is less clear: we do not have an authoritative analysis as to why the IRA called the ceasefire of 1994, nor why Sinn Féin signed the GFA. It cannot be asserted, with confidence, that the hurting stalemate in the full sense of an acceptance of politics had been reached: it would appear, however, that it had, and indeed that the IRA leadership, or the more far-sighted elements within it, had come to this conclusion ten or more years previously.[23] The element of doubt about this, and the continuing uncertainty about IRA intentions associated with the decommissioning issue, in effect a mechanism for the stalling of political rather than military utility, leaves this question open.[24] It remains, however, the key question.

Fourth, in Ireland, as elsewhere, it is important not to lose sight of the inertia which a conflict of this kind creates. The majority of the people in Ireland may well be tired of the war, but there is a minority for whom, emotionally and economically, the war is a way of life – through employment in military and security forces, through the funds available from grants and through racketeering. One of the central problems in building peace in former war-torn societies – Lebanon, Guatemala, El Salvador – has been that of providing employment for former paramilitaries. In societies where the drugs trade is linked to guerrilla opposition the financial obstacles to peace-building may be even greater.

Fifth, and more broadly, there is a special problem about bringing peace in societies that are ethnically fragmented, as Ireland is, as distinct from riven by predominantly social divisions, as was the case in, for example, Central America. In fragmented societies, war creates or reinforces – more the latter in the Irish case – a deep suspicion and cleavage in the society which no rush of optimism or agreement, let alone international involvement, can overcome. Here we also find that displacement of conflict and demand from the fundamental issues – land, discrimination, violence – to secondary but now no less acute ones – prisoners, investigative commissions, nomenclature and symbolism. What the French call *l'évolution des esprits*, a broad change of mind, is much slower to come than initial enthusiasm might suggest. The voting patterns after Good Friday 1998 and the wary respect which politicians of all stripes have paid to the concerns of their communities indicate that the past, for all that people are tired of its negative side, weighs heavily on the present, stoked up, of course, by those with an interest in preserving it.

This suggests, by way of conclusion, that a comparative study of peace processes and agreements must include the possibility of failure, as well as success. Indeed, based on the record of the 1990s, one can suggest a set of four categories of peace process:

- those that are broadly successful;
- processes where political discussion continues, but with protracted and initially unanticipated delays and disappointments;
- processes where a suspension of military hostilities is accompanied by a complete political stalemate, usually policed by external forces; and
- those that break down and return to the previous levels of conflict.

The first category would include Namibia and El Salvador; the second, Palestine, Cambodia, Haiti and Ireland; the third, Bosnia, Cyprus, Nagorno-Karabagh and Western Sahara; and the fourth, Afghanistan, Sri Lanka, Sudan, Angola and Colombia.

It may be important to maintain the division between the second and third categories: the failure to reach the full implementation of an agreement does not equate to a return to the anterior situation, prior to the signing of such an agreement. This is why the most relevant parallels for Ireland may, in addition to the post-1998 Basque Country, be Palestine and South Africa: in the former the Oslo Accords of 1993 were meant to have led, by May 1999, to a final status settlement and an independent Palestinian State; in the latter the transition to multi-racial rule and the advent of the ANC to power in 1994 were meant to usher in an era of political stability and economic prosperity. Given these goals, the longer term outcome of both is still in balance; but to say that the broad goals of the initial agreement were not met does not mean that the situation has, or is likely to, return to the *status quo ante*. A slippage from the second to the third category does not equate to return to the wars of earlier years. If there is no deterministic time-table for peace, some kind of historical ratchet nonetheless operates.

This is all the more evident if these cases of stalled peace processes, of which Ireland is also one, are contrasted with the real regressions of the fourth category or with cases where a ceasefire holds but without *any* significant political or economic progress. In this perspective, and even allowing for some controlled return to paramilitary action, Ireland remains, with Palestine, in the second of the four categories of peace process – stalled, but not paralysed or collapsed. As ever, Ireland is not alone, or unique, whatever its nationalists, as well as those who despair of it overcoming its nationalisms, may sometimes assert.

Notes

An earlier version of this chapter was given as a paper to the United Nations Training School, the Curragh November 1995. My thanks to the participants in that seminar, and to contributors to the Twenty-First Century Trust conference on global governance, October 1995, for suggestions and comments.

1 See, *inter alia*, Brendan O'Leary and John McGarry, *The Politics of Antagonism: Understanding Northern Ireland* (London: Athlone Press, 1993); Ian Lustick, *Unsettled States, Disputed Lands* (Ithaca, NY: Cornell University Press, 1993); Adrian Guelke, *Northern Ireland: The International Perspective* (Dublin: Gill & Macmillan, 1988); Frank Wright, *Northern Ireland: A Comparative Analysis* (Dublin: Gill & Macmillan, 1987).

2 I have gone into this in greater detail in 'Irish Problems in International Perspective: A Personal View', *Irish Studies in International Affairs*, vol. 7, 1996, and 'Irish Nationalism in Comparative Perspective', Torkel Opsahl Memorial Lecture, 1997, Democratic Dialogue, Belfast.

3 I have written on this in 'Letter from Dublin', *Middle East Research and Information Project Reports* (Washington, DC: MERIP, 1991).

4 Cesareo R. Aguiler de Prat, 'Stormont en Euskadi?' *Mundo*, November 1998. De Prat, one of the leading Spanish students of the Irish conflict, warns, in particular, of the dangers of imposing numerical majorities in fragmented societies, but stresses that the big difference between the Basque Country and Northern Ireland is the division between communities in the latter.

5 I have gone into this in greater detail in 'Irish Neutralism in Cold War Politics: A Harder Look', Sheffield Papers in International Studies, Department of Politics, University of Sheffield, 1990.

6 Michael Cox, 'Bringing in the "International": The IRA Ceasefire and the End of the Cold War', *International Affairs*, vol. 73, no. 4, October 1997; Roger MacGinty, 'American Influences on the Northern Ireland Peace Process', *Journal of Conflict Studies*, vol. 17, no. 2, fall 1997.

7 I have drawn here on the informative analysis by a former UN participant in the Guatemala process: Peter Barwick, 'Multi-Dimensional Peacekeeping in Guatemala: Mixed Success', MSc dissertation, Department of International Relations, London School of Economics, 199.

8 In response to Iraqi pressure, the Security Council delayed for several days before passing a resolution of any kind, and then failed either to name the agressor or to call for a return to the pre-conflict boundaries.

9 Critics made much of 'double standards' in the action to support Kuwait, and cases were cited where the UN had failed to act: Palestine, Cyprus, Kashmir, Tibet, Sahara, Timor. These were, however, cases of territories that had not yet attained independence and international recognition which were occupied prior to their establishhment of a substantive independence.

10 For discussion see James Mayall (ed.) *The New Interventionism 1991–1994: United Nations' Experience in Cambodia, Former Yugoslavia and Somalia* (Cambridge: Cambridge University Press, 1996); Adam Roberts, *Humanitarian Action in War: Aid, Protection and Impartiality in a Policy Vacuum* (London: International Institute for Strategic Studies, 1996).

11 Boutros Boutros-Ghali, *Agenda for Peace*, 2nd edn (New York: United Nations, 1995).

12 For a comprehensive and perceptive account of the shift from *lucha armada* to democratic politics in Latin America, see Jorge Castañeda, *Utopia Unarmed* (New York: Knopf, 1993).

13 International Institute of Strategic Studies, *The Military Balance 1998–9* (London: Oxford University Press, 1996), table 46, pp. 295–300.

14 For documentation of recent and current wars see, amid a large literature, Dan Smith, *The State of War and Peace Atlas* (London: Penguin, 1997); Thomas Rabehl, *Das Kriegsgeschehen 1998* (Opladen: Leske & Budrich, 1999), and Mariano Aguirre (ed.) *Anuario CIP* (Madrid: CIP, 1992 and 1993).

15 Alain Minc, *Le Nouveau moyen age* (Paris: Gallimard, 1993); Robert Harvey, *The Return of the Strong: The Drift to Global Disorder* (London: Macmillan, 1995).

16　Robert Kaplan, 'The Coming Anarchy', *Atlantic Monthly*, February 1994.

17　Michael Ignatieff, *Blood and Belonging: Journeys into the New Nationalism* (London: Chatto & Windus, 1993), esp. pp. 1–2, where he argues: 'The key narratve of the new world order is the disintegration of nation states into ethnic civil war; the key architects of that order are warlords; and the key language of our age is ethnic nationalism.' Among the *new* nationalists are Germans, Quenecois, Kurds and Northern Irish; see also *The Warrior's Honour* (London: Chatto & Windus, 1998).

18　Mary Kaldor, *New and Old Wars: Organized Violence in a Global Era* (Cambridge: Polity Press, 1999); Mary Kaldor and Basker Vashee (eds.), *New Wars* (London: Pinter 1999).

19　UN, NATO, OSCE, WEU, Council of Europe, EU, Partnership for Peace.

20　'An Atrocity Too Far for Spain', *The European*, pp. 17–23, 1997. I am grateful to Keda Sodupe, Bernardo Atxaga, Jose Maria Montero and Bob Sutliffe for providing background on the role of social movements in the Basque peace progress: interviews San Sebastian/Donostia July 1991, Bilbao/Bilbo, July 1996. For critiques of ETA see *Cuadernos de CIP* (Madrid: CIP, June 1997), including Mariano Aguirre, 'Sobre las Pequeñas Patrias'.

21　'The whole map of Europe has been changed … but as the deluge subsides and the waters fall short we see the dreary steeples of Fermanagh and Tyrone emerging once again': *Hansard*, 16 February 1922, col. 1270.

22　William Zartman, *Elusive Peace: Negotiating an End to Civil Wars* (Washington, DC: Brookings Institution, 1995).

23　Kevin Bean, 'The New Departure: Recent Developments in Irish Republic Ideology and Strategy', *Occasional Papers in Irish Studies*, no. 6, Institute of Irish Studies, University of Liverpool, 1994.

24　Michael Cox makes this point well in 'Bringing in the "International"'.

27

Rethinking the international and Northern Ireland: a critique

PAUL DIXON

Internationalising Northern Ireland

The emergence of the peace process and the interest of international relations scholars have precipitated a welcome and growing body of literature emphasising the importance of the international dimension in the politics of Northern Ireland. Leading figures in the field, Frank Wright, Adrian Guelke and Michael Cox, have challenged the insularity of much analysis of the conflict by setting it in a comparative and international perspective.[1] The international dimension has been said to play a key role in the emergence of the Northern Irish peace process. It is argued that the ending of the Cold War changed the international climate and precipitated moves to end anti-imperialist conflicts in South Africa and the Middle East. These developments made it far more difficult for the Provisional IRA to continue its anti-imperialist military campaign and facilitated the ceasefire. The ending of the Cold War also prompted the British Government to moderate significantly its attitude to Northern Ireland, making possible an accommodation with republicans. The end of superpower rivalry allowed the US to ignore the 'special relationship' with the UK and interfere in the internal affairs of its closest ally. The US was able to overcome British intransigence and push the process forward. The acceleration of European integration broke down mistrust between the British and Irish governments and provided models for overcoming conflict. Northern Ireland could not escape the 'irresistible logic of globalisation'.[2] This comparative account tends to reinforce the nationalist and republican discourses on the peace process.[3]

The international dimension *has* played a significant role in the Northern Ireland conflict. The debate here is not about whether the international dimension has influenced the conflict; rather it concerns, firstly, how much weight is to be attached to the international dimension, and, secondly, what the mechanisms are by which the international dimension has played a role. These issues are not easy to resolve, but it is possible to show that the arguments of some international relations theorists overemphasise the international dimension. In this chapter, more weight is placed on the internal (Northern Ireland) and *national* (UK and Ireland) dimensions of the conflict.

The argument presented here contends, firstly, that British policy towards Northern Ireland since 1972 has been marked by continuity and *tactical adjustments*, with the international dimension having little impact on its trajectory. International pressure is thought not to have played a significant role in making the British Government negotiate the power-sharing compromise reached at Sunningdale with the Republic of Ireland and the Northern Irish parties in 1973 (power-sharing plus Council of Ireland). This suggests that international pressure was not necessary, although it may have been helpful, in bringing about the similar but more complex GFA in 1998 (power-sharing, plus an Irish dimension, plus an east–west dimension). If international influence was unnecessary to produce the Sunningdale settlement of 1973 (arguably a more pro-nationalist agreement than the GFA), why was it necessary to produce the GFA of 1998 (famously referred to by Séamus Mallon as 'Sunningdale for slow learners')? International pressure may, from time to time, influence British policy, but the continuity of policy is largely explained by the internal and *national* constraints operating on it.

Secondly, it is argued that important developments which led to the peace process were already underway prior to the ending of the Cold War and that it is shifts in the republican movement rather than the international climate that largely explain the peace process.

Thirdly, the Sinn Féin leadership did use a 'script' about the changing international climate to persuade grassroots republicans to give up the armed for an unarmed struggle. This script included stories about the ending of the Cold War, the development of peace processes in South Africa and the Middle East, the role of the US in the 'pan-nationalist front' and the development of European integration.

Fourthly, the international dimension has been used by political actors to choreograph a settlement in Northern Ireland, creating a theatrical performance to persuade diverse constituencies to accept accommodation. The US president played a role in the choreographing of the peace process but in a way that was probably often welcomed rather than opposed by the British Government. Choreography is, therefore, an important mechanism for the influence of the international on the peace process.

Fifthly, the continuities and similarities between the Sunningdale Agreement and the GFA suggest that the influence of European integration on the peace process has also been exaggerated.

Finally, the impact of the international and discourses about the role of the international on unionism and the peace process are considered. The exaggeration of the impact of the international on the peace process has been in the interests of 'pan-nationalism', and this may have exacerbated unionists' insecurities about their isolation and the outcome of any peace process.

Bringing in the international

The key texts analysed here are two papers by Michael Cox.[4] The four key areas of argument are considered in what follows.

The Provisional IRA: from insularity to anti-imperialism

Cox 'does not reject "internalist" explanations for the end of the IRA war but suggests that we cannot isolate the "peace process" in the North from changes taking place in the wider international system'; 'the winding down of the "armed struggle" was also the result of transnational pressures upon the most immediate reason for the conflict: the Provisional IRA'. The Provisional IRA built its movement on 'traditional and authentically Irish lines', and so 'there was no need for republicans to look outside of Ireland for inspiration or guidance', and it was only later that they built international links, particularly with the PLO and the ANC.[5]

The end of the Cold War, the receding tide of global radicalism after 1989 and the apparent movement toward the resolution of conflicts in the Middle East and South Africa created an international climate that made the resolution of the conflict in Northern Ireland 'far more likely': 'In effect, having become part of a wider revolutionary project, Irish republicanism could hardly avoid being affected by its collapse in the latter half of the 1980s.' Cox states that his 'purpose here … is … to explain how and why the end of a larger competition, which apparently had very little to do with the local conflict in Northern Ireland, has such a big impact upon the theory and practice of the Irish republican movement'.[6]

Cox argues that 'the conclusion of the Cold War made it far more difficult for the IRA to continue with its military campaign – not because the organisation did not have the capacity to do so, but rather because in the post-Cold War era, its campaign of violence could no longer be so readily justified'.[7] Moreover, 'the fact that the Cold War had drawn to a conclusion made a ceasefire far more likely'; and 'by altering completely the global framework within which the IRA campaign had hitherto been conducted, the end of the Cold War made it far more difficult for the organization to legitimize a strategy which by the late 1980s had already reached a dead end'.[8] After the collapse of communism, republican explanations for Britain's continuing presence in Northern Ireland had less credibility.

Britain: 'no selfish strategic or economic interest'

The end of the Cold War and the collapse of communism in Eastern Europe in 1989 and in the USSR in 1991 posed enormous problems for the republican movement's analysis of British interests in Northern Ireland. Traditionally, republicans had argued that Britain had political, strategic and economic interests in keeping Northern Ireland part of the Union. Britain had a historical attachment to the Union as part of the British nation, and its economic control over Ireland was facilitated by occupation of the North. This also secured Britain's strategic interests by preventing the emergence of a united and neutral Ireland outside of the NATO alliance. British Secretary of State for Northern Ireland Peter Brooke made a 'significant intervention' in a 'remarkable speech', declaring in November 1990 that Britain had 'no selfish strategic or economic interest in Northern Ireland'. According to Cox, the IRA ceasefire 'would have been unthinkable' without this declaration.[9]

The US: no Cold War, no special relationship?

The ending of the Cold War also made it possible for the US to play a far more decisive role in Northern Irish affairs. Because the probability of the Conservative Government helping to bring the republican movement into a peace process 'was never likely to be high', the role of the US in the early stage of the process 'was to be crucial'. The US backed a 'fairly high level fact-finding delegation to Ireland' and played a 'crucial back stage role supporting Dublin against London in the difficult negotiations that in the end led to the signing of the Downing Street Declaration'. Clinton then gave his support for the granting of a US visa to Adams in January 1994 against British wishes.[10]

The EU: the road to post-nationalism?

The changing position of Ireland in Europe and changes in the structure of Europe 'as much as anything else … made the peace process possible'. Until Britain and Ireland joined the EEC (European Economic Community, forerunner of the EU) in 1973 they had few real incentives for co-operating over the management of the conflict in Northern Ireland. Joining the EEC helped to break down mistrust between the two countries. The 1985 Anglo-Irish Agreement and the 1993 Downing Street Declaration could not have occurred 'without the longer term revolution that had transformed Anglo-Irish relations after Ireland and the UK joined the EC back in 1972'. The European example also showed Northern Ireland how 'apparently permanent divisions could be overcome by peaceful means'.[11] Elizabeth Meehan, reviewing the impact of the EU on Northern Ireland, argued that 'the language and conventions of EU policy-making have helped to open up a space for contending parties to talk about solutions to old problems in a new way – and to act upon that'.[12]

Change within continuity: the first and second peace processes

At the heart of the critique of this nationalist discourse is an argument about the continuity of British policy on Northern Ireland since the early 1970s. The second peace process (1994–present) during the recent Troubles in Northern Ireland is too seldom seen in the context of the first peace process (1972–74), which produced the Sunningdale Agreement (1973). The Good Friday, or Belfast, Agreement (1998) is a more sophisticated document than Sunningdale's, but the two are comparable in that at the heart of both lies, firstly, power-sharing and, secondly, the all-Ireland dimension.[13]

In the case of the first peace process it is usually argued that the international dimension – influences outside Britain and Ireland – played little part in bringing about the Sunningdale Agreement.[14] On the other hand, it is claimed that the international dimension played an important, even vital, role in the second peace process. The question remains: why, if the international dimension is so important, did the British and Irish governments manage to reach agreement in 1973 but the British had to be coerced by the international dimension into the 1998 GFA?

The British did not have to be coerced into the Sunningdale Agreement because – regardless of international influence – this was the likely ground on which a stable settlement to the conflict was to be found. British policy on Northern Ireland since the early–mid-1970s can be seen to have been characterised by a considerable degree of continuity in the pursuit of this twin-track (power-sharing–Irish dimension) settlement but with tactical adjustments.[15] There was no radical departure in British policy in the late 1980s or early 1990s. Peter Brooke's speeches merely reiterated in a stark way what had been stated before: that there was no purely military solution to the conflict and that Britain had no selfish, strategic or economic interest in Northern Ireland.[16] The British Government played an active role in the peace process, and recent evidence suggests that there were exchanges between Gerry Adams and the British Government dating back to 1986.[17] There is further evidence of British determination in the back-channel contacts with Sinn Féin (1990–93) and the overtures of Brooke and his successor Peter Mayhew to the republicans. The signing of the Downing Street Declaration (1993), the Joint Framework Document (1995) and the GFA (1998) are all evidence of British determination to do this. The problem for the British was how to push the process forward without alienating the unionists, who would have to be brought to the negotiating table with Sinn Féin.

British policy and the Government's approach to conflict resolution in the first and second peace processes had similarities.

- The British made assumptions about the existence of a moderate silent majority in Northern Ireland.
- Contrary to myth, the British Government did conduct negotiations with paramilitaries to bring them into the democratic process.
- The British declared that they would accept the will of the majority in Northern Ireland if it favoured Irish unity and effectively disavowed any selfish, strategic or economic interests.
- There was also close co-operation between the British and Irish governments at Sunningdale, to the extent that unionists were probably pushed too far in the negotiations.
- The British were caught between reassuring unionists of their support for the Union and declaring themselves neutral between the contending parties.
- This conflict of interest arose out of a perceived need to *balance* unionist and nationalist claims in order to reach an agreement.[18]

The continuities in British policy on Northern Ireland suggest that the impact of the international dimension was less significant than has been suggested. It may also be that the international dimension is important less for its impact on the conflict than for the way actors in the conflict, particularly the Sinn Féin/IRA leadership, have used it to legitimise their tactics to the republican grassroots.

The internationalisation of the Provisional IRA?

Although the republican movement was not short of home-grown heroes,[19] there is evidence that throughout the recent conflict republicans looked abroad to anti-imperialist movements for inspiration and propaganda for what they saw as their war against the British. The successes of anti-imperialist movements – at their height in the 1960s and 1970s – in forcing Britain's withdrawal from the empire and the victory of the Viet Cong over the USA in Vietnam seemed to suggest that anti-imperialism was surfing the wave of history and British defeat in Northern Ireland was inevitable. According to Stephen Howe,

> To link the Ulster conflict with Third World anticolonial struggle was to associate it with revolutionary glamour, with movements which commanded massive sympathy amongst the young and radical in advanced capitalist states including Britain itself, with new and imaginative models of social development, perhaps above all with success.[20]

The republicans attempted to depict Northern Ireland as Britain's Vietnam. Seán Mac Stiofáin, the Provisional IRA's chief of staff during 1970–72, saw the struggle as an anti-imperialist one: 'the struggle for Ireland's freedom was only part of the worldwide struggle against imperialism. Therefore I and other Republicans rejoiced at the successes of any other movement fighting a true revolutionary war, and we mourned their defeats.' He took heart from the battle of Dien Bien Phu (the defeat of the French colonial power by the Vietnamese in 1954): 'we knew what it meant. The tide of history was beginning to turn, and the decaying colonial powers could not hope to brazen out humiliating military defeat like that for very long … The colonial era appeared to be doomed, but it would not be finally destroyed without fierce fighting and bitter sacrifice.' Mac Stiofáin had been imprisoned with Cypriot 'terrorists' in the 1950s and had learnt from them methods of opposing British rule; he was also an observer of other anti-imperialist struggles.[21] According to Maria Maguire, the main examples followed by the Provisional IRA in its terrorist campaign against the British Army were Cyprus and Aden.[22] There was a belief among the Provisionals that, like other anti-imperialist movements, if they could inflict sufficient casualties on the British Army, they could provoke a withdrawal. Republican hopes and unionist fears of forcing a British withdrawal were not without some substance.[23] Martin McGuinness negotiated on behalf of the IRA in London in 1972; he refused accommodation with unionists, arguing that they had to get rid of the British. This was best achieved by violence, 'as proved all over your Empire. You will get fed up and go away.'[24] According to Liam Ó Ruairc, during the 1970s Sinn Féin made common cause with Third World countries, including Tanzania, Cuba and Algeria. In the 1980s Sinn Féin showed interest in Nicaragua, SWAPO (South West African People's Organisation) in Namibia and Angola, North Korea and South Africa.[25] Libya provided important materiel support to the IRA.

The propaganda war was seen as integral to the Provisional IRA's struggle against 'British imperialism'. The portrayal of republicans as part of an international and successful anti-imperialist movement was likely to be useful in bolstering republican morale and determination as well as increasing pressure on the British Government, but was it necessary to sustain the campaign? If republicans were, as Cox argues, insular at the beginning of the 1970s, then they were able to sustain their endeavour during the height of the violence without international legitimacy. The faltering Middle Eastern peace process could persuade republicans to return to violence. The South African peace process has left the ANC the dominant force in South Africa, while in Northern Ireland Sinn Féin has but been one element in a power-sharing coalition. In other words, is it that the fate of these other peace processes impinges on the republican movement or is it the republican leadership's use of these international examples, and the international dimension, to justify its political strategy that is important here?

The origins of the peace process?

To search for a single point of origin for the peace process is probably misguided. The peace process is more usefully seen as the result of an unfolding dynamic that cannot be separated off from previous developments. Nevertheless, there are good reasons for thinking that the developments which resulted in the peace process were already under way well before the ending of the Cold War. These include:

- Sinn Féin's shift to the 'long war' in the late 1970s, setting the Republican movement on a more political path;
- the further emphasis on political and electoral struggle during and after the hunger strikes (1981), leading to the 'ballot box and armalite' strategy;
- the Anglo-Irish Agreement, which gave the Irish Government a say in the running of Northern Ireland. The British Government's determination to face down unionist resistance to the Agreement suggested that unionists were not simply the dupes of British imperialism;
- in terms of republican ideology Sinn Féin's decision to end abstentionism in 1986 was a major development, provoking a split in the movement and the formation of republican Sinn Féin;
- the Irish Government's contacts with Sinn Féin (1987);
- by the mid- to late 1980s there was evidence that the republican movement had fought its way, politically and militarily, into a stalemate with the British Government;[26]

- the Hume–Adams talks (1988) initiated a debate within nationalism, with the SDLP arguing that the British had no military or economic interests in Northern Ireland and were effectively neutral. They proposed a 'pan-nationalist front' to bring national and international pressure to bear on the British to persuade unionists into a united Ireland.

In other words, there were major developments in republican thinking prior to the ending of the Cold War, whether this is dated from 1989 and the collapse of communism in Eastern Europe or from 1991 and the demise of the Soviet Union. The end of the Cold War was unexpected, so developments in republican thinking were not even in anticipation of the collapse of communism, and Sinn Féin was not an advocate of Soviet-style socialism.

The end of the Cold War did appear to have some impact on the willingness of British Prime Minister Margaret Thatcher to make overtures to the republican movement. In November 1989 Peter Brooke, secretary of state for Northern Ireland, gave an important interview in which he claimed that, although the security forces could contain the IRA, he found it 'difficult to envisage' the Provisionals' military defeat. He indicated that the British would negotiate if the IRA stopped its violence. Twelve months later Brooke declared that Britain 'had no selfish strategic or economic interest in Northern Ireland'. Margaret Thatcher had approved Brooke's last speech, whereas before the end of the Cold War she had had reservations about such a declaration. She also gave her personal approval to secret talks with Sinn Féin in October 1990 in order to find out what was happening in the republican movement.[27]

Whether Thatcher's attitude regarding the end of the Cold War and towards Britain's strategic interests in Ireland was more widely reflected in British ruling circles may be doubted. In the early to mid-1970s the British Government's willingness to contemplate withdrawal (and Irish unity or independence) suggests that it was unlikely that Britain had overriding strategic 'Cold War' interests in Northern Ireland that necessitated military occupation. The 'Cold War' argument misses the continuities of British policy and exaggerates the significance of developments in British policy in 1989–90. The British had long accepted that there was no purely military solution and that Britain had 'no selfish strategic or economic interest' in Northern Ireland. This had been argued by the SDLP since the early 1970s and was accepted by some leading Provisionals by the mid-1970s.[28] Brooke's speeches in 1989–90 were restatements of British policy rather than major developments. But the content of these speeches, in the light of the end of the Cold War, may have been deliberately presented as signalling a new departure, and they were anyway important in stimulating further ideological developments among Republican activists.

Public knowledge of developing peace processes in South Africa (1990, the lifting of the ban on the ANC and the release of Nelson Mandela) and the Middle East (1993, the Oslo Accords) also came after significant moves in the Northern

Ireland peace process. The emphasis placed on these fellow national liberation movements in republican ideology – particularly in the more propaganda-friendly case of South Africa – may well have accelerated an ideological rethink, but they have to be seen in the context of developments prior to 1989. The apparent upsurge of 'ethnic conflict' following the end of the Cold War provided an alternative explanation of the conflict in Northern Ireland, though one less flattering to the republican movement, because comparisons with former Yugoslavia and other 'ethnic conflicts' suggested that the IRA was engaged in a communal war rather than a movement for national liberation.

The argument that British policy shifted with the ending of the Cold War was also useful for the Sinn Féin leadership to deploy in trying to convince republicans that the way forward was unarmed struggle. The leadership could claim that it had remained strong but that the British had made the first important concession, and in response to a shift in British policy it could now contemplate a new unarmed strategy.[29] This discourse disguises the fact that the British and the SDLP had long claimed that the British had no selfish strategic or economic interest in Northern Ireland. Conservative Prime Minister Edward Heath, in his Guildhall speech on 15 November 1971, stated:

> Many Catholics in Northern Ireland would like to see Northern Ireland unified with the South. That is understandable. It is legitimate that they should seek to further that aim by democratic and constitutional means. If at some future date the majority of the people in Northern Ireland want unification and express that desire in the appropriate constitutional manner, I do not believe any British Government would stand in the way.

This was underlined in the Green Paper of October 1972, in which the British Government stated that: 'No UK Government for many years has had any wish to impede the realisation of Irish unity, if it were to come about by genuine and freely given mutual agreement and on conditions acceptable to the distinctive communities.'[30]

The British did not seem to have any overriding strategic interest in Northern Ireland that could not have been accommodated by an Irish government in the event of a united Ireland. The interests of Britain seem primarily to have been in the stability of Ireland, and it was prepared to contemplate any settlement likely to achieve that. This was apparent after Bloody Sunday and again in the mid-1970s, when even Conservative politicians were willing to consider a range of options, including repartition and Irish unity, if they were likely to stabilise Ireland.[31] In fact there was considerable continuity in British policy arising from what were perceived to be the requirements of conflict resolution.[32] There is evidence that the republican leadership's thinking on British interests in Northern Ireland developed after Margaret Thatcher had taken on unionist opposition to the Anglo-Irish Agreement in 1985 rather than just at the end of the Cold War.[33] Republican ideology had generally portrayed unionists as the dupes of British imperialism, but the conflict between the British Conservative (and Unionist) Government and Ulster unionism again casts doubt on this assumption.

The US dimension

The influence of the USA was not required to bring about Sunningdale in 1973; it is possible to argue, therefore, that, while it may have been helpful, it was not essential for the negotiation of the GFA in 1998. The Conservative Government had played an important role in pushing forward the peace process well *before* US pressure was brought to bear. The problem for the British is that publicly claiming this role was likely to destabilise the unionist population of Northern Ireland, who have been highly sceptical of the peace process and *interference* from outside. British Secretary of State for Northern Ireland Tom King had 'contacts' with the Sinn Féin leadership dating from 1986.[34] It was Margaret Thatcher who, shortly before her resignation in 1990, authorised back-channel contacts with Sinn Féin and had tolerated Brooke's overtures to the republican movement. Brooke's speech and the operation of the back channel both pre-date Clinton's influence and 'the Greening of the White House'.[35] The succeeding British Prime Minister John Major developed the process, with conciliatory speeches from Secretary of State for Northern Ireland Patrick Mayhew and the continuation of the back channel. In spite of a diminishing majority, Major signed the Downing Street Declaration in 1993 and the Joint Framework Document in 1995 – the latter, more particularly, being seen as a pro-nationalist document.

While the US undoubtedly played a more active role *during* the peace process (although it had previously involved itself in Northern Ireland), it may be that this had been, to some extent, with the connivance of the British Government. Had the British wanted to see the peace process move forward they had an interest in helping the Sinn Féin leadership persuade its grassroots of the importance of pursuing unarmed struggle. This was partly to be achieved by creating the illusion of a pan-nationalist front in which the US played an important symbolic role. The pan-nationalist front was principally a charade constructed by the Irish Government, the SDLP and the US Government to persuade republicans that they could pursue their goals more effectively through unarmed rather than armed struggle. The power of the pan-nationalist front was to be demonstrated by *apparent* victories over the British Government, such as the granting of Gerry Adams's first visa to visit the USA. The British Government also created the illusion of a pan-unionist front to counter the image of pan-nationalism and to reassure unionists that their interests would be protected in any peace process.[36] As a 'senior British source' explained: 'It is the job of the British government to push the Unionists to a line beyond which they will not go; it is the job of the Irish government to pull the Republicans to a line beyond which they will not come.'[37]

There is evidence that the decision to grant Gerry Adams a visa to enter the US in 1995 was choreographed, the charade being acted out by the British and US governments to reassure important interests in Northern Ireland and take the peace process forward. In 1995, six months after the ceasefire, Adams wanted to visit the US again, this time to raise funds for Sinn Féin. The British again *publicly* opposed such a move and wanted the US Government to use its leverage with Sinn Féin to make progress on the decommissioning of IRA weapons before all-party talks could take place. In private, however, Mayhew told US officials that he wanted Sinn Féin to 'seriously discuss decommissioning' rather than there being a hand-over of weapons before they could enter talks. Nancy Soderberg, deputy national security adviser, described 'a complete disconnect' between what Mayhew asked of the US Government in private and his stronger public statements for decommissioning later the same day when he announced the 'Washington Three'.[38]

Patrick Mayhew's failure to emphasise to the Americans the importance of an arms' hand-over could be seen as a complete blunder, or else the British Government may have believed that it had room to push unionists farther by taking steps to water-down the conditions necessary to bring Sinn Féin into talks. *Privately*, the British Government may not have been too distressed at the decision by the US president to lift the ban on Adams and allow him to raise funds, as this decision would bolster the credibility of the Sinn Féin leadership's unarmed strategy in the eyes of the republican grassroots. The ceasefire would be entrenched by appearing to demonstrate the support of the most powerful government in the world for pan-nationalism. As the British secretary of state had said to a private meeting: 'To some extent we have got to help Mr Adams carry with him the people who are reluctant to see a ceasefire.'[39]

The British Government's publication of the Joint Framework Document and its weakening of the decommissioning conditions in the 'Washington Three' resulted in rising unionist and Conservative backbench dissent. In view of this, John Major needed to reassure the former by playing his role as 'champion of the Union'. Major made a public show of his fury at Clinton's decision over the Adams visa and refused to take the US president's telephone calls for five days. Shortly thereafter, Clinton praised Major for taking 'brave risks' in making peace 'within the context in which he must operate'.[40] According to a source close to Clinton, within weeks 'the President had developed a genuine respect for Major and figured he was trying to do the right thing and understood why Major might need to make a gesture by not taking a phone call'.[41]

The US president's high-profile rejection of the British Government underlined the potential power of the pan-nationalist front and seemed to show republicans the influence they could have through 'unarmed struggle'. At the same time, Major's public display of anger at Clinton demonstrated to unionists that the British Government was fighting its corner and maintaining pan-unionist unity. The US Government was believed to have gained for Adams his first visa to the US, in 1994. But, as the former Taoiseach Albert Reynolds commented, it was the *appearance* of a pan-nationalist victory that was more important than the reality: '*if we could be seen* to win a diplomatic argument [over the British] on the world stage, supported by Washington ... it would have been a big step forward' (my emphasis).[42] Reynolds commented later on the granting of the first visa:

> John Major told me he was taking a very strong stand on it, and I could understand that. Let Washington decide who they want to support. I convinced Washington that it was important as part of the demonstration [to republicans] of the strategy of non-violence, that it could succeed, of having a few victories here and there. Having said that, John had to be seen to be winning at times as well. We all recognised that.[43]

The image of the US president coercing the British Government into the peace process against its will appears to be far from accurate. The dynamics of the peace process were already under way long before Clinton's presidency. While US influence may have exerted some pressure on the British, particularly over Adams's first visa application, its effect has been deliberately exaggerated.[44] The key role played by the US president was symbolic, in giving credence to the Sinn Féin leadership's strategy that the republican movement could more effectively advance its goals through the pan-nationalist front (including the USA) and by unarmed rather than armed struggle.[45] Clinton appears to have moderated his pro-nationalist stance after 1995, perhaps as he came to acknowledge the importance of addressing (or appearing to address) both republican and unionist concerns if there was to be a successful outcome to the peace process. The GFA was one of Clinton's major foreign policy successes. As Will Hazelton concludes:

> Despite Irish America's nationalist sympathies and aspirations, one-sided intervention supporting Irish unification would have not only damaged US relations with Britain but also proved highly destabilising given Northern Ireland's volatile divisions and counter-productive for further Anglo-Irish cooperation. More limited and impartial involvement, aimed at helping the parties edge toward a consensus, avoided the twin pitfalls of having to assume responsibility for a potentially costly situation or of engaging in empty rhetoric and symbolic posturing to appease a largely domestic audience. Moreover, close and friendly relations with both Ireland and Britain meant that the US, for one, was neither required nor expected to be the senior partner.[47]

The EU

There are at least three ways in which the EU is held to have impinged on the peace process:

- The British and Irish governments joined the EEC in 1973, and this gave them incentives to co-operate over Northern Ireland, which helped to break down mistrust between the two countries. This brought about a transformation in British–Irish relations.
- The example of the EU and the institutions themselves provided an illustration to Northern Ireland of the ways in which conflict could be overcome by peaceful means.

- The process of European integration has had an ameliorating impact on identity in Northern Ireland and has helped to create an environment in which a peace process could come to a successful conclusion.

These arguments are questionable, given the experience of the early 1970s. Firstly, during this period there was close co-operation between the British and Irish governments in their unsuccessful attempt to construct a power-sharing settlement. In September 1971 the British prime minister met the taoiseach, symbolising Britain's recognition of the Republic's legitimate interests in northern affairs. The Green Paper of October 1972 maintained that 'it was clearly desirable that any new arrangements for Northern Ireland should, whilst meeting the wishes of Northern Ireland and Great Britain, be, so far as possible, acceptable to and accepted by the Republic of Ireland'.[47] In fact, there is evidence that British–Irish co-operation was even too close. The London correspondent of the *Irish Times* reported that the Irish 'entered enthusiastically into negotiations, and from this point onwards the British kept them very closely informed, usually in advance, of their proposals. Relations, recently so chilly, soon became warm, even excessively cosy.'[48] There appears to have been a cooling in British–Irish relations from 1974 to 1979. After the Dublin summit of 1980 a new activism developed in the relationship, which has produced the Anglo-Irish Agreement, giving the South role in the affairs of the North, the Downing Street Declaration, the Joint Framework Document and the GFA.

The second claim for EU influence is its impact on the construction of the institutions of the GFA, yet little evidence is produced to support this claim, and the British already had experience of setting up power-sharing institutions in the retreat from empire. The Sunningdale Agreement, it has been argued, bears a close resemblance to the GFA. As no one has argued that the EEC influenced the structure of the Sunningdale institutions, it seems more likely that the general institutional framework of the GFA (power-sharing and an Irish dimension) was influenced more by what are perceived to be the requirements of conflict resolution than the example of the European Union.

The third aspect of European influence, its impact on identity in Northern Ireland, is difficult to prove or disprove. Modernisation theory and 'hyper-globalisers' have argued that functional co-operation and integration, of the type promoted by the EU, will replace national identity or else dissipate national identities as a European identity emerges alongside them. Some have argued that Northern Ireland is moving into a post-nationalist or postmodern era. There appears to be little evidence to support the idea that European integration is ameliorating the conflict. The peace process has been elite-driven: opinion polls and surveys do not suggest that politicians are being compelled by any movement from below toward accommodation. The spectre of European integration has been used by nationalists to claim the inevitability of Irish unity. Unionists have tended to accept these functionalist assumptions and consequently have come to oppose European integration and be very sceptical of the EU. Although the republican movement is highly sceptical of European integration and modernising assumptions that it will result in Irish unity, it is another discourse that the leadership can use to sell the peace process to its grassroots. During the secret back-channel contacts between Sinn Féin and the British Government, the British representative claimed that European integration made Irish unity inevitable.[49]

The development of the EU may well have had an impact on the conflict; the problem is in attempting to assess the extent of this impact. It is difficult to be precise, but doubt can be cast on some of the excessive claims of the 'Euro-enthusiasts', whose aspirations – attractive as they might be – have clouded their analysis of the problems facing the realisation of those aspirations, resulting in an over-optimistic view of the demise of the state and nationalism. In 1988 Guelke surveyed the impact of Europe on the conflict, concluding: 'The Community dimension has failed to transcend sectarianism ... The EEC, far from dissolving the conflict, has internationalised it. This has worked politically to the benefit of constitutional nationalism, though not from the bottom up, but from the top down.'[50]

In the British general election of June 2001 John Hume and his brand of 'post-nationalism' were defeated by the Euro-sceptical nationalists of Sinn Féin, one of the few parties in the Republic to oppose the Nice Treaty and therefore be on the winning side in the referendum. Similarly, the extremely Euro-sceptical DUP is gaining ground on the merely Euro-sceptical UUP. The depth of the Republic's Europhilia has been thrown into question by the rejection of the Nice Treaty in 2001, although that verdict was overturned in 2002. Euro-enthusiasts have exaggerated the impact of the EU on the conflict in Northern Ireland. They have confused prescription with description: they may desire to see a post-nationalist future, but that should not be mistaken for a belief that that future has arrived.

Conclusion: internationalisation and unionist isolation

The argument presented here is that the international dimension *does* have an impact on the conflict in Northern Ireland. While there are great difficulties in assessing the impact of the international, doubt can at least be cast on some of the more excessive claims for its influence. The mechanisms by which this influence is felt are not always clearly specified. The aspect of international influence emphasised in this chapter has been the way it has been used to provide a nationalist discourse for deployment in the propaganda war and to persuade an important republican constituency to support unarmed struggle to achieve their objectives. This has stressed the influence of the international dimension and relegates the role of internal factors on the Northern Ireland peace process. The strength with which this case has been argued is an important corrective to insularity, but it has exaggerated the role of the international dimension and the power of the pan-nationalist front. The British Government has been reluctant to counter this nationalist argument, first, because it has been useful in sustaining republican involvement in the peace process, and second, because to emphasise the role of the British Government in choreographing the peace process could well raise unionist fears of other 'backstage' manoeuvres by 'perfidious Albion'.

The exaggeration of international influence on the peace process may have had a benign impact on republicans, encouraging them to suspend the armed struggle. But it could also have raised unionist fears that the internationalisation of the conflict has resulted in a process that is biased against an increasingly powerless and isolated unionism, with the British Government as the untrustworthy guarantor of the place of unionists within the Union. This may have inhibited the ability of pro-Agreement unionists to sustain involvement in the peace process and accommodation with nationalists.[51]

This raises the intriguing question as to whether the exaggeration of the role of the international dimension has hindered rather than helped the peace process? To what extent has the beneficial effect on nationalism been outweighed by the adverse effect on unionism?

Unionists have long feared that the process of European integration would undermine the Union between Great Britain and Northern Ireland rather than bring the Republic back into the Union. Europeans have tended to be more sympathetic to the nationalist cause than that of unionism.[52] The interventions of US presidents in Northern Ireland have been stacked in favour of the nationalist community, tending to have more of an electoral interest in appeasing the Irish-American community by making overtures to nationalists than in supporting unionist demands. Traditionally, the Irish-Americans voted for the Democratic Party, and Jimmy Carter's presidency saw a more active role for the US on Northern Ireland, as indicated by his statement on 30 August 1977, signalling a significant departure in US policy and establishing a precedent for future interventions. It attacked republican supporters in the USA and offered economic aid in the event of a solution to the conflict. Republican President Ronald Reagan sought to woo Irish-Americans away from the Democrats. US pressure was thought to have played some role in bringing about the signing of the Anglo-Irish Agreement in 1985.[53] President Clinton's involvement in Northern Ireland was, then, part of a pattern of interventions that favoured nationalists, although some effort was made to maintain contacts with unionists.[54] As Dumbrell concludes:

> To sections of unionist opinion, however … [their] … worst nightmare seemed to have been realised: an American-driven process, geared to American security interests, seemed likely to generate cross-border institutions and, eventually, a united Ireland in which Northern Protestants would be abandoned. By the same token, Clinton's actions raised unrealistic hopes in nationalist circles.[55]

Opinion polls suggested that Catholics were more favourably disposed than Protestants towards US interest in Northern Ireland. A poll for the *Sunday Times* in September 1996 found that 75 per cent of Catholics and 26 per cent of non-Catholics interviewed thought American interest in Northern Ireland was a help towards a settlement, while 64 per cent of non-Catholics and 14 per cent of Catholics thought it a hindrance.[56] A survey conducted in 1998 found that 93 per cent of Catholics found the US Government to be 'very or quite helpful' in the search for peace compared to 55 per cent of Protestants.[57] Both principal unionist parties have been highly sceptical of the role of the US in Northern Ireland and have attempted to counteract what they see as its pro-nationalist bias.

The election of George W. Bush to the US presidency and the terrorist attacks on the World Trade Center on 11 September 2001 have, arguably, made the international climate more supportive of unionism. The IRA's alleged links with the FARC movement in Colombia, its gun-running, refusal to disarm and association with other international 'terrorist' groups have not endeared it to the US president or to Irish-America.[58] The pan-nationalist front has demanded further IRA moves on disarmament as payback from republicans for the 'leg-up' into democratic politics which has seen Sinn Féin emerge as the principal nationalist party in Northern Ireland, while making significant gains in the Republic. Unionist support for the GFA has slipped, but Bush's right-wing presidency may provide some reassurance to Ulster's unionists that the nationalist, or at least republican, tide in the US is ebbing.[59]

Notes

I thank the panelists and participants at the session 'Northern Ireland: The International Dimension' at the British International Studies Association Conference, Edinburgh, 2001. In particular, I thank Michael Cox for generously acting as discussant and for encouraging the development of the paper I presented at that session into this chapter.

  1 Frank Wright, *Northern Ireland: A Comparative Analysis* (Dublin: Gill & Macmillan, 1987); Adrian Guelke, *Northern Ireland: The International Perspective* (Dublin: Gill & Macmillan, 1988); Michael Cox, Adrian Guelke and Fiona Stephen (eds), *A Farewell to Arms? From 'Long War' to Long Peace in Northern Ireland* (Manchester: Manchester University Press, 2000).
  2 Michael Cox, '"Cinderella at the Ball": Explaining the End of the War in Northern Ireland', *Millennium*, vol. 27, no. 2, 1998, p. 340.
  3 Paul Dixon, *Northern Ireland: The Politics of War and Peace* (Basingstoke: Palgrave, 2001).
  4 Michael Cox, '"Bringing in the International": The IRA Ceasefire and the End of the Cold War', *International Affair*, vol. 73, no. 4, 1997; and Cox, '"Cinderella at the Ball"'.
  5 Cox, '"Cinderella at the Ball"', pp. 329, 330 and 331.
  6 *Ibid.*, pp. 332 and 330–1.
  7 *Ibid.*, p. 330.
  8 Cox, '"Bringing in the international"', pp. 676 and 677.
  9 Cox, '"Cinderella at the Ball"', p. 334.
  10 *Ibid.*, pp. 335 and 336.
  11 *Ibid.*, pp. 337 and 339.
  12 Elizabeth Meehan, '"Britain's Irish Question: Britain's European Question?" British–Irish relations in the Context of European Union and the Belfast Agreement', *Review of International Studies*, vol. 26, 2000, p. 96.
  13 Dixon, *Northern Ireland*, p. 285.
  14 John Dumbrell, *A Special Relationship: Anglo-American Relations in the Cold War and After* (Basingstoke: Palgrave 2001), pp. 199–201; Joseph E. Thompson, *American Policy and Northern Ireland* (London: Praeger, 2001).

15 Paul Dixon, 'British Policy towards Northern Ireland 1969–2000: Continuity, Tactical Adjustment and Consistent "Inconsistencies"', *British Journal of Politics and International Relations*, vol. 3, no. 3, 2001, pp. 340–68.

16 Dixon, *Northern Ireland*, pp. 285 and 144–7.

17 Ed Moloney, *A Secret History of the IRA* (London: Allen Lane, 2002), p. 246.

18 Dixon, 'British Policy towards Northern Ireland 1969–2000'.

19 Joanne Wright, *Terrorist Propaganda: The Red Army Faction and the Provisional IRA, 1968–86* (London: Macmillan, 1991), p. 223.

20 Stephen Howe, *Ireland and Empire* (Oxford: Oxford University Press, 2000), p. 170.

21 Seán Mac Stiofáin, *Memoirs of a Revolutionary* (Edinburgh: Cremonesi, 1975), pp. 52–3, 70 and 52.

22 Maria Maguire, *To Take Arms: A Year in the Life of the Provisional IRA* (London: Macmillan, 1973), p. 74.

23 Dixon, *Northern Ireland*, chapter 5.

24 Peter Taylor, 'McGuinness Was "Man to Watch" in 1972', *Daily Mail*, 3 May 2001.

25 See Ó Ruairc's series of interesting articles at http://lark.phoblacht.net.

26 Henry Patterson, *The Politics of Illusion* (London: Serif, 1997), p. 210.

27 Anthony Seldon, *John Major* (London: HarperCollins, 1997); *Guardian*, 16 October 1999.

28 Dixon, *Northern Ireland*, chapters 5 and 6.

29 Quoted in Cox, '"Cinderella at the Ball"', pp. 334–5.

30 Northern Ireland Office, *The Future of Northern Ireland: A Paper for Discussion* (Belfast: NIO, 1972), para. 52.

31 Dixon, *Northern Ireland*, pp. 120 and 158–62.

32 Dixon, 'British Policy towards Northern Ireland 1969–2000'.

33 Eamonn Mallie and David McKittrick, *The Fight for Peace* (London: Mandarin, 1997).

34 Moloney, *A Secret History of the IRA*, p. 246.

35 Sinn Féin, *Setting the Record Straight* (Belfast: Sinn Féin, 1994).

36 Paul Dixon, 'Political Skills or Lying and Manipulation? The Choreography of the Northern Ireland Peace Process', *Political Studies*, vol. 50, no. 3, 2002, pp. 725–41.

37 *Observer*, 5 February 1995.

38 Conor O'Clery, *The Greening of the White House* (Dublin: Gill & Macmillan, 1996), p. 191.

39 *Irish Times*, 9 January 1995.

40 *Daily Telegraph*, 18 April 1995.

41 O'Clery, *The Greening of the White House*, p. 219.

42 *Endgame in Ireland*, BBC2 Television, 8 July 2001.

43 Cited in Eamonn O'Kane, 'The Republic of Ireland's Policy towards Northern Ireland: The International Dimension as a Policy Tool', *Irish Studies in International Affairs*, vol. 13, 2002, pp. 127–8.

44 Dumbrell, *A Special Relationship*, pp. 210–11.

45 Dixon, 'Political Skills or Lying and Manipulation?'

46 Will Hazelton, 'Encouragement from the Sidelines: Clinton's Role in the Good Friday Agreement', *Irish Studies in International Affairs*, vol. 11, 2000, p. 117; Andrew J. Wilson, 'The Billy Boys Meet Slick Willy: The Ulster unionist Party and the American Dimension to the Northern Ireland Peace Process, 1994-99', *ibid.*

47 NIO, *The Future of Northern Ireland*, para. 78.

48 James Downey, *Britain, Ireland and the Northern Question* (Dublin: Ward River Press, 1983), p. 125.

49 Paul Dixon, 'European Integration and Irish Unity?', in Sean Byrne and Cynthia L. Irwin (eds), *Turning Points in Ethnopolitical Conflict* (West Hartford, CT: Kumarian Press, 2000), pp. 174–89.

50 Guelke, *Northern Ireland*, p. 164.

51 Paul Dixon, 'Internationalization and unionist Isolation: A Response to Feargal Cochrane', *Political Studies*, vol. 43, 1995.

52 Guelke, *Northern Ireland*, p. 172.
53 Dixon, *Northern Ireland*, p. 199.
54 Wilson, 'The Billy Boys Meet Slick Willy'.
55 John Dumbrell, 'The United States and the Northern Irish Conflict 1969-94: From Indifference to Intervention', *Irish Studies in International Affairs*, vol. 6, 1995.
56 Quoted in *Irish Political Studies*, vol. 12, p. 190.
57 Quoted in R. MacGinty and J. Darby, *Guns and Government: The Management of the Northern Ireland Peace Process* (Basingstoke: Palgrave, 2002), p. 117.
58 See the hostility of the *New York Post* editorial of 10 November 2002 to the republican movement.
59 *Guardian*, 12 January 2002.

28

Rethinking the international and Northern Ireland: a defence

MICHAEL COX

Introduction

How do we account for, let alone make sense of, one of the least likely peace processes of more recent times, namely that which occurred in Northern Ireland in the second half of the 1990s? This question has preoccupied, indeed baffled, many commentators for one rather obvious reason: like many other significant events of the late twentieth century, hardly anyone expected the Troubles to come to an end. On the contrary, the overwhelming consensus was that the war in Northern Ireland would persist, either because the two communities remained deeply divided, or because the conflict had developed its own particular dynamic, or because it was not really costing enough. There was, though, another reason for pessimism: an assumption that the ending of the Cold War, which was helping to bring to an end other intractable conflicts elsewhere in the world, could not have any real influence in Northern Ireland.[1] The fall of the Berlin Wall may have been welcome, as was the overcoming of the larger East–West divide in Europe. Indeed, some in the North of Ireland even hoped that if the war between the blocs could be resolved, then the conflict in Northern Ireland could be too? But these were lone voices in a bleak wilderness, and as one grisly year gave way to another after 1989, few really believed or expected that events in Europe, Germany and the world at large would influence developments in the North. Thus in the early 1990s it very much looked at least as if this most singular of local conflicts – fed, it was argued, by factors that had more to do with the seventeenth than with the twentieth century – would go on and on, presumably until one of the two sides either collapsed or triumphed over the other.

It was this pessimism based on such a reading of the relationship between Northern Ireland and the larger East–West conflict that I set out to challenge in a number of interventions, beginning in 1997, three years after the IRA announced its first ceasefire and a year before the GFA itself.[2] In these I advanced an argument that some even graced with the title 'thesis', one which when boiled down to essentials advanced two simple propositions: that a long-term peace in Northern Ireland was more likely than was prolonged war – not a fashionable position to defend at the time; and that one of the reasons for this was the larger shifts in the international system brought about by the end of the Cold War. Few, however, seemed prepared to go along with this upstart effort to bring in the 'international'; some, in fact, took great pleasure in trying to knock it down. I found this most odd. After all, had not other historians in the past not pointed to a relationship, say, between events in Ireland in the 1790s and the French revolution? Had they not shown a connection, too, between what happened in Ireland in 1914–21 and British imperial policy in the world at large? Had they not also pointed to a connection between Northern Ireland's role in the Second World War and its much closer integration into the UK after the war – even between British strategic interests in the early years of the Cold War and Northern Ireland's geographical proximity to Atlantic sea-lanes?

So why all the fuss now about trying to show an association (no more) between a development as historically crucial as the end of the Cold War and the unexpected turn of events in Northern Ireland? Was Northern Ireland a place apart, standing, so to speak, outside of history? If my several critics were to be believed, then the answer to this question, it seemed, was an unambiguous and most definite, 'Yes'.

People of different backgrounds objected to my thesis. First, there were mainstream political scientists, to whom my argument was not only lacking in parsimony (which I took to mean that it complicated the picture by introducing one variable too many) but focused on the wrong thing – the international – when all one needed to do was concentrate on the domestic, the true terrain of analysis where, according to at leasat some political scientists, the truth was bound to be located.[3] This theoretical scepticism often went hand in hand with a refusal to think of Northern Ireland in anything other than the terms in which it was understood by most local actors. Thus if those on the ground thought the end of the Cold War did not matter, then, quite obviously, it did not matter. There was also a much bigger and more varied group who tried to meet me half way.[4] The international should not be ignored, they conceded, but, when all was said and done, it was still local factors, from people power,[5] war weariness and British intelligence successes,[6] to the formation of a new Catholic middle-class in the North, that really mattered. There was no need therefore to make too much of the global when the explanation for what happened in Northern Ireland in the 1990s could be found in Northern Ireland itself, in Ireland more generally or in the changing relationship between Ireland and the UK.[7]

My initial response to these varied criticisms was less one of hostility than one of surprise that, on the one hand, so many had been kind enough to take my own, rather puny, efforts so seriously and, on the other, that they (with one or two exceptions) had made me sound much more of an international extremist than I really was. After all, I had never tried to suggest that the peace process was a result of the ending of the Cold War alone.[8] Nor, of course, had I ever tried to deny the central importance of internal factors. My one, indeed my only, goal was altogether more modest: namely, to add something to our understanding of Northern Ireland by trying to talk about a relationship that had in my view been ignored by those seeking to understand why this most unexpected of peace processes ever took place.[9] Nor did I think I was I tilting, Don Quixote-like, at windmills of my own imagining. Indeed, judging by more recent work, the tendency to explain the transition from war to peace in largely localist terms persists, with authors still going on in great detail about who said what to whom, when and where in Dublin, Belfast and London, and rarely venturing outside the local bar, the Stormont meeting room or the west Belfast rendezvous to explain what, to many outsiders at least, seems self-evident: that however we try to measure influence or weigh contributing factors, a part of the story *has* to involve the outside world, what was happening in it, and how this then impacted on Northern Ireland.

Part of my problem, of course, was that the conflict in Northern Ireland seemed so parochial that few could imagine it had had any relationship at all to what was going on elsewhere. Another was that as the debate unfolded it became clear that what I understood by 'the Cold War' differed considerably from what others understood by the term. This difference crystallised when one of my erstwhile critics (a very senior Irish politician) asked me quite pointedly whether or not I really believed all this stuff about the end of the Cold War and its influence on the situation in the North? He was himself unconvinced. As he pointed out to one whom he evidently saw as a rather naive academic from across the water (at the time I was living in Wales), I didn't know the half of it. But one thing of which he was certain, having read the files, was that the Provos had never been run by the Russians. So, how could the end of the Cold War have had any impact on the peace process? As I mused at the time, this wasn't quite the point I was trying to make. The Cold War, as I had explained elsewhere and at great length – though obviously with insufficient clarity for the Irish politician in question – had not just been about two superpowers slugging it out with missiles, spies and proxies. Rather, it had been something much wider, a system in its own right, that had impacted on politics, influenced ideological debate, shaped the way we thought about economics, underpinned alliances, defined the Third World, and fed in many subtle ways into the way we all thought about the world around us. All of this, and not just bi-polarity in some very formal sense, is what had come to an end in the late 1980s; and what I had set out to show was how this quite revolutionary transformation in the international landscape – the end of history, no less, according to Fukuyama – fed into the situation in Northern Ireland more generally and into IRA thinking more specifically. This was the critical connection. The IRA may well have been a quint-essentially Irish phenomenon. However, it could not escape the world or ignore what was happening outside of Ireland. Nor, I think, did it try to. Indeed, as a leading figure in Irish republicanism later conceded, 'the end of the Cold War and its effects on the strategic and the regional interests of the West made it possible for a number of peace processes' to take place, including, he implied, the one then beginning to unfold in Northern Ireland.[10]

Of course, this connection was not made by all militants within the republican movement. As Richard English has shown in his quite magnificent study, *Armed Struggle*, republicanism was a very broad ideological church. It also had different constituencies, including those who happened to be in the prisons and those who were not. One can even show – and Richard does – that the origins of what became known as the peace process actually predate the fall of the Berlin Wall. So why assign such importance to the international? All fair points. But they hardly do major damage to my argument. After all, I had never meant to suggest that all republicans were internationally minded, only that some of them, the more crucial individuals, were, and they then went on to do the business in the 1990s. Nor was I trying to deny that the sources of the peace process could be traced back in time – that would be absurd.

Yet, as even my more critical opponents would have to admit, it was only in the 1990s, once the Cold War had actually come to an end, that the process reached a successful conclusion; and I do not think that this was a coincidence. Indeed, we do not even have to guess the point. As a number of senior republicans at the time and since have argued, the struggle within Ireland was part of something much bigger and wider, and when the world started to change beyond recognition after 1989, this could not but have an impact on their thinking. It did so, in the first instance, by showing that there might be other ways of achieving one's goals than through revolutionary violence; it did so, secondly, by weakening the republican move-ment's rationale for fighting the British presence in Ireland; thirdly, the ending of the Cold War made it possible for a 'third party', the USA, to play a far more decisive role in Northern Irish affairs; and, finally, it was inevitable that the gradually retreating tide of global radicalism after 1989 would have an impact on the thinking of the IRA, a self-proclaimed revolutionary movement with a project of building socialism in Ireland. Indeed, there is strong evidence that as the cause of revolution around the world began to ebb in the 1990s, this had a marked influence on a number of key figures in the republican movement; enough, it seems, to have forced at least some of them to rethink what they had been doing since the heady days of the 1970s.

I turn now to the key issues and ways in which the winding down of the Cold War impacted on Northern Ireland, and the theory and practice of modern Irish republicanism.[11]

Farewell to national liberation

The Provisional IRA began life in 1970 not as as a fully formed guerrilla organisa-tion, but as a poorly equipped group who saw its first task to be the defence of the besieged Catholics of the North against the perceived threat posed by the Protestant majority.[12] Those who created the Provisionals also saw their job as rebuilding a movement along traditional and authentically Irish lines. Thus, according to the early 'Provos', there was no need for republicans to look outside of Ireland for inspiration or guidance. Indeed, at a time when national liberation movements around the world were eliciting the sympathies and support of student radicals in Western Europe and the USA, the Provisional leadership seemed almost to go out of its way to distance itself and the new IRA from those other struggles – especially if they were led by revolutionary Marxists.

In spite of this apparent narrowness of outlook, however, the IRA was impelled by both military necessity and a genuine sense of political solidarity to forge links with other movements of national liberation. In part, the move was hastened by the collapse of the IRA's original scenario of quick victory over the British.[13] This not only forced a shift in its tactics, but led also to the emergence of those in the organisation more sympathetic to socialist ideas and more inclined to build serious bridges to other revolutionary groups and regimes. This hardly made the republican movement agents of the USSR, as some on the conservative right argued at the time.[14] On the other hand, its continuing campaign against the USA's most special ally – the UK – certainly made the USSR sympathetic to the IRA's cause. It would be something of an exaggeration to talk, as one writer has done, of the IRA now becoming 'Pravda's Provos'.[15] Nevertheless, Soviet coverage of the situation in Northern Ireland remained broadly sympathetic to the republican cause and only changed significantly following the collapse of the USSR itself in 1991.

Nor was it just the USSR that looked favourably on the struggle in Ireland: revolutionaries from nearly every other part of the world viewed the Irish situation through the larger prism of anti-imperialism, insisting that they were all engaged in a larger project that would ultimately conclude in victory for the oppressed and the exploited. Their radical Irish comrades could only agree; indeed they expressed this most forcefully in statement after revolutionary statement which looked not only to the more obvious examples of national liberation in South Africa, the Middle East and Central America, but even to Cuba itself. Indeed, for some within the movement, Cuba was something of a beacon. Its leaders, after all, had been marginal and persecuted figures, like themselves; they had, however, succeeded, and, having overthrown imperialism, they went on to build a more pluralistic version of offshore island socialism that some in Ireland found particularly attractive. Not for nothing did many of the younger republicans see in Che a potent symbol of resistance and ultimate sacrifice, while in Fidel they saw the revolutionary turned principled statesman who had more than his fair share of admirers in republican ranks – one of whom happened, significantly, to be Gerry Adams.

There was and is no simple or direct connection between the settlement of other regional conflicts after the Cold War and the change of strategy by the IRA. As a leading figure in the republican movement noted at the time, 'only a fool would argue that there are direct parallels' between the situation in Northern Ireland and those of other Third World conflicts.[16] However, as another significant figure has conceded, those who had already gone through the difficult transitional process leading, elsewhere, from war to peace, might have something to teach the Irish; he even admitted that those who had made peace in other countries had given 'tremendous support' to those in Ireland trying to do the same.[17] Sinn Féin's president Gerry Adams made much the same general point. Ireland, he accepted, was different and it would be a 'mistake' to think otherwise. On the other hand, if conflicts as apparently intractable as those in the Middle East and South Africa could be resolved, then this obviously held out hope for the people of Ireland. Furthermore, because these other conflicts had been brought to an end, according to Adams 'an international climate' was created which made the resolution of all conflicts, including the one in Northern Ireland, far more likely. Northern Ireland's conflict might have been different from the others, but it was neither unique nor immune to change taking place in the wider international system.[18]

In effect, having become identified with and made cause alongside other national liberation movements, Irish republicanism could hardly avoid being affected by their effective collapse in the latter half of the 1980s. Logistically of course the republicans could fight on, as they did most effectively with weapons supplied by another anti-imperialist – Libyan leader, President Qadaffi. Having the capacity to bomb and shoot, however, was hardly the same as being part of a broad movement whose larger aim was nothing less than the destruction of imperialism as a system. Inevitably, as that movement began to retreat, republicans in Ireland started to lose their various points of ideological and political reference around the world. Even more crucially, perhaps, those who earlier had extended solidarity to their 'Irish brothers and sisters' now began to advise them to follow the path of peace. It was one thing to have your enemies suggest that you abandon the armed struggle; it was something else altogether to have those with enormous moral standing in the republican movement – figures like Mandela and Arafat – tell you the same.[19]

The Soviet threat and after

If post-Cold War events in the Third World increased the IRA's sense of isolation, developments in the larger strategic landscape helped undermine its analysis of why it was necessary to fight the British. To explain why this should have been so, we have to understand the republican movement's explanation of the presence of the British in Ireland.[20]

According to republicans, Britain remained because Northern Ireland provided them with a vital (albeit costly) platform from which to exercise economic control over Ireland as a whole. As a Sinn Féin document of 1988 argued, though the annual British subvention to the North was high, it would be quite 'wrong to conclude that this level of spending negates any British economic interest in Ireland'. But economics was only one part of a complex set of ties linking the two countries. Of even greater importance was an abiding British fear of what might happen were Ireland ever to be united. For locked, as it was, into what seemed like a permanent Cold War conflict with Russia, Britain – according to republicans – stayed on in the North to secure one part of Ireland for NATO and to prevent the creation of a united and neutral Ireland outside of the NATO alliance. Economics may have been important in maintaining the Union. There was even something to be said for the argument that the 'British establishment' had a historical attachment to the Union, if not necessarily to unionists themselves. But these were second-level explanations of why Britain went to such lengths to remain. As one republican source put it before the Berlin Wall came tumbling down, though Britain's 'continuing involvement in Ireland' was based on a number of calculations, including an exaggerated fear of Ireland becoming a 'European Cuba', by far the 'most important' consideration 'now' was its concerns about Irish neutrality and the serious threat which that posed to NATO and Britain's 'strategic interests'.[21]

The collapse of communism in Eastern Europe in 1989, followed two years later by the implosion of the USSR itself, clearly posed considerable problems for the republican movement's analysis of why Britain hung on to Northern Ireland. After all, with no USSR, there could be no Soviet threat; and this inevitably left Sinn Féin in desperate need of a new argument to explain both the British presence and why force was needed to remove it. It also created an intellectual opening for John Hume, leader of the SDLP. Hume was already involved in detailed negotiations with Gerry Adams about the best way of resolving the situation in the North. Significantly, part of these negotiations had revolved around the critical issue of British intentions. Adams, not surprisingly, insisted that the British had powerful reasons for staying in Ireland, and the only way to get them to go was therefore by physical means. Hume, on the other hand, believed that the British were either agnostic about or indifferent to Irish unity; in fact, as he pointed out to Adams, they had already indicated as such in Article 1 of the Anglo-Irish Agreement of November 1985 where it was clearly stated that if a majority in Northern Ireland wanted a united Ireland, the Government of the United Kingdom would not stand in the way. Now, four years later, with Soviet power in retreat across Europe and the Warsaw Pact in free-fall, it seemed to Hume that the republican argument (and the strategy which flowed from it) was more than ever quite fatally flawed.[22]

In a quite deliberate move designed to support Hume in his discussions with Adams, Secretary of State for Northern Ireland Peter Brooke made a significant intervention. In London in November 1990 he outlined British policy on Ireland in a remarkable speech in the course of which he both displayed a genuine sensitivity to nationalist history and insisted that the Government itself had no 'selfish strategic or economic interest in Northern Ireland'.[23] The response of Sinn Féin to this very real challenge was to cast doubts on Brooke's motives and his analysis. Nonetheless, that display of bombast could not hide its very real uncertainty about what to do next. Indeed, in private, at least some of its leaders were beginning to accept the possibility that Britain's declared neutrality 'might be real and that the IRA might, therefore, be open to persuasion on the merits of armed struggle'.[24]

In and of itself, the collapse of the Soviet threat would not have induced an IRA ceasefire. That said, it would wrong to underestimate the impact which the change in the wider East–West relationship had on the republican movement; and, in particular, on the leadership's ability to persuade sceptics that because of new global realities there was not much point fighting an enemy who might anyway want to go now that it had no reason for staying. Martin McGuinness in particular played a crucial role in convincing the hard-liners about the need for a deal; and one of the ways in which he did so was by stressing that he too was now certain that 'in the new European and post-Cold War situation, Britain no longer had any strategic interests in Ireland'.[25] Furthermore, once it became apparent to the two governments, in London and Dublin, that the question of British interests was critical, they did everything in their power to address the issue in an attempt to convince republicans that violence was no longer necessary. It was no coincidence, of course, that the crucial Downing Street Declaration of December 1993 reiterated the now familiar post-Cold War line that the British Government had 'no selfish strategic or economic interests in Northern Ireland'.[26] It would be plainly absurd to suggest that the inclusion of this phrase led directly to the first IRA ceasefire. Yet, without it, a cessation of violence would have been unthinkable

No longer 'special?'

Taken together the collapse of the Warsaw Pact and the disintegration of the wider revolutionary project created a set of international conditions which made the peace process more likely. There was always a possibility, however, that despite this critical convergence of circumstances one of the key actors would fail to act decisively. The Conservative Government in particular had good reason to be cautious: after all, on two occasions the IRA had tried to kill its key leaders and had murdered two of Mrs Thatcher's closest friends. Many in the Government also doubted whether Adams and McGuinness could deliver a ceasefire; and, even were they able to do so, whether such a ceasefire would last. Moreover, they feared that to include Sinn Féin in the political process now would create enormous political problems in terms of their relations with the main unionist parties at Westminster. Finally, as formal guardians of the Union and keepers of the faith on law and order, the Conservative Government could hardly be expected to be enthused about negotiating with those whose method was murder and whose primary aim was the destruction of the link between one part of the UK and the rest.

The likelihood of a Conservative Government seizing the opportunity and pushing ahead with some sort of agreement was never likely to be high, which is why the role of the US in the early stages of the peace process was to be crucial.[27] The details of what happened are now fairly well known. As a presidential candidate, Bill Clinton had forged a close alliance with the Irish-American lobby, a fact which did not go unnoticed by Sinn Féin. Naturally enough, this lobby expected him to play a more active role over Northern Ireland than had his predecessor. He did not disappoint them. First, in the autumn of 1993 he backed an important, and fairly high level, fact-finding delegation to Ireland. Significantly, it was while the delegation was in Ireland that the IRA announced a temporary ceasefire. In December 1993, the US then played what many regard as a vital back-stage role supporting

Dublin against London in the difficult negotiations that, in the end, led to the signing of the Downing Street Declaration. Finally, and crucially, in January 1994, President Clinton reversed an earlier decision and, against the advice of the State Department, the CIA and the FBI, personally sanctioned a visa for Gerry Adams to visit the USA. Though a crushing defeat for the British Government, this decision and the extraordinary visit which followed in February was of great importance in the peace process – certainly, without it, the IRA would not have declared a ceasefire six months later.[28]

It might well be argued that Clinton's decisive intervention on Northern Ireland had very little to do with the end of the Cold War as such, and was simply another example of an American president playing the Irish card for reasons of domestic politics. Clinton's activism might also be read (and indeed has been) as reflecting the growing influence in the US of a new type of Irish-American: powerful instead of poor, organised in the boardrooms and not just in the Democratic precincts of Chicago and New York, and desperately keen to help Ireland in a constructive way rather than sending money to Ireland to help 'the boys'. It could also be seen as a measure of the power of the Kennedy family – including that of the new ambassador to Ireland, Mrs Jean Kennedy Smith. Some have even argued that Clinton's intervention was a act of sheer revenge against his political enemies in the British conservative establishment who had done everything in their power to get one George Bush and not William J. Clinton elected to the White House back in 1992.

Though there is clearly *some* truth in all these varied explanations of Clinton's Irish policy, they do not add up to the whole story. They can hardly explain, for instance, why Clinton was prepared to ignore the advice of key foreign policy officials over the decision to admit Adams into the US; nor do they really help us understand why he tilted as far as he did towards Dublin. Most importantly of all, they cannot account for a series of decisions which seemed almost designed to alienate the one country which many still regarded – even in the post-Cold War era – as the USA's special ally. And alienated the British Government undoubtedly felt. Hence, when John Major was informed of the White House decision to allow Adams into the US he is reliably reported to have been 'furious', and for a short time thereafter refused to talk to Clinton. A campaign of vilification against Clinton in the British press rumbled on for months thereafter. In fact, well over two years later, Clinton's policy on Ireland was cited on the front page no less of *The Times* as an important indication of his general foreign policy ineptitude.[29] Even in Ireland itself many were genuinely astonished by how far Clinton had been prepared to go. As one highly astute and well-placed analyst later put it, there is little doubt that the 'US input' on the North was 'tough for [the] British to swallow'.[30]

Of course Clinton's intervention, though critical in bringing about the first IRA ceasefire, could not in the end prevent it breaking down, and it was to take a good deal of effort by a new and energetic Labour Government in Britain to persuade Irish republicans to restore the peace in July 1997. But with or without 'New' Labour and Clinton's close personal ties to Tony Blair, the US was still going to pursue its own agenda in Northern Ireland. No longer would it defer to London or treat the question of Northern Ireland (as it had done until 1989) as an internal British affair. Moreover, even with a new UK administration in control of Northern Ireland, the peace process continued to require the support of the US. Indeed, a key player in brokering the peace deal in April 1998 was none other than the former Senate majority leader, George Mitchell.[31] It was not just Senator Mitchell, however, who made the GFA possible.[32] It was Clinton, too. In fact, it was only a 'last-minute appeal by Clinton' to the Irish Prime Minister Bertie Ahern, to Unionist leader David Trimble and, finally to Gerry Adams that broke the deadlock on 10 April and made the historic agreement possible. Little wonder that Blair later praised the US president for his 'unswerving support and commitment to the peace'. [33]

Europe and Ireland

Finally, any analysis of the republican decision to halt its campaign of violence has to take account of the changing position of Ireland in Europe and changes in the very structure of Europe itself.[34] In fact, it might well be argued that it was those changes, as much as anything else, that made the peace process possible. To understand why, we have to return beyond 1989 to 1972 and the Irish Republic's original decision join the EEC.

Initially motivated by a recognition of the failure of economic nationalism to bring genuine prosperity, Ireland's decision to 'join' Europe transformed the country in myriad ways. In straightforward material terms, of course, it made Ireland altogether more prosperous and far less dependent on the British market. But, more subtly, it brought about an important alteration in what has been termed the Irish national project.[35] Hitherto, Irish politics and culture was dominated by the idea of Irish unity and opposition to British rule in the North. After 1972, as a result of deeper integration within Europe, this project seemed to make a good deal less sense. Indeed, as Ireland became more a part of Europe, the old nationalist dream of making the country whole once again looked increasingly irrelevant. Certainly, in the minds of most Irish people, it seemed far less important than the Common Agricultural Policy, getting large amounts of aid from Brussels, or proving to its European neighbours that it had at last become a developed society.[36] Moreover, as the dreary military campaign in the North continued unabated, many in the South began to think about the costs of running the other part of Ireland, and wondered, too, whether or not their new found prosperity in Europe would be threatened by unification; and, having concluded that it might be, began to revise their views about Ireland's traditional claims to the 'six [heavily subsidised] counties' of Antrim, Down, Tyrone, Fermanagh, Armagh and Derry.[37]

Joining Europe thus transformed Ireland, and in the process created a widening gap between traditional nationalist, or republican, aspirations and new Irish realities. Hence, whereas old-style nationalists may have dreamt of fighting for Ireland (as they were still doing in the North) more and more citizens in the Irish Republic itself saw their future to be in acquiring an education and working either in Europe or possibly at home. Equally, whereas it had once been normal to call for the protection of Irish industries, in the new Ireland the State itself now made every effort to encourage foreign investment. Naturally, this was anathema to classical republicans who argued that this would both undermine a particular way of life and mean the loss of economic independence. The new political class in Dublin and the overwhelmingly mass of the Irish people brushed aside such objections. The more cynical among the Irish intelligentsia even suggested that there was only one thing worse than being 'exploited' by multinational corporations which introduced new skills and new jobs into Ireland, and that was not being exploited at all! This may have been a poor joke, but in the Irish context it was not an insignificant one and reflected an important shift in the wider debate about the nature of imperialism and its impact on Ireland.[38]

If Ireland's accession into the wider European space undercut old republican truths, it also changed the nature of the Anglo-Irish relationship. Until joining Europe and becoming a partner of Britain, Ireland had had few real incentives in co-operating with the UK in the management of the North. However, the experience of partnership in Europe actually forced Dublin and London together. This did not change their differing perspectives on the North. Nevertheless, by uniting the countries in the same organisation it did help break down the mistrust which had previously poisoned relations between the two. It led them also to the fairly obvious conclusion that their division had contributed to the conflict in Northern Ireland and that the disturbances in the North posed a serious threat to Ireland as a whole. Thus both – it was now clear – had to work in tandem to ensure that instability in Northern Ireland did not spill over and render Ireland itself ungovernable. This, of course, was the true meaning of the Anglo-Irish Agreement and the Downing Street Declaration. While both statements were designed to deal in the short term with the political and military threat posed by Sinn Féin and the IRA, neither could have happened without the longer term revolution that had transformed Anglo-Irish relations after Ireland and the UK joined the EEC back in 1972.[39]

Finally, if dynamic change in Europe and in Ireland's relationship with Britain did much to weaken the appeal of traditional republicanism, developments after 1989 seemed to undermine the republican case altogether. It did so, firstly, by showing that deep and apparently permanent divisions could be overcome by peaceful means. Moreover, as many were quick to point out at the time, if it was possible to heal the scars that had once disfigured Europe, was it not feasible that the same could happen in Northern Ireland itself? Indeed, according to those engaged in trying to persuade the IRA to give up the armed road (notably, the influential John Hume), until the chasm between the two communities in the North had been bridged, there was little point in fighting for Irish unity. It was also left to Hume to draw another lesson from the events in Europe. Borders in the new post-Cold War

Europe, he argued, were becoming increasingly irrelevant. Hence, what exactly was the purpose of a military campaign aimed at eliminating something that was, in effect, just an imaginary line across the Irish countryside? Hume was quite blunt in his assessment. In an increasingly integrated Europe, he argued – where the very notion of *sovereignty* itself was being brought into question – the IRA campaign and the pre-modern assumptions which underpinned it were basically irrelevant.[40] Furthermore, what exactly were republicans fighting for? Prior to 1989 the movement could at least claim (and key figures like Adams and Morrison regularly did) that its objective was to build an Irish form of socialism on the island of Ireland. But with the left now in headlong retreat across Europe, that project seemed like a pipe-dream, a product of old thinking rendered irrelevant by the disintegration of the old European system.

Again, the extent to which these varied changes played a part in transforming republican theory and practice is not easy to measure precisely. However, there is strong evidence that key figures in the leadership were not insensitive to the fact that irreversible alterations in the European landscape posed a series of difficult questions which traditional republicanism could not easily answer. A key figure in Sinn Féin indeed conceded that one of the factors that made the peace process possible was (to use his own words), 'the Single European Act and the dominance of the EU on the island of Ireland'.[41] Certainly, the highly revisionist Sinn Féin programme of 1992 bore witness to the influence which changes in Europe was having on republican thinking. One can also detect the same processes at work in the less radical language that key figures in the movement began to employ. Though a few remained clearly committed to their vision of a socialist Ireland standing outside of the capitalist club of Europe, most began to sound decidedly less enthusiastic about constructing what amounted to a siege economy in opposition to the European Union. Many also started to wonder about the wisdom of struggling for something in Ireland that had apparently failed elsewhere. As one of their number pointed out, though republicanism had traditionally been a movement of economic resistance, by the mid-1990s its attitude to the market and private enterprise had undergone a good deal of change. He expressed the point rather pithily (at a time when Adams himself was trying to convince American multinationals to invest in Catholic West Belfast), that republicans no longer had a serious 'problem with capitalism'.[42] Prior to the ideological earthquake of 1989 such thoughts would have been considered pure heresy in an organisation devoted to liberating the 'men of no property'. With the passing of the old Europe and the collapse of planning across the Continent, this was no longer the case. Neither Ireland, it seemed, nor those who had fought for over twenty-five years to unite it by violent means could escape the irresistible dynamic of globalisation.

Conclusion

I have been concerned to show how and why a particularly brutal and lengthy military campaign, conducted by one of the most established guerilla organisations of the twentieth century against one of the more effective democratic states finally came to an end. Whether the 'war' would have come to an end of its own accord – the result, in the last analysis, of a military stalemate between the British State and Irish republicanism – is, of course, an open question.[43] Evidently many of my critics would seem to think so. I am not so sure. Domestic factors may indeed have started the ball rolling before the ending of the Cold War; indeed, the critical Anglo-Irish Agreement was in the process of being drafted even before Gorbachev came to power! But one agreement in 1985 and a host of other events (including the IRA's decision to go political in the early 1980s) do not a peace process make. And that is where I think the 'international' did make a significant contribution to the final winding down of the Troubles. Born of the turbulent 1960s, sustained indirectly by the Cold War in the 1970s and 1980s, they finally – though not inevitably – came to a conclusion in the settling 1990s – along with a number of other conflicts which had drawn more direct inspiration from the larger struggle between East and West.

Yet even though the 'war' in the North has come to an end,[44] that does not in itself mean that the underlying sources of the conflict have completely disappeared.[45] It is one thing to make peace; it is quite another to construct a stable society in which all can unite around the same institutions. It has not happened in the Middle East; it has not happened in Bosnia, and there is a strong chance it will not happen in the North of Ireland either. As others in this volume have shown only too graphically, although we may have moved into a new era as a result of the peace process and the GFA, this has neither eliminated sectarianism, nor overcome identity differences nor resolved deeply divisive issues such as decommissioning, police reform and the establishment of serious North–South bodies – problems which, added together, have done much to erode support for the Northern Ireland Executive established in 1998. In fact, the wonder is not that the executive finally fell when it did, but that it lasted as long as it did.

Many questions remain unresolved therefore. That said, Northern Ireland has managed to travel a considerable distance from where it had been in the 1980s to where it is now, in the first decade of the twenty-first century. Of course, times have changed. When I wrote my initial piece, we were still living in what was generally referred to as the post-Cold War era, when many things seemed possible. Now, as we are so often reminded, that moment has passed, to be replaced by a new era of insecurity and new forms of terrorism associated with Islam and what one writer has termed the 'Occidental' hatred of all things Western. To some, there is no great difference between previous forms of terror – normally associated with the Cold War – and these more catastrophic forms. Indeed, what we are seeing today, it is argued, is merely old terrorist wine in some new theological bottles. I would beg to differ. Ruthless though old forms of terrorism may have been, their instigators were still compelled to operate in a world not of their own, other-worldly, fantasies composed of infidels and paradise, but one shaped by the logic of a larger ideological conflict that in the main involved rational actors, rational ends and the possibility of negotiated settlements. Indeed, it was precisely that rationality which in the end drew Irish republican leaders to the inescapable conclusion that under conditions where the chances of national liberation were rapidly receding, in a world where history was decidedly not moving in its direction, it was high time to rethink their strategy. Those dealing with a very different kind of terrorist threat today face an altogether more difficult situation, and may be allowed the momentary luxury of thinking that those who had to deal and finally come to terms with the Provisional IRA had a relatively easy time of it. Jihad-ists may not be inter-nationally ignorant; in fact, in many ways, they seem to have a better grasp of global realities than those who tried to destroy Northern Ireland by force. Yet one very much doubts if they will be influenced in the same way as an earlier generation of Irish revolutionaries appear to have been by something so well defined as the Cold War, whose conclusion in the 1980s provided a space which, other things being equal, made some form of peace settlement possible. Clearly, we all live in more dangerous times, even those now enjoying the fruits of a well-deserved peace in Northern Ireland.

Notes

1 See Adrian Guelke, 'The Peace Process in South Africa, Israel and Northern Ireland: A Farewell to Arms?', *Irish Studies in International Affairs*, vol. 5, 1994, pp. 93–106.
2 See Michael Cox, 'Bringing in the "International": The IRA Ceasefire and the End of the Cold War', *International Affairs*, vol. 73, no. 4, 1997, pp. 671–93.
3 See Paul Dixon, 'International Influence on Northern Ireland?' *Irish Studies in International Affairs*, vol. 13, 2002, pp. 105–20.
4 See the serious attempt to deal with my argument by Richard English in his magisterial, *Armed Struggle: A History of the IRA* (London: Macmillan, 2003), pp. 303–15.
5 See Feargal Cochrane, 'Unsung Heroes or Muddle-Headed Peaceniks? A Profile and Assessment of NGO Activity in the Northern Ireland "Peace Process", *Irish Studies in International Affairs*, vol. 12, 2001, pp. 97–112.
6 See for example Peter Taylor, *Behind the Mask: The IRA and Sinn Féin* (New York, TV Books, 1998).
7 The role of the Anglo-Irish Agreement of 1985 in creating peace in the 1990s is most forcefully articulated perhaps in Arwell Ellis Owen, *The Anglo-Irish Agreement: The First Three Years* (Cardiff: University of Wales Press, 1994).
8 See my '"Cinderella at the Ball": Explaining the End of War in Northern Ireland', *Millennium*, vol. 27, no. 2, 1998, pp. 325–42.
9 Though see Garrett FitzGerald and Paul Gillespie, 'Ireland's British Question' *Prospect*, vol. 12, October 1996, pp. 25–6.
10 Interview with Mitchell McLaughlin, 23 July 1996.
11 Aside from the now definitive study by Richard English, the three most useful guides to the IRA and the peace process are Brendan O'Brien, *The Long War. The IRA & Sinn Féin: From Armed Struggle to Peace Talks* (Dublin: O'Brien Press, 1993); Eamonn Mallie and David McKittrick, *The Fight for Peace: The Secret Story Behind the Irish Peace Process* (London: Heine-mann, 1996); and Ed Moloney, *A Secret History of the IRA* (London: Penguin Books, 2002).

12 On the IRA in war see Patrick Bishop and Eamonn Mallie, *The Provisional IRA* (London: Heinemann, 1987); Tim Pat Coogan, *The IRA* (London: Fontana, 1987); Henry Patterson *The Politics of Illusion: Repubicanism and Socialism in Modern Ireland* (London: Hutchinson Radius, 1989); M. L. R. Smith, *Fighting for Ireland? The Military Strategy of the Irish Republican Movement* (London: Routledge, 1995); Martin Dillon, *25 Years Of Terror: The IRA's War Against the British*, reprinted (London: Bantam edition reprinted, 1997).

13 Thus, according to a leading Irish republican in the early 1970s: 'if we could continue to inflict high British casualties and step up the sabotage campaign, it would be difficult for them to bear the strain and drain on their economy and no government could be prepared to continue indefinitely in such a situation': Sean MacStiofain, *Memoirs of a Revolutionary* (Edinburgh: Gordon Cremonesi, 1975), p. 261.

14 Claire Sterling, *The Terror Network: The Secret War of International Terrorism* (New York: Holt, Rinehart & Winston, 1981).

15 See Chris Skillen, '"Pravda's Provos": Russian and Soviet Manipulation of News from Ireland', *Irish Political Studies*, vol. 8, 1993, pp. 73–88.

16 Interview with Mitchell McLaughlin.

17 *Ibid.*

18 See Gerry Adams, *Selected Writings* (Dingle: Brandon, 1997), pp. 274–5.

19 Both Arafat and Mandela visited Dublin in the early 1990s and had extensive discussions with the leadership of Sinn Féin; a delegation from Sinn Féin also visited South Africa in 1995: see *An Phobacht/Republican News*, no. 363, July–August 1995. For a fine discussion of the impact of the peace process in South Africa on Sinn Féin see Adrian Guelke, 'Comparatively Peaceful: The Role of Analogy in Northern Ireland's Peace Process', *Cambridge Review of International Affairs*, vol. 11, no. 1, summer–fall 1997, pp. 28–45

20 On the strategic dimension in Anglo-Irish relations see G. R. Sloan, *The Geopolitics of Anglo-Irish Relations in the Twentieth Century* (London: Leicester University Press, 1997).

21 The information in this paragraph is drawn from the discussion in Mallie and McKittrick, *The Fight for Peace*, p. 83.

22 See John Hume, 'A New Ireland in a New Europe', in Dermot Keogh and Michael H. Haltzel (eds), *Northern Ireland and the Politics of Reconciliation* (Washington, DC: Woodrow Wilson Centre Press, 1993), pp. 228–9.

23 Speech by Peter Brooke, secretary of state for Northern Ireland, London, 9 November, 1990.

24 O'Brien, *The Long War*, p. 212.

25 *Ibid.*, p. 305.

26 Joint Declaration, Downing Street, London, 15 December 1993.

27 For important background see the excellent study by *Irish Times* journalist Conor O'Clery, *The Greening of the White House* (Dublin: Gill & Macmillan, 1997).

28 Paul Arthur, 'American Intervention in the Anglo-Irish Peace Process: Incrementalism or Interference', *Cambridge Review of International Affairs*, vol. 11, no. 1, summer–fall 1997, pp. 46–62.

29 'US Links with Britain "Worst Since 1773"', *The Times*, 16 August, 1996.

30 See Garret FitzGerald, *Irish Times*, 9 December, 1995.

31 For details on the role of George Mitchell between 1993 and 1996 see the numerous entries in Paul Bew and Gordon Gillespie (eds), *The Northern Ireland Peace Process, 1993–1996* (London: Serif, 1996).

32 After the agreement, David Trimble praised George Mitchell 'whose patience and fairness won universal praise': David Trimble, 'Ulster Should Say 'Yes', *Daily Telegraph*, 13 April 1998. The US senator also became something of a star figure among the British media: see the profile on him by Nicola Jennings, 'George Mitchell: Man in the middle', *Guardian*, 6 April 1998.

33 *Financial Times*, 11–12 April 1998, p. 1.

34 This section on Europe draws heavily on excellent work by Professor Elizabeth Meehan: see in particular 'British–Irish Relations in the Context of the European Union', *Review of International Studies*, vol. 26, no. 1, January 2000.

35 See Richard Kearney, *Postnationalist Ireland – Politics, Culture, Philosophy* (London: Routledge, 1997).

36 By the end of 1995, total net transfers to Ireland from Europe amounted IR£18.45 billion, the bulk coming from the Common Agricultural Policy and the Structural Funds: see *Challenges and Opportunities Abroad: White Paper on Foreign Policy* (Dublin: Department of Foreign Affairs, 1996), p. 59.

37 On the rise of historical revisionism in Ireland see John Whyte, *Interpreting Northern Ireland* (Oxford: Clarendon Press, 1996), pp. 119–33.

38 For a guide to Ireland in Europe see Patrick Keatinge (ed.), *European Security: Ireland's Choices* (Dublin: Institute of European Affairs, 1996), and Paul Gillespie (ed.), *Britain's European Question – the Issues for Ireland* (Dublin: Institute of European Affairs, 1996).

39 See the essays on Ireland's place in the new Europe collected in *Irish Studies in International Affairs*, vol. 8, 1997.

40 See *Derry Journal*, 18 February, 1994, p. 10.

41 Interview with Mitchell McLaughlin.

42 Quoted in Suzanne Breen, 'Sword in the Stone', *Fortnight*, no. 340, June 1995, p. 7.

43 See Anthony McIntyre, 'Modern Irish Republicanism: The Product of British State Strategies', *Irish Political Studies*, no. 10, 1995, pp. 97–121.

44 Fred Ikle, *Every War Must End* (New York: Columbia University Press, 1977).

45 Karin Aggestam and Christer Jonsson, '(Un)Ending Conflict: Challenges in Post-War Bargaining', *Millennium*, vol. 26, no. 3, 1998, p. 792.

Conclusion:
peace beyond the GFA?

ADRIAN GUELKE, MICHAEL COX
AND FIONA STEPHEN

By 2004 it was evident that if a way could be found out of Northern Ireland's political impasse, it would be likely to involve considerable change to the workings of the GFA. Indeed, this was reflected in the fact that even British and Irish governments, which had previously resisted the notion that there could be any alternative to the GFA, spoke of retaining its fundamental principles, rather than upholding it in its existing form. What was in doubt, as the formal review of the operation of the GFA began, was whether any basis could be found for the restoration of devolved government in the context of the outcome of the Northern Ireland Assembly elections in November 2003. In the elections, the two most radical parties on either side of the sectarian divide had emerged victorious. The polarisation of opinion is graphically illustrated by comparing the percentage share of votes and the seats won by the five biggest parties in the assembly elections in 2003 compared to those of 1998 (table 1).

Table 1 Assembly elections of 2003 and 1998: results for the five main parties in terms of percentage of first preference votes and seats

Party	% vote in 2003	Seats in 2003	% vote in 1998	Seats in 1998
DUP	25.71	30	18.01	20
Sinn Féin	23.52	24	17.63	18
UUP	22.68	27	21.25	28
SDLP	16.99	18	21.96	24
APNI	3.67	6	6.50	6

In 1998 the party most closely associated with the principles on which the GFA was based, as well as the most unequivocal supporters of its terms, the SDLP, topped the poll in terms of first preference votes. Admittedly, the UUP won more seats. By contrast, in 2003 the SDLP came fourth in both its share of first preference votes and in seats. For the first time in more than thirty years, the SDLP could no longer claim to represent a majority among nationalists in Northern Ireland. The political wing of the Provisional IRA, Sinn Féin, could now claim to represent a clear majority of the province's Catholic minority. At the same time, the DUP, which had strongly opposed the GFA, topped the poll in 2003. Even that understated the strength of the anti-GFA opinion in the Protestant community, as a number of those who had stood as UUP candidates were also opposed to the GFA. In January 2004, three UUP MLAs, including Jeffrey Donaldson, defected to the DUP, putting that party in an even more dominant position, should the suspension of the political institutions be lifted.

What accounts for this polarisation of opinion and for the seeming failure of the GFA? Further, what is the relationship between polarisation of opinion and the implementation of the GFA? Since the defeat of his party in the assembly elections, the former first minister, David Trimble, has argued that disillusionment has not been with the terms of the GFA itself. Rather, he argues, it has stemmed from the failure of paramilitary organisations, but most especially the Provisional IRA, to fulfil their obligations under the GFA. In support of this viewpoint, he has highlighted opinion poll evidence indicating that unionist support for the GFA goes up markedly in the context of the IRA carrying out the acts of completion demanded of it by, among others, the British Government. The argument is quite persuasive in accounting for the radicalisation of unionist opinion: opinion polls do indeed show that unionists believe that the implementation of the GFA has been one-sided. However, what it does not explain is why nationalist opinion has become radicalised in the opposite direction. In large part this was a product of how the main pro-GFA party, the UUP, approached its implementation.

On the very day George Mitchell announced that the parties had reached agreement, the British Prime Minister Tony Blair wrote to David Trimble to offer unionists reassurance on the implementation of the GFA. Blair made clear the British Government's view that 'the process of decommissioning should begin straightaway'. He also promised that if after six months the provisions for removing from office a party that was not complying with the GFA failed because their implementation required a cross-community majority in the assembly, then he would act. In particular, the British Government would 'support changes to these provisions to enable them to be made properly effective in preventing such people from holding office'. It was hardly surprising that Blair's letter was widely understood to mean that if the IRA failed to start decommissioning immediately, then the British Government would support Sinn Féin's exclusion from the Northern Ireland Executive, regardless of the SDLP's stance on the issue.

The obvious difficulty was that this did not correspond with the GFA's wording on decommissioning. The relevant clause – 7(3) – read:

> All participants accordingly reaffirm their commitment to the total disarmament of all paramilitary organisations. They also confirm their intention to continue to work constructively and in good faith with the Independent Commission, and to

use any influence they may have, to achieve the decommissioning of all paramilitary arms within two years following endorsement in referendums North and South of the agreement and in the context of the implementation of the overall settlement.[1]

While this set a target date for the completion of the process of decommissioning by paramilitaries on both sides of the sectarian divide, it did not lay down that decommissioning had to begin by a particular date.

In the run-up to the referendum on the GFA, the UUP ran its own supportive campaign, interpreting the GFA's terms as a total victory for unionism. The nature of UUP campaigning contrasted sharply with that of the non-party 'Yes' campaign that treated the GFA as the embodiment of political accommodation between unionism and nationalism. There were further warning signs that Trimble did not intend to operate the GFA as a deal between the forces of moderate unionism and moderate nationalism. Despite the overwhelming vote in favour of the GFA in the referendum, the UUP approached the assembly elections as simply another round in the contest between unionism and nationalism in which the distinction between the two remained of far greater importance than did support for or opposition to the GFA. This was reflected in the fact that anti-GFA unionists were permitted to stand as UUP candidates.

Throughout all his subsequent battles on the issue within his party, Trimble consistently downplayed the significance of the differences between the pro- and anti-GFA factions of the UUP. He argued that the differences, for the most part, concerned not the basic principles but the tactics. By contrast, Trimble's opponents inside his own party did regard the GFA as a fundamental question on which compromise was impossible. Trimble's willingness to embrace the GFA stemmed from the belief that unionists had been poorly served by the negative stance of his predecessor towards previous political initiatives. He believed that unionist interests could be advanced by a policy of constructive engagement. That entailed a readiness to compromise on the understanding that unionists had to give ground on some issues in order to gain on others. However, his acceptance that it was in the interests of unionists to enter into negotiations and to make deals was not accompanied by any ideological commitment to the idea of political accommodation between unionism and nationalism.

Trimble's behaviour after the GFA was in marked contrast to that of the unionist leader, Brian Faulkner, after the Sunningdale Agreement in December 1973. Whereas Faulkner behaved after Sunningdale as if the leader of the SDLP, Gerry Fitt, had just become his closest political ally, Trimble's approach was quite different. The election of David Trimble as first minister and Séamus Mallon as deputy first minister, which required the support of both of the UUP and the SDLP, did not prove to be the foundation of a new partnership of the centre. Relying on Blair's assurances, the UUP attempted to force on the other pro-GFA parties an interpretation of the terms as requiring IRA decommissioning ahead of Sinn Féin's entry to the Northern Ireland Executive. When, in November 1998, Mallon declared that if the IRA had not commenced decommissioning by May

2000, the SDLP would be prepared to support Sinn Féin's exclusion from the executive, the UUP showed no interest in his offer.

By treating the SDLP as irrelevant to the solution of the problem of decommissioning, the UUP undercut the position of the party among nationalist voters. Nationalists tended to view the UUP's refusal to support the formation of an executive in the first eighteen months of the operation of the GFA as evidence of unionists' reluctance to share power with Catholics. At the same time, they were inclined to see the constant efforts of the unionists to disqualify Sinn Féin from participating in any executive as an effort to disadvantage the nationalist community as a whole by reducing the latter's input to the governance of Northern Ireland. After failing to force the IRA to commence decommissioning or the British Government to introduce legislation to disqualify Sinn Féin from office, the UUP ultimately had little alternative but to 'jump first', as it was popularly phrased. That is to say, the UUP agreed to the formation of the Executive, with Sinn Féin participation ahead of IRA decommissioning, at the end of 1999. This followed a review of the operation of the GFA under the chairmanship of former US Senator George Mitchell.

Though the Mitchell review had not resulted in the publication of a formal agreement, the UUP's understanding was that IRA decommissioning would follow shortly. When it failed to occur by the end of January 2000, Trimble indicated that he and the other UUP ministers would resign from office and thus bring about the collapse of the Northern Ireland Executive. To prevent this eventuality, Secretary of State for Northern Ireland Peter Mandelson suspended the operation of the institutions, a controversial action as such a step was not provided for in the GFA and clearly lay outside its terms. Though the action was motivated by the wish to preserve the GFA in the long run, it was opposed both by nationalists in Northern Ireland and by the Irish Government because it implied that the British Government had the power to act outside of the GFA. Suspension put pressure on the republican movement to address the issue of decommissioning, the more especially as the SDLP remained ready to consider Sinn Féin's exclusion on the basis of the May 2000 deadline in the GFA.

In the light of this pressure, the IRA adopted a significant confidence-building measure in May 2000. It permitted independent international monitors to inspect a number of its arms dumps, a step towards the requirement that arms be permanently put out of use. On the basis of this initiative the UUP agreed to the re-establishment of the Northern Ireland Executive with Sinn Féin participation. However, this did not solve the problem of decommissioning. In particular, the UUP regarded the inspection of arms dumps as merely a confidence-building measure and not as a substitute for the actual decommissioning which the party required. Consequently, the executive functioned during the next year under the threat that in due course Trimble and the other UUP ministers would bring about its collapse unless decommissioning occurred. Trimble duly resigned on 1 July 2001 following the UK's general election of the previous month that had been delayed due to the foot and mouth crisis affecting British agriculture. In Northern Ireland the DUP and Sinn Féin gained seats at the expense of the UUP and the SDLP. Prolonged talks followed Trimble's resignation. Through the device of one-day suspensions, which bought time for further negotiations, the British Government succeeded in preventing the collapse of the executive while a solution to the problem was being sought.

External events had a considerable influence on the ultimate outcome of this process. In August three members of the republican movement were arrested in Colombia, a development that damaged Sinn Féin's relations with the Bush Administration. Then on 11 September, al-Qaeda's attack on America had a profound impact on the international climate of opinion in relation to political violence by sub-state groups. This put even further pressure on the republican movement to act to avoid being caught up in the war against terrorism by being blamed for the breakdown of the GFA. On 23 October 2001 the IICD confirmed that it had witnessed a significant act of decommissioning by the IRA, and that event paved the way for the Northern Ireland Assembly to meet and to re-elect Trimble as first minister, with the new SDLP leader Mark Durkan as the deputy first minister. There was a further act of decommissioning in April 2002 ahead of a general election in the Republic of Ireland, a gesture that contributed to the election of five Sinn Féin TDs.

Despite progress on decommissioning, however, unionists remained divided on the continued functioning of the GFA and dissatisfied that the IRA continued to function as a paramilitary organisation, as demonstrated, in their eyes, by the violence that was taking place at sectarian interfaces in Belfast, as well as by other events. Trimble's opponents within the UUP demanded that he make the dismantling of the IRA a condition for the continued functioning of the GFA. In September the UUC set January 2003 as a deadline for steps in that direction, but before that point was reached police raids on Sinn Féin's offices at Stormont in an investigation of alleged spying by republicans on the NIO created a more immediate crisis in the functioning of the GFA. To forestall the collapse of the executive through unionist resignations, the British Government once again announced the indefinite suspension of the institutions and restored direct rule from Westminster.

Following suspension, Tony Blair visited Belfast and set out the Government's thinking on the future of the GFA. He argued that the peace process had reached 'a fork in the road' that required 'acts of completion' by the paramilitaries and not just incremental steps to restore confidence. This formed the basis of the negotiations that took place during the first four months of 2003. Sinn Féin's response to Blair's speech had been to put forward the party's own demands for 'acts of completion' from the British Government. There followed protracted bargaining between the two sides. From the unionists' perspective it seemed that every time the British Government sought to secure the republicans' compliance with the GFA they were obliged to offer the republicans more concessions in exchange for any movement on their part. By contrast, from the nationalists' perspective, republicans were demanding simply that the British Government fulfil its obligations under the GFA.

Iraq was the centre of the British Government's attention during this period, with the consequence that the timetable for agreement slipped, forcing the British Government to delay the elections to the Northern Ireland Assembly that had been due to take place at the beginning of May. In April Blair held a war summit with Bush in Northern Ireland. The intention was that it should also form the backdrop for a deal on reviving the institutions under the GFA. To that end, Ahern joined Blair and Bush at Hillsborough, and the three leaders issued a statement in support of the peace process. In particular, they commended the Joint Declaration that the British and Irish governments were due to issue later that week. In fact, the declaration was not published that week, and Blair and Ahern called off the summit they had been due to hold. The choreography had floundered over the refusal of the republican movement to accept the terms of the Joint Declaration. The nub of the matter was paragraph 13, which read:

> Paramilitarism and sectarian violence, therefore, must be brought to an end from whichever part of the community they come. We need to see an immediate, full and permanent cessation of all paramilitary activity, including military attacks, training, targeting, intelligence gathering, acquisition or development of arms or weapons, other preparations for terrorist campaigns, punishment beatings and attacks and involvement in riots. Moreover, the practice of exiling must come to an end and the exiled must feel free to return in safety. Similarly, sectarian attacks and intimidation directed at vulnerable communities must cease.[2]

A war of words between the British Government and Sinn Féin followed the cancelled summit in April. However, because the Joint Declaration had not been published, it was hard for the public to make sense of the dispute between the two sides. It was only in May, after it decided to indefinitely suspend the holding of the Northern Ireland Assembly elections, that the British Government published the Joint Declaration. A further attempt to provide a basis for reviving the institutions in advance of the elections was made in the autumn of 2003. By this point the British Government had concluded that, regardless of the outcome of such nego- tiations, the elections could be delayed no longer. That put pressure on the UUP: it was evident that if elections went ahead in the absence of agreement and with the institutions in suspension, the UUP would fare poorly in the polls. The centrepiece of this attempt to restore confidence in the GFA was direct talks between the UUP and Sinn Féin.

Progress towards a deal was certainly made, but to judge from Taoiseach Bertie Ahern's subsequent comment that he had considered not making the trip to Hillsborough, it seems that the details were not fully tied down. Nevertheless, the parties initiated a sequence of steps that were intended to make possible the restoration of the institutions. A first step in the process was the announcement by the British Government on 21 October that new Northern Ireland Assembly elections would take place on 26 November. This was followed by a speech by the president of Sinn Féin according to which the republican movement would regard the full implementation of the GFA as providing closure of the conflict. Then

General de Chastelain announced that a third substantial act of decommissioning had taken place, though he provided few details beyond that bald statement, in accord with the IRA's insistence on confidentiality. At this point, David Trimble halted the sequence of actions on the grounds that the Provisional IRA's act of decommissioning fell short of the UUP's requirement of greater transparency.

At the time both Blair and Ahern were in Hillsborough, Northern Ireland, to lend their weight to the promise of a new beginning. The response of the two leaders was to argue that the interruption of the sequence represented a hitch and to deny that the deal had collapsed beyond hope of repair. In this context, Blair suggested, on the basis of the information available to the Government, that people in Northern Ireland would have been satisfied if they had been given the full details. He repeated this view in the House of Commons on 22 October and added that the Government was working to find a way to make further information available to the public. The following day the IICD issued a statement in the wake of a meeting with DUP leader Ian Paisley declaring that if the commissioners were forced to disclose the inventory of what had been decommissioned without the IRA's agreement they would have no alternative but to resign. The statement also denied that such an inventory had been disclosed to the two governments.

Despite the breakdown of the deal between the UUP and Sinn Féin, the British Government did not seek to further delay the holding of the assembly elections. The circumstances for an election – the middle of winter and with the institutions suspended – strongly favoured the radical parties on either side of the sectarian divide. The direct negotiations between the UUP and Sinn Féin had sidelined the SDLP. At the same time, Sinn Féin could claim that it was not responsible for the breakdown of the October 2003 deal and that the party had done its best to create the conditions for the restoration of the institutions. By contrast, from the perspective of unionists, the outcome of the negotiations exposed the UUP as incompetent in its dealings with Sinn Féin. A badge sported by Ian Paisley cruelly highlighted the impression many unionists had of Trimble's leadership: alongside Trimble's head on the body of a cockerel was the slogan: 'Cock-a-doodle-do – Didn't the IRA make a fool out of you?' (*Irish Times*, 28 November 2003). In addition, the UUP went into the election as a party divided, with Jeffrey Donaldson taking every opportunity to emphasise his disaffection with Trimble's leadership and his opposition to the GFA. The assumption that the two radical parties would prevail in the election contributed further to their triumph, as electors on either side sought to counter the impact of the expected victory of the other side's radicals – what might be called the seesaw principle of Northern Ireland politics. Ironically, the SDLP helped to reinforce this assumption by basing its campaign on the slogan of stopping the DUP.

The DUP's displacement of the UUP as the largest unionist party was followed by the defection of a number of UUP members to the DUP, including Jeffrey Donaldson and two other MLAs. That further strengthened the position of the DUP in the assembly, though with the assembly suspended this had more symbolic than practical meaning. The DUP proclaimed that its victory had put paid to the GFA. By contrast, Sinn Féin insisted that there could be no renegotiation of the GFA. The British Government, as had been expected prior to the assembly elections, initiated a review of the operation of the GFA to address the political impasse. Political commentators differed over whether the DUP would modify the stance it had taken during the elections so as to be able to enjoy the fruits of its victory. However, even those who believed that ultimately there would be a political deal between the DUP and Sinn Féin did not expect that agreement would be reached quickly or easily. Indeed, it could be argued that the two parties did not need a deal in order to make further gains in elections due (or likely) to take place in 2004 and 2005 in both the UK and the Republic of Ireland. In fact, a deal open to criticism by the UUP and the SDLP might actually damage their electoral prospects.

Another factor pointing to a prolonged period of stalemate was the absence of a crisis in the peace process comparable to that in the political process. The Northern Ireland Assembly elections had taken place against a generally peaceful background and while paramilitary activities had not ceased, there was, by and large, greater confidence than there had been in 1998 in the durability of the peaceful conditions that prevailed in most areas of the province. In particular, confidence that the IRA's war is over has grown with the passage of years. In most other respects, however, a comparison of the situation in 2004 with that in 1998 underlines the difficulties that both the peace process and the political process face. A variety of factors made the GFA possible, as it had seemed at the time:

- There was the assumption among pro-agreement unionists that the alternative to the GFA could only be far worse for unionists.
- The GFA could be seen as reward for the efforts of civil society in Northern Ireland to promote a political settlement to underwrite the peace.
- The development of Britain as a post-imperial society that saw its future in integration in the European Union provided a favourable context for the acceptance of the GFA's approach to issues of sovereignty.

Each of these factors looks very different in 2004. One of Trimble's strongest arguments for accepting the GFA was that if unionists said 'No' once again to a political initiative, they would find most of the GFA items they liked least imposed on them while getting none of those for which they wished. As of 2004, the unionist position seems much stronger, with the alternative to the GFA not being joint sovereignty but simply the continuation of direct rule. This makes the situation comparable to that of 1974 when the Sunningdale Agreement collapsed because unionists preferred direct rule to power-sharing plus an Irish dimension. That the default option to the full operation of the GFA was direct rule first became apparent with the Mandelson suspension of February 2000. Dublin objected strongly because suspension meant that that the choice was no longer the GFA under British or Irish sovereignty (depending on the choice of 50 per cent plus 1 of the Northern Ireland electorate) but something quite different. In defence of the

British Government's position, it can be argued that the change reflects where it puts the blame for the obstruction of political progress. Thus, at the time of the GFA, the unionists constituted in British eyes the main obstacle to a settlement. By contrast, the suspensions of February 2000 and October 2002 were a result of actions or non-actions by republicans. Just as it required hints of joint sovereignty to secure unionist acquiescence in 1998, the argument goes, so to get Republicans to move requires direct rule. The obvious difficulty is that, in part, at least, because of unionist actions, few in the Catholic community are disposed to blame the republicans for the impasse in the process.

People used to have great hopes that civil society, in the form of the voluntary and community sector aided by business and trade unions, could lead the way in enabling Northern Ireland to overcome its sectarian divisions – some rosier interpretations of the GFA itself saw it as a product of the activities of civil society. From the vantage point of 2004, the pertinent question seems to be 'Whatever happened to civil society? Is there any role left for it against the backdrop of the political polarisation that has occurred since the GFA?' In retrospect, it is apparent that the main political parties resented the influence of civil society under direct rule and were determined to reduce it under devolved government. Yet, curiously, appeals to civil society still take place – and in the oddest of circumstances. The extraordinary statement on Northern Ireland of Bush, Blair and Ahern on 8 April 2003 contained an appeal to civil society to support the Joint Declaration that the British and Irish governments were due to issue two days later but in fact did not. Since the two governments' initiative depended on what the Provisional IRA agreed to do, as became apparent very quickly, quite what the point was in appealing to civil society remained unclear. Did the governments imagine that the IRA Army Council could be moved by the forces that civil society might mobilise?

The view of Britain as a post-imperial society now seems far-fetched against the backdrop of Blair's wars and most particularly his participation in the US invasion of Iraq. Admittedly, the position of junior partner in an imperialist enterprise, acting as Greece to the USA's Rome, does not represent a full return to Britain's imperial past. Further, the role that Irish-American groups play in US politics complicates the picture, so that the consequences for unionists of the global assertion of US power may not turn out to be entirely beneficial for their vision of the future of Northern Ireland. Nevertheless, the apparent return to a world in which some states assert the doctrine that they are more equal than others and are not bound by the international norms that apply to other states has generally been reassuring to unionists. They also welcome the fact that this has occurred in the context of a war against terrorism, though they remain angry that the situation in Northern Ireland has not been included within its compass. In the run-up to the GFA, the position of Washington had appeared to be equidistant from Dublin and London, so that Britain's special relationship seemed balanced by a special relationship between the USA and the Republic of Ireland. Blair's relationship to the Bush Administration as a consequence of Iraq now makes such a claim seem ridiculous.

At the same time, the progress of European integration seems to have stalled in the wake of European disagreement over the war to overthrow Saddam Hussein. The EU seems more preoccupied with the consequences of the expansion of its membership than with further steps to deepen co-operation. Further, the public mood in a number of countries, including Britain, appears to have turned against such steps. In particular, the prospect of Britain's adopting the euro as its currency has receded and any pressure to do so has been reduced by Sweden's rejection of the euro in a referendum. Consequently, the notion that European integration might provide an impetus for extending co-operation between the two parts of Ireland under the GFA no longer seems persuasive. Of course, it is by no means impossible that external circumstances will change. In the light of the difficulties that the coalition occupying Iraq have encountered, enthusiasm for imperialist adventures may diminish in both the USA and Britain. Expansion of its membership may re-invigorate the European Union and its relevance to political accommodation in Ireland may regain credibility, particularly if the former is credited with resolving ethnic conflict in other places, such as Cyprus.

At this juncture in Northern Ireland's affairs, there seems to be greater uncertainty over the external context than the domestic setting of the Irish question. While the future of the GFA in its present form is uncertain, a return to the Troubles seems unlikely. The republican movement has gained far too much from the peace process to contemplate going back to the strategy of the long war. That does not rule out activities short of a breach of the cessation of the war against the British presence in Ireland and these may well be the source of continuing controversy and of political difficulty. However, the British Government is unlikely to want to place the larger IRA ceasefire at risk by any measures it takes against the republican movement. Of course, miscalculation by the Government or the republican movement could destabilise the peace process. What seems most likely, however, is that Northern Ireland will remain suspended for some time between, on the one hand, a state of conflict and, on the other, full normalisation. Sinn Féin has profited politically from presenting itself as the party of peace both in Northern Ireland and in the Republic of Ireland, and that would be put in jeopardy by either a return to violence or a situation in which peace was no longer seen as the issue of paramount importance. Furthermore, other forces, including those of loyalism and dissident republicanism, provide formidable barriers to the complete removal of the threat of violence from the politics of Northern Ireland.

Notes

1   The full text of the GFA is reproduced in Michael Cox, Adrian Guelke and Fiona Stephen (eds), *A Farewell to Arms? From 'Long War' to Long Peace in Northern Ireland* (Manchester: Manchester University Press, 2000); extract is from p.317; see also Appendix 2, this volume.

2   The full text of the Joint Declaration by the British and Irish governments of April 2003 is given in Appendix 4 to this book.

Appendices

APPENDIX 1

Chronology of Northern Ireland from war to peace

1968

5 October: clashes between civil rights demonstrators and the police in Londonderry/Derry after protest march is banned by Minister of Home Affairs William Craig, an event often taken to mark the start of Northern Ireland's troubles.

1969

14 August: British troops deployed in Northern Ireland in aid of the civil power.
28 December: announcement of the formation of the Provisional IRA.

1971

9 August: introduction of internment (detention without trial).
September: formation of the UDA.

1972

30 January: thirteen civil rights demonstrators killed by the Parachute Regiment in Londonderry/Derry; another person subsequently died of injuries.
24 March: direct rule from Westminster imposed on Northern Ireland.

1973

9 December: Sunningdale Agreement, under which parties to share power in a new devolved government in Northern Ireland agree to establish a Council of Ireland to provide an Irish dimension to the political settlement.

1974

28 May: collapse of power-sharing Northern Ireland Executive following general strike organised by the UWC.

1985

15 November: signature of the Anglo-Irish Agreement under which the British

Government undertook to consult the Government of the Republic of Ireland on its policies in Northern Ireland.

1988

14 October: talks in Duisburg, West Germany, among representatives of the UUP, the DUP, the SDLP and the APNI.

1990

9 November: Secretary of State for Northern Ireland Peter Brooke declared that Britain has no selfish strategic or economic interest in Northern Ireland.

1991

26 March: the terms of agreement among the province's constitutional parties to enter into talks on the future of Northern Ireland are announced by Peter Brooke.

1992

17 February: launch of the Sinn Féin publication *Towards a Lasting Peace in Ireland*.
10 April: Provisional IRA bombs in the City of London, the day after the British general election, cause massive damage.
10 November: Brooke–Mayhew talks among the constitutional parties end in deadlock.

1993

24 April: John Hume, leader of the SDLP, and Gerry Adams, president of Sinn Féin, issue first joint statement.
15 December: British and Irish governments issue Joint Declaration.

1994

31 August: Provisional IRA proclaims ceasefire.
13 October: CLMC proclaims ceasefire.

1995

22 February: launch of Framework Documents by British and Irish governments.
7 March: Decommissioning of some weapons set as condition for Sinn Féin's entry into all-party talks by Secretary of State for Northern Ireland Sir Patrick Mayhew.
30 November: Bill Clinton visits Northern Ireland.

1996

24 January: publication of the Report of the International Body on Arms Decommissioning.
9 February: Provisional IRA ended ceasefire with the bombing of Canary Wharf in London.
30 May: elections for the Northern Ireland Forum.
10 June: start of the multi-party negotiations.

1997

20 July: resumption of Provisional IRA ceasefire.

1998

12 January: British and Irish governments issued the document Propositions of Heads of Agreement.

10 April: GFA announced at conclusion of talks between the eight parties to the multi-party negotiations.

22 May: referenda in Northern Ireland and the Republic of Ireland massively endorsed GFA.

25 June: elections to the Northern Ireland Assembly.

15 August: twenty-nine people were killed in Omagh by a bomb placed by dissident republican group the RIRA.

1999

15 March: human rights lawyer Rosemary Nelson assassinated by loyalists.

2 July: British and Irish governments issue Joint Statement intended to provide a way forward on the establishment of the Northern Ireland Executive and the decommissioning of weapons. Publication of the Report of the IICD.

15 July: UUP boycotted formation of the executive, bringing about its collapse and resulting in the invocation of the procedures for reviewing the implementation of the GFA. Resignation of Deputy First Minister Seamus Mallon.

6 September: start of Mitchell review of the implementation of the GFA.

9 September: publication of the Report of the Patten Commission on policing.

18 November: George Mitchell issued concluding report of his review.

23 November: award of the George Cross to the RUC.

27 November: UUC supports implementation of the deal agreed between the UUP and Sinn Féin in the Mitchell review of the implementation of the GFA, subject to the proviso of a final decision by the UUC in February 2000.

29 November: Northern Ireland Assembly votes to annul resignation of Seamus Mallon as deputy first minister. Election of ministers of the Northern Ireland Executive.

2 December: transfer of powers to devolved institutions in Northern Ireland; first meeting of the Northern Ireland Executive. Anglo-Irish Agreement replaced by new British–Irish Agreement. Amendments to articles 2 and 3 of the Irish constitution put into effect.

13 December: inaugural meeting of the North–South Ministerial Council in Armagh.

17 December: inaugural meeting of the British–Irish Council in London.

2000

11 February: suspension of the Northern Ireland Executive by Secretary of State for Northern Ireland Peter Mandelson, following the failure of the Provisional IRA to

start decommissioning of its weapons or to indicate a date by which a start to decommissioning would be made.

25 March: David Trimble defeated South Belfast MP Rev. Martin Smyth by 457 votes to 348 (57-43 per cent) in challenge to his leadership of the UUP.

5 May: British and Irish governments issued implementation plan.

6 May: statement by the Provisional IRA that, in the context of the full implementation of the GFA and of the two governments' statement, it would initiate a process that would 'completely and verifiably put IRA arms beyond use'. The statement also committed the Provisional IRA to permitting the third-party inspection of some of its arms dumps.

27 May: UUC voted to support David Trimble on the issue of re-entering the power-sharing executive with Sinn Féin by 459 votes to 403 (53-47 per cent).

30 May: restoration of devolved government to Northern Ireland.

1 June: meeting of the Northern Ireland Executive.

26 June: announcement that the first inspection of Provisional IRA arms dumps had occurred.

21 September: UUP loses South Antrim by-election.

12 December: third visit to Northern Ireland by President Clinton.

2001

24 January: Peter Mandelson resigned; his replacement as Secretary of State for Northern Ireland was John Reid.

7 June: UK general election.

1 July: David Trimble resigned as first minister.

9–14 July: Weston Park talks.

6 August: decommissioning body accepted the Provisional IRA plan to put weapons beyond use.

11 August: first one-day suspension of the institutions.

14 August: Arrest of three republicans in Colombia.

21 September: second one-day suspension announced.

12 October: Reid 'specified' that UDA–UFF and LVF ceasefires were over.

18 October: resignation of unionist members from the Northern Ireland Executive announced.

23 October: IIDC confirmed that it had witnessed significant disposal of arms by the Provisional IRA.

24 October: renomination of UUP members of the Northern Ireland Executive.

4 November: RUC renamed Police Service of Northern Ireland (PSNI).

6 November: Trimble re-elected as first minister and Mark Durkan elected as deputy first minister.

11 November: Durkan became the leader of the SDLP.

28 November: dissolution of the UDA's political wing, the UDP.

2002

17 March: break-in at Special Branch offices in Castlereagh Police Station.

8 April: second act of Provisional IRA decommissioning announced.

17 May: general election in the Republic of Ireland; five Sinn Féin TDs elected.

5 June: Alex Maskey of Sinn Féin elected mayor of Belfast.

21 September: as a result of meeting of the UUC, UUP leaders signal that they will withdraw from the Northern Ireland Executive unless progress is made on party demands of the republican movement by 18 January 2003.

4 October: police raid on Sinn Féin's offices at Stormont in connection with investigation of spying by republicans on the NIO.

14 October: announcement of the indefinite suspension of the Northern Ireland governmental institutions and the restoration of direct rule from Westminster.

17 October: speech by Prime Minister Tony Blair in Belfast on the 'fork in the road' in the peace process.

19 December: publication of religious breakdown from 2001 census: Protestant community at 53.1 per cent (58 per cent in 1991), Catholic community at 43.8 per cent (42 per cent in 1991).

2003

10 January: Johnny Adair sent back to prison.

1 February: murder of John Gregg in loyalist feud.

6 February: Adair's supporters fled to Scotland.

5 March: elections for Northern Ireland Assembly postponed until 29 May.

7&8 April: President George Bush in Northern Ireland.

1 May: indefinite postponement of the Northern Ireland Assembly elections and publication of Joint Declaration.

17 June: Trimble emerged victorious in UUC confrontation with Donaldson.

6 September: Trimble again secured UUC vote in another confrontation with Donaldson.

21 October: third act of IRA decommissioning announced in the context of failed sequence of actions to restore institutions.

26 November: fresh elections held to Northern Ireland Assembly, after further attempt at settlement broke down, resulted in victories for radical parties, the DUP securing more seats than the UUP and Sinn Féin more seats than the SDLP.

2004

5 January: Jeffrey Donaldson and two other UUP MLAs joined the DUP after having resigned from the UUP on 18 December 2003.

3 February: start of the review of the operation of the GFA.

APPENDIX 2

The Good Friday Agreement (Belfast Agreement)

AGREEMENT REACHED IN THE MULTI-PARTY NEGOTIATIONS, 10 APRIL 1998

TABLE OF CONTENTS

11. Validation, Implementation and Review
    Validation and Implementation
    Review Procedures Following Implementation

ANNEX: Agreement between the Government of the United Kingdom of Great Britain and Northern Ireland and the Government of Ireland

1. DECLARATION OF SUPPORT

1. We, the participants in the multi-party negotiations, believe that the agreement we have negotiated offers a truly historic opportunity for a new beginning.
2. The tragedies of the past have left a deep and profoundly regrettable legacy of suffering. We must never forget those who have died or been injured, and their families. But we can best honour them through a fresh start, in which we firmly dedicate ourselves to the achievement of reconciliation, tolerance, and mutual trust, and to the protection and vindication of the human rights of all.
3. We are committed to partnership, equality and mutual respect as the basis of relationships within Northern Ireland, between North and South, and between these islands.
4. We reaffirm our total and absolute commitment to exclusively democratic and peaceful means of resolving differences on political issues, and our opposition to any use or threat of force by others for any political purpose, whether in regard to this agreement or otherwise.
5. We acknowledge the substantial differences between our continuing, and equally legitimate, political aspirations. However, we will endeavour to strive in every practical way towards reconciliation and rapprochement within the framework of democratic and agreed arrangements. We pledge that we will, in good faith, work to ensure the success of each and every one of the arrangements to be established under this agreement. It is accepted that all of the institutional and constitutional arrangements – an Assembly in Northern Ireland, a North–South Ministerial Council, implementation bodies, a British–Irish Council and a British–Irish Intergovernmental Conference and any amendments to British Acts of Parliament and the Constitution of Ireland – are interlocking and interdependent and that in particular the functioning of the Assembly and the North/South Council are so closely interrelated that the success of each depends on that of the other.
6. Accordingly, in a spirit of concord, we strongly commend this agreement to the people, North and South, for their approval.

2. CONSTITUTIONAL ISSUES

1. The participants endorse the commitment made by the British and Irish Governments that, in a new British–Irish Agreement replacing the Anglo-Irish Agreement, they will:
(i) recognise the legitimacy of whatever choice is freely exercised by a majority of the people of Northern Ireland with regard to its status, whether they prefer to continue to support the Union with Great Britain or a sovereign united Ireland;
(ii) recognise that it is for the people of the island of Ireland alone, by agreement between the two parts respectively and without external impediment, to exercise their right of self-determination on the basis of consent, freely and concurrently given, North and South, to bring about a united Ireland, if that is their wish, accepting that this right must be achieved and exercised with and subject to the agreement and consent of a majority of the people of Northern Ireland;

(iii) acknowledge that while a substantial section of the people in Northern Ireland share the legitimate wish of a majority of the people of the island of Ireland for a united Ireland, the present wish of a majority of the people of Northern Ireland, freely exercised and legitimate, is to maintain the Union and, accordingly, that Northern Ireland's status as part of the United Kingdom reflects and relies upon that wish; and that it would be wrong to make any change in the status of Northern Ireland save with the consent of a majority of its people;

(iv) affirm that if, in the future, the people of the island of Ireland exercise their right of self-determination on the basis set out in sections (i) and (ii) above to bring about a united Ireland, it will be a binding obligation on both Governments to introduce and support in their respective Parliaments legislation to give effect to that wish;

(v) affirm that whatever choice is freely exercised by a majority of the people of Northern Ireland, the power of the sovereign government with jurisdiction there shall be exercised with rigorous impartiality on behalf of all the people in the diversity of their identities and traditions and shall be founded on the principles of full respect for, and equality of, civil, political, social and cultural rights, of freedom from discrimination for all citizens, and of parity of esteem and of just and equal treatment for the identity, ethos, and aspirations of both communities;

(vi) recognise the birthright of all the people of Northern Ireland to identify themselves and be accepted as Irish or British, or both, as they may so choose, and accordingly confirm that their right to hold both British and Irish citizenship is accepted by both Governments and would not be affected by any future change in the status of Northern Ireland.

2. The participants also note that the two Governments have accordingly undertaken in the context of this comprehensive political agreement, to propose and support changes in, respectively, the Constitution of Ireland and in British legislation relating to the constitutional status of Northern Ireland.

ANNEX A

Draft Clauses/Schedules for Incorporation in British legislation

1. (1) It is hereby declared that Northern Ireland in its entirety remains part of the United Kingdom and shall not cease to be so without the consent of a majority of the people of Northern Ireland voting in a poll held for the purposes of this section in accordance with Schedule 1.

   (2) But if the wish expressed by a majority in such a poll is that Northern Ireland should cease to be part of the United Kingdom and form part of a united Ireland, the Secretary of State shall lay before Parliament such proposals to give effect to that wish as may be agreed between Her Majesty's Government in the United Kingdom and the Government of Ireland.

2. The Government of Ireland Act 1920 is repealed; and this Act shall have effect notwithstanding any other previous enactment.

SCHEDULE 1

Polls for the Purpose of Section 1

1. The Secretary of State may by order direct the holding of a poll for the purposes of section 1 on a date specified in the order.

2. Subject to paragraph 3, the Secretary of State shall exercise the power under paragraph 1 if at any time it appears likely to him that a majority of those voting

would express a wish that Northern Ireland should cease to be part of the United Kingdom and form part of a united Ireland.

3. The Secretary of State shall not make an order under paragraph 1 earlier than seven years after the holding of a previous poll under this Schedule.

4. (Remaining paragraphs along the lines of paragraphs 2 and 3 of existing Schedule 1 to 1973 Act.)

ANNEX B

Irish Government draft legislation to amend the Constitution

Add to Article 29 the following sections:

7. 1. The State may consent to be bound by the British–Irish Agreement done at Belfast on the … day of … 1998, hereinafter called the Agreement.

2. Any institution established by or under the Agreement may exercise the powers and functions thereby conferred on it in respect of all or any part of the island of Ireland notwithstanding any other provision of this Constitution conferring a like power or function on any person or any organ of State appointed under or created or established by or under this Constitution. Any power or function conferred on such an institution in relation to the settlement or resolution of disputes or controversies may be in addition to or in substitution for any like power or function conferred by this Constitution on any such person or organ of State as aforesaid.

3. If the Government declare that the State has become obliged, pursuant to the Agreement, to give effect to the amendment of this Constitution referred to therein, then, notwithstanding Article 46 hereof, this Constitution shall be amended as follows:

i. the following Articles shall be substituted for Articles 2 and 3 of the Irish text:
'2. [Irish text to be inserted here]
3. [Irish text to be inserted here]
(ii) the following Articles shall be substituted for Articles 2 and 3 of the English text:

Article 2

It is the entitlement and birthright of every person born in the island of Ireland, which includes its islands and seas, to be part of the Irish nation. That is also the entitlement of all persons otherwise qualified in accordance with law to be citizens of Ireland. Furthermore, the Irish nation cherishes its special affinity with people of Irish ancestry living abroad who share its cultural identity and heritage.

Article 3

1. It is the firm will of the Irish nation, in harmony and friendship, to unite all the people who share the territory of the island of Ireland, in all the diversity of their identities and traditions, recognising that a united Ireland shall be brought about only by peaceful means with the consent of a majority of the people, demo-cratically expressed, in both jurisdictions in the island. Until then, the laws enacted by the Parliament established by this Constitution shall have the like area and extent of application as the laws enacted by the Parliament that existed immediately before the coming into operation of this Constitution.

2. Institutions with executive powers and functions that are shared between those jurisdictions may be established by their respective responsible authorities for stated purposes and may exercise powers and functions in respect of all or any part of the island.'

iii. the following section shall be added to the Irish text of this Article:
'8. [Irish text to be inserted here]'
and

iv. the following section shall be added to the English text of this Article:
'8. The State may exercise extra-territorial jurisdiction in accordance with the generally recognised principles of international law.'

4. If a declaration under this section is made, this subsection and subsection 3, other than the amendment of this Constitution effected thereby, and subsection 5 of this section shall be omitted from every official text of this Constitution published thereafter, but notwithstanding such omission this section shall continue to have the force of law.

5. If such a declaration is not made within twelve months of this section being added to this Constitution or such longer period as may be provided for by law, this section shall cease to have effect and shall be omitted from every official text of this Constitution published thereafter.

3. STRAND ONE

Democratic Institutions in Northern Ireland

1. This agreement provides for a democratically elected Assembly in Northern Ireland which is inclusive in its membership, capable of exercising executive and legislative authority, and subject to safeguards to protect the rights and interests of all sides of the community.

The Assembly

2. A 108-member Assembly will be elected by PR(STV) from existing Westminster constituencies.

3. The Assembly will exercise full legislative and executive authority in respect of those matters currently within the responsibility of the six Northern Ireland Government Departments, with the possibility of taking on responsibility for other matters as detailed elsewhere in this agreement.

4. The Assembly – operating where appropriate on a cross-community basis – will be the prime source of authority in respect of all devolved responsibilities.

Safeguards

5. There will be safeguards to ensure that all sections of the community can participate and work together successfully in the operation of these institutions and that all sections of the community are protected, including:

(a) allocations of Committee Chairs, Ministers and Committee membership in proportion to party strengths;

(b) the European Convention on Human Rights (ECHR) and any Bill of Rights for Northern Ireland supplementing it, which neither the Assembly nor public bodies can infringe, together with a Human Rights Commission;

(c) arrangements to provide that key decisions and legislation are proofed to ensure that they do not infringe the ECHR and any Bill of Rights for Northern Ireland;

(d) arrangements to ensure key decisions are taken on a cross-community basis;

(i) *either* parallel consent, i.e. a majority of those members present and voting, including a majority of the unionist and nationalist designations present and voting;

(ii) *or* a weighted majority (60%) of members present and voting, including at least 40% of each of the nationalist and unionist designations present and voting.

Key decisions requiring cross-community support will be designated in advance, including election of the Chair of the Assembly, the First Minister and Deputy First Minister, standing orders and budget allocations. In other cases such decisions could be triggered by a petition of concern brought by a significant minority of Assembly members (30/108).

(e) an Equality Commission to monitor a statutory obligation to promote equality of opportunity in specified areas and parity of esteem between the two main communities, and to investigate individual complaints against public bodies.

Operation of the Assembly

6. At their first meeting, members of the Assembly will register a designation of identity – nationalist, unionist or other – for the purposes of measuring cross-community support in Assembly votes under the relevant provisions above.

7. The Chair and Deputy Chair of the Assembly will be elected on a cross-community basis, as set out in paragraph 5(d) above.

8. There will be a Committee for each of the main executive functions of the Northern Ireland Administration. The Chairs and Deputy Chairs of the Assembly Committees will be allocated proportionally, using the d'Hondt system. Membership of the Committees will be in broad proportion to party strengths in the Assembly to ensure that the opportunity of Committee places is available to all members.

9. The Committees will have a scrutiny, policy development and consultation role with respect to the Department with which each is associated, and will have a role in initiation of legislation. They will have the power to:
    *   consider and advise on Departmental budgets and Annual Plans in the context of the overall budget allocation;
    *   approve relevant secondary legislation and take the Committee stage of relevant primary legislation;
    *   call for persons and papers;
    *   initiate enquiries and make reports;
    *   consider and advise on matters brought to the Committee by its Minister.

10. Standing Committees other than Departmental Committees may be established as may be required from time to time.

11. The Assembly may appoint a special Committee to examine and report on whether a measure or proposal for legislation is in conformity with equality requirements, including the ECHR/Bill of Rights. The Committee shall have the power to call people and papers to assist in its consideration of the matter. The Assembly shall then consider the report of the Committee and can determine the matter in accordance with the cross-community consent procedure.

12. The above special procedure shall be followed when requested by the Executive Committee, or by the relevant Departmental Committee, voting on a cross-community basis.

13. When there is a petition of concern as in 5(d) above, the Assembly shall vote to determine whether the measure may proceed without reference to this special procedure. If this fails to achieve support on a cross-community basis, as in 5(d)(i) above, the special procedure shall be followed.

Executive Authority

14. Executive authority to be discharged on behalf of the Assembly by a First Minister and Deputy First Minister and up to ten Ministers with Departmental responsibilities.

15. The First Minister and Deputy First Minister shall be jointly elected into office by the Assembly voting on a cross-community basis, according to 5(d)(i) above.

16. Following the election of the First Minister and Deputy First Minister, the posts of Ministers will be allocated to parties on the basis of the d'Hondt system by reference to the number of seats each party has in the Assembly.

17. The Ministers will constitute an Executive Committee, which will be convened, and presided over, by the First Minister and Deputy First Minister.

18. The duties of the First Minister and Deputy First Minister will include, inter alia, dealing with and co-ordinating the work of the Executive Committee and the response of the Northern Ireland administration to external relationships.

19. The Executive Committee will provide a forum for the discussion of, and agreement on, issues which cut across the responsibilities of two or more Ministers, for prioritising executive and legislative proposals and for recommending a common position where necessary (e.g. in dealing with external relationships).

20. The Executive Committee will seek to agree each year, and review as necessary, a programme incorporating an agreed budget linked to policies and programmes, subject to approval by the Assembly, after scrutiny in Assembly Committees, on a cross-community basis.

21. A party may decline the opportunity to nominate a person to serve as a Minister or may subsequently change its nominee.

22. All the Northern Ireland Departments will be headed by a Minister. All Ministers will liaise regularly with their respective Committee.

23. As a condition of appointment, Ministers, including the First Minister and Deputy First Minister, will affirm the terms of a Pledge of Office (Annex A) undertaking to discharge effectively and in good faith all the responsibilities attaching to their office.

24. Ministers will have full executive authority in their respective areas of responsibility, within any broad programme agreed by the Executive Committee and endorsed by the Assembly as a whole.

25. An individual may be removed from office following a decision of the Assembly taken on a cross-community basis, if (s)he loses the confidence of the Assembly, voting on a cross-community basis, for failure to meet his or her responsibilities including, inter alia, those set out in the Pledge of Office. Those who hold office should use only democratic, non-violent means, and those who do not should be excluded or removed from office under these provisions.

Legislation

26. The Assembly will have authority to pass primary legislation for Northern Ireland in devolved areas, subject to:

(a) the ECHR and any Bill of Rights for Northern Ireland supplementing it which, if the courts found to be breached, would render the relevant legislation null and void;

(b) decisions by simple majority of members voting, except when decision on a cross-community basis is required;

(c) detailed scrutiny and approval in the relevant Departmental Committee;

(d) mechanisms, based on arrangements proposed for the Scottish Parliament, to ensure suitable co-ordination, and avoid disputes, between the Assembly and the Westminster Parliament;

(e) option of the Assembly seeking to include Northern Ireland provisions in

United Kingdom-wide legislation in the Westminster Parliament, especially on devolved issues where parity is normally maintained (e.g. social security, company law).

27. The Assembly will have authority to legislate in reserved areas with the approval of the Secretary of State and subject to Parliamentary control.

28. Disputes over legislative competence will be decided by the Courts.

29. Legislation could be initiated by an individual, a Committee or a Minister.

Relations with Other Institutions

30. Arrangements to represent the Assembly as a whole, at Summit level and in dealings with other institutions, will be in accordance with paragraph 18, and will be such as to ensure cross-community involvement.

31. Terms will be agreed between appropriate Assembly representatives and the Government of the United Kingdom to ensure effective co-ordination and input by Ministers to national policy-making, including on EU issues.

32. Role of Secretary of State:
   (a) to remain responsible for NIO matters not devolved to the Assembly, subject to regular consultation with the Assembly and Ministers;
   (b) to approve and lay before the Westminster Parliament any Assembly legislation on reserved matters;
   (c) to represent Northern Ireland interests in the United Kingdom Cabinet;
   (d) to have the right to attend the Assembly at their invitation.

33. The Westminster Parliament (whose power to make legislation for Northern Ireland would remain unaffected) will:
   (a) legislate for non-devolved issues, other than where the Assembly legislates with the approval of the Secretary of State and subject to the control of Parliament;
   (b) to legislate as necessary to ensure the United Kingdom's international obligations are met in respect of Northern Ireland;
   (c) scrutinise, including through the Northern Ireland Grand and Select Committees, the responsibilities of the Secretary of State.

34. A consultative Civic Forum will be established. It will comprise representatives of the business, trade union and voluntary sectors, and such other sectors as agreed by the First Minister and the Deputy First Minister. It will act as a consultative mechanism on social, economic and cultural issues. The First Minister and the Deputy First Minister will by agreement provide administrative support for the Civic Forum and establish guidelines for the selection of representatives to the Civic Forum.

Transitional Arrangements

35. The Assembly will meet first for the purpose of organisation, without legislative or executive powers, to resolve its standing orders and working practices and make preparations for the effective functioning of the Assembly, the British–Irish Council and the North/South Ministerial Council and associated implementation bodies. In this transitional period, those members of the Assembly serving as shadow Ministers shall affirm their commitment to non-violence and exclusively peaceful and democratic means and their opposition to any use or threat of force by others for any political purpose; to work in good faith to bring the new arrangements into being; and to observe the spirit of the Pledge of Office applying to appointed Ministers.

Review

36. After a specified period there will be a review of these arrangements, including the details of electoral arrangements and of the Assembly's procedures, with a view to agreeing any adjustments necessary in the interests of efficiency and fairness.

ANNEX A

Pledge of Office

To pledge:

(a) to discharge in good faith all the duties of office;

(b) commitment to non-violence and exclusively peaceful and democratic means;

(c) to serve all the people of Northern Ireland equally, and to act in accordance with the general obligations on government to promote equality and prevent discrimination;

(d) to participate with colleagues in the preparation of a programme for government;

(e) to operate within the framework of that programme when agreed within the Executive Committee and endorsed by the Assembly;

(f) to support, and to act in accordance with, all decisions of the Executive Committee and Assembly;

(g) to comply with the Ministerial Code of Conduct.

Code of Conduct

Ministers must at all times:

- observe the highest standards of propriety and regularity involving impartiality, integrity and objectivity in relationship to the stewardship of public funds;
- be accountable to users of services, the community and, through the Assembly, for the activities within their responsibilities, their stewardship of public funds and the extent to which key performance targets and objectives have been met;
- ensure all reasonable requests for information from the Assembly, users of services and individual citizens are complied with; and that Departments and their staff conduct their dealings with the public in an open and responsible way;
- follow the seven principles of public life set out by the Committee on Standards in Public Life;
- comply with this code and with rules relating to the use of public funds;
- operate in a way conducive to promoting good community relations and equality of treatment;
- not use information gained in the course of their service for personal gain; nor seek to use the opportunity of public service to promote their private interests;
- ensure they comply with any rules on the acceptance of gifts and hospitality that might be offered;
- declare any personal or business interests which may conflict with their responsibilities. The Assembly will retain a Register of Interests. Individuals must ensure that any direct or indirect pecuniary interests which members of the public might reasonably think could influence their judgement are listed in the Register of Interests;

4. STRAND TWO

North/South Ministerial Council

1. Under a new British–Irish Agreement dealing with the totality of relationships, and related legislation at Westminster and in the Oireachtas, a North/South Ministerial

Council to be established to bring together those with executive responsibilities in Northern Ireland and the Irish Government, to develop consultation, co-operation and action within the island of Ireland – including through implementation on an all-island and cross-border basis – on matters of mutual interest within the competence of the Administrations, North and South.

2. All Council decisions to be by agreement between the two sides. Northern Ireland to be represented by the First Minister, Deputy First Minister and any relevant Ministers, the Irish Government by the Taoiseach and relevant Ministers, all operating in accordance with the rules for democratic authority and accountability in force in the Northern Ireland Assembly and the Oireachtas respectively. Participation in the Council to be one of the essential responsibilities attaching to relevant posts in the two Administrations. If a holder of a relevant post will not participate normally in the Council, the Taoiseach in the case of the Irish Government and the First and Deputy First Minister in the case of the Northern Ireland Administration to be able to make alternative arrangements.

3. The Council to meet in different formats:
(i) in plenary format twice a year, with Northern Ireland representation led by the First Minister and Deputy First Minister and the Irish Government led by the Taoiseach;
(ii) in specific sectoral formats on a regular and frequent basis with each side represented by the appropriate Minister;
(iii) in an appropriate format to consider institutional or cross-sectoral matters (including in relation to the EU) and to resolve disagreement.

4. Agendas for all meetings to be settled by prior agreement between the two sides, but it will be open to either to propose any matter for consideration or action.

5. The Council:
(i) to exchange information, discuss and consult with a view to co-operating on matters of mutual interest within the competence of both Administrations, North and South;
(ii) to use best endeavours to reach agreement on the adoption of common policies, in areas where there is a mutual cross-border and all-island benefit, and which are within the competence of both Administrations, North and South, making determined efforts to overcome any disagreements;
(iii) to take decisions by agreement on policies for implementation separately in each jurisdiction, in relevant meaningful areas within the competence of both Administrations, North and South;
(iv) to take decisions by agreement on policies and action at an all-island and cross-border level to be implemented by the bodies to be established as set out in paragraphs 8 and 9 below.

6. Each side to be in a position to take decisions in the Council within the defined authority of those attending, through the arrangements in place for co-ordination of executive functions within each jurisdiction. Each side to remain accountable to the Assembly and Oireachtas respectively, whose approval, through the arrangements in place on either side, would be required for decisions beyond the defined authority of those attending.

7. As soon as practically possible after elections to the Northern Ireland Assembly, inaugural meetings will take place of the Assembly, the British–Irish Council and the North/South Ministerial Council in their transitional forms. All three institutions will meet regularly and frequently on this basis during the period between the

elections to the Assembly, and the transfer of powers to the Assembly, in order to establish their modus operandi.

8. During the transitional period between the elections to the Northern Ireland Assembly and the transfer of power to it, representatives of the Northern Ireland transitional Administration and the Irish Government operating in the North/South Ministerial Council will undertake a work programme, in consultation with the British Government, covering at least 12 subject areas, with a view to identifying and agreeing by 31 October 1998 areas where co-operation and implementation for mutual benefit will take place. Such areas may include matters in the list set out in the Annex.

9. As part of the work programme, the Council will identify and agree at least 6 matters for co-operation and implementation in each of the following categories:
(i) Matters where existing bodies will be the appropriate mechanisms for co-operation in each separate jurisdiction;
(ii) Matters where the co-operation will take place through agreed implementation bodies on a cross-border or all-island level.

10. The two Governments will make necessary legislative and other enabling preparations to ensure, as an absolute commitment, that these bodies, which have been agreed as a result of the work programme, function at the time of the inception of the British–Irish Agreement and the transfer of powers, with legislative authority for these bodies transferred to the Assembly as soon as possible thereafter. Other arrangements for the agreed co-operation will also commence contemporaneously with the transfer of powers to the Assembly.

11. The implementation bodies will have a clear operational remit. They will implement on an all-island and cross-border basis policies agreed in the Council.

12. Any further development of these arrangements to be by agreement in the Council and with the specific endorsement of the Northern Ireland Assembly and Oireachtas, subject to the extent of the competences and responsibility of the two Administrations.

13. It is understood that the North/South Ministerial Council and the Northern Ireland Assembly are mutually inter-dependent, and that one cannot successfully function without the other.

14. Disagreements within the Council to be addressed in the format described at paragraph 3(iii) above or in the plenary format. By agreement between the two sides, experts could be appointed to consider a particular matter and report.

15. Funding to be provided by the two Administrations on the basis that the Council and the implementation bodies constitute a necessary public function.

16. The Council to be supported by a standing joint Secretariat, staffed by members of the Northern Ireland Civil Service and the Irish Civil Service.

17. The Council to consider the European Union dimension of relevant matters, including the implementation of EU policies and programmes and proposals under consideration in the EU framework. Arrangements to be made to ensure that the views of the Council are taken into account and represented appropriately at relevant EU meetings.

18. The Northern Ireland Assembly and the Oireachtas to consider developing a joint parliamentary forum, bringing together equal numbers from both institutions for discussion of matters of mutual interest and concern.

19. Consideration to be given to the establishment of an independent consultative forum appointed by the two Administrations, representative of civil society, comprising the social partners and other members with expertise in social, cultural, economic and other issues.

ANNEX

Areas for North–South Co-operation and Implementation
may include the following:

1. Agriculture – animal and plant health.
2. Education – teacher qualifications and exchanges.
3. Transport – strategic transport planning.
4. Environment – environmental protection, pollution, water quality, and waste management.
5. Waterways – inland waterways.
6. Social Security/Social Welfare – entitlements of cross-border workers and fraud control.
7. Tourism – promotion, marketing, research, and product development.
8. Relevant EU Programmes such as SPPR, INTERREG, Leader II and their successors.
9. Inland Fisheries.
10. Aquaculture and marine matters
11. Health: accident and emergency services and other related cross-border issues.
12. Urban and rural development.

Others to be considered by the shadow North/South Council.

5. STRAND THREE

British–Irish Council

1. A British–Irish Council (BIC) will be established under a new British–Irish Agreement to promote the harmonious and mutually beneficial development of the totality of relationships among the peoples of these islands.
2. Membership of the BIC will comprise representatives of the British and Irish Governments, devolved institutions in Northern Ireland, Scotland and Wales, when established, and, if appropriate, elsewhere in the United Kingdom, together with representatives of the Isle of Man and the Channel Islands.
3. The BIC will meet in different formats: at summit level, twice per year; in specific sectoral formats on a regular basis, with each side represented by the appropriate Minister; in an appropriate format to consider cross-sectoral matters.
4. Representatives of members will operate in accordance with whatever procedures for democratic authority and accountability are in force in their respective elected institutions.
5. The BIC will exchange information, discuss, consult and use best endeavours to reach agreement on co-operation on matters of mutual interest within the competence of the relevant Administrations. Suitable issues for early discussion in the BIC could include transport links, agricultural issues, environmental issues, cultural issues, health issues, education issues and approaches to EU issues. Suitable arrangements to be made for practical co-operation on agreed policies.
6. It will be open to the BIC to agree common policies or common actions. Individual members may opt not to participate in such common policies and common action.
7. The BIC normally will operate by consensus. In relation to decisions on common policies or common actions, including their means of implementation, it will operate by agreement of all members participating in such policies or actions.
8. The members of the BIC, on a basis to be agreed between them, will provide such financial support as it may require.

9. A secretariat for the BIC will be provided by the British and Irish Governments in co-ordination with officials of each of the other members.

10. In addition to the structures provided for under this agreement, it will be open to two or more members to develop bilateral or multilateral arrangements between them. Such arrangements could include, subject to the agreement of the members concerned, mechanisms to enable consultation, co-operation and joint decision-making on matters of mutual interest; and mechanisms to implement any joint decisions they may reach. These arrangements will not require the prior approval of the BIC as a whole and will operate independently of it.

11. The elected institutions of the members will be encouraged to develop interparliamentary links, perhaps building on the British–Irish Interparliamentary Body.

12. The full membership of the BIC will keep under review the workings of the Council, including a formal published review at an appropriate time after the Agreement comes into effect, and will contribute as appropriate to any review of the overall political agreement arising from the multi-party negotiations.

British–Irish Intergovernmental Conference

1. There will be a new British–Irish Agreement dealing with the totality of relationships. It will establish a standing British–Irish Intergovernmental Conference, which will subsume both the Anglo-Irish Intergovernmental Council and the Intergovernmental Conference established under the 1985 Agreement.

2. The Conference will bring together the British and Irish Governments to promote bilateral co-operation at all levels on all matters of mutual interest within the competence of both Governments.

3. The Conference will meet as required at Summit level (Prime Minister and Taoiseach). Otherwise, Governments will be represented by appropriate Ministers. Advisers, including police and security advisers, will attend as appropriate.

4. All decisions will be by agreement between both Governments. The Governments will make determined efforts to resolve disagreements between them. There will be no derogation from the sovereignty of either Government.

5. In recognition of the Irish Government's special interest in Northern Ireland and of the extent to which issues of mutual concern arise in relation to Northern Ireland, there will be regular and frequent meetings of the Conference concerned with non-devolved Northern Ireland matters, on which the Irish Government may put forward views and proposals. These meetings, to be co-chaired by the Minister for Foreign Affairs and the Secretary of State for Northern Ireland, would also deal with all-island and cross-border co-operation on non-devolved issues.

6. Co-operation within the framework of the Conference will include facilitation of co-operation in security matters. The Conference also will address, in particular, the areas of rights, justice, prisons and policing in Northern Ireland (unless and until responsibility is devolved to a Northern Ireland administration) and will intensify co-operation between the two Governments on the all-island or cross-border aspects of these matters.

7. Relevant executive members of the Northern Ireland Administration will be involved in meetings of the Conference, and in the reviews referred to in paragraph 9 below to discuss non-devolved Northern Ireland matters.

8. The Conference will be supported by officials of the British and Irish Governments, including by a standing joint Secretariat of officials dealing with non-devolved Northern Ireland matters.

9. The Conference will keep under review the workings of the new British–Irish Agreement and the machinery and institutions established under it, including a formal published review three years after the Agreement comes into effect. Representatives of the Northern Ireland Administration will be invited to express views to the Conference in this context. The Conference will contribute as appropriate to any review of the overall political agreement arising from the multi-party negotiations but will have no power to override the democratic arrangements set up by this Agreement.

6. RIGHTS, SAFEGUARDS AND EQUALITY OF OPPORTUNITY

Human Rights

1. The parties affirm their commitment to the mutual respect, the civil rights and the religious liberties of everyone in the community. Against the background of the recent history of communal conflict, the parties affirm in particular:
   - the right of free political thought;
   - the right to freedom and expression of religion;
   - the right to pursue democratically national and political aspirations;
   - the right to seek constitutional change by peaceful and legitimate means;
   - the right to freely choose one's place of residence;
   - the right to equal opportunity in all social and economic activity, regardless of class, creed, disability, gender or ethnicity;
   - the right to freedom from sectarian harassment; and
   - the right of women to full and equal political participation.

United Kingdom Legislation

2. The British Government will complete incorporation into Northern Ireland law of the European Convention on Human Rights (ECHR), with direct access to the courts, and remedies for breach of the Convention, including power for the courts to overrule Assembly legislation on grounds of inconsistency.

3. Subject to the outcome of public consultation underway, the British Government intends, as a particular priority, to create a statutory obligation on public authorities in Northern Ireland to carry out all their functions with due regard to the need to promote equality of opportunity in relation to religion and political opinion; gender; race; disability; age; marital status; dependants; and sexual orientation. Public bodies would be required to draw up statutory schemes showing how they would implement this obligation. Such schemes would cover arrangements for policy appraisal, including an assessment of impact on relevant categories, public consultation, public access to information and services, monitoring and timetables.

4. The new Northern Ireland Human Rights Commission (see paragraph 5 below) will be invited to consult and to advise on the scope for defining, in Westminster legislation, rights supplementary to those in the European Convention on Human Rights, to reflect the particular circumstances of Northern Ireland, drawing as appropriate on international instruments and experience. These additional rights to reflect the principles of mutual respect for the identity and ethos of both communities and parity of esteem, and – taken together with the ECHR – to constitute a Bill of Rights for Northern Ireland. Among the issues for consideration by the Commission will be:
   - the formulation of a general obligation on government and public bodies fully to respect, on the basis of equality of treatment, the identity and ethos of both communities in Northern Ireland; and

- a clear formulation of the rights not to be discriminated against and to equality of opportunity in both the public and private sectors.

New Institutions in Northern Ireland

5. A new Northern Ireland Human Rights Commission, with membership from Northern Ireland reflecting the community balance, will be established by Westminster legislation, independent of Government, with an extended and enhanced role beyond that currently exercised by the Standing Advisory Commission on Human Rights, to include keeping under review the adequacy and effectiveness of laws and practices, making recommendations to Government as necessary; providing information and promoting awareness of human rights; considering draft legislation referred to them by the new Assembly; and, in appropriate cases, bringing court proceedings or providing assistance to individuals doing so.

6. Subject to the outcome of public consultation currently underway, the British Government intends a new statutory Equality Commission to replace the Fair Employment Commission, the Equal Opportunities Commission (NI), the Commission for Racial Equality (NI) and the Disability Council. Such a unified Commission will advise on, validate and monitor the statutory obligation and will investigate complaints of default.

7. It would be open to a new Northern Ireland Assembly to consider bringing together its responsibilities for these matters into a dedicated Department of Equality.

8. These improvements will build on existing protections in Westminster legislation in respect of the judiciary, the system of justice and policing.

Comparable Steps by the Irish Government

9. The Irish Government will also take steps to further strengthen the protection of human rights in its jurisdiction. The Government will, taking account of the work of the All-Party Oireachtas Committee on the Constitution and the Report of the Constitution Review Group, bring forward measures to strengthen and underpin the constitutional protection of human rights. These proposals will draw on the European Convention on Human Rights and other international legal instruments in the field of human rights and the question of the incorporation of the ECHR will be further examined in this context. The measures brought forward would ensure at least an equivalent level of protection of human rights as will pertain in Northern Ireland. In addition, the Irish Government will:

- establish a Human Rights Commission with a mandate and remit equivalent to that within Northern Ireland;
- proceed with arrangements as quickly as possible to ratify the Council of Europe Framework Convention on National Minorities (already ratified by the UK);
- implement enhanced employment equality legislation;
- introduce equal status legislation; and
- continue to take further active steps to demonstrate its respect for the different traditions in the island of Ireland.

A Joint Committee

10. It is envisaged that there would be a joint committee of representatives of the two Human Rights Commissions, North and South, as a forum for consideration of human rights issues in the island of Ireland. The joint committee will consider, among other matters, the possibility of establishing a charter, open to signature by all democratic political parties, reflecting and endorsing agreed measures for the protection of the fundamental rights of everyone living in the island of Ireland.

Reconciliation and Victims of Violence

11. The participants believe that it is essential to acknowledge and address the suffering of the victims of violence as a necessary element of reconciliation. They look forward to the results of the work of the Northern Ireland Victims Commission.

12. It is recognised that victims have a right to remember as well as to contribute to a changed society. The achievement of a peaceful and just society would be the true memorial to the victims of violence. The participants particularly recognise that young people from areas affected by the troubles face particular difficulties and will support the development of special community-based initiatives based on international best practice. The provision of services that are supportive and sensitive to the needs of victims will also be a critical element and that support will need to be channelled through both statutory and community-based voluntary organisations facilitating locally-based self-help and support networks. This will require the allocation of sufficient resources, including statutory funding as necessary, to meet the needs of victims and to provide for community-based support programmes.

13. The participants recognise and value the work being done by many organisations to develop reconciliation and mutual understanding and respect between and within communities and traditions, in Northern Ireland and between North and South, and they see such work as having a vital role in consolidating peace and political agreement. Accordingly, they pledge their continuing support to such organisations and will positively examine the case for enhanced financial assistance for the work of reconciliation. An essential aspect of the reconciliation process is the promotion of a culture of tolerance at every level of society, including initiatives to facilitate and encourage integrated education and mixed housing.

Economic, Social and Cultural Issues

1. Pending the devolution of powers to a new Northern Ireland Assembly, the British Government will pursue broad policies for sustained economic growth and stability in Northern Ireland and for promoting social inclusion, including in particular community development and the advancement of women in public life.

2. Subject to the public consultation currently under way, the British Government will make rapid progress with:

   (i) a new regional development strategy for Northern Ireland, for consideration in due course by the Assembly, tackling the problems of a divided society and social cohesion in urban, rural and border areas, protecting and enhancing the environment, producing new approaches to transport issues, strengthening the physical infrastructure of the region, developing the advantages and resources of rural areas and rejuvenating major urban centres;

   (ii) a new economic development strategy for Northern Ireland, for consideration in due course by the Assembly, which would provide for short and medium term economic planning linked as appropriate to the regional development strategy; and

   (iii) measures on employment equality included in the recent White Paper ('Partnership for Equality') and covering the extension and strengthening of anti-discrimination legislation, a review of the national security aspects of the present fair employment legislation at the earliest possible time, a new more focused Targeting Social Need initiative and a range of measures aimed at combating unemployment and progressively eliminating the differential in unemployment rates between the two communities by targeting objective need.

3. All participants recognise the importance of respect, understanding and tolerance in relation to linguistic diversity, including in Northern Ireland, the Irish language, Ulster-Scots and the languages of the various ethnic communities, all of which are part of the cultural wealth of the island of Ireland.

4. In the context of active consideration currently being given to the UK signing the Council of Europe Charter for Regional or Minority Languages, the British Government will in particular in relation to the Irish language, where appropriate and where people so desire it:

   • take resolute action to promote the language;
   • facilitate and encourage the use of the language in speech and writing in public and private life where there is appropriate demand;
   • seek to remove, where possible, restrictions which would discourage or work against the maintenance or development of the language;
   • make provision for liaising with the Irish language community, representing their views to public authorities and investigating complaints;
   • place a statutory duty on the Department of Education to encourage and facilitate Irish medium education in line with current provision for integrated education;
   • explore urgently with the relevant British authorities, and in co-operation with the Irish broadcasting authorities, the scope for achieving more widespread availability of Teilifís na Gaeilge in Northern Ireland;
   • seek more effective ways to encourage and provide financial support for Irish language film and television production in Northern Ireland; and
   • encourage the parties to secure agreement that this commitment will be sustained by a new Assembly in a way which takes account of the desires and sensitivities of the community.

5. All participants acknowledge the sensitivity of the use of symbols and emblems for public purposes, and the need in particular in creating the new institutions to ensure that such symbols and emblems are used in a manner which promotes mutual respect rather than division. Arrangements will be made to monitor this issue and consider what action might be required.

7. DECOMMISSIONING

1. Participants recall their agreement in the Procedural Motion adopted on 24 September 1997 'that the resolution of the decommissioning issue is an indispensable part of the process of negotiation', and also recall the provisions of paragraph 25 of Strand 1 above.

2. They note the progress made by the Independent International Commission on Decommissioning and the Governments in developing schemes which can represent a workable basis for achieving the decommissioning of illegally-held arms in the possession of paramilitary groups.

3. All participants accordingly reaffirm their commitment to the total disarmament of all paramilitary organisations. They also confirm their intention to continue to work constructively and in good faith with the Independent Commission, and to use any influence they may have, to achieve the decommissioning of all paramilitary arms within two years following endorsement in referendums North and South of the agreement and in the context of the implementation of the overall settlement.

4. The Independent Commission will monitor, review and verify progress on decommissioning of illegal arms, and will report to both Governments at regular intervals.

6. Both Governments will take all necessary steps to facilitate the decommissioning process to include bringing the relevant schemes into force by the end of June.

8. SECURITY

1. The participants note that the development of a peaceful environment on the basis of this agreement can and should mean a normalisation of security arrangements and practices.

2. The British Government will make progress towards the objective of as early a return as possible to normal security arrangements in Northern Ireland, consistent with the level of threat and with a published overall strategy, dealing with:
    (i) the reduction of the numbers and role of the Armed Forces deployed in Northern Ireland to levels compatible with a normal peaceful society;
    (ii) the removal of security installations;
    (iii) the removal of emergency powers in Northern Ireland; and
    (iv) other measures appropriate to and compatible with a normal peaceful society.

3. The Secretary of State will consult regularly on progress, and the response to any continuing paramilitary activity, with the Irish Government and the political parties, as appropriate.

4. The British Government will continue its consultation on firearms regulation and control on the basis of the document published on 2 April 1998.

5. The Irish Government will initiate a wide-ranging review of the Offences Against the State Acts 1939-85 with a view to both reform and dispensing with those elements no longer required as circumstances permit.

9. POLICING AND JUSTICE

1. The participants recognise that policing is a central issue in any society. They equally recognise that Northern Ireland's history of deep divisions has made it highly emotive, with great hurt suffered and sacrifices made by many individuals and their families, including those in the RUC and other public servants. They believe that the agreement provides the opportunity for a new beginning to policing in Northern Ireland with a police service capable of attracting and sustaining support from the community as a whole. They also believe that this agreement offers a unique opportunity to bring about a new political dispensation which will recognise the full and equal legitimacy and worth of the identities, senses of allegiance and ethos of all sections of the community in Northern Ireland. They consider that this opportunity should inform and underpin the development of a police service representative in terms of the make-up of the community as a whole and which, in a peaceful environment, should be routinely unarmed.

2. The participants believe it essential that policing structures and arrangements are such that the police service is professional, effective and efficient, fair and impartial, free from partisan political control; accountable, both under the law for its actions and to the community it serves; representative of the society it polices, and operates within a coherent and co-operative criminal justice system, which conforms with human rights norms. The participants also believe that those structures and arrangements must be capable of maintaining law and order including responding effectively to crime and to any terrorist threat and to public order problems. A police service which cannot do so will fail to win public confidence and acceptance. They believe that any such structures and arrangements should be capable of delivering a policing service, in constructive and inclusive partnerships with the community at

all levels, and with the maximum delegation of authority and responsibility, consistent with the foregoing principles. These arrangements should be based on principles of protection of human rights and professional integrity and should be unambiguously accepted and actively supported by the entire community.

3. An independent Commission will be established to make recommendations for future policing arrangements in Northern Ireland including means of encouraging widespread community support for these arrangements within the agreed framework of principles reflected in the paragraphs above and in accordance with the terms of reference at Annex A. The Commission will be broadly representative with expert and international representation among its membership and will be asked to consult widely and to report no later than Summer 1999.

4. The participants believe that the aims of the criminal justice system are to:
   - deliver a fair and impartial system of justice to the community;
   - be responsive to the community's concerns, and encouraging community involvement where appropriate;
   - have the confidence of all parts of the community; and
   - deliver justice efficiently and effectively.

5. There will be a parallel wide-ranging review of criminal justice (other than policing and those aspects of the system relating to the emergency legislation) to be carried out by the British Government through a mechanism with an independent element, in consultation with the political parties and others. The review will commence as soon as possible, will include wide consultation, and a report will be made to the Secretary of State no later than Autumn 1999. Terms of Reference are attached at Annex B.

6. Implementation of the recommendations arising from both reviews will be discussed with the political parties and with the Irish Government.

7. The participants also note that the British Government remains ready in principle, with the broad support of the political parties, and after consultation, as appropriate, with the Irish Government, in the context of ongoing implementation of the relevant recommendations, to devolve responsibility for policing and justice issues.

ANNEX A

Commission on Policing for Northern Ireland

TERMS OF REFERENCE

Taking account of the principles on policing as set out in the agreement, the Commission will inquire into policing in Northern Ireland and, on the basis of its findings, bring forward proposals for future policing structures and arrangements, including means of encouraging widespread community support for those arrangements.

Its proposals on policing should be designed to ensure that policing arrangements, including composition, recruitment, training, culture, ethos and symbols, are such that in a new approach Northern Ireland has a police service that can enjoy widespread support from, and is seen as an integral part of, the community as a whole.

Its proposals should include recommendations covering any issues such as retraining, job placement and educational and professional development required in the transition to policing in a peaceful society.

Its proposals should also be designed to ensure that:

- the police service is structured, managed and resourced so that it can be effective in discharging its full range of functions (including proposals on any necessary arrangements for the transition to policing in a normal peaceful society);
- the police service is delivered in constructive and inclusive partnerships with the community at all levels with the maximum delegation of authority and responsibility;
- the legislative and constitutional framework requires the impartial discharge of policing functions and conforms with internationally accepted norms in relation to policing standards;
- the police operate within a clear framework of accountability to the law and the community they serve, so:
  * they are constrained by, accountable to and act only within the law;
  * their powers and procedures, like the law they enforce, are clearly established and publicly available;
  * there are open, accessible and independent means of investigating and adjudicating upon complaints against the police;
  * there are clearly established arrangements enabling local people, and their political representatives, to articulate their views and concerns about policing and to establish publicly policing priorities and influence policing policies, subject to safeguards to ensure police impartiality and freedom from partisan political control;
  * there are arrangements for accountability and for the effective, efficient and economic use of resources in achieving policing objectives;
  * there are means to ensure independent professional scrutiny and inspection of the police service to ensure that proper professional standards are maintained;
- the scope for structured co-operation with the Garda Siochana and other police forces is addressed; and
- the management of public order events which can impose exceptional demands on policing resources is also addressed.

The Commission should focus on policing issues, but if it identifies other aspects of the criminal justice system relevant to its work on policing, including the role of the police in prosecution, then it should draw the attention of the Government to those matters.

The Commission should consult widely, including with non-governmental expert organisations, and through such focus groups as they consider it appropriate to establish.

The Government proposes to establish the Commission as soon as possible, with the aim of it starting work as soon as possible and publishing its final report by Summer 1999.

ANNEX B

Review of the Criminal Justice System

TERMS OF REFERENCE

Taking account of the aims of the criminal justice system as set out in the Agreement, the review will address the structure, management and resourcing of publicly funded elements of the criminal justice system and will bring forward proposals for future criminal justice arrangements (other than policing and those aspects of the system relating to emergency legislation, which the Government is considering separately) covering such issues as:

- the arrangements for making appointments to the judiciary and magistracy, and safeguards for protecting their independence;
- the arrangements for the organisation and supervision of the prosecution process, and for safeguarding its independence;
- measures to improve the responsiveness and accountability of, and any lay participation in the criminal justice system;
- mechanisms for addressing law reform;
- the scope for structured co-operation between the criminal justice agencies on both parts of the island; and
- the structure and organisation of criminal justice functions that might be devolved to an Assembly, including the possibility of establishing a Department of Justice, while safeguarding the essential independence of many of the key functions in this area.

The Government proposes to commence the review as soon as possible, consulting with the political parties and others, including non-governmental expert organisations. The review will be completed by Autumn 1999.

10. PRISONERS

1. Both Governments will put in place mechanisms to provide for an accelerated programme for the release of prisoners, including transferred prisoners, convicted of scheduled offences in Northern Ireland or, in the case of those sentenced outside Northern Ireland, similar offences (referred to hereafter as qualifying prisoners). Any such arrangements will protect the rights of individual prisoners under national and international law.
2. Prisoners affiliated to organisations which have not established or are not maintaining a complete and unequivocal ceasefire will not benefit from the arrangements. The situation in this regard will be kept under review.
3. Both Governments will complete a review process within a fixed time frame and set prospective release dates for all qualifying prisoners. The review process would provide for the advance of the release dates of qualifying prisoners while allowing account to be taken of the seriousness of the offences for which the person was convicted and the need to protect the community. In addition, the intention would be that should the circumstances allow it, any qualifying prisoners who remained in custody two years after the commencement of the scheme would be released at that point.
4. The Governments will seek to enact the appropriate legislation to give effect to these arrangements by the end of June 1998.
5. The Governments continue to recognise the importance of measures to facilitate the reintegration of prisoners into the community by providing support both prior to and after release, including assistance directed towards availing of employment opportunities, re-training and/or re-skilling, and further education.

11. VALIDATION, IMPLEMENTATION AND REVIEW

Validation and Implementation

1. The two Governments will as soon as possible sign a new British–Irish Agreement replacing the 1985 Anglo-Irish Agreement, embodying understandings on constitutional issues and affirming their solemn commitment to support and, where appropriate, implement the agreement reached by the participants in the negotiations which shall be annexed to the British–Irish Agreement.
2. Each Government will organise a referendum on 22 May 1998. Subject to Parliamentary approval, a consultative referendum in Northern Ireland, organised under

the terms of the Northern Ireland (Entry to Negotiations, etc.) Act 1996, will address the question: 'Do you support the agreement reached in the multi-party talks on Northern Ireland and set out in Command Paper 3883?'. The Irish Government will introduce and support in the Oireachtas a Bill to amend the Constitution as described in paragraph 2 of the section 'Constitutional Issues' and in Annex B, as follows: (a) to amend Articles 2 and 3 as described in paragraph 8.1 in Annex B above and (b) to amend Article 29 to permit the Government to ratify the new British–Irish Agreement. On passage by the Oireachtas, the Bill will be put to referendum.

3. If majorities of those voting in each of the referendums support this agreement, the Governments will then introduce and support, in their respective Parliaments, such legislation as may be necessary to give effect to all aspects of this agreement, and will take whatever ancillary steps as may be required including the holding of elections on 25 June, subject to parliamentary approval, to the Assembly, which would meet initially in a 'shadow' mode. The establishment of the North–South Ministerial Council, implementation bodies, the British–Irish Council and the British–Irish Intergovernmental Conference and the assumption by the Assembly of its legislative and executive powers will take place at the same time on the entry into force of the British–Irish Agreement.

4. In the interim, aspects of the implementation of the multi-party agreement will be reviewed at meetings of those parties relevant in the particular case (taking into account, once Assembly elections have been held, the results of those elections), under the chairmanship of the British Government or the two Governments, as may be appropriate; and representatives of the two Governments and all relevant parties may meet under independent chairmanship to review implementation of the agreement as a whole.

Review Procedures Following Implementation

5. Each institution may, at any time, review any problems that may arise in its operation and, where no other institution is affected, take remedial action in consultation as necessary with the relevant Government or Governments. It will be for each institution to determine its own procedures for review.

6. If there are difficulties in the operation of a particular institution, which have implications for another institution, they may review their operations separately and jointly and agree on remedial action to be taken under their respective authorities.

7. If difficulties arise which require remedial action across the range of institutions, or otherwise require amendment of the British–Irish Agreement or relevant legislation, the process of review will fall to the two Governments in consultation with the parties in the Assembly. Each Government will be responsible for action in its own jurisdiction.

8. Notwithstanding the above, each institution will publish an annual report on its operations. In addition, the two Governments and the parties in the Assembly will convene a conference 4 years after the agreement comes into effect, to review and report on its operation.

AGREEMENT BETWEEN THE GOVERNMENT OF
THE UNITED KINGDOM OF GREAT BRITAIN
AND NORTHERN IRELAND
AND THE GOVERNMENT OF IRELAND

The British and Irish Governments:

Welcoming the strong commitment to the Agreement reached on 10th April 1998 by themselves and other participants in the multi-party talks and set out in Annex 1 to this Agreement (hereinafter 'the Multi-Party Agreement');

Considering that the Multi-Party Agreement offers an opportunity for a new beginning in relationships within Northern Ireland, within the island of Ireland and between the peoples of these islands;

Wishing to develop still further the unique relationship between their peoples and the close co-operation between their countries as friendly neighbours and as partners in the European Union;

Reaffirming their total commitment to the principles of democracy and non-violence which have been fundamental to the multi-party talks;

Reaffirming their commitment to the principles of partnership, equality and mutual respect and to the protection of civil, political, social, economic and cultural rights in their respective jurisdictions;

Have agreed as follows:

ARTICLE I

The two Governments:

(i) recognise the legitimacy of whatever choice is freely exercised by a majority of the people of Northern Ireland with regard to its status, whether they prefer to continue to support the Union with Great Britain or a sovereign united Ireland;

(ii) recognise that it is for the people of the island of Ireland alone, by agreement between the two parts respectively and without external impediment, to exercise their right of self-determination on the basis of consent, freely and concurrently given, North and South, to bring about a united Ireland, if that is their wish, accepting that this right must be achieved and exercised with and subject to the agreement and consent of a majority of the people of Northern Ireland;

(iii) acknowledge that while a substantial section of the people in Northern Ireland share the legitimate wish of a majority of the people of the island of Ireland for a united Ireland, the present wish of a majority of the people of Northern Ireland, freely exercised and legitimate, is to maintain the Union and accordingly, that Northern Ireland's status as part of the United Kingdom reflects and relies upon that wish; and that it would be wrong to make any change in the status of Northern Ireland save with the consent of a majority of its people;

(iv) affirm that, if in the future, the people of the island of Ireland exercise their right of self-determination on the basis set out in sections (i) and (ii) above to bring about a united Ireland, it will be a binding obligation on both Governments to introduce and support in their respective Parliaments legislation to give effect to that wish;

(v) affirm that whatever choice is freely exercised by a majority of the people of Northern Ireland, the power of the sovereign government with jurisdiction there shall be exercised with rigorous impartiality on behalf of all the people in the diversity of their identities and traditions and shall be founded on the principles of full respect for, and equality of, civil, political, social and cultural rights, of freedom from discrimination for all citizens, and of parity of esteem and of just and equal treatment for the identity, ethos and aspirations of both communities;

(vi) recognise the birthright of all the people of Northern Ireland to identify themselves and be accepted as Irish or British, or both, as they may so choose, and accordingly confirm that their right to hold both British and Irish citizenship is accepted by both Governments and would not be affected by any future change in the status of Northern Ireland.

ARTICLE 2

The two Governments affirm their solemn commitment to support, and where appropriate implement, the provisions of the Multi-Party Agreement. In particular there shall be established in accordance with the provisions of the Multi-Party Agreement immediately on the entry into force of this Agreement, the following institutions:

(i) a North/South Ministerial Council;
(ii) the implementation bodies referred to in paragraph 9 (ii) of the section entitled 'Strand Two' of the Multi-Party Agreement;
(iii) a British–Irish Council;
(iv) a British–Irish Intergovernmental Conference.

ARTICLE 3

(1) This Agreement shall replace the Agreement between the British and Irish Governments done at Hillsborough on 15th November 1985 which shall cease to have effect on entry into force of this Agreement.

(2) The Intergovernmental Conference established by Article 2 of the aforementioned Agreement done on 15th November 1985 shall cease to exist on entry into force of this Agreement.

ARTICLE 4

(1) It shall be a requirement for entry into force of this Agreement that:
(a) British legislation shall have been enacted for the purpose of implementing the provisions of Annex A to the section entitled 'Constitutional Issues' of the Multi-Party Agreement;
(b) the amendments to the Constitution of Ireland set out in Annex B to the section entitled 'Constitutional Issues' of the Multi-Party Agreement shall have been approved by Referendum;
(c) such legislation shall have been enacted as may be required to establish the institutions referred to in Article 2 of this Agreement.

(2) Each Government shall notify the other in writing of the completion, so far as it is concerned, of the requirements for entry into force of this Agreement. This Agreement shall enter into force on the date of the receipt of the later of the two notifications.

(3) Immediately on entry into force of this Agreement, the Irish Government shall ensure that the amendments to the Constitution of Ireland set out in Annex B to the section entitled 'Constitutional Issues' of the Multi-Party Agreement take effect.

In witness thereof the undersigned, being duly authorised thereto by the respective Governments, have signed this Agreement.

Done in two originals at Belfast on the 10th day of April 1998.

Tony Blair
Marjorie ('Mo') Mowlam
For the Government
of the United Kingdom of
Great Britain and Northern Ireland

Bertie Ahern
David Andrews
For the Government
of Ireland

ANNEX I

The Agreement Reached
in the Multi-Party Talks

ANNEX 2

Declaration on the Provisions of
Paragraph (vi) of Article 1
In Relationship to Citizenship

The British and Irish Governments declare that it is their joint understanding that the term 'the people of Northern Ireland' in paragraph (vi) of Article 1 of this Agreement means, for the purposes of giving effect to this provision, all persons born in Northern Ireland and having, at the time of their birth, at least one parent who is a British citizen, an Irish citizen or is otherwise entitled to reside in Northern Ireland without any restriction on their period of residence.

APPENDIX 3

Extract from 'Towards a Lasting Peace', Sinn Féin Document, 1992

ARMED STRUGGLE

Armed struggle has, throughout history and in all parts of the globe, been seen as a legitimate component of peoples' resistance to foreign oppression. In Ireland, it was armed struggle which created the conditions for the removal of British jurisdiction over the 26 Counties and the emergence of a separate (if truncated) Irish state.

However, armed struggle is recognised by republicans to be an option of last resort when all other avenues to pursue freedom have been attempted and suppressed.

It must be recognised that there has been no consistent constitutional strategy to pursue a national democracy in Ireland. Certainly, there has been no consistent and principled strategy advanced during the last 20 years of continuous conflict.

Objective evaluations of the armed struggle, including those of the British government, recognise that its history to date indicates that it is likely to be sustained for the foreseeable future.

In these circumstances there is an onus on those who proclaim that the armed struggle is counter-productive to advance a credible alternative. Such an alternative would be welcomed across the island but nowhere more than in the oppressed nationalist areas of the Six Counties which have borne the brunt of British rule since partition and particularly for over 20 years past. The development of such an alternative would be welcomed by Sinn Féin.

APPENDIX 4

Joint Declaration on Peace (Downing Street Declaration), 15 December 1993

The following is the text of the 'Joint Declaration on Peace' also known as the 'Downing Street Declaration'. This declaration was issued on 15 December 1993 by John Major, then British Prime Minister, and Albert Reynolds, then Taoiseach, on behalf of the British and Irish governments

1. The Taoiseach, Mr. Albert Reynolds, TD and the Prime Minister, the Rt Hon. John Major MP, acknowledge that the most urgent and important issue facing the people of Ireland, North and South, and the British and Irish Governments together, is to remove the conflict, to overcome the legacy of history and to heal the divisions which have resulted, recognising the absence of a lasting and satisfactory settlement of relationships between the peoples of both islands has contributed to continuing tragedy and suffering. They believe that the development of an agreed framework for peace, which has been discussed between them since early last year, and which is based on a number of key principles articulated by the two Governments over the past 20 years, together with adaptation of other widely accepted principles, provides the starting point of a peace process designed to culminate in a political settlement.

2. The Taoiseach and the Prime Minister are convinced of the inestimable value to both their peoples, and particularly for the next generation, of healing divisions in Ireland and of ending a conflict which has been so manifestly to the detriment of all. Both recognise that the ending of divisions can come about only through the agreement and co-operation of the people, North and South, representing both traditions in Ireland. They therefore make a solemn commitment to promote co-operation at all levels on the basis of the fundamental principles, undertakings, obligations under international agreements, to which they have jointly committed themselves, and the guarantees which each Government has given and now reaffirms, including Northern Ireland's statutory constitutional guarantee. It is their aim to foster agreement and reconciliation, leading to a new political framework founded on consent and encompassing arrangements within Northern Ireland, for the whole island, and between these islands.

3. They also consider that the development of Europe will, of itself, require new approaches to serve interests common to both parts of the island of Ireland, and to Ireland and the United Kingdom as partners in the European Union.

4. The Prime Minister, on behalf of the British Government, reaffirms that they will uphold the democratic wish of the greater number of the people of Northern Ireland on the issue of whether they prefer to support the Union or a sovereign united Ireland. On this basis, he reiterates, on the behalf of the British Government, that they have no selfish strategic or economic interest in Northern Ireland. Their primary interest is to see peace, stability and reconciliation established by agreement among all the people inhabit the island, and they will work together with the Irish Government to achieve such an agreement, which will embrace the totality of relationships. The role of the British Government will be to encourage, facilitate and enable the achievement of such agreement over a period through a process of dialogue and co-operation based on full respect for the rights and identities of both traditions in Ireland. They accept that such agreement may, as of right, take the form of agreed structures for the island as a whole, including a united Ireland achieved by peaceful means on the following basis. The British Government agree that it is for the people of the island of Ireland alone, by agreement between the two parts respectively, to exercise their right of self-determination on the basis of consent, freely and concurrently given, North and South, to bring about a united Ireland, if that is their wish. They reaffirm as a binding obligation that they will, for their part, introduce the necessary legislation to give effect to this, or equally to any measure of agreement on future relationships in Ireland which the people living in Ireland may themselves freely so determine without external impediment. They believe that the people of Britain would wish, in friendship to all sides, to enable the people of Ireland to reach agreement on how they may live together in harmony and in partnership, with respect for their diverse traditions, and with full recognition of the special links and the unique relationship which exist between the peoples of Britain and Ireland. The Taoiseach, on behalf of the Irish Government, considers that the lessons of Irish history, and especially of Northern Ireland, show that stability and well-being will not be found under any political system which is refused allegiance or rejected on grounds of identity by a significant minority of those governed by it. For this reason, it would be wrong to attempt to impose a united Ireland, in the absence of the freely given consent of the majority of the people of Northern Ireland. He accepts, on behalf of the Irish Government, that the democratic right of self-determination by the people of Ireland as a whole must be achieved and exercised with and subject to the agreement and consent of a majority of the people of Northern Ireland and must, consistent with justice and equity, respect the democratic dignity and the civil rights and religious liberties of both communities, including: – the right of free political thought; – the right of freedom and expression of religion; – the right to pursue democratically national and political aspirations; – the right to seek constitutional change by peaceful and legitimate means; – the right to live wherever one chooses without hindrance; – the right to equal opportunity in all social and economic activity, regardless of class, creed, sex or colour. These would be reflected in any future political and constitutional arrangements emerging from a new and more broadly based agreement.

5. The Taoiseach however recognises the genuine difficulties and barriers to building relationships of trust either within or beyond Northern Ireland, from which both traditions suffer. He will work to create a new era of trust, in which suspicion of the motives and actions of others is removed on the part of either community. He considers that the future of the island depends on the nature of the relationship

between the two main traditions that inhabit it. Every effort must be made to build a new series of trust between those communities. In recognition of the fears of the Unionist community and as a token of his willingness to make a political contribution to the building up of that necessary trust, the Taoiseach will examine with his colleagues any elements in the democratic life and organisation of the Irish State that can be represented to the Irish Government in the course of political dialogue as a real and substantial threat to their way of life and ethos, or that can be represented as not being fully consistent with a modern democratic and pluralist society, and undertakes to examine any possible ways of removing such obstacles. Such an examination would of course have due regard to the desire to preserve those inherited values that are largely shared throughout the island or that belong to the cultural and historical roots of the people of this island in all their diversity. The Taoiseach hopes that over time a meeting of hearts and minds will develop, which will bring all the people of Ireland together, and will work towards that objective, but he pledges in the meantime that as a result of the efforts that will be made to build mutual confidence no Northern Unionist should ever have a fear in future that this ideal will be pursued either by threat or coercion.

6. Both Governments accept that Irish unity would be achieved only by those who favour this outcome persuading those who do not, peacefully and without coercion or violence, and that, if in the future a majority of the people of Northern Ireland are so persuaded, both Governments will support and give legislative effect to their wish. But, notwithstanding the solemn affirmation by both Governments in the Anglo-Irish Agreement that any change in the status of Northern Ireland, would only come about with a consent of the majority of the people of Northern Ireland, the Taoiseach also recognises the continuing uncertainties and misgivings which dominate so much of Northern Unionist attitudes towards the rest of Ireland. He believes that we stand at a stage of our history when the genuine feelings of all traditions in the North must be recognised and acknowledged. He appeals to both traditions at this time to grasp the opportunity for a fresh start and a new beginning, which could hold such promise for all our lives and the generations to come. He asks the people of Northern Ireland to look on the people of the Republic as friends, who share their grief and shame over all the suffering of the last quarter of a century, and who wants to develop the best possible relationship with them, a relationship in which trust and new understanding can flourish and grow. The Taoiseach also acknowledges the presence in the *Constitution of the Republic* of elements which are deeply resented by Northern Unionists, but which at the same time reflect hopes and ideals which lie deep in the hearts of many Irish men and women North and South. But as we move towards a new era of understanding in which new relationships of trust may grow and bring peace to the island of Ireland, the Taoiseach believes that the time has come to consider together how best the hopes and identities of all can be expressed in more balanced ways, which no longer engender division and the lack of trust to which he has referred. He confirms that, in the event of an overall settlement, the Irish Government will, as part of a balanced constitutional accommodation, put forward and support proposals for change in the *Irish Constitution* which would fully reflect the principle of consent in Northern Ireland.

7. The Taoiseach recognises the need to engage in dialogue which would address the honesty and integrity the fears of all traditions. But that dialogue, both within the North and between the people and their representatives of both parts of Ireland, must be entered into with an acknowledgment that the future security and welfare

of the people of the island will depend on an open, frank and balanced approach to all the problems which for too long have caused division.

8.   The British and Irish Governments will seek, along with the Northern Ireland constitutional parties through a process of political dialogue, to create institutions and structures which, while respecting the diversity of the people of Ireland, would enable them to work together in all areas of common interest. This will help over a period to build the trust necessary to end past divisions, leading to an agreed and peaceful future. Such structures would, of course, include institutional recognition of the special links that exist between the peoples of Britain and Ireland as part of the totality of relationships, while taking account of newly forged links with the rest of Europe.

9.   The British and Irish Governments reiterate that the achievement of peace must involve a permanent end to the use of, or support for, paramilitary violence. They confirm that, in these circumstances, democratically mandated parties which establish a commitment to exclusively peaceful methods and which have shown that they abide by the democratic process, are free to participate fully in democratic politics and to join in dialogue in due course between the Governments and the political parties on the way ahead.

10. The Irish Government would make their own arrangements within their jurisdiction to enable democratic parties to consult together and share in dialogue about the political future. The Taoiseach's intention is that these arrangements could include the establishment, in consultation with other parties, of a Forum for Peace and Reconciliation to make recommendations on ways in which agreement and trust between both traditions can be promoted and established.

11. The Taoiseach and the Prime Minister are determined to build on the fervent wish of both their peoples to see old fears and anomalies replaced by a climate of peace. They believe the framework they have set out offers the people of Ireland, North and South, whatever their tradition, the basis to agree that from now on their differences can be negotiated and resolved exclusively by peaceful political means. They appeal to all concerned to grasp the opportunity for a new departure. That step would compromise no position or principle, nor prejudice the future of either community. On the contrary, it would be an incomparable gain for all. It would break decisively the cycle of violence and the intolerable suffering it entails for the people of these islands, particularly for both communities in Northern Ireland. It would allow the process of economic and social co-operation on the island to realise its full potential for prosperity and mutual understanding. It would transform the prospects for building on the progress already made in the Talks process, involving the two Governments and the constitutional parties in Northern Ireland. The Taoiseach and the Prime Minister believe that these arrangements offer an opportunity to lay the foundation for a more peaceful and harmonious future, devoid of the violence and bitter divisions which have scarred the past generation. They commit themselves and their Governments to continue to work together, unremittingly, towards that objective.

APPENDIX 5

A personal message from Rt Hon. Sir Patrick Mayhew, December 1993

A PERSONAL MESSAGE FROM RT HON. SIR PATRICK MAYHEW, QC, MP,
SECRETARY OF STATE FOR NORTHERN IRELAND

The Prime Minister and the Taoiseach made a Joint Declaration on 15 December. Because of the importance of its message, I have tried to make it as widely available as possible, through this booklet. I am also taking this opportunity to set out some of the key features of the Declaration.

The Declaration, which complements and underpins the Talks process and the search for a comprehensive political settlement, has been made following discussions between the two Governments, since early last year, on a framework for peace. It challenges those who use or support violence to stop now.

The Declaration sets out constitutional principles and political realities which safeguard the vital interests of both sides of the community in Northern Ireland. It reflects the beliefs of both Governments, but compromises the principles of neither. It makes no prejudgements.

The text both reiterates Northern Ireland's statutory constitutional guarantee and reaffirms that the British Government will uphold the democratic wish of a greater number of the people of Northern Ireland, on the issue on whether they prefer to support the Union or a sovereign united Ireland. On this basis the British Government reiterates that they have no selfish strategic or economic interest in Northern Ireland. They agree that it is for the people of the island of Ireland alone, by agreement between the two parts respectively, to exercise their right of self-determination on the basis of consent, freely and concurrently given, North and South, to bring about a united Ireland, if that is their wish.

For their part, the Irish Government accept that it would be wrong to attempt to impose a united Ireland, in the absence of the freely given consent of a majority of the people of Northern Ireland and that the democratic right of self-determination by the people of Ireland as a whole must be achieved and exercised with and subject to the agreement and consent of a majority of Northern Ireland.

In short, the consent of a majority of the people in Northern Ireland is required before any constitutional change could come about.

The Irish Government also confirm that in the event of an overall settlement, they will, as part of a balanced constitutional accommodation, put forward and support proposals for change in the Irish Constitution, which would fully reflect the principle of consent in Northern Ireland.

The Declaration reinforces the firm foundation for future political development, on the same three stranded basis that the main constitutional parties in Northern Ireland and the two Governments have already accepted. Both Governments reiterate that, following a cessation of violence, democratically mandated parties which establish a commitment to exclusively peaceful methods, and which have shown that they abide by the democratic process, are free to participate fully in democratic politics and to join in dialogue in due course between Governments and the political parties on the way ahead.

The Joint Declaration represents a sound platform for the Talks process and a realistic core for lasting peace. It shows the British and Irish Governments working together; for democracy and against violence. As such, I commend it to you.

APPENDIX 6

The TUAS document circulated by the republican leadership, summer 1994

The briefing paper of April deals with strategic objectives and events to that date in more detail than this paper. However, a brief summary is helpful. Our goals have not changed. A united 32-county democratic socialist Republic.

The main strategic objectives to move us towards that goal can be summarised thus. To construct an Irish nationalist consensus with international support on the basis of the dynamic contained in the Irish peace initiative. This should aim for:

a The strongest possible political consensus between the Dublin government, Sinn Féin and the SDLP.
b A common position on practical measures moving us towards our goal. A common nationalist negotiation position.
c An international dimension in aid of the consensus (mostly USA and EU).

The strategic objectives come from prolonged debate but are based on a straightforward logic: that republicans at this time and on their own do not have the strength to achieve the end goal. The struggle needs strengthening; most obviously from other nationalist constituencies led by SDLP, Dublin government and the emerging Irish-American lobby, with additional support from other parties in EU rowing in behind and accelerating the momentum created.

The aim of any such consensus is to create a dynamic which can:

1. Effect [*sic*] the domestic and international perception of the republican position, i.e. as one which is reasonable.
2. To develop a northern nationalist consensus on the basis of constitutional change.
3. To develop an Irish national consensus on the same basis.
4. To develop Irish-America as a significant player in support of the above.
5. To develop a broader and deeper Irish nationalist consensus at grassroots level.
6. To develop and mobilise an anti~imperialist Irish peace movement.
7. To expose the British government and the unionists as the intransigent parties.
8. To heighten the contradictions between British unionist and 'Ulster Loyalism'.
9. To assist the development of whatever potential exists in Britain to create a mood/climate/party/movement for peace.
10. To maintain the political cohesion and organisational integrity of Sinn Féin so as to remain an effective political force.

Present British intentions are the subject of much debate and varied opinion. However, what can be said is that sometime [*sic*] preceding the DSD (Downing Street Declaration) of December '93 a deal was done with the UUP (Ulster Unionist Party) to keep the Conservatives in power. This becomes an obstacle to movement.

The DSD does not hold a solution.

Republicans are not prepared to wait around for the Brits to change, but as always we are prepared to force their hand.

It is nonetheless important to note that there has been no recent dialogue between the Brit government and Republican representatives since November '93.

The republican position is that if the Brits want to talk they should do it through normal political channels.

At the end of the April briefing it states: 'Our (strategic) objectives should guide all our actions. Given that these are our guidelines we must now look at what our options are and what initiatives we can undertake.'

After prolonged discussion and assessment the Leadership decided that if it could get agreement with the Dublin government, the SDLP and the Irish-American lobby on basic republican principles which would be enough to create the dynamic that would considerably advance the struggle, then it would be prepared to use the TUAS option.

We attempted to reach such a consensus on a set of principles which can be summarised briefly thus;

1. Partition has failed.
2. Structures must be changed.
3. No internal settlement within 6 counties
4. British rule breaches the principle of NSD (national self-determination).
5. The Irish as a whole have the right to NSD without external impediment.
6. It is up to the Dublin/London governments with all parties to bring about NSD in the shortest time possible.
7. The unionists have no veto over discussions involved or their outcome.
8. A solution requires political and constitutional change.
9. An agreed united and independent Ireland is what republicans desire. However an agreed Ireland needs the allegiance of varied traditions to be viable.

Contact with the other parties involved have been in that context. There are of course differences of opinion on how a number of these principles are interpreted or applied.

In particular: on British rule breaching the principle of NSD; on the absolute right of the Irish to NSD without external impediment; or interpretation of what veto and consent mean; on the issue of timescales.

Nevertheless, differences aside, the leadership believes there is enough in common to create a substantial political momentum which will considerably advance the struggle at this time. Some substantial contribution factors which point towards now being the right time for an initiative are:

- Hume is the only SDLP person on the horizon strong enough to face the challenge.
- Dublin's coalition is the strongest government in 25 years or more.
- Reynolds has no historical baggage to hinder him and knows how popular such a consensus would be among grassroots.
- There is potentially a very powerful Irish-American lobby not in hock to any particular party in Ireland or Britain.
- Clinton is perhaps the first US President in decades to be substantially influenced by such a lobby.

- At this time the British government is the least popular in the EU with other EU members.

It is the first time in 25 years that all the major Irish nationalist parties are rowing in roughly the same direction. These combined circumstances are unlikely to gel again in the foreseeable future.

The leadership has now decided that there is enough agreement to proceed with the TUAS option. It has been stated from the outset that this is a risky strategy. Its success will depend greatly on workload. All activists must be pro-active. Those who continue their present work need to double effect. If you find yourself idle help in another field.

TUAS has been part of every other struggle in the world this century. It is vital that activists realise the struggle is not over. Another front has opened up and we should have the confidence and put in the effort to succeed on that front. We have the ability to carry on indefinitely. We should be trying to double the pressure on the British.

For various reasons, which include the sensitivity of discussions up to this point, communication up and down the organisation has been patchy. Since we are now entering a more public aspect to the initiative communication should be a less encumbered matter and therefore more regular than before.

APPENDIX 7

IRA Ceasefire Statement, 31 August 1994

Recognising the potential of the current situation and in order to enhance the democratic process and underlying our definitive commitment to its success, the leadership of the IRA have decided that as of midnight, August 31, there will be a complete cessation of military operations. All our units have been instructed accordingly.

At this crossroads the leadership of the IRA salutes and commends our volunteers, other activists, our supporters and the political prisoners who have sustained the struggle against all odds for the past 25 years. Your courage, determination and sacrifice have demonstrated that the freedom and the desire for peace based on a just and lasting settlement cannot be crushed. We remember all those who have died for Irish freedom and we reiterate our commitment to our republican objectives. Our struggle has seen many gains and advances made by nationalists and for the democratic position.

We believe that an opportunity to secure a just and lasting settlement has been created. We are therefore entering into a new situation in a spirit of determination and confidence, determined that the injustices which created this conflict will be removed and confident in the strength and justice of our struggle to achieve this.

We note that the Downing Street Declaration is not a solution, nor was it presented as such by its authors. A solution will only be found as a result of inclusive negotiations. Others, not the least the British government[,] have a duty to face up to their responsibilities. It is our desire to significantly contribute to the creation of a climate which will encourage this. We urge everyone to approach this new situation with energy, determination and patience.

APPENDIX 8

Combined Loyalist Military Command Ceasefire Statement, 13 October 1994

After a widespread consultative process initiated by representations from the Ulster Democratic and Progressive Unionist Parties, and after having received confirmation and guarantees in relation to Northern Ireland's constitutional position within the United Kingdom, as well as other assurances, and, in the belief that the democratically expressed wishes of the greater number of people in Northern Ireland will be respected and upheld, the CLMC will universally cease all operational hostilities as from 12 midnight on Thursday 13th October 1994.

The permanence of our ceasefire will be completely dependant upon the continued cessation of all nationalist/republican violence, the sole responsibility for a return to War lies with them.

In the genuine hope that this peace will be permanent, we take the opportunity to pay homage to all our Fighters, Commandos and Volunteers who paid the supreme sacrifice. They did not die in vain. The Union is safe.

To our physically and mentally wounded who have served Ulster so unselfishly, we wish a speedy recovery, and to the relatives of these men and women, we pledge our continued moral and practical support.

To our prisoners who have undergone so much deprivation and degradation with great courage and forbearance, we solemnly promise to leave no stone unturned to secure their freedom.

To our serving officers, NCOs and personnel, we extend our eternal gratitude for their obedience of orders, for their ingenuity, resilience and good humour in the most trying of circumstances, and ... we commend them for their courageous fortitude and unshakeable faith over the long years of armed confrontation.

In all sincerity, we offer to the loved ones of all innocent victims over the past twenty years, abject and true remorse. No words of ours will compensate for the intolerable suffering they have undergone during the conflict.

Let us firmly resolve to respect our differing views of freedom, culture and aspiration and never again permit our political circumstances to degenerate into bloody warfare.

We are on the threshold of a new and exciting beginning with our battles in future being political battles, fought on the side of honest, decency and democracy against the negativity of mistrust, misunderstanding and malevolence, so that, together, we can bring forth a wholesome society in which our children, and their children, will know the meaning of true peace.

APPENDIX 9

The Framework Documents, 22 February 1995

A NEW FRAMEWORK FOR AGREEMENT

A shared understanding between
the British and Irish Governments
to assist discussion and negotiation involving
the Northern Ireland parties

1. The Joint Declaration acknowledges that the most urgent and important issue facing the people of Ireland, North and South, and the British and Irish Governments together, is to remove the causes of conflict, to overcome the legacy of history and to heal the divisions which have resulted.

2. Both Governments recognise that there is much for deep regret on all sides in the long and often tragic history of Anglo-Irish relations, and of relations in Ireland. They believe it is now time to lay aside, with dignity and forbearance, the mistakes of the past. A collective effort is needed to create, through agreement and reconciliation, a new beginning founded on consent, for relationships within Northern Ireland, within the island of Ireland and between the peoples of these islands. The Joint Declaration itself represents an important step towards this goal, offering the people of Ireland, North and South, whatever their tradition, the basis to agree that from now on their differences can be negotiated and resolved exclusively by peaceful political means.

3. The announcements made by the Irish Republican Army on 31 August 1994 and the Combined Loyalist Military Command on 13 October 1994 are a welcome response to the profound desire of people throughout these islands for a permanent end to the violence which caused such immense suffering and waste and served only to reinforce the barriers of fear and hatred, impeding the search for agreement.

4. A climate of peace enables the process of healing to begin. It transforms the prospects for political progress, building on that already made in the Talks process. Everyone now has a role to play in moving irreversibly beyond the failures of the past and creating new relationships capable of perpetuating peace with freedom and justice.

5. In the Joint Declaration both Governments set themselves the aim of fostering agreement and reconciliation, leading to a new political framework founded on

consent. A vital dimension of this three-stranded process is the search, through dialogue with the relevant Northern Ireland parties, for new institutions and structures to take account of the totality of relationships and to enable the people of Ireland to work together in all areas of common interest while fully respecting their diversity.

6. Both Governments are conscious of the widespread desire, throughout both islands and more widely, to see negotiations underway as soon as possible. They also acknowledge the many requests, from parties in Northern Ireland and elsewhere, for both Governments to set out their views on how agreement might be reached on relationships within the island of Ireland and between the peoples of these islands.

7. In this Framework Document both Governments therefore describe a shared understanding reached between them on the parameters of a possible outcome to the Talks process, consistent with the Joint Declaration and the statement of 26 March 1991. Through this they hope to give impetus and direction to the process and to show that a fair and honourable accommodation can be envisaged across all the relationships, which would enable people to work constructively for their mutual benefit, without compromising the essential principles or the long-term aspirations or interests of either tradition or of either community.

8. Both Governments are aware that the approach in this document presents challenges to strongly-held positions on all sides. However, a new beginning in relationships means addressing fundamental issues in a new way and inevitably requires significant movement from all sides. This document is not a rigid blueprint to be imposed but both Governments believe it sets out a realistic and balanced framework for agreement which could be achieved, with flexibility and goodwill on all sides, in comprehensive negotiations with the relevant political parties in Northern Ireland. In this spirit, both Governments offer this document for consideration and accordingly strongly commend it to the parties, the people in the island of Ireland and more widely.

9. The primary objective of both Governments in their approach to Northern Ireland is to promote and establish agreement among the people of the island of Ireland, building on the Joint Declaration. To this end they will both deploy their political resources with the aim of securing a new and comprehensive agreement involving the relevant political parties in Northern Ireland and commanding the widest possible support.

10. They take as guiding principles for their co-operation in search of this agreement:
    (i) the principle of self-determination, as set out in the Joint Declaration;
    (ii) that the consent of the governed is an essential ingredient for stability in any political arrangement;
    (iii) that agreement must be pursued and established by exclusively democratic, peaceful means, without resort to violence or coercion;
    (iv) that any new political arrangements must be based on full respect for, and protection and expression of, the rights and identities of both traditions in Ireland and even-handedly afford both communities in Northern Ireland parity of esteem and treatment, including equality of opportunity and advantage.

11. They acknowledge that in Northern Ireland, unlike the situation which prevails elsewhere throughout both islands, there is a fundamental absence of consensus about constitutional issues. There are deep divisions between the members of the two main traditions living there over their respective senses of identity and allegiance, their views on the present status of Northern Ireland and their vision of future relationships in Ireland and between the two islands. However, the two Governments

also recognise that the large majority of people, in both parts of Ireland, are at one in their commitment to the democratic process and in their desire to resolve political differences by peaceful means.

12. In their search for political agreement, based on consent, the two Governments are determined to address in a fresh way all of the relationships involved. Their aim is to overcome the legacy of division by reconciling the rights of both traditions in the fullest and most equitable manner. They will continue to work towards and encourage the achievement of agreement, so as to realise the goal set out in the statement of 26 March 1991 of 'a new beginning for relationships within Northern Ireland, within the island of Ireland and between the peoples of these islands'.

13. The two Governments will work together with the parties to achieve a comprehensive accommodation, the implementation of which would include interlocking and mutually supportive institutions across the three strands, including:

(a) Structures within Northern Ireland (paragraphs 22 and 23) – to enable elected representatives in Northern Ireland to exercise shared administrative and legislative control over all those matters that can be agreed across both communities and which can most effectively and appropriately be dealt with at that level;

(b) North/South institutions (paragraphs 24–38) – with clear identity and purpose, to enable representatives of democratic institutions, North and South, to enter into new, co-operative and constructive relationships; to promote agreement among the people of the island of Ireland; to carry out on a democratically accountable basis delegated executive, harmonising and consultative functions over a range of designated matters to be agreed; and to serve to acknowledge and reconcile the rights, identities and aspirations of the two major traditions;

(c) East–West structures (paragraphs 39–49) – to enhance the existing basis for co-operation between the two Governments, and to promote, support and underwrite the fair and effective operation of the new arrangements.

Constitutional Issues

14. Both Governments accept that agreement on an overall settlement requires, inter alia, a balanced accommodation of the differing views of the two main traditions on the constitutional issues in relation to the special position of Northern Ireland.

15. Given the absence of consensus and depth of divisions between the two main traditions in Northern Ireland, the two Governments agree that such an accommodation will involve an agreed new approach to the traditional constitutional doctrines on both sides. This would be aimed at enhancing and codifying the fullest attainable measure of consent across both traditions in Ireland and fostering the growth of consensus between them.

16. In their approach to Northern Ireland they will apply the principle of self-determination by the people of Ireland on the basis set out in the Joint Declaration: the British Government recognise that it is for the people of Ireland alone, by agreement between the two parts respectively and without external impediment, to exercise their right of self-determination on the basis of consent, freely and concurrently given, North and South, to bring about a united Ireland, if that is their wish; the Irish Government accept that the democratic right of self-determination by the people of Ireland as a whole must be achieved and exercised with and subject to the agreement and consent of a majority of the people of Northern Ireland.

17. New arrangements should be in accordance with the commitments in the Anglo-Irish Agreement and in the Joint Declaration. They should acknowledge that it

would be wrong to make any change in the status of Northern Ireland save with the consent of a majority of the people of Northern Ireland. If in future a majority of the people there wish for and formally consent to the establishment of a united Ireland, the two Governments will introduce and support legislation to give effect to that wish.

18. Both Governments recognise that Northern Ireland's current constitutional status reflects and relies upon the present wish of a majority of its people. They also acknowledge that at present a substantial minority of its people wish for a united Ireland. Reaffirming the commitment to encourage, facilitate and enable the achievement of agreement over a period among all the people who inhabit the island, they acknowledge that the option of a sovereign united Ireland does not command the consent of the unionist tradition, nor does the existing status of Northern Ireland command the consent of the nationalist tradition. Against this background, they acknowledge the need for new arrangements and structures – to reflect the reality of diverse aspirations, to reconcile as fully as possible the rights of both traditions, and to promote co-operation between them, so as to foster the process of developing agreement and consensus between all the people of Ireland.

19. They agree that future arrangements relating to Northern Ireland, and Northern Ireland's wider relationships, should respect the full and equal legitimacy and worth of the identity, sense of allegiance, aspiration and ethos of both the unionist and nationalist communities there. Consequently, both Governments commit themselves to the principle that institutions and arrangements in Northern Ireland and North/South institutions should afford both communities secure and satisfactory political, administrative and symbolic expression and protection. In particular, they commit themselves to entrenched provisions guaranteeing equitable and effective political participation for whichever community finds itself in a minority position by reference to the Northern Ireland framework, or the wider Irish framework, as the case may be, consequent upon the operation of the principle of consent.

20. The British Government reaffirm that they will uphold the democratic wish of a greater number of the people of Northern Ireland on the issue of whether they prefer to support the Union or a sovereign united Ireland. On this basis, they reiterate that they have no selfish strategic or economic interest in Northern Ireland. For as long as the democratic wish of the people of Northern Ireland is for no change in its present status, the British Government pledge that their jurisdiction there will be exercised with rigorous impartiality on behalf of all the people of Northern Ireland in their diversity. It will be founded on the principles outlined in the previous paragraph with emphasis on full respect for, and equality of, civil, political, social and cultural rights and freedom from discrimination for all citizens, on parity of esteem, and on just and equal treatment for the identity, ethos and aspirations of both communities. The British Government will discharge their responsibilities in a way which does not prejudice the freedom of the people of Northern Ireland to determine, by peaceful and democratic means, its future constitutional status, whether in remaining a part of the United Kingdom or in forming part of a united Ireland. They will be equally cognizant of either option and open to its democratic realisation, and will not impede the latter option, their primary interest being to see peace, stability and reconciliation established by agreement among the people who inhabit the island. This new approach for Northern Ireland, based on the continuing willingness to accept the will of a majority of the people there, will be enshrined in British constitutional legislation embodying the principles and commitments in the Joint Declaration and this Framework Document,

either by amendment of the Government of Ireland Act 1920 or by its replacement by appropriate new legislation, and appropriate new provisions entrenched by agreement.

21. As part of an agreement confirming the foregoing understanding between the two Governments on constitutional issues, the Irish Government will introduce and support proposals for change in the Irish Constitution to implement the commitments in the Joint Declaration. These changes in the Irish Constitution will fully reflect the principle of consent in Northern Ireland and demonstrably be such that no territorial claim of right to jurisdiction over Northern Ireland contrary to the will of a majority of its people is asserted, while maintaining the existing birthright of everyone born in either jurisdiction in Ireland to be part, as of right, of the Irish nation. They will enable a new Agreement to be ratified which will include, as part of a new and equitable dispensation for Northern Ireland embodying the principles and commitments in the Joint Declaration and this Framework Document, recognition by both Governments of the legitimacy of whatever choice is freely exercised by a majority of the people of Northern Ireland with regard to its constitutional status, whether they prefer to continue to support the Union or a sovereign united Ireland.

Structures in Northern Ireland

22. Both Governments recognise that new political structures within Northern Ireland must depend on the co-operation of elected representatives there. They confirm that cross-community agreement is an essential requirement for the establishment and operation of such structures. They strongly favour and will support provision for cross-community consensus in relation to decisions affecting the basic rights, concerns and fundamental interests of both communities, for example on the lines adumbrated in Strand 1 discussions in the 1992 round-table talks.

23. While the principles and overall context for such new structures are a recognised concern of both Governments in the exercise of their respective responsibilities, they consider that the structures themselves would be most effectively negotiated, as part of a comprehensive three-stranded process, in direct dialogue involving the relevant political parties in Northern Ireland who would be called upon to operate them.

North/South Institutions

24. Both Governments consider that new institutions should be created to cater adequately for present and future political, social and economic inter-connections on the island of Ireland, enabling representatives of the main traditions, North and South, to enter agreed dynamic, new, co-operative and constructive relationships.

25. Both Governments agree that these institutions should include a North/South body involving Heads of Department on both sides and duly established and maintained by legislation in both sovereign Parliaments. This body would bring together these Heads of Department representing the Irish Government and new democratic institutions in Northern Ireland, to discharge or oversee delegated executive, harmonising or consultative functions, as appropriate, over a range of matters which the two Governments designate in the first instance in agreement with the parties or which the two administrations, North and South, subsequently agree to designate. It is envisaged that, in determining functions to be discharged or overseen by the North/South body, whether by executive action, harmonisation or consultation, account will be taken of:

(i) the common interest in a given matter on the part of both parts of the island; or

(ii) the mutual advantage of addressing a matter together; or

(iii) the mutual benefit which may derive from it being administered by the North/South body; or

(iv) the achievement of economies of scale and the avoidance of unnecessary duplication of effort.

In relevant posts in each of the two administrations participation in the North/South body would be a duty of service. Both Governments believe that the legislation should provide for a clear institutional identity and purpose for the North/South body. It would also establish the body's terms of reference, legal status and arrangements for political, legal, administrative and financial accountability. The North/South body could operate through, or oversee, a range of functionally-related subsidiary bodies or other entities established to administer designated functions on an all-island or cross-border basis.

26. Specific arrangements would need to be developed to apply to EU matters. Any EU matter relevant to the competence of either administration could be raised for consideration in the North/South body. Across all designated matters and in accordance with the delegated functions, both Governments agree that the body will have an important role, with their support and co-operation and in consultation with them, in developing on a continuing basis an agreed approach for the whole island in respect of the challenges and opportunities of the European Union. In respect of matters designated at the executive level, which would include all EC programmes and initiatives to be implemented on a cross-border or island-wide basis in Ireland, the body itself would be responsible, subject to the Treaty obligations of each Government, for the implementation and management of EC policies and programmes on a joint basis. This would include the preparation, in consultation with the two Governments, of joint submissions under EC programmes and initiatives and their joint monitoring and implementation, although individual projects could be implemented either jointly or separately.

27. Both Governments envisage regular and frequent meetings of the North/South body:

- to discharge the functions agreed for it in relation to a range of matters designated for treatment on an all-Ireland or cross-border basis;
- to oversee the work of subsidiary bodies.

28. The two Governments envisage that legislation in the sovereign Parliaments should designate those functions which should, from the outset, be discharged or overseen by the North/South body; and they will seek agreement on these, as on other features of North/South arrangements, in discussion with the relevant political parties in Northern Ireland. It would also be open to the North/South body to recommend to the respective administrations and legislatures for their consideration that new functions should be designated to be discharged or overseen by that body; and to recommend that matters already designated should be moved on the scale between consultation, harmonisation and executive action. Within those responsibilities transferred to new institutions in Northern Ireland, the British Government have no limits of their own to impose on the nature and extent of functions which could be agreed for designation at the outset or, subsequently, between the Irish Government and the Northern Ireland administration. Both Governments expect that significant responsibilities, including meaningful functions at executive level, will be a feature of such agreement. The British Government believe that, in

principle, any function devolved to the institutions in Northern Ireland could be so designated, subject to any necessary savings in respect of the British Government's powers and duties, for example to ensure compliance with EU and international obligations. The Irish Government also expect to designate a comparable range of functions.

29. Although both Governments envisage that representatives of North and South in the body could raise for discussion any matter of interest to either side which falls within the competence of either administration, it is envisaged, as already mentioned, that its designated functions would fall into three broad categories:

consultative:

the North/South body would be a forum where the two sides would consult on any aspect of designated matters on which either side wished to hold consultations. Both sides would share a duty to exchange information and to consult about existing and future policy, though there would be no formal requirement that agreement would be reached or that policy would be harmonised or implemented jointly, but the development of mutual understanding or common or agreed positions would be the general goal;

harmonising:

in respect of these designated responsibilities there would be, in addition to the duty to exchange information and to consult on the formulation of policy, an obligation on both sides to use their best endeavours to reach agreement on a common policy and to make determined efforts to overcome any obstacles in the way of that objective, even though its implementation might be undertaken by the two administrations separately;

executive:

in the case of these designated responsibilities the North/South body would itself be directly responsible for the establishment of an agreed policy and for its implementation on a joint basis. It would however be open to the body, where appropriate, to agree that the implementation of the agreed policy would be undertaken either by existing bodies, acting in an agency capacity, whether jointly or separately, North and South, or by new bodies specifically created and mandated for this purpose.

30. In this light, both Governments are continuing to give consideration to the range of functions that might, with the agreement of the parties, be designated at the outset and accordingly they will be ready to make proposals in that regard in future discussions with the relevant Northern Ireland parties.

31. By way of illustration, it is intended that these proposals would include at the executive level a range of functions, clearly defined in scope, from within the following broad categories:

- sectors involving a natural or physical all-Ireland framework;
- EC programmes and initiatives;
- marketing and promotion activities abroad;
- culture and heritage.

32. Again, by way of illustration, the Governments would make proposals at the harmonising level for a broader range of functions, clearly defined in scope (including, as appropriate, relevant EU aspects), from within the following categories:

aspects of:
- agriculture and fisheries;

- industrial development;
- consumer affairs;
- transport;
- energy;
- trade;
- health;
- social welfare;
- education; and
- economic policy.

33. By way of example, the category of agriculture and fisheries might include agricultural and fisheries research, training and advisory services, and animal welfare; health might include co-operative ventures in medical, paramedical and nursing training, cross-border provision of hospital services and major emergency/accident planning; and education might include mutual recognition of teacher qualifications, co-operative ventures in higher education, in teacher training, in education for mutual understanding and in education for specialised needs.

34. The Governments also expect that a wide range of functions would be designated at the consultative level.

35. Both Governments envisage that all decisions within the body would be by agreement between the two sides. The Heads of Department on each side would operate within the overall terms of reference mandated by legislation in the two sovereign Parliaments. They would exercise their powers in accordance with the rules for democratic authority and accountability for this function in force in the Oireachtas and in new institutions in Northern Ireland. The operation of the North/South body's functions would be subject to regular scrutiny in agreed political institutions in Northern Ireland and the Oireachtas respectively.

36. Both Governments expect that there would be a Parliamentary Forum, with representatives from agreed political institutions in Northern Ireland and members of the Oireachtas, to consider a wide range of matters of mutual interest.

37. Both Governments envisage that the framework would include administrative support staffed jointly by members of the Northern Ireland Civil Service and the Irish Civil Service. They also envisage that both administrations will need to arrange finance for the North/South body and its agencies on the basis that these constitute a necessary public function.

38. Both Governments envisage that this new framework should serve to help heal the divisions among the communities on the island of Ireland; provide a forum for acknowledging the respective identities and requirements of the two major traditions; express and enlarge the mutual acceptance of the validity of those traditions; and promote understanding and agreement among the people and institutions in both parts of the island. The remit of the body should be dynamic, enabling progressive extension by agreement of its functions to new areas. Its role should develop to keep pace with the growth of harmonisation and with greater integration between the two economies.

East–West Structures

39. Both Governments envisage a new and more broadly based Agreement, developing and extending their co-operation, reflecting the totality of relationships between the two islands, and dedicated to fostering co-operation, reconciliation and agreement in Ireland at all levels.

40. They intend that under such a new Agreement a standing Intergovernmental Conference will be maintained, chaired by the designated Irish Minister and by the Secretary of State for Northern Ireland. It would be supported by a Permanent Secretariat of civil servants from both Governments.

41. The Conference will be a forum through which the two Governments will work together in pursuance of their joint objectives of securing agreement and reconciliation amongst the people of the island of Ireland and of laying the foundations for a peaceful and harmonious future based on mutual trust and understanding between them.

42. The Conference will provide a continuing institutional expression for the Irish Government's recognised concern and role in relation to Northern Ireland. The Irish Government will put forward views and proposals on issues falling within the ambit of the new Conference or involving both Governments, and determined efforts will be made to resolve any differences between the two Governments. The Conference will be the principal instrument for an intensification of the co-operation and partnership between both Governments, with particular reference to the principles contained in the Joint Declaration, in this Framework Document and in the new Agreement, on a wide range of issues concerned with Northern Ireland and with the relations between the two parts of the island of Ireland. It will facilitate the promotion of lasting peace, stability, justice and reconciliation among the people of the island of Ireland and maintenance of effective security co-operation between the two Governments.

43. Both Governments believe that there should also be provision in the Agreement for developing co-operation between the two Governments and both islands on a range of 'East–West' issues and bilateral matters of mutual interest not covered by other specific arrangements, either through the Anglo-Irish Intergovernmental Council, the Conference or otherwise.

44. Both Governments accept that issues of law and order in Northern Ireland are closely intertwined with the issues of political consensus. For so long as these matters are not devolved, it will be for the Governments to consider ways in which a climate of peace, new institutions and the growth of political agreement may offer new possibilities and opportunities for enhancing community identification with policing in Northern Ireland, while maintaining the most effective possible deployment of the resources of each Government in their common determination to combat crime and prevent any possible recourse to the use or threat of violence for political ends, from any source whatsoever.

45. The Governments envisage that matters for which responsibility is transferred to new political institutions in Northern Ireland will be excluded from consideration in the Conference, except to the extent that the continuing responsibilities of the Secretary of State for Northern Ireland are relevant, or that cross-border aspects of transferred issues are not otherwise provided for, or in the circumstances described in the following paragraph.

46. The Intergovernmental Conference will be a forum for the two Governments jointly to keep under review the workings of the Agreement and to promote, support and underwrite the fair and effective operation of all its provisions and the new arrangements established under it. Where either Government considers that any institution, established as part of the overall accommodation, is not properly functioning within the Agreement or that a breach of the Agreement has otherwise occurred, the Conference shall consider the matter on the basis of a shared commitment to arrive

at a common position or, where that is not possible, to agree a procedure to resolve the difference between them. If the two Governments conclude that a breach has occurred in any of the above circumstances, either Government may make proposals for remedy and adequate measures to redress the situation shall be taken. However, each Government will be responsible for the implementation of such measures of redress within its own jurisdiction. There would be no derogation from the sovereignty of either Government; each will retain responsibility for the decisions and administration of government within its own jurisdiction.

47. In the event that devolved institutions in Northern Ireland ceased to operate, and direct rule from Westminster was reintroduced, the British Government agree that other arrangements would be made to implement the commitment to promote co-operation at all levels between the people, North and South, representing both traditions in Ireland, as agreed by the two Governments in the Joint Declaration, and to ensure that the co-operation that had been developed through the North/South body be maintained.

48. Both Governments envisage that representatives of agreed political institutions in Northern Ireland may be formally associated with the work of the Conference, in a manner and to an extent to be agreed by both Governments after consultation with them. This might involve giving them advance notice of what is to be discussed in the Conference, enabling them to express views to either Government and inviting them to participate in various aspects of the work of the Conference. Other more structured arrangements could be devised by agreement.

49. The Conference will also be a framework for consultation and coordination between both Governments and the new North/South institutions, where the wider role of the two Governments is particularly relevant to the work of those institutions, for example in a coordinated approach on EU issues. It would be for consideration by both Governments, in consultation with the relevant parties in the North, or with the institutions after they have been established, whether to achieve this through formal or ad hoc arrangements.

Protection of Rights

50. There is a large body of support, transcending the political divide, for the comprehensive protection and guarantee of fundamental human rights. Acknowledging this, both Governments envisage that the arrangements set out in this Framework Document will be complemented and underpinned by an explicit undertaking in the Agreement on the part of each Government, equally, to ensure in its jurisdiction in the island of Ireland, in accordance with its constitutional arrangements, the systematic and effective protection of common specified civil, political, social and cultural rights. They will discuss and seek agreement with the relevant political parties in Northern Ireland as to what rights should be so specified and how they might best be further protected, having regard to each Government's overall responsibilities including its international obligations. Each Government will introduce appropriate legislation in its jurisdiction to give effect to any such measure of agreement.

51. In addition, both Governments would encourage democratic representatives from both jurisdictions in Ireland to adopt a Charter or Covenant, which might reflect and endorse agreed measures for the protection of the fundamental rights of everyone living in Ireland. It could also pledge a commitment to mutual respect and to the civil rights and religious liberties of both communities, including:

- the right of free political thought,
- the right to freedom and expression of religion,
- the right to pursue democratically national and political aspirations,
- the right to seek constitutional change by peaceful and legitimate means,
- the right to live wherever one chooses without hindrance,
- the right to equal opportunity in all social and economic activity, regardless of class, creed, gender or colour.

52. This Charter or Covenant might also contain a commitment to the principle of consent in the relationships between the two traditions in Ireland. It could incorporate also an enduring commitment on behalf of all the people of the island to guarantee and protect the rights, interests, ethos and dignity of the unionist community in any all-Ireland framework that might be developed with consent in the future, to at least the same extent as provided for the nationalist community in the context of Northern Ireland under the structures and provisions of the new Agreement.

53. The Covenant might also affirm on behalf of all traditions in Ireland a solemn commitment to the exclusively peaceful resolution of all differences between them including in relation to all issues of self-determination, and a solemn repudiation of all recourse to violence between them for any political end or purpose.

Conclusion

54. Both Governments agree that the issues set out in this Framework Document should be examined in the most comprehensive attainable negotiations with democratically mandated political parties in Northern Ireland which abide exclusively by peaceful means and wish to join in dialogue on the way ahead.

55. Both Governments intend that the outcome of these negotiations will be submitted for democratic ratification through referendums, North and South.

56. Both Governments believe that the present climate of peace, which owes much to the imagination, courage and steadfastness of all those who have suffered from violence, offers the best prospect for the Governments and the parties in Northern Ireland to work to secure agreement and consent to a new political accommodation. To accomplish that would be an inestimable prize for all, and especially for people living in Northern Ireland, who have so much to gain from such an accommodation, in which the divisions of the past are laid aside for ever and differences are resolved by exclusively political means. Both Governments believe that a new political dispensation, such as they set out in this Framework Document, achieved through agreement and reconciliation and founded on the principle of consent, would achieve that objective and transform relationships in Northern Ireland, in the island of Ireland and between both islands.

57. With agreement, co-operation to the mutual benefit of all living in Ireland could develop without impediment, attaining its full potential for stimulating economic growth and prosperity. New arrangements could return power, authority and responsibility to locally elected representatives in Northern Ireland on a basis acceptable to both sides of the community, enabling them to work together for the common welfare and interests of all the community. The diversity of identities and allegiances could be regarded by all as a source of mutual enrichment, rather than a threat to either side. The divisive issue of sovereignty might cease to be symbolic of the domination of one community over another. It would instead be for decision

under agreed ground-rules, fair and balanced towards both aspirations, through a process of democratic persuasion governed by the principle of consent rather than by threat, fear or coercion. In such circumstances the Governments hope that the relationship between the traditions in Northern Ireland could become a positive bond of further understanding, co-operation and amity, rather than a source of contention, between the wider British and Irish democracies.

58. Accordingly the British and Irish Governments offer for consideration and strongly commend these proposals, trusting that, with generosity and goodwill, the peoples of these islands will build on them a new and lasting agreement.

Extract from the Mitchell Principles, January 1996

Extract from the Report of the Independent International Commission
on Decommissioning:
Principles of Democracy and Non-Violence, January 1996

20. Accordingly, we recommend that the parties to such negotiations affirm their total and absolute commitment:

   a To democratic and exclusively peaceful means of resolving political issues;
   b To the total disarmament of all paramilitary organizations;
   c To agree that such disarmament must be verifiable to the satisfaction of an independent commission;
   d To renounce for themselves, and to oppose any effort by others, to use force, or threaten to use force, to influence the course or the outcome of all-party negotiations;
   e To agree to abide by the terms of any agreement reached in all-party negotiations and to resort to democratic and exclusively peaceful methods in trying to alter any aspect of that outcome with which they may disagree; and
   f To urge that 'punishment' killings and beatings stop and to take effective steps to prevent such actions.

21. We join the Governments, religious leaders and many others in condemning 'punishment' killings and beatings. They contribute to the fear that those who have used violence to pursue political objectives in the past will do so again in the future. Such actions have no place in a lawful society.

APPENDIX 11

IRA Ceasefire Statement, 19 July 1997

On August 31, 1994 the leadership of Oglaigh na hEireann (IRA) announced their complete cessation of military operations as our contribution to the search for lasting peace.

After 17 months of cessation in which the British government and the unionists blocked any possibility of real or inclusive negotiations, we reluctantly abandoned the cessation.

The IRA is committed to ending British rule in Ireland. It is the root cause of divisions and conflict in our country. We want a permanent peace and therefore we are prepared to enhance the search for a democratic peace settlement through real and inclusive negotiations.

So having assessed the current political situation, the leadership of Oglaigh na hEireann are announcing a complete cessation of military operations from 12 midday on Sunday 20 July, 1997.

We have ordered the unequivocal restoration of the ceasefire of August 1994. All IRA units have been instructed accordingly.

APPENDIX 12

'Propositions on Heads of Agreement', issued by the British and Irish governments, 12 January 1998

Balanced constitutional change, based on commitment to the principle of consent in all its aspects by both British and Irish governments, to include both changes to the Irish Constitution and to British constitutional legislation.

Democratically elected institutions in Northern Ireland, to include a Northern Ireland assembly, elected by a system of proportional representation, exercising devolved executive and legislative responsibility over at least the responsibilities of the six Northern Ireland departments and with provisions to ensure that all sections of the community can participate and work together successfully in the operation of these institutions and that all sections of the community are protected.

A new British–Irish agreement to replace the existing Anglo-Irish Agreement and help establish close co-operation and enhance relationships, embracing:

- An intergovernmental council to deal with the totality of relationships, to include representatives of the British and Irish governments, the Northern Ireland administration and the devolved institutions in Scotland and Wales, with meetings twice a year at summit level.
- A North–South ministerial council to bring together those with executive responsibilities in Northern Ireland and the Irish Government in particular areas. Each side will consult, co-operate and take decisions on matters of mutual interest within the mandate of, and accountable to, the Northern Ireland assembly and the Oireachtas respectively. All decisions will be by agreement between the two sides, North and South.
- Suitable implementation bodies and mechanisms for policies agreed by the North–South council in meaningful areas and at an all-island level.
- Standing intergovernmental machinery between the Irish and British governments, covering issues of mutual interest, including non-devolved issues for Northern Ireland, when representatives of the Northern Ireland administration would be involved.

Provision to safeguard the rights of both communities in Northern Ireland, through arrangements for the comprehensive protection of fundamental human, civil, political, social, economic and cultural rights, including a Bill of Rights for Northern Ireland supplementing the provisions of the European Convention and to achieve full respect for the principles of equity of treatment and freedom from discrimination, and the cultural identity and ethos of both communities. Appropriate steps to ensure an equivalent level of protection in the Republic.

Effective and practical measures to establish and consolidate an acceptable peaceful society, dealing with issues such as prisoners, security in all its aspects, policing and decommissioning of weapons.

APPENDIX 13

The Hillsborough Statement, 1 April 1999

TEXT OF THE DECLARATION
ISSUED BY BRITISH AND IRISH GOVERNMENTS,
1 April 1999
(The Hillsborough Statement)

The following is the text of the declaration issued by the Taoiseach, Mr Ahern, and the British Prime Minister, Mr Blair, at Hillsborough Castle yesterday.

Working draft, 1 April Declaration

It is now one year since the Good Friday Agreement was concluded. Last May it was emphatically endorsed by the people, North and South, and as such it now represents their democratic will.

The Agreement, in its own words, offers a truly historic opportunity for a new beginning. It gives us a chance, in this generation, to transcend the bitter legacy of the past and to transform relationships within Northern Ireland, between North and South, and between these islands.

All parties firmly believe that the violence we have all lived through must be put behind us. Never again should we or our children have to suffer the consequences of conflict. It must be brought to a permanent end. In partnership together we want to ensure a future free from conflict.

The realisation of that future places a heavy obligation on us all, individually and collectively. The implementation in full of the Agreement is inevitably a lengthy and complex process, involving continuing effort and commitment on all our parts.

It is encouraging and important that, even though much remains to be done, very substantial progress has already been made in turning the promise of the Agreement into a reality. We must not forget or underplay how far we have come.

Balanced changes to both the Irish Constitution and to British constitutional legislation based on the principle of consent have been approved and are now ready to take effect.

The Northern Ireland Assembly was elected last June and has since been preparing for devolution. The international agreement signed in Dublin on 8 March provides for the establishment of the North–South ministerial council and implementation bodies, the British–Irish Council and the British–Irish Intergovernmental Conference.

The Northern Ireland Human Rights Commission has been established and its members appointed, and the new Equality Commission has been legislated for. Comparable steps by the Irish Government are well under way.

The needs of victims of violence, and their families, including those of the disappeared, are being addressed in both jurisdictions, though we acknowledge that for many their pain and suffering will never end.

The commitments in the Agreement in relation to economic, social and cultural issues, including as regards the Irish language, are being carried forward, though much of this work is inevitably long term.

Steps have been taken towards normalisation of security arrangements and practices, while the Commission on Policing for Northern Ireland and the review of criminal justice are both well advanced in their vital work.

Numerous prisoners, in both jurisdictions, have benefited from mechanisms providing for their accelerated release.

Against this background there is agreement among all parties that decommissioning is not a precondition but is an obligation deriving from their commitment in the Agreement, and that it should take place within the time-scale envisaged in the Agreement, and through the efforts of the Independent International Commission on Decommissioning.

Sinn Féin have acknowledged these obligations but are unable to indicate the time-scale on which decommissioning will begin. They do not regard the Agreement as imposing any requirement to make a start before the establishment of the new institutions.

The UUP do not wish to move to the establishment of the new institutions without some evident progress with decommissioning.

It would be a tragedy if this difference of view about timing and the sequence of events prevented the implementation of the Agreement from advancing.

We believe that decommissioning will only happen against a background where implementation is actively moving forward. Continued progress in establishing the new institutions will in itself create confidence. On the other hand, it is understandable that those who take the next steps in implementation should seek to be assured that these steps are not irrevocable if, in the event, no progress is made with decommissioning.

We therefore propose the following way forward.

On [date to be set] nominations will be made under the d'Hondt procedure of those to take up office as ministers when powers are devolved.

At a date to be proposed by the Independent International Commission on Decommissioning but not later than [one month after nomination date] a collective act of reconciliation will take place. This will see some arms put beyond use on a voluntary basis, in a manner which will be verified by the Independent International Commission on Decommissioning, and further moves on normalisation and demilitarisation in recognition of the changed situation on security.

In addition to the arrangements in respect of military material, there will at all times be ceremonies of remembrance of all victims of violence, to which representatives of all parties and the two governments, and all churches, will be invited.

Around the time of the act of reconciliation, powers will be devolved and the British–Irish Agreement will enter into force.

The following institutions will then be established: the North–South Ministerial

Council, the North–South Implementation Bodies, the British–Irish Council and the British–Irish Intergovernmental Conference.

By one month after nomination date, the Independent International Commission on Decommissioning will make a report on progress. It is understood by all that the successful implementation of the Agreement will be achieved if these steps are taken within the proposed time-scales; if they are not taken, the nominations mentioned above will fall to be confirmed by the Assembly.

APPENDIX 14

'The Way Forward': Joint Statement by the British and Irish governments at Stormont, 2 July 1999

After five days of discussion, the British and Irish Governments have put to all the parties a way forward to establish an inclusive Executive, and to decommission arms.

These discussions have been difficult. But as they conclude, the peace process is very much alive, and on track.

The Good Friday Agreement presents the best chance of peace and prosperity in decades.

It is clear from our discussions that nobody wants to throw that opportunity away.

We believe that unionist and nationalist opinion will see that our approach meets their concerns, and will support it accordingly.

The way forward is as follows:

1. All parties reaffirm the three principles agreed on 25 June

    - an inclusive Executive exercising devolved powers;
    - decommissioning of *all* paramilitary arms by May 2000;
    - decommissioning to be carried out in a manner determined by the International Commission on Decommissioning.

2. The D'Hondt procedure to nominate Ministers to be run on 15 July.
3. The Devolution Order to be laid before the British Parliament on 16 July to take effect on 18 July. Within the period specified by the de Chastelain Commission, the Commission will confirm the start to the process of decommissioning, that start to be defined as in their report of 2 July.
4. As described in their report today, the commission will have urgent discussions with the groups' points of contact. The commission will specify that actual decommissioning is to start within a specified time. They will report progress in September and December 1999, and in May 2000.
5. A 'failsafe' clause: the governments undertake that, in accordance with the review provisions of the agreement, if commitments under the agreement are not met, either in relation to decommissioning or to devolution, they will automatically, and with immediate effect, suspend the operation of the institutions set up by the agreement.

In relation to decommissioning, this action will be taken on receipt of a report at any time that the commitments now being entered into, or steps which are subsequently laid down by the commission are not fulfilled, in accordance with the Good Friday Agreement. The British government will legislate to this effect.

All parties have fought very hard to ensure their basic concerns have been met. This means that we are now closer than ever to a fulfilling the promise of the Good Friday agreement:

- a government for Northern Ireland in which the two traditions work together in a devolved administration;
- new North–South and British–Irish institutions;
- the decommissioning of paramilitary arms;
- constitutional change;
- equality, justice, human rights and the normalisation of Northern Ireland society.

All sides have legislative safeguards to ensure that commitments entered into are met. This is an historic opportunity. Now is the time to seize it.

APPENDIX 15

Statement issued by the IRA, 21 July 1999

The argument that the present political process can deliver real and meaningful change has been significantly undermined by the course of events over the past 15 months.

This culminated in the failure last week to establish the political institutions set out in the Good Friday agreement.

The agreement has failed to deliver tangible progress and its potential for doing so has substantially diminished in recent months.

The credibility and motivation of unionist leaders who signed up to the agreement is clearly open to question. They have repeatedly reneged on the commitments they made in signing the agreement and successfully blocked the implementation of its institutional aspects.

It is clearly their intention to continue their obstructionist tactics indefinitely. There is irrefutable evidence that the unionist political leadership remains, at this time, opposed to a democratic peace settlement.

Recent events at Stormont cannot obscure the fact that the primary responsibility for the developing political crisis rests squarely with the British government. They have once again demonstrated a lack of political will to confront the unionist veto.

Over the past five years we have called and maintained two prolonged cessations of military operations to enhance the peace process and underline our definitive commitment to its success. We have contributed in a meaningful way to the creation of a climate which would facilitate the search for a durable settlement.

The first of these cessations floundered on the demand by the Conservative government for an IRA surrender. Those who demand the decommissioning of IRA weapons lend themselves, in the current political context, inadvertently or otherwise, to the failed agenda which seeks the defeat of the IRA. The British government have the power to change that context and should do so.

It remains our view that the roots of conflict in our country lie in British involvement in Irish affairs. Responsibility for repairing the damage to the argument that the present political process can deliver real change rests primarily with the British government.

APPENDIX 16

Statement by Senator George Mitchell in Belfast concluding the Review of the Northern Ireland Peace Process, 18 November 1999

I indicated in my last statement on 15 November that I expected to be in a position to issue a concluding report on the review soon after the publication of the assessment of the Independent International Commission on Decommissioning (IICD) and of the parties' positions on the issues which we have been considering together in the review.

Those steps have now been taken. Together they represent a set of extremely positive developments.

I welcome the statements from the parties, which should further build mutual confidence in each other's commitment to the full implementation of the Good Friday Agreement and to the three principles as agreed on 25 June, namely:

- An inclusive executive exercising devolved powers.
- Decommissioning of all paramilitary arms by May 2000.
- Decommissioning to be carried out in a manner determined by the IICD.

I also welcome the IICD assessment of how it can best achieve the mandate under the agreement. I share its conclusion that:

Decommissioning is by definition a voluntary act and cannot be imposed. To bring decommissioning about, the Commission will need the co-operation and support of the political parties, using all the influence they have, together with the wholehearted commitment of paramilitary organisations.

While decommissioning is an essential element of the agreement, the context in which it can be achieved is the overall implementation of that agreement. All participants have a collective responsibility in this regard.

In response to the IICD assessment, the parties have made clear that the IICD is the agreed mechanism for achieving decommissioning, under the terms of the Good Friday Agreement.

In the light of these and other encouraging developments, including the proposed appointment of authorised representatives of paramilitary organisations to the IICD, I believe that a basis now exists for devolution to occur, for the institutions to be established, and for decommissioning to take place as soon as possible.

Devolution should take effect, then the executive should meet, and then the paramilitary groups should appoint their authorised representatives, all on the same day, in that order.

I hereby recommend to the governments and the parties that they make the necessary arrangements to proceed, and call on them to do so without delay. That completes the review, and with it my role in this process. I conclude with some personal comments.

Not long ago, the Ulster Unionists and Sinn Féin did not speak directly. In the early weeks of the review, their exchanges were harsh and filled with recrimination. But gradually, as one of them put it, 'trust crept in'.

It may not be trust yet, but it is an important start, and the discussions did become serious and meaningful.

For that credit goes to the leaders, David Trimble and Sir Reg Empey; and Gerry Adams and Martin McGuinness. They, and the other leaders of their parties, set aside their hostility for the good of their society.

The Social Democratic and Labour Party, led by John Hume and Seamus Mallon, provided crucial insight and involvement. It will play an important role in the executive.

The leaders of the other pro-agreement parties were strongly supportive: Sean Neeson and Seamus Close of Alliance, David Ervine and Billy Hutchinson of the Progressive Unionist Party, Monica McWilliams and Jane Morrice of the Northern Ireland Women's Coalition, and Gary McMichael and David Adams of the Ulster Democratic Party; and all of their colleagues.

They and their parties were essential to the Good Friday Agreement. They are indispensable to its full implementation. It cannot and will not be done without them.

The prime ministers of the United Kingdom and Ireland, Tony Blair and Bertie Ahern, and President Clinton, played important roles in this effort, as did Mo Mowlam, David Andrews and Liz O'Donnell.

The new Secretary of State, Peter Mandelson, is a strong and effective leader who, in a short time, has had an enormous positive impact.

I also would like to recognise two superb officials, Bill Jeffrey for the British, and Dermot Gallagher for the Irish. With their colleagues, they provided me with invaluable assistance, for which they have my gratitude.

As a result of all of these efforts, neither side will get all it wanted and both will endure severe political pain.

But there is no other way forward. Prolonging the stalemate will leave this society uncertain and vulnerable.

If this process succeeds, the real winners will be the people, who want their political leaders to work out their differences through democratic dialogue.

I have been involved in this effort for nearly five years. I cannot say that I've enjoyed every minute of it.

But while on occasion it has been difficult, it has also been one of the most meaningful times of my life.

I am totally committed to the cause of peace and reconciliation in Northern Ireland.

Admiration

And I can say that the longer I've been here the more I have come to admire and like and believe in the people.

They are energetic and productive, warm and generous. I have been treated here as though I were at home.

In a sense I am at home, because my emotions and a part of my heart will be here forever, even though I will not always be physically present.

My thanks to you ladies and gentlemen of the press for your courtesy, to the prime minister and taoiseach for inviting me to take part in this process, to the party leaders with whom I have spent these past few months and who I respect for their courage, and, finally, to the people for their warmth and hospitality.

I hope to return often, in other capacities. My fervent prayer is that it will be to a society in which hope and opportunity are alive and where a durable peace, tolerance and mutual respect are not distant dreams, but rather are the reality of daily life for all of the people.

Irish Republican Army (IRA) Statement on Arms Inspections, 26 June 2000

The following statement was received from Oglaigh na hÉireann, the IRA, by An Phoblacht on 25 October 2000.

The leadership of Óglaigh na hÉireann is committed to a just and lasting peace.

In recent years we have engaged in an unprecedented series of substantial and historic initiatives to enhance the peace process.

The record shows that we have honoured every commitment we have made.

In this context, and despite the abuse of the peace process by those who persist with the aim of defeating the IRA and Irish republicanism, and the obvious failure of the British government to honour its obligations under the terms of the Good Friday agreement and the commitments made at Hillsborough, the leadership of the IRA has decided:

To honour all the commitments entered into by us and to underpin the peace process. All undertakings by us were premised clearly on the speedy and full implementation of the commitments made by the two governments on 5 May and the commitments made under the Good Friday agreement.

The British government has thus far not honoured its undertakings. Despite this the IRA leadership has decided that the reinspection of a number of arms dumps will be repeated to confirm that our weapons remain secure.

In many ways this reinspection is more important than the first inspection.

We have also decided to resume discussions with the IICD when we are satisfied that the peace process will be advanced by those discussions. On 25 June we re-established contact with the commission. Because the British government has yet to honour its undertakings, we have not resumed discussions with the IICD. Neither have we broken off contact.

These actions announced by us today represent clear and irrefutable evidence of the IRA's commitment to a just and equitable peace settlement.

The significance of these decisions should not be underestimated or undervalued, not least because of developments since another initiative by us resulted in the political institutions being established on 2 December after 18 months of impasse.

Less than three months later the British government suspended these institutions.

This was despite the IICD February report which welcomed our belief that the 'state of perpetual crisis' can be averted and that the issue of arms can be resolved.

The IICD recognised that the IRA provides no threat to the peace process. It also accepted the importance of the IRA's contribution and support for the process as issues of considerable significance for peace.

The IICD reported that all of this held out the real prospect of an agreement which would enable it to fulfil the substance of its mandate.

Despite the bad faith involved in the British government's suspension of the institutions, within weeks the Sinn Féin leadership put to us and to the two governments ideas that had the potential to overcome this crisis.

Following this on 5 May the British and Irish governments issued a joint letter and a joint statement setting out commitments by the two governments to the full implementation of the Good Friday agreement by June 2000.

The British government publicly and privately committed itself to deal with a range of matters including human rights, equality, justice, demilitarisation and policing.

Our commitment to a just and permanent peace was underlined once again when we announced our initiative of 6 May.

We said that we will initiate a process that will completely and verifiably put IRA arms beyond use. We explained the context for this:

'The full implementation, on a progressive and irreversible basis, by the two governments, especially the British government, of what they have agreed will provide a political context, in an enduring political process, with the potential to remove the causes of conflict and in which Irish republicans and unionists can, as equals, pursue our respective political objectives peacefully.'

And importantly we announced that we were prepared to put in place a confidence-building measure to confirm that our weapons remained secure. This was widely welcomed and recognised as a huge and historically unprecedented departure by us.

Finally we committed ourselves to resume contact with the IICD and to further discussions with the commission on the basis of the IRA leadership's commitment to resolving the issue of arms.

On Monday 26 June in a public statement we confirmed that the commitments made by us on 6 May had been fulfilled. At that point the British government had not delivered on its commitments.

Now months later the British government has yet to honour its commitments. The IRA are doing our best to enhance the peace process. This is not our responsibility alone. Others also must play their part.

The political responsibility for advancing the current situation and making progress rests with the two governments, especially the British government.

APPENDIX 18

Joint Statement by the British and Irish governments, 25 June 2004

Our discussions today with the Northern Ireland parties were guided by two fundamental objectives: the need to see an end now to all forms of paramilitary activity; and the imperative of restoring as soon as possible a stable and inclusive partnership government in Northern Ireland.

We recognise the constructive spirit in which the parties have approached these discussions and the ongoing Review of the operation of the Agreement. Nevertheless, we believe that the effort to achieve our two objectives needs to be stepped up if those discussions are to be brought to a successful conclusion and the current stalemate ended.

With that in mind, intensive political dialogue, led by the two Governments, will resume at the beginning of September to finalise agreement on all outstanding matters with a view to restoring the full and inclusive operation of the political institutions as soon as possible. Agreement is required on:

- a definitive and conclusive end to all paramilitary activity;
- the decommissioning, through the IICD, of all paramilitary weapons, to an early timescale and on a convincing basis;
- a clear commitment on all sides to the stability of the political institutions and to any changes to their operation agreed within the Review; and
- support for policing from all sides of the community, and on an agreed framework for the devolution of policing.

We recognise that reaching agreement will not be easy. But we cannot allow matters to drift on. Further delay is not in the interest of the people of Northern Ireland. We are determined that agreement should be reached on these key issues at the latest by the autumn. The Review will resume in September to complete its work. We urged the parties today to maintain their engagement over the summer with a view to advancing progress on these issues and to prepare their respective communities for the substantial steps that will be required in order to reach overall agreement.

Meanwhile, the two Governments remain committed to the continuing implementation of their commitments under the Joint Declaration, including in particular measures to end sectarianism, safeguard rights and to promote equality and reconciliation. The next meeting of the British–Irish Intergovernmental Conference on 7 July will review progress in this area, as well as wider issues.

We believe that the parties understand and accept the responsibility that their electoral mandates have placed on them to resolve the current impasse. This responsibility requires all parties to demonstrate a commitment to reaching the fundamental accommodation we all wish to see. It is critical that Northern Ireland enjoys a summer free from violence and tension on the streets. We hope that all parties will work to ensure that events over the coming months create the right atmosphere for successful talks in the autumn.

Gerry Adams: Review of the Good Friday Agreement, 3 February 2004

The review as set out in the Good Friday Agreement is about improving the delivery of the Agreement. It was never envisaged that it would take place during a suspension of institutions – indeed the British government had no right to suspend the institutions, and had to step outside the Agreement to unilaterally take that power on themselves and I do not accept for one second the British Secretary of State's defence of this action.

The reality at this time is that instead of stable political institutions with the people's elected representatives making decisions on important issues, which affect all our lives, across a range of social and economic issues; instead of a fully operational Assembly and all-Ireland institutions leading the delivery of change, advancing the equality agenda and championing human rights based society; we have continuing impasse.

It is almost three months since elections to the Assembly.

Those results show that the Good Friday Agreement continues to enjoy the substantial support of the majority of the people. Those who voted did so in the expectation that those they elected would be part of working institutions.

We are entitled therefore to ask the British Government to explain at this point the inconsistency between their assertion that the Agreement cannot be renegotiated and their failure to restore the political institutions which are the democratic core of the Agreement.

We are entitled also to ask the Democratic Unionist Party to explain how they intend to contribute to discussion on how best to implement the Agreement when they have declared their intention to subvert it.

The answers to such questions will at least allow the emergence of some clarity with respect to both the nature of and the likely outcome of the review. The review was never meant to deal with a process which is on hold so it is vital from the outset that we do not lend to any ambiguity about the purpose or expected outcome.

The review is not a renegotiation of the Good Friday Agreement. It is an opportunity to accelerate the process of change promised in the Agreement. It is an opportunity to re-endorse the Agreement. And yet we have parties to this review who are either in breach of the Agreement, ambiguous about the Agreement or determined to destroy it. But you are we welcome. Your presence here is implicit recognition of how, despite our differences, we can discuss these issues.

Sinn Féin is bringing a positive attitude to the review and we will proactively listen to the views of the other parties. We submitted a comprehensive agenda for discussion to the governments and have prepared detailed positions across these; including, the political institutions, the suspension powers, participation in NSMC [North–South Ministerial Council] and expansion of the Implementation Bodies, an All-Ireland Inter-Parliamentary Forum and All-Ireland Consultative Forum, the transfer of powers on policing and justice and many other matters.

The Review must address in particular the lack of progress on the equality and human rights front, identify the causes of this and seek a commitment from all to put it right.

It must address the failure of those in Ministerial Office to adhere to their Pledge of Office. It must deal with the need to define the duties of Ministerial Office, to include a requirement to attend Executive meetings or meetings of the North–South Ministerial Council.

And of course it should also reflect on what is working well. It must consider for example the improvements recommended by the Procedures Committee and subsequently endorsed by the Assembly, including all the parties here.

Sinn Féin intends also to raise matters such as electoral registration, collusion, including the refusal of the British Government to publish the Cory report, and the absence in many deprived areas, both unionist and nationalist working class neighbourhoods, of a real social economic peace dividend. These are matters directly linked to the Good Friday Agreement and which require focus and discussion and action taken.

Sinn Féin is prepared to play our full part in facing up to our responsibilities. I have set a peaceful direction for all republicans to follow and I reiterate that today.

There is also a heavy responsibility on the two governments – and especially on the Taoiseach and the British Prime Minister – to provide the essential political leadership required to move the overall process on. As the leaders of the two governments and the joint and co-equal guarantors of the Agreement, it falls to them to marshal the pro-Agreement forces and implement a strategy to do this. That is the unambiguous desire of the electorate in returning 74 pro-Agreement candidates out of a total of 108.

Of course, Sinn Féin has its own responsibilities in this as the largest pro-Agreement party. The electorate has made clear in successive votes since 1998 that they oppose efforts to turn the clock back or to sustain a status quo, which is not an option. There is an onus on the British Government to lift the suspension of the institutions and allow the process defined in the Agreement to take its course.

It also means that the two governments have to honour their obligations made in the Agreement, made in last year's Joint Declaration and made in subsequent discussions. In order to advance this entire process of change the British Government needs to press ahead with all its commitments to secure peoples rights and entitlements. This has not happened. Instead the tactical approach of the last 5 years has encouraged the rejectionists.

This cannot continue.

To be effective this review must defend and accelerate the process of change promised in the Good Friday Agreement. And we, sitting around this table must not lose sight of the fact that the Agreement, which as the culmination of an enormous effort by the two governments and the parties to tackle the causes of conflict, continues to hold the promise of a new beginning for everyone.

We should also take encouragement from the fact that we collectively, whatever about our differences, have transformed the situation. There has been huge progress made, not least through the efforts of the people in this room and those who support us on this island.

Speech by David Trimble at the UUP Annual Conference, 27 March 2004

This has been a long week. People sometimes ask me why I want to continue to lead our Party, why I endure the relentless criticism. To be honest, my life – and Daphne's – would be less stressful if I stepped down now. I stay, because there is a job to be done – a job to be seen through.

The Ulster Unionist Party has an historic role. It is to protect and promote the Union of the British people. We in this room wish to add to the distinction of being Ulster Men and Ulster Women, the glory of being British. To achieve that end is not always easy. For all our Leaders, going back to Lord Carson and Sir James Craig, it has always involved difficult compromises which unsettled significant elements in the Party and community. But we have stuck to our task and vision. This Ulster Unionist Council was founded 100 years ago next year. Through all the dark days and years, especially the years of terrorism, this Council is what has embodied decency and commonsense in Ulster politics. It has defended the Union successfully. The decisions it has made today continue in that tradition.

There is a comparison to be made between the years since the Agreement and the years which surrounded another Agreement made in 1921. Many people then felt it was a compromise too far. The creation of an independent Ireland, Ulster reduced from six counties to nine, and devolution intended to put us on the window ledge of the Union. Moreover, Sir James Craig was willing to work a North–South Council of Ireland administering a wide range of all Ireland services. Those were really difficult decisions. But this party had the courage to face up to the realities.

And here we are nearly a century later when few then believed our struggle would endure for more than a decade or two.

This Council again made a profound decision in April 1998 that the Union is best guaranteed through a system of partnership in Northern Ireland and good co-operative relations with our neighbour.

Last November some people pretended that there was some other possible way of achieving devolution and securing the Union. They perpetrated a fraud on the Ulster electorate – a fraud the electorate has begun to notice.

Martin McGuinness frequently has a problem telling the truth but even he cannot help himself sometimes. When he said on Radio Ulster earlier this week that the DUP's talk of excluding Sinn Féin was a mere camouflage for their acceptance of the power-sharing executive model, he highlighted the reality of the DUP's position.

There is a joke in West Belfast: Question: What is the difference between the Provos and the Official IRA? Answer: 25 years. That is how long it took the Republican Movement to learn the futility of violence.

Today's version is, What is the difference between the UUP and the DUP? Answer: six years. That is how long it took the latter to begin to come to terms with reality.

Imitation is the sincerest form of flattery. But it was not the DUP that has carried the burden. It is this Party which forced a partitionist settlement on Sinn Féin. No-one should underestimate the scale of that achievement. No-one should forget the received wisdom eight years ago. It was that Sinn Féin would never accept a return to Stormont; never accept the removal of Articles 2 and 3; never accept a Unionist First Minister; never accept an implicit Unionist veto on the constitutional issue. It was common place that they would resume their campaign before accepting those defeats for republicanism.

Who would have imagined then that the major focus now would not be on the existence of the Border but on making the IRA add the end of its paramilitary and racketeering activities to the now decade long cessation of its 'military' campaign?

Our Party, by taking the right decisions, has made it politically impossible for the IRA to return to its so-called 'war'. By refusing to be bullied out of the Talks in 1996-1998 this Party robbed Republicans of any excuse for refusing to tread the democratic path. It has been an infuriatingly slow journey but it is a journey in the right direction. In the view of this Party it is a journey that has to be completed before Sinn Féin can play a full role in the politics of our Province.

We have been on a long journey. Like John Bunyan's Pilgrim we could have chosen the wide path of populism but our duty to our people and our country has taken us on the narrow path of adversity where we have been subject to all manner of attacks and where friends fell by the wayside. But, like Pilgrim, our faith and conviction in our ultimate destination remains rock solid.

A decade ago when this party started on this journey we were virtually alone. But we are alone no longer. The Prime Minister, the Taoiseach, every major party in Britain and Ireland all concur in the demand for an end to all paramilitary activity. Last week George Bush told the White House reception which included Adams and McGuinness, that there was no place for paramilitaries in a democracy and that if it happened in the US 'we would root them out and bring them to justice'. Even Senator Kennedy and the 'Friends of Ireland' in their St Patrick's Day statement devoted their first three points to the ending of all paramilitary activity and referred to the special responsibility for republicans to give a lead in bringing that about.

We have been joined too by another party nearer home. The ground which the Ulster Unionist Party staked out in 1997-8 is now the ground upon which DUP stands today. For all of the rant and roar about our supposed treachery, they have, nevertheless, stolen our clothes – stolen them because they know that there is nothing else to fit the political realities.

Read 'Devolution Now'. Among its proposals is the corporate Assembly, the 12-person Executive replaced by a 108-person Executive, but operating on all key matters on a cross-community basis. They are in de facto negotiations with Sinn Féin. The DUP is champing at the bit to take office and co-operate with Sinn Féin in the day-to-day governance of Northern Ireland.

The DUP has performed a triple somersault from the positions outlined in their election manifesto.

And we have not overlooked the irony of the position of the Member for Lagan

Valley. He convened crisis meeting after defining moment to oppose in this Party that which he is bending over backwards to endorse in the DUP. And let's not forget he brought this Party to a crisis point – and even to the High Court – last summer because he wanted to oppose the legislation giving effect to the International Monitoring Commission. Yes, the very same IMC the DUP are now trying to claim credit for!

We in this Party pride ourselves, and rightly so, on being a broad church – not in harness to one particular denomination. But we cannot be so broad a church that we tolerate competing gospels, ministers, congregations and choirs. We cannot be so democratic that our own members use the freedom granted by our culture and constitution to exploit and undermine our institutions.

Membership of this party is not enforced. It is voluntary. But membership of the party brings certain responsibilities; foremost of which is a willingness to accept the decisions endorsed by a majority of your fellow members. No one is denied the right to express their opinion – be it at branch, constituency, council, executive, or officer level. In return for that individual right, must be the collective right of the party to expect collective loyalty.

The Ulster Unionist Party is not the personal property of any individual or cabal. It is the collective property of you, its members. I know there is despair when new squabbles break out. We all want unity and a sense of purpose. We need to see the party operating as a team. This Council represents those members. This Council has given me the task of leading.

Leading is about staking out new ground and building a better future. It is time for an end to the introspection that has consumed us for too long.

The challenges are well known to us. They do not need to be identified again and again. But they are not insuperable challenges. We can overcome them.

The first among them is to restore our Party's electoral fortunes. Our Party has lost out in the past but it has always come back because it represents the commonsensical attitudes of the unionist people. They are never comfortable with self-righteous demagogues and slick salesmen.

But we cannot sit back and assume it will all work out in our favour. We have had a wake up call. We need to revitalise ourselves. Today we are the second unionist party so we need to recall the car hire firm's slogan, 'We're number two, we try harder'. Above all we must focus on the task in hand.

That immediate challenge is the European election, just two months away. In Jim Nicholson we have the only candidate going before the Ulster people with real experience, real tried- and-tested ability to deliver for this Province. He has won great respect for our Party and our Province at the heart of the European institutions. But how many in Ulster know that it is Jim who the European Parliament chose to lead for it in relations with the United States, Europe's biggest trading partner.

Let us be realistic. Sinn Féin will mobilise single-mindedly for June. The SDLP will be fighting for its political life. There is a danger of complacency in Unionist Ulster.

That is why the campaign begins here. It is not the Jim Nicholson campaign; it is a campaign for this whole Party; a campaign for no less than Ulster itself.

Jim and his campaign team cannot be expected to shoulder the burden alone. It is the patriotic duty of every constituency association, every branch, every member of this Party to rally support for Jim.

Beyond the European election there are further challenges. We are making a start today, giving our Party a modern structure for the 21st Century. Next month our Party HQ will have a new dynamism with the appointment of a new Chief Executive, whose job will be to make us as effective and efficient as possible.

We must harness the enthusiasm which in North Down led to us winning such a famous victory in the last General Election. It is the spirit which I detected three weeks ago at the Lagan Valley AGM – new members, new money, new drive at long last. It is that kind of spirit that can take us forward in constituencies like East Belfast, East Londonderry, Fermanagh and South Tyrone, and Strangford. We are in striking distance in East Belfast for the first time in a generation. It is not the time to lose focus and to let Peter Robinson escape.

So I say, don't remain in this party if your only ambition is to undermine and destroy it. But stay. Stay and help rebuild this party, reshape it, so we retake our position as the primary vehicle of unionism.

I am not a quitter. I don't take the scenic route or the easy option. That is not leadership.

I am ready to lead from the front. But, I have always consulted with all levels and at all stages.

We have won the policy war. The DUP, the three governments, nationalism and republicanism – they are all now on the ground that we staked out.

We have secured and strengthened the Union. We have laid the foundation for a peaceful, stable and lasting settlement.

If we stick to the job, rebuild internally, reconnect externally, we will regain our position as the party for the pro-Union electorate.

That is my ambition as leader of this great party.

And that is our collective duty to the people of Northern Ireland.

Extracts from 'Devolution Now', the DUP's Concept for Devolution, 5 February 2004

INTRODUCTION: THE DUP SUPPORTS DEVOLUTION
FOR NORTHERN IRELAND

We believe that it should be *stable, accountable, effective* and *efficient.*

The Belfast Agreement failed to deliver for the people of Northern Ireland and a new form of devolution is required.

This document sets out how new arrangements for the governance of Northern Ireland can be achieved […]

Over the last few years the DUP has published a number of documents setting out its policy for devolution. Since 2001 we have produced our 'Seven Principles' for devolution, released our critique of the Belfast Agreement in 'Towards a New Agreement', published our 'Vision for Devolution', set out our 'Seven Tests' and dealt with the issues in our 'Fair Deal Manifesto'.

Our proposals flow from the policies on which we fought the election.

The DUP proposals are based on policies which have been endorsed by a substantial majority of unionists in Northern Ireland.

Our proposals for Strand 2 and Strand 3 matters will be dealt with separately as will our proposals on other issues such as Policing, Justice and Human Rights. In relation to Strand 1, this document represents only our concept for devolution and deals in general terms with the issues which need to be addressed. During the negotiating process we will publish further details on this and other issues in the process.

These proposals take account of political realities in Northern Ireland and are predicated on the basis that only those who are committed to exclusively peaceful and democratic means should exercise any Cabinet-style Ministerial responsibility. They allow for change in the nature of any administration in the light of prevailing circumstances; are devised to avoid the collapse of the Assembly even in extreme circumstances; always leave the ultimate authority and accountability with the Northern Ireland Assembly and give equal opportunity and value to all parties in accordance with their mandates. Nationalists and Republicans have attempted to suggest that some unionists 'do not want to have a Fenian about the place'. These proposals demonstrate the sound democratic and accurate position that 'we do not want to have a terrorist about the place'. We believe that these proposals offer a real opportunity to get devolution up and running in Northern Ireland quickly.

If the issues in Strand 1 can be resolved quickly then the other issues could be resolved in parallel with the institutions up and running or by commissions set up to deal with identified areas of concern.

OUR SEVEN PRINCIPLES

1. The DUP is a devolutionist party. We believe in democratic, fair and accountable government.
2. No negotiating with the representatives of terrorism but we will talk to other democratic parties.
3. Those who are not committed to exclusively peaceful and democratic means should not be able to exercise unaccountable executive power.
4. Terrorist structures and weaponry must be removed before the bar to the Stormont Executive can be opened.
5. Any relationship with the Republic of Ireland should be fully accountable to the Assembly.
6. The DUP will work to restore the morale and effectiveness of the police force.
7. We will strive to ensure genuine equality for all including equality in funding [...]

OUR SEVEN TESTS

1. Any Agreement must command the support of both Nationalists and Unionists.
2. Any Assembly must be democratic, fair and accountable. Any executive power must be fully accountable to the Assembly.
3. Only those committed to exclusively peaceful and democratic means should exercise any Cabinet-style Ministerial responsibility.
4. Within any new Agreement any relationship with the Republic of Ireland must be fully accountable to the Assembly.
5. A new settlement must be able to deliver equality of opportunity to unionists as well as nationalists.
6. Agreed arrangements must be capable of delivering an efficient and effective administration.
7. The outcome must provide a settlement within the UK, not a process to a united Ireland. It must provide stable government for the people of Northern Ireland and not be susceptible to recurring suspension [...]

A NEW AGREEMENT MUST BE

Stable: The Belfast Agreement was not stable and was incapable of delivering stable government. An alternative needs to be established which takes cognisance of parties behaviour but is sufficiently robust to withstand pressure.

Accountable: Ministers were not accountable to the Assembly for their decisions. A mechanism for holding individual Ministers to account must be established.

Effective: The Agreement failed to provide clear direction or effective decision making thus rendering the process cumbersome. The alternative is a system which is responsive, removing unnecessary levels of bureaucracy.

Efficient: Political bureaucracy spiralled out of control under the Agreement. The alternative must provide value for money and cut back the costs of government [...]

PROPOSALS

- We believe that there should be a 72 Member Assembly elected by the Single Transferable Vote form of Proportional Representation with four members from each Westminster constituency. The method of election could be reviewed following a period of stability for the Assembly.
- In the Assembly cross-community support would be required by means of Key Vote majorities.
- The Assembly would have executive and legislative responsibility for the areas which were the responsibility of the six Northern Ireland Departments before 1999 with the exception that responsibility for Social Security would rest at Westminster and responsibility for the Human Rights Commission and Equality Commission would be devolved to Northern Ireland. Other issues should only be transferred to Northern Ireland with the consent of Parliament and a Key Vote of a Northern Ireland Assembly.
- There should be a maximum of eight Government Departments in Northern Ireland and functions should be determined to best deliver services to the community.
- We propose the abolition of the Civic Forum.
- The Assembly, by Key Vote, would determine how executive power was exercised.

A number of models which could deliver effective decision making could be agreed by the parties to facilitate this consideration.

This could take account of the prevailing circumstances in Northern Ireland and would allow the Assembly to proceed with the most extensive and collective form of devolution which could be facilitated at any time […]

- The administration could either be in some form of an Executive or an arrangement where the Assembly would be a Corporate Body responsible for decision making in an agreed manner.
     The Executive could be either a voluntary coalition (as in Scotland with collective cabinet responsibility) or a mandatory coalition with arrangements for accountability and effective decision making. This Executive would be subject to a vote of confidence at any time and would require a Key Vote majority to survive.
- If an Executive could not be formed or if an Executive collapsed powers would be transferred from the Executive/Ministers to the Assembly.
     On the basis of a Key Vote the Assembly could make arrangements for the exercise of that executive power.
- There would be a fixed four year term for the Assembly.
- Arrangements would need to be put in place to ensure a smooth change over from the previous arrangements to the new arrangements.
- We propose that an Efficiency Commission be established to make recommendations about the value for money of all aspects of the devolved institutions. This would enable an earlier return to devolution and allow matters which are not primarily divisive political issues to be dealt with in a practical manner.
- Pending the implementation of the findings of the Efficiency Commission and subject to other agreements by Key Vote the existing Government Departments would remain in place.
- As a default, executive power would be exercised by the Departments subject to the direction and control of the Assembly. Clearly the Assembly would wish to find the most appropriate and effective manner of doing so […]

EFFICIENCY OF DEVOLVED INSTITUTIONS

A Commission should be established to make recommendations about the efficiency of every aspect of the devolved institutions. This would include the number of Assembly Members, the number of Government Departments, the functions of Government Departments and the Civic Forum. This Commission would report in time to enable changes to take effect before the next Assembly election.

Our proposals - which are consistent with our policy set out in *'Rates Time Bomb'* - to the Commission will include:

- Alteration of the size of the Assembly from 108 to 72 members.
- Reduction in the maximum number of Government Departments to 8.
- Streamlining of OFMDFM (including removing duplication with other Departments).
- Reorganisation of functions in Government Departments.
- Abolition of Civic Forum.

The Commission's remit might include the remaining work to be done in the Review of Public Administration. The Commission should report to the Assembly within a stipulated period making its recommendations. If the Assembly can agree by Key Vote these or other arrangements then Westminster should give the Assembly powers (if necessary) to legislate for these changes. In the absence of agreement HMG would legislate for the necessary changes at Westminster [...]

VOTING IN THE ASSEMBLY

- There should be two categories of votes, Normal Votes and Key Votes.
- Normal Votes would simply require a majority of Assembly Members present and voting to pass.
- Key Votes would be either important votes such as the formation of an administration, changes to Assembly procedure or votes which were triggered by a petition of concern which would need 30 MLAs in a 108 member Assembly and proportionately less for a smaller Assembly.
- A Key Vote could only be passed in one of two ways:
  —Either it would require more than seventy percent of Assembly Members present and voting, or
  —it would require a majority of Assembly Members which also included a majority of designated unionists and a majority of designated nationalists.
- Designations should be mandated by the electorate and fixed for the Assembly term to prevent abuse of the system [...]

MODELS OF ADMINISTRATION

1 Voluntary coalition model

This form of administration would be established by a Key Vote of the Assembly. Any vote of confidence would also require to attain a Key Vote majority. The Cabinet would be formed following negotiations between the parties on whatever basis could attain a Key Vote majority. Such an agreement is likely to address the distribution and arrangement of Ministerial Offices as well as a Programme for Government. The Cabinet would act by way of collective responsibility and ultimate power would rest with the Cabinet as opposed to the individual Departments.

We believe that this is likely to be the most effective administration and we would be prepared to form a Voluntary Coalition with other democratic parties.

2 Mandatory coalition model

This form of administration would be established by allocating the Departments on a proportionate basis. To ensure that Ministers were accountable, legislative change would be required to ensure that ultimate power would rest with the Executive as opposed to the individual Departments. In addition decisions of the Executive could be challenged by the Assembly and would require a Key Vote of the Assembly to stand. Arrangements would be made to allow each designation to elect to the positions of First Minister and Deputy First Minister as appropriate.

We would not be prepared to support these arrangements whilst those who would be entitled to Ministerial seats were not committed to exclusively peaceful and democratic means. The Prime Minister has set out the tests which need to be passed to enable such parties to participate in any Executive.

3 Corporate assembly model

In this model the Assembly would be responsible for all Executive functions of the Northern Ireland Departments by way of Key Vote approval.

There are a significant number of ways in which this could be achieved including practices which are adopted in Great Britain. In all cases the ultimate power and authority would rest with the Assembly and be subject to the will of the Assembly by Key Vote. The question of terrorist-related parties exercising executive power would therefore not arise.

TRIED AND TESTED

The decision making process advocated in the Corporate Assembly Model is not inconsistent with the modus operandi in local government. In that context democratic parties have, for many years, been able to represent their constituents within a political structure where, despite an absence of trust, decisions have been taken without the requirement to act in partnership with those associated with terrorism [...]

FORMING AN EXECUTIVE

During the lifetime of the old Agreement the Ulster Unionist Party entered government with Sinn Féin before any decommissioning was carried out.

On two further occasions they re-entered government with Sinn Féin in parallel with an IRA decommissioning stunt – the extent of which is known to no one other than the IRA and the Decommissioning Body.

Just before the November 2003 election a step by step choreographed deal was unfolding that again was to have the UUP entering government with Sinn Féin on the back of a further 'gesture' from the IRA.

The Prime Minister has set out in clear terms the requirements that Sinn Féin/IRA must meet.

He called them 'acts of completion'.

The DUP, unlike the UUP, will not take the IRA on its word nor accept an incremental process. For the DUP no instalment will satisfy.

Completion is what we require and no move to include Sinn Féin in an Executive or granting them executive power will precede the full delivery of the Blair Necessities.

If at any time there is a Key Vote in favour of forming an Executive the Assembly can determine to bring this about. Equally, if an Executive is in place and for whatever reason cannot command the support of the Assembly by Key Vote it would fall and revert to another model. This gives the arrangements the flexibility to react to changed circumstances and the voters the opportunity to make decisions at election time. These arrangements represent both a launch pad and a safety net.

THE PROCESS

The DUP will not operate the Mandatory Coalition with Sinn Féin before it meets the Blair Necessities but will operate the Voluntary Coalition with parties including the SDLP immediately.

If the SDLP is unwilling to operate a Voluntary Coalition in the absence of SF then we would be willing to operate the Corporate Assembly Model until either the SDLP agree to operate a Voluntary Coalition or SF/IRA deliver on the Blair Necessities.

THE BLAIR NECESSITIES

Pledge to the people of Northern Ireland, Wednesday 20 May 1998:

'I pledge to the people of Northern Ireland: Those who use or threaten violence excluded from the Government of Northern Ireland.'

Balmoral, 14 May 1998:

'Those who have used the twin tactics of ballot box and the gun must make a clear choice. There can be no fudge between democracy and terror.'

Belfast NewsLetter, 22 May 1998:

'Representatives of parties intimately linked to paramilitary groups can only be in a future Northern Ireland Government if it is clear that there will be no more violence and the threat of violence has gone. That doesn't just mean decommissioning, but all bombing, killings, beatings, and an end to targeting, recruiting and all the structures of terrorism.'

Belfast Harbour Commissioners Speech, 17 October 2002:

'Another inch by inch negotiation won't work. Symbolic gestures, important in their time, no longer build trust.'

'It's time for acts of completion.'

'Republicans to make the commitment to exclusively peaceful means, real, total and permanent. For all of us, an end to tolerance of paramilitary activity in any form. A decision that from here on in, a criminal act is a criminal act. One law for all, applied equally to all.' [...]

House of Commons, 27 November 2002:

Rev. Ian Paisley (North Antrim): The Prime Minister is aware that in the past two days my party has met the Minister with responsibility for security in Northern Ireland and the Secretary of State for Northern Ireland.

We put one question to both: what is an act of completion? Does it consist of IRA–Sinn Féin repudiating and ceasing violence and being disbanded, or does it simply mean that they make a statement that they will give up violence?

Can the Prime Minister tell us what he believes it means?

The Prime Minister: I can. It is not merely a statement, a declaration or words. It means giving up violence completely in a way that satisfies everyone and gives them confidence that the IRA has ceased its campaign, and enables us to move the democratic process forward, with every party that wants to be in government abiding by the same democratic rules [...]

Statement, Prime Minister, 1 May 2003:

'What part of no activities do they not understand? Well the answer to that I am afraid is very clear. The answer is, the activities listed in Paragraph 13, because that's what we have asked for. Will those activities continue to be authorised or not by the IRA? Yes or no? It's not a desperately complicated situation, but it is one that requires a very clear answer.

We need to see an immediate, full and permanent cessation of all paramilitary activity, including military attacks, training, targeting, intelligence-gathering, acquisition or development of arms or weapons, other preparations for terrorist campaigns, punishment beatings, and attacks and involvement in riots.

Moreover the practice of exiling must come to an end, and the exiled must feel free to return in safety. Similarly, sectarian attacks and intimidation directed at vulnerable communities must cease.'

Prime Minister's Briefing, 15 January 2004:

'In respect of the Republican Party – Sinn Féin – is there a clear understanding that we cannot have a situation where any party that is in government is associated with active paramilitary organisations?'

'And we cannot have a situation where people are expected to sit in government with political parties attached to active paramilitary organisations. When people say to me, well you said people wouldn't be in government if they were linked to active paramilitary organisations, that is precisely the reason we have not had a functioning devolved government in Northern Ireland, because we have not been satisfied about that.'

'It has got to be clear, you cannot expect after five and a half years of the Good Friday Agreement, you cannot expect people to sit down in government unless they are all playing by the same rules, and there is no way round that.'

House of Commons, 21st January 2004:

'I would like to say that any criminal activity of the sort he has described is completely unacceptable - we cannot have a situation in which people are expected to sit in government with political parties that are attached to active paramilitary organisations.'

Index